Thought & Knowledge:
An Introduction to Critical Thinking
Fourth Edition

Thought & Knowledge:
An Introduction to Critical Thinking
Fourth Edition

Diane F. Halpern
Berger Institute for Work, Family, & Children
Claremont McKenna College

LEA **LAWRENCE ERLBAUM ASSOCIATES, PUBLISHERS**
2003 Mahwah, New Jersey   London

#50065032

Editor:	Bill Webber
Textbook Marketing Manager:	Marisol Kozlovski
Editorial Assistant:	Erica Kica
Cover Design:	Robert Perine
Textbook Production Manager:	Paul Smolenski
Full-Service & Composition:	UG / GGS Information Services, Inc.
Text and Cover Printer:	Hamilton Printing Company

This book was typeset in 10/12 pt. Palatino, Bold, and Italic
The heads were typeset in Americana Extra Bold, and Palatino Bold.

Lawrence Erlbaum Associates, Inc., Publishers
10 Industrial Avenue
Mahwah, New Jersey 07430

Library of Congress Cataloging-in-Publication Data
Halpern, Diane F.
    Thought and knowledge : an introduction to critical thinking / Diane F. Halpern.—4th ed.
        p. cm.
Includes bibliographical references and indexes.
    ISBN 0-8058-3965-8 (alk. paper)—ISBN 0-8058-3966-6 (alk. paper)   1. Critical thinking. I. Title.
    BF441 .H25 2003
    153—dc21

                                                                    2002024594

Books published by Lawrence Erlbaum Associates are printed on acid-free
paper, and their bindings are chosen for strength and durability.

Printed in the United States of America
10 9 8 7 6 5 4 3 2 1

This book is dedicated to the loving memory of
Dr. Katharine D. Newman—
author, professor, friend, aunt, and so much more.
She loved people and she loved learning.
What better tribute is there?

Contents

Preface to Fourth Edition

Based on the belief that it's good for kids to have married parents, some states in the United States are paying a marriage bonus to couples receiving Temporary Aid to Needy Families (TANF, formerly known as welfare). When I discussed this novel approach to social engineering with the students in my college classes, many thought it was a good idea. However, no one thought that unmarried couples who receive TANF should have to pay an "unmarried penalty"; none of the students thought that if couples decided NOT to marry that they should be "fined" or "punished" financially for their decision. The funny thing about this discussion was that the students did not immediately understand that if the government provides more money for couples who get married, it is also paying less money to couples who don't get married. Whether we call it a "marriage bonus" or "unmarried penalty" is just a matter of framing—the way we present the information. In one frame (marriage bonus), it seems like a much better idea than the other frame (unmarried penalty). There are countless similar examples where a change in the way information is presented produces large changes in how people feel about the information. But, with some training in critical thinking, we can learn to recognize framing and thus not fall prey to attempts to influence what we think by manipulating the way information is presented.

There are so many other examples where critical thinking skills are important— ranging from decisions about politics and the environment to personal choices about whom and when to marry and whether or when to have children. If I say that only a stupid person would agree with a particular position or that everyone else agrees with me, it is often easy to sway individual and public opinions against or for the same position. I can even persuade many people that one brand of soap is a "good buy" (buy two bars and get one free) or that crime is or isn't a major threat to your safety by describing the same set of facts as "crime rates are up by 300%" versus "only five crimes have been committed in a major metropolitan area this year." Surely crime seems more menacing with the first statistical statement than the second, even though both can be true.

With the deluge of information on the internet, especially unreliable and even false information, the need to enhance one's ability to think critically is more critical than ever before. I hope that you will find the information in the fourth edition of *Thought & Knowledge: An Introduction to Critical Thinking* useful and informative. Over the years, many readers have written to me with real-life examples of the ways they have used the critical thinking skills that are presented in this book. Please keep those e-mails coming (Diane.Halpern@claremontmckenna.edu), and have fun with this book!

ACKNOWLEDGMENTS FOR THE FOURTH EDITION

This is the best part—where I get to thank the wonderful people who have helped to make the fourth edition the best one (so far). Sincere thanks to Dr. Bill Buskist at Auburn University and Dr. Mark Haviland at the Loma Linda University School of Medicine for their insightful comments on every chapter. The book has benefited greatly from their insightful comments and very hard work. I also thank the many students who have used this book (in earlier editions) over the last 20 years for their helpful insights. I hope that the many new examples and clarifications will make it more user-friendly than ever before. Finally, thanks to my wonderful family—my husband, Sheldon; daughter, Jaye; son, Evan; and daughter-in-law, Karen. You make it all worthwhile.

1

Thinking: An Introduction

Contents

Many people would sooner die than think. In fact they do.

—Bertrand Russell (quoted in Macmillan, 1989)

"Think about it!" How many times have you heard this phrase or said it yourself? Look around you. Watch a student solving a calculus problem, or a programmer "debugging" a computer program, or a politician arguing that the Strategic Defense Initiative will not work. Watch a child absorbed in a fairy tale, or an architect designing a skyscraper, or a senior citizen planning to live on a fixed income. What are they doing that makes their faces appear so serious, so quizzical—so much like Rodin's famous statue, "The Thinker," which inspired the pose for the beautiful woman thinker on the cover of this book? They are all "lost in thought," yet lost seems like a strange word to describe the process of thinking—maybe "creating knowledge in thought" would be a more appropriate phrase.

THE NEED FOR CRITICAL THINKING SKILLS

Although the ability to think critically has always been important, it is a vital necessity for the citizens of the 21st century. Every generation needs more education than the one that came before because the world is becoming increasingly technical and complex. In his award-winning book, Earl Hunt (1995) examined the skills that will be needed by our workforce in the early decades of this century and asks, "Will we be smart enough?" Our quality of life, perhaps even the future of our planet, depends on how we answer this question. The workforce is one critical place where we can witness the dizzying pace of change. There is an increased demand for a new type of worker—the "knowledge worker" or the "symbol analyst," a phrase that is used by the United States secretary of labor to describe someone who can carry out multistep operations, manipulate abstract and complex symbols and ideas, acquire new information efficiently, and remain flexible enough to recognize the need for continuing change and for new paradigms for lifelong learning. Workers in almost every job category can expect to face novel problems in a workplace that is changing repeatedly. Familiar responses no longer work, and even newly acquired ones won't work for long.

   The information explosion is yet another reason why we need to provide specific instruction in thinking. It has been estimated that "The world's total yearly production of print, film, optical, and magnetic content would require roughly 1.5 billion gigabytes of storage. This is the equivalent of 250 megabytes per person for every man, woman, and child on earth" (Regents of the University of California, http://www.sims.berkeley.edu/how-much-info/, January 30, 2001). The sheer magnitude of the information glut is a good example of how much the world is changing because quantities of knowledge are no longer measured in number of words or pages, but in units that most people can only vaguely comprehend. (I suppose that millions of gigabytes of magnetic content is larger than anything I can imagine.)

   We now have an incredible wealth of information available, quite literally at our fingertips, via the Internet and other remote services with only a few minutes of "search time" on the computer and a few clicks of a mouse. The quantity of data that is available is overwhelming, creating a "paralysis of analysis" as we make choices about how to select information from this ever-expanding database (Davidson, 1996). Relevant, credible information has to be selected, interpreted, digested, evaluated, learned, and applied or it is of no more use on a computer screen than it is on a distant library shelf. If we cannot think intelligently about the myriad of issues that confront us, then we are in danger of having all of the answers, but still not knowing what they mean. The twin abilities of knowing how to learn and knowing how to think clearly about the rapidly proliferating information that we must select from are the most important intellectual skills for the 21st century.

The information glut and the constantly changing workplace are not the only reasons why critical thinking is more critical now than at any previous time in history. For the first time in history, we have the ability to destroy all life on earth. The decisions that we make as individuals and as a society regarding the economy, conservation of natural resources, and the development of nuclear weapons will affect future generations of all people around the world.

We are called upon to make decisions on a wide range of important local and personal topics. For example, in a recent election, voters had to decide if they favored or opposed an increase in property taxes, the construction of a canal that would divert water from one part of the state to another, mandatory AIDS testing for criminals, and a rent control ordinance, in addition to deciding which candidate they preferred for diverse political offices including governor, state treasurer, county commissioner, and trustee of the local library system. Consumers need to decide if irradiated foods pose a health risk, if the public school system is providing an adequate education, and whether health plans that allow you to choose your physician are preferable to plans that do not. Because every citizen is required to make countless important decisions, it may seem obvious that, as a society, we should be concerned with the way these decisions are made. Surprisingly, it is only within the last 10 to 20 years that educators, politicians, and the general public have begun to address this topic in a serious manner.

GRIN AND BEAR IT   by Lichty & Wagner

Courtesy of NAS, INC.

6-15

"Fifty cents for my thoughts?"

In the United States, the topic of critical thinking gained widespread attention when the (U.S.) National Education Goals Panel established educational goals that the United States would strive to achieve by the year 2000 and beyond. Panel members realized that our best hope for a strong global economy and for citizens who can participate in the democratic process is to produce college graduates with a broad knowledge base and strong critical thinking skills. An educated, thinking citizenry is the best way, perhaps the only way, to ensure world peace and adequate resources. Accordingly, one of the educational goals that they set for the year 2000 and beyond was that:

> The proportion of college graduates who demonstrate an advanced ability to think critically, communicate effectively, and solve problems will increase substantially. (National Education Goals Panel, 1991, p. 237)

Unfortunately, this goal was the only one of the national education goals that was never funded, despite bipartisan support from both George Bush (the elder) and Bill Clinton, a fact that led some to cynically suggest that politicians really do not want a thinking public.

Numerous national reports over the last 25 years have shown that instruction designed to improve the thinking process is desperately needed. In one of the earliest reports on this problem, the United States was been described as a "nation at risk" because we are failing to provide students with the most essential component of education—instruction that fosters the development of the ability to think (National Commission of Excellence in Education, 1983). College faculty from a variety of academic disciplines list critical thinking (and problem solving) along with communicating, interpersonal skills, and computer literacy as the "the basic competencies or skills that every college graduate [should] have" (Diamond, 1997). Adult workers agree, with 81% of the over 1,000 who responded to a national survey, reporting that critical thinking, literacy, and communication skills are "very important" compared to only 50% who rated computer skills as "very important" (The Chronicle of Higher Education, 2000). Politicians of every persuasion, blue-ribbon panels, workers, and students all recognize the critical importance of critical thinking as the primary objective of education.

International studies repeatedly paint a gloomy picture of the current status of critical thinking. Izawa and Hayden (1993) summarized the results from an international comparison in which the best students from the United States scored lower than the worst Japanese students in mathematical problem solving; abysmal results were also obtained for reading skills and knowledge of history. Neubert and Binko (1992), using data from a different study, concluded that only 39% of 17-year-olds can find, summarize, and explain information. And, in what may be the most horrifying tale ever told by the prolific science fiction writer, Isaac Asimov (1989) reported on the true state of scientific understanding and knowledge by Americans. In a telephone survey conducted by the Public Opinion Laboratory at Northern Illinois University, Asimov noted that the researchers found that only 20% of the more than 200 adults surveyed believe that the sun revolves around the earth. Why, asks Asimov, over 400 years since the scientific community agreed on the fundamental scientific fact that the earth revolves around the sun, are the vast majority of adults still unaware of a basic fact that is "taught" in grammar school science? The depressingly long list of findings and reports by prestigious panels that conclude that many adults do not have adequate thinking and learning skills shows that it is time to stop issuing reports and time to start acting in ways that promote these skills.

Numerous other countries have recognized that the world community is growing smaller and the need for a citizenry that can think critically is imperative in every country. Such was the conclusion of a panel of experts on higher education that met in Mexico. They agreed that "the job of the university today is to turn out students who can think in a rapidly changing world" (De Lopez, 1992, p. B4). News reports from Pakistan and many different countries in Eastern Europe and Asia also document phenomenal growth in the number of college courses designed to help their students become better thinkers (Bollag, 1997; Cohen, 2000; Collett, 1994).

If the conclusions of national and international study groups don't convince you of the need for critical thinking instruction, consider this: Most people will finish their formal education between the ages of 18 and 22. Today's young adults are expected to have the longest average life span in the history of the world, with most living into their 70s and many living into their 80s and 90s. We can only guess what life will be like in the years 2060 or 2070 or beyond, years that many of you who are reading this book will live through. One likely guess is that many of today's young adults will be working at jobs that currently don't exist and dealing with technologies that dwarf the imagination of present-day science fiction writers. What do they need to learn during their first two decades of life that will prepare them for their remaining 50+ years?

It is difficult to imagine any area where the ability to think clearly is not needed. Yet, few of us have ever received explicit instructions in how to improve the way we think. Traditionally, our schools have required students to learn, remember, make decisions, analyze arguments, and solve problems without ever teaching them how to do so. There has been a tacit assumption that adult students already know "how to think." Research has shown, however, this assumption is wrong. Psychologists have found that only 25% of first-year college students possess the skills needed for logical abstract thought—the type of thought needed to answer "what would happen if. . ." questions and to comprehend abstract concepts (McKinnon & Renner, 1971). The situation is succinctly summed up by Brock, formerly the Republican Party chairman and currently an international consultant, who, after reading a recent report on the low level of learning and thinking skills of college graduates, exclaimed, "It ought to terrify everybody" (quoted in Frammolino, 1993, p. A41).

Thought and Knowledge

Knowledge will forever govern ignorance: And a people who mean to be their
own Governours, must arm themselves with the power which knowledge gives.

—James Madison
(Texas Library Association, http://www.txla.org/groups/godort/kip-award.html)

One of the elementary schools that I attended as a child had the words "Knowledge Is Power" chiseled into a concrete block above its front door. If I were asked to amend this maxim based on my experiences over the many years since I last past through those doors, I would edit the concrete block to read "Thought and Knowledge Are Power," because knowledge is powerful only when it is applied appropriately, and thought is powerful only when it can utilize a large and accurate base of knowledge.

This is a book about thought and knowledge and the relationship between these two constructs. It is about thinking in ways that allow us to use previous knowledge to create new knowledge. Everything we know, and everything everyone else knows—that is, all existing knowledge—was created by someone. When we learn Euclidean geometry, we are learning about knowledge created by the great mathematician, Euclid. Similarly, other eminent inventions and insights such as the wheel, shoes, video games, toilet paper, $E = mc^2$, and the "discovery" of America all represent knowledge created by people. Knowledge is not something static that gets transferred from one person to another like pouring water from one glass to another. It is dynamic. Information becomes knowledge when we make our own meaning out of it. Of course, it is silly to think that we should all start from "scratch" and re-create the wheel. We build on the knowledge created by others to create new knowledge.

We also create knowledge every time we learn a new concept. The newly acquired information is used to construct our own internal knowledge structures. ("Knowledge structures" is a technical term used by cognitive psychologists to describe all of the interrelated concepts that each of us has about different subjects.) Knowledge is a "state of understanding" that exists only in the mind of the individual knower (King, 1994, p. 16). We use our existing knowledge when we receive new information in order to make sense of the new information, thus the acquisition of knowledge is an active mental process. Each individual builds "extensive knowledge structures" that connect new ideas to what is known so that knowledge is always personal and somewhat idiosyncratic. These knowledge structures or **schemata** are our personal internal representations about the nature of the world. When we recombine them in new ways with other schemata, we are creating new knowledge. This idea was expressed more eloquently by Resnick (1985, p. 130) when she said: "Knowledge is no longer viewed as a reflection of what has been given from the outside; it is a personal construction in which the individual imposes meaning by relating bits of knowledge and experience to some organizing schemata."

A Working Definition of Critical Thinking

Ultimately, it is not we who define thinking, it is thinking that defines us.

—Carey, Foltz, & Allan (*Newsweek*, 1983, February 7)

Although many psychologists and others have proposed definitions for the term "critical thinking," these definitions tend to be similar in content. In a recent review of the critical thinking literature, Fischer and Spiker (2000) found that most definitions for the term "critical thinking" include reasoning/logic, judgment, metacognition, reflection, questioning, and mental processes. Jones and his colleagues (Jones, Dougherty, Fantaske, & Hoffman, 1995; Jones, Hoffman, Moore, Ratcliff, Tibbetts, & Click, 1995) obtained consensus from among 500 policymakers, employers, and educators, who agree that critical thinking is a broad term that describes reasoning in an open-ended manner and with an unlimited number of solutions. It involves constructing a situation and supporting the reasoning that went into a conclusion.

Here is a simple definition that captures the main concepts: **Critical thinking is the use of those cognitive skills or strategies that increase the probability of a desirable outcome. It is used to describe thinking that is purposeful, reasoned, and goal directed—the kind of thinking involved in solving problems, formulating inferences, calculating likelihoods, and making decisions, when the thinker is using skills that are thoughtful and effective for the particular context and type of thinking task.** Critical thinking is more than merely thinking about your own thinking or making judgments and solving problems—it is using skills and strategies that will make "desirable outcomes" more likely. Decisions as to which outcomes should be desirable are embedded in a system of values (Halpern, in press; Sternberg, in press).

One of my favorite definitions of critical thinking was published over 40 years ago (1960) and comes very close to this contemporary notion of critical thinking as a learnable skill: "Critical thinking then is the process of evaluation or categorization in terms of some previously accepted standards . . . this seems to involve attitude plus knowledge of facts plus some thinking skills" (Russell, cited in d'Angelo, 1971, p. 6). In short, Russell's equation is:

Attitude + Knowledge + Thinking Skills = Intelligent Thinking

What's Critical About Critical Thinking?

The "critical" part of critical thinking denotes an evaluation component. Sometimes the word "critical" is used to convey something negative, as when we say, "She is a critical person." However, evaluation can and should be a constructive reflection of positive and negative attributes. When we think critically, we are evaluating the outcomes of our thought processes—how good a decision is or how well a problem has been solved. Critical thinking also involves evaluating the thinking process—the reasoning that went into the conclusion we've arrived at or the kinds of factors considered in making a decision. Critical thinking is sometimes called **directed thinking** because it focuses on obtaining a desired outcome. Daydreams, night dreams, and other sorts of thinking that are not engaged in for a specific purpose are not subsumed under the critical thinking category. Neither is the type of thinking that underlies our routine habits, which, although goal directed, involve very little conscious evaluation, such as getting up in the morning, brushing our teeth, or taking a usual route to school and work. These are examples of **nondirected or automatic thinking**. Other examples of *noncritical thinking* include the rote recall of information (e.g., listing state capitals) or the failure to consider evidence that might support a conclusion that you do not like.

In thinking about critical thinking, consider, for example, someone in need of money who decides to remedy this problem with a trip to the racetrack where she bets on a pretty filly named "Handsome Singer." There is some (small) chance that she will "win big" if her horse comes in, but this is not an example of critical thinking, even if she reflected on her actions and "Handsome Singer" was the first to cross the finish line. The most likely outcome is that she will lose the money she bet, surely an undesirable outcome. On the other hand, suppose that she invested her money in a "blue-chip" stock instead of betting it on "Handsome Singer." There is some chance that she will lose her money with this strategy, but on average in the long run, the likelihood of the desirable outcome of having more money is much higher with the stock investment. The investment is a rational or reasoned course of action, but it cannot guarantee a desirable outcome. The future is always unknown and there can never be guarantees about the future, even for the best of thinkers. A substantial increase in the likelihood of a desirable outcome is the best that critical thinking can promise, and it is the best hope for the future that anyone can offer.

The focus of this book is on the development and improvement of those skills that characterize clear, precise, purposeful thinking. It is a practical book, based primarily on applications of cognitive psychology to memory, reasoning, problem solving, creativity, language, and decision making. Despite the fact that some critics have claimed that critical thinking is just a "fad" that will surely go out of style, it has a very long history in psychology and education. John Dewey, the pioneering American educator, identified "learning to think" as the primary purpose of education in 1933. Besides, it is difficult for me to consider that the need to think well is a "passing fancy" that will soon be out of style, much like the Rubik's cube, "big hair," and bell-bottom jeans.

Although psychology has been concerned with the way people think for much of its 100+ years of existence as an academic discipline, cognitive psychology, the branch of psychology that is concerned with thought and knowledge, has virtually dominated scientific psychology for the past 30 years. Cognitive psychologists are concerned with learning about the skills and strategies used in problem solving, reasoning, and decision making and the way these abilities relate to intelligence. All of this interest in human thinking processes has given birth to a new area of psychology that has come to be known as **cognitive process instruction**. Its goal is to utilize the knowledge we have accumulated about human thinking processes and mechanisms in ways that can help people improve how they think. For example, by examining correct and incorrect responses in a variety of situations, psychologists have found that most people's spontaneous and intuitive approaches to solving problems are frequently wrong. Furthermore, psychologists can often predict when an incorrect response will be made either because of the nature of the problem or because of common biases that a problem solver may bring to the problem. This knowledge is already being put to use to solve a host of applied problems that range from providing military personnel with map-reading skills to designing "user-friendly" computer programs.

Changing How People Think: Should It Be Done?

We know that the average American, because of changes in the economy at home and abroad, will change work seven or eight times in a lifetime. . . . If that is true, it is clear that we need an agenda as a people for lifetime learning.

—U. S. President Bill Clinton ("Clinton's message," 1994, p. 6A)

The whole idea of influencing the way people think may seem scary. It suggests terms like "mind control" and "propaganda," or perhaps even a "Big Brother," like the one in Orwell's chilling novel *1984*, who knew what you were thinking. In reality, though, critical thinking is an antidote to the kind of mind control that worried Orwell. Learning the skills of clear thinking can help everyone recognize propaganda and thus not fall prey to it, analyze unstated assumptions in arguments, realize when there is deliberate deception, consider the credibility of an information source, and think a problem or a decision through in the best way possible.

When I discuss the topic of critical thinking with students and other people with whom I come in contact, I am sometimes told that there is no such thing as critical thinking because different viewpoints are "all a matter of opinion" and that everyone has a right to his or her own opinion. They argue that a "better way to think" does not exist. I certainly agree that we all have the "right" to our own opinion; however, some "opinions" are better than others. If, for example, you believe that heavy alcohol consumption is good for pregnant women, you had better be able to back up this belief with sound reasoning. (There isn't any.) The opposite belief, that pregnant women should drink very little, if at all, can be supported with carefully controlled laboratory studies that document the deleterious effect of alcohol on a developing fetus.

Similarly, everyone has the right to believe in phenomena such as astrology and extra-sensory perception, but there is no sound evidence to support the existence of these phenomena. James Randi, a magician and escape artist who is now best known for his work in debunking claims of psychics and others, has a certified $1 million fund that will be given to anyone who can legitimately demonstrate paranormal ability under test conditions. The $1 Million Paranormal Challenge is still unclaimed (James Randi Educational Foundation, http://www.randi.org/research/index.html). All beliefs are *not* equally good.

Let's consider some examples of the need to think critically. A good place to start is with commercials. Sponsors pay substantial sums for the opportunity to persuade customers to purchase their products. An advertising campaign is rated as successful if more of the product is sold after the advertisement, and the additional sales more than cover the cost of the advertisement. One of my favorite examples is cigarette advertisements. As you undoubtedly know, every cigarette advertisement in the United States must carry a message like this one: "Warning: The U.S. Surgeon General has determined that cigarette smoking is dangerous to your health." It would seem that this message would conjure up visions of hacking coughs, stained teeth, and lung cancer, and thus reduce the effectiveness of any cigarette advertisement. To counter the surgeon general's warning, many cigarette advertisements show smokers in natural outdoor surroundings with crystal lakes, clear blue skies, and tall, green pine trees. One cigarette advertisement reads, "Come to where the clean is." Another classic cigarette ad reads, "Alive with pleasure"—an attempt to counteract the association of smoking with premature death.

Have you ever stopped to consider the association of cigarette smoking and the beauty of an outdoor scene? Does cigarette smoking seem healthier when it is associated with beautiful people in beautiful settings? One brand of cigarettes is called "Malibu." The advertisements depict the soft white sand and foamy blue ocean at Malibu Beach in California, which is probably the ultimate setting for "beautiful people." The beautiful setting that is brought to mind by the name of this brand of cigarettes is designed to counteract images of sickly people gasping under oxygen tents—a more probable associate of cigarette use.

Another example of the need for critical thinking comes from a conversation I once had with a cab driver. Our conversation got around to the way laundry products are advertised. He told me that he never paid any attention to advertisements and that they had no effect on his decision about which product to buy. He went on to say that he always buys the blue liquid detergent that is good at getting out "ring around the collar." Do you see the inconsistency in his statements? Although he believed that he was not allowing the advertising claims to influence him, in fact, they were directly determining his buying habits. I doubt if many people worried about "ring around the collar," "waxy-yellow build-up" on their kitchen floor, "fresh smelling carpets," or "soft elbows" before commercials told us that we were remiss and socially undesirable unless we attended to these details. The unstated assumption in these commercials is that the "problems" they identify (dark lines on the inside neck portion of shirts, or floors that aren't as clear as new ones) are important ones that can be remedied if you purchase the advertised products. The cab driver, for example, accepted the problem of ring around the collar as a valid concern and then purchased the advertised product without any conscious awareness of the ways his thoughts and behaviors had been influenced.

In every political campaign, candidates tell voters that they are opposed to waste, fraud, pollution, crime, and overpaid bureaucrats. These speeches are inevitably followed with loud cheering and applause. (Pay attention to this when you watch the next political convention—regardless of the party.) What's wrong with these speeches? The candidates never really say anything. I've never heard any candidate claim to be *for* waste, fraud, pollution, crime, or overpaid bureaucrats. Voters should ask them to be more explicit about their goals, how they would accomplish them, and where the money would come from to finance political plans.

Here's another example. The following problem was posed to 9-year-olds in the United States: "Jason bought three boxes of pencils. What else do you need to know to find out how many pencils he bought?" (Solorzano, 1985). Only 35% of the youngsters realized that the missing information was how many pencils were in each box. Here is a problem that was presented to a large sample of 13-year-olds: "An army bus holds 36 soldiers. If 1,128 soldiers are being bussed to their training site, how many busses are needed?" (Chance, 1986, p. 26). Most of the students tested had no trouble carrying out the computations. The problem came in using the answer in a meaningful way. Many rounded the answer they received to the nearest whole number and concluded that 31 busses were needed. Others gave a decimal answer (31.33) or showed the remainder from their long division. The problem was not one of basic computational skills, but of thinking about the kind of answer that the problem required and using a strategy that was different from one that was taught in school, namely rounding "up" to the next highest whole number rather than rounding to the nearest whole number. Perhaps, simple examples like this one provide the most convincing answer to the question of whether critical thinking should be taught. America's most precious commodity is thinking, educated people. We must make this the goal of education.

EMPIRICAL EVIDENCE THAT THINKING CAN BE IMPROVED

Everyone agrees that students learn *in college, but whether they learn to* think *is more controversial.*

—Wilbert J. McKeachie (1992, p. 3)

If you've been thinking critically about the idea of improving how you think, then you've probably begun to wonder if there is any evidence that thinking can be improved. Although there has been some debate about whether it is possible to produce long-lasting enhancements in the ability to think effectively (Block, 1985; Bruer, 1993; Facione, Facione, & Giancarlo, 2000; Glaser, 1984; Halpern & Nummedal, 1995; Norris, 1992), we now have a considerable body of evidence that thinking skills courses and thinking skills instruction that is embedded in other courses can have positive effects that are transferable to many situations. Numerous qualitatively different forms of outcome evaluations for thinking courses provide substantial evidence for the conclusion that it is possible to use education to improve the ability to think critically, especially when instruction is specifically designed to encourage the transfer of these skills to different situations and different domains of knowledge. In fact, it is difficult to identify any aspect of critical thinking that could not be taught and learned. We learn mathematics in the belief that mathematical skills can be used in real-world contexts in which they are needed; similarly, we learn writing and speaking skills in the belief that learners will use these skills when they write or speak in any context. When students take courses designed to improve their ability to work with numbers, write, or speak, most students show improvements. There is no reason why we should believe that instruction in critical thinking would not show the same positive effects.

Here is a brief summary of some of the findings that support the conclusion that critical thinking skills can be learned in educational settings and later used in other contexts:

1. A formal evaluation of a nationwide thinking skills program in Venezuela showed that students who had participated in classes designed for instruction in thinking skills showed greater gains in orally presented arguments and in answering open-ended essay questions than a comparable control group (Herrnstein, Nickerson, de Sanchez, & Swets, 1986). This study is particularly notable because the researchers used an experimental design that allowed them to conclude that it was the instruction and not some extraneous factor that caused students in the experimental group to improve in their ability to think critically. Students were assigned at random either to receive the thinking skills instruction or some other "control" instruction. Additionally, the oral arguments and writing samples were graded blind; that is, the graders did not know if the students they were assessing had received the thinking skills instruction or were in the control group. The results showed that the targeted thinking skills were transferred and used appropriately with novel topics. Students who received the thinking skills instruction showed greater gains than the control group students on tests of general aptitude (sometimes called intelligence tests), problem solving, decision making, reasoning, creative thinking, and language. This experiment provides strong support for the conclusion that improvements in thinking are possible when instruction is designed for this purpose. Unfortunately, because of a change in government support for this program, there are no long-term follow-up data from the Venezuela project, but at least in the short-term, it does seem that better thinking can be learned.

2. Self-reports by college students show that the overwhelming majority believe that they have made substantial gains in their ability to think critically after completing a thinking skills course (e.g., Block, 1985). Students rate themselves higher on numerous self-report scales including the willingness to suspend judgment, ability to evaluate conflicting claims, use of likelihood and uncertainty, and utilization of numerous problem-solving heuristics such as working backward from the goal, eliminating useless information, and evaluating the credibility of an information source. Of course, believing that you have improved in the ability to think critically is not the same as actually demonstrating improvements in critical thinking, but at least student self-assessments are in agreement with other sorts of data. Taken together with the other data presented later, self-reports add to our confidence in concluding that long-lasting enhancements in the ability to improve how we think can result from instruction in critical thinking.

3. Other researchers have used a Piagetian cognitive developmental approach to determine if critical thinking instruction was associated with greater developmental gains when compared to a control group. They found that adult students who received the critical thinking instruction showed greater gains in their level of cognitive development than a matched group that received standard college-level coursework (Fox, Marsh, & Crandall, 1983). This is an impressive improvement in light of

the finding that only 25% to 50% of first-year college students possess the skills needed for abstract logical thought when this ability is assessed with Piagetian measures (McKinnon & Renner, 1971).

In another study that used a cognitive developmental approach to determine the effectiveness of critical thinking instruction, Leming (1998) and Kronholm (1993) taught college students how to think critically about controversial public policy issues. They used the Reflective Judgment Interview that was developed by King and Kitchener (1994) to measure gains in critical thinking. The Reflective Judgment Interview is a standardized instrument in which students are presented with situations that call for the evaluation of evidence, expert opinion, and the adequacy of the argument. Leming and Kronholm found that the students who participated in the year-long project designed to develop their thinking skills showed significantly greater gains on the Reflective Judgment Interview than the students who had standard instruction. The authors believe that advancement in cognitive developmental stages is a better way to measure improvements in critical thinking because it can index incremental growth based on each student's starting point prior to instruction.

4. A theoretically advanced means of assessing changes in thinking ability is to study how a body of knowledge undergoes changes in mental representation. Although the theoretical rationale for this technique is beyond the scope of this book, the findings of these sorts of studies are easily comprehended. Schoenfeld and Herrmann (1982), for example, found that when college students were taught general thinking skills, they demonstrated substantial improvement in problem solving relative to students who received more traditional instruction. In addition, these students organized their mental representation of the content matter in ways that were more similar to an expert's mental representation than a control group did.

5. Using a skills approach, Facione (1991; Facione, Facione, & Giancarlo, 2000) found that college students who received coursework in critical thinking scored significantly higher on a multiple-choice test of thinking skills than comparable students who had not taken such a course. Other studies have also documented improvements on multiple-choice tests of critical thinking. For example, Lehman, Lempert, and Nisbett (1988) found that graduate-level college students improved significantly on a critical thinking test that included short scenarios about realistic situations. They concluded that training with general "rules" of thinking is generalized to other contexts.

6. The strongest support for beneficial outcomes from critical thinking instruction comes from a collection of studies by Nisbett and his colleagues (Nisbett, 1993). For example, in one study, Nisbett and his coauthors phoned students at their home after the coursework was completed, under the guise of conducting a survey. They found that students spontaneously applied the thinking skills that they had been taught in school when they encountered novel problems, even when the school-related context cues were absent (Fong, Krantz, & Nisbett, 1986). In a different study, inductive reasoning tasks were taught to college students using realistic scenarios from many different domains. Students were able to use these skills on a later test. The authors concluded that critical thinking is "a skill" and that "it is transferable" (Jepson, Krantz, & Nisbett, 1993, p. 82). Nisbett's (1993) edited book contains 16 chapters that show that rules of logic, statistics, causal deduction, and cost-benefit analysis can be taught in ways that will generalize to a variety of settings. A similar conclusion about the positive effects of courses designed to promote critical thinking was reached in another independent review of the literature (Bruer, 1993; Chance, 1986).

7. Additional support was reported by Kosonen and Winne (1995), who studied the transfer of critical thinking skills to a novel domain in a study that used college

students, secondary school students, and middle-school students as participants. Like Nisbett, they found that when students learned general rules about reasoning and practiced these skills with everyday "ill-structured" problems, the thinking skills transferred to new contexts and different domains. Most recently, Lovett and Greenhouse (2000) (building on the work of Paas, 1992, and others) reported similar results. Lovett and Greenhouse found that when students learned to solve multiple problems using "varied" problem sets during learning, the initial learning took significantly longer, but the students who learned with a variety of examples performed better on transfer problem sets than students who practiced only on similar problems. Thus, it seems that critical thinking skills are learned best and are most likely to transfer to novel situations when they are taught using a variety of different examples. Principles derived from empirical studies like these (and others) that show the successful transfer of critical thinking skills can serve as a model for instructional design. Many important principles from cognitive psychology are applied in this text to encourage effective learning that lasts.

All of the diverse findings (and many others that are not reviewed here because the relevant research literature is huge) point to the same conclusion: Adult students can learn to think more critically when they receive instruction that is designed for this purpose. The assessment studies that used comparison groups suggest that gains are most pronounced when instruction is specifically designed for the promotion of critical thinking. Critical thinking does not automatically result as a by-product of standard instruction in a content area. A systematic educational effort to improve thinking is needed to obtain these positive effects (Baron, 1990). Critical thinking instruction needs to focus overtly and self-consciously on the improvement of thinking, and the learning experience needs to include multiple examples across domains in order to maximize transfer.

Transfer of Training

Why Johnny can't read was one of the central questions raised about American education in the 1970s. Why Johnny can't think replaced it in the 1980s.

—A. L. Brown and J. C. Campione (1990, p. 108)

All of these studies that attest to the effectiveness of critical thinking instruction are studies of the generalizability or transfer of critical thinking skills. The real goal of any instruction to improve thinking is **transfer of training**. What I mean by transfer is the use of critical thinking skills in a wide variety of contexts. The whole enterprise of learning how to improve thinking would be of little value if these skills were used only in the classroom or only on problems that are very similar to those presented in class. Ideally, critical thinking skills should be used to recognize and resist unrealistic campaign promises, circular reasoning, faulty probability estimates, weak arguments by analogy, or language designed to mislead whenever and wherever it is encountered. Critical thinkers should be better able to solve or offer reasonable solutions to real-world problems, whether it is the problem of nuclear war or how to set up a new video recorder. These skills should also be long lasting and useful for the many decades of critical thinking that most of us will face. Admittedly, these are lofty goals, but they are important ones. The best way to promote the kind of transfer I'm advocating is with the conscious and deliberate use of the skills that you learn in a wide variety of contexts. Students can actively enhance transfer by looking for instances that call for critical thinking skills and using them.

The problems and review exercises that are provided in the exercise book that accompanies this text, *Thinking Critically About Critical Thinking*, are designed to maximize transfer. A variety of different types of problems are presented about different topics. By working through these problems, you will increase the likelihood that you will recall and use the thinking skills that are presented in the text and in real life when you really need them. There are many variables that affect how likely you are to transfer a thinking skill from one area of study to another, but we do know that transfer can and does occur (Klaczynski, 1993). Be sure to be on the lookout for other instances when these thinking skills are needed, and be sure to use them!

LEARNING TO THINK CRITICALLY:
A FOUR PART MODEL

The model that I have proposed for critical thinking instruction consists of four parts (Halpern, 1998, in press):

1. Explicitly learn the skills of critical thinking
2. Develop the disposition for effortful thinking and learning
3. Direct learning activities in ways that increase the probability of transcontextual transfer (structure training)
4. Make metacognitive monitoring explicit and overt

Let's consider each of these parts.

A Skills Approach to Critical Thinking

As you work your way through the chapters in this book, you will come across many different thinking skills, with each chapter containing those skills that are especially useful in thinking about the chapter topic. For example, the thinking skills used in understanding likelihood and uncertainty are presented in that chapter. You may be wondering what a "thinking skill" is. Some examples should help. Here is a list of generic skills that are important in many situations.

A critical thinker can

- Recognize semantic slanting and guilt by association.
- Seek out contradictory evidence.
- Use the metacognitive knowledge that allows novices to monitor their own performance and to decide when additional help is needed.
- Make risk: benefit assessments.
- Generate a reasoned method for selecting among several possible courses of actions.
- Give reasons for choices as well as varying the style and amount of detail in explanations depending on who is receiving the information.
- Recall relevant information when it is needed.
- Use skills for learning new techniques efficiently and relating new knowledge to information that was previously learned.
- Use numerical information including the ability to think probabilistically and express thoughts numerically.

- Understand basic research principles.
- Demonstrate an advanced ability to read and write complex prose.
- Present a coherent and persuasive argument on a controversial, contemporary topic.
- Provide complex instructions in language that is appropriate for the audience.
- Use matrices and other diagrams for communication.
- Synthesize information from a variety of sources.
- Determine credibility and use this information in formulating and communicating decisions.

Critical thinking instruction is predicated on two assumptions: (a) that there are clearly identifiable and definable thinking skills that students can be taught to recognize and apply appropriately, and (b) if recognized and applied, the students will be more effective thinkers. Thus, one part of the model for learning to become a better thinker is learning how to use the skills of critical thinking and how to recognize when a particular skill or skills are needed.

The Disposition for Effortful Thinking and Learning

All our dignity lies in thought.

—Blaise Pascal (1623–1662)

No one can become a better thinker just by reading a book or even by just learning a set of thinking skills that would be useful, if they were used. An essential component of critical thinking is developing the attitude or disposition of a critical thinker. Good thinkers are motivated and willing to exert the conscious effort needed to work in a planful manner, to check for accuracy, to gather information, and to persist when the solution isn't obvious or requires several steps.

Performance-Competence Distinction

Very often there is an important distinction between what people *can* do and what they actually do. This is called the **performance-competence distinction**. It is of no value to learn a variety of critical thinking skills if you never use them. Developing a **critical thinking attitude** is at least as important as developing thinking skills. Sears and Parsons (1991) described critical thinking as an "ethic" in order to emphasize the importance of attitude to good thinking. Facione, Facione, and Giancarlo (2000) found that students who had positive attitudes toward critical thinking showed the greatest gains from critical thinking instruction. Many errors occur not because people can't think critically, but because they don't. One of the major differences between good and poor thinkers, and correspondingly between good and poor students, is their attitude. A critical thinker will exhibit the following dispositions or attitudes:

1. Willingness to Plan

If everybody thought before they spoke, the silence would be deafening.

—George Barzan
(Cybernation International; http://www.cyber-
nation.com/victory/quotes/thoughtsandthinking.html)

I've watched thousands of students (literally) take exams. There are always some students who begin to write as soon as the exam hits their desk. They just plow ahead and begin writing before they begin thinking. Not surprisingly, the results are a disoriented jumble that often bears little relation to the questions being asked. When asked a question in class, they will often answer with the first idea that comes to mind. These students need to learn to check their impulsivity and plan their response. They should be outlining or diagramming the structure of a response before they begin to write. Planning, the invisible first step in critical thinking, is essential. With repeated practice, anyone can develop the **habit of planning**.

2. Flexibility

In a classic old book, Rokeach (1960) talks about rigidity and dogmatism as the characteristics of a "closed mind." A person with a closed mind responds negatively to new ideas by stating, "That's the way I've always done it." Another common retort that shows the unwillingness to consider new ideas is the well-worn phrase, "If it ain't broke, don't fix it." This sort of close-minded response cuts off consideration of new ideas. By contrast, an attitude of flexibility is marked by a willingness to consider new options, try things a new way, reconsider old problems. An open-minded person is willing to suspend judgment, gather more information, and attempt to clarify difficult issues. This does not mean that all opinions are equally good or that judgment should take a backseat to openness. It does mean, though, that a critical thinker is willing to think in new ways, review evidence, and stick with a task until all reasonable options have been considered.

3. Persistence

"You may be disappointed if you fail, but you are doomed if you don't try."

—Beverly Sills (quoted in James Rogan, *Bits & Pieces*, 1993, p. 7)

Baron (1987), in an excellent essay on the significance of attitudes, emphasized the importance of persistence to academic success. Closely related to persistence is the willingness to start or engage in a thoughtful task. Some people look at a seemingly difficult task and opt not to even begin the thinking process. They're defeated at the start. Others will start working on a task and stop before it is completed. Good thinking is hard work that requires diligent persistence. Critical thinking is usually effortful: It can make you as tired as any physical labor, but can be much more rewarding. In a comparison of students who were unsuccessful in mathematics with those who were successful, researchers found that much of the difference in success rates was directly attributable to differences in attitudes. The unsuccessful students believed that if a problem could not be solved in less than 10 minutes, then they would not be able to solve it. By contrast, the successful students persisted in working on difficult problems (Schoenfeld, 1985).

4. Willingness to Self-Correct, Admit Errors, and Change Your Mind When the Evidence Changes

In science it often happens that scientists say, "You know that's a really good argument; my position is mistaken," and then they would actually change their minds and you never hear that old view from them again. They really do it. It

doesn't happen as often as it should, because scientists are human and change is
sometimes painful.

—Carl Sagan
(The Review: Science and Pseudoscience Review in Mental Health;
http://www.pseudoscience.org/definitions-pseudo.html)

We all make mistakes. In fact, creative thoughts and actions would not be possible if we were unwilling to make mistakes, at least some of the time. Instead of becoming defensive about errors, good thinkers can acknowledge them and learn from them. People with good critical thinking attitudes utilize feedback, try to figure out what went wrong, and try to recognize the factors that led to the error. They recognize ineffective strategies and abandon them in order to improve the thinking process. Critical thinkers are also able to change their mind or the conclusion that they reached, when new information warrants such a change. They do not need to hold onto an old idea that is no longer justified.

It is interesting to note that the general public usually does not like it when a public figure changes his or her mind, especially when the change is away from a conclusion that was popular. However, if a person is open to a fair evaluation of new information, sometimes that information will lead to a different conclusion. It would be foolish to hold to an old conclusion or belief when it is no longer warranted. The ability to change one's conclusion when new or better information becomes known is not "waffling" or some other negative term that is used to describe someone whose views change as readily as the shifting direction of the wind. What is needed is a new term that has positive connotations to be used for critical thinkers who are willing to change conclusions when sound evidence warrants a change. The progress of science depends on such people, although unfortunately this is one attitude of critical thinking that is still all too rare.

5. Being Mindful

In order to develop basic thinking skills, it is necessary to direct your attention to the processes and products of your own thoughts. Langer (2000) defines **mindfulness** as "the simple act of drawing novel distinctions" (p. 220). It is the opposite of the "automatic pilot" that we use for routine tasks like setting the dinner table, getting to school or work every day, or watching television in the evening. According to Langer, learning requires a mindful engagement with the task and materials. She told a humorous personal story about a case of mindlessness that makes this point well (Langer, 1989). When shopping one day, the clerk told her that she had not signed the back of the credit card she was using. Langer signed the card, then handed it back to the clerk. The clerk then processed the sale and had Langer sign the credit slip. Then, dutifully, as she had no doubt been instructed, the clerk checked the signature on the back of the newly signed credit card with the signature on the credit slip. She never realized that she had just seen Langer sign both!

As long as we respond in a mindless or routinized way, problems worth solving will never be recognized, and creative solutions will be missed.

6. Consensus Seeking

Committee and group organizational structures are most often the norm in the world of work. Critical thinkers need to be predisposed to seek ways in which consensus among group members can be achieved. They maintain an awareness of the social realities that need to be overcome so that thoughts can become actions. Consensus seekers need high-level communication skills, but they also need to find ways to compromise and to achieve agreement. Without this disposition and related interpersonal skills, even the most brilliant thinkers will find that they cannot convert thoughts to actions.

Transfer of Training

In becoming a better thinker, it is important to have a large repertoire of critical thinking skills and to be willing to engage in the effortful process of using them. The third component of this model involves recognizing when critical thinking is needed, so that you can select the most appropriate skills for the situation. This is the Achilles' heel of transfer. The problem in learning thinking skills that are needed in multiple contexts is that there are no obvious cues in the context to trigger the recall of the thinking skill. Critical thinkers need to create the recall cues from the structural aspects of the problem or argument, so that when the structural aspects are present, they can serve as cues for retrieval. A similar point was made by Hummel and Holyoak (1997), who said, "First, thinking is structure sensitive. Reasoning, problem solving, and learning . . . depend on a capacity to code and manipulate relational knowledge."

When critical thinking skills are learned so that they transfer appropriately and spontaneously, critical thinkers can focus on the structure so the underlying characteristics become salient instead of the domain-specific surface characteristics. An example should help here because the idea of transferring skills to novel areas is highly abstract.

Suppose that you understand the way contrast effects can influence one's judgment. For this example, suppose that you know that if you are offered several part-time jobs that pay $6 an hour, $8.50 an hour will seem like more money than if you had been offered several part-time jobs that pay $10 an hour. Even if you know that contrast effects can influence judgments, will you be able to recognize the power of contrast effects on your judgment in a totally different situation, such as when your friend begins a story about his "brush with the law" by telling you about all of the people from your old high school class who are now in jail? His "brush with the law" will seem much less serious when it is told after stories about people you know who committed serious crimes than it would if he had told it after stories about people you know who are successful and have not committed any crimes. In this example, your hypothetical friend is making his own crime seem less bad by contrasting it with more serious ones. How can you recognize that the same principle of contrast is affecting your judgment in both situations (judgments about pay per hour and seriousness of a crime)? If you can recognize that the same principle is at work, you could use the same critical thinking skills to prevent the effect of contrast from influencing how you think. In other words, how can you learn to apply your knowledge about contrast effects in different sorts of situations?

There is an old saying in psychology that "the head remembers what it does." It is important to direct your own learning so that the skills of critical thinking are learned (encoded) in a way that will facilitate their recall in novel situations. It is what learners do that determines what gets learned. Here are some examples of thinking tasks that are designed to help with the transfer of critical thinking skills.

They require readers to perform certain tasks or answer carefully crafted questions that draw attention to structural aspects of the problem or argument: If you complete the exercises in the workbook that accompanies this text (*Thinking Critically About Critical Thinking*), you will

- Draw a diagram or other graphic display that organizes the information.
- List additional information you would want before answering a question.
- Explain why a particular multiple-choice alternative was selected. Which is second best? Why?
- State the problem in at least two ways.
- Identify which information is most important. Which information is least important? Why?
- Categorize the findings in a meaningful way.
- List two solutions for problems.
- Identify what is wrong with an assertion that was made in the question.
- Present two reasons that support the conclusion and two reasons that do not support the conclusion.
- Identify the type of persuasive technique being used.
- Present two actions you would take to improve the design of a study that was described.

Tasks like these require learners to focus on structural aspects of the problems so that the learner can identify and use an appropriate critical thinking skill.

Metacognitive Monitoring

Metacognition refers to our knowledge of what we know (or what we know about what we know) and the use of this knowledge to direct further learning activities. When engaging in critical thinking, you will need to monitor your thinking process, check whether progress is being made toward an appropriate goal, ensure accuracy, and make decisions about the use of time and mental effort. There is good evidence that you can become a better thinker and learner by developing the habit of monitoring your understanding and by judging the quality of your learning (Cohen, Freeman, & Wolf, 1996). Metacognition is the executive or "boss" function that guides how adults use different learning strategies and make decisions about the allocation of limited cognitive resources. Numerous studies have found that good learners and thinkers engage in more metacognitive activities than poor learners and thinkers, and that the skills and attitudes of metacognitive activities can be taught and learned so that students can direct their own learning strategies and make judgments about how much effort to allocate to a cognitive task.

For example, when learners are required to provide reasons and evidence to support a conclusion and counterreasons and conflicting evidence that refutes the conclusion, they must focus on the quality of their thinking. The giving of reasons forces thinkers to "tickle their memory." By this I mean they have to access information stored in memory. They also have to consider both positive and negative evidence. It is well documented that we tend to weigh evidence much more heavily when it favors a belief that we hold over evidence that disconfirms a personal belief (Stanovich & West, 1997). Numerous studies have found that good learners and thinkers engage in more metacognitive activities than poor learners and thinkers,

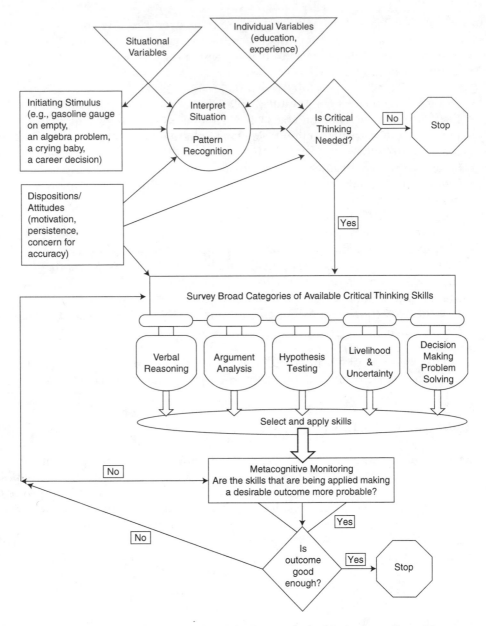

FIG. 1.1 A schematic model of the critical thinking process. Notice how dispositions, individual background variables, and situational variables all influence the way a situation is interpreted and the decision as to whether or not it requires the effortful process of critical thinking. If critical thinking is needed, then individuals select the critical thinking skills that are most likely to be appropriate for the situation. Five categories of skills are shown in this diagram. Good critical thinkers have a large repertoire of critical thinking skills to choose from and are skilled at making selections that are appropriate for the situation. (Critical thinking skills and the selection of the appropriate skill are learned.) Metacognitive monitoring is repeatedly cycled as individuals determine if the skills they are using are increasing the likelihood of a desirable outcome or if other skills are needed. When a "good enough" outcome is achieved, the process is stopped.

and that the skills and attitudes of metacognitive activities can be taught and learned so that students can direct their own learning strategies and make judgments about how much effort to allocate to a cognitive task (Nelson, 1996; Swanson, 1990).

A schematic diagram of the critical thinking process, including individual differences and situation variables is shown in Figure 1.1. Notice how dispositions and attitudes influence the process at multiple points, beginning with recognizing patterns in the environment that may require critical thinking (e.g., a gas gauge pointing to empty or a career decision that needs to be made) and ending with the decision when to end the thinking process. The skills of critical thinking are selected and applied as individuals monitor their progress toward a desirable outcome. Good instruction with structure training will make all of the stages of the process more efficient and more likely to be successful.

One of the most frequently asked questions concerning thinking skills instruction is whether learning to be a critical thinker can make someone more intelligent. As noted earlier (and in numerous other reviews, see for example, Perkins & Grotzer, 1997), substantial evidence exists that instruction in critical thinking really can help people think better and that improved thinking will transfer to novel contexts. Can critical thinking improve intelligence? The answer to this important question depends upon how intelligence is defined.

Before you read further, stop for a minute to think about your own definition of intelligence. If a program of instruction can help learners to think better, have they become more intelligent?

INTELLIGENCE AND THINKING SKILLS

If we want to improve America's schools, we will have to apply in the classroom what we know about humans as intelligent, learning, thinking cultures.

—Bruer (1993, p. 1)

One of the most frequently asked questions concerning thinking skills instruction is whether learning to be a critical thinker will make someone more intelligent. The answer to this important question depends on how intelligence is defined.

The Nature of Intelligence

Solving problems is the specific achievement of intelligence.

—George Polya (1957)

Intelligence is one of the most controversial topics in psychology. It is a basic topic in thinking because intelligence is the "stuff" of which thought is made. It is difficult to imagine a context in which intelligence is not manifested or needed. The term intelligence is used commonly in everyday language. Most people believe that they are at least about average or above average in intelligence (Brim, 1966). (Despite Garrison Keillor's assurances to the contrary, you should realize that this is mathematically absurd because most people can't be above average.)

Psychologists continue to debate exactly what the term "intelligence" *should* mean (Ceci, 1996; Herrnstein & Murray, 1994; Neisser et al., 1996). Think for a minute about your own definition of intelligence. A dictionary won't be much help, because dictionaries define difficult multifaceted concepts like intelligence with a few simple words that reflect some expert's opinion of what a word means. What *should* we mean when we refer to intelligence? This question leads to another and even more important question, "Who is the appropriate authority to decide what it means to be intelligent?" (The importance of thinking about definitions is a critical thinking skill that is presented in more detail in Chapter 3, "The Relationship Between Thought and Language.") When Robert Sternberg (1982), a psychologist known for his research on understanding the concept of intelligence, asked people to list the characteristics of an intelligent person, the following answers were frequently given: "reasons logically and well," "reads widely," "keeps an open mind," and "reads with high comprehension." Most people share these intuitive notions of intelligence. These everyday notions of intelligence are consistent with the definition of critical thinking. Thus, for most people, intelligent thinking is very similar to the idea of critical thinking.

Sternberg's (1999) own definition of intelligence is concerned with the way people "achieve success in life, given one's personal standards, within one's sociocultural context" (http://spider.apa.org:80/ftdocs/gpr/1999/december/gpr34292.html). Sternberg's theory of Successful Intelligence is composed of analytic, practical, and creative intelligences. Each of these three components of Successful Intelligence can be measured separately, and most tasks involve some combination of two or three of these intelligences. Sternberg and his colleagues developed a program for teaching successful intelligence to middle-school students (Williams, Blythe, White, Li, Sternberg, & Gardner, 1996) that they evaluated in many different settings (Gardner, Krechevsky, Sternberg, & Okaguki, 1994). They reported that students taught with their three-part intelligence program outperformed control groups that did not receive this instruction. Thus, they concluded that they successfully taught the children to be more intelligent.

Sternberg is not alone in his belief that intelligence can be enhanced with programs specifically designed for this purpose, although the various researchers do disagree about the appropriate content for programs designed to enhance intelligence and about the components that make up intelligence. Perkins and Grotzer (1997) describe a program of instruction that is similar to the approach being used in this text, with specific instruction in thinking skills, dispositions, metacognition, and transfer of training. They concluded that "intelligence can be taught to at least a limited extent, with more research required to determine the extent to which intelligence can be increased. Instruction can help people to enhance reflective intelligence with significant generality and persistence" (p. 1125).

The idea that intelligence can be taught is not new. The notion of intelligence as learning and thinking was articulated early in this century by the famous Russian psychologist, Lev Vygotsky (1978). He offered an alternative to the static view of human learning and intelligence as a "fixed quantity" that could be observed and assessed in laboratory settings. According to Vygotsky, intelligence is best indexed by the way in which people learn, especially when they receive feedback about their learning, rather than in the level of learning they have achieved at some point in time. This emphasis is not surprising in light of Vygotsky's work with disadvantaged populations in the aftermath of the Russian Revolutionary war, in which many children never had the opportunity to develop their intelligence because of the severe privations of war. These same children often learned new skills and knowledge very quickly when they were given the opportunity to learn, demonstrating a level of intelligence that could not have been predicted by any standardized measure that might have been used to test them. Thus, it was their ability to learn from their experiences that Vygotsky used to define and measure intelligence, not a score on a test or similar other measure.

Several contemporary psychologists have suggested that conceptualizations of intelligence need to include emotional aspects of life's success, such as having rewarding relationships, empathy, good self-esteem, and optimism (Goleman, 1995; Mehrabian, 2000; Salovey & Sluyter, 1997). One way of linking the literature on emotional intelligence to critical thinking is to consider interpersonal situations as contexts that call on critical thinking skills. For example, an interpersonal problem at work is no different from any other problem in that it requires good problem statements, generation of many possible solutions, and selection of a solution that maximizes a desired outcome—steps that are used to solve any problem, regardless of contexts.

Perhaps the most famous definition of intelligence was offered by E. G. Boring many years ago in response to the question, "What is intelligence?" He replied: "intelligence is what the tests test" (1932, p. 35). The "tests" he was referring to are, of course, standardized intelligence tests. The way psychologists have measured intelligence has had a direct effect on the way they have come to think about intelligence.

The Measurement of Intelligence

As you can imagine, the measurement of intelligence has proven to be a difficult task. The underlying idea is that intelligence exists, and because it exists, it exists in some quantity (in each individual), and because it exists in some quantity, it can be measured. The only difficulty with this line of reasoning is: "How?"

There is an obvious need to be able to quantify or measure intelligence. Historically, intelligence tests were designed for a very practical reason. In the early part of this century, the French government realized the need to know which children should receive regular classroom instruction and which should receive remedial or accelerated instruction. Alfred Binet and Theodore Simon were given the job of designing a test that could be used to place children in the appropriate educational setting. Modern intelligence tests are still used for this purpose.

Binet and Simon recognized that the type of question that an intelligent 4-year-old can answer correctly is very different from the type of question that an intelligent 8-year-old can answer correctly. Thus, they devised a test with items that varied in difficulty for each age level. The tests designed in France by Binet and Simon have been revised many times. The most popular revision was undertaken by Lewis Terman, a psychologist at Stanford University. Terman's revision of the earlier intelligence test is commonly referred to as the Stanford-Binet. Another popular battery of intelligence tests was written by David Wechsler. He authored two separate tests, the Wechsler Intelligence Scale for Children (WISC) and Wechsler Adult Intelligence Scale (WAIS) designed for adults over 15 years of age. Wechsler's intelligence tests yield three IQ scores—one based on verbal test items, one based on performance test items, and one based on all of the test items, called full-scale IQ. Following are some test items written to be similar to the ones found in the WAIS (Jensen, 1980, pp. 144–145).

Verbal Test Items
1. At what temperature does water freeze?
2. Who wrote *The Republic*?
3. Why is gold worth more than copper?
4. How many inches are there in 3 1/2 feet?
5. If six men can finish a job in 3 days, how many men would be needed to finish it in 1 day?
6. In what way are sperm and ovum alike?
7. Repeat a series of digits after the test administrator recites them. (For example, a test taker would hear "8175621" and then repeat the digits either in the same order they were given or in reverse order.)
8. Explain the meaning of strange.
9. Explain the meaning of adumbrate.

Performance Test Items
Test takers are asked to:
10. Translate the numerals 1 to 9 into code symbols (e.g., 1 = [, 2 = }, 3 = #, etc.).
11. Tell what is missing from familiar objects or scenes (e.g., a clock without hands).
12. Use wooden cubes painted red and white to duplicate a design shown on cards.
13. Arrange a series of cartoons into a logical sequence.
14. Assemble jigsaw puzzles.

The actual test items vary in difficulty and are presented in increasing difficulty within each type of test. The IQ score that an individual receives is determined by calculating how many questions she or he answered correctly relative to the average person in the standardization group.

As you can see from these items, intelligence is measured with a variety of questions. The general knowledge verbal questions tap information that most people would be expected to learn as a member of our society. For most of us, answering questions about the temperature at which water freezes involves only memory retrieval, but it assumes that we had the opportunity to learn this information. Some of the more difficult ones, like "Who wrote *The Republic*?" would obviously favor those with a good academic background. Abstract reasoning about the nature of supply-and-demand is needed to answer the question "Why is gold worth more than copper?" The ability to use numbers as well as the knowledge that there are 12 inches in one foot is needed to answer the fourth question. The answer to question number 6 is difficult because the differences between sperm and ovum may be more salient than their similarities. Of course, you also need to know what these terms mean, again favoring anyone with a good (and standard) academic background. Repeating a series of digits forward or backward requires good memory skills. If you practice the memory aids (mnemonics) discussed in the memory chapter, you can go off the top of the scale on this question. The eighth and ninth questions are standard vocabulary questions.

The performance items are more difficult to categorize. Because most of the tests are timed, speed is an important factor in determining performance IQ. Changing numerals to code symbols involves a careful balance of speed and accuracy in order to finish as many numerals to code transformations as possible with few errors. Question 11 tests your knowledge of common objects. The ability to duplicate designs is a spatial ability. Arranging a series of cartoons in a logical sequence requires the test taker to generate hypotheses about the actions depicted. It is necessary to be able to see a whole object from its parts, a spatial ability, to put jigsaw puzzles together. Intelligence tests assume that the test taker is motivated to perform well (which is often not true) and that the test taker has had the sorts of experiences that are assumed to be "normative," another assumption that is often unwarranted. The notion of intelligence that is embedded in standardized tests is that intelligence is a fixed quantity.

Not surprisingly, intelligence testing yields lower scores for minority groups and any low-income population because these groups have not had the same learning experiences that are assumed by the writers of the IQ tests. Readers are probably aware of the recent, acrimonious controversies surrounding some of these issues, many of them generated by the publication of a massive book entitled *The Bell Curve* (Herrnstein & Murray, 1994). The authors argue that intelligence is largely inherited, that it is measured fairly by standard intelligence tests, that it remains fairly constant from childhood into old age, and that it is affected only marginally by education. I disagree with all of these points (Halpern, 1995).

LEARNING TO BE INTELLIGENT

Cognitive science enables us to go beyond intelligence tests and understand how the human mind solves problems.

—Robert Sternberg (1992, p. 53)

Thus far, we have considered several different notions of what it means to be intelligent and some of the problems in determining how intelligent someone is. Because this text is concerned with thinking and helping you to learn how to improve your thinking, it seems reasonable to return to the question posed at the beginning of this section: "Will learning to be a critical thinker make you more intelligent?" For those psychologists who view intelligence as a fixed quantity that can measured with test items that depend, in part, on the opportunities that are afforded to individuals (e.g., the rich have more and better educational opportunities than the poor), then their answer will be "no." However, along with an increasing number of psychologists, I believe that the static notion of intelligence is wrong and damaging. If any individual can learn to be a better thinker and subsequently can use newly acquired thinking skills across a wide variety of contexts, then I believe that, by definition, that person has learned to be more intelligent. There will always be some people who are more intelligent than others. There are individual differences and limits on how well each of us can think and reason, and certainly intelligence is also determined, in part, by genetics. However, we all have some amount of undeveloped potential; everyone can make substantial gains in his or her intellectual abilities. Even though we can't all be geniuses, we can all learn to think more intelligently.

Many contemporary psychologists agree that intelligence is comprised of skills that can be enhanced with training (deGroot, 1983; Nickerson, 1986; Perkins & Grotzer, 1997). Sadler and Whimbey (1985), pioneers in the area of thinking skills improvement, echoed these sentiments when they defined intelligence as "a complex of skills" (p. 44). The same basic idea can be seen in deGroot's (1983) definition of intelligence as a mental program consisting of heuristics and in Nickerson's (1987) advice to teachers that they teach for tactics. Skills, strategies, heuristics, and tactics are all different words for the same idea—learnable components of intelligent thought.

BECOMING A BETTER THINKER: THE QUICK AND EASY WAY

"A sucker is born every minute."

—P. T. Barnum (cited in Bartlett, 1980, p. 460)

As I raced through the supermarket after work one day, I was surprised to see a candy bar called "Think!" Just what I needed, a candy bar with "mind-enhancing ingredients." And to think (oops, pardon the pun) that I was working hard to learn better thinking skills when all I had to do was eat a candy bar. Apparently, I am not the only one to wonder about "Think!" candy bars. The Center for Science in the Public Interest, a nonprofit organization of health and science professionals, investigated this candy bar in a recent issue of *Nutrition Action HealthLetter* (Science in the Public Interest, 2000). They contacted the candy bar company for evidence to back up the claim that the ingredients in "Think!" can help you "stay sharp." Here's the company's response: "'We're not claiming that it helps you think,' insists Garret Jennings, the inventor of Think!, the 'Food for Thought' bar. . . . But, if somebody feels great after a Think! Bar,' asks Jennings, 'who cares if that is just a placebo effect?'" (p. 12).

I hope that your response to the question posed at the end of the last paragraph is, "I do." A placebo is used as a control or comparison whenever drugs are tested—it is the condition that contains no active drugs—you may know it as a "sugar pill." Sometimes just the belief that we are taking a "drug" that will improve the ability to think can lead us to believe that we really are thinking better, even when we are not. But then, I guess this thinking-candy is targeted at consumers who are not good thinkers in the first place. Of course, it is possible that there are some ingredients that could enhance the ability to think. The question for thoughtful consumers is "What is the evidence that this product does what the manufacturer claims?" According to Science in the Public Interest, the answer is "none."

Unfortunately, there are no quick and easy programs that will make you a better thinker, despite some unscrupulous claims that you can think better instantly, without really trying. One article in a supermarket-checkout-line "newspaper" claimed that pregnant women could make their as yet unborn children more intelligent by listening to fine music and reading classical literature during their pregnancy. Other ludicrous schemes for better thinking include breathing into paper bags and listening to subliminal tapes. A large-scale study by The National Academy of Sciences concluded that there is no scientific evidence to support the claim that biofeedback, "neurolinguistic programming," subliminal learning, or other commercial "super learning" techniques can improve your thinking (Gillette, 1987; Greenwald, Spangenberg, Pratkanis, & Eskenazi, 1991; Hostetler, 1988). In a second major study, the National Research Council (1994) found that there is no evidence to support claims that sleep-learning is possible, even though most of us believe that it sure would be nice. A trip through most so-called "health food stores" will reveal a wide variety of products and pseudo-medicines that claim or suggest that they can improve your memory, enhance your thinking, or do whatever else is desirable (e.g., make you thin, sexy, strong, and smart). However, there is usually little or no valid evidence that any of these products can bring about their promised effects.

THINKING ABOUT THINKING

You are today where your thoughts have brought you; you will be tomorrow where your thoughts take you.

—James Allen (Cybernation International,
http://www.cybernation.com/victory/quotes..subjects/
quotes_thoughtsandthinking.html)

There are many different ways to conceptualize the thinking process. From the perspective of a neuropsychologist or biologist, thinking is the activation of groups of neurons. Other researchers study the medium of thought, that is, the conscious and unconscious use of symbols, images, and words. Another approach is to conceptualize thinking as the flow and transformation of information through a series of stages. As I think about using the brain to think about the way the brain works, I am reminded about a joke I once heard: A comedian commented that he never eats tongue, a common food in many cultures, because he wonders if the tongue he is eating is tasting him while he is tasting it. Similarly, I wonder if we can use our brain to reveal its own mysteries?

Thinking as a Biological Process

The brain exists in order to construct representations of the world.

—Philip Johnson-Laird (quoted in Restak, 1988, p. 235)

Researchers from many fields have spent their lifetimes trying to understand what people do when they think. Brain researchers are interested in understanding how the brain and other parts of the nervous system work. Every time you have a thought, feel an emotion, or receive information through your senses, your nervous system is involved. If you could examine your own brain, you would no doubt be surprised to find that it looks like a giant mushy walnut with the consistency of a soft-boiled egg. There is nothing in its appearance to even suggest that it is the foundation of human thought.

The capacity of the human brain is awesome. "If each of the brain's 10 to 15 billion neurons is capable of only two states, on or off, the capacity of the brain would be 2^{10} billionth power. To write out this number at the rate of one digit per second would take ninety years" (The Chronicle of Higher Education, 1987, p. A2). Even if these figures are off by a few billion or so, it is clear that we each have some undeveloped potential. The human brain has remained essentially unchanged since the dawn of modern history, yet during that time humans have used this amazing mass to develop advanced technologies that include the ability to visit distant planets and have more than doubled the average expected life span. What has changed is "the information that is going into the brain and the processing it receives" (Machado, cited in Walsh, 1981, p. 640.) It is the ability to learn and to think that has changed the world.

Although brain researchers have discovered fascinating links between the physiology and anatomy of the brain and intellectual skills, there is still much to learn. Everything that we are or ever will be can, at least on one level, be attributed to patterns of neurons that communicate via chemical messengers. The connections among neurons change as a function of experience (and genetically coded information). Experience is the major architect of the brain (Gazzaniga, Ivry, & Magnun, 1998). We can change our brains by selecting different sorts of experiences. Every time you learn something new, you have changed your brain. If you have learned anything new since you started reading this book, you are already a changed person—I have "messed with" your brain. I hope you will agree that I left it better than it was before you started reading. As a discipline, brain research is still in its infancy.

Thus far, biologists have discovered that factors like malnutrition, lead poisoning, and some drugs can impair the capacity for higher level thought. Current science fiction notions about brain transplants, pills to make us smarter, or miracle foods that prolong neural life remain in the realm of late-night movies, Saturday afternoon matinees, and research laboratories. Learning is the best way to rewire the brain.

Thinking as Imagery and Silent Speech

Thinking is the talking of the soul with itself.

—Author Unknown
Found in a Fortune Cookie

Psychologists at the beginning of the century believed that thinking was composed of mental images. Later, other psychologists hypothesized that thinking was simply a form of "silent speech," much like talking to yourself without vocalization. In order to test these hypotheses, psychologists would ask subjects to describe what they did when responding to certain questions. Let's try some examples. As you answer each question posed below, try to be aware of what you did as you "thought about it."

1. How many windows are in your living room?
2. What does your mother look like?
3. What letter comes after N in the alphabet?

THE FAMILY CIRCUS.   **By Bil Keane**

12-2
Copyright 1982
The Register and Tribune
Syndicate, Inc.

"Thinking is when the picture is in your head
with the sound turned off."

4. Name a word that rhymes with "shoe."
5. How much is 2 + 3?
6. Can you define "critical thinking"?

As you answered these questions, were you aware of the use of images and/or words? Most people find that when they are asked to describe some concrete object, like the number of windows in their living room or their mother, they are aware of picture-like images. In fact, it seems almost impossible to answer these questions without generating an internal representation or utilizing **imagery** in some way. Can you describe your mother or anyone else without creating an image? Questions like 3 or 4, which involve the order of letters in the alphabet and the sounds of words, usually require an individual to recite the items silently. (Did you sing "l-m-n-o-p" to yourself in order to answer Question 3?) When answering questions like 5 and 6, people are often unable to say how they arrived at an answer. (By the way, if your answer to Question 6 was "no," you should go back and reread the beginning sections in this chapter.) Most people feel that the answers just seemed to "pop into their heads" without their being conscious of the "medium" or "stuff" of thought.

Currently, research psychologists are debating whether the "true" medium of thought involves imagery, or sentence-like propositions, or both. For most people, the question is moot, as almost everyone reports that, at least under some circumstances, they are aware of both mental images and "silent speech" during the thought process. Most of the time, however, we have little or no conscious awareness of what happens when we think.

Sometimes, thinking can be improved if we "work at" generating an image or using speech-like thought. Albert Einstein often credited his ability to solve difficult problems to his extensive use of imagery. The most famous use of imagery was recorded by the chemist Kekule. He knew that if he could understand the structure of a benzene molecule he would have hit on one of the most important discoveries in organic chemistry. Kekule knew that most chemical molecules are long strands of atoms, and that the structure of a benzene molecule had to be different. In order to solve this problem, Kekule practiced generating visual images that might help him to find the right one. His hard work was rewarded when the historic answer came to him this way:

> Again the atoms were gamboling before my eyes . . . My mental eye . . . could now distinguish larger structures . . . all twining and twisting in a snakelike motion. But look! What was that! One of the snakes had seized hold of its own tail, and the form whirled mockingly before my eyes. As if by a sudden flash of lightning I awoke (Kekule, quoted in Rothenberg, 1979, pp. 395–396).

The image of a snake biting its own tail led Kekule to the discovery that the benzene molecule was structured as a closed ring and not like strands of the other molecules. Thus, he was able to use visual imagery to direct his thoughts about a complex topic.

Words also serve to direct and stimulate thought. Although it may be obvious that thoughts are usually communicated with language, it is also true that language helps to generate thoughts. The generative role of language can be seen in an experiment by Glucksberg and Weisberg (1966). They used a classic problem in the psychology literature that was originally devised by Duncker (1945). In this problem, subjects are required to attach a candle to a wall so that it could be lit. They are given a candle, a box of matches, and some thumbtacks. Stop now and think how you would go about solving this problem if you were given only these materials (Fig 1.2). Don't go on until you've thought about it.

The best solution is to dump the matches from their box, tack the box to the wall, and set the candle in the box. Most subjects have difficulty with this task because they fail to think of the box as part of the solution—they see it only as a "box of matches." Glucksberg and Weisberg had people solve this problem under one of two conditions. The items were either labeled ("box," "tacks," "candle," and "matches") or they were not labeled. Subjects in the labeled condition solved the problem in about 1 minute, while those in the unlabeled condition took an average of 9 minutes. The labels directed attention to the relevant items and changed how the subjects in the first group solved this problem.

Let's consider a different example of the way language directs thought. There is a popular riddle that goes something like this:

> A young boy and his father went for a Sunday drive. A drunken driver swerved in front of their car, killing the father on impact. The young boy was rushed to the nearest hospital where the chief of neurosurgery was summoned to perform an operation. Upon seeing the boy, the chief of neurosurgery cried out, "I can't operate on him, he's my son!" How is this possible?

When I've posed this riddle to students, they have sometimes replied: "The chief of neurosurgery is the boy's stepfather"; "The real father didn't die"; or "It's impossible." Have you guessed the correct answer? The answer is that the chief of neurosurgery is the boy's mother. The reason for the difficulty is that, in our society, when we hear terms like "chief of neurosurgery" we tend to consider only males. The words we use can determine the kinds of thoughts we think. (This concept is developed more fully in Chapter 3.)

Have you ever listened to two professionals in the same field discussing their work? Most professionals have highly developed specialized terms to communicate their thoughts. Often, these specialized terms also serve to guide the way the professionals think:

FIG. 1.2   Using only the materials shown in this figure, how would you attach the candle to the wall so that it can be burned?

How did the surgeon acquire his knowledge of the structure of the human body? . . . It has taken hundreds of dissections to build up the detailed and accurate picture of the structure of the human body that enables the surgeon to know where to cut. A highly specialized sublanguage has evolved for the sole purpose of describing this structure. The surgeon had to learn this jargon of anatomy before the anatomical facts could be effectively transmitted to him. Thus, underlying the "effective action" of the surgeon is an "effective language." Learning this anatomical language was a prerequisite to the transmission of the factual information that is needed here for effective action. (Bross, 1973, p. 217)

As this author points out, technical jargon not only facilitates communication among professionals, it is an inherent part of the development of ideas in a specialized discipline. As you will see, I stress the learning of specialized terms in every chapter in this book because the terms carry much of the meaning that is being conveyed.

The use of jargon can serve as an efficient shorthand for communication among professionals. Specialized terms, however, can also serve as a barrier that keeps laypersons from understanding. Have you ever gone to a physician and found you were unable to communicate with her because you didn't understand the technical terms she used? A physician with a clear understanding of the problem should be able to communicate the nature of your problem in plain language. Beware of anyone who scatters terms indiscriminately or uses them as labels for simple phenomena.

A friend of mine once went to an allergy specialist who, after extensive tests, announced that my friend had "chronic rhinitis." Although my friend found this diagnosis alarming, with further questioning, she learned this means "runny nose," a diagnosis she could have made by herself.

Preferred Modes of Thought

Even though most people report that they are aware of the use of imagery and silent speech, at least some of the time there is good evidence that individuals have **preferred modes of thought**. That is, some people seem to think more fluently or easily with one of these types of internal representation than the other. Suppose that I was giving you directions to a building on a college campus. Consider the two types of directions shown in Figure 1.3. Do you prefer the map that conveys information in a spatial array or the verbal directions (e.g., "Take the second left after you pass Lake Avenue")? There also seems to be individual differences in preferred sensory modes. Some students report that they comprehend difficult material best when they read it; others prefer to listen to difficult material.

There is more than just anecdotal evidence in support of the notion that people have preferred modes of thought. Gardner (1983) provided considerable evidence for the concept of "multiple intelligences." There is abundant evidence that some people prefer to think "spatially" while others prefer to think verbally (Halpern, 2000; Halpern & Collaer, in press). For example, college students with low verbal ability performed much higher on their tests when they were instructed with a knowledge map, which is a spatial representation of information, than when they were instructed in the usual manner that relies more heavily on verbal skills (Patterson, Dansereau, & Wiegmann, 1993). There are also some tasks that are particularly well suited for a particular thinking mode. Imagery, for example, is usually a better strategy when dealing with spatial problems like those commonly

Driving Directions:
1. Take Embarcadero Road exit from the Bayshore Freeway.
2. Make a right at the exit (South) and continue straight for approximately 2 miles.
3. When you cross El Camino Real the street name changes to Galvez Street. Continue on Galvez to the next large street, which is Campus Drive.
4. Make a left on Campus Drive. (This is a curvy street. Follow it around as it curves to the right.)
5. Make a right onto Mayfield Avenue.
6. Take the first right, which is Lagunita Drive.
7. Park in the second lot on the left.

FIG. 1.3 Consider the map and accompanying verbal directions. Which would you prefer if you had to find your way?

encountered in geometry, the building trades, and architecture. Deliberately switching from one mode to another is often a critical thinking strategy. I'll be returning to this notion several times throughout this book. I will suggest that you write out in words the procedures and solutions to mathematics and science problems and use imagery and spatial techniques when comprehending complex prose. Comprehension and problem solving can often be enhanced with the deliberate use of different thinking modes. Even if you are particularly proficient with one mode, it is good to develop less-preferred modes as well.

CRITICAL THINKING: HOLLYWOOD STYLE

Unfortunately, critical thinking sometimes has a pejorative connotation. This is especially true in common media depictions of the good thinker as someone who is cold and calculating. The quintessential example of stereotype is the pointy-eared Mr. Spock of *Star Trek* fame. As you probably know, Mr. Spock is a fictitious character from the popular television series and movies about space travel in the distant future. Spock, as he is most commonly called, is only half-human, a fact that is revealed by his pointy-ears. The other half of his bi-species heritage is Vulcan, a species of being whose thinking is totally rational. In fact, he is so reasoned that he is unable to understand the mushy and sentimental emotions that seem to plague mere humans—emotions like love and hate, which have no rational counterpart. The media depiction of this popular fictitious character presents the message that rational thought is cold and incompatible with human feelings.

Other times, the media depicts the "good thinker" or good student as the "nerd." The good thinker is rarely the attractive beauty queen or the athletic stud. More typically, this character is ridiculed for wearing thick glasses (often held together with tape), wiping at or sniffing with chronic rhinitis, and expressing a predilection for plaid clothing. This negative message about good thinking is a common theme in movies made for the huge teen market. In many ways, the idea that thinking reflectively or following a reasoned plan of action instead of an emotional one is made to appear "uncool." The impulsive and dashing bubbleheads who are portrayed as the heroes in this genre of immensely profitable movies are as ludicrous a stereotype as the nerdy good thinker. Perhaps if the movies showed the lives of these stereotyped teens a few years later, when the impulsive bubblehead is working at a low-paying job (or in jail) and the nerdy thinker is doing interesting work for a better salary, critical thinking would suddenly look very "cool." As long as these stereotyped movie images make money, it will be difficult to correct these negative stereotypes and make critical thinking a desirable goal.

The negative image of thinking is not just restricted to teen movies. After every televised presidential debate, a small army of "spin masters" come on the air to tell the American public what the candidates just said. Their task is to put a positive "spin" on their preferred candidate (e.g., He provided a clear vision for America . . . blah, blah, blah) and a negative spin on the opponent (e.g., He was perspiring and did not smile enough . . . blah, blah, blah). In one retelling of what the candidates just said, a prominent spin master faulted the opposition candidate for providing too much information and for hesitating before answering complex questions! It seems to be the expected format that candidates will provide quotable snippets that are completely unrelated to reasoned responses about immensely important issues (e.g., I knew John Kennedy and you're no John Kennedy; Read my lips!) and short answers that reduce complex issues to one liners. The general public often responds negatively when candidates give thoughtful, intelligent responses to complex questions, perhaps because we have been conditioned to associate this sort of response with the "loser" image that Hollywood and the other media seem to enjoy.

Critical thinking has been unfairly portrayed as cold and unemotional. The desirable goal of a problem or decision is often based on values, feelings, and predilections. In addition, one frequently recommended skill in improving an outcome is to try to "see" the issue from the perspective of other individuals. This sort of perspective taking should increase empathy rather than decrease it. In addition, critical thinking, because of its roots in psychology, takes into account the intimate connection between thinking and feeling. Most psychotherapies involve the use of cognitive processes—thinking, communicating, and understanding—as a way to alter emotional responses. Empathy, imagination, and value setting are all part of critical thinking.

NON SEQUITUR © Wiley Miller. Dist. By UNIVERSAL PRESS SYNDICATE. Reprinted with permission. All rights reserved.

A FRAMEWORK FOR THINKING

Thinking . . . is continuous, a series of informed improvisations more like those of a jazz musician than the playing of a classical musician performing a set piece of music from a score.

—Restak (1988, p. 233)

Unfortunately, there is no simple "how to" formula that can be used in every situation that calls for critical thought. You already know about the importance of planning as one of the attitudes or predispositions for critical thinking, but knowing that it's important to plan is of little value if you don't know how to plan. Consider the following advice about wilderness survival that appeared in a phone directory:

Wilderness Survival
Things you must NOT do:

- Wear brand new boots.
- Leave an open fire unattended.
- Panic. If you meet trouble, stop and think.

I'm sure that the first two recommendations are excellent, but I'm less sure about the value of telling someone to think without any instructions about how to go about it. The following is a general, all-purpose framework or guide that can be used to direct the thinking process. It's not a sure-fire guarantee to good thinking (there are none), but it is a way of getting started and ensuring that the **executive processes** needed in thinking—planning, monitoring, and evaluating—are being used in a reflective manner. You can probably guess why these are called executive processes. They function like the "boss" in a busy office by directing the flow of work and deciding where to put the available resources. The framework is a series of questions, some of which may be repeated several times during the thinking process, which are general enough to be useful in a wide variety of applications, including reasoning from premises, analyzing arguments, testing hypotheses, solving problems, estimating probabilities, making decisions, and thinking creatively. These questions follow from the flow diagram in Figure 1.1. Although the framework will remain the same for all of these thinking tasks, the actual skills used will vary somewhat with the nature of the task. The proposed framework is an adaptation of the problem-solving procedures originally proposed by the brilliant mathematician and scholar George Polya in 1945. Polya's model is presented in Chapter 9, "Development of Problem-Solving Skills."

As you progress through each of the following chapters in this book, you will gain experience in applying this framework in different contexts and different knowledge domains. The thinking skills you acquire as you work through this book will transfer to other contexts if you acquire the habit of *using* the framework. The purpose of presenting the framework now is to provide an introduction and overview of what's to come. It's an easy-to-use guide that, through repeated practice, should become automatic. The following questions will be used to guide the thought process:

1. What Is the Goal?

Critical thinking was defined earlier in this chapter as the use of those cognitive skills or strategies that increase the probability of a desirable outcome. This term is used to describe thinking that is purposeful, reasoned, and goal directed. The first step in improving thinking is to be clear about the goal or goals. What is it that you want to do? Real-life problems are messy. Sometimes there are multiple goals, and sometimes we'll return to this question several times, as our understanding of the goal will often change after we've worked on it for a while. A clearly articulated goal will provide direction to the thinking process and allow you to make better decisions about the skills you will need to use. In the course of thinking about real-world problems, you may need to change direction and redefine the problem and the desired outcome several times, but it's still important to have an outcome in mind to provide some focus. After all, if you don't know where you're going, you can never be sure if you've arrived.

There are a large variety of possible goals. Goals can include deciding among a set of possible alternative solutions, generating a novel solution, synthesizing information, evaluating the validity of evidence, determining the probable cause of some event, considering the credibility of an information source, and quantifying uncertainty.

Are you making a decision about whether to have a heart transplant or what flavor ice cream to select from the corner store? Impulsive thinking about ice cream flavors is not a bad thing and does not require critical thinking; impulsive thinking about life-and-death decisions does. Not everything we do in life requires critical thought. The way you identify the goal should help you plan the time and effort required by the situation.

2. What Is Known?

This is the starting point for directed thinking. While this may seem fairly straightforward now, when we actually use this framework on real problems, you'll find that you may have to return to the "knowns" several times as you interpret and reinterpret the situation. Some information will be known with certainty, other information may be only probably true or partially known. This step will also include recognizing gaps in what's known and the need for further information gathering.

3. Which Thinking Skill or Skills Will Get You to Your Goal?

Once you have some idea of where you are (the knowns or givens) and where you're going (the goal or purpose), you're better able to plan goal-directed thinking processes. Knowing how to get from where you are to where you want to be is the power of critical thinking. These are the thinking skills or strategies that have been alluded to throughout this chapter. Just as there are many different possible goals, there are many different strategies for attaining them. Let's consider the "thinking is like a map" analogy a little further because it can help to clarify some abstract concepts by making them more concrete. Suppose you are about to go on a trip to visit two old friends. One has become a Buddhist monk and lives high on a mountaintop in the Himalayas. The other has become a surfing champion and is living on the beautiful island of Hawaii. You'd have to use a different method of travel to reach each destination, one time scaling a mountain, the other deciding between a plane or boat. Similarly, you'll have to use different thinking skills with different types of thought problems.

This step will involve generating and selecting the appropriate strategy to reach the goal. If you've given any thought to how you will reach a Himalayan mountaintop (I'm assuming that this is a novel thought for most of you), you'll start to generate several options. You'll probably have to cross an ocean, which means deciding between a plane or boat of some sort, and then travel by train and/or car, and then travel by foot and/or animal (which one?). Of course, you'll probably need a guide. What are the vaccination requirements for someone traveling to Tibet? Oh yes, will you need a visa? I think you've gotten the idea by now that traveling to a Himalayan mountaintop is a lot like other quests for knowledge. It will take time and careful planning. By contrast, your trip to visit your surfer friend will be easier and cheaper. Some problems are like that.

4. Have You Reached Your Goal?

I've taught statistics for more than 20 years now. I must have asked students if they've checked their work as often as I've said my name. A concern with accuracy is probably the biggest predictor of success. Does your solution make sense? Did you get to your mountaintop in Tibet or are you on an anthill in Iowa? Was your goal the right one or should it really have been "where shall I travel this summer?" If it really should have been the latter goal, then you can forget Tibet and consider Paris or Japan or the rugged beauty of Newfoundland. What have you learned on the way that you can use again?

Becoming a Better Thinker: A Skills Approach

Critical thinking skills are those strategies for finding ways to reach a goal. Of course, dividing the thinking process, which is fluid and continuous, into discrete skills is artificial, but it is necessary to break the massive topic of critical thinking into manageable pieces. Although I have divided the topic of critical thinking into several chapters, each of which focuses on a different type of problem (e.g., reasoning, analyzing arguments, testing hypotheses, making decisions, estimating likelihoods), these problems are not easily separable in real life. You will often need to estimate likelihoods when making a decision or generate possible solutions in a reasoning task. The division is necessary for teaching and learning and is not meant to imply that critical thinking can be cut into neat packages.

The development of critical thinking skills requires specific instruction, practice in a variety of contexts, feedback, and time to develop. I hope that working your way through this book will be mostly enjoyable and well worth all of the effort. An important part of learning is applying the skills of critical thinking to the many different examples that appear throughout the book. I hope that you will be using the workbook that accompanies this text, *Thinking Critically About Critical Thinking*, so that you can practice, practice, practice. As the old joke goes, it is the only way to get to Carnegie Hall. So, please get comfortable, prepare for some interesting work, and enjoy this book.

CHAPTER SUMMARY

1. The rapidly accelerating pace of change that marks the opening of the 21st century has made the ability to think critically more important than at any other time in history.

2. Critical thinking can be defined as the use of those cognitive skills or strategies that increase the probability of a desirable outcome. It is used to describe thinking that is purposeful, reasoned, and goal-directed.

3. There is considerable empirical evidence from a variety of sources that cognitive skills can be learned from instruction specifically designed to teach these skills and that these skills transfer to real-world settings when they are practiced in multiple contexts.

4. Developing a critical thinking attitude and disposition is at least as important as developing the skills of critical thinking. The skills are useless if they are not used. The attitude of a critical thinker must be cultivated and valued.

5. Metacognition refers to people's knowledge of their own thought processes. We often have little conscious awareness of how we think. Self-monitoring your own thought processes is one way to improve how you think.

6. Many contemporary psychologists conceptualize intelligence as made up of component parts, which include acquiring and using knowledge, executive processes that guide the thinking and learning process. These components can all be improved and developed with instruction and practice. We all have some undeveloped potential and can learn to think more intelligently.

7. People report that thinking sometimes seems to rely on visual imagery and sentence-like propositions. There are individual differences and task differences in the use of these modes of thought.

8. A general, all-purpose framework for thinking was presented. It consists of four questions that should be asked whenever you're faced with a critical thinking task. It will serve as a guide for the thinking process.

9. Remember, you are what (and how) you think! Have fun with this book.

TERMS TO KNOW

You should be able to define the following terms and concepts. A good way to review and check your comprehension is to cover up the definition, then try to define each term, then uncover the definition and compare your answer with the brief one that is provided. (Your answer is expected to be more complete than the one presented in this review.) The goal is not to memorize the terms; instead you should be sure that your definition captures the meaning of the term. Be sure to cover the definition because it is easy to believe you know it when the answer is in front of you, but hard to fool yourself when you have to generate your own answer. If you find that you're having difficulty with any term, be sure to reread the section in which it is discussed.

Schemata. Internal representations of knowledge. The way we organize our knowledge about the world.

Critical Thinking. The use of those cognitive skills or strategies that increase the probability of a desirable outcome. It is purposeful, reasonable, and goal directed. Also known as directed thinking. Compare with nondirected thinking.

Directed Thinking. Critical thinking or thinking that is goal directed.

Nondirected Thinking. Daydreams, night dreams, and rote memorization. Compare with directed (or critical) thinking.

Cognitive Process Instruction. Instruction based on cognitive theories and research that is designed to help people improve how they think.

Transfer of Training. The spontaneous use of skills that are learned in one context in a different context.

Performance-Competence Distinction. The difference between what a person does (performance) and what that person is able to do (competence).

Critical Thinking Attitude. The willingness to plan, flexibility in thinking, persistence, willingness to self-correct, mindful attention to the thought process, and the seeking of consensus. It is not possible to be a critical thinker without this sort of attitude.

Habit of Planning. The repeated and automatic use of plans.

Mindfulness. The act of drawing novel distinctions. Mindful engagement with material is needed for good learning.

Metacognition. Our knowledge about our memory and thought process. Colloquially, what we know about what we know.

Imagery. The use of an internal picture-like representation while thinking.

Preferred Modes of Thought. Individual preferences for different types of internal representations.

Executive Processes. The oversight or planning and monitoring processes in thinking.

2

Memory: The Acquisition, Retention, and Retrieval of Knowledge

Many years ago I read a story about a beautiful young woman who, because of a terrible fear of growing old, made an interesting deal with the Devil. She agreed to sell her soul to him. In return, he promised that she would spend her old age in complete happiness. The Devil kept his promise. When the woman grew old, she became totally senile. Her old age was spent in the memories of her youth, visiting with friends who had long since died, totally oblivious of life around her. The memory of this story has stayed with me for a long time. I wonder if she would have made this deal if she had known that her happiness would be bought with senility and would consist of a life among her memories. I would like to be able to tell you who wrote this story and give you the title, so that you can read it for yourself, but I can't. I've forgotten where I read it. Although I believe that I can remember accurately many of the details of the story, I can't remember where I read it or who wrote it.

MEMORY AS THE MEDIATOR
OF COGNITIVE PROCESSES

*How wonderful, how very wonderful the operations of time, and the changes of
the human mind! . . . If any one faculty of our nature may be called more
wonderful than the rest, I do think it is memory.*

—Austen (quoted in Powell, 1985, p. 403)

Ulric Neisser (1982), a cognitive psychologist, once asked, "What do we use the past for?" (p. 13). This may seem like a strange question, but a good way to begin our quest to understand memory is by examining its function. According to Neisser, we use the past to define ourselves. If you are a fan of the soap operas, you'll recognize this as one of the favorite themes. Soap opera plots often involve memory loss (amnesia) in one of the protagonists. The usual sequence of events consists of a sudden blow to the head of a leading man or woman followed by a peculiar loss of memory in which the identity of family members is forgotten. While this is rare in real life, it does point out the essential role of memory. It tells you who you are, where you're from, and where you're going.

Try to imagine what life would be like if you had no memory. For most of us, this is a frightening thought. A loss of memory is a kind of death. If we had no memory for our past, the people we are would no longer exist, even if our bodies continued to function. Our memories are our most valuable possession. I don't know anyone who would sell the memories he or she has accumulated over a lifetime, no matter how much money was offered. Life without memory is unfathomable.

All intelligent systems (e.g., humans, computers, dogs, cockroaches) have the ability to learn and remember. These abilities play a crucial role in all of our lives. Most important, they are inevitable consequences of living. For humans, the ability to learn and remember well often determines the quality of life, economic status, and sometimes even survival. Because the ability to think clearly depends, in large part, on how well we can utilize past experiences, memory is a central topic in developing thinking skills. Thinking is a cognitive process—what and how we think depends on what we know—on the contents of our memories. In this chapter, we consider current views of how memory works, why forgetting occurs, when memory can be misleading, and ways to improve memory.

All thinking skills are inextricably tied to the ability to remember. As you proceed through the chapters in this book, you will repeatedly find evidence of the pervasive influences of memory on how and what we think. Consider, for example, the perception of risk. Psychologists have found that hazards that are unusually memorable such as a recent disaster or a sensationalized depiction in a film or televised newscasts (e.g., stories about teenagers who kill their parents and knife-wielding wives who mutilate their husbands) distort people's perception of risk. Most people rate dramatic causes of death such as earthquake or shark attack as many times more likely than they actually are, and less memorable causes of death are routinely underestimated (Lichtenstein et al., 1978).

The distortion in perceived risk is due to the sorts of events that people can think of when they make judgments about risk. Public opinion polls show that crime is a major concern for most Americans. But, is there really a crime wave, or just the perception of a rapid increase in the rate of crime? The Center for Media and Public Affairs reviewed 573 television shows, movies, and music videos that were released from 1998 to 1999. They found an average of 31 acts of violence were depicted per hour of viewing time, which is approximately one act of violence every two minutes; the three major television networks in the United States showed more crimes per show every year for the last several years—even though the crime rate had not changed (Center for Media and Public Affairs, http://www.cmpa.com/archive/viol98.htm). Why are television news shows increasing their coverage of crime? In part, a few violent crimes dominated the news, but it is also possible that the major networks are trying to compete with the tabloid-type shows that feature violent crime. It is not surprising that a recent poll taken in the city of Milwaukee found that 80% of the people surveyed believe that crime had increased or stayed the same, when in fact, crime in Milwaukee has been steadily declining (Fletcher, March 25, 2000). The point being is that many people think about crime when they are asked their concerns. Why crime? To answer this question, we need to understand why crime is what "comes to mind" and not something else like poverty, the environment, or education, when people search through their memory stores and retrieve "crime" as their primary concern. The perception that crime is rising, which is at odds with the actual data, would be expected to influence how people think about crime-related issues like mandatory sentences for offenders, willingness to fund the construction of new prisons, and whether to buy burglar alarms or own hand guns.

A related media-made impression of a crime wave can arise from reporting increases without ever stating the actual number of crimes. For example, although it was true that the killing of tourists in Florida went up 300% in a two-year period, it helps to mention the actual number that have been killed: The number increased from three deaths to eight deaths—hardly a crime wave, even though many people now believe that it is not safe to travel to Florida! It is not surprising then that people would conclude that there has been a rapid rise in the rate of crime—after all, this is what is shown and reported on news shows, and what we are likely to recall when deciding about the risk of crime. In Chapter 7 on likelihood and probability, I will describe the confusion between percentages and frequencies in the context of thinking with numbers, but the point I want to make here is that it is the huge increase in the percentage of crimes that most people will remember and use when making judgments about crime. Few people will ever think to ask about the number of tourists who were killed, so frequency information will not be "available" in memory for use in helping them decide if a place is safe or unsafe.

Another example of the centrality of memory to the thinking process can be seen in decision making by juries. The jury process is at the heart of the U.S. legal system.

It is one of our most cherished rights as citizens. A group of strangers is cloistered in a small room for the sole purpose of evaluating evidence pertaining to the guilt or innocence of an accused. The synthesis, analysis, and weighing of evidence that is often contradictory is a complex cognitive process, which, like all cognitive processes, depends on what is remembered. In a simulated study of how juries reach decisions, Reyes, Thompson, and Bower (1980) varied the vividness (and, therefore the memorability) of the evidence provided during a mock trial. In half of the cases, the prosecution presented the more vivid information; in the other half, the defense presented the more vivid information. Judgments of guilt paralleled the differential recall of the prosecution and defense arguments. When the information favoring the defendant was more vivid, he was more likely to be acquitted (found not guilty), and when the information favoring the plaintiff was more vivid, the defendant was more likely to be found guilty. The "jurors" based their decision about guilt or innocence on the information available to them from their memories of the trial. The vivid information was more memorable, more available, and therefore more likely to be utilized in the jury deliberations. The influence of the availability of information in decision making will be considered again in Chapter 8.

The Time Line

The relationship among learning, retaining, and recalling involves the passage of time. Let's clarify this with an example. It is reasonable to expect that during a college career, students will take many, many exams. When you finish reading this section of the book, you should be able to answer a question like: "What is the relationship among learning, retaining, and recalling?" If you write the correct answer on an exam, your professor will infer that sometime before the exam you learned the relevant material, you retained it (kept it in memory), and you were able to recall it (retrieve it from memory) when it was needed (on the exam). Learning and retaining are not observable behaviors. They must be inferred from the activity of recall, which is inferred from some other behavior, such as writing the correct answer on a test. A friend can watch you while you move your eyes across the lines of print that appear in a book propped up in front of you, but she can't see you learn. In the example presented here, writing the correct answer on an exam is the behavior that allows the inference that learning and retention have occurred. Learning and retention are **hypothetical constructs**, terms that have been made up to help psychologists study and understand the mind and, thus, they have been called "convenient fictions." Learning and retention are like perception, motivation, thirst, sex drives, hallucinations, and many other terms in that they have no external physical reality. They are only known by inference, and they are helpful in understanding the processes of the mind.

Learning and retention are usually inferred together. If I asked you what notable event occurred in Australia in 2000, and you answered correctly, then I would infer that you learned, retained, and recalled that Australia was the site of the 2000 Olympic Games. If you are unable to answer this question, then either: (a) you never learned the fact in question; or (b) you learned it, but forgot it; or (c) you could recall it in some other situation, maybe with some recall cues.

The relationship between learning and memory is a temporal one (time-based) and is depicted on the time line in Fig. 2.1. Something happens at Time 1 that we call learning or the acquisition of information. Following Time 1 is an interval, which

FIG. 2.1. A time line depicting the relationship among learning, memory, and retrieval.

can be as short as a few thousandths of a second or as long as a lifetime. Retention of information during this time interval is attributed to memory, but indexed by retrieval. At Time 2 (some time after Time 1), the individual exhibits some behavior, like correctly answering an exam question that allows us to infer that the material was both learned and remembered.

Varieties of Memory

Thought and memory are closely related, for thought relies heavily on the experiences of life.

—Norman (1988, p. 115)

The goal of good remembering is to learn information that may be useful in the future and to learn it in a way that makes it easy and likely to be recalled when it is needed. By gaining some insight into the way memory works, you should be able to use this knowledge to improve your ability to remember.

In the first chapter, I provided a working definition for "critical thinking" and the more general term "thinking." A key idea is that **thinking** is the manipulation or transformation of some internal representation (Hunt, 1989; Reisberg, 2001). Our internal representations are manipulated or transformed in symbolic ways, so that the knowledge we have can be used to solve problems and make decisions. Notice that I use the term "knowledge" whenever I refer to an internal representation. Information exists in the world. When we learn information—that is, **acquisition** or the incorporation—of information into our existing mental structures, it becomes meaningful—it becomes knowledge. When we think, we use our knowledge to accomplish some goal. When we think in deliberate ways that increase the probability of obtaining that goal, we are engaging in critical thinking.

Memory is not a single process. It is a series of processes or systems, each of which has its own operating principles. Psychologists do not agree about the number of separate processes that comprise memory because there are many dimensions to memory and many different ways to conceptualize the remembering processes. I like to think of it as different ways to cut the "memory pizza." (I was a pizza waitress when I was in college, and I frequently tried to cut the pizza in novel ways. I'm not sure why I recalled this experience as I searched for an analogy for memory, but this is what I remembered. I hope that this is a useful way to understand this discussion. At least, the pizza analogy should provide food for thought.)

For example, memory operates differently when you learn a motor skill like skiing than it does when you study for a history test. Therefore, you would not use the same methods to learn to ski as you would to learn about an event in history. Similarly, what you do during the **retention interval**, the time interval between the acquisition of new information and its retrieval. **Retrieval** is the act of remembering information at recall. The length of the retention interval also governs what and how you learn and recall. If you had to remember the date of the Civil War for only 5 seconds, you would engage in different remembering activities during the retention interval than if you had to remember it for 5 months. What you already know about skiing or history is also an important determinant of the way in which you go about adding to that knowledge. Similarly, the complexity of the information and the context in which you learn and remember also play a role in the selection of the best strategies for learning and remembering. Intuitively, we all know about some of these differences, but an improved understanding of the operating principles of memory should help to use it more efficiently.

Perhaps another analogy would be useful at this point because the concept of memory systems is so abstract. Think about the many interrelated components in an automobile engine. If you understand that pumping too much gas into a stalled car can "flood" the engine, then you can avoid this problem. Similarly, if you understand that the battery can lose its charge if you run the heater, lights, and radio for a long time when the motor is off, you can also use this knowledge to avoid the problem of a dead battery. The many systems of memory also have operating rules, and if you acquire, retain, and recall information with these rules in mind, you should be a better driver of your own memory system.

Here are some of the distinctions that have been made to differentiate among memory systems: **Episodic memory** is the memory we have for events in which we can recall our own participation—when and where we learned them (Tulving, 1972). Examples of episodic memory include remembering where you spent your 17th birthday, recalling the plot from a movie you saw last week, and remembering the day you graduated from high school. This sort of memory is fairly easy to acquire because it seems to happen without much effort on your part. **Semantic memory** is the memory that we have for facts like the multiplication table and word meanings. You probably cannot remember where and when you learned that $7 \times 9 = 63$ or the definition of "chauvinist pig," but these are parts of your memory system. You probably can recall all of the trouble you had learning the multiplication tables. It is easy to talk about the knowledge contained in episodic and semantic memory. For this reason, these two systems are part of a larger grouping in memory that is called **declarative memory**.

Motor memory, as you might expect, pertains to remembering motor skills. Let's suppose that you are an excellent outfielder in baseball. You can get your glove to the place where the ball is going and throw it in the right direction within fractions of a second. This is certainly an impressive skill, but it is very difficult to verbalize exactly how you do it. You are able to call on your knowledge when it is needed, but can't exactly say what it is that you do. If you wanted to teach me to be a great outfielder (lots of luck), you could not just tell me what you do. It would be of little use for you to describe your activities, "I catch the ball instead of missing it, then throw it where it is most needed, instead of somewhere else." On the other hand, if you wanted to teach me the multiplication tables, you could do that in words.

Procedural memory, or remembering how to do something, shares some features with motor memory. The difference is that the procedure does not necessarily have to involve motor skills. For example, if you are as old as I am (unlikely), then you once learned how to use a slide rule. (For those of you who grew up in the age of cheap and efficient calculators, a slide rule is a device that looks like a ruler and can be used to perform mathematical calculations.) This is a kind of "knowing how" that is often differentiated from declarative tasks that involve "knowing that."

Another way of dividing memory depends on how hard you have to "work" in order to remember. This distinction is between automatic and effortful memory. How many movies have you seen in the last two months? Even avid movie-goers can almost always answer this question (Hasher & Zacks, 1984). Frequency information is one type of learning and remembering that occurs fairly automatically; that is, with little conscious awareness or practice. For this reason, it is often called **automatic memory**. By contrast, suppose that you need to remember a series of dates for a history exam. Unfortunately, this sort of information will require that you work at remembering—most probably you would repeat the dates until you could recite them without looking. This is an example of **effortful memory**. Some types of memory will require hard work, others will be easy, but with repeated practice and the acquisition of additional information, effortful processing will become more automatic. Perhaps one way of thinking about education is that it makes hard "things" easy. Experts in any area—history buffs, computer programmers, skilled athletes—have all done the hard work of learning and now make "it look so easy," so automatic. Now they have more attentional and memory resources for the more advanced aspects of their work.

Other, totally different ways of "slicing the memory pizza" depend on the length of the retention interval. If the retention interval is up to one or two minutes, then the best ways to ensure recall will be different than when the interval is longer (up to an entire lifetime). Simple rehearsal, such as repeating a phone number that needs to be remembered long enough to dial it, will work well for short retention intervals. If you needed to learn your new phone number so that you can recall it months or years from now, you could not spend the retention interval repeating your phone number. You need to engage in activities that are appropriate for long-term retention.

Memory can also be categorized by the type of recall task that will be performed. If you only have to recognize the correct response, you will need less effort at acquisition than if you actually have to generate the response with few cues. Students frequently tell me that they study differently when they are expecting a multiple-choice test (recognition) than an essay test, (recall with few cues). There is experimental evidence that when students expect a multiple-choice test, they perform better on this type of test than on a recall test and when students expect an essay test, they perform better on essay tests than multiple-choice tests (Tversky, 1973). When preparing for a test, students engage in **intentional learning** activities and do something to help them remember the material. Learning that occurs without deliberate effort is called **incidental**, for example, your memory for the plot of a television sitcom that you saw last night. I often hear from students who come to my office for academic advising that they "can't do math" or "can't do science" or "can't write well." I think that what they really mean is that the learning of math (or science or writing—we all have different skills and abilities) is effortful. Of course, with hard work, they can. I think that if they understood that some kinds of learning are effortful and some are easy, then they would not be so quick to conclude that they "can't do it," when in fact what they need to do is exert conscious effort and do the hard cognitive work of intentional learning.

Like learning, recall can be effortful or easy, and sometimes, automatic. I don't know why I remembered my years as a pizza waitress when I was thinking about ways to explain the abstract concept of memory. It came to me spontaneously. Several different ways of conceptualizing the multiple processes of memory, or, as I have been calling it, cutting the memory pizza, are shown in Fig. 2.2.

Varieties of Memory

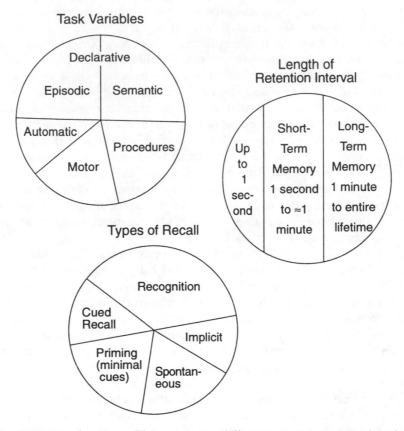

FIG. 2.2.   Varieties of memory. There are many different ways to conceptualize the types of memory processes. I suggested that you think of it as ways to cut up a pizza—in this case, a memory pizza. Each of these "pieces" or categories of memory has its own set of operating principles.

As you can see, there are many ways to categorize the multiple processes of memory. What you need to remember from this discussion is that you will have to consider what you need to remember and when and why you will need it, and what you already know about the topic when you engage in activities that promote remembering. But, whatever the nature of the memory task, a consistent theme throughout this book is that the knowledge we retain in that amazing organ that perches on top of our spines, directs the mental processes that we call thinking. A strong base of knowledge and good thinking skills operate together in the critical thinker (Champagne, 1992; Lawson, 1999). However, it is important to bear in mind that although an excellent memory may direct and influence thinking, a head full of good facts does not make someone a good thinker. One of the saddest sights in college is the student whose memory is an encyclopedic compendium of unintegrated factoids. Just as great thinking skills with a head that contains no knowledge is worthless, so is a head full of information without the thinking skills, unless you aspire to be a game-show contestant! Thought and knowledge—sounds to me like a great title for a book.

Memory Without Awareness

Few judges are psychologists, or they would realize that nothing can be stricken out of a human consciousness after being let in. Judges seem to be quite unaware that it is a hard task to put anything into the average mind and, once in, an impossible one to take it out.

—Clarence Darrow (1932, p. 145)

One kind of memory that has fascinated many psychologists during the last decade is memory for information that we do not know we know. It's hard to understand how something that we do not know we know could be called memory, so an example should help. Suppose that I write a two-word phrase in such small type that you couldn't read it. If I asked you to recall the phrase, you would say that you never saw it or it was so small you could not read it. Additionally, suppose that I devised a task that demonstrated that, in fact, you did have some memory for that two-word phrase, even though you had no conscious knowledge of ever reading it. The memory test for unconscious memory could be a word fragment task, where you fill in the blanks to form a two-word phrase, for example, _ _ s _ s _ pp _ _ e. If you filled in the blanks to read "just suppose," and I found that none or very few people who had not been exposed to this two-word phrase in small print could fill in the blanks, then I would have evidence for memory without conscious knowledge. In fact, there is good evidence for just such a memory system. Because it is a memory that we cannot access by the usual methods of responding, it is called **implicit memory** (Graf & Komatsu, 1994; Greenwald, 1992; Roediger, 1990). By contrast, **explicit memory** is memory for information that can be discussed or described.

Here is another example—suppose that your family always spoke Italian in the home when you were a small child, and now that you are an adult, you cannot seem to remember a single word of Italian. Yet, if you took a class in Italian, you would find that the words that you thought you didn't know come back to you so that you are speaking Italian with less effort than other students who did not grow up in a home where Italian was spoken. This is a kind of implicit memory because you had no conscious awareness of the fact that you knew some Italian, yet you found that you did.

If we can show that we "remember" information that we did not know that we know, can this unconscious information influence how we think without our being consciously aware of their effect? It seems that these memories that we do not know about consciously can have an effect on how we feel about the objects of these memories. The effect of unconscious memories are seen when people are asked about preferences. For example, imagine that you are participating in an experiment where a word is repeated a few times, but you do not really know what the word is because it may have been spoken too softly for you to hear, or it was spoken in a noisy room, or it was a word or picture that was shown so badly out of focus that you cannot say what was shown. Suppose also that some time later, you hear the word or see the picture. It is probable that you will indicate that you prefer the stimulus that you never knew was heard or said. Similarly, if you see the name of some unknown person but you have no conscious memory of seeing that name, you are more likely to judge that it is the name of a famous person when you encounter it some time later than if you had not previously been exposed to the name (Seamon et al., 1995). It seems that these stimuli that reside in a memory system that you have no conscious knowledge of "feel familiar" even though you do not know why.

Memories "feel" different from new information, and we use these feelings about memory as a basis for judgments, without knowing that familiarity is causing us to make the judgments that we do.

The Illusion of Truth.   What would happen if I told you a lie, and you have no conscious memory that I told you this lie? Here's one possibility: Did you know that the president of your college was caught shoplifting at Sears? Sure, this is a lie; I don't know anything about the president of your college; in fact, I don't really know you, and you may never have attended college. Let's further suppose that you forgot that I told you this lie, and some time later you hear that there was a crime on campus and the president of your university is a possible suspect. It seems that the information linking the president and crime will "feel familiar," even though you don't recall where you heard it before, and you are more likely to judge the statement that your president committed a crime as the truth than if I had not previously told you the lie that she was caught shoplifting at Sears. Can you see why this phenomenon is called the **"illusion of truth"**? Information that was encountered previously, even if at the time you knew it might be a lie, makes it more likely that you will believe the information when it is encountered a second time than if you had not been told the original lie (Wegner, Wenzlaff, Kerker, & Beattie, 1981).

So what should I do if I want to influence how you evaluate information—if I want you to believe my lie? I could repeat the information that I want you to believe several times, then allow some time to pass so that you don't recall where you heard it. When you hear the information at some time in the future, it will seem familiar, so you will assume it is true. (It would have a "familiar ring" to it.) Based on the illusion of truth, can you understand why rumors are effective, even when they are known to be lies? Have you ever heard the expression, "there is no such thing as bad publicity"? It seems that people often forget exactly what they heard, but when they encounter a person's name for a second (or more) time, the name seems familiar. We tend to interpret this feeling of familiarity in a way that gives it meaning. So, an actor or politician who is not well known, but was involved in some scandal or was in the news for some other reason, will be judged as more famous than one whose name does not have the same "familiar feel."

Classical Conditioning.   Another kind of memory without awareness is the result of classical conditioning. If you have had an introductory class in psychology, then you probably learned about the pioneering work of Ivan Pavlov. He was able to get dogs to salivate to the sound of a bell by repeatedly pairing the sound of a bell with the presentation of food. In human terms, that is like getting you to respond to the sound of a bell in much the same way that you would respond to the sight and smell of a thick, juicy steak sizzling on a grill. (If you are a vegetarian, then think of a juicy veggieburger or whatever the appropriate mouth-watering meal is for you.) Classical conditioning can occur without conscious awareness, and clever propagandists have used this technique to influence how people think.

There is a striking example of the use of classical conditioning to influence thoughts and actions on display at the Museum of Tolerance in Los Angeles, California, which is a museum that is dedicated to documenting and explaining the origins and consequences of prejudice and intolerance. In one display, old movies that were shown in Nazi Germany depict the repeated pairing of revolting scenes of rats streaming out of sewers and running over garbage and other waste. Virtually everyone responds with disgust to these repulsive scenes. Exaggerated pictures of

Jews were flashed onto the screen so that the long noses of the disgusting rats are superimposed over the exaggerated facial features of Jews. It does not take long before the facial features evoke feelings of disgust, which were learned through the repeated pairing of the repulsive rat scenes and the faces. For people who viewed these movies, the feeling of disgust can be elicited at some time later when similar facial features are encountered, without the viewer ever being aware of where or how this association was learned. This is a powerful and frightening example of the way memory without awareness can support a conscious program of prejudice and discrimination. As the learner (viewer of the films), you would attribute the feeling of disgust to some other reason or source, a fact that makes its effect so pernicious.

In one of the controversies that erupted during the presidential match between Al Gore and George W. Bush, two candidates for president of the United States in 2000, a controversial television advertisement criticized Gore's health plan as a plan that would be run by "bureaucrats." There is nothing unusual in this because name-calling is a common political technique used to persuade voters not to vote for the other candidate. What was unusual in this advertisement was that the word "RATS" was briefly flashed on the television screen as the announcer said the word "bureaucrats." This advertisement can be seen on the Internet at a site that is maintained by "Political Ad Critic" (http://political.adcritic.com). The television screen is reproduced in Fig. 2.3. In thinking about the effect of this advertisement, remember that the word "RATS" was flashed very quickly. I do not know what the intent of the advertising agency was, although I can guess at their intent. George W. Bush claimed that he had no knowledge of the advertisement.

Look closely at Fig. 2.4. This picture is taken from a picture book of Mother Goose Tales. It was published in 1942, during World War II. This is a series of pictures about what may be the world's most famous egg, Humpty Dumpty. Does Humpty Dumpty look vaguely familiar to you? It will, if you are a history buff. He bears an uncanny resemblance to Adolf Hitler, leader of the Nazi forces during World War II. Does his fall and his inability ever to rise again (be put together again) suggest that a message is being sent that the reader might learn without conscious awareness?

ACQUISITION

In 1935, *Time Magazine* featured the predictions of Ralph S. Willard, a Hollywood chemist who claimed to be able to freeze monkeys and resuscitate them. Willard suggested that this process could be used with prisoners because it was cheaper than jail, the unemployed, who could be kept frozen until the economy produced more jobs, and even the depressed, who could remain in the freezer until a cure was found. By the way, it is clear that "Willard was a humbug" who disappeared into science fiction history. (Harris, 1993, p. 55)

Unless you already knew this, you have just acquired new information. You can answer questions that you couldn't answer a few moments ago. You are a changed person, and you will never be the same again. The knowledge you have embedded in memory pertaining to *Time Magazine*, cryogenics (freezing people), and strange ideas from the 1930s is altered. So it is with all new information that causes you to change what you know and how you think.

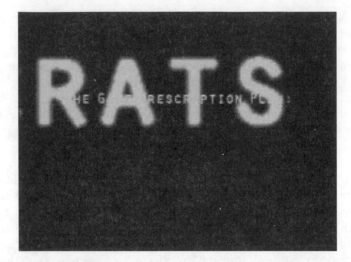

FIG. 2.3. A reproduction of the television screen that was used during an anti-Gore commercial during the presidential campaign in 2000. (From http://political.adcritic.com.)

You may have heard the term "information explosion," which refers to the tremendous increase in the amount of information we have to deal with in contemporary society—information that has to be acquired, retained, and retrieved if we are to function in an increasingly complex world. Consider, for example, the documentation that soldiers have to master in order to learn and perform maintenance on military tanks. There are more than 40,000 pages of instructions, and the tools required for maintenance could fill a large truck (Brooks, Simutis, & O'Neil, 1985). The soldiers who are responsible for the tanks need to know how to learn and recall large amounts of technical information in order to perform well at this highly complex task. As more of us log on to electronic networks, we are privy to staggering quantities of information. We need to know how to search selectively and how to navigate through a sea of databases, bulletin boards, discussion groups, and "buying opportunities."

We are surrounded every moment by more information than we could possibly acquire. Stop some friends some time during the day and ask them to close their eyes. Ask them questions about the room they're in (for example, which pots are on the stove, if they're in the kitchen), or the book they're reading (like whether there are headings on the page they're reading or what is shown on the book cover), or the person they're with (like whether a friend parts her hair on the side or down the middle). You'll be surprised how much of this potentially available information is not known. We are selective about the nature of the information we acquire.

Strategies That Promote Learning

There is no substitute for the serene pleasure that learning can bring.

—Izawa (1993, p. 43)

Although there are many different kinds of memory processes and contexts, several general rules have emerged that can promote the learning of new information. There is an old saying that goes something like this, "the head remembers what it

Humpty Dumpty

Humpty Dumpty sat on a wall,
Humpty Dumpty had a great fall;

All the King's horses
and all the King's men

Cannot put Humpty Dumpty
together again.

FIG. 2.4. An illustration taken from *The Tall Book of Mother Goose*. Pictures by Feodor Rojankovsky. (1942). New York: Harper & Row. Look closely at Humpty Dumpty. He looks too much like Adolph Hitler for the message of his sudden downfall and inability to rise again to be a coincidence.

does." (I really like this saying and use it a few times in this book.) Embarrassingly, I once again have to admit that I don't remember where I first heard it, but I do recall the message: What you do at acquisition (when you are learning something) is an important determinant of what you will remember. Simply put, if you engage in activities that promote learning, you will improve your memory.

Pay Attention.   One of the primary determinants of what we know is what we attend to. Think back to the last time you were at a large, noisy party with people standing around in small groups talking to each other. Imagine that you're standing with two acquaintances discussing the weather. There are several small groups of people standing nearby who are also carrying on conversations. If someone near you, but not talking to you, mentions your name or something of interest (e.g., "Did you hear the latest news about Debbie and Stanley?"), this will attract your attention. If, however, the same person standing at the same distance from you, speaking in the same voice, is discussing tree blight, you probably would never notice, unless you have a special interest in tree blight. Think about what will happen to the conversation you've been having about the weather. If your answer is "Not much," you're correct. When you switched your attention to the more interesting conversation, you lost most of the meaning of the original conversation. If, at this point, the person who has been talking to you suddenly stops and asks, "What do you think about it?" you'd become embarrassed, because you would have no knowledge of what she had been saying.

The phenomenon described here is called the **Cocktail Party Effect**. Most people can think of an episode where they've experienced this effect. It demonstrates several basic properties of attention.

1. If you don't pay attention, you won't acquire information. Let's consider the scenario a little more closely. When you were attending to the weather conversation, you knew very little or nothing about the other conversations around you. When you switched your attention to the more interesting conversation, you could not say what was happening in the weather conversation. Thus, attention will be a major factor in what gets remembered, because it determines what gets into the human information system.
2. There are limitations on your ability to process information. All of the conversations going on around you are not processed equally well.
3. There are individual differences in what is attended to. If you had no interest in "the latest news about Debbie and Stanley," but found the weather fascinating, then you would not have switched your attention and could have responded with more than a sheepish grin to the question, "What do you think about it?"

If you're interested in knowing more about memory so that you can improve your own, then you'll have to pay attention to attention. Many people complain that they forget the names of people soon after they've been introduced. It is likely that they never paid attention to the name at the time of introduction. If information is not acquired, then it can never be remembered. When meeting someone, it is a good idea to repeat the person's name aloud to be certain that you've heard it correctly and to be certain that you've paid attention. Saying the name, rather than just hearing it, is an important aid for remembering. If you cannot say the name soon after hearing it, you can be sure that you won't remember it some time later. You need to develop the habit of monitoring your attention. If your eyes are moving across a text, but your mind is somewhere else, you need consciously to be aware of the fact that you're not attending, so that you can redirect your effort to the material to be learned. It's been said that a good politician remembers names. This is also true of successful salespeople, teachers, waiters, and waitresses. Even if you'll never be a politician, salesperson, teacher, or waiter or waitress, it is a good social skill that is well worth the effort.

When learning a name (for a person, a concept, or object) immediately repeat and then "do" something to help you fix it in your memory—say it out loud a second time, spell it, associate it with something that can help you remember the name such as a person's features, or just explain what it means in your own words. The effect of generating the name (saying it from your own memory) will help with recall. I tried to explain this principle to the manager at a sandwich shop where I frequently stop. Often the order is wrong, which costs money and hurts business. I suggested that he have the people taking the order repeat it back to the customer to ensure its accuracy and to help the order-taker or sandwich-maker remember the order as he or she works on it. The manager looked unimpressed with this sage advice. It's unfortunate because this simple generative task would significantly reduce the number of wrong orders and unhappy customers.

In case you're unimpressed with the rule that unless you attend to something you won't know it, let's try a demonstration. Most people will admit that they like money and have worked hard to earn it. In Fig. 2.5 there are several drawings of a U.S. penny.

Only one is correct. If you're like most people, you won't be able to recognize the correct penny because you never attended to its details. Although you've dealt with pennies numerous times (if you are a resident of the United States), you learned only enough of the details to tell it apart from other coins. You probably never acquired a detailed memory of pennies. To find the "correct" answer, check it with a real penny, but be certain that you attend to all of the details carefully. If you're still dubious, try drawing a telephone keypad from memory or name the letters on the second row of your computer keyboard. Few people find that they know which numbers and letters go together, yet we have all dialed telephones thousands of

FIG. 2.5. Fifteen drawings of a U.S. penny. Which one is correct? (From Nickerson and Adams, 1979).

times, and few can name the letters, yet we can use them, often without looking. These actions have become so automatic that we no longer pay conscious attention to them and without attention, they cannot be recalled.

The need to pay attention in school should be obvious. John Holt (1964), a respected educator and author of the book *How Children Fail*, believes that many children fail in school because they don't pay attention. Think about how your mind sometimes seems to wander when reading textbooks or during lectures. Most students are not even aware when they're not paying attention. It should be obvious by now that in order to develop better memory skills, you will also have to develop attentional skills.

Monitor Meaning. Comprehension and memory are closely related concepts because memory is enhanced when the material is meaningful, and meaningful information is retained more easily than material that is low in meaning. If you are learning in a classroom setting, from a textbook, or some similar setting in which the information is complex prose and you need to be able to recall it some time later, you need to monitor how much and what you are understanding. Stop at the end of each section, and state or write in your own words, without looking at the text, what you just read. This is important because it provides practice at remembering, but you still need to practice your remembering after some time has passed since reading the text.

If you cannot meaningfully summarize each section just after reading it, then you will not be able to summarize it at some later date. You need to be aware of what you are learning, and take action if you have "lost it." This is a concrete way to check on your attention. If you finished a section in a text and have no idea what you just read, you need to go back and attend to the content. Additional suggestions for monitoring meaning are given later in this chapter in the section on metamemory and in Chapter 3 where questioning strategies are presented.

Stop now, cover this section of your book and say aloud or write out in two or three sentences about what this section on memory is conveying.

To demonstrate the powerful influence of meaning on memory, look at A, B, and C in Fig. 2.6 for a few seconds, then cover the figures and reproduce them from memory. Try this now.

You probably remembered some parts of the figures shown in Fig. 2.6, but didn't remember them perfectly. Suppose I now tell you that Fig. 2.6A is a soldier walking his dog behind a picket fence (Do you see the dog's tail and the end of the soldier's rifle?), and that Fig. 2.6B is a washerwoman scrubbing the floor (Do you see her water bucket and the bottoms of her shoes?). If you recognized Fig. 2.6C as a bear behind a tree, then you drew it more accurately than if it seemed more like abstract art. Making the figures meaningful will enhance how well they are remembered. You can test this with friends by telling them what the figures are, uncovering them briefly, and then comparing how much your friends remembered to your own drawings.

Your elementary school teachers recognized the role that meaning plays in memory when they told you to "read for meaning." We can add meaning to information by elaborating on it. For example, when you are learning something, try to relate it to something that you already know (Connor-Greene, 2000). Put the topic in context or make your own summary of the information (Davis & Hult, 1997). The idea is to exert the effort and spend the time needed to relate new material to something that is already known so that you won't remember it as an isolated bit of information.

In a clever demonstration of the principle that anything that improves comprehension will improve memory, two psychologists (Bransford & Johnson, 1972)

FIG. 2.6. A demonstration of the effect of meaningfulness on memory. Look at these figures for a few seconds, then cover them and reproduce them from memory. (Figures A and B are adapted from Osgood, 1953. Figure C is adapted from Hanson, 1958).

presented college students with the following passage to read. Read it for yourself and then see how much you can remember.

> The procedure is actually quite simple. First you arrange things into different groups depending on their makeup. Of course, one pile may be sufficient depending on how much there is to do. If you have to go somewhere else due to lack of facilities that is the next step, otherwise you are pretty well set. It is important not to overdo any particular endeavor. That is, it is better to do too few things at once than too many. In the short run this may not seem important, but complications from doing too many can easily arise. A mistake can be expensive as well. The manipulation of the appropriate mechanisms should be self-explanatory, and we need not dwell on it here. At first the whole procedure will seem complicated. Soon, however, it will become just another facet of life. It is difficult to foresee any end to the necessity for this task in the immediate future, but then one never can tell. (p. 722)

You probably did not remember very much of this passage. I also doubt that you found it very understandable.

I'd like you to read the passage again, this time keeping the title "Washing Clothes" in mind. It should seem much more memorable because the title provided a context or a framework for understanding the passage. When information is provided before a person reads a text or learns about a topic, the reader is better able to assimilate the incoming information. The **advance organizers**—the preliminary information—act as a guide or framework that helps the learner to anticipate information and to relate it to other topics. This is the rationale behind the outlines that appear at the beginning of each chapter in this book and the reason why each chapter in the accompanying exercise book begins with a series of questions that requires you to think about the topics in the chapter you are about to read.

Distribute Learning.   In plain English, this strategy means, "Don't cram." You will learn material in a way that is more resistant to forgetting if you space out the learning sessions. This seems to hold true whether you are learning a motor skill, like how to return the ball with a strong back hand in tennis, the derivation of chemistry formulas, or how to use a new piece of equipment. Spread out the study sessions for maximal benefit (Cull, 2000; Donovan & Radosevich, 1998). If you can allocate only 5 hours to studying for an exam, spread it out over 3 or 4 days, instead of spending the entire time at one sitting. Of course, study periods also need to be long enough to allow for integration of the information you're reading. The ideal study period depends on many factors including the difficulty of the material, your own attentional capacities, and how much has to be learned. In fact, it seems that the more variability you use when learning, the better able you are to recall information in a wide variety of settings, so study for different lengths of time with different intervals between study sessions for the longest lasting memories.

Get Organized.   "Clean up your room!" I don't think that there is a person alive who hasn't heard (or spoken) these words. The idea that "you'll never be able to find anything in this mess" may also apply to how you store information in memory. Although the similarity between memory and a messy room is obviously a gross oversimplification, organization does make it easier both to find a pair of socks that match and retrieve information from memory.

I'd like to demonstrate this point with two lists of words. Read one list, at a rate of approximately one word per second, cover the list, and write down as many of the words as you can remember, then repeat this process with the second list.

Girl
Heart
Robin
Purple
Finger
Flute
Blue
Organ
Man
Hawk
Green
Lung
Eagle
Child
Piano

Stop now, cover the above list, and write down as many words from this list as you can remember.

Now read the next list, cover it, and then write down as many of the words that you can remember from this list.

Green
Blue
Purple
Man
Girl
Child
Piano
Flute
Organ
Heart
Lung
Finger
Eagle
Hawk
Robin

Stop now, cover the above list, and write down as many words from this list as you can remember.

Undoubtedly, you recalled correctly more words from the second list than from the first. You may not have realized that the lists were identical except for the order in which the words were presented. You might expect that you did better the second time because you already had a chance to practice the words once. This is true. The additional time spent studying the words can partially account for the improvement in recall. However, most of the improvement on the second list came from the organization provided by presenting words in categories. Research has shown that when lists of words are presented in categories, recall of material is two to three times better than when the same list of words is randomly presented (Bower & Clark, 1969). When words are presented in random order, as in the first list, recall is improved when subjects have enough time to generate their own categories (Bousfield, 1953).

You can apply this memory principle by organizing material that you need to learn. If you are learning a classification system for a biology course or the properties of metals for a course in science, study one group or category at a time. See how the groups relate and note similarities and differences within and between categories. Impose a structure or organization on the material to be learned. Interrelate the items so that they become coherent. I'll be presenting several strategies for organizing complex prose passages in Chapter 3. Organizational strategies are as important in the recall of prose passages as they are in the recall of lists.

Generate Multiple Cues for Retrieval.   I've seen it happen many times. A good student, who works hard, finds that he can't remember an answer on an exam, and then soon after turning in his paper, the answer seems to pop into his head. Or, similarly, as soon as he hears the answer, he realizes that he "knew" it, but couldn't remember it when it was needed. These are frustrating experiences that can have dire consequences if you can't recall, for example, the CPR (cardio pulmonary resuscitation) you learned in high school or the emergency procedures for those times when you run low on air in the middle of a deep sea dive. Knowledge that you can't recall when it is needed is called **inert knowledge**. Later, in Chapter 10 on creative thinking, we will consider ways to help you think of new solutions for new problems. "Think of" is really the same as activating inert knowledge. Memory is central to all thinking. Psychologists know a great deal about remembering and forgetting, including some ways to make information that you "know" available when you need it. We know that what you do when you are learning something will have a strong effect on whether you are able to recall it when it is needed.

When you recall something, it is in response to some cue. For example, "name some strategies that promote recall." In this example, the terms "strategies to promote recall" are the cues for what is to be remembered. You would not answer with a statement like "Al Pacino is a great actor," although this might be your answer to the question, "Name a great actor." When you learn something, you need to learn it along with the cues that are likely to be present at recall. Ask questions about causes and consequences of the material you are learning. How does the newly acquired information relate to other concepts? What I am describing is the principle of **encoding specificity**, the idea that material is most likely to be recalled when you are presented with the same cues that were available when you learned it.

You can use the principle of encoding specificity to improve your memory by generating a rich variety of cues whenever you learn. A "deep" understanding will help to prevent the problem of inert knowledge. By asking why, when, and how questions and developing interconnected knowledge structures in which you relate what is learned to what you already know, you will be able to respond to a greater variety of retrieval cues (The Cognition and Technology Group at Vanderbilt, 1993). Learning that encourages a "deep" or extensive knowledge will help to make the information spontaneously available in those situations when you need it (Van Haneghan et al., 1992). Be sure to concentrate on cues that you are most likely to encounter when you have to remember something. You can also use external memory aids as cues to recall, a topic I will discuss later in this chapter.

Overlearn.   When can you stop studying? Well, if this question is applied to a specific example, like studying for a literature exam, then the best answer is when you know the material perfectly over several different sessions. Consider what happens when a child learns her multiplication tables. At some point, she gets through the entire pack of dreaded "flash cards" (remember them?) without an error. If she stopped learning there, you would find that the next time she went through the deck of flash cards, a few errors would "creep" in. She needs to overlearn, that is, go through the pack of cards without errors many times, with sessions spaced out over time, to ensure accurate recall when these arithmetic facts are needed.

Be Aware of Noncognitive Factors.   There are many factors that can affect your ability to learn that has little to do with cognition but you do need to be able to recognize them so that you can find ways to eliminate them. Suppose that you are trying to learn something (anything), but are exhausted from lack of sleep or from excessive exercise (say, the marathon you just ran); your ability to attend, encode, and retain information will suffer. Your ability to learn can also be adversely affected by drugs (prescription and nonprescription varieties), an extremely anxious or depressed emotional state ("I'll never learn this, then I will flunk out, then everyone will know I am dumb, then I will have to sell hamburgers for the rest of my life," etc.), a lack of time for learning, a poor background in the subject area, and many more factors. Did you know that lack of sleep can be as detrimental to your ability to think and respond as being drunk? Sleep deprivation is a major cause of accidents. The scary part of sleep deprivation is that the sleep-deprived person has little knowledge of how poorly he or she is thinking. You will probably not allow friends to drive drunk, but will think nothing of allowing them to drive when they are overtired, a condition that can be just as dangerous. These are just a few of many possible behaviors that depress your ability to learn. I hate to sound like your mother, but take care of yourself, eat right, exercise, get enough sleep, and get help with physical and emotional problems. There is little point in working on the thinking skills that are presented throughout this book if you are going to be spending much of your life strung out on drugs, half-asleep, or too anxious to learn.

RETENTION

The art of remembering is the art of thinking . . . our conscious effort should not be so much to impress *or* retain *(knowledge) as to* connect *it with something already there.*

—William James (1890)

The term "retention" is sometimes used synonymously with memory. Unfortunately, this term suggests that memory is like a vast storage tank or library where memories are stored and something like miniature pictures of events are retrieved when we need to recall an event. This notion of memory is wrong.

The Constructive Nature of Memory

Many of the popular notions people hold about memory are wrong. For example, in a story by the famous mystery writer Agatha Christie, the witness to a crime had her memory of it "covered over" by a series of events that followed the crime so that she was unable to remember what happened. As the years passed and the witness grew old, the distracting and confusing information was forgotten until only the "true" memory remained. The notion of how our memory works makes for great fiction, but is a wrong account of what psychologists have learned about memory. In fact, the reverse of this account of memory is more accurate. If we encounter new information after an event takes place, we are likely to confuse the new information with our original memory; the original memory does not become "clearer" or better with time.

In a study of memory for the O. J. Simpson trial, college students were asked about their memory for the verdict in this famous murder trial 3 days after it was announced and then again 15 and 32 months later (Schmolck, Buffalo, & Squire, 2000). It is surprising that at 32 months after the verdict was announced, few of the students even remembered filling out a questionnaire about their memory of the O. J. Simpson trial soon after it happened. At 32 months, many major errors in memory occurred, with many students answering questions to which they had earlier responded that they didn't know. They filled in the missing pieces in their memory after the fact, and had high confidence in their memory for the event, even when their memory was wrong.

Several important facts about memory are demonstrated in this study: (a) memories are frequently inaccurate and sometimes completely wrong; (b) we tend to fill in missing information in memory with information that "fits" with our belief system or was acquired after the event occurred; (c) there is very little relationship between memory accuracy and confidence—we are often highly confident that we are remembering an event exactly as it happened, when, in fact, the memory is partly or wholly wrong. These are important points to remember about memory because we all rely on information stored in memory to make decisions and understand events, and we mostly believe that our own memory is highly accurate.

Prior Knowledge. Your ability to learn and remember new material depends on what you already know. You certainly wouldn't take an advanced course in nuclear physics if you never had a basic course in physics. However, you probably never realized that prior knowledge, the information you already know, influences how you think and how you remember new information in almost any context. You can read a passage about a familiar topic more quickly than you can read a passage of (objectively) comparable difficulty regarding an unfamiliar topic because your prior knowledge about a known topic facilitates comprehension. Later in this book, I consider the differences between novices and experts in how they solve problems. The expert is better able to comprehend a problem and to remember important aspects of the problem because of her prior knowledge of the field.

Stereotypes and Prejudice

Stereotyping is a category based cognitive response to another person.

—Fiske (1993, p. 623)

An interesting experimental demonstration of the idea that prior knowledge influences what people will remember was conducted by two psychologists, Snyder and Uranowitz (1978). Two groups of college students served as subjects. Students in both groups read the same story about a woman named Betty. The story contained information about her life. Among the information presented was the fact that she occasionally dated men. Up to this point, everything was the same for the students in both groups. After reading the story, one group of students was told that Betty had become a lesbian, while the other group of students was told that she was leading a heterosexual lifestyle. The question of interest was whether this would influence what they remembered about Betty's life story. One week later, all of the students returned to the laboratory to answer questions about the story they had read. They were asked many questions, but the critical question was;

In high school, Betty:
(a) occasionally dated men
(b) never went out with men
(c) went steady
(d) no information provided

Can you guess the results of this experiment? The group of students who were told that Betty is now a lesbian were much more likely to "remember" (b) as the correct answer than the group of students who were told that Betty is a heterosexual. The students who had been told that Betty is a lesbian believed that they remembered something that hadn't occurred. Their prejudices and beliefs about lesbians caused them to remember events that never transpired.

In an experiment designed to determine how sex role stereotypes influence memory (Halpern, 1985), high school students were given dull, boring stories to read about the life of a main character who was either a male ("David") or a female ("Linda"). The events described in the story were those commonly engaged in by both women and men. Female high school students who read stories with Linda as the protagonist remembered the story better than other female students who read the same story with David as the protagonist; whereas, male high school students remembered the story better when David was the protagonist. It seems that the high school students were able to identify with the main character when his or her sex was the same as their own, and this resulted in better memory for the details of the story. In addition, errors in memory were biased toward conformity with sex role stereotypes.

Our beliefs about lesbians, women, men, and other groups, especially racial and ethnic groups, exert strong influences on what we will remember about members of these groups. People may honestly believe that they are recalling something that, in fact, never occurred because their beliefs about what must have happened bias how they recall the events.

Experiments like the ones just described have important implications for understanding the nature of prejudice. Let's return to the earlier example and suppose that Betty was a real person whom you knew while growing up. There may be many things that you can remember about Betty. You now learn that she is a lesbian. Suppose further that you have a stereotype of lesbians as women who drive trucks, crush beer cans with one hand, and hate men. Because this stereotype, like most, contains very little truth about any hypothetical "average" lesbian, you would be forced either to change your stereotype or to change what you remember about Betty. It seems that it is our specific memories that change, not the more abstract memory information underlying our stereotypes. You might selectively remember information like the fact that she always liked to play basketball and forget other information about Betty that is inconsistent with your stereotype, like the fact that she also liked to cook and plant flowers. Allport (1954), in a classic book on prejudice wrote, "It is possible for a stereotype to grow in defiance of all evidence . . . " (pp. 189–190). This is an important point that I want to reiterate. Our beliefs are not easily changed; instead, we tend to change our memory for what we saw and heard so that the memory is made consistent with the beliefs. Most often, memory is altered without conscious awareness that the information is being recalled in a way that does not match the event. This is why stereotypes are so resistant to change, and the need to understand how we think and remember is so important. The critical need to understand and reduce stereotyping and prejudice was concisely summarized by Fiske (1993, p. 621), "Without stereotypes there would be less need to hate, exclude, exterminate."

Stereotypes act as maps that simplify the world for all of us. They allow us to make predictions about people, and they also lead us to often exaggerate group differences (Klauer & Meiser, 2000). In general, most people recall more positive and fewer negative characteristics for their own group with the reverse for memory about other groups.

Inference and Distortion. Memory is malleable. Our memory depends on how we encoded or interpreted events, not the events themselves. What we remember changes over time (Schacter, 1999). When our knowledge and experience change, our memories also change (Bartlett, 1932). There are additions made to memories so that we remember events that never occurred and deletions made so that we forget other events that did. Often, people cannot distinguish between their own thoughts and their perceptions (Johnson & Raye, 1981). Have you ever wondered," Did she really say that or did I think she said that?" At your next high school or college re-union get together with friends to remember old times. You may be surprised to find that the same events are remembered differently by each of you, and each will have memories that others don't have. Furthermore, each of several people who shared a common event and remembered it differently will be highly confident that his or her memory is highly accurate. Overconfidence about our ability to remember is another pervasive psychological trait that bears almost no relationship to how accurate the memory really is.

Eyewitness Testimony.   Seeing is believing, or so they say. Nowhere is this adage held as strongly as in our legal system. Very often eyewitness testimony is the determining factor between a conviction and an acquittal. Defendants with credible, plausible alibis have been convicted by an eyewitness's identification. Should we be placing so much faith in the accounts given by eyewitnesses?

If we use the theoretical framework provided earlier, then recall of the event depends on acquisition, retention, and retrieval. Information can never be recalled correctly unless it was attended to at the time it occurred. This would not seem to be a problem if we're interested in memory for a crime, because it would seem to demand our attention. In fact, witnesses and victims fail to notice many important details because of a narrowing of attention that occurs under stress. If there is a gun or other weapon used during the crime, then the victim focuses on the weapon. Other details that are needed for correct identification, like whether the assailant had a moustache, may go unnoticed (Loftus, 1979).

There are many alterations of the memory of the event that occur during the retention interval, which in this case is the time between the crime and the recollection of it at trial. Discussions of the crime after it occurred can be incorporated into memory so that the individual may honestly believe that she is recalling the crime, while what is really being recalled is a discussion of the crime.

A notorious example of the fallibility of human memory was seen in a highly publicized case involving a Catholic priest who was positively identified as an armed robber by several different witnesses. The trial ended abruptly when a much younger and taller man confessed, offering details of the crime that could only have been known by the real robber, because they were never publicized. The witnesses had not lied. Each honestly believed that he or she remembered seeing the priest as the robber. It is important to realize that although memory can sometimes be astonishingly accurate, it can also be astonishingly wrong.

Real and False Memories.   An explosive controversy involving memory has shaken public confidence in many accounts of memories that were not recalled for long periods of time and then suddenly emerged, often during psychotherapy sessions. These memories usually involve traumatic events such as witnessing a murder or experiencing sexual or other physical abuse. Some psychologists believe that these memories are quite accurate and that they were not available for recall because they were repressed as a protective mechanism for the individual who could not deal with the trauma. Other psychologists believe that even though some of these memories may be accurate accounts of real events, many are likely to be "false" memories for events that either did not occur or were very different from the way they were remembered (Loftus, 1993; Roediger & Bergman, 1998).

Memories can be accurate or inaccurate and there is no way to distinguish between the two. In some cases, there is corroborating evidence showing that the memory is "true" (e.g., physical evidence of abuse), and in other instances, there is evidence that these "memories" were "suggested" by therapists and others, and thus, never occurred. But, in many cases, there is no scientific or other way to detect the differences among a highly accurate memory, an altered memory that is partly accurate and partly inaccurate, and a completely false memory. There have been many highly publicized cases involving prominent figures in which some horrible deed was alleged to have happened. Unfortunately, some innocent people have been accused of horrible crimes. One such case involved Cardinal Bernardin, a respected Catholic leader, who was accused of abusing a young man. The young man remembered the abuse for the first time many years after it allegedly occurred. The young man later decided that he didn't really remember such abuse. On the other hand, memories of abuse and other tragic events are sometimes accurate. The evidence must be considered on a case-by-case basis, which is how our legal system works.

RETRIEVAL

What is your mother's maiden name? Unless you happened to be sitting here thinking about your mother's name, the name seemed to "pop" into your mind. The answer must have been stored in some way that allowed it to be retrieved with a simple question. In fact, it seems almost impossible not to remember your mother's maiden name, when you are asked this question. Now try this one: What are the names of the Seven Dwarfs in *Snow White and the Seven Dwarfs*? If you did not grow up in America or another Western culture, then you may have responded to this question with, "Huh?" Of course, you cannot remember something that you never learned. If you grew up in North America or another Western culture, then you probably saw the movie and read this old fairy tale, and now you are having trouble with this question, even though you probably heard their names and read them several times. Forgetting can be a frustrating experience for everyone. How can we understand the retrieval process when it works so well sometimes and so poorly other times? (P.S. Are you ready to give up? Their names are Bashful, Sneezy, Sleepy, Grumpy, Happy, Doc, and Dopey.)

Forgetting

Happiness lies in good health and a bad memory.

—Ingrid Bergman (quoted in Smith, 1992, p. A1)

One of the major theories of forgetting is that events interfere with each other in memory. This is called the **interference theory of forgetting**. Suppose that you are studying French and Spanish in college. You'd probably find that you sometimes get them confused because what you've learned about one language "interferes" with what you've learned about the other. In general, the more similar two events are (or in this case languages), the more interference there will be. Knowing this, can you think of a way to reduce interference and improve memory? In the example just given, one way would be to take the courses in different semesters to minimize the interference, or at least one course early in the morning and the other in the evening. By keeping the French and Spanish courses as separate as possible, you can reduce some of the interference.

Thinking and Forgetting. By definition, we can't recall what we have forgotten. Often, we will have partial information about the forgotten information, such as the frustrating, "I know that I know the answer, but I can't remember it now." Psychologists call this experience the "tip of the tongue" phenomena because of the maddening way the information seems to be right on the tip of the tongue, but can't quite be recalled. Other times, we simply do not know what we have forgotten. Researchers have found that most often people treat the absence of information as though it is evidence that there is none. Let me explain with an example. Should you marry your significant other? Suppose that you can think of ("thinking of" is the same as recalling) two reasons why you should and none why you shouldn't. Because you cannot recall any reasons that run counter to this decision, you rely on what can be recalled to guide your decision. The problem, of course, is that we cannot know what we have forgotten. However, it is possible to spend some time and effort considering what sort of evidence might have been forgotten and overlooked. Did you forget to consider that she picks her nose and this really bothers you, or that he is a sloppy housekeeper, a trait that drives you "crazy"? The need to generate information so that it can be evaluated is discussed in several places throughout this book. For now, think of it as a forgetting problem that can be lessened, but not eliminated, with conscious effort to consider what might have been forgotten. Because we cannot recall any reasons why we may be making the wrong decision, people tend to be overconfident about the quality of their decisions. A second reason for the overconfidence that we have in our thinking and remembering processes is that we can only act on one decision (e.g., marry or not), and we can never know if another decision would have been better.

Recall Errors. It is clear that we store knowledge (or generate it) in highly organized ways. Sometimes, the errors we make can provide clues to how it is organized. Has your father or mother ever called you by your sibling's name? Most people respond, "Yes." But, few people report that their father or mother called them by the name of the family dog. Intuitively, this would be insulting (unless they really love the dog) because it suggests some underlying facts about how your parent thinks about you. Similarly, if your boyfriend or girlfriend called you by the name of a former significant other, this is also perceived as insulting because it suggests that he or she was thinking about the former boyfriend or girlfriend or that information about you and the former love are stored together in memory.

I can think of several examples where these "slips of the tongue" have revealed some telltale signs about the way people store information in memory. In one embarrassing example, a university administrator kept mixing up the names of two African-American deans. This painful mix-up showed how he had stored information about them in memory and tended to think about them as "African-American deans" instead of some other grouping or as individuals.

Stop now, and answer the two questions in the following box. After you write in the answer for each question, rate how confident you are that your answer is correct. Use the numbers 1 to 7 to rate your confidence with 1 = not at all confident, 7 = completely confident, and 4 = middle level of confidence.

---

1. How many animals of each kind did Moses take on the ark?
   _____Confidence rating (1–7)

2. In the biblical story, what was Joshua swallowed by?
   _____Confidence rating (1–7)

Look over your confidence ratings and compare with them with the ratings of other students. If you responded like most people, you were very confident and very wrong. Did you respond with the "2" to the first question? If you did, you were wrong because Moses didn't have an ark; you were thinking about Noah. What about the second question? Were you confident that the answer is a "whale?" If so, you were wrong again because it wasn't Joshua who was swallowed by a whale. Demonstrations like this one show how memory works. When you read about animals on an ark, you activated your knowledge for the biblical ark story and never noticed that Moses was named in the question. The same thing happened with your knowledge of the biblical whale story. Reflect on what this shows us about human memory—the way it is organized and used and the way we can be completely confident and completely wrong. Try this demonstration with your family and friends and then explain to them what you have learned about remembering.

Retrieval Cues

As you recall (I hope, I hope) a strategy for good learning is to generate multiple cues when you are learning new information that should be useful at recall. Let's consider how these cues operate at recall. Have you ever heard a song on the radio and then thought about the time you first heard it? ("They're playing our song.") Where did these memories come from? Something in the environment acted as a retrieval cue so that the memory was brought into conscious awareness.

Let's try a demonstration of the powerful effect retrieval cues can have on memory. Below is a list of words I'd like you to read. Go through the list once at a rate of approximately one word per second, or have someone read them aloud to you. See how many words you can remember.

Winter
Green
Foot
Pencil
Sweater
Jupiter
Chicago
Bible
French
Violin
Lunch
Russia
Collie

Spaghetti
Melrose Place
Newsweek

Stop now, cover the above list, and see how many of the list items you can recall in any order. Be sure to try this exercise before you go on. **Don't look back at the list when you are finished**.

_____

If you didn't remember all 16 words, what happened to the words you forgot? Are they permanently lost or could you remember them with the proper retrieval cues?

Here is a list of cues. See how many of the "forgotten" words you can recall.

A season of the year
A color
A part of the body
A writing instrument
An article of clothing
A planet
A name of a city
A type of book
A language
A musical instrument
A meal
A country
A breed of dog
A food
A television show
A magazine

Certainly you can remember many more of the items on the list with the appropriate retrieval cues, and this improvement can't be attributed simply to guessing. Generating your own cues while you are trying to learn something in order to facilitate recall is one good way to improve memory when the cues that you use at learning are those that are likely to be available at recall. The cues act like "hooks" in memory so that information is more accessible and can be more readily remembered.

Many of the strategies to improve memory "work" by providing retrieval cues. Have you ever had the frustrating experience of struggling to recall the name of your best friend or your favorite author and then remembered it *after* you embarrassed yourself by forgetting such obvious information? As discussed in the section on generating multiple cues at the time of learning (encoding cues), the fact that you may have the knowledge needed in a situation does not guarantee that access to that knowledge will occur. Retrieval cues help us to locate relevant information that is stored in memory; they allow us to use what we know. The ability to access stored knowledge is an "important hallmark of intelligence" (Bransford, Sherwood, Vye, & Rieser, 1986).

WORKING MEMORY

A common theme among researchers who study memory is that memory has a limited capacity; that is, we cannot remember everything that we would like. Nor can we keep too many different "pieces" of information in an active form in memory so that we can use them all simultaneously. If I asked you to recite the alphabet backwards while solving calculus problems, you would object because there is simply not enough "space" or "effort" or whatever term you want to use to execute these two tasks simultaneously, although either one alone can be performed. The cognitive resources that are used to execute mental operations and to remember the outcomes of these processes are available only in a limited supply. The "place" where conscious thought occurs is called **working memory** because it is the hypothetical space where we perform the work of thinking. One goal of an efficient cognitive system is to make the work of thinking easier, or, metaphorically to reduce the amount of space or effort needed in working memory.

Baddeley (1986, 1992) has proposed a view of working memory that includes a "central executive" or "boss" that directs the activities we engage in while thinking, and other systems that involve visual and verbal modes of thought. Often without awareness, we make decisions about how to spend the limited resources of working memory. One of these decisions is to use external aids. For example, instead of trying to remember my shopping list, I write it down. I know that it is not worth the mental effort of committing this list to memory. We also categorize information to reduce the load on memory. I could remember to buy "stuff" for the dog (dog food, biscuits, flea powder) and "stuff" for the kids' lunches (sandwich makings, apples, lunch bags), etc. This strategy would reduce the number of items that I would have to recall and make forgetting less likely.

Another way we manage our memory is by making decisions about what information we need to use and how much mental effort to "spend" on a particular task. For example, suppose that you had to make a decision concerning a complex issue. You could decide to omit technical information that is difficult to understand, and therefore uses a great deal of working memory. If you had to decide if there is danger from the nuclear waste dump that is next to your house, you might decide to deal with only a subset of the information to simplify the difficult task of understanding nuclear risk. Unfortunately, you could also reduce the mental workload by seeking simple explanations for complex issues such as crime (it's caused by unemployment), truancy (it's caused by bad parents), or economic downturns (it's caused by some minority group that is different from you). These simple purported causes for difficult problems help to reduce the amount of information that is used to reach a conclusion, but they are also a detriment to good thinking because complex problems do not have simple, single causes.

Chunking

As you can see, the strategies that we use to reduce the effort of thinking and remembering can lead to biases and errors. What is needed is an efficient way to reduce the demands on working memory that will not have a negative effect on what and how we think. Multiple studies of the ways that experts think have shown that one of the major differences between people with expertise in some field and those without the expertise is in the efficient way that the experts organize and recall information that is specific to their specialty. The experts are able to perceive large, meaningful patterns of information, which reflects the highly organized nature of the information in their memories. They also know how to search for answers to problems using information available in the environment and knowledge that they have stored in memory. Experts keep the goal clearly in mind, and regulate their thinking process (Glaser, 1992). These highly compact memory "units" and efficient search strategies place fewer demands on working memory. Interestingly, these advantages are specific to the expert's specialization. They approach cognitive tasks in other domains much like the rest of us, a fact that suggests that the real advantage is not in a generally superior mind or memory, but in the highly developed knowledge structures and search procedures that correspond to one's area of expertise (Chi, Glaser, & Farr, 1988).

Meaningfulness and familiarity can account for some individual differences in the ability to utilize highly compact memory units. Have you ever wondered how a good poker or pinochle or chess player is able to remember which cards have been played or which moves have been made? In a classic study of chess players' memories for the positions of chess pieces on a board, deGroot (1966) found that chess masters could remember chess positions that actually occurred in a game after looking at the board for only 5 seconds. Novice chess players had much more difficulty in remembering where the chess pieces had been. Does this mean that really good chess players have extraordinary memories? To answer this question, deGroot placed the pieces randomly on the board and asked master and novice players to view the board for 5 seconds and then recall the positions of the pieces. In the random placement condition, both groups performed about the same. It seems that the master players remembered more than the novices only when the board positions were highly meaningful.

It seems likely that good card players remember which cards have already been played because each hand is highly meaningful to them. For example, John Moss (1950, a pseudonym for the author of *How to Win at Poker*) describes a series of possible hands that a player can be dealt along with several possible cards that could be drawn. It would be easy for him or another poker shark to remember a "four of diamonds in the hole with a four of hearts, six of diamonds and ace of spades exposed." He could remember this as a single familiar hand, while a novice player would have to remember four separate cards. For the good players, this hand would represent a single chunk in memory. Reducing a large number of items to a single item to be remembered is called **chunking**. (No, it is not a brand of Chinese food.) It is a subtle and ubiquitous memory process that allows us to recall whole sentences instead of words and whole words instead of letters. As material becomes increasingly meaningful, we can reduce the number of items that need to be remembered. Master chess players and card players seem to have this memory advantage.

Look quickly at the row of letters and numbers presented below, and then cover them and try to remember as many as you can:

IB   MF   BI   TW   AJ   FK
816   44   93   62   51   69   41

If you had difficulty with this task, the reason may be that the information was not chunked or grouped into meaningful units. Suppose I reorganize the letters by changing the spacing but not their order. They now become IBM, FBI, TWA, JFK. You should have no difficulty remembering all of the letters now. The amount of information hasn't changed, but the cognitive demand has. It is much easier to recall information that is chunked into meaningful units. Consider the row of numbers. Suppose I tell you that this series, if regrouped, is the sequence 9^2, 8^2, 7^2, etc. Again, by relating the input to what's known to make it meaningful, a difficult memory task can be made trivial. The notion that meaning is important in memory will be raised again, later in this chapter, when we consider strategies for improving memory.

Working Memory and Problem Solving

Working memory is the "place" where we manipulate information so that we can use the information to perform some task. When solving a problem or making a decision, many different strategies or alternatives need to be considered simultaneously. One bottleneck in these processes is the limited capacity of working memory. After all, we cannot consider 20 different options at the same time or apply several different strategies in our mind to decide which will work. We will return to the limited capacity of working memory in several of the following chapters because it is easier to solve problems or make decisions when we can reduce the load on working memory (Reber & Kotovsky, 1997).

METAMEMORY

If one has poor insights into the inner workings of their cognitive system, this should inhibit their performance on virtually all tasks, because it is hard to imagine a single cognitive task that does not require some level of metacognitive awareness for its successful completion.

—Ceci and Ruiz (1993, p. 175)

The term **metamemory** refers to one's personal knowledge of his or her own memory system. It seems that much of the difference between good and poor learners can be attributed to metamemory. Bransford (1979) has summarized this:

> . . . (E)ffective learners know themselves what they need to know and do in order to perform effectively; they are able to monitor their own levels of understanding and mastery. These active learners are therefore likely to ask questions of clarification and more efficiently plan their study activities. Such activities are quite different from passively accepting (yet momentarily actively processing) the particular information that a person or text presents. (p. 248)

In Chapter 3, I will build on this theme and emphasize the importance of asking questions as a metamemory strategy.

This quote from Bransford brings up the important concept of active learning. Very little, if anything, can be learned passively (American Psychological Association, 1992; Bransford, Brown, & Cocking, 1999). You need to deal actively with material if you want to remember it. Good learners know when they understand the material and when they do not understand it; poor learners don't seem to notice the difference. Good learners know what they have to do to facilitate learning. These are the executive processes that keep the learner mindful of what and how much is being learned. For example, good learners may spontaneously link new information to information previously learned or think of possible applications for the new materials they are learning. As you read this paragraph, you may be applying this learning "device" by noting the similarity of this concept with one you learned in the section entitled organization, that imposing additional organization on material by activities like these will result in improved comprehension.

An interesting study has shown that students who are having academic problems in college approach their text assignments differently from good students (Whimbey, 1976). The less successful college students read difficult material straight through without seeming to notice when they didn't understand the material and without rereading the difficult sections. Good students know these strategies. Whimbey found that he could improve performance for the poorer students by teaching them how to organize the material and how to become aware of what they were understanding and what they weren't. Too often college students and others believe that they know some material because they've read or heard it. They're surprised to find that they can't answer basic questions about the material they thought they knew.

Nelson and Narens (1990) provided a list of tasks that are used in experimental settings to assess metamemory. This list can easily be adapted as a way to enhance metamemory. For example, before you begin a learning task, carefully assess the ease with which you expect to achieve the learning, called **ease of learning judgments**. If you are a senior in college who has majored in sociology, you might decide that the material presented in an introductory psychology text would be easy for you to learn. Alternatively, you could decide that a course in Asian philosophy would be relatively difficult to learn. The reason for making ease of learning judgments is that they require you think about the to-be-learned material, considering what you already know about the topic, your ability in the area, and the learning context. These reflections will prepare you to allocate the necessary time and mental resources to accomplish the task.

While you are learning, consider how well you know the material—that is, make judgments of how well you are learning—**quality of learning judgments**. If you can determine that it is not going well, then you can redirect your learning activities and seek help. After learning, think about how well you know and understand what has just been learned—**feelings of knowing judgments**. Finally, when you are using the material in a response, make **degree of confidence judgments** about your answers. Taken together, these four tasks will provide an ongoing monitor of learning and memory, and they can help with the selection of control procedures such as allocating more time and effort, trying another study mode, and stopping the learning session.

These four metamemory tasks are summarized in Table 2.1.

Confidence

The idea that we can be highly confident about the accuracy of our memories and completely wrong has already been mentioned in several places in this chapter. It is clear that, in some ways, we can be misled by our own assessments of how well we can remember. For example, if students are asked to judge how likely they are to recall information about a topic right after they studied it, they tend to overestimate the likelihood that they will recall the information correctly at some later time (Benjamin, Bjork, & Schwartz, 1998). It seems that immediately after learning, the information is easily recalled, so we assume that it will be easy to recall at some later time. A more accurate estimate of how likely students are to recall information would come from judgments that are not made while the newly learned information is so "fresh." It seems that we should be less confident about the accuracy of our memories and the likelihood of recalling something in the future, even when the memory "feels" accurate and recall seems easy.

TABLE 2.1.
Self-Reflective Tasks That Can Serve as a Guide for Monitoring
the Process of Remembering

When	What	How
Before learning	Ease of learning judgments	Look over the material that is to be learned and judge the ease with which you will learn it. Consider what you already know about the topic, the reason why you are learning it, and your own abilities.
While learning	Quality of learning judgments	As you learn, monitor how well you are understanding the information or performing a motor skill. Can you summarize in your own words what is being learned? Are you generating multiple cues and using techniques that foster deep learning?
After learning	Feeling of knowing judgments	When the learning task is completed, reflect on how well you learned the material. Have you overlearned for maximal retention and used distributed practice? Will you be able to recall the material some time in the future?
At recall	Degree of confidence judgments	When you are recalling the information, consider how confident you are in your recall.

MNEMONICS

In an episode of the popular children's television show, *Sesame Street*, Bert and Ernie, two lovable Muppets, discussed an intriguing memory phenomenon. Bert noticed that Ernie had tied a piece of string around his finger to help him remember something. In fact, Ernie tied string around each of his eight fingers (apparently Muppets have eight fingers) to be really sure that he didn't forget. After some prompting from Bert, Ernie recalled that the string was supposed to help him remember he should buy more string, because they had run out of string.

Although this story is humorous, it illustrates some fundamental assumptions and problems encountered by humans (and Muppets) in dealing with their memory. The wide range of activities from tying a string around one's finger to the more elaborate procedures presented later are called **mnemonic devices**. They are techniques for organizing and elaborating information so that it can be more easily remembered. Many students use mnemonic devices to prepare for exams and some of the techniques are so common that we usually don't think of them as mnemonics.

During the summers when I was in college, I worked as a waitress at a resort in the Catskill Mountains of New York. The resort had a nightclub with the usual array of singers, dancers, jugglers, and animal acts. (The kitchen help were not allowed to attend the nightclub, so, of course, we would sneak in as often as we could.) One particular act that amazed me was a memory act by Harry Lorayne. He went around the audience recalling people's names. His memory seemed limitless. I was also surprised at how much the audience enjoyed his performance and that an amazing memory would qualify as a nightclub act. After all, no one ever asked me to demonstrate the amazing powers of critical thinking as a nightclub act! (Perhaps there is a reader who books nightclub acts, who is just looking for this sort of late-night crowd-pleasing entertainment.) Harry Lorayne later wrote two books on this topic (Lorayne, 1975; Lorayne & Lucas, 1974). The mnemonic principles he used are presented here along with several others.

Most mnemonics are based on a few simple memory principles. They all force you to pay attention to the items to be remembered, and they provide either an organization scheme or a meaningful context for unrelated items. The user is often required to organize the material and to use the mnemonic as an efficient retrieval cue. The use of mnemonics also requires metacognitive monitoring—keeping track of what you know. They are intentional strategies, ones that you can use when you decide that you want to remember something. Thus, from what you've already learned about memory earlier in this chapter, you can see that mnemonics are not mere theatrical tricks. They work because they represent applications of basic principles of memory.

We all employ memory aids everyday. The most common aids are **external memory aids**, such as the sticky notes that are popular, calendars in which we write appointments and other activities that we want to remember, timers to remind us to turn off the stove, and shopping lists. Mnemonics that are designed to help us retrieve information from memory are called **internal memory aids**. In this chapter, I present four basic types of internal memory aids—keywords and images, rhymes, method of places, and first letters. Each will be discussed in turn followed by some guidelines for selecting the appropriate mnemonic for the type of material to be learned.

Keywords and Images

The following demonstration was presented as an anecdote by Donald Norman (1976, p. 134). I have used it as a class demonstration many times, and students are always surprised at how well it works. The use of this mnemonic depends on first learning **keywords**, which serve as "hooks" for information that is learned later. In this case, the keywords are in the form of a simple poem to learn. Spend a minute or two learning this poem:

> One is a bun,
> Two is a shoe,
> Three is a tree,
> Four is a door,
> Five is a hive,

Six are sticks,
Seven is heaven,
Eight is a gate,
Nine is a line, and
Ten is a hen.

Do you have this memorized? If not, go over the poem again.

Now, I'm going to present a list of words to be remembered. You have to form an image or association between the listed items and the items in the poem you just learned. For example, the first item on the list is ashtray. Image an ashtray with a bun in it, since the bun was the first item in the poem. You could imagine something like a large hamburger bun sitting in a dirty ashtray. Read the items on the list one at a time, allowing enough time to form an image.

1. ashtray
2. firewood
3. picture
4. cigarette
5. table
6. matchbook
7. glass
8. lamp
9. shoe
10. phonograph

Now, cover the list of words and answer the following questions:

What is number eight?
What number is cigarette?

If your experience was like the one Norman described or the ones my students report, then you've been surprised to find that the answers were easily available. In this case you learned a list of rhyming keywords and then used imagery to relate the words to be learned to the keywords. Research has shown that images are best when they're interacting (e.g., the bun is in the ashtray and not just next to it) and when they are vivid and detailed (the bun that I was imaging was a hamburger bun and the ashtray was glass) (Baddeley & Andrade, 2000; Bower, 1972). The deliberate use of both verbal and imagery modes of thought was introduced in Chapter 1. We'll use this strategy again in Chapters 9 and 10 on creativity and problem solving. Of course, you're probably thinking, "Why not just write the list down on paper?" If paper and pencil are allowable and available, this is certainly the best and cheapest mnemonic that you can find, but often we need to commit lists to memory. If you are an anatomy student, you have to learn long lists of the names of nerves, bones, and other organs. Chemists need to learn complex formulas, and it would not instill confidence in me if I found that my surgeon kept a written list of body parts above the operating table (but, it might not be a bad idea). There are many real-life in-stances when we need to learn long lists of material in as efficient a way as possible.

In a recent survey, college students were asked about the strategies that they used to help them remember material for exams (Soler & Ruiz, 2000). Most of the college students, like the 10th graders who were also surveyed, responded that they used low-level strategies like repetition, a strategy that is very inefficient if the goal is long-term remembering. Few reported that they used more effective strategies like deliberately forming vivid images of the material they were learning.

Images can also be used alone (without keywords). They are especially advantageous when you want to remember names and faces. This is the technique that Harry Lorayne (1975) uses. Change the names you want to remember to a concrete noun; pick out a distinctive feature of the face and image the two as interacting. He suggests that you pay special attention to cheeks, lips, facial lines, forehead, nose, eyebrows, and eyes. For example, if you meet Ms. Silverstein and you notice that she has wide-set eyes, you could image a silver beer mug (stein) between her eyes. Mr. Dinter could be changed to dinner and an entire dinner could be imaged on his large forehead. Try this at the next party you attend. You'll find it fun, and you may surprise yourself with your new abilities.

A keyword mnemonic system has been developed especially for learning a second language (Atkinson, 1975). Suppose you are learning French and are faced with the following three vocabulary words with their English translations to learn:

French	English
homme	man
etoile	star
legume	vegetable

Students begin by generating their own keywords. The keyword should sound like the foreign vocabulary word. Thus, for the word *homme*, I'd generate "home," for *etoile*, I'd use "a towel," and for *legume*, I'd use "lagoon."

The second step makes use of imagery by linking an image of the keyword with the correct translation of the foreign word. I'd visualize a man entering a large home, a towel with a star painted on it, and vegetables floating in a lagoon. (It's best when the items are interacting.) When the foreign words *homme*, *etoile*, and *legume* are encountered, students would then automatically recall the images and retrieve the correct translations.

Atkinson claims that as facility with the foreign language develops the need to remember the images diminishes and students can extract the intended meaning without the use of imagery. Students who are taught to use this method consistently recall more correct English translations (72% compared with 46%) than students who use the usual rote rehearsal method of repeating the words until they "stick." Furthermore, this method seems to work best when students generate their own keywords and images. The need for active participation in learning and the payoff from the effortful work of learning are general rules for improving memory. This is a mnemonic that is well worth using if you are studying a foreign language.

Rhymes

We also use rhymes to help us remember. For example, there are few people who haven't heard:

I before E, except after C.
or
Thirty days hath September, April, June, and November.

Answer this question quickly. What letter comes after N? Most people find that they need to sing that portion of the alphabet (l, m, n, o, p) to answer this question. Like rhymes, the rhythm established in songs help to deter forgetting.

Rhymes are useful when order is important because mistakes in order will usually destroy the rhyme. Notice that the first keyword poem I presented relied on keywords, images, and rhymes (one is a bun, etc.). This is an especially easy mnemonic to use, probably because several mnemonic devices are employed in the same poem to guard against forgetting.

Methods of Places

Before I describe how "places" work as a mnemonic device, I'd like you to remember my back-to-school shopping list. Read the list through slowly once, then see how many items you can recall.

Pencils
Ruler
Notebook
Marking pens
Compass
Tape
Paper
Scissors
Sharpener
Reinforcements
Tablet
Glue

How many items on this list did you remember?

Now I'll show you how the **method of places** (or method of loci) could improve your recall for this list. Pick a familiar route, like the one from your house to school. Now imagine each of the items on this list placed somewhere along this route. The pencils could be very tall and form a fence around your front lawn, the ruler could be sitting across your car, the notebook could be the stop sign at your corner, etc. Try this now with the back-to-school shopping list just presented. Once the images are formed, you should be able to remember every item by "mentally walking through" your route and noticing the items you've imagined along the way.

I once went to an introductory lesson for a very expensive memory improvement course. The method of places was the demonstration they used to convince potential students that the course was valuable. For months afterward, I received letters in the mail asking me if I "forgot" to send my money and to register for their course. The expensive (there are no cheap ones) memory improvement courses teach the same methods presented in this chapter. They have no magic secrets that are unavailable in the psychology literature.

The Greeks, who were famous for giving long speeches from memory, have left us with many tips on how to best use this method. For example, the same route can be used repeatedly for different lists, but we should be careful not to put more than one item at the same place (Ross & Laurence, 1968). They also suggested that the places should not be too much alike (e.g., don't use only stop signs along your route) and that they should not be too brightly lit (or there will be glare) nor too dimly lit (or the objects will be difficult to see). This is a good method to use when events need to be remembered in a particular order, since the route can be mentally traversed forward or backward.

Research with the elderly has shown that they can perform as well as much younger college students when they are taught and use this mnemonic. This is important because America is an aging society, and many elderly fear a loss of memory. If you are elderly, or if you know someone who is, many of the simple mnemonics presented in this chapter such as the method of places and use of visual imagery can be used as an aid to memory and thus, postpone or reduce cognitive aging effects. It is also particularly useful to assist the elderly with the use of external memory aids such as medication boxes that have an alarm to signal the time for the medication, calendars, and timers (Park, 1992). External aids have the advantage of helping those with failing (or poor) memory recall the tasks that are important. The internal mnemonics offer the benefit of helping the elderly retain their own cognitive abilities.

First Letters

First letter mnemonics are probably most commonly used in preparing for tests. To use this technique, take the first letter of each term to be learned, insert vowels and other letters if necessary, and make a word. When you need to remember the list, you recall the word you formed and then use each letter as a retrieval cue for each item on the list. Many of us learned to remember the names of the Great Lakes as HOMES (Huron, Ontario, Michigan, Erie, and Superior). If you never learned this before, you'll never forget it again.

The first letter mnemonic organizes unrelated terms into a single word. You already know how important good organization is for memory. I can remember using this technique when I was a college student. The class had been told to be prepared to answer a long essay question that was to be written during an in-class exam. There were six points that I wanted to make in the essay, and I wanted to be sure that I included all of them in order. I took the first letter of each of the points, made up a word using these letters and used this word to help me remember all of the points for the exam. (It worked well.) This technique is also especially useful when you have to speak in front of people without notes. Select one word that can stand for each point you want to make and use the first letter of each word to form a single retrievable word. Even though good speeches may appear unrehearsed, good speakers practice with techniques like this one. It helps them to present their speech in a confident and professional manner.

A related mnemonic that doesn't fit clearly into any of the categories is the one used to recall the value of pi. I'm presenting it in this section because even though it doesn't involve first letters, it is a letter-based technique. Read the following sentence:

May I have a drink, alcoholic, of course.

By counting the letters in each word, you can read off the digits for pi, which are 3.1415926. It is easier to remember a single meaningful sentence than it is to recall eight digits.

Mnemonic Principles

Mnemonic devices can be powerful aids for memory. They are also paradoxical because it seems that to remember better you need to remember more. The first letter mnemonic requires that you remember the new word you created with the first letters as well as each of the words. The keyword systems require that you learn a keyword system, and the rhymes present you with a song or poem to be learned. They each necessitate work. Acquiring a good memory means working at it, but it is work that pays off in lifelong dividends. There are hundreds of studies that demonstrate that the deliberate use of mnemonics improves recall (McCormick & Levin, 1987).

There is probably no field that requires more rote memory, in addition to other sorts of remembering, as medicine. There are thousands of mnemonics to help students in the medical fields recall the names of anatomical parts and their connections. Here is one that I learned in biology class many years ago: "On Old Olympus Towering Tops, A Finn And German Viewed Some Hops." Some readers will recognize this mnemonic as a way to recall the 12 cranial nerves in order: Olfactory, Optic, Occulomotor, Trochlear, Trigeminal, Abducens, Facial, Auditory [or Vestibulocochlear], Glossopharyngeal, Vagus, Accessory [or Spinal root of the accessory], Hypoglossal. As you can probably guess, there is a Web site dedicated to medical mnemonics (http://www.medicalmnemonics.com).

Let's try to develop a mnemonic that could help you to remember the types of mnemonics. First, let's review what they are: keywords and images, rhymes, method of places, and (first) letters. Although you could use the method of places and image each of these terms along a route, or associate them with a keyword, or make up a poem, my choice for a list like this one is the first letter mnemonic. Start by listing the first letter of each term: K, R, MP, L. You can modify the first letter technique by using each letter to begin a word in a sentence, since incorporating these letters in a single word may be difficult. Try it. The sentence one of my students came up with is "Kind Round Men, Please Listen." Use imagery also to aid recall. Imagine a round (fat) man with a kind face and very big ears (for listening). Make your images detailed and vivid. (Can you see his round tummy and elephant-size ears?) If you're asked to recall the mnemonic devices, you can list each one, and by remembering the name of each, all of the information you've learned about them should also be easily retrieved.

Many people find it difficult to remember how to spell the word "mnemonics." Another student suggested this one: *Memory Never Explains MONey and Ice Cream Sandwiches.* Be sure to think about this mnemonic. Can you generate an image to go along with this sentence? You should never have difficulty spelling this word correctly again.

External Memory Aids

External memory aids, which are sometimes called "cognitive prostheses," are also valuable in helping with the multitude of remembering tasks that we all encounter. If you have to remember to do something, use a kind of remembering called **prospective memory** because it is memory for a future event—setting an alarm, posting a note, tying a string on your finger, or leaving something in an obvious and unavoidable place (e.g., the waste basket in front of the door; Herrmann & Gruneberg, 1999).

Some people have acquired specialized and specific external memory aids. I was impressed with such a system when I was attending a ballet at the grand Bolshoi Theatre in Moscow. Like many cities with very cold weather, it is customary to check your coat when you arrive at the theater. In addition, many people also check bags, boots, and large hats. The workers at the wardrobe have to be able to dispense hundreds of possessions very quickly when the ballet is over. In addition, the checkers also rent binoculars and need to remember who rented the binoculars so as to be certain that the binoculars are returned. I found that the checkers had devised a simple external mnemonic system. The coat hooks are numbered (into the hundreds at each station). When someone checks a bag with the coat, the checker uses a number that ends in 4 (14, 24, 34, etc.). Then, when the claim ticket is presented at the end of the show, a 4 in the last digit means that the checker should look below for a package. If a person rents binoculars, then a chalk line is marked above the coat hook number. Then, if a coat is retrieved and there is a chalk mark above the number, the checker knows that binoculars are to be returned. This simple system, which has probably developed over many years, helps to get a large number of people out of the wardrobe area and reduces the time spent in line. This last point is critical to Russians who often have to wait in long lines. If only such a system could be used to reduce the other lines as well.

Remembering Events

Most often we need to remember events rather than lists or related concepts. Much of the work done in the area of event memory has been conducted by psychologists trying to assist victims and witnesses of crime with recall of the criminal activity. We can borrow the mnemonic techniques that they use to improve memory.

The Cognitive Interview. "Information is the lifeblood of a criminal investigation" (Stewart, 1985). How can eyewitnesses to an event be helped to remember what happened so that they can provide law enforcement officers with the needed information? One way to improve the quantity and quality of what gets remembered is with the use of a memory aid for events known as the **cognitive interview** (Fisher, 1995). The cognitive interview is based on principles derived from cognitive psychology about how information is organized and the types of retrieval cues that can work to prime recall. It seems that the unflappable Sergeant Friday from the old television show *Dragnet* was wrong when he asked for, "just the facts, ma'am." The accuracy and completeness of recall is improved by elaboration, especially about objects and activities that occurred near the crime in time or space. Geiselman and Fisher (1985) have found that recall for events can be enhanced by using the following strategies:

1. Start by recalling ordinary events that occurred before the target event (i.e., the crime). Visualize the circumstances. Think about the layout of the room, weather, traffic flow, or any other aspect of the scene. Think about your mood at the time.
2. Be as complete as possible in your recall. Don't edit your report or exclude something because you think that it might not be important.
3. Recall the event in both forward and backward order, or start from the middle and recall both forward and backward in time from some central incident.

4. Change your perspective. Try to recall the event as though you were some other person such as a spectator (real or imaginary) or you were the perpetrator of a crime.

There are additional techniques that can be useful for recall of specific types of information. If you are trying to remember the physical appearance of someone, does someone else whom you know come to mind? Why? In what ways are they similar? If you can't recall a name, recite the alphabet to see if a particular letter can "jog" your memory. Sometimes partial information like the number of syllables in a name can be recalled. If numbers are involved (e.g., a license plate), try to recall the number of digits or some physical characteristic of the digits like their size or color.

The techniques of the cognitive interview can be used anytime you need to remember an event. There are several studies showing that it can help children and adults remember events. Imagine, for example, that there has been a recent rash of burglaries in your neighborhood. Suppose further that you hid a valuable piece of jewelry as a deterrent to theft, but later realize that you can't remember where you hid it. Or, more commonly, suppose you can't remember where you left your car keys. This can be a very frustrating type of forgetting. In this case you would try to retrace your steps and try to recall the last time you used them. Systematic and deliberate use of these techniques should be helpful in recall.

BIASES IN MEMORY

All of the mnemonics or strategies for remembering presented thus far in this chapter have been concerned with the *deliberate* use of memory strategies. Much of what we remember was acquired incidentally, that is, without the use of a conscious, deliberate scheme. If you go to the movies, you can later recall the plot and actors as well as the name of the theater you were sitting in, without deliberately creating images or using rhymes. It's fortunate that we don't always have to work at remembering.

Unfortunately, our memories are subject to certain biases. All items stored in memory are not equally likely to be recalled, and when memory errors occur, they are not random. Because all thinking relies on memory, it is important to recognize the ways in which memory can be biased.

Confirmation Bias

One type of bias that was already discussed is the effect of stereotypes. Stereotypes alter memory in predictable ways. The influence of stereotypes is just one instance of a more general bias to remember more easily information that confirms our hypotheses than information that contradicts them (Beyth-Marom, Dekel, Gombo, & Shaked, 1985). In an interesting study of this effect, college students were told that their dreams would be interpreted by a clinical psychologist (Mazzoni, Loftus, Seitz, & Lynn, 1999). The psychologist, who was a collaborator in the study, gave the students false information about the meaning of their dreams, telling, for example, that their dreams revealed that they had been bullied before the age of 3. A large proportion of the students came to "remember" this incident, which never happened.

Additionally, students who believed in the validity of dream interpretation before the experiment were more likely to remember the incident suggested by the clinical psychologist than those who did not. Thus, prior beliefs about what we believe to be true influence memory, so that we tend to remember events that are consistent with our beliefs.

Pollyanna Effect in Memory

Recall is also biased in that we tend to remember events in ways that reflect positively on us. If you want to try this out, stop now and list the grades you received in high school (or if you are in high school now, list the grades you received in middle school). It seems that most people remember getting very good grades (Bahrick, Hall, & Berger, 1996). Like previous studies, it also seems that there is little relationship between how confident someone is about the memory for one's grades and the accuracy of that memory.

Vivid, Dramatic, Personal, and Familiar

We also know that there is a recall advantage to information that is well known, familiar, prominent (generally important or personal), recent, vivid, and dramatic. Having said this, we also know that, over time, memory for even these sorts of events will become inaccurate, even though it continues to "feel" like an accurate memory (Schacter, 1999). There is also the frustrating problem of inert knowledge, which occurs when we do not recall information at a time when it is needed. In addition, general knowledge about events is sometimes mistaken as memory for a specific event because people cannot tell the difference between events as they were experienced and events that they constructed from general knowledge (Jacoby, Kelley, & Dywan, 1989). These biases in memory have profound effects on how people think. For this reason, I'll be returning to biases in memory several times throughout this book.

LONG-TERM ACCURACY IS SOMETIMES EXCELLENT

Before you despair completely, you will be happy to know that memory can also be fairly good. For example, if you were wondering, "Why bother learning this, if I will soon forget it and not even know that I forgot," there are several good reasons to keep studying. It seems that memory for information learned in a cognitive psychology class was still fairly good for main concepts and important ideas, even 12 years after learning, although memory for many of the names of the theorists tended to be forgotten in about three years (Conway, Cohen, & Stanhope, 1991) and memory for high school math was almost perfect decades later for students who continued learning and took math in college (Bahrick & Hall, 1991). In a study of memory for Spanish that was learned in high school or college (students for whom Spanish was not their native language), researchers found that rapid forgetting occurred during the first six years from the date the formal language learning was completed, but approximately 60% of what was learned was remembered through the adult years and up until the 60s and 70s when age-related forgetting began to occur (Schmidt, Peeck, Paas, & van Breukelen, 2000). The original level of learning is important in determining how well something will be remembered over time, with higher levels of learning associated with better long-term memory. Similarly, memory for the neighborhood in which adults grew up was also marked with a short period of forgetting followed by good memory (for what was not forgotten) for 40 or more years (Schmidt, Peeck, Paas, & van Breukelen, 2000). As in the other studies, good remembering was associated with overlearning and spacing of learning episodes. Thus, the more you learn, the better you remember information related to the topic of your learning, with broad principles and concepts generally well remembered for a lifetime.

You can take advantage of these operating principles of memory in two ways. First, you could use them to improve memory by considering information that you want to remember by overlearning and spacing learning sessions over time. In addition, make the material to-be-learned familiar and prominent, generate encoding cues, use organizational strategies, and elaborate by connecting the new information to knowledge you have already acquired. Perhaps, even more importantly, you can be aware of the ways your memory is likely to be biased and engage in deliberate attempts to debias your recollections.

APPLYING THE FRAMEWORK

A general framework for thinking was presented in Chapter 1. Let's see how we can apply it to the topic of memory.

1. What Is the Goal?

At least three different types of thinking goals involve memory. The first is how to acquire (learn) something so that it can be more readily recalled at a later time. This is an **encoding (or acquisition) goal**. A second type is a **retrieval goal** in which the desired outcome is recall of some item that was previously stored. Finally, there is a **debiasing goal**. This involves examining your recall for evidence of bias so that you can recognize the possibility that a memory may not be veridical and correct for it.

The first step in applying the framework is to determine what the appropriate goal is for a given situation. Are you learning new material, trying to recall something accurately, or examining your recollections for possible bias?

2. What Is Known?

This is a question about where to start. Is there a list of foreign vocabulary words sitting in front of you that you have to learn? Can you remember seeing your wallet this morning, but can't remember what you did with it after that? Can you remember most of the battles fought in Europe during the 19th century, but can't get the order straight? Are you considering your own thinking about a contemporary issue like gays in the military or "three strikes and you're out?" If so, then you will need to consider where your beliefs and attitudes came from and the ways in which they may be biased or even completely wrong, even when they "feel" right. Different skills would be used in each of these situations. By paying careful attention to what is known or given, you can use this information as a guide for selecting the appropriate skill for each situation.

3. Which Thinking Skill or Skills Will Get You to Your Goal?

Several different strategies to improve memory were presented in this chapter. You have to select among them for ones that are most likely to help you attain your goal. The selection is based on the nature of the goal, what is known, and how much effort you are willing to put into goal attainment. For example, if your goal is to remember the names of the people you meet during a business meeting or during the course of interviewing with many different people, you would select Harry Lorayne's imaging technique for associating names and faces. Similarly, if you were able to take notes during the interviews, you would review your notes. You could use the method of places for subject areas like history and social sciences for which knowing the correct sequence of events is crucial to understanding them. Similarly, if you are thinking through your beliefs and attitudes about complex issues, you need to select skills that will help you evaluate them for bias, distortion, and error.

The following memory skills were presented in this chapter. Review each skill and be sure that you understand how to use each one.

- Monitoring your attention
- Developing an awareness of the influence of stereotypes and other beliefs on what we remember
- Making abstract information meaningful as an aid to comprehension and recall
- Using advance organizers to anticipate new information and to prepare for reading
- Organizing information so that it can be recalled more easily
- Overlearning because you know that it will increase the probability and accuracy of recall
- Recognizing that although you may be very confident that you are recalling an event accurately, there is also a high probability that your memory is not as accurate as it feels
- Generating retrieval cues at both acquisition and retrieval
- Practicing recall for information that you are intentionally trying to learn
- Monitoring how well you are learning
- Using external memory aids
- Employing keywords and images, rhymes, places, and first letters as internal memory aids
- Applying cognitive interview techniques
- Developing an awareness of biases in memory so that you can consider the way your own beliefs, attitudes, and background knowledge could be influencing what and how you remember

4. Have You Reached Your Goal?

Suppose that you selected the keyword mnemonic for foreign language learning to learn a list of technical terms in a course in physics. You go through the list, generate familiar English words that sound like the ones you're trying to learn, etc. (You cleverly adapted the technique for use with words that may as well be from a foreign language as far as you're concerned.) The effort doesn't stop there. Go over the list "cold" (without your notes and with their definitions covered). Distribute your learning and overlearn. Do you know the words? If not, go through the technique as many times as needed to pass this quality assurance test. As mentioned in Chapter 1, parts of this framework may have to be reiterated. You may need to select a different mnemonic if the first one isn't getting you to your goal. Try singing the words and their definitions. (Sure, your roommate will think you're strange. So what?) These steps call for careful monitoring of progress, persistence, and flexibility until you find a strategy that works.

If the goal is to examine your own memories for bias, then you would need to think about your personal beliefs about the situation or person being recalled, any information that you may have learned after the event occurred that could influence your memory, and other biasing factors. You can never know how accurate your memory is unless there is some external record, like a videotape that was taken at the time of the to-be-remembered incident. But, you can develop a healthy dose of humility about the accuracy of your own memories and understand the way in which the memories, and consequently the thoughts, of others can also be biased.

CHAPTER SUMMARY

1. Memory was described as the mediator of cognitive processes because all of our thoughts depend upon the ability to use what we have stored in memory.

2. There are many different varieties of memory, and what and how you learn and remember will depend on the type of information to-be-remembered, what you already know, the length of the retention interval, and noncognitive factors like health and motivation.

3. By engaging in the hard work of effortful learning, you can make whatever is being learned easier and more automatic, so there is a real payoff in effort for those who are willing to work at their learning.

4. There are many learning strategies that reflect the fact that all learning is not the same. Good learners will know what they have to do to learn and remember, and they will do it.

5. It is important to attend to information that you want to learn and to monitor how well you are learning.

6. The "illusion of truth" refers to the memory phenomenon in which we forget the source and sometimes even the content of a message, but when we encounter the name of a person who was part of the forgotten message, the "feeling of familiarity" is interpreted as "the new message must be true." Of course, this occurs without conscious awareness, so all we can do is be aware of the possibility that it is happening and be less willing to believe rumors or innuendos.

7. Our memories are not perfect true "copies" of events that have occurred. Prior knowledge, subsequent knowledge, stereotypes, and meaningfulness of the material all influence what will be remembered. These distortions and biases occur without conscious awareness, so we need to be vigilant for the ways in which personal beliefs and experiences could be influencing memory.

8. Memory can be improved with appropriate retrieval cues and good organization. Generation of to-be-remembered information (with minimal or varied cues) spaced over time will result in enhanced recall relative to passive or massed rehearsal.

9. Working memory is the term used for the "place" in which we consciously think. It has a seriously limited capacity that we can control by deciding which information to attend to and how much effort a particular task is worth. When learning is difficult, we need to reduce the load on working memory. This can be done by writing information on paper, making it more automatic, or attending to the information to-be-learned.

10. Mnemonics improve recall because they utilize the basic memory principles of attention, organization, meaningfulness, and chunking. The mnemonics presented were keywords and images, rhymes, method of places, and first letters. (Remember: *Kind Round Men, Please Listen.*)

11. Memory for events can be improved with the cognitive interview technique, which uses elaboration at recall to improve memory.

12. Although it is difficult to believe, even those memories in which we are very confident can be completely wrong. This is difficult for most people to accept because our phenomenological sense is that our own memories are "true."

13. Our memories are biased in predictable ways. Examine your own recall for the possible influence of biases related to stereotypes, general knowledge, positive reflections on oneself, or for information characteristics such as being well known, familiar, prominent, recent, vivid, and/or dramatic.

TERMS TO KNOW

You should be able to define or describe the following terms and concepts. If you find that you're having difficulty with any term, be sure to reread the section in which it is discussed.

Hypothetical Constructs. Terms like learning, memory, and perception that are used as labels for the theoretical processes that underlie human thought and behavior.

Thinking. The manipulation or transformation of some internal representation.

Acquisition. Used to describe learning. Also known as encoding, or putting information into memory.

Retention Interval. The time interval between the acquisition of new information (learning) and its retrieval.

Retrieval. The act of recalling or remembering information that had been previously acquired (learned).

Episodic Memory. Memory for events in which we can remember our own participation.

Semantic Memory. Memory for facts like word meanings and the multiplication tables.

Declarative Memory. Knowledge that can be verbalized easily.

Motor Memory. Memory for the performance of motor skills like swimming or riding a bicycle.

Procedural Memory. Memory for accomplishing some task such as using a slide rule or operating equipment.

Automatic Memory. Remembering that seems effortless such as the memory for the frequency of events.

Effortful Memory. Remembering that requires the deliberate and conscious use of strategies such as memory for a series of dates.

Intentional Learning. Used to describe learning efforts and activities that are engaged in when a learner is deliberately trying to learn something so that it can be recalled later.

Incidental Learning. Learning that occurs without any deliberate effort, such as learning the plot of a television show or the habits of family members.

Implicit Memory. Memory about which we have little conscious knowledge.

Explicit Memory. Memory for information that can be discussed and described. Compare with implicit memory.

Illusion of Truth. When a message is forgotten and the name of a person (or an event) that was in the forgotten message is encountered at some time in the future, this person (or event) feels familiar. People look for reasons why it would feel familiar and decide that the new message must be true. This illusion operates without conscious awareness.

Cocktail Party Effect. Information that is being attended to will be remembered, while information that is not being attended to will be forgotten or never learned. Phenomenon is named for the way people switch their attention among different simultaneous conversations at large parties.

Advance Organizers. Outlines or other summaries that are used before learning to assist with the process of acquisition.

Inert Knowledge. Knowledge that isn't recalled when it is needed.

Encoding Specificity. The cues that are available at learning (or encoding) will be useful if they are also available at retrieval.

Interference Theory of Forgetting. A theory of how we forget that attributes forgetting to "interference" or displacement of the to-be-remembered items by other material that has been previously or subsequently learned.

Working Memory. The "place" where knowledge is consciously manipulated or transformed. Thinking is constrained because working memory has a limited capacity.

Chunking. A memory process in which a number of related items are stored and retrieved as a unit in order to facilitate memory.

Metamemory. A person's knowledge about his or her own memory system; for example, knowing that you have to repeat a series of digits in order to maintain them in memory.

Ease of Learning Judgments. Individual estimates of how easy or difficult it will be to learn a skill or information. This type of judgment is made before the learning process.

Quality of Learning Judgments. Individual estimates of how well material is being learned. This type of judgment is made during the learning process.

Feelings of Knowing Judgments. Individual estimates of how well something is known. This type of judgment is made after the learning process.

Degree of Confidence Judgments. Individual estimates of whether a particular response is correct. This type of judgment is made at the time of retrieval.

Mnemonic Devices. Memory aids or techniques that are utilized to improve memory.

External Memory Aids. The deliberate use of lists, timers, calendars, and similar devices to remind an individual to do something.

Internal Memory Aids. Mnemonic devices or memory aids that rely on plans or strategies to make retrieval easier and more likely.

Keywords. A mnemonic device or memory aid in which a previously learned list of words or rhymes serve as associates or "hooks" for the to-be-remembered items.

Method of Places. (Also known as method of loci.) A mnemonic device or memory aid in which a familiar route is selected and the to-be-remembered items are imaged at intervals along the route. At recall, the individual "mentally traverses" the route to retrieve the items.

First Letter Mnemonics. A mnemonic device or memory aid in which the first letters of each word to be learned are combined into a single word.

Prospective Memory. Remembering to do something at some time in the future.

Cognitive Interview. A technique for recalling events that uses principles of cognitive psychology to guide the retrieval process.

Encoding Goal. Recognizing that you want to learn something—use the strategies for promoting learning.

Retrieval Goal. Recognizing that you want to recall something—use the strategies for improving recall.

Debiasing Goal. A conscious attempt to recognize the ways in which memory can be biased and engaging in activities that are designed to minimize the bias such as continuing to search for additional information and reflecting on stereotypes.

3

The Relationship Between Thought and Language

Contents

There is an old story about three umpires that goes something like this:

> Three umpires were unwinding at a local pub after a very tough day. All three had endured abusive shouts like, "Kill the Umpire" and had numerous offers for new pairs of eyeglasses. After a few mugs of brew, they began discussing how they would decide to call balls and strikes. The first umpire, Jim, explained that it was really quite simple. "I simply call them as I see them."
>
> Donnie, the second umpire, disagreed when he said, "I see them as I call them."
>
> Neil, the third umpire emphatically shook his head in disagreement with the other two. "You're both wrong," he said, slurring his words somewhat. "They don't even exist until I call them."

Neil had a good point. Whether a ball whizzing past home plate is a ball or strike depends on what the umpire labels it. The words he uses both interpret and define reality.

THOUGHT AND LANGUAGE

The development of mind, thought, and language is simply a nexus in which it is impossible to separate one from the other.

—Michael Studdert-Kennedy (quoted in Restak, 1988, p. 231)

How do you express your thoughts in words and sentences? How influenced are you by your particular language? You will have difficulty answering these questions because you use both so automatically and because you have no conscious awareness of the way your thoughts give rise to the words you use to express them. In fact, if you try to monitor your speaking process, you'll find yourself stuttering and interfering with the fluid speech that you normally create so easily. It's as though speech emerges automatically and preformed. Conscious attention directed at the process tends to interfere with it.

Psycholinguistics

Communication is primarily an exercise in thinking.

—Pitt and Leavenworth (1968, p. viii)

Psycholinguistics is the field of psychology concerned with how we acquire and use language. Language is a complex cognitive activity that all normal humans perform with apparent skill and ease. As speakers, we select the words we want to use and produce them in a (mostly) grammatically correct form. As listeners, we use the information in another's utterance to share the expressed thoughts. What do we know about the way speakers and listeners share thoughts through the medium of language?

Underlying Representation and Surface Structure

Language appears to be simply the clothing of naked thought.

—Miller (1972, p. 43)

The comprehension of language is a process in which the message is used to construct a representation of the information referred to in the message (Resnick, 1985).

The sequence of sounds that we produce must correspond to our intended meaning if we are to communicate successfully. The "sender" and the "receiver" also must share a common knowledge of word meanings and grammar. Because language is always incomplete, the receiver must rely on prior knowledge, context, and other cues to comprehension to construct a correct representation.

Psychologists who are concerned with the way people use and understand language divide language into two structures or types of representations. The **underlying representation** of language refers to the meaning component of language—it's the thought you want to convey. **Surface structure** refers to the sounds of the verbal expression that you use or its written form on paper, a computer monitor, or some other writing surface. Look carefully at Fig. 3.1, which depicts this process. As you can see, the thought in the mind of the "sender" is the underlying or deep structure. The thought is private and known only to the sender. The problem in producing language is deriving surface structure from the underlying representation in the sender's mind, and the problem in comprehending language is getting from the surface structure back to the speaker's (or writer's) underlying representation. Language is integral in these processes because it is the medium with which thoughts and emotions are most often expressed and interpreted (although other media such as dance, mime, and visual arts are sometimes used to express thoughts and emotions).

A communication is "successful" when the underlying representation constructed by the receiver matches the underlying representation of the sender. The receiver's representation of the meaning is constructed over time because using language is a sequential process with words uttered or read one after the other. All strategies for improving comprehension involve ways of building representations so that they will most nearly match the one intended by the sender. It is the representation of knowledge about the world, the "architecture of the cognitive system," that mediates comprehension (Bower & Cirilo, 1985).

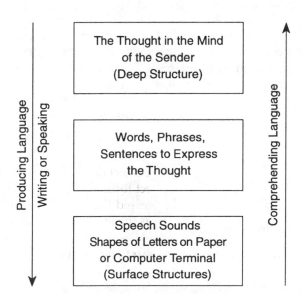

FIG. 3.1. The problem of comprehension. The sender has a thought that she wants to communicate to a receiver. The thought (deep structure) is private and known only to the sender. It is transformed by speech sounds or the shapes of letters (surface structure), which are used by the receiver to reconstruct the meaning expressed by the sender's words.

When language is ambiguous, the surface structure can have more than one meaning or underlying representation. Some examples of ambiguous sentences are:

- Visiting professors can be boring. (This can be interpreted to mean either that it is boring to visit the offices of professors or that it is boring when professors visit campus.)
- They are kissing fish. (This can be interpreted to mean either that they are a variety of fish called "kissing fish," or that they are a variety of fish who kiss, or that at least two people have their mouths in the fish bowl and are engaging in the somewhat kinky behavior of kissing fish.)
- He cooks carrots and peas in the same pot. (I won't explain the two possible interpretations, but you will need to read this one aloud.)
- Each sentence is ambiguous because there is a single surface structure (the sound of the sentence) and at least two possible underlying representations or interpretations. Clear communications are unambiguous. With only a little effort, an ambiguous statement can be made clear so that it corresponds to only one underlying representation. For example, the first sentence can be made unambiguous with simple changes:
  It is boring to visit professors.
  or
  Professors who visit campus are boring.

When there is a problem in the communication process, it is often difficult to know if the problem stems from the sender's thinking, the sender's use of language, the receiver's use of language, or the receiver's thinking. For example, consider a conversation that I had with a 5-year-old girl with whom I spent a very long afternoon. She asked me to buy her a hamburger, which I was glad to do. While standing in line to order her food, she let me know in a very loud voice that she wanted her hamburger "with no meat." Obviously puzzled, I thought perhaps she didn't understand that the brown patty on the roll, the "hamburger," was meat. I patiently tried to explain this concept to her. Adamantly, and even louder, she screamed that she wanted her hamburger without meat. Aha, I thought, she must want plain cheese on a bun—sort of a cheeseburger without the burger. But no, she rejected this possibility and began a full-scale tantrum at this point. What was the problem? Was the problem with language—did she not know the meaning of the words "hamburger" or "meat"? Was the problem in her thinking, which was illogical? Was I the problem? Perhaps my background knowledge of what constitutes a hamburger did not match hers. In other words, did the problem stem from faulty thinking or faulty use of language, or, possibly both? I never did find out she had wanted. We beat a hasty exit from the restaurant as the other customers and the servers gave us very disapproving looks. By the way, I took a regular hamburger with us, which she happily ate in the car as I drove her home.

Implications and Inference

Communication depends as much on information that is implied as it does on the words that are explicitly stated. Comprehension of meaningful material will always require the listener or reader to make inferences by going beyond the words uttered.

Consider this very simple three-sentence story:

> Matt inherited a great deal of money.
> Bertha loves diamonds and furs.
> Bertha married Matt.

Although very little factual information was provided, it is a meaningful story. Readers infer that Bertha married Matt for his money and that she will use his money to buy diamonds and furs, although this interpretation may not be correct. All communication requires the receiver to fill in gaps between given bits of information to understand the intended meaning. Much of the meaning people convey goes beyond the meaning of the words they utter (Dews & Winner, 1999). Has anyone ever said to you, "You're a big help!" when they mean exactly the opposite? Sarcasm, as in this example, can only be interpreted by NOT using the words as spoken to determine their meaning. To know when "You're a big help!" means the exact opposite, we rely on context and the tone and expression used. The fact that we often assume a meaning that does not correspond to the definition of the words used is why psychologists conceptualize the acquisition of knowledge as a process of construction that is built by integrating new information with what is already known by both receiver and sender. Many decades ago, Bruner (1957) succinctly defined thinking as "going beyond the information given." Understanding language by making inferences is a prime example of this definition of thinking.

The Role of Inference in Advertisements

When you produce speech, the intended meaning is implied or suggested by the words you use, the context in which it is embedded, and verbal and nonverbal expressions. It is possible to say one thing and to communicate something quite different. This technique is often used by advertisers who want to persuade you to buy their products, yet have legal restrictions on the kinds of statements they can make.

A television commercial for American Express Travelers Cheques goes something like this:

> "Oh, no, we've lost our travelers cheques! What will we do?" (Couple wrings their respective hands at this point, obviously looking distressed.)
> The voice of a distinguished actor comes on, "What kind were they?"
> Distressed couple responds, "American Express."
> The distinguished actor calmly reassures them, "Good thing you have American Express Travelers Cheques. You can get a refund at their conveniently located office across the street."
> The now-smiling couple walk off the screen to the tune of "Don't leave home without them."

Other traveler check companies have complained about this advertisement because it implies that people who lose other brands of travelers' checks may not get a refund. Notice that although this is never stated, the advertiser assumes that it is a reasonable inference from the information offered.

Perhaps you're familiar with a popular advertisement for Listerine, a brand of mouthwash. An apparently middle-class mother bundles her children in warm clothing while discussing colds and flu. She earnestly states how much she dislikes "scratchy sore throats" and "runny noses." To keep her family healthy, she sees that they eat right, get plenty of rest and exercise, and "gargle with Listerine." Of course, she never says that Listerine will prevent or cure colds. This would be a false claim because there is no evidence that it does. Yet, this information is implied. Studies with fictitious commercials have shown that viewers do infer from advertisements like this one that mouthwash will protect against colds (Harris, 1977).

Carefully selected words in advertisements are used to create an inference that something is true when it is not. Airlines and other businesses often boast:

"Nobody beats our fares."

They expect that readers will infer that this means that they have the lowest fares. Of course, they never state that they have the lowest fares because that would be false. Nobody beats their fares because nearly all of the fares are the same. They could have said, "Our fares are the same as our competitors." But, if they said it that way, it would not mislead readers into believing that they have the lowest fares, and consumers would correctly conclude that it doesn't matter which airline they book with if cost is the sole determining factor. Always consider the distinction between the linguistic content of the message and the inference you draw from it.

When you start reading and listening critically to advertisements, you may be surprised to find appalling attempts to create impressions that can change beliefs. It is instructive to read the advertisements for supposed weight loss products (e.g., cellulite creams, sauna suits, herbal wraps, vitamins, magic formula pills). Even the ubiquitous "before and after" photos are designed to create the inference that you will lose "30 or more pounds in two weeks" while eating anything you want and without "tedious" exercise.

Harris (1977) found that people remember the implied meaning of a message, and not the actual statements that were made. If you have already read the chapter on the development of memory skills, this shouldn't be surprising to you. Meaningful information is more easily remembered than nonmeaningful information. We rarely remember statements verbatim. Thus, our memory of events depends on the interpretations we give them when they occur.

Rules for Clear Communication

"When I use a word," Humpty Dumpty said, in a rather scornful tone, "it means just what I choose it to mean—neither more or less."
"The question is," said Alice, "whether you can make words mean so many different things."
"The question is," said Humpty Dumpty, "which is to be master—that's all."

—Lewis Carroll (*Through the Looking Glass*, 1872, p. 190)

To communicate effectively, you need to know a great many things in addition to the thought being communicated and the words being used as the vehicle for the communication: What is the purpose of the communication? What are your listener's characteristics—what is your listener's age and social status? How much does the listener know or want to know about the topic? The answers to all of these questions shape the nature of communications. We implicitly change the way we speak or write, depending on how we answer these questions, and we make these changes without realizing the extent to which the listener shapes our use of language. Communication is governed by rules that we all obey, although you may never have consciously considered them.

Rule 1: Tell listeners what you believe they want to know

Consider how you would answer a simple question like, "Where do you live?" If I met you in Europe and asked you this question, you would probably respond, "in the United States." If I asked you this question in New York, you would respond with the name of a state, "in Pennsylvania." If I asked you the same question on your college campus, you might respond, "in the dorms." If I asked you this question while we were in the dorms, you might respond, "in Wing D, Room 331." And, if I asked you this question in your dorm room, you would probably reply by giving the name of your hometown. The same question could be asked each time, yet you would give a different answer that depended on the context in which the question is asked and what you thought I wanted to know. The level of information you choose to convey depends on the purpose of the communication.

Rule 2: Don't tell listeners what they already know

In Chapter 1, I began by introducing the topic of thinking and the need for the development of critical thinking skills. You probably did not think that this was unusual. Suppose I started every chapter in this book the same way. You would not only think that this was unusual, you may also question my mental status.

When you present information to an audience, you balance the amount of new information that you present with the old or already known information. If you present too much new information at once, listeners will be lost and will not be able to extract the intended meaning; if you present too much old or known information, listeners will be bored. The relative proportion of old information to new information is known as the **given/new distinction** (Clark & Haviland, 1977).

The ratio of given or known information to new information is a determinant of the difficulty of a communication. If a passage (spoken or written) contains too much new material for a listener or reader, it will be difficult to comprehend. No one would take an advanced course in biochemistry without first obtaining the requisite background in biology and chemistry. The educational process, if successful, fosters the transformation of new information into the students' systems of known information.

Rule 3: Vary the style of your communication, depending upon the knowledge, age, and status of the listeners

Suppose you are an expert computer programmer given the task of describing the operations of a computer center to a group of visitors. You would vary the way you convey the necessary information for each of the following: a group of politicians; a group of children from an elementary school; your history professor; a close friend; or an expert programmer from another university.

Your communication would be more or less technical depending on what you believe your listener knows about the topic. You might tell the politicians about the high costs of maintaining a computer center; the elementary school children might simply be told about the general use of computers; you might explain to your history professor how computers can be used in research; your close friend might be told that you feel you're being underpaid; and the visiting programmer might be told about the capacity of the computers and the steps you've taken to prevent the spread of computer viruses.

The readability of text or ease with which spoken language is understood depends, in large part, on the match between the text and the reader. The reason so many of us find income tax and legal documents so difficult is that they are written by and for accountants and lawyers—people with highly differentiated underlying representations of the topics referred to in these documents. The rest of us have to make many more inferences and more memory searches to understand the concepts because our underlying representations of these concepts are relatively sparse. This is why whenever we're engaged in communication; it is important to consider the characteristics of the reader or listener. This is a more formal way of saying that the beliefs, knowledge, and expectations of the intended audience for a communication should determine how much detail goes into a communication and which words are used. The difficulty of a text does not reside in the text itself, but in the reader-text interaction.

The idea that what people understand depends on what they already know was beautifully made in a book aptly titled, "How People Learn" (Bransford, Brown, & Cocking, 1999). They tell about a fish who gets to learn about the world above the sea as it is explained to him by a friendly bird. When the bird tells of humans who walk upright, we see the fish's mental image of walking fish. The story goes on to show how each description of the dry world would be interpreted by a learner who only knew of the water world. No matter how accurate the description, the fish's understanding was limited strictly by his own life experiences and knowledge of the world.

Rule 4: Tell the truth

When we communicate with each other, it is assumed that the information being conveyed is truthful. This is an imperative for meaningful communication. Of course, sometimes people lie. How do you process information when you believe that the speaker is lying? All components of the communication are scrutinized. In general, the communication process breaks down when the listener suspects that the speaker is violating this rule. This loss of communication is eloquently described by Chang (1993) in her description of life during Mao's reign over communist China, a time when no one dared to speak the truth: "The whole nation slid into doublespeak. Words became divorced from reality, responsibility, and people's real thoughts. Lies were told with ease because words had lost their meaning" (p. 298).

Rule 5: Use a simple straightforward style

Mark Twain said this best when he said, "Eschew surplusage." Information is transmitted best when simple and precise language is used. Some people think that use of multisyllabic words and intricate sentence structures is a sign of intelligence. This is not true. It is a far more difficult task to express complex thoughts in simple language than to express simple thoughts in complex language. The transformation of our private thoughts into easily understood language is the benchmark of human cognition. Sloppy thinking can never be made good even with the most flowery language.

Rule 6: Use manner and context to clarify meaning

Meaning depends not only on the words that we use, but also on the context and the manner we use to convey it. Have you ever had the experience of having someone say, "I'll be happy to do that for you" in a manner that clearly showed that she was most unhappy?

Context is a critical aid for comprehension. "The food is on the table" can be an invitation to eat or a simple descriptive statement, depending on the context. Context is also used to decide which of two possible meanings is the intended meaning for ambiguous sentences. The intended meaning of "They are kissing fish" is usually straightforward when spoken in context. One way that context directs comprehension is by influencing the way we process incoming language.

Ekman (1992) speaks of "lying truthfully," that is, literally telling the truth while leaving the listener with the opposite impression. For example, he tells about a man who had been unfaithful to his wife for years without getting caught! He had, on several occasions, taken money from her purse to buy flowers for other women. Each time he did this, she noticed the missing money and innocently commented to him: "I could have sworn I had an extra $50 in my purse; I must have lost it." Finally, one day she suspects that her partner has been unfaithful to her because she finds matches from a local hotel in his coat when she takes it to the cleaners. When she confronts him about this, he "honestly lies," by retorting: "Right. I've been having a torrid affair during my lunch breaks; and do you remember those times you thought you had lost money? Well, you didn't. I've been stealing your money to buy my noon-time lovers gifts. And, let me see, what other ignominities have I omitted?" This man just made a complete confession, yet the intent was to mislead his wife by casting it in irony. Intonation matters!

Figure 3.2 is a visual demonstration of the context effect. You'll find that you have no difficulty reading any of the words in Fig. 3.2. Now look carefully at the letters that make up the words. The "H" in "the" is the same form as the "A" in "cat," yet you may not have noticed this unless I pointed it out to you. Similarly, the way we perceive the other "inky" letters depends on the rest of the letters that make up the

TAE CAT

RED

SROT

EISH

DEBT

FIG. 3.2. Examples of the ways context influences meaning.
Notice, for example, that the "D" in "RED" is identical to the "B" in "DEBT." (Adapted from Rumelhart, D. E., McClelland, J. L., and the PDP Research Group. (1986). *Parallel distributed processing*. Cambridge, MA: The MIT Press, p. 8.)

word context. Context provides strong cues that guide the way we construct knowledge about the nature of the world.

Analogy and Metaphor

*Midway between the unintelligible and the commonplace, it is metaphor which
most produces knowledge.*

—Aristotle (*Rhetoric III*, 1410b)

One exception to the rule that the words used to convey a message should correspond to their intended meaning is the use of analogy and metaphor. (The English grammatical distinction among analogy, metaphor, and simile is not being considered here because it is irrelevant in this context.) If I tell you that "Myrtle is a hard-headed woman," the literal translation is not the one intended. In this case, the receiver must use his knowledge about the referent topic (hard surfaces) and "map" the relevant knowledge onto his knowledge of Myrtle. Although you certainly have never met Myrtle, and you may never have heard the expression "a hard-headed woman," you can probably tell me that she is a stubborn, strong-willed person. You came to this understanding by taking your knowledge of hard surfaces, selecting characteristics of hard surfaces that might be relevant to a description of a person, and transferring that knowledge to what you already know about Myrtle.

Using Analogies as an Aid to Understanding

Analogies are pervasive in human thought. Whenever we are faced with a novel situation, we seek to understand it by reference to a known familiar one. When we think by analogy, we map the underlying structure of a known topic onto the target or unknown topic. This mental process is known as "structure mapping" (Halpern, Hansen, & Riefer, 1990; Gentner & Gentner, 1983). Structure mapping assumes network-like representations of concepts in memory in which underlying structural relationships and surface attributes (physical characteristics) are coded along with each concept. For example, when we read that an atom is like a miniature solar system, the implication is that the solar system and the atom have similar relationships among their component parts—smaller bodies revolving around a larger one in fixed path patterns. Other aspects, such as surface similarity (e.g., the sun is hot and large and contains burning gases) is not implied. Analogies can be a useful tool in the comprehension and recall of scientific passages (Halpern, 1987; Halpern, Hansen, & Riefer, 1990). When students read technical passages that contained appropriate analogies to familiar topics, they scored higher on tests of comprehension and recall than a control group of students who read the same passage without the analogy.

All analogies and metaphors state that two concepts are alike in some way. Good analogies have similar underlying structures even when the topics are highly dissimilar. They maintain much of their underlying structure in the transfer from base (known) to target (unknown) domains while surface features are of minimal importance. Poor analogies are ones in which only surface or superficial characteristics are similar. If I said that Myrtle is like milk because they both start with the letter *m*, I would be using a very poor analogy. Whenever you encounter an analogy, you need to consider the nature of the similarity relationship. Are the two concepts similar in their underlying structure so that relevant information about one concept can be used to understand the other concept, or is the similarity trivial? The paradox in thinking with analogies is that the best analogies usually differ in their surface features. Blasko (1999) described analogical thinking as the "interaction of two dissimilar concepts" (p. 1676).

Using Analogies as Problem-Solving Aids

What do you do when you are faced with a problem that has no obvious solution? I address this question in more detail in Chapter 9 on problem solving, but one strategy that is appropriate to consider here is the use of a solution that is borrowed from a problem with a similar structure, often from a very different domain of knowledge. The conditions under which people do and don't recognize and use analogous solutions for problems from very distant domains of knowledge has been the subject of much research (e.g., Vosniadou & Orotony, 1989). In order for this strategy to "work," the problem solver must recognize that the essential characteristics of the two problems are similar, despite the fact that the topics may be very different.

Consider, for example, the problem of bonding (gluing) two surfaces during dental surgery. All bonding substances require a dry surface for bonding, and the mouth is a wet environment. How can this problem be solved? The use of the small towels or "teeth driers" do not work well during oral surgery, which can involve profusive bleeding and the production of much saliva. Some creative dental surgeon looked for similar problems in other domains. He or she (I don't know the identity of this unsung critical thinker) studied the way barnacles attach themselves to piers and other surfaces in the ocean. The adaptive barnacle displaces the water (sort of moves it aside) from the small area to which it is attaching. This displacement of fluids has been modified for use in dentistry. If you're like most people, you will agree that any discovery that makes dental surgery quicker and more successful is a welcome advance. In this example, the problem solver considered the similarities in the two problems of bonding in wet environments and then adapted a solution from one domain (barnacles in the ocean) to a very different one (dental bonding). In this way, an analogy was used to solve a problem.

When cognitive psychologists study the use of analogies to solve problems, they are usually disappointed to find that most of the analogies are only superficially similar to the problem people are given to work on (Tweney & Chitwood, 1995). Laboratory studies of the use of analogies to solve problems are not encouraging. Recently, Dunbar (2001) investigated the use of analogies in real-life settings where experts in a field solve real problems, not the artificial ones that cognitive psychologists create. He found very different results. Real experts involved in solving problems that are important to them use analogies that share "deep structural features" (p. 126). Scientists generate anywhere from between 3 to 15 analogies in a one-hour laboratory meeting, with the majority coming from the domain in which they are working. Dunbar concluded that analogies focusing on relational features are frequently used to help solve problems.

Using Analogies to Persuade

In the popular movie, *Dead Poets Society*, the unlikely hero, Robin Williams, who plays a high school teacher of English, asks his class of young men, "What is the purpose of language?" After a short period of silence, a student yells out the obvious answer, "to communicate." Of course, this is not the correct answer in the movie. The hero-English-teacher-character responds that the purpose of language is to "woo women." An important point is made in this fictional exchange between student and teacher. The purpose of language is to persuade—to change how and what people think. We use language to persuade others to like or date us (as expressed in this movie), to alter or maintain political beliefs (e.g., capitalism is good), or to convince someone to make a purchase (e.g., a particular brand of jeans).

We frequently use analogies to persuade someone that X is analogous to Y, therefore what is true for X is also true for Y. A good example of this sort of "reasoning by analogy" was presented by Bransford, Arbitman-Smith, Stein, and Vye (1985). They described a legal trial in the book, *Till Death Us Do Part* (Bugliosi, 1978). Much of the evidence presented at the trial was circumstantial. The attorney for the defense argued that the evidence was like a chain, and like a chain, it was only as strong as its weakest link. He went on to argue that there were several weak links in the evidence; therefore, the jurors should not convict the accused. The prosecutor also used an analogy to make his point. He argued that the evidence was like a rope made of many independent strands. Several strands can be weak and break, and you will still have a strong rope. Similarly, even though some of the evidence was weak, there was still enough strong evidence to convict the accused. (The prosecutor won the case.)

Can you see how the use of analogies can guide how we think? In the trial example, different sorts of outcomes depend on which of the analogies you found more compelling. Let's consider another example. At a meeting of county administrators, several people who were receiving welfare argued that there should be welfare recipients on the county board. They argued that welfare recipients were in the best position to understand the problems of life on welfare and therefore should be part of the group that makes decisions about welfare. One of the board members said that was an absurd proposition. He argued that having welfare recipients on the county board was like putting residents of an "insane asylum" on the committee that makes the rules for the asylum. What do you think of this analogy? In what ways are people on welfare like the residents of an insane asylum? How are they different? Are they different in ways that makes the board member's conclusions invalid? The insane are unable to think rationally, by definition. This is not true for the poor. I don't believe that this was a good analogy and would not have been persuaded by it. (In fact, I find it insulting.)

Several different sorts of analogies were used in an attempt to persuade the judge and the public during an antitrust lawsuit against Microsoft (*Time*, 1998, June 1). Bill Gates, who argued that it was not a monopoly to bundle only Microsoft products (e.g., Internet Explorer and not Netscape) with its Windows Operating System, made this analogy—"Forcing Microsoft to include Netscape's competing software in our operating system is like requiring Coca-Cola to include three cans of Pepsi in every six-pack it sells" (p. 25). The response from *Time* magazine to this analogy was, ". . . . Coke doesn't control the system that distributes all drinks" (p. 25). Analogies flowed from both sides of the case. Roberta A. Katz, lawyer for Netscape responded, "It's as if one of the networks was also producing the inner workings of the TV set, and every TV was wired so that network was the one you saw" (p. 25). *Time* responded to these anti-Microsoft analogies as well, ". . . at least the Windows user can stick the Microsoft browser in the trash and download Netscape" (p. 25). One thing is clear: Both sides of this heated, high stakes case believed that they could alter the outcome of the case by the use of judicious analogies that would make their point. In case you are wondering about the outcome of this contentious court case, Microsoft was ordered to break into at least two main divisions. As I am writing this, the case is wending its way through a maze of appeals. (Additional analogies from this court case are presented in *Thinking Critically About Critical Thinking*, the workbook that accompanies this text.)

Some analogies are just plain bad—sometimes hilariously funny. I have an unattributed e-mail that claims to contain the winners of a high school contest for the "worst analogy." I don't know if there ever was such a contest, or if these are winning entries, but they are certainly worthy of that dubious honor. Here are two attributed to "unknown": "Her vocabulary was as bad as, like, whatever" and "The red brick wall was the color of a brick-red Crayola crayon."

Here is another bad analogy taken from a magazine advertisement: The advertisement states that "new research" suggests that we have two brains—the one in our head and a second one, "which can override" the one in our head. The second one is our intestines. I hope your initial response to this analogy is to ask questions like, "What recent research? Who did it? Where was it published?" The picture in the ad shows the convoluted outer portion of a brain and intestines drawn to sort of look like the brain. The analogy continues to point out that both have nerve cells (so do sea slugs—is this a critical similarity?). Like the brain in your head, your intestines "is wise"; therefore, you should buy (you knew the ad was to convince you to buy something) healthy bacteria. Whenever you see an attempt to persuade you to buy something or to think a certain way based on analogy, consider the nature of the analogy. Is the analogy sound? How does that analogy relate to its purpose? Even if the "healthy bacteria" are a good idea to purchase and consume, how do they relate to the brain analogy? Just because it is possible to draw the intestines in a way that "looks like" a brain does not mean that they are similar in ways that should be selling the advertised product.

Analogies are used to sell more than "healthy bacteria" for a "brain-like intestines." They are used to sell political candidates and even wars. The 1991 Persian Gulf Crisis offers numerous examples. Was the situation (from the perspective of the United States) like the beginning stages of World War II with Hussein emerging as Hitler (as the hawks would have us believe) or was it like the beginning stages of Vietnam trapping us into an unpopular and protracted war (as the doves would have us believe; Gentner & Holyoak, 1997; Spellman & Holyoak, 1992)? "It would not be an exaggeration to say that the United States went to war over an analogy" (Spellman & Holyoak, 1992, p. 913). These competing analogies were used to persuade the general public about the best response for the situation.

As a final example of the power of analogies to persuade, consider the following speech by Bishop Desmond Tutu (1986), an eloquent leader in the political movement that ended apartheid in South Africa:

> Sometimes you get the notion that people try to inject into your heart that what you do is insignificant; it cannot make a difference. Let me disabuse you of that notion. When people see a colossal problem, they wonder whether they could do anything that makes a difference. They need to keep remembering what they are told about how you eat an elephant—one piece at a time. (p. 216)

Analogies are useful thinking strategies in many different contexts. The deliberate use of analogies as an aid to solving problems and enhancing creativity is discussed in greater detail in later chapters.

WORDS AND THEIR MEANINGS

Eight years after resigning as president, Richard Nixon denied lying *but
acknowledged that he, like other politicians, had* dissembled.

—Paul Ekman (1992, p. 25)

Is alcoholism an illness or is it the lack of willpower by weak people who could stop
drinking if they really wanted to? Is drunkenness a crime that requires punishment
or a mental health condition that needs treatment? I have frequently been asked
questions like these, especially by students who are worried about or disgusted with
a loved one who has a drinking problem. There are many important aspects to this
question. First, the answer to the question of whether alcoholism is an illness depends on how the term "illness" is defined, and more importantly, who gets to do
the defining. Second, it is possible that alcoholism would fit a definition of illness
and be controllable by the individual. The way this question is posed reveals many
unstated assumptions by the person asking the question regarding the nature of
illness and alcoholism. The ramifications of the way we classify alcoholism are important. If we decide that it is a disease, then it is destigmatized and treatment
would be paid for medical insurance plans. If it is a criminal offense, then alcoholics
can expect to "do" jail time, or at least fall under the criminal justice system. Medical
insurance does not cover crimes. The answer to this vexing question has varied over
different geographical locations and throughout history.

Words often have both cognitive and emotional meanings. If I name my brand of
cookies, "Mother's Cookies," then presumably I am activating some of the emotional attachment you feel toward your mother when you think about my cookies.
Furthermore, if I believe that most people will have positive emotions toward their
own mothers (at least when mentioned in the context of cookies), then "Mother's
Cookies" would be a good name for my cookies. Of course, you probably know that
most store-bought cookies are baked in huge factories by people who may or may
not be mothers. I suppose most people like to think that a mother-like figure or perhaps a group of playful elves are baking something tasty for them. The popularity of
these marketing strategies suggests that it is good business to arouse positive emotional reactions toward a product.

Here are some new corporate names, which have no cognitive meaning, but suggest positive emotions. According to Juge (2000, March 9), here is the suggested
meaning of some of the nearly 3000 American companies who changed names in
2000:

- Verizon   "Are they trying to court fans of the band Vertical Horizon (whose
  name itself is an oxymoron)—maybe to show that with Verizon, anything is
  possible?" (p. B4)
- Cingular   "evokes singular, a sign of the company's attempt to sell itself as
  promoters of individuality. Cingular is about you and your individual needs
  and the celebration of your own self expression." (p. B4)
- Accenture   "plays on the belief that parts of the word mean something." (p. B4)

Like all marketing, these names were devised to sell an identity, in this case with
made-up words. It's funny that the name designed to make you think about your individuality (Cingular) is really asking you to be one of their 19 million clients! (Juge,
2000, March 9).

Definitions and the Control of Thought

An amazing event occurred in 1973—millions of mentally ill people were suddenly cured! Well, not exactly suddenly cured. What happened in 1973 was that the American Psychiatric Association removed "homosexuality" from its list of official mental disorders, with the result that the millions of homosexuals were no longer considered by the psychiatric establishment as mentally ill. The American Psychiatric Association maintains the powerful position of deciding which categories of human behavior and emotion should be defined as mental illnesses. This is an immense power because the human behaviors and emotions that are listed in the official "handbook" of mental disorders, the Diagnostic and Statistical Manual (American Psychiatric Association, 1994), determine whether an individual will receive medical funding for treatment, whether a judge will decide to commit an individual to a mental facility or to a prison, and whether people label themselves and others as "normal."

For most of everyday transactions, definitions do not pose a problem. We do not normally have to decide what is meant by terms like *desk, book, house*, etc., unless the particular desk, book, or house is so unusual that there might be doubt about how well it fits our notions of what these terms mean. Of course, we cannot define every term that we use—this would be a tedious and pointless exercise. However, the problem of definition can be critical when words are used as a means of persuasion.

Consider the disastrous situation that occurred when Americans were held against their will in Iran during Jimmy Carter's term (1976–1980) as president of the United States. At first, the Americans were described as *detainees*, but the term quickly changed to *interees*. Soon, the Americans were being referred to as *prisoners* and then *hostages*. Each time, the word used to describe their status escalated in its emotional impact. The label *detainees* suggests that there is nothing to worry about; *hostage* is a "fighting term" that will cost lives and means armed conflict is likely. Americans can be convinced that military action is need to free *hostages*, but people are unlikely to be willing to kill or die for *detainees*. It is of little value to try to decide which of these terms is the most correct; more importantly, who gets to decide which term is used?

This is an important point because the words used to describe a situation become more warlike as a prelude to armed conflict. For example, in 1985, Philadelphia police dropped a bomb on the home and headquarters of a black militant group called "MOVE." It destroyed two city blocks and left over 200 people homeless. How could this happen? According to Wagner-Pacifici, a professor at Swarthmore College, as the confrontation heated up, the words used to describe this group changed from more neutral terms like "zealots" to more inflammatory terms like "terrorists." The language used to frame the problem was a major factor in the action taken by the police. She concluded that, "If you end up talking about an action you're going to take against a group in military terms, you begin to think and operate as if you are in a war" (quoted in The Chronicle of Higher Education, April 20, 1994, p. A8).

Let's take a simple concept, like death. When is a person dead? It is now possible to maintain an individual on machines that breathe for her and tubes that carry nutrients into the body and wastes out. Is such an individual dead? How do you know? We think very differently about an individual who is dead than one who is not. We bury the dead and not the living, but how can we know what to do if we cannot decide whether an individual is living or dead? New technologies and medical advances have made even simple concepts like death more complex.

Terms that are heavily laden with emotional impact often elicit strong images. If you have already read Chapter 2 on memory, then you recall (I hope) that imagery helps to maintain a concept in memory, a factor that is related to its ability to elicit strong emotions. This fact is well known by propagandists who want to convince the masses to act in extreme ways. In *Mein Kampf*, Adolph Hitler used expressions like "racial brew," "purity of the blood," "poisoning of the blood," and "bastardization" in his successful attempt to convince millions of people to participate in the killing of millions of other people who differed from them in their religious beliefs. Hitler even offered the "final solution," which means that he found a way to solve a problem: His solution was to massacre an entire religious group. Hitler and his compatriots also used actual visual images to reinforce these emotions. Pictures of Jews were alternated with revolting pictures of sewer rats and roaches crawling over filth so that the images of Jewish faces and the vermin would become associated in people's minds. It is interesting to note that the Nazis studied American advertising in the 1920s to develop their persuasive techniques. If you are thinking that no contemporary person would fall prey to such blatant tactics designed to increase racism, you have not read the papers lately.

Stop now and consider the way in which you would define the term *crime*, if you had the power to write the definitions.

(Did you really stop and try to define what you think the word *crime* should mean?) Don't go on until you try this simple exercise.

According to Peck, there was a famous inmate in a federal jail, a gangster named Louis Lepke. In the cell next to his was a young conscientious objector from Iowa, named Lowell Naeve. Mr. Naeve tried to explain what a conscientious objector was to Mr. Lepke. Lepke replied incredulously, "You mean they put you in here for *not* killing?" (quoted in Peck, 1986, p. 146). Lepke then laughed and laughed. Did your definition of crime include the crime of refusing to go to war? Is Mr. Naeve a criminal?

Definitions are not static "truths." Meanings change over time as a function of technological development, changing social mores, and a drift in the way words are used. However, it is not true that a word can mean anything that anyone wants it to. There is an advertisement in a large city newspaper for a plastic surgeon who "specializes in nose reduction, breast enlargement and reduction, liposuction, baggy eyes, weak chins, face lifts, and saddlebag thighs." Putting aside the obnoxious idea that every body part needs "fixing," this surgeon claims to be able to do it all. How then, can he claim to be a "specialist"? The word is being misused to convey the idea that he has great depth of knowledge and experience in *all* aspects of plastic surgery. If he can perform many types of plastic surgery, he is a generalist. By definition, he can't specialize in everything.

Similarly, I bristle at offers for "free gifts with purchase." This is a marketing scheme based on the idea that we all love gifts and bargains. A gift is free, or it is not a gift. Consider the great deal that I saw advertised for soap.

Buy three bars, get one free.

The cost of the four bars of soap was $2.00. How does this differ from buying soap at its regular price of $.50 a bar? Do I really believe that the soap manufacturer has a "gift" for me? It is not "free" nor is it a "gift," if I have to pay money to receive it. Every brand of vitamins in the store near my home offers 30 "free" vitamins with the purchase of a bottle of 100 vitamins. (The free vitamins are packaged separately in a small bottle, thus adding to production costs and increasing waste and the cost of the vitamins.) Wouldn't it be more honest to state instead that the price shown is the cost for 130 vitamins? I promise to buy such a brand, if I ever find one that is honest in advertising its cost. Also, if I ever meet up with the advertising giant who devised this particular scheme to separate consumers from their money, I will have a "free gift" for her or him.

The Power of Labels and Categories

As I sat with friends drinking coffee at my kitchen table, someone yelled, "Kill it, kill it," as a very large bug darted across the floor. "Yuk, it's a cockroach." But on further inspection, we found that it was not a cockroach, but a "cute little cricket." A friend scooped up the cricket in a paper cup and gently released it outdoors, while my daughter ran after it trying to feed it lettuce and grass. Why was it disgusting and in need of immediate extermination when we believed it to be one type of bug—a cockroach—and cute and in need of saving when it turned out to be another—a cricket?

The process of categorization is essential in understanding the world and guiding our responses. When we see a bug, or a baby, or an old person, or a professor, we use our knowledge about the categories to which they belong to make inferences about how they are likely to act. We know that a baby will share some essential features with all babies. It will sometimes cry for reasons that we cannot understand; it will need to have its diaper changed; it will slobber and coo. Of course, every baby is unique, but, fortunately, we can use our knowledge of category membership to know something about every baby. This is fortunate because it reduces the load on memory and allows us to understand and predict what will happen when interacting with any baby. The process of categorization is an example of **cognitive economy**, which means that it is a process that reduces the mental workload and makes thinking less effortful. Instead of having to learn a set of new expectations for every stimulus with which we come in contact, we can use category membership to reduce the uncertainty in the situation.

Although categories are necessary in dealing with the large variety of objects in the world, they also can be the cause of serious errors. Not all members of a category are the same, and often a stimulus is miscategorized. Stereotypes result from several cognitive and noncognitive processes, but one clear reason that they persist is due to the effect of categorical thinking. Think about a racial or religious group that is different from your own. Describe the members of that group. You will find that general terms emerge that clearly do not apply to all group members, and may not even apply to any group members. When you think about members of your own race or religion, you will tend think of them as much more individualized than members of other groups. As long as we classify individuals into racial and religious groups and label the members of these groups with certain attributes, stereotypical beliefs will be maintained.

Every year U.S. park rangers report that someone is seriously mauled by a bear in one or more of our national parks. Often, the injured person was trying to feed or even hug a large, wild bear. Why? Because many Americans have categorized bears along with dogs as friendly animals with which we can play. After all, the only bears that most of us know personally are Yogi Bear (a lovable and dim-witted cartoon character), Smokey the Bear (the spokesbear for fire prevention, also a cartoon character), teddy bears (popular stuffed animals), and possibly the highly trained, human-like bears that we see riding bicycles and playing ball in zoo and circus acts.

Non Sequitur © Wiley Miller. Dist. By UNIVERSAL PRESS SYNDICATE. Reprinted with permission. All rights reserved.

These artificial situations lead many people to miscategorize bears as cuddly animals instead of dangerous ones.

Similarly, people decide what is natural or right based on their categorical systems. In Western countries, dead cows and chickens are acceptable foods. The Vietnamese traditionally consider dogs and monkeys to be food, yet many Westerners cringe at this "unnatural" food choice. Many Japanese find raw seafood to be a delicacy, and the French often enjoy eating snails and frog's legs. (I have often wondered what happens to frog arms. Yes, this is a feeble attempt at a joke. Do I get points for just trying?) In times of severe famine, people have been known to eat old shoes, the bark of trees, and even other humans. The point of this stomach-turning paragraph is that what seems to be a natural category, like what is a food, often turns out to be culturally bound and arbitrary, when it is inspected more closely. We use the same processes of categorical thinking when we determine which behaviors are natural for women and men and other groups, such as old people and the disabled, based on experiences in our own culture. Most of us are completely unaware of the extent to which culture influences our thinking by creating categories and determining what belongs in each category.

Prototypical Thinking

At the local baseball game, the final score was 8–9, yet no man on either team ever crossed home plate.

How is this possible?

You should be able to solve this riddle fairly easily because it has the same structure and answer as a riddle that I posed in Chapter 1. I repeat it here to make a point. We tend to think in terms of **prototypes** or best examples of a category. Not surprisingly this is called **prototypical thinking**. Give up? The game was played in an all-women league. For those of you who could not solve this problem, it is probably because you automatically think of males when you think of baseball players, just as in the first chapter, many people did not think of a woman when the physician was described as a neurosurgeon. Even if you had heard the neurosurgeon puzzle before, did you recognize that the same principle was affecting your thinking when I changed the riddle so that it pertained to baseball players? Of course, you know that women play baseball, but this does not readily "come to mind."

Although I have never met you, I already know a great deal about what and how you think. Let me demonstrate this with an exercise devised by Decyk (1994). For each of the following categories, give a good example. In fact, give the first example that comes to mind:

1. A bird
2. A color
3. A triangle (a picture is okay)
4. A motor vehicle
5. A sentence
6. A hero
7. A heroic action
8. A game
9. A philosopher
10. A writer

Are you finished? Here is a list of your most likely answers: (1) for a bird you probably named robin or sparrow, or possibly eagle; (2) for a color you most likely said red or blue; (3) for your triangle you either drew or named an equilateral triangle; (4) for a motor vehicle you probably listed a car; (5) for an example of a sentence you probably wrote a short declarative sentence (e.g., The girl ran home.); (6) the hero you named is most likely one of the following males—Superman, Batman, or possibly a fireman; (7) the heroic action you named probably involved a single act by a male such as a rescue by a fireman; (8) most likely you listed Monopoly as an example of a game, or some other board game; (9) for a philosopher you probably named Socrates or Aristotle; (10) and finally, for a writer you probably named Stephen King, but if you named someone else, it is very probably a white male author.

What is the point of this demonstration? People tend to think in terms of prototypes or "best examples" of a category. Our prototypes vary from culture to culture, but they are relatively standard within a culture. If you live in Australia, you might name a "kiwi" as an example of a bird, a response that would be very unusual for Americans or Chinese. Thinking in terms of prototypes biases how and what we think. When we think about members of a category, only the most typical exemplars (examples of a category) readily come to mind. Consider the implications of the finding that most people name only living white males as an example of a writer. It means that we carry a standardized "picture" or "definition" of those characteristics that writers share and these characteristics are restricted with regard to time, race, and sex. Of course, different answers would be expected from people from countries other than the United States or, possibly, other cultural groups within the same country. Most Russians would probably name Puskin, or less probably, Tolstoy or Chekhov, if they were asked to give an example of a writer. But, regardless of what the particular prototype is, the reliance on the most typical member of a category limits thinking. Few people will name an older person or a child or a dog when asked to think of a hero, yet old people and children and even dogs (e.g., Lassie) can and do perform heroic acts. The most commonly named philosophers are dead, Greek males. With prototypes like this, few people will "think of" philosophy as a popular, contemporary profession that is open to all ages and races.

If you maintain a conscious awareness of the way prototypes restrict thinking, it is possible to reduce their effect (Decyk, 1994). Practice giving unusual answers to the category questions asked above. With a little thought, you can think of ways to subdivide the categories and expand the possibilities that you develop. For example, Monopoly is a board game. Name some other types of games (e.g., ball games, card games, jacks). Think about games played alone (e.g., solitaire) and games played with others (e.g., hangman). What about games from other countries, games from other times in history, and games played by children (e.g., pat-a-cake and peek-a-boo)? With very little effort, you can generate a wide variety of games that differ from your prototype. The deliberate use of giving unusual examples of categories is one way of making a wider array of information that is stored in memory more accessible, so that you can use the knowledge that you already have acquired when you need it.

LANGUAGE: TOOL OR MASTER OF THOUGHT?

Learn a new language and get a new soul.

—Czech proverb

We use language not only to convey our thoughts, but also to mold and shape them. Language and thought are inextricably related concepts that exert mutual influences on each other. Some psychologists believe that language, at least in part, influences thought. Examples of this concept were presented earlier in this chapter in the section on labeling and the way labels affect how we think. The hypothesis that the language we use affects how we think is called the **Sapir-Whorf hypothesis of linguistic relativity**, or more informally, the Sapir-Whorf hypothesis (Sapir, 1960; Whorf, 1956).

"How do I know what I mean until I see what I say?" (Miller, 1972, p. 43). In a humorous way, this question examines the relationship between thought and language. Although it seems clear to most people that our thoughts influence the language that we use, it is sometimes more difficult to understand the reciprocal nature of the relationship. Anthropologists and psychologists have studied whether people who speak different languages also think differently. Perhaps you have had the experience of translating a passage from one language to another and had difficulty conveying exactly the same meaning. Jokes are a good example of this. Ethnic jokes that are told in their native language frequently lose their humor when they are told in translation. Could this indicate that ways of thinking, as reflected in language, differ across cultures?

Some chilling implications of the Sapir-Whorf hypothesis appeared in George Orwell's classic book written in 1949, which he entitled *1984*. In *1984*, he wrote about a repressive society that was able to control the thoughts of its citizenry by redefining some words and removing others from the language. By gaining control of the language, this futuristic society dictated which thoughts were possible and which were not.

The Orwellian example is an extreme interpretation of the Sapir-Whorf hypothesis that language absolutely determines thought. According to this view, if a term does not exist within a language, speakers do not have the corresponding thought. Do you believe that if the word *love* didn't exist in our language, then people wouldn't be able to feel the emotion represented by the word? Most people would disagree with the strong form of the Sapir-Whorf hypothesis. Cross-cultural research that has examined the way different languages influence thought has not supported the strong version of the Sapir-Whorf hypothesis (Berlin & Kay, 1969; Rosch, 1977). A weaker version of the Sapir-Whorf hypothesis is that language influences but does not determine thinking. As an example of this, consider the following terms carefully and decide if each elicits a different thought: senior citizen; old man; golden-ager. Did each term connote a different thought? Did you think about a different type of person with each word? Most people agree that they did. (See Fig. 3.3.)

The Direction and Misdirection of Thought

All words are pegs to hang ideas on.

—Henry Ward Beecher (1812–1887)

Proverbs from Plymouth Pulpit (cited in Drysdale 1887, p. 33)

Senior Citizen   Old Man   Golden Ager

FIG. 3.3.   The words we use influence how we think. Compare the different thoughts that are evoked by the terms "senior citizen," "old man," and "golden-ager."

Given that language will influence what we think, it is only a short leap to suggest that language can be used in deliberate ways to shape thinking so that it conforms to a particular ideology or point of view. It also seems likely that if we understand how language is used to direct how we think, then an awareness of the ways in which this occurs should help us to resist the automatic type of thinking that goes along with an uncritical approach to communication.

Emotional Language and Name Calling

As described in the earlier section on labeling, the same event can be described in several different ways. Yet, the words we use to describe an event are not interchangeable in the meaning they convey. Language that is highly emotional has a different effect on readers and listeners than more mundane ways of conveying the intended meaning. This is the weaker version of the Sapir-Whorf hypothesis—although language may not *determine* thought, it directs, and sometimes misdirects, it. Consider the heated debate between those for and against abortion. The faction opposed to abortion realized that it is better to be for something than against something and therefore decided to call their stance "pro-life" rather than "anti-choice." On the other side, those who favored abortion certainly didn't want to be called "anti-life" and decided to label their stance "pro-choice." They hoped that people would think differently about a position that is "pro-choice" than they would about one that is "anti-life." Of course, the position hasn't changed—only its label or name has changed, but presumably the way the position is labeled influences how people think about it. One "pro-lifer" told a colleague that the best way to win a debate on this topic is to use frequently the words *kill* and *baby* in the same sentence (Kahane, 1992). The juxtaposition of these two words is sure to bring about an emotional response.

Another example of the deliberate choice of words to create a carefully planned impression concerns the "rewriting" of history. All history texts (indeed, everything) were written by someone with a particular point of view. Recently, the word *aggression* was taken out of Japanese history books that described World War II invasions. Do the same descriptions of an act seem "better" in some sense when they are not modified by the word *aggressive*? The contemporary Japanese historians who asked for this deletion apparently think so. Similarly, Russian historians are now using harsher terms to describe Stalin's role when he was the leader of the former Soviet Union. They now know and are free to say that Stalin slaughtered millions of innocent Russians whose "crime" was to disagree with his policies. Such people were officially labeled "enemies of the state," a label that was meant to instill fear in the individual who received such a label and to convey to everyone else that disagreement with Stalin's official policies would be considered an act of treason. History is also being rewritten in nonverbal ways in the new capitalist Russia. A massive number of statues of Lenin and Stalin are now being sold as scrap metal with new statues of Peter the Great and other Romanovs (members of the former ruling family) now standing on the pedestals that held the bronze busts of communist leaders for most of the 20th century. With the advent of advertising in the new capitalist Russia, images of the "Marlboro Man" puffing away on imported cigarettes are now more numerous than depictions of the formerly ubiquitous Lenin. It is clear that emotionally laden words and inspiring visual displays both reflect and influence how people think.

The lesson is clear: When you want to influence how people think, choose your words and images carefully. You also need to be aware of the ways in which other people attempt to manipulate your thoughts by the labels they use. The deliberate use of words designed to create a particular attitude or foster certain beliefs is called **semantic slanting**. The meaning or semantics is slanted so that the listener's thoughts will be directed in some way. It's fairly easy to find examples of this around election time when issues and groups label themselves with favorable terms and others with negative terms (name calling). During a recent election, a group called "Citizens for Sane Laws" opposed a proposition, and another group called "Citizens for Better Government" favored it. The political advertisements continued to broadcast these group names and the message to vote "No on 10" or "Yes on 10," depending on who financed the advertisement. Very little meaningful information was ever given on the merits or problems of the proposition. Be wary of attempts to influence your thinking through the use of positive and negative labels, especially on the important issues that concern social and political policies. I received a political solicitation that may be among the most blatantly slanted in the choice of words that it used. The outside of the envelope read, "The bloated, blathering bottom-feeders of big government hope that you'll never uncover *these* secrets." For some reason, I didn't expect to find reasoned and impartial information inside the envelope. Would you?

Ambiguity, Vagueness, and Equivocation

The thinking process can also be misled when words are imprecise or misused. Words are **ambiguous** when they can have multiple meanings depending on context, and the appropriate meaning is unclear in a given context. The problem here, as in the sentences described earlier, is one of determining the intended meaning or underlying representation. A good example of this was provided by von Oech (1983). According to von Oech, J. Edgar Hoover, the former director of the FBI, was reviewing a typed copy of a letter he had dictated to his secretary. He didn't like the margin widths she had used for the letter and wrote, "Watch the borders" on the letter and asked her to retype the letter and send copies to top FBI agents. For the next two weeks, FBI agents were put on special alert along the Canadian and Mexican borders.

Another humorous example of ambiguity was provided by Fogelin (1987). Compare the following two sentences:

Mary had a little lamb; it followed her to school.
Mary had a little lamb; and then a little broccoli.

The word *had* is ambiguous. It is used to mean *owned* in the first sentence and *ate* in the second sentence. Its meaning is not clarified until the second half of each sentence. A clever example of ambiguity can be found in the title of a classic book by Phyllis Chesler (1972), *Women and Madness*, in which she meant madness to mean both anger and insanity. I also deliberately used ambiguity in the title of my edited book *Changing College Classrooms* (Halpern, 1994). The word *changing* could refer to the fact that college classrooms are changing or that we should engage in activities to change them. I meant the word in both senses; hence I made deliberate use of ambiguity. Often, a situation is ambiguous and you are not sure how to respond or which of several definitions is appropriate. Although this sort of ambiguity can lead to errors, not all ambiguity is negative. Sometimes, creative interpretations of the intended meaning and creative responses are the result of ambiguous situations.

Although ambiguous words have multiple meanings, vague words have imprecise meanings. **Vagueness** refers to a lack of precision in a communication. If your friend Martha told you to bake a cake in a hot oven, you'd probably ask her how hot it should be. In this context, the word *hot* is too vague and needs to be specified further. Consider the "clarification" provided by Justice Brennan of the U.S. Supreme Court when he provided a working definition that would assist those in the legal process of determining the sort of punishment that is cruel and unusual. As you probably know, punishment that is cruel and unusual is prohibited by the U.S. Constitution. But, we have little guidance for determining what makes a punishment cruel and unusual. He offered, "a punishment is cruel and unusual . . . if it does not comport with human dignity." Such a definition will not help a judge or jury decide whether a particular punishment is cruel and unusual. Justice Brennan's comments are much too vague to be useful. It is not easier to determine which actions do not comport with human dignity than it is to decide if they are cruel and unusual. A communication is vague if it does not specify enough details for its intended purpose.

There is legislation in California that requires warning notices to be posted in all places where the public may come in contact with cancer-causing chemicals. The sign designed for gas stations is shown in Fig. 3.4.

As you can see, the new signs are too vague to be of value. There is no information about the level of risk, or the likelihood of developing cancer, or how long you would have to be exposed to these chemicals to reach some level of risk. There is no way to use this information to make a meaningful decision about whether the risk is so high the area should be avoided. This is a clear example of a deliberately unclear communication. The gasoline companies were opposed to this law and have registered their complaint by posting the required signs, but not providing the public with interpretable information.

Vagueness is sometimes a socially polite way of handling an unpleasant situation. If you ask someone about her divorce, you may get a vague response like "We were incompatible," rather than a more precise, but less acceptable, "The stinking rat cheated every chance he could get."

FIG. 3.4. An example of vagueness. California law requires that warning signs be posted in all places where consumers come in contact with cancer-causing chemicals. Signs like this one are being used at all gas stations. The information they convey is too vague to be meaningful.

Equivocation occurs when the meaning of a word is changed in the course of the same discussion, and thus is different from vagueness or ambiguity. Consider the following "line of reasoning" (Reasoning will be considered more fully in the next chapter.):

1. Man is the only rational animal.
2. No woman is a man.
3. Therefore, no woman is rational. (Damer, 1987)

The meaning of the word *man* changed from the first to the second sentence. In the first sentence, *man* stood for all of humanity—both female and male. In the second sentence, it was used as a sex-specific term, with females conveniently omitted.

Etymology and Reification

These two terms both concern word meanings. **Etymology** is the study of word origins. It's often interesting to learn how language evolved and developed. However, it is wrong to conclude that a word has a particular meaning or nuance based on the word from which it was derived. Consider, for example, the use of the word *gay* to refer to homosexual men. The word is commonly used today to denote pride and other positive attributes of male homosexuals. The origin of the word was quite different. The word *gay* was derived from a definition meaning "wanton and licentious." It would be wrong to conclude that gays are therefore wanton and licentious. Language is a living entity and word definitions evolve and change. Returning to a word's origins to find its contemporary meaning is like studying the writings of Karl Marx to understand how modern communism is practiced in Cuba.

Reification is a more difficult concept to explain. Reification occurs when something abstract is given a name and then treated as though it were a concrete object. Consider the Freudian notion of the "ego." According to Freudian theory, the ego is that portion of the personality that deals with reality. Sometimes, therapists forget that it is an abstract concept and start treating it as though it were tangible. If a physician suggested that you take vitamins or engage in exercise to strengthen your ego, you should run quickly from his office. The ego is not something that can be physically altered because it is an abstract concept, not a physical body part. Perhaps the most obvious case of reification involves the concept of intelligence, where intelligence tests yield "IQ" scores that are said to measure it, and then IQ is used as though it were the physical embodiment of intelligence.

Bureaucratese and Euphemism

Two language barriers to comprehension are bureaucratese and euphemism. **Bureaucratese** is the use of formal, stilted language that is unfamiliar to people who lack special training. The same information can be expressed better with simpler terms. Bureaucratese is different from the use of precise technical terms that may be needed in specialized disciplines; in bureaucratese, the style and language hinders our understanding instead of aiding it. The legal profession is often guilty of bureaucratese. I once read a legal document that began with the term "Witnesseth." Of course, I questioned what meaning was being conveyed with the use of this term, which is standard on many legal forms. The answer was "very little." It could have been deleted altogether or replaced with "Notice" or "Read this document," both of which would have been more meaningful than the obscure "Witnesseth." Ditto for other obscure terms like "party of the first part" and "party of the second part," not to mention the archaic Latinisms that riddle the law (e.g., "ex parte" and "corpus delecti").

Euphemism is the substitution of a desirable term for a less desirable or offensive one. Although there is nothing inherently wrong with polite conversation, the result is often a loss of communication. Euphemism is common in hospital and medical facilities where bodily functions need to be discussed. Hospital personnel may ask a patient if he has "voided his bladder." Many patients do not realize that this refers to urination. In fact, it has been shown that a majority of patients do not understand the language that is commonly used in their interactions with medical staff. Many patients do not understand words like *malignant*, *benign*, *terminal*, and *generic*. You can imagine a solemn physician telling a patient that she is "terminal," with the patient then brightly inquiring when she'll get better. It is easy to see how the use of euphemisms can lead to misunderstandings.

Euphemisms abound in advertisements of all sorts. Do "bathroom tissue" and "feminine hygiene products" seem more desirable and glamorous than toilet paper and menstrual pads? Euphemisms often obscure the intended meaning. Although polite speech is a necessary rule of society, euphemistic terms that are not commonly used interfere with the communication of ideas, and thus should be avoided.

Euphemisms are designed to change the affect or emotion that we feel when we confront topics that we may find repugnant. The idea is that feelings will be less negative if a phenomenon is given a more acceptable name. For example, many people have complained that "beauty pageants," like the "Miss America Pageant," are demeaning to its participants whose value is determined by their appearance—much like a horse or cow at an auction. Officials and sponsors of these pageants disagree. They argue that these pageants are opportunities for the contestants to demonstrate their talents and to win money and other prizes that can be used to finance an education or to launch a career. Those who believe that such displays are demeaning reply that the bathing suit competition, in which women march around in skimpy bathing suits and high-heel shoes, should not be a requirement for scholarship money for a college education. This argument has continued heatedly for years, mostly centering around the bathing suit competition. In recognition of the fact that a contestant's appearance when clad in scanty clothing probably is unrelated to her talent, academic potential, or scholarship, the officials of the Miss America Pageant decided to remedy this situation. They renamed the competition. Women still parade in scanty swimsuits and high heels, but now it is called "health and fitness in a swimsuit" (Leive, 1994). This is a strange euphemism for the portion of the competition that leads the contestants to resort to starvation diets and plastic surgery—neither of which promotes health and fitness.

Probably the biggest perpetuators of euphemisms are politicians. In response to public protests over tax increases, we now have "revenue enhancement" bills. Abortion is now sometimes called "pregnancy termination," and sex education classes are often called "family education." One of my favorite examples is in the change of a class title that was offered in a junior high school. Based on the idea that boys as well as girls need to know about cooking, nutrition, and similar topics, a teacher offered a course called "home economics for boys." It had zero enrollment. She then got wise and retitled the course "bachelor living." So many boys wanted to take the class with this new name, there was a waiting list. With very little effort, you should be able to find other examples where the change of a label changed how people think.

Framing with Leading Questions, Negation, and Marked Words

Framing occurs when a question is asked in a way that suggests what the correct response should be. The reader is "led" into assuming a particular perspective or point of view.

Consider the following problem:

Imagine that the United States is preparing for the outbreak of an unusual disease, which is expected to kill 600 people. Two alternative programs to combat the disease have been proposed. Assume that the exact scientific estimate of the consequences of the programs are as follows:

If Program A is adopted, 200 people will be saved.

If Program B is adopted, there is 1/3 probability that 600 people will be saved, and 2/3 probability that no people will be saved.

Which of the two programs would you favor? (Tversky & Kahneman, 1981, p. 453)

Now consider the same problem, and select between the following two programs:

If Program C is adopted, 400 people will die.

If Program D is adopted there is 1/3 probability that nobody will die, and 2/3 probability that 600 people will die.

Which of these two programs would you favor?

When this problem was presented to college students, 72% of those given the first set of choices selected Program A, and 78% of those given the second set of choices selected Program D. Look closely at the choices. Program A and C are effectively identical—they differ only in that A is described in terms of the numbers of lives saved, but C is described in terms of the number who will die. Programs B and D are also identical, differing only in the language used to describe the outcomes. It seems that most people are **risk adverse**, which means that they prefer options that do not involve loss. When an alternative makes a potential loss prominent (e.g., focuses on the number that die), people will reject that alternative. It is clear that when an option is stated in terms of a loss, it is judged more negatively than a mathematically identical statement about gains. This is an important result, showing that human judgments and preferences can be readily manipulated by changes in the way questions are asked or framed. If I tell you that a new medical treatment has a 50% success rate, you will be more likely to endorse its use than if I tell you that it has a 50% failure rate. The only difference is whether the information was presented in a positive (success rate) frame or a negative (failure rate) frame (Halpern & Blackman, 1985; Halpern, Blackman, & Salzman, 1989).

Framing is one of those topics that appears in several different chapters in this text because it can be used to influence thinking in many different contexts. A frame creates a particular perspective on a issue—"it manipulates salience in order to influence subsequent judgment" (Rhoads, http://www.influenceatwork.com/retrieved February 10, 2002). The underlying idea is that we can be made to think about the same subject in different ways, depending on what it is about that subject that we are focusing on. For example, if I asked you if you think that the president is doing a good job, you might think about the state of the economy and come up with one answer or think about international relations and come up with another. If I can get you to focus on one of these variables (the economy or international relations) by making it more salient in your thinking, then I could influence the way you assess the president. Framing effects are ubiquitous—good salespeople use them to get us to focus on positive aspects of their products and good lawyers and others use them to persuade juries and the rest of us about the guilt or innocence of their client.

Framing effects can be powerful. If you understand how they work, you can use framing to your advantage and recognize when others are using it to their advantage. Suppose you are interviewing for a job and you have gotten to the "sticky" issue of negotiating salary. If you said to the prospective employer that you really wanted $50,000 a year, but you are willing to take $45,000, the employer begins to see this offer as a gain of $5000. Similarly, if the prospective employer were to say that she was ready to offer $40,000 but is willing to go as high as $45,000 (after all you studied critical thinking and should be worth more salary), then you would have the "feeling" of having gained $5000. The first figure mentioned set a frame (or anchor—a topic considered later in this chapter) for interpreting the salary (Pinkley & Northcraft, 2000).

Another example of the influence of language on thought comes from a study by Loftus (1975, p. 561). Forty people were asked questions about their headaches. A key question was posed in one of two ways:

"Do you get headaches frequently, and, if so, how often?"
or
"Do you get headaches occasionally, and, if so, how often?"

Can you anticipate the results of this study? The respondents who answered the first question reported an average of 2.2 headaches per week, whereas those who answered the second question reported an average of .7 headaches per week. It seems that if people are asked questions with the word *frequently*, they will believe they have experienced more headaches than if they are asked the same question with the word *occasionally*. Note that although this example does not seem to contain any deliberate attempts to mislead or direct respondents' answers, the changes in wording have accomplished exactly that end. Pay careful attention to the way that questions are posed. Always consider if slight changes in the language used would result in different responses. Try rephrasing a question or information for yourself and remain alert for ways in which slight changes in phrasing could be producing large differences in responses.

Salespeople know that leading questions can be good for business. If I am showing you some household items, a good sales technique is to ask "How many will you take?" The assumption here is that the sale is made, and it is only a matter of how many you will buy, not whether you will buy. Similarly, a car salesperson who is ready to "close the deal" will ask "What color do you want?" This question makes it clear that you have already decided that you will buy the car and the only decision left is that of color.

Advertisers and merchants like to price their wares in uneven amounts, like $19.99 and $24.95. Have you ever wondered why they don't simplify matters and price garments to the nearest dollar so that $19.99 would be labeled $20.00 and $24.95 would become $25.00? The frame or perspective being induced here is one of considering the price as "less than $20.00." Of course, the one-cent difference is negligible, but it does seem to change how people think about the price.

Listeners can also be framed or misled with **negation**. Suppose you read that a prominent politician is not a drunk. Suppose further that this is absolutely true; she is not a drunk. Most people would infer that there was some question about her sobriety and the truth of the assertion. The pragmatic function of negation is to deny something that is plausible (Carroll, 1986). Thus, listeners will infer the plausibility of that which was denied. President Richard Nixon hadn't considered this psycholinguistic principle when he uttered the now-famous words in response to his Watergate debacle—"I am not a crook." Most people took this to mean that it is plausible that he is a crook. Thus, the denial of some act often has the paradoxical result that people now believe it is more likely to be true than they would have if no denial had been made.

Contrast and Context

Are you making a good salary? How is your health? Is the new love in your life intelligent and kind? Do you approve of the current president? The way you are likely to answer all of these questions depends on what you are comparing them to and the context in which the comparison is being made. Contrast and context provide meaning to cognitive activities like judging and evaluating. In a classic study, Parducci (1968) asked subjects to decide how bad it is to "pocket the tip that the previous customers left for the waitress." Half the subjects were asked to judge this event along with the following mild infractions: stealing a loaf of bread from a store when you are starving; playing poker on Sunday; cheating at solitaire. The other half of the subjects were asked to judge the same event (pocketing the tip that the previous customers left for the waitress) along with the following infractions: spreading rumors that an acquaintance is a sexual pervert; putting your deformed child in the circus; murdering your mother without justification or provocation.

Taking a waitress' tip was judged to be a more serious offense when it was presented along with milder infractions than when it was presented among a list of serious infractions. The event (pocketing a tip) was exactly the same in each case, and the wording was identical. Changes in the context in which it was presented created changes in the way it was evaluated. Context is an important determinant of the meaning we assign to events.

Judgments and evaluations are always made relative to some frame of reference. Suppose that your friend has just moved into a small one-room apartment near campus. This apartment will seem like heaven, if he has moved from an even smaller one-room apartment that he shared with four people he did not like, and it will seem awful if he moved from a large swanky penthouse in the best part of the city. The object being evaluated (the apartment) and the evaluator are the same in both scenarios. The only change is the frame of reference that is being used. Contrast is a powerful determinant of the way in which we evaluate an alternative.

I recall reading a book when I was a child entitled *Cheaper by the Dozen* (Gilbreth, 1963). It was a (mostly) true story about a family with 12 children, hence the title, and their parents, who were psychologists. The father knew very well about the power of contrast effects. After he purchased a new home for his family, he took them out to see it for the first time. He drove around the city, stopping at various run-down houses in bad neighborhoods, while he pretended to be lost. Finally, he pulled up to the home he had purchased, which looked like a palace in comparison to the decaying shacks he had stopped at earlier. The family was delighted with their luxurious new home, which certainly seemed even better when compared to the others that they had just seen. This principle is used quite well in the letter that is reprinted from a delightful book by Cialdini (1993) and shown in Fig. 3.5.

Contrast can be used effectively in a wide range of situations. For example, Zimbardo and Leippe (1991) offer this advice when you want to borrow money from a friend or parent. They suggest that you first ask for a large sum that you are fairly

Dear Mother and Dad:

Since I left for college I have been remiss in writing and I am sorry for my thoughtlessness in not having written before. I will bring you up to date now, but before you read on, please sit down. You are not to read any further unless you are sitting down, okay?

Well, then, I am getting along pretty well now. The skull fracture and the concussion I got when I jumped out the window of my dormitory when it caught on fire shortly after my arrival here is pretty well healed now. I only spent two weeks in the hospital and now I can see almost normally and only get those sick headaches once a day. Fortunately, the fire in the dormitory, and my jump, was witnessed by an attendant at the gas station near the dorm, and he was the one who called the Fire Department and the ambulance. He also visited me in the hospital and since I had nowhere to live because of the burntout dormitory, he was kind enough to invite me to share his apartment with him. It's really a basement room, but it's kind of cute. He is a very fine boy and we have fallen deeply in love and are planning to get married. We haven't got the exact date yet, but it will be before my pregnancy begins to show.

Yes, Mother and Dad, I am pregnant. I know how much you are looking forward to being grandparents and I know you will welcome the baby and give it the same love and devotion and tender care you gave me when I was a child. The reason for the delay in our marriage is that my boyfriend has a minor infection which prevents us from passing our pre-marital blood tests and I carelessly caught it from him. I know that you will welcome him into our family with open arms. He is kind and, although not well educated, he is ambitious. Although he is of a different race and religion than ours, I know your often expressed tolerance will not permit you to be bothered by that.

Now that I have brought you up to date, I want to tell you that there was no dormitory fire, I did not have a concussion or skull fracture, I was not in the hospital, I am not pregnant, I am not engaged, I am not infected, and there is no boyfriend. However, I am getting a "D" in American History, and an "F" in Chemistry and I want you to see those marks in their proper perspective.

Your loving daughter,

Sharon

FIG. 3.5. This fictitious letter is a good example of the use of context to influence judgments of "how bad" different events are perceived. From Cialdini, R. B. (1993). *Influence: Science and Practice* (3rd edition). HarperCollins: NY.

certain will be refused. (Hey, can you loan me $75?) Follow this by asking for the smaller sum that you really need. (No, well, how about $25?) They found that you are more likely to receive the smaller amount when it follows a large request than when it is requested without the larger request being made first. Zimbardo and Leippe reported that charitable contributions are also more likely when the requester asks for any amount—"even a penny will help." When solicitors for charities request "even a penny," people are more likely to give larger sums of money to the charity than to charitable appeals that do not emphasize that "even small amounts will help."

Anchoring

When we have little basis for making a meaningful decision, we often rely on whatever information is available, even when we know it is probably worthless. For example, compare these two questions (Mussweiler & Strack, 2000):

Is the average price of a new car higher or lower than $22,000?
Is the average price of a new car higher or lower than $11,000?

You probably answered lower to the first question and higher to the second. Now, suppose I ask you to estimate the price of the average new car. If you had only been asked the first question, you are likely to give a higher estimate than if you had only been asked the second question. The price asked served as an **anchor**—a figure that you used as a beginning point or comparison for making your estimate. Anchors influence our thinking, but they operate without conscious awareness unless we are vigilant for them. Suppose you are judging something important like the severity of a crime. Think how you might respond to "Should the defendant serve life in jail without the possibility of parole?" compared to "Should the defendant be sentenced to three years on probation and community service?" Without knowing anything else, like the nature of the crime, can you see that most people would use these examples of sentences as anchors and tend to suggest much more severe sentences if they are asked the first sentence than if they are asked the second?

Have you ever wondered why solicitations for charities or political organizations have check boxes that you are supposed to check to indicate the amount of your contribution? Almost always, the highest values are listed first. The next time you receive a solicitation, look at the reply card. It is likely to read something like:
___ $1000 ____ $ 500 ____ $200 ____ $ 100

The implied message is clear—start by thinking about giving us $1000. The high start rate should anchor your contributions so that they will be closer to $1000 than they would have been without these suggested levels of "giving."

Barometers of Thought

Public opinion polls are often used to provide information to policymakers who want to know how a sample from a population of interest will react to some action like a tax cut or a military response in a troubled place in the world. Suppose that you want to know how average American citizens will think about a controversial issue. It is impossible to provide a straightforward answer to the question "What do Americans think?" Not only is there the obvious problem that Americans are quite diverse in their thinking, there is also the problem of assessing what any individual thinks. The kind of answers that people give to opinion questions depends on the way the questions are asked. Read the following two opinion polls, which gave very different indices of what the American people thought about the controversial U.S. policy in the former Yugoslavia (Brennan, 1993, p. A5).

Gallup Poll:
"As you may know, the Bosnian Serbs rejected the United Nations peace plan and Serbian forces are continuing to attack Muslim towns. Some people are suggesting the United States conduct air strikes against Serbian military forces, while others say we should not get militarily involved. Do you favor or oppose U.S. air strikes?"

The Results:
Favor: 36%
Oppose: 55%

Depends: 3%
No Opinion   6%

ABC News Poll:
"Specifically, would you support or oppose the United States along with its allies in Europe, carrying out air strikes against Bosnian Serb artillery positions and supply lines?"

The Results:
Support: 65%
Oppose: 32%
No Opinion   3%

What is the difference between these two opinion polls, which were taken on the same day, yet yielded very different results? In the Gallup Poll, no mention was made of joining with our European allies, whereas in the ABC News Poll, the action was described as working with our allies. Well, what did Americans *really* think about the American role in Bosnia-Herzegovina on this particular day in 1993? Like all difficult questions in life, the answer is "It depends." In this case, it depends on how and what is asked. It is fairly easy to deliberately slant the results of an opinion poll by carefully selecting wording that will favor one position or another. In fact, it may not be possible to find any wording that would be unbiased. Try this one for yourself:

Are you in favor of a national program that ensures good quality, affordable day care for infants and young children whose parents work outside of the home?
YES   NO   NO OPINION
Are you in favor of programs that are paid for with your tax dollars that place infants and young children in child care institutions for 9 to 10 hours each day?
YES   NO   NO OPINION

Can you see how it would be easy to present data to Congress and other decision-making bodies that either support or refute the idea that most Americans are in favor of or opposed to a program of national day care? Before you interpret the results from any poll or respond to one, consider very carefully the way in which the questions were posed. What sort of background information was given and what words were used?

COMPREHENSION: THE REASON FOR LANGUAGE

Language is the first medium of the rational mind.

—Ferguson (1981, p. 120)

A student once told me that despite the fact that she really wanted to understand the material in her textbook, she found that the information went "in one eye and out the other." In other words, it "didn't stick" or seem to involve her brain at all. Although her "eyes" read every word, she was unable to understand or remember the material. We can sympathize with her because we've all had this experience at one time or another. Comprehension failures often result from the language used to express an idea and not from the difficulty of the idea itself. Good teachers know how to communicate complex ideas so that they can be easily understood, but poor teachers could talk or write for days without conveying the ideas to their students.

Strategies for Comprehension

What can you do to enhance your ability to comprehend? There are many comprehension strategies or skills designed to help make information that is presented in natural (everyday) language more understandable. These strategies aid in discovering, retaining, and utilizing the information in speech and written prose. They all involve ways of building a meaningful representation that matches the one used by the "sender" (i.e., speaker or writer).

The process of comprehension may be best described with an analogy. Imagine that a friend has a large jungle gym (child's climbing toy) in his backyard, and that he is giving it to you as a present. Because it is too large to transfer in its assembled state, you need to take it apart to move it to your home. Once you get it home, you need to reassemble it. To do so, you have to identify which part is the base and then add component parts to it. When it is reassembled, it should look the same as it did in your friend's yard.

The same is true of comprehension. If your friend has a complex knowledge structure in his head, he would transfer the information to you via language. You would have to identify the main ideas (or base) in order to build your own mental representation. You would also have to understand the relationships among the parts of the information so that you can graft them onto the main ideas in the correct way. Comprehension is attained when your knowledge structure "looks the same as" the one your friend has in his head. In other words, you would both have the same underlying representation for the transferred information. All comprehension strategies are activities that aid in the transfer of underlying structures. They provide guides for identifying main ideas and determining the relevance of various components of the message. They assist the comprehender in discovering the underlying relationships among the constituent parts of the message.

What do you do when you comprehend a passage? Most people respond that they have no idea what they do to aid their understanding, yet they can say what they do when they study. Remember, any cognitive activity that aids comprehension will also aid memory, so any effective comprehension strategy is also a memory strategy.

Re-representation

In understanding complex phenomena—anything ranging from planetary motions to our beliefs about racial and ethnic groups—we rely on mental models. These models are connected knowledge structures that help us to make sense out of our experiences. They guide what we see, how we interpret events, and how we remember them. For example, if I believe that boys are more aggressive than girls, then I may interpret a scuffle on the playground between two boys as being more aggressive than the same scuffle if it had involved two girls. In addition, I may remember details that are consistent with this interpretation (e.g., torn clothing) even when they did not occur. It seems that we are often more likely to alter our memory for events in ways that are consistent with our mental models than we are to alter the models. Our goal is to maintain models or beliefs about the world that are as accurate as possible, but it seems that we are better at preserving faulty mental models than we are at altering them to reflect true experiences.

Consider this: In a random telephone survey conducted by the Public Opinion Laboratory at Northern Illinois, 21% of the over 2,000 adults who responded to the survey believe that the sun revolves around the earth, and an additional 7% did not know which revolves around which. Didn't most of these adults learn somewhere that for over 400 years the scientific community unanimously determined that the earth revolves around the sun? Although we cannot be sure, I would guess that most of these adults learned this fact, but never altered their mental models of planetary motion because their everyday observations don't support it. We see the sun "moving" across the sky as morning turns into night. The earth-centric view of the universe makes sense according to the naive model that is easily constructed and tested on a daily basis. To change an individual's mental model, we need to understand the ones that exist prior to instruction and design instruction so that the errors in naive models are exposed and the benefits of the new model are obvious. This principle applies in multiple contexts including the way we understand the physical and social world. There are numerous demonstrations that students can write a correct answer on an exam or recognize a correct answer among a list of foils, without ever changing the nature of their understanding. To challenge the way we understand the world, we need to create situations where our beliefs are tested against other models. To do this, we need to be open to the way in which we "connect information." A good way to make our models explicit is to use comprehension processes that require **re-representation**. We need to represent our beliefs in multiple ways—to draw concept maps and other spatial layouts that represent ideas visually when information is highly verbal and to use verbal strategies when the information is highly spatial.

Questioning and Explaining

Good thinkers are good questioners.

—Alison King (1994, p. 18)

There have been numerous demonstrations of the beneficial effects of posing questions to oneself and others as part of the learning process. Palincsar and Brown (1984), for example, found that when students were required to formulate relevant questions for their peers they were better able to comprehend new passages than a control group of students who never practiced posing questions. The best-known technique for studying from text is based on the process of asking good questions about the material being read and then demonstrating comprehension by answering the questions. When students generate and answer their own questions about a text, comprehension and recall improves (e.g., Heiman & Slomianko, 1986).

One of the best-known methods based on the combination of questioning and paraphrase is **SQ3R**, which stands for Survey, Question, Read, Recite, Review (Adams, Carnine, & Gersten, 1982). The first thing to do when you begin reading complex text is to *S*urvey the chapter (or some other manageable unit of text). When you survey, you look at section headings and subheadings to gain an overview about what you will be reading. This tactic will allow you to anticipate related topics as you read. It also forms a skeletal framework for the mental representation you will be building that can be used to interpret and organize incoming information. Before you read each section (approximately one or two pages is usually a good length), turn the section heading into a *Q*uestion.

The single most important variable in promoting long-term retention and transfer is "practice at retrieval"—students need to generate responses, with minimal retrieval cues, repeatedly over time. For example, the main heading for this section of text is "strategies for comprehension." A good question that you should be able to answer when you finish this section is "What are some strategies for comprehension, and how do they work?" If you can't answer this question, with the book closed, when you finish this section, then you do not know the information presented. A good question for this subsection on "questioning and explaining" is "How are questioning and explaining used to improve comprehension?"

The first of the 3Rs is "Read." Reading is the third step; it is not the first thing you do when learning from text. It is often useful to take notes at this time. For these notes to be beneficial, they need to **paraphrase** or restate in *your own words* the information. The "Recite" portion is the answering of the questions you previously posed. This needs to be done without reference to the book or your notes—practice at recall. It is too easy to believe that you know the material when it is sitting in front of you, only to discover later that you really don't "own" it when away from the book or your notes. At this point, you need to monitor the quality of your response by assessing how well you can answer the questions. It's a good idea to recite the answer aloud or to write out an answer. Cognitive psychologists know that "one of the most demanding tests of people's comprehension of a text is to have them summarize it, distilling and abstracting it into a few sentences" (Bower & Clapper, 1989, p. 293). If you can't answer the questions, you need to go back and recycle through the material. Reread the section, reconsider the questions you've posed, and review the structure of the information. The final "R" is for *Review*. Go over the material again—practice spaced over time is a powerful strategy for successful recall. Psychologists call this **overlearning**. Overlearning is an important part of the process of understanding and learning because it ensures that newly acquired information will be available when it is needed. Recall becomes increasingly automatic, accurate, and less effortful, with overlearning.

King (1989, 1992, 1994) conducted a series of studies that clearly demonstrate the value of **reciprocal peer questioning**, a technique in which learners learn to pose thoughtful questions, which they then take turns answering. She concluded that the ability to ask thoughtful questions is a skill that needs to be learned because most people tend to ask "low-level" simple recall questions (e.g., What is the date of . . . Who did . . .) and not those that require a meaningful analysis of complex information, if they are not trained in the formulation of thoughtful questions. King has devised a series of **generic questions**, which can be used with modifications in almost any context. Look at the generic questions that are presented in Table 3.1.

When learners completed these questions using information from a lecture or text, they showed better recall and comprehension than control groups who were instructed either to study independently, engage in group discussions, generate summaries, or ask questions without training in how to ask good questions (King, 1992). More importantly, King found that when students become proficient at using higher-level questioning, they spontaneously ask these questions in a variety of other learning situations (King, 1994). These studies provide further support for the conclusion that I presented in the first chapter: Critical thinking skills transfer to novel contexts when instruction emphasizes the need to practice and use these skills in many contexts. Thus, there are very strong indications that you can improve your comprehension and memory by using the generic questions that appear in Table 3.1. Here are some examples applied to the information in this chapter:

- How does context affect judgment?
- Compare underlying structure with surface structure with regard to their role in the process of communication.

TABLE 3.1
Guiding Thought-Provoking Questioning

Generic Questions	Specific Thinking Skills Induced
What is a new example of . . . ?	Application
How could . . . be used to . . . ?	Application
What would happen if . . . ?	Prediction/hypothesizing
What are the implications of . . . ?	Analysis/inference
What are the strengths and weaknesses of . . . ?	Analysis/inference
What is . . . analogous to?	Identification and creation of analogies and metaphors
What do we already know about . . . ?	Activation of prior knowledge
How does . . . affect . . . ?	Activation of relationship (cause-effect)
How does . . . tie in with what we learned before?	Activation of prior knowledge
Explain why . . .	Analysis
Explain how . . .	Analysis
What is the meaning of . . . ?	Analysis
Why is . . . important?	Analysis of significance
What is the difference between . . . and . . . ?	Comparison–contrast
How are . . . and . . . similar?	Comparision–contrast
How does . . . apply to everyday life?	Application—to the real world
What is the counterargument for . . . ?	Rebuttal argument
What is the best . . . and why?	Evaluation and provision of evidence
What are some possible solutions to the problem of . . . ?	Synthesis of ideas
Compare . . . and . . . with regard to . . .	Comparision–contrast
What do you think causes . . . ? Why?	Analysis of relationship (cause–effect)
Do you agree or disagree with this statement: . . . ? What evidence is there to support your answer?	Evaluation and provision of evidence
How do you think . . . would see the issue of . . . ?	Taking other perspectives

Note. A list of generic questions provided by King (1994). These question stems can be used in almost any context. Research has shown that comprehension and memory are improved when students learn to ask and answer thoughtful questions based on these stems. More important, students use these generic questions in novel contexts, showing that transfer of critical thinking skills occurs when students understand that transfer is the goal of activities that improve thinking.

- Explain how analogies can be useful in enhancing comprehension.
- How does anchoring apply to everyday life?
- What is the difference between ambiguity and vagueness?
- What is the meaning of the term "generic questions"?

Can you answer these questions?

Concept Maps

An oft-repeated theme in this book is to utilize both verbal and spatial-like strategies as thinking aids. **Concept maps**, sometimes called graphic organizers, are spatial arrays that require learners to attend explicitly to the underlying structure in a passage. They can provide a picture of a learner's knowledge structures and show the way in which new information is incorporated into information that is already known. Mayer (1987) calls the deliberate use of graphic organizers "structure training techniques" because they force the learner to focus on the structure of a text. There are several varieties of concept maps, but all of them use spatial representations to make efficient use of the information in a text.

Linear Arrays.   Sometimes, the best way to understand a topic is to represent the information in a **linear array**. This is useful when the information presented is fairly linear or straight-line-like in its structure. An example of this would be a very simple "line" of events occurring one after the other: The girl hit the boy. He started to cry. The teacher heard the boy's cry. She ran into the room. She punished the girl. The girl was sent to the principal's office, etc. This rather boring story is a straightforward sequence of events that followed each other in a strict temporal ordering. A simple linear representation would adequately capture all of the relevant information.

girl hit boy
boy cried
teacher arrived
teacher punished girl
girl to principal's office
etc.

Another example when a modified linear array would be a good choice of representation is in representing any parts or processes that are aligned linearly in the physical world. Vaughan (1984) taught medical students how to utilize graphic organizers when learning from medical texts. The digestive system is aligned in a fairly linear manner beginning with the mouth and ending with the rectum. Students who read about the digestive system listed the parts of the digestive system in linear order and noted along with each part its purposes in the digestive process and its components. The resulting linear array is shown in Fig. 3.6. Vaughan reported that the medical students who learned to use graphic organizers like this one showed significant improvement in their comprehension of medical school texts.

Time lines that are commonly used in history are helpful in providing a visual picture of and appreciation for time spans and the co-occurrence of events. When the distance between events is proportional to the time between their occurrence, a much more accurate understanding of the importance of time as the key underlying dimension of history is possible than with any verbal description. This is another situation in which a linear array can foster comprehension.

Hierarchies

Most of the information we deal with is considerably more complex than simple linear chains. An alternative structural form for information is that of **hierarchies** or tree structures in which information is organized around class inclusion rules. Class inclusion rules are those rules in which something is a part of or a type of something else. Examples of class inclusion rule are the classification of toes as part of the foot and roses as a type of flower. Information of this sort can usually be categorized into levels, with higher levels dividing into lower levels according to some rule. Biological classification systems are a good example of hierarchically organized information. Bower (1970) studied organizational factors in memory using hierarchically

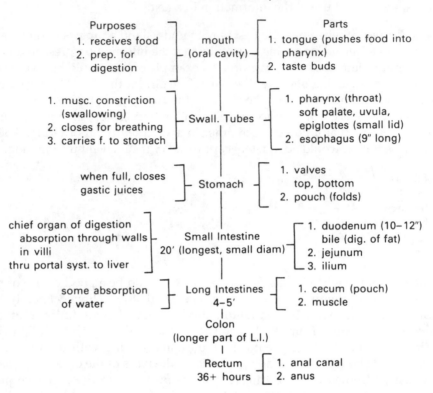

FIG. 3.6.   Modified linear array depicting the purposes and parts of the digestive system. A linear array is a good spatial arrangement for this information because, like the array, the digestive system is linear. Adapted from Vaughan (1984).

arranged information about minerals. Figure 3.7 depicts this hierarchy. Bower found that when subjects organized information this way, they had significantly better recall than a group of control subjects. He also found that when a "node" or branch of the hierarchy was forgotten, subjects failed to recall the entire portion of the "tree" that was below it. I'll be returning to these results later in this book in Chapter 9 on problem solving because hierarchies or tree diagrams are sometimes used as problem-solving aids.

Networks

The relationships among ideas in a communication are not usually based on simple class inclusion rules. Concepts can be related to each other in numerous other ways, and it is the depiction of the correct relationship among concepts that is central to all graphic organizing techniques. **Networks** are graphic organizers in which several different types of relationships are made explicit. Much of the work in this area has been conducted by Dansereau and his colleagues. He developed a

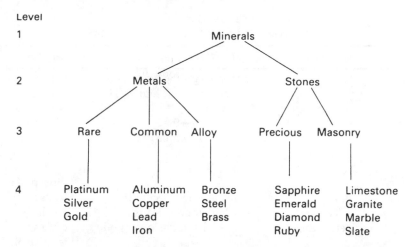

Level

1

2

3

4

FIG. 3.7. Hierarchy of minerals. An example of a hierarchical graphic organizer. Hierarchies are particularly useful when the information is organized according to class inclusion rules. Adapted from Bower (1970).

training manual and program for counselors in substance abuse programs where concept maps (he calls them guide maps) are used to create treatment plans and to assess progress in the program (Dees & Dansereau, 2000). He found that these maps promote organized thinking in the messy real world of drug treatment.

When students learn the technique of networking, they are taught to focus on and identify six different types of relationships or links among concepts (Holley, Dansereau, McDonald, Garland, & Collins, 1979; Dansersau, 1995). Two of these relationships are the *class inclusion* rules of hierarchies: X is a part of Y (e.g., France is a part of Europe), and X is a *type of* Y (e.g., mangoes are a type of fruit). The third relationship is called a *leads to link*. This type of relationship occurs whenever X leads to Y (e.g., stealing leads to jail). The other three relationships or links are *analogy*, X is like Y (e.g., a paw is like an arm); *characteristic*, X is a characteristic or feature of Y (e.g., brilliance is a characteristic of diamonds); and *evidence*, X is evidence that Y occurred (e.g., antibodies are evidence of infection). These six relationships are described more fully in Table 3.2.

As you can see from Table 3.2, networking requires students to consider the nature of the relationship among concepts in a text and then to categorize them into six different possible types. The relationships are then depicted in a network-like array with all of the relationships labeled. Eylon and Linn (1988) reported that errors in understanding often result from inappropriate links among concepts. When learners construct networks, they must consciously consider the relationships among concepts, a strategy that leads to greater comprehension. Research with both younger and older adults has shown that when they learned to identify structural relationships in a passage, such as descriptions, sequences, cause, problem-solution, comparisons, and listings, comprehension and retention was improved (Meyer & Poon, 2001).

An example of a completed network is shown in Fig. 3.8. The network shows the relationships among concepts in a nursing text on wounds. Look carefully at this figure. "Types of wounds" and the "process of healing" are *parts* of the discussion of wounds. "Open," "closed," "accidental," and "intentional" are *types* of wounds. In the process of healing, the "lag phase" *leads to* the "fibroplasia phase," which *leads to* the

TABLE 3.2
Six Types of Links Used in Networks

Type	Example	Structure	Key Words
Part of link	hand | p finger	*Hierarchy*—the lower node is part of the higher node	is a part of is a segment of is a portion of
Type of/ example of link	school | t private	*Hierarchy*—the lower node is an example of the higher node	is a type of is in the category is an example of is a kind of three procedures are
Leads to link	practice | l perfection	*Chain*—the object of the higher node leads to or results in the lower node	leads to results in causes is a tool of produces
Analogy link	school <u>a</u> factory	*Cluster*—the content of one node is analogous to the other node	is similar to is analogous to is like corresponds to
Characteristic link	sky <u>c</u> blue	*Cluster*—the content of one mode is a trait of the other node	has is characterized by feature is property is trait is aspect is attribute is
Evidence link	broken <u>e</u> x-ray arm	*Cluster*—the content of one node is evidence for the other node	indicates is illustrated by is demonstrated by supports documents is proof of confirms

Note. This table is adapted from Holley et al. (1979). Notice how the "key words" suggest the type of link that is being described.

contraction phase. "Soft, pink, and friable" is *a characteristic of* tissue continuity. The other two types of relationships, analogy and evidence, are not used in this network.

Identification and use of these six types of relationships or links and their combination in a unified network requires considerable practice. This is an effortful strategy, which, like some of the mnemonic techniques, pays off once it is well learned. Holley and associates (1979) found that when subjects were well trained in this technique, they performed significantly better on subsequent tests than control students who did not learn this technique, with the biggest improvement for students with low grade point averages. It seems that the students who were doing very well in school were already attending to the relationships among concepts. Then it was the poorer students who benefited most from explicit instruction and practice in identifying, labeling, and diagramming the relationships among concepts.

Look carefully at the generic "fill-in-the-blank" concept map that can be used to understand any theory that is shown in Fig. 3.9 (Dansereau, 2001). If you take this

FIG. 3.8. Example of a network of a chapter from a nursing text on wounds (Holley et al., 1979). The use of linking relationships force the learner to consider the way concepts are related.

Legend: p is a "part of" link
t is a "type of" link
l is a "leads to" link
c is a "characteristic of" link

ACADEMIC GUIDE MAP
FOR "THEORIES"

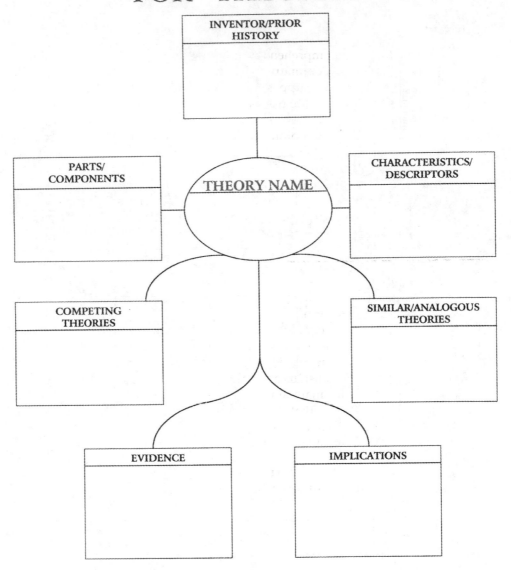

FIG. 3.9. A generic fill-in-the-blank concept map that can be used to understand any theory in any domain of knowledge. Descriptive information could be filled in the circles with the links labeled as the type of information. When you fill in the various "boxes"—for example, giving evidence for and against the theory—you will be developing a "deep" knowledge of the theory (Dansereau, 2001).

generic map for understanding theories to any class in which theories are being taught, you can think of yourself as being "armed" with an information aid. As you fill in the boxes and circles, you will develop an enhanced understanding of the theory you are learning.

Matrices

When the material to be comprehended involves comparisons of several topics along a number of dimensions, a **matrix** is the representation of choice. (The word *matrices* is the plural of matrix.) Suppose, for example, that you are reading a passage about wars. The purpose of the passage is to compare and contrast various antecedent conditions of war and to consider their effect. Suppose further that the wars being considered are the Revolutionary War, World War I, World War II, the Korean Conflict, and the Vietnam Conflict. In order to understand the nature of these wars, you need to organize the information so that commonalities and distinctions will emerge. A suggested matrix for this information is shown in Table 3.3.

By filling in the empty cells in Table 3.3, selected categories of information can readily be compared and similarities and differences can easily be spotted. A coherent "pattern" of information about these wars can then be extracted. The framework can be applied to other wars involving other countries to determine, for example, if there are universal commonalities for all wars. Similarly, matrices can be useful when a judgment has to be made about products or courses of action that differ along multiple dimensions. If you are familiar with the way in which the magazine *Consumer Reports* provides information about products to consumers, you will recognize that this is the technique that they use. For example, if you want to buy a refrigerator, you will find that *Consumer Reports* rates several different brands and models of refrigerators along many dimensions. The models would be listed in the left-hand column and the dimensions across the top, such as cost to operate, ease of opening the door, how well it maintains a set temperature, storage space built into the door, and the other features that differ among refrigerators. The ratings in each cell are pictorial (colored circles) that help to convert a large amount of information to a format that is comprehensible in a single glance. A similar technique was used

TABLE 3.3
Example of a Matrix Graphic Organizer

	War				
	Revolutionary War	World War I	World War II	Korean Conflict	Vietnam Conflict
Major precipitating events					
U.S. justification for the war					
"Other side" justification for the war					
Number of lives lost—each side					
Major battles					
Resolution					
Types of weapons					
Relationship to later war, if any					

Note. Matrices are particularly good spatial arrays when the information involves several different topics (e.g., wars) that are being compared on several dimensions (e.g., characteristics of war).

Goal	20% Voluntary Subsidy	Simple Mandate	Play-or-Pay Mandate
Decreased number of uninsured	Somewhat	Somewhat	Well
Increase efficiency	Not at all	Not at all	Well
Limit costs for workers	Somewhat	Not at all	Well
Control small business costs	Well	Not at all	Somewhat
Contain government costs	Somewhat	Well	Not at all

| ■ Well | ▨ Somewhat | □ Not at all |

FIG. 3.10.   A shaded matrix that compares three possible health care plans compared on five "goals." The use of shading with a matrix allows for an easier comparison among the plans. Adapted from RAND (1992). Health care and the uninsured: Who will pay? *RAND Research Review, XVI*, pp. 6–8.

by the RAND Corporation (1992, p. 7) in their analysis of three different plans for financing health insurance. Look at this matrix, which is presented in Fig. 3.10.

As you can see, the RAND Corporation listed five desirable goals for any health care plan. These are listed under "goal." The three health care plans they compared are a 20% voluntary subsidy, a simple mandate or law that would require employers to provide health insurance, and a play-or-pay plan that would allow employers to shop for the best plan for their employees. The degree of shading in a square is an indication of how well the particular plan satisfies a goal. Which plan seems the best given their evaluation and the way they presented the data? It is easy to see that the third option meets three goals very well, one goal somewhat, and one goal not at all. Thus, it would seem that the third plan is the best overall, but this conclusion is only warranted if all of the goals are equal in importance. If the containment of government costs is much more important than any of the others, then the third plan is not a good one because it does not satisfy this goal. The relative importance of each goal depends on individual judgment that, ideally, is informed by knowledge of the issues.

Matrices can also be used to organize information so that it can be used more easily. Day, Rodin, and Stoltzfus (1990) investigated the effect of changing the representation of information on the ease with which it is used. A medication schedule that was given to a (real) patient is shown in Fig. 3.11. The list format shown on the left side of Fig. 3.11 is the way that the physician presented the medication schedule to the patient. The matrix format shown on the right provides the same information, but is clearly easier to use. Not surprisingly, Day, Rodin, and Stoltzfus found that both young and old subjects were more accurate in their understanding of and memory for the medication schedule when it was provided in a matrix format. It is clear that some representations will facilitate the use of information and

LIST FORMAT	
Inderal	- 1 tablet 3 times a day
Lanoxin	- 1 tablet every a.m.
Cafafate	- 1 tablet before meals and at bedtime
Zantac	- 1 tablet every 12 hours (twice a day)
Quinaglute	- 1 tablet 4 times a day
Coumadin	- 1 tablet a day

MATRIX FORMAT

	Breakfast	Lunch	Dinner	Bedtime
Inderal	✓	✓	✓	
Lanoxin	✓			
Cafafate	✓	✓	✓	✓
Zantac		✓		✓
Quinaglute	✓	✓	✓	✓
Coumadin				✓

FIG. 3.11. Two representations of medication schedules for an elderly patient. The list on the left is the format that was given to the patient. The matrix on the right was devised by Day, Rodin, and Stoltzfus (1990). Adapted from Day, R. S., Rodin, G. C., and Stoltzfus, E. R. (1990). Alternative representations for medication instructions: Effects on young and old adults. Paper presented at the 3rd Cognitive Aging Conference, Atlanta, GA.

others will hinder it. One goal is to understand which representation matches the underlying structure of the information being conveyed.

General Guidelines and Principles

In a study of "at-risk students" (those identified as being at risk of failing and not completing their education), Pogrow (1992) concluded that these students have academic difficulties because "they do not understand 'understanding'" (p. 90). What he means by this is that these students do not know what they need to do to ensure that information is acquired in a way that is meaningful and resistant to forgetting. Many ideas about learning and knowing are foreign to them such as: complex information will contain multiple interacting concepts; learners need to understand how concepts relate to one another; difficult material has to be questioned, explained, drawn, and discussed; and comprehension needs to be continually monitored. There is ample empirical evidence that more of these "at-risk" students could complete their education if they were taught how to improve their comprehension.

Techniques that promote understanding are critically important in our complex world. The ability to comprehend difficult material is empowering because it allows us to understand and act intelligently on a wide range of issues including the purchase of a new refrigerator, understanding how AIDS is transmitted, or deciding how to vote on a variety of health insurance initiatives. We all need a society in which citizens think and respond thoughtfully, if we are to prosper, or even survive, in a time of skyrocketing complexity.

All of the strategies for comprehension require learners to monitor their understanding of the information. They are all active cognitive strategies that facilitate the construction of meaningful representations. The graphic organizers offer ways to transform text into explicit spatial representations that display relationships among concepts. They all make abstract concepts more concrete. Like all good cognitive strategies, they require the learner to relate new information to prior knowledge in a way that makes remembering most efficient. Like many of the other thinking skills presented in this book, they require effort and must be practiced in order to be useful. It is not enough to read about them. They have to be used in a variety of situations to ensure transfer.

Although most of this chapter has been concerned with the process of comprehension, which is going from surface structure to underlying structure, many of the principles can be used in language production or going from underlying structure to surface structure. The task of writing involves transforming your internalized meaning into words. Many people have difficulty with writing because they find that this is a difficult translation. Kellogg (1990) compared the quality of persuasive papers written by college students who either prepared an outline before they began their papers (a linear display) or used a clustering technique in which associated ideas were first generated from memory and then connected with lines that showed how the ideas were related. He found that the students who were required to outline before they wrote improved in their organization and writing style (writing is a mostly linear activity), and the students who used clustering produced a larger number of ideas than those who used outlines. I will return to these results in Chapter 10 on creativity where I discuss the generation of ideas.

Graphic organizers, like clustering or flowcharts, or matrices, can be terrific aids in the writing process. Suppose you were to write an essay about acquired immune deficiency syndrome (AIDS). You could begin the planning process by considering the kinds of links employed in networking (type of, part of, leads to, evidence for, characteristics of, and analogy). What "types of" people are most and least at risk? What is the "evidence for" AIDS (laboratory tests, symptoms)? What are the "characteristics of" at-risk groups or risky activities? Some people have called for quarantine, which is "analogous to" the way the way society has responded to other dread diseases. Once you have considered the information you want to present, the relationship among the facts can be depicted in a network. The network offers a nonlinear alternative to outlines when planning the writing process. Thus, by "running comprehension strategies backward," they can be used to produce language (spoken or written) instead of their more usual role in comprehending language.

APPLYING THE FRAMEWORK

1. What Is the Goal?

The thinking goal addressed in this chapter is how to enhance comprehension when the medium for communication is natural language. A more formal way of saying the same thing is that the goal is to create an accurate underlying representation (i.e., re-presentation of the underlying message) from the surface structure provided in speech and written text. The newly acquired knowledge will ideally be stored in memory in a way that will make it easily accessible when it is needed.

2. What Is Known?

This step requires determining where you are before selecting the appropriate thinking skill. Are you in a situation in which there is likely to be deliberate attempts to bias your thinking on an issue (e.g., consumer decisions, political rhetoric)? Do you have to learn from a text that contains information on which you will soon be tested? Is the information particularly complex? Do you already have good background knowledge? What is the structure of the information and the reason why you need or want to understand it? Will a graphic presentation help with comprehension? If so, does the material match a structure such as a linear array, hierarchy, matrix, network or flowchart?

3. Which Thinking Skill or Skills Will Get You to Your Goal?

The skills described in this chapter are those involved in comprehending language. As with every list of skills, users need to monitor their comprehension to determine what is and what isn't being understood. The process of skill use often requires trying a different skill if the one being used is not promoting understanding. The following comprehension skills were presented in this chapter. Review each skill and be sure that you understand when and how to use each one.

- Recognizing and defending against the inappropriate use of emotional language, labeling, name calling, ambiguity, vagueness, and arguments by etymology
- Developing the ability to detect misuse of definitions, reification, euphemism, and bureaucratese
- Thinking about the reason for a communication, the background knowledge of the listener, and the context when deciding what and how to communicate
- Understanding the use of framing with leading questions, and negation
- Using analogies appropriately, which includes examining the nature of the similarity and its relationship to the conclusion
- Deliberately giving a variety of examples when thinking about members of a category so that you are not thinking about category members in terms of a prototype (e.g., thinking about many ways to be successful, not just the most common examples like making a high salary)
- Recognizing the emotional components of some words and the way word choices can affect how you think and feel
- Recognizing when an anchor may be biasing your judgments about a quantity or cost and deliberately trying other values that could be alternative anchors
- Employing questioning and explaining as a skill for text comprehension
- Practicing at retrieval of information so that remembering becomes more accurate and easier with spaced practice
- Selecting and using graphic organizers (linear arrays, hierarchies, networks, matrices, flowcharts)

4. Have You Reached Your Goal?

Have you been monitoring your understanding? Can you paraphrase a passage with the book closed? Did you systematically consider all of the ways in which we can be misled with language that were presented in this chapter? Did you consider the reason for the communication and have you satisfied that reason?

CHAPTER SUMMARY

1. Psycholinguistics is the branch of psychology that is concerned with understanding how people produce and comprehend language.

2. Psychologists view language as comprising two components or levels: a meaning component (underlying representation) and a speech sound component (surface structure). The problem of comprehension is moving from a thought by the sender (underlying structure) through language and then reconstruction of the thought by the receiver.

3. Language is ambiguous when a single surface structure has two or more possible underlying representations.

4. Language and thought exert mutual influences on each other with our thoughts determining the language we use and, in turn, the language we use reshaping our thoughts.

5. Six rules of communication were presented. Every time we attempt to communicate with others, we utilize these rules to determine what information we will convey and how to express the information.

6. Language comprehension requires that the listener make many inferences. The kinds of inferences we make depends on context, manner, and the words selected to convey the message.

7. There are many ways that words can be used to mislead the listener deliberately. Several ways that the choice of words can influence thought were presented. The deliberate use of emotional and nonemotional words is designed to influence how you think about a topic.

8. Emotional words often elicit strong mental images. Because images are highly resistant to forgetting, they are readily available when the topic is mentioned.

9. Prototypes, or the most typical member of a category, are usually thought of first when we think about an example of a category. These prototypes bias what we think. This bias can be overcome with deliberate practice at generating examples that are not typical.

10. A value that is easily available in memory can unconsciously serve as an anchor or starting point that we use to estimate quantities or cost. We need to think consciously of many different possible values that could serve as anchors as a way of reducing the effect of anchors.

11. The way in which we judge or evaluate a situation depends on the context in which it is embedded and the way it contrasts with similar recent events. Our judgments are strongly determined by recent experiences.

12. Strategies to improve the comprehension of text were described. They all require learners to attend to the structure of the information and to make the relationships among concepts explicit. Multiple representations—both visual spatial displays and verbal strategies—are used as aids to comprehension.

TERMS TO KNOW

You should be able to define or describe the following terms and concepts. If you find that you're having difficulty with any term, be sure to reread the section in which it is discussed.

Psycholinguistics. The branch of psychology that is concerned with the acquisition, production, comprehension, and usage of language.

Underlying Representation. The meaning component of language. It's the thought that you want to convey with an utterance. Compare with surface structure.

Surface Structure. The sounds of an utterance or the outward appearance of a language expression. Compare with underlying representation.

Given/New Distinction. The ratio of known (given) information to new information in a communication. It is a primary determinant of the difficulty of a communication.

Cognitive Economy. Any process that reduces the mental workload and makes thinking or remembering less effortful.

Prototype. The best or most typical example of a category. For example, dog is the prototype for the category "animal."

Prototypical thinking. Using the most typical member in a category as a guide to making inferences about other members of that category.

Sapir-Whorf Hypothesis of Linguistic Relativity. The hypothesis that language, at least in part, determines or influences thought.

Semantic Slanting. The deliberate use of words designed to create a particular attitude or foster certain beliefs.

Ambiguous. An utterance is ambiguous when it can have more than one meaning or underlying representation.

Vagueness. A lack of precision in a communication. A communication is vague if it does not specify enough details for its intended purpose.

Equivocation. A change in the meaning of a word in the course of the same discussion.

Etymology. Reference to the origin of a word in order to determine its meaning.

Reification. Occurs when an abstract concept is given a name and then treated as though it were a concrete object.

Bureaucratese. The use of formal, stilted language that is often unfamiliar to people who lack special training.

Euphemism. The substitution of a desirable term for a less desirable or offensive one.

Framing. Occurs when a question is asked in a way that suggests what the correct response should be. The reader is "led" into assuming a particular perspective or point of view.

Risk Adverse. A general preference for options that do not involve possible loss over options that involve possible gain, even when the expected value is higher for the option that describes a loss.

Negation. The use of denial to imply that a fact is plausible.

Anchoring. The unconscious use of a value that is easily accessible in memory as a "starting point" for making a judgment about a quantity or cost.

Re-representation. The deliberate use of multiple ways to represent information—concept maps, spatial arrays, and verbal strategies—as a means of enhancing comprehension and memory.

SQ3R. A strategy for comprehension that requires the use of questioning and paraphrase. The letters stand for **S**urvey, **Q**uestion, **R**ead, **R**ecite, and **R**eview.

Paraphrase. Restating ideas in your own words.

Overlearning. Reviewing material after it is learned so that recall becomes automatic and less effortful.

Reciprocal Peer Questioning. The process of having learners pose thoughtful questions that they take turns answering.

Generic Questions. Question "stems" that can be modified and applied to many different topics.

Concept Maps (sometimes called graphic organizers). The use of spatial displays to organize information.

Linear Arrays. A graphic organizer in which information is presented in a list format.

Hierarchies. A type of graphic organizer that uses a tree structure. Most useful when information is organized according to class inclusion rules.

Networks. Graphic organizers in which types of relationships among concepts are depicted.

Matrix. A rectangular array that is useful when the information presented involves comparisons along several dimensions.

4

Reasoning: Drawing Deductively Valid Conclusions

Contents

As far as Joan's opponent was concerned, the debate wasn't going well. It was clear from the sea of nodding heads and sounds of "uh huh" and "yeah" that Joan was scoring points and convincing the audience; whereas, he seemed to be losing support every time he spoke. He wasn't surprised; he had been warned. Joan had studied reasoning and now knew how to make people believe anything. Soon she would have everyone convinced that the war was justified and what was wrong was right. The way she's going, she could probably make people believe that day is night. It certainly wasn't fair, but what can you expect from someone who studied reasoning?

This fictional vignette was taken from a real-life incident. I was present at a debate where one debater accused the other of cheating by using reasoning. At the time, I thought that this was pretty funny because I had come to think of reasoning as an important critical thinking skill—the sort of skill that you would use to make valid conclusions when dealing with information that is complex and emotional. To the losing side of this debate, it was a trick. Trick, skill, or strategy, reasoning is the best way to decide whom and what to believe.

LOGICAL AND PSYCHOLOGICAL

The trick, of course, is to reason well. It isn't easy and it isn't automatic.

—Kahane (1980, p. 3)

Reasoning is often taken to be the hallmark of the human species. Colloquially, reasoning tells us "what follows what." When we reason, we use our knowledge about one or more related statements that we can reasonably believe are true to determine if another statement, the conclusion, is true. A **conclusion** is an inferential belief that is derived from other statements. The ability to reason well is a critical thinking skill that is crucial in science, mathematics, law, forecasting, diagnosing, and just about every other context you can imagine. In fact, I can't think of an academic or "real-world" context in which the ability to reason well is not of great importance.

Many definitions of the term *critical thinking* identify reasoning as central to the concept as seen in the definition that was derived from three rounds of rankings by school administrators in the United States. The procedure they used to derive their preferred definition of critical thinking is called the delphi technique, which refers to a method for achieving agreement among experts in some field. In this case, definitions were circulated among all participants three times. They agreed that "critical thinking is . . . cohesive, logical reasoning patterns" (Stahl & Stahl, 1991, p. 84).

Pragmatism and Logic

When we reason logically, we are following a set of rules that specify how we "ought to" derive conclusions. **Logic** is the branch of philosophy that explicitly states the rules for deriving valid conclusions. The laws of logic provide the standard against which we assess the quality of someone's reasoning (Garnham & Oakhill, 1994). According to logic, a conclusion is **valid** if it necessarily follows from some statements that are accepted as facts. The factual statements are called **premises**. Conclusions that are not in accord with the rules of logic are **illogical**. Although we maintain that the ability for rational, logical thought is unique to humans, all too often we reach invalid or illogical conclusions. This fact has led Hunt (1982, p. 121) to award "A flunking grade in logic for the world's only logical animal."

Psychologists who study reasoning have been concerned with how people process information in reasoning tasks. The fact is that, in our everyday thinking, the psychological processes quite often are not logical. In a classic paper on the relation between logic and thinking, Henle (1962) noted that even though everyday thought does not generally follow the formal rules of logic, people use their own imperfect rules. If we were not logical, at least some of the time, we wouldn't be able to understand each other, "follow one another's thinking, reach common decisions, and work together" (Henle, 1962, p. 374). To demonstrate this point, stop now and work on one of the problems Henle posed to her subjects in one of her studies:

> A group of women were discussing their household problems. Mrs. Shivers broke the ice by saying: "I'm so glad we're talking about these problems. It's so important to talk about things that are in our minds. We spend so much of our time in the kitchen that, of course, household problems are in our minds. So it is important to talk about them." (Does it follow that it is important to talk about them? Give your reasoning.) (p. 370)

Do not go on until you decide if it is valid to conclude that Mrs. Shivers is correct when she says that it is important to talk about household problems. Why did you answer as you did?

When Henle posed this problem to graduate students, she found that some students arrived at the wrong answer (as defined by the rules of logic); whereas others arrived at the right answer for the wrong reasons. Consider the following answer given by one of her subjects: "No. It is not important to talk about things that are in our minds unless they worry us, which is not the case" (p. 370). Where did this subject go wrong? Instead of deciding if the conclusion followed logically from the earlier statements, she added her own opinions about what sorts of things it is important to talk about. Thus, even though the answer is incorrect as evaluated by the standard rules of logic, it is correct by the subject's own rules. Consider this answer: "Yes. It could be very important for the individual doing the talking and possibly to some of those listening, because it is important for people to 'get a load off their chest,' but not for any other reason, unless in the process one or the other learns something new and of value" (p. 370). This time, the participant gave the correct answer, but for the wrong reasons. This participant, like the first one, added her own beliefs to the problem instead of deriving her conclusions solely on the basis of the information presented. Henle has termed this error in reasoning the **failure to accept the logical task**.

It seems that in everyday use of reasoning, we don't determine if a conclusion is valid solely on the basis of the statements we are given. Instead, we alter the statements we're given according to our beliefs and then decide if a conclusion follows from the altered statements. We function under a kind of **personal logic** in which we use our personal beliefs about the world to formulate conclusions about related issues.

Psychologists and philosophers have puzzled over the finding that for some everyday and formal reasoning tasks, most people seem to behave as though they are using the rules of logic, but for other reasoning tasks, there seems to be little evidence that the laws of logic are being followed. In other words, whether most of us appear logical depends on the type of reasoning problem that is being studied. Simon and Kaplan (1989) do not find this state of affairs surprising. They believe that "intelligent behavior is adaptive and hence must take on strikingly different forms in different environments" (p. 38). More recent studies support the conclusion that people have more than one way of reasoning, sometimes following the laws of logic and sometimes twisting or abandoning them. For example, Rips (2001, p. 133) concluded that "arguments have different roles and purposes, and people assess them differently depending on which purpose they have in mind."

The word **pragmatic** refers to anything that is practical. In real life, people have a *reason for reasoning*, and sometimes the laws of logic are at odds with the setting, consequences, and commonly agreed on reasons and rules for deriving conclusions. As Henle's participants showed in the previous example, in real life, we add our own beliefs and knowledge to the facts we are given when we determine if a conclusion is supported by the premises. In most everyday settings, this is a pragmatic or practical approach to reasoning problems.

Inductive and Deductive Reasoning

Actual thinking has its own logic; it is orderly, reasonable, reflective. √

—Dewey (1933, p. 75)

A distinction is often made between inductive and deductive reasoning. (See Chapter 6, "Thinking as Hypothesis Testing" for a related discussion of this topic.) In **inductive reasoning** observations are collected that support or suggest a conclusion. It is a way of projecting information from known examples to the unknown (Heit, 2000). For example, if every person you have ever seen has only one head, you would use this evidence to support the conclusion (or suggest the hypothesis) that everyone in the world has only one head. Of course, you can't be absolutely certain of this fact. It's always possible that someone you've never met has two heads. If you met just one person with two heads, your conclusion must be wrong. Thus, with inductive reasoning you can never *prove* that your conclusion or hypothesis is correct, but you can disprove it.

When we reason inductively, we collect facts and use them to provide support or disconfirmation for conclusions or hypotheses. It's how we discover what the world is like. Lopes (1982) described induction this way: "Scientists do it; lay people do it; even birds and beasts do it. But the process is mysterious and full of paradox . . . induction cannot be justified on logical grounds" (p. 626). We reason inductively both informally in the course of everyday living, and formally in experimental research. For this reason, hypothesis testing is sometimes described as the process of inductive reasoning. When we reason inductively, we generalize from our experiences to create beliefs or expectations. Sometimes inductive reasoning is described as reasoning "up" from particular instances or experiences in the world to a belief about the nature of the world.

In **deductive reasoning**, we begin with statements known or believed to be true, like "everyone has only one head," and then conclude or infer that Karen, a woman you've never met, will have only one head. This conclusion follows logically from the earlier statement. If we know that it is true that everyone has only one head, then it must also be true that any specific person will have only one head. This conclusion necessarily follows from the belief; if the belief is true, the conclusion *must* be true. Deductive reasoning is sometimes described as reasoning "down" from beliefs about the nature of the world to particular instances. Rips (1988) argues that deduction is a general-purpose mechanism for cognitive tasks. According to Rips, deduction "enables us to answer questions from information stored in memory, to plan actions according to goals, and to solve certain kinds of puzzles" (p. 117). The notion of "reasoning up" from observations and "reasoning down" from hypotheses is schematically shown in Fig. 4.1.

© King Features Syndicate, Courtesy KFS, INC.

Although it is common to make a distinction between inductive and deductive reasoning, the distinction may not be a particularly useful description of how people reason in real life. In everyday contexts, we switch from inductive to deductive reasoning in the course of thinking. Our hypotheses and beliefs guide the observations we make, and our observations, in turn, modify our hypotheses and beliefs. Often, this process will involve a continuous interplay of inductive and deductive reasoning. Thinking in real-world contexts almost always involves the use of multiple thinking skills.

LINEAR ORDERING

Reasoning is simply a matter of getting your facts straight.

—B. F. Anderson (1980, p. 62)

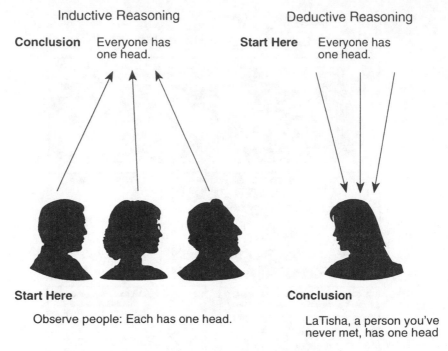

Inductive Reasoning

Conclusion   Everyone has
                one head.

Start Here
Observe people: Each has one head.

Deductive Reasoning

Start Here   Everyone has
                one head.

Conclusion
LaTisha, a person you've
never met, has one head

FIG. 4.1. A pictorial distinction between deductive (reasoning "down" from premises) and inductive reasoning (reasoning "up" from examples). In most real-world settings, we use both types of reasoning recursively.

Joel is stronger than Bill, but not as strong as Richard. Richard is stronger than Joel, but not as strong as Donald. Who is strongest and who is second strongest?

Although I'm sure that you've never met Joel, Donald, Richard, and Bill, I'm also sure you could answer this question. The premises or statements in this problem give information about the orderly relationship among the terms; hence, it is called a **linear ordering** or **linear syllogism**. Like all deductive reasoning problems, the premises are used to derive valid conclusions—conclusions that must be true if the premises are true. In linear ordering problems, we're concerned with orderly relationships in which the relationships among the terms can be arranged in a straight-line array.

Linear Diagrams

How did you solve the problem about Joel, Donald, Richard, and Bill? Most people work line by line, ordering the people as specified in each line:

"Joel is stronger than Bill, but not as strong as Richard" becomes:

Strong

—Richard
—Joel
—Bill

Not Strong

"Richard is stronger than Joel, but not as strong as Donald" adds Donald to the previous representation:

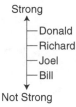

Strong

—Donald
—Richard
—Joel
—Bill

Not Strong

Thus, it is easy to "see" that Donald is strongest and Richard is second strongest.

Research with linear syllogisms has shown that people rely, at least in part, on spatial imagery or some sort of spatial representation to answer the question.

Work through the following pairs of linear syllogisms. Try to decide if one member of each pair is easier to solve than the other:

1. A. Julio is smarter than Diana.
    Diana is smarter than Ellen.
    Who is smartest? Julio, Diana, Ellen, or don't know.
    or
   B. JoAnne is taller than Susan.
    Rebeccah is taller than JoAnne.
    Who is shortest? JoAnne, Susan, Rebeccah, or don't know.

2. A. Pat is not taller than Jim.
    Jim is shorter than Tiffany.
    Who is tallest? Pat, Jim, Tiffany, or don't know.
    or
   B. Les is worse than Moshe.
    Harold is worse than Moshe.
    Who is worst? Les, Moshe, Harold, or don't know.

3. A. Stuart doesn't run faster than Louis.
    Louis doesn't run slower than Dena.
    Who is slowest? Stuart, Lois, Dena, or don't know.
    or
   B. Howard is fatter than Ace.
    Ace is thinner than Kyla.
    Who is thinnest? Howard, Ace, Kyla, or don't know.

As you worked through these problems, did some seem more difficult to you than others? You probably found problem 1A to be the easiest. Research has shown that when the second term in the first premise is the first term in the second premise (Diana in problem 1A), and when the comparison terms are congruent (smarter, smarter, smartest), the linear ordering is fairly easy to solve. Problem 1B does not follow this simple form. The comparisons are between JoAnne and Susan and Rebeccah and Susan. In addition, the comparison terms are not congruent (taller, taller, shortest). The correct answer is 1A for Julio. The correct answer for 1B is Susan.

Problem 2A contains the negation term "not," which adds to the complexity of the problem. In addition, information is given in terms of both taller and shorter, which makes this a difficult problem. The correct answer is Tiffany. (Pat could be the same height or shorter than Jim.) You can represent this relationship graphically as:

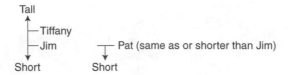

Although problem 2B contains all congruent comparison terms (worse, worse, worst), some people find it tricky because we don't know if Les or Harold is worst. In addition, research has shown that it is more difficult to comprehend terms like "worse" than it is to use terms like "better" because it denotes that all three are bad, whereas "better" is a more neutral term. (The correct answer is "don't know.") Problem 3A contains two negative terms as well as incongruent comparison terms (faster, slower, slowest). From the information given, we can't determine who is slowest. Problem 3B is somewhat easier because it doesn't contain negatives, but it does contain incongruent comparison terms (fatter, thinner, thinnest). The answer as to who is thinnest is Ace.

As you worked through these problems, you should have discovered some of the following psychological principles of linear orderings:

1. Orderings are easiest to solve when comparison terms are congruent (e.g., short, shorter, shortest).
2. Solutions will be facilitated if the second term in the first premise is the first term in the second premise (A is better than B; B is better than C).
3. Negations make the problem more difficult (e.g., A is not hairier than B).
4. Comparisons between adjacent terms (e.g., Julio and Diana in problem 1A) are more difficult than comparisons between end terms (Julio and Ellen) (Potts, 1972).
5. *When you are faced with a difficult syllogism of any sort, a good strategy for solving it is to draw a spatial array. With a linear syllogism, draw a linear array, so that the relationships among the terms can be inspected visually.*
6. Comparison terms that limit the meaning of a sentence, like worse and dumber, are more difficult to process than more general and neutral terms like better and smarter. The adjectives that connote a bias (e.g., worse, dumber) are called **marked adjectives**, whereas the neutral adjectives are called **unmarked adjectives**.

These summary remarks can be used as an aid for clear communication of linearly ordered information. When you want someone to understand a linear ordering, use congruent terms, make the second term in the first premise the first term in the second premise, and avoid negations and marked adjectives. These few rules for communicating linear information show a basic cognitive principle: Negative information (no, not) is more difficult to process than positive information, in part because it seems to place additional demands on working memory (Matlin, 2002). There are many advantages to using diagrams when dealing with verbal information, including reducing the load on working memory and making relationship obvious and visible.

Confusing Truth and Validity

*Knowing is only part of being educated, thinking and reasoning with what we
know completes it.*

—Schauble and Glaser (1990, p. 9)

Logically, the rules for deciding if a conclusion is valid are the same no matter what
terms we use. In the first example in this section, I could provide the premise that
Donald is stronger than Richard or I could substitute any name that I wanted (Igor
is stronger than Yu-Chin or any letter or symbol, C is stronger than A). The truth is
not important in these examples, because the premises are treated as though they
were true. This probably bothered some of you. Suppose I said,

> Your sister is uglier than the wicked witch in the Wizard of Oz.
> *You are uglier than your sister.*
> Therefore, you are uglier than the wicked witch in the Wizard of Oz.

You'd probably protest this conclusion. You may not even have a sister, but given
the premises, the conclusion is valid. Test it for yourself. However, that doesn't
make it true. Chapter 5 will address the issue of determining the truth or believability of the premises. So far, we've only considered the question of validity: whether
a conclusion must be true if the premises are true. People very often have trouble
separating truth from validity. This is particularly difficult when the conclusion
runs counter to cherished beliefs or strong emotion.

Although the rules of logic dictate that content is irrelevant to the conclusions we
formulate, in most real-life situations, content does influence how we choose valid
conclusions. It is possible to construct deductive reasoning problems so that the beliefs most people maintain conflict with logical conclusions. **Belief bias** or **confirmation bias** occurs when an individual's beliefs interfere with her or his selection of
the logical conclusion. This effect has been demonstrated many times and is so pervasive that it interferes with good thinking in almost every context (Nickerson,
1998). We all seem to have difficulty in thinking critically when the reasoned conclusion is one that we do not believe to be true. Consider this example, which dates
back to 1944 (Morgan & Morton). Obviously, most Americans in 1944 had very
strong beliefs about World War II, which clearly influenced their reasoning process.
When presented with deductive reasoning problems, Americans were more likely
to select conclusions that agreed with their belief biases than conclusions that ran
counter to their belief biases.

It should come as no surprise to you that human reasoning becomes illogical
when we are discussing emotional issues. This is true for people in every strata of
society, even for justices of the United States Supreme Court. When Justice William
O. Douglas was new to the Supreme Court, Chief Justice Charles Evans Hughes
gave him these words of advice, "You must remember one thing. At the constitu-
tional level where we work, ninety percent of any decision is emotional. The rational part of us supplies the reasons for supporting our predilections" (Hunt, 1982,
p. 129). Unfortunately, appellate legal proceedings are sometimes exercises in politics, with decisions changing as frequently as the political climate. Legal "reasoning" has sometimes served as a framework to persuade others that a conclusion is
valid. If you understand how to formulate valid inferences, you'll be able to with-
stand and recognize its misuse by those who would use it to their advantage.

IF, THEN STATEMENTS

Reason, of course, is weak, when measured against its never-ending task. Weak, indeed, compared with the follies and passions of mankind, which, we must admit, almost entirely control our human destinies, in great things and small.

—Albert Einstein (1879–1955)

If, then statements, like the other examples of reasoning presented in this chapter, use premises that are known or believed to be true to determine if a valid conclusion follows. If, then statements are concerned with **contingency relationships**—some events are dependent or contingent on the occurrence of others. If the first part of the contingency relationship is true, then the second part must also be true. If, then statements are sometimes called **conditional logic** or **propositional logic**. Work through the four following if, then statements. Decide if the third statement is a valid conclusion.

1. If she is rich, she wears diamonds.
   She is rich.
   Therefore, she wears diamonds.
   Valid or Invalid?

2. If she is rich, she wears diamonds.
   She isn't wearing diamonds.
   Therefore, she isn't rich.
   Valid or Invalid?

3. If she is rich, she wears diamonds.
   She is wearing diamonds.
   Therefore, she is rich.
   Valid or Invalid?

4. If she is rich, she wears diamonds.
   She isn't rich.
   Therefore, she isn't wearing diamonds.
   Valid or Invalid?

In each of these problems, the first premise begins with the word *if*; the *then* is not explicitly stated, but can be inferred ("then she wears diamonds"). The first part of this premise ("If she is rich") is called the **antecedent**; the second part ("she wears diamonds") is called the **consequent**.

Tree Diagrams

Like the other types of deductive reasoning problems, conditional statements can be represented with a spatial display. **Tree diagrams**, diagrams in which the critical information is represented along "branches," like a tree, are used in several chapters in this book, and can be used to determine validity with if, then deductive reasoning problems. Tree diagrams are very handy representational forms in many situations and are well worth the trouble of learning to use. We will use tree diagrams in

Chapter 7 on understanding likelihood, Chapter 9 on problem solving, and Chapter 10 on creativity.

Tree diagrams are easy to begin. Every tree diagram begins with a "start" point. A start point is a dot on the paper that you label "start." Everyone finds the first step easy.

Start

The dots are more formally called nodes, and branches (lines) come out from nodes. The branches represent everything that can happen when you are at that node. In if, then problems, there are two states that are possible from the start node. In this example, either she is rich or she is not rich. There are two possibilities, so there will be two branches coming from the start node. The antecedent is the first event on the "tree" with a second branch representing the consequent. The validity of the conclusion can be determined by examining the branches. Let's try this with the first problem.

"If she is rich" becomes:

"She wears diamonds" is added as a second set of branches by showing that the "rich" node is always followed by "diamonds," but the "not rich" node may or may not be followed by "diamonds." We put both possibilities on the branches leading from "not rich" because we are not given any information about the relationship between being "not rich" and "wearing diamonds."

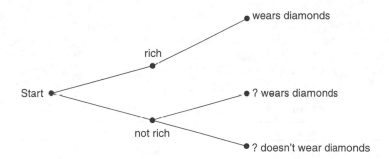

When we are told that "She is rich," circle the branch or branches that has this label and move along the branches from the "rich" node and conclude that she "wears diamonds." There is only one node in this diagram that represents the possibility that she is rich, and this node has only one branch attached from it—the branch that leads to "wears diamonds." Once you locate the "rich" node, the only possible consequent is "wears diamonds." Thus, the conclusion to problem number 1 is valid. The technical term for this problem is **affirming the antecedent**. In this case, the second premise affirms or indicates the antecedent is true; therefore, its consequent is true.

Problem 2 also contains a valid conclusion. The tree diagram is exactly the same as in the first problem because the same if, then statements are made. In determining the validity of the conclusion, we begin with "She isn't wearing diamonds," which is represented at only one node, so we trace this back to the "not rich" node. Because the second premise indicates that the consequent is not true, this sort of problem is technically called **denying the consequent**.

Many people are willing to conclude that problem 3 is also valid when, in fact, it is not. Although it must be assumed to be true that if she is rich, she wears diamonds, it is also possible that poor people wear diamonds. I have found that intelligent college students (and yes, many of their professors also) have difficulty with this problem. Because the second premise states that the consequent has occurred, this sort of problem is called **affirming the consequent**. It is fallacious (i.e., wrong) to believe that because the consequent is true, the antecedent must also be true. "If," in these reasoning problems, doesn't mean "if and only if," which is how many people interpret it. Of course, she may be rich, it may even be more likely that she is rich, but we cannot conclude that she is rich just because she is wearing diamonds. You can see this on the tree diagram. There are two different nodes labeled "wears diamonds," one connected to the "rich" node and one connected to the "not rich" node. We cannot determine which must be true because either is possible.

The fallacy of affirming the consequent is one type of deductive reasoning error called **illicit conversion**. Illicit conversions, in if, then statements occur when people believe that "If A, then B" also means "If B, then A."

Problem 4 is also invalid, although it is tempting to conclude that if she isn't rich, she isn't wearing diamonds. Can you guess the technical term for this sort of problem? It is called **denying the antecedent** because premise 2 states that the antecedent is false. Again, by starting at the "not rich" node, you can see that it is connected to both "wears diamonds" and "doesn't wear diamonds," so either is possible.

A summary of these four kinds of reasoning, with examples of each, is shown in Table 4.1.

Several popular advertisements take advantage of people's tendencies to make invalid inferences from if, then statements. There is a commercial for yogurt that goes something like this:

Some very old people from a remote section of the former Soviet Union are shown. We're told that it is common for people in this remote region to live to be 110 years old. We're also told that they eat a great deal of yogurt. The conclusion that the advertisers want people to make is that eating yogurt will make you live 110 years.

TABLE 4.1
Four Kinds of Reasoning with If, Then Statements

	Antecedent	*Consequent*
Affirming	*Affirming the Antecedent* *Valid Reasoning* *Example:* If I am dieting, then I will lose weight. I am dieting.	*Affirming the Consequent* *Invalid Reasoning* *Example:* If Harry went to the supermarket, then the refrigerator is full. The refrigerator is full.
	Therefore, I will lose weight.	Therefore, Harry went to the supermarket.
Denying	*Denying the Antecedent* *Invalid Reasoning* *Example:* If it is raining, then my hair is wet. It is not raining.	*Denying the Consequent* *Valid Reasoning* *Example:* If Judy and Bruce are in love, then they are planning to marry. They are not planning to marry.
	Therefore, my hair is not wet.	Therefore, Judy and Bruce are not in love.

Implicitly, we're being told that if we eat yogurt, then we'll live to be 110 years old. Of course, it's possible to live to be 110 without ever tasting yogurt, and we have no reason to believe that yogurt added years to their lives. There is no basis for making a causal inference for believing that eating yogurt can *cause* anyone to live a long time. These remote Russians engage in strenuous physical labor most of their lives and do not come into contact with many outsiders who carry potentially contagious diseases. Either of these facts, or countless others, including heredity, could account for their longevity. (It is also possible that the longevity claim is subject to question.) The advertisers are obviously hoping that the viewers will fall prey to the fallacy of affirming the consequent and say to themselves, "If I eat yogurt, I will live to a very old age."

If, Then Reasoning in Everyday Contexts

In questions of science, the authority of a thousand is not worth the humble reasoning of a single individual.

—Galileo Galilei (The Quoteaholic, http://*www.quoteaholic.com.*
Retrieved Jan. 15, 2002)

If, then statements, like linear orderings, appear implicitly in standard prose. Of course, we seldom find them neatly labeled "premise and conclusion." Yet, they are often the basis for many common arguments. The fallacies of denying the antecedent and affirming the consequent in everyday contexts are quite common.

There is currently an acrimonious debate over the issue of providing junior and senior high school students with contraceptive information. The pro side argues that if students are given this information, then they will act responsibly when engaging in intercourse. Formally, this becomes: If students receive contraceptive information, then they will engage in "protected" intercourse. The con side argues that students should not engage in intercourse (whether protected or not); therefore, they should not receive contraceptive information. This is an example of the fallacy of denying the antecedent. It does not follow that if they are not given contraceptive information, then they will not engage in intercourse.

Here's another example, virtually verbatim, from this morning's news. The specific details are not important because examples of this sort probably can be gleaned from the news on any day of the week. Viewers were told that if the president of the United States handled a tense situation with Communist China well, then a tense international situation would be resolved without escalation of hostilities. The situation was resolved well (hostilities did not escalate), so the commentator concluded that the president handled the tense situation well. Of course, it is possible that the information in the if, then statement is really not true, and even if the president did a good job, the situation could get worse. When we reason deductively with the laws of logic, we assume that the propositions are true, so let's put aside the very real possibility that we should not assume it to be true and apply the principles of if, then reasoning.

When the situation is drawn out in a decision tree, it is easy to see that it could have been resolved well, even if the president had not handled the tense situation well.

A point that has been made repeatedly throughout this chapter is that people often do not reason according to the laws of formal logic without instruction in reasoning. This is an example where using the laws of logic would help us understand the situation better.

In everyday (practical) reasoning, we use information that is not stated in the premises in order to decide if the conclusion follows from the premises. One sort of knowledge we rely on is our knowledge about the content of the premises. The following two sentences demonstrate this point (Braine, 1978, p. 19):

> If Hitler had had the atomic bomb in 1940, he would have won the war.
> and
> If Hitler had had one more plane in 1940, he would have won the war.

Although logic dictates that people should be able to reason identically with both of these premises and should avoid the fallacies of affirming the consequent and denying the antecedent, in fact most people find it easier to reason correctly with the first premise than the second. As with all of the forms of deductive reasoning that will be covered in this chapter, the content of the premises and our own belief biases influence the way we determine what sorts of conclusions we are willing to accept as valid. When we interpret if, then statements in everyday contexts, we rely on our knowledge about the content to decide if a conclusion follows. According to the rules of formal logic, we should be able to reason in ways that are independent of content. We should all arrive at identical, logically correct conclusions, no matter what the content is. Of course, humans are not perfect logic machines and there are important individual differences in the sorts of models people use to solve reasoning problems (Bucciarelli & Johnson-Laird, 1999). We do and should determine if the premises are true before deciding if a conclusion follows. (This point will be emphasized in Chapter 5.)

Negation

As seen in the previous section on linear reasoning, the use of negatives ("no," "not") in a reasoning problem makes it much more difficult to solve (Wason, 1969). These difficulties are apparent in the following examples in which either the antecedent or consequent is negative.

> If the light is not green, I will go to Rome.
> *It is not true that the light is not green.*
> What, if anything, can you conclude?

> If the letter is B, then the number is not 4.
> *The number is not 4.*
> What, if anything, can you conclude?

These are difficult to deal with because of the use of negation and its affirmation or denial. The first statement denies the negative antecedent (not (not green)). This is called a **double negation**. You can't assume anything about the consequent when the antecedent is denied, even when the antecedent itself is negative. Look at the second example. Most people incorrectly decide that it is correct to conclude from the second example that "The letter is B." You should recognize this as an example of affirming the consequent. If you are having difficulty answering these questions, draw the corresponding tree diagrams, and the answer will "appear."

I once heard a politician make a statement similar to these. He said, "It is not true that I do not favor the legislation." It took me a few seconds to realize that he implied that he favored the legislation. He could have meant that he was neutral with respect to the legislation, neither favoring nor opposing it, but in the context, I interpreted his statement to mean that he favored the legislation. This is an example in which I used context to clarify intended meaning. When negative information is given, people take longer to solve reasoning problems and are less accurate, probably because the negative information (not or no) adds to the burden of working memory (Garnham & Oakhill, 1994; Noveck & Politzer, 1998).

Confirmation Bias

Confirmation bias, the predilection to seek and utilize information that supports or confirms your hypotheses or premises, can be seen in this classic problem (Johnson-Laird & Wason, 1970):

Four cards are lying face up on a table in front of you. Every card has a letter on one side and a number on the other. Your task is to decide if the following rule is true, "If a card has a vowel on one side, then it has an even number on the other side." Which card or cards do you need to turn over in order to find out whether the rule is true or false? You may turn over only the minimum number necessary to determine if this rule is true. Please stop now and examine the cards below to determine which ones you would want to turn over. Don't go on until you have decided which cards you would want to turn over.

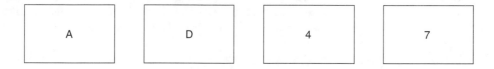

Few people select the correct cards in this problem, which has become known as the **four-card selection task**. It is a widely studied task that is popular in the literature of cognitive psychology. Most people respond "A only" or "A and 4." The correct answer is "A and 7." Can you figure out why? The best way to solve this reasoning problem is to draw a tree diagram that corresponds to the statement, "If a card has a vowel on one side, then it has an even number on the other side." It should look like this:

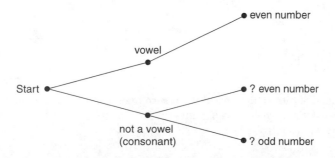

If A doesn't have an even number on the other side, the rule is false. Similarly, if 7 has a vowel on the other side, the rule is false. What about D and 4? D is a consonant. It doesn't matter if there is an even or odd number on the back because the rule says nothing about consonants. Because 4 is an even number, it doesn't matter if there is a vowel or consonant on the back. The reason that this is such a difficult problem is that people interpret the rule to also mean "If a card does not have a vowel on one side, then it does not have an even number on the other side" or, without negatives, "If a card has a consonant on one side, then it has an odd number on the other side." These alternate interpretations are incorrect. Do you recognize the error as denying the antecedent? This is a robust (strong) effect. It is an extremely difficult task because of the crucial role of disconfirmation. People fail to appreciate the importance of a falsification strategy. That is, we need to think of ways to show that a hypothesis may be false, instead of looking for evidence that would show that a hypothesis may be correct. This is exacerbated with the incorrect assumption that the converse of the rule is also true. The only correct way to solve this problem is to select only cards that can falsify the rule.

Part of the difficulty people have with this task may be related to the abstract nature of the problem. After all, there is very little we do in our everyday life that relates vowels and even numbers. Try out a more realistic and less abstract version of this task (adapted from Johnson-Laird, Legrenzi, & Legrenzi, 1972):

In order to understand this task, you may need some background information (depending on your age). Many years ago, the United States Post Office had two different postage rates known as first-class and second-class mail. You could pay full postage, which was 5 cents, if you sealed your letter (first class), or you could pay a reduced, 3-cent rate, if you merely folded the flaps closed and didn't seal them (second class). (First-class mail had priority for delivery over second-class mail.)

Suppose you are a postal employee watching letters as they move across a conveyor belt. The rule to be verified or disconfirmed is: "If a letter is sealed, then it has a 5 cent stamp on it." Four letters are shown in Fig. 4.2. Which ones would you have to turn over to decide if the rule is true?

Stop now and work on this problem. Don't go on until you've decided which letters (at a minimum) you would have to turn over to test this rule.

Did you notice that this is the same task that was posed earlier? The correct answer is the first sealed envelope and the last envelope (the one with the 3 cent stamp). This is an easier problem than the more abstract one because people find it easier to understand that a letter that is not sealed could also have a 5 cent stamp on it than it is to understand that if the letter is not a vowel it could also have an even

FIG. 4.2. Which of these letters would you turn over to decide if the following rule is true: "If a letter is sealed, then it has a 5-cent stamp on it." (Adapted from Johnson-Laird, Legrenzi, & Legrenzi, 1972.)

number on the back. Your tree diagram should look like this:

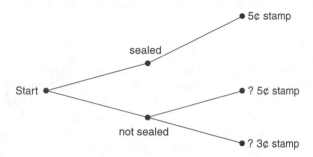

Johnson-Laird and Wason (1977) found that when the problem is presented in this realistic manner, 22 out of 24 subjects were able to solve the problem. Johnson-Laird and Wason concluded that our everyday experiences are relevant in determining how we reason.

Permission and Obligation Schemata

Many researchers have tried to understand why so many people have so much difficulty with the four-card selection task (I also find it very confusing), but have little difficulty when it is rephrased in the stamped-letter example. These are identical problems from the perspective of logic—the rules for reasoning are the same in the two problems.

Cheng and Holyoak (1985) explored the basic differences in how people think about these two problems. They postulated that when people use if, then reasoning for pragmatic purposes, they usually involve either the permission to do something, called **permission schema** (if something is true, then you have permission to do something else) or they involve an obligation or contractual arrangement, called **obligation schema** (if something is true, then you have an obligation to do something else). In real life, these are the two most common situations in which people use if, then reasoning. Instead of using the rules of formal logic, people tend to develop abstract general rules that work well in specific situations and help them to achieve their goals. Cheng and Holyoak found that the permission and obligation schemata operate across domains. In other words, it does not matter if the topic concerns stamped letters, an agreement to perform a job, or permission to borrow the car. Here is an example of each:

If a passenger has been immunized against cholera, then he may enter the country. (permission schema)

If you pay me $100,000, then I'll transfer ownership of this house to you. (obligation schema)

When if, then statements involve permission or obligation, then people make few reasoning errors. Furthermore, when most people understand the rules of permission and obligation, the content of the statement doesn't matter—people apply the rules appropriately across domains. Cheng and Holyoak (1985) also found that when they included a rationale for the rule, most of the people they asked to solve this problem had no difficulty with it. In the sealed envelope problem, they added the following rationale for the rule, "The country's postal regulation requires that if a letter is sealed, then it must carry a 20-cent stamp" (p. 400). Thus, a rule that was extremely difficult to apply when it was presented in an abstract form was easily used by most people when it was used in a familiar context with an explanation.

If, and Only If

Certain contexts seem to require that we understand them in a way that is inconsistent with the laws of logic. Suppose you are told: "If you mow the lawn, I'll give you five dollars" (Taplin & Staudenmeyer, 1973, p. 542). This statement invites the interpretation, "If you do not mow the lawn, I won't give you five dollars." In the everyday inference we make from language, this is a valid conclusion, although it is erroneous from the perspective of formal logic. In understanding statements of the "If p, then q" variety, the conclusions that we are willing to accept as valid depend very much on what p and q are. In this lawn-mowing example, the intended meaning is "if, and only if you mow the lawn, then I'll give you five dollars." In dealing with real-world if, then statements, you need to decide whether the intended message is "if p, then q" or "if, and only if p, then q." The important point of this example is that context is irrelevant to the laws of logic, which are the same whether you are talking about pay for mowing a lawn or turning over a card to check an abstract rule. It is not surprising that people vary their thinking depending on context because context is important in real-life settings.

Chained Conditionals

We can make things just a little more complicated (just what you were hoping for), by building on if, then statements and making them into longer chains. A **chained conditional** occurs when two if, then statements are linked so that the consequent of one statement is also the antecedent of the other statement. In skeleton form, or fill-in-the-blank form, this becomes:

If A, then B. If B, then C.

As before, it doesn't matter what we use to fill in for A, B, and C, if we are reasoning according to the laws of logic. For example, "If Jodi wants to be a physicist, then she will study calculus. If she is studying calculus, then she has a final exam on Wednesday." With this conditional chain, we can conclude that she has a final exam on Wednesday, if we learn that she wants to be a physicist.

Don't be tempted to assume that every time you have three terms, you have a chained conditional. Consider this example.

If she wants to be a physicist, then she will study calculus.
If she wants to be a physicist, then she will have an exam on Wednesday.

These are two conditional statements, but they do not have the chained structure because the consequent of one statement is not the antecedent of the other statement.

If, Then Reasoning in Legal Contexts

Consider the sad saga of an American star who was accused of killing his ex-wife and her friend. The specifics of this American tragedy are not relevant because there are always similar crimes in which the key to the defense or prosecution hinges on if, then reasoning. In this particular case, the suspect had an excellent alibi from 11 p.m. and later on the night of the killing. In other words,

If the murder occurred any time from 11 p.m. or later, the defendant is innocent.
The prosecutor attempted to show that the murder occurred prior to 11 p.m. Suppose that she was successful in convincing the jury that the murder occurred at 10:30. What can we conclude about the guilt or innocence of the defendant?

To make it easier for you, I have drawn the tree diagram that corresponds to this real-life situation.

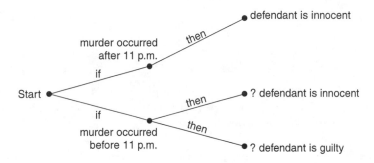

I hope that you determined that if the murder occurred at 10:30, we do not know if the defendant is guilty or innocent. Unless there is other evidence that "proves beyond a reasonable doubt" that the defendant committed these grisly murders, then the jury must acquit him. They cannot convict a man because of the error of denying the antecedent. If anyone tries to tell you that this critical thinking stuff is a "bunch of bunk" (or some more colorful phrase), then give him or her this example in which misunderstanding could lead to a wrongful conviction. Whom would you want on a jury that decides your guilt or innocence—people who think critically or those who rush to a hasty decision and are easily misled with persuasive techniques?

COMBINATORIAL REASONING

We recognize the gravity of the challenge to get our students to think, to think critically, and even to think scientifically. Certainly it is abundantly clear to me that science education fails if it doesn't tackle the matter of thinking.

—Munby (1982, p. 8)

One approach to enhancing reasoning skills is based on a model of intelligence that was proposed by the Swiss psychologist Jean Piaget. Piaget was primarily concerned with the way people acquire knowledge and the way cognitive processes change throughout childhood and early adulthood. According to Piaget, there are four broad developmental periods (each broken into stages). As people move from infancy into adolescence, their cognitive abilities mature in qualitatively distinct stages culminating with the ability to think in orderly, abstract ways. Piaget's examples of abstract thought involve thinking skills that are needed to understand scientific concepts. One of the scientific reasoning skills that Piaget believed to be important is **combinatorial reasoning**, which is use of systematic and orderly steps

FIG. 4.3. Mixing colorless liquids

when making combinations so that all possible combinations are formed. Here is a classic task that involves this skill:

Mixing Colorless Chemicals. This task involves mixing chemicals until a yellow color is obtained. Suppose that you were given four bottles of odorless, colorless liquids. They appear to be identical except for being labeled 1, 2, 3, and 4. You are also given a fifth beaker labeled X, which is the "activating solution." The activating solution is always needed to obtain the yellow color, which results from a chemical reaction. How would you go about finding which of the chemicals in combination will yield the yellow color?

Some rules: The amount of each chemical is not important, nor is the order in which you combine them. It may help you in working on this problem to visualize the materials as presented in Fig. 4.3.

Stop now and think about how you would approach this problem. Do not go on until you have written down all of the tests you would perform.

How did you approach this problem? Did you realize that you needed an organized plan or did you begin by randomly mixing the liquids? The best approach to this task is a very methodical one. It must include mixing each liquid separately with the activating solution (1 + X, 2 + X, 3 + X, 4 + X), then carefully mixing two liquids at a time with X (1 + 2 + X, 1 + 3 + X, 1 + 4 + X, 2 + 3 + X, 2 + 4 + X, 3 + 4 + X), then three at a time with X (1 + 2 + 3 + X, 1 + 2 + 4 + X, 1 + 3 + 4 + X, 2 + 3 + 4 + X), then all four at once (1 + 2 + 3 + 4 + X), being careful to observe which combinations would yield the yellow color. Look over the way the chemicals were combined in a systematic manner so that no combinations would be missed or duplicated. This technique of systematic combinations will be needed to perform the reasoning tasks in the next section.

SYLLOGISTIC REASONING

Nothing intelligible ever puzzles me.
Logic puzzles me.

—Lewis Carroll (1832–1898)

Syllogistic reasoning is a form of reasoning that involves deciding whether a conclusion can properly be inferred from two or more statements. One type of syllogistic reasoning is categorical reasoning. **Categorical reasoning** involves **quantifiers** or terms that tell us how many. Quantifiers are terms like "all," "some," "none," and "no." The quantifiers indicate how many items belong in specified categories.

A **syllogism** usually consists of two statements that are called premises and a third statement called the conclusion. In categorical syllogisms, quantifiers are used in the premises and conclusion. The task is to determine if the conclusion follows logically from the premises.

The premises and conclusion of a syllogism are classified according to **mood**. (The word *mood* has a special meaning in this context that is unrelated to its more usual meaning about how someone feels.) There are four different moods, or combinations of positive and negative statements with the terms "all" or "some." The four moods are:

Mood	Abstract Example	Concrete Example
Universal Affirmative	All A are B.	All students are smart.
Particular Affirmative	Some A are B.	Some video games are fun.
Universal Negative	No A are B.	No smurfs are pink.
Particular Negative	Some A are not B.	Some democrats are not liberals.

As you can see from this table, a statement is universal if it contains the terms "all" or "no"; it is particular if it contains the term "some"; it is negative if it contains "no" or "not"; and it is affirmative if it is not negative. Thus, it should be easy to classify the mood of any statement by identifying the key terms.

Several syllogisms are presented here. Each consists of two premises and a conclusion. Work through each syllogism and decide if the conclusion is valid (V) or invalid (I). To be valid, the conclusion must *always* be true given its premises. In other words, when you decide that a syllogism is valid, you are saying "if the premises are true, then conclusion must be true." In other words, "Does the conclusion 'follow from' the premises?" *If you can think of one way that the conclusion could be false when the premises are true, then it is invalid.* Don't go on until you have worked through these syllogisms.

1. Premise #1:   All people on welfare are poor.
   Premise #2:   *Some poor people are dishonest.*
   Conclusion: Some people on welfare are dishonest.   Valid or Invalid?

2. Premise #1:   No parents understand children.
   Premise #2:   *Some teachers understand children.*
   Conclusion: No parents are teachers.   Valid or Invalid?

3. Premise #1:   Some lawyers are not smart.
   Premise #2:   *Some smart people are rich.*
   Conclusion: Some lawyers are rich.   Valid or Invalid?

4. Premise #1:   All physics students are good in math.
   Premise #2:   *Some coeds are physics students.*
   Conclusion: Some coeds are good in math.   Valid or Invalid?

5. Premise #1:   All Americans need health insurance.
   Premise #2:   *Everyone who needs health insurance should vote for it.*
   Conclusion: All Americans should vote for health insurance.   Valid or Invalid?

According to the rules of logic, it should not matter if the syllogisms are presented in abstract terms of A's and B's (e.g., Some A's are not B's), nonsense terms like zev and creb (All zev are creb), or meaningful terms like lawyers and cool (No lawyers are cool). The logical rules for deciding if a conclusion can be validly inferred from the premises remain the same. We're really saying "All _____ are _____." It should make no difference how we fill in the blanks; any letters, nonsense or meaningful words, or even fancy pictures should be handled in the same way. However, from a psychological perspective, there are important content differences, and people have difficulty using the rules of syllogistic reasoning when the conclusion is not one that they believe to be true, even if logically it follows from the premises. One way to avoid the problem of having one's biases affect how we reason with quantifiers is to use circle diagrams, which, like linear diagrams and tree diagrams, alleviate the limitations of short-term memory and make relationships obvious and visible.

How did you go about deciding if the conclusions were valid? There are two different types of strategies that can be used with syllogisms to determine if a conclusion follows from its premises. If you've been reading the chapters in order, then you know that a common approach to improving thinking is the deliberate use of both spatial and verbal strategies. The same two approaches apply here. First, I will present a spatial method for testing conclusions, then I will provide some verbal rules that can also be used. Either method will "work," but you'll probably find that you prefer one method over the other. I have been teaching this material to college students for many years and have found that individual students have very strong preferences for either circle diagrams or verbal rules.

Circle Diagrams for Determining Validity

One way of determining if a conclusion is true is with the use of circle diagrams that depict the relationships among the three terms (A, B, C or whatever we used to fill in the blanks). The degree to which the circles overlap depicts the inclusion or exclusion of the categories.

There are several different methods of drawing diagrams to depict the relationships among the terms in a syllogism. One of these methods is known as Venn Diagrams, named for a 19th century English mathematician and logician who first introduced them. These are the same diagrams that you probably used in mathematics classes if you ever studied set theory. (This was a very popular way to teach the "new math," before it was abandoned and replaced with the "old math.") A second method of diagramming relationships is known as Euler Diagrams. According to popular lore, this method was devised by Leonard Euler, an 18th century Swiss mathematician, who was given the task of teaching the laws of syllogistic reasoning to a German princess. Because the princess was having difficulty understanding the task, Euler created a simple procedure that could be used to understand the relationships among the terms and to check on the validity of inferences. A third method is called the ballantine method because of its use of three overlapping circles. In all of these methods, circles are used to indicate category membership. The differences among these methods is not important here, and the general strategy of checking conclusions with circle drawings will be referred to as **circle diagrams**. If you've learned a different method of circle diagrams in another context (e.g., a class on set theory or a logic class), then continue to use that method as long as it works well for you.

Look very carefully at Fig. 4.4.

Universal Affirmative All A are B. (All angels are bald.)	All A are B, *and* some B are not A.	or	All A are B, *and* all B are A.

Particular Affirmative Some A are B. (Some angels are bald.)	All A are B, *and* some B are not A.	or	All A are B, *and* all B are A.	or
	All B are A, *and* Some A are not B.	or	Some A are B *and* some B are A. *Also* some A are not B, *and* some B are not A.	

Universal Negative No A are B. (No angels are bald.)	No A are B, and no B are A.

Particular Negative Some A are not B. (Some angels are not bald.)	No A are B, and no B are A.	or	All B are A, *and* some A are not B.	or
	Some A are B, and some B are A. Also some A are not B, and some B are not A.			

FIG. 4.4. Circle diagrams depicting correct interpretations of the premises used in syllogisms. Note that "all" can have two correct interpretations, "some" can have four correct interpretations, "no" has one correct interpretation, and "some-not" can have three correct interpretations.

The four moods that statements in syllogisms can have are listed in the left-hand column of Fig. 4.4. Next to each statement are circle diagrams that are correct depictions of the relationships in the statement. Stop now and look very carefully at Fig. 4.4. One circle represents everything that is A, and a second circle represents everything that is B. For the purposes of deductive reasoning, it does not matter what A and B are. In the example in Fig. 4.4, A is used to stand for angels and B is used to stand for bald, but it could be anything. I could just as easily used A to stand for college students and B to stand for punk rockers.

Look at the way the circles are combined so that they form a "picture" of what is being said in words. Let's start in the middle of the figure, with "universal negative," the easiest example. When we say, "No A are B," this means that nothing that is in category A is also in category B. This is depicted by drawing a circle labeled A and one labeled B that do not touch or overlap in any way. There is only one way to draw this relationship. Notice that when we say, "No A are B," we are also saying that "No B are A." Can you see that from the circle diagram? Every time you have a universal negative, the relationship will be "pictured" with two circles that do not overlap—one for things that are A and one for things that are B.

Consider now universal affirmative, "All A are B." Again we use two circles—one labeled A and one labeled B. And again, we want to draw the two circles so that they represent the relationship in which everything that is A is B. As you can see in Fig. 4.4, there are two different ways of depicting this relationship because there are two possible correct ways of understanding what it means. By drawing the A circle inside the B circle, we are depicting the case where "All A are B," but there are some B that are not A (some bald people are not angels). The second drawing shows the case where "All A are B," and "All B are A" (all bald people are angels). Either of these two interpretations could be true when we are told that "All A are B."

Don't be discouraged if this seems difficult to you. It will soon be easier as it becomes more meaningful and you work your way through the examples. Look at the other two possibilities in Fig. 4.4. There are three possible ways to depict particular negative (Some A are not B) and four possible ways to depict particular affirmative (Some A are B). Now look at all of the moods and notice the different ways that two circles can be combined. There are five different possible ways to combine two circles, and each combination represents a different meaning!

1. A and B do not overlap:

2. A and B are the same circle:

3. A is inside B:

4. B is inside A:

5. A and B partially overlap:

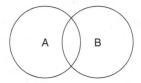

Let's draw circle diagrams to depict the relationships in Syllogism 1. The first two sentences are the premises. Write out each premise and next to each premise, draw the appropriate circle diagrams. For example, the first premise states, "All people on welfare are poor." In skeletal form, it is "All A are B" with A standing for "people on welfare" and B standing for "poor." You should recognize this as universal affirmative. Go to Fig. 4.4, look across from universal affirmative, and you will see that there are two possible ways to draw circles that correspond to this premise. Repeat this with the second premise: Some poor people are dishonest. You already decided that A = people on welfare, and B = poor. The new term, dishonest, can be represented by C. The second premise then becomes "Some B are C." This is an example of particular affirmative. Look across from particular affirmative on Fig. 4.4 and you will see that there are four possible ways to draw circles to represent this relationship. The only difference is that for Premise 2, we are using the letters B and C to stand for the categories. Thus, the first two premises will look like this:

A = people on welfare; B = poor; C = dishonest.

1. All people on welfare are poor.
   (All A are B.)

Premise 1a   Premise 1b

2. Some poor people are dishonest.
   (Some B are C.)

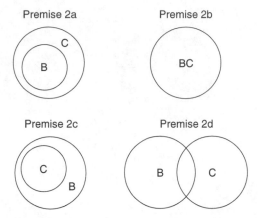

To determine if the conclusion is valid, we systematically combine each of the figures in the first premise with each of the figures in the second premise. If we find one
combination that would not correspond to the conclusion, then we can stop and decide that the conclusion is invalid. If we make all possible combinations of figures
from Premise 1 and figures from Premise 2, and they are all consistent with the conclusion, then the conclusion is valid. In other words, if all combinations of Premise 1
with Premise 2 support the conclusion, then the conclusion is valid. The first few
times you work on these, it may seem laborious, but you will soon "see" the answers
and find ways to shortcut the process of working through all the combinations.

Here is the conclusion:

Some poor people on welfare are dishonest.

(Some A are C).

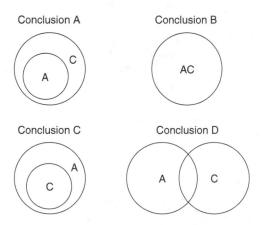

Premise 1 has two possible drawings and Premise 2 has four possible drawings.
You can see that I labeled the two Premise 1 drawings 1a and 1b and the four
Premise 2 drawings 2a, 2b, 2c, and 2d. To work systematically, you need to use the
combinatorial reasoning rules that were presented in the last section. Start with 1a
and combine it with 2a, then 1a and 2b, 1a and 2c, 1a and 2d. Then repeat the pattern
by combining 1b with 2a, then 1b with 2b, then 1b with 2c, and finally 1b with 2d. Of
course, you hope that you won't have to go through this entire procedure because

you can stop as soon as you find one combination that violates the conclusion that "Some A are C." Work along with me.

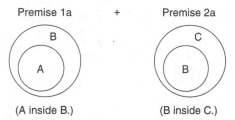

Premise 1a   +   Premise 2a

(A inside B.)   (B inside C.)

When I combine these two depictions, I will get a figure with A inside B and B inside C:

This combination shows a result that is consistent with the conclusion that "Some A are C." Go on!

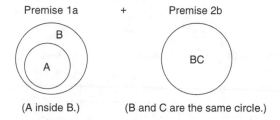

Premise 1a   +   Premise 2b

(A inside B.)   (B and C are the same circle.)

When I combine 1b and 2b, I get a depiction where A is inside the B/C circle.

This is consistent with the conclusion that "Some A are C." Go on!

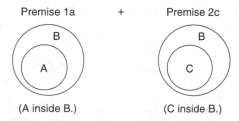

Premise 1a   +   Premise 2c

(A inside B.)   (C inside B.)

This gets a little tricky here, because *there are several different ways to combine 1a and 2c and we have to try all of them* until we run out of combinations or find one that is not consistent with the conclusion. Here we draw all ways that A can be inside B and C can be inside B.

A and C are the same circle inside B.

This is still consistent with "Some A are C." Go on!
A and C partially overlap inside B.

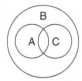

This is still consistent with "Some A are C." Go on!
A and C are two circles inside B.

This does not agree with the conclusion that "Some A are C."
Stop here!

I know that this seems like a lot of work, but after you work a few problems, you can spot the combinations that will make a conclusion invalid, so you will not need to try every possible combination. Until then, work systematically through all combinations. A list of steps for checking the validity of conclusions with circle diagrams is shown in Table 4.2. Stop now and look over the steps. Refer back to them as we work through the rest of the syllogisms.

TABLE 4.2
Steps for Determining the Validity
of Conclusions Using Circle Diagrams

---

1. Write out each premise and the conclusion of the syllogism.
2. Next to each statement, draw all correct diagrams using the diagrams shown in Fig. 4.1.
3. Systematically combine all diagrams for Premise 1 with all diagrams for Premise 2. Try Premise 1a (the first diagram for Premise 1) with Premise 2a (the first diagram for Premise 2). Continue combining Premise 1a with all Premise 2 diagrams, then go on and combine all Premise 1b with all Premise 2 diagrams. Continue in this manner (Premise 1c with all Premise 2 diagrams, then Premise 1d with all Premise 2 diagrams) until
4. You find *one* diagram in which the conclusion is invalid or
5. You have tried all combinations of Premise 1 and Premise 2 diagrams.

Note. Sometimes there will be more than one way to combine diagrams from the two premises. Be sure to try all combinations.

When trying out all combinations, remember that there are five possible ways to combine two circles: (a) A inside B, (b) B inside A, (c) A and B overlapping partially, (d) A and B with no overlap (two separate circles), and (e) A and B represented by one circle (A and B are the same circle). These five possibilities are shown below.

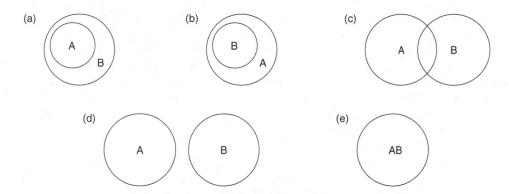

Let's try Syllogism 2.
A = parents; B = understand children; C = teachers.
No parents understand children.
(No A are B.)

Premise 1a

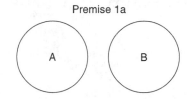

Some teachers understand children.
(Some C are B.)

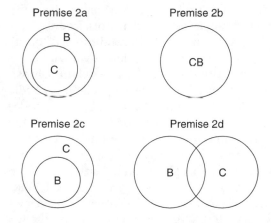

Premise 2a Premise 2b

Premise 2c Premise 2d

No parents are teachers.
(No A are C.)

Conclusion A

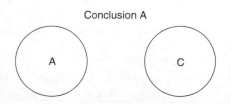

The two circles that depict the first premise are only one figure because it is Universal Negative, and two separate circles are needed to depict this relationship. It is labeled 1a. The second premise is Particular Affirmative, which is depicted with four figures (2a, 2b, 2c, 2d). The conclusion is Universal Negative, so it is also depicted with one figure consisting of two separate circles. Now combine 1a + 2a, 1a + 2b, 1a + 2c, and 1a + 2d. You can stop as soon as you find one combination that is not consistent with the conclusion and decide that it is invalid, or try all combinations and then decide that it is valid.

As you work through all combinations of the circle drawing that can be combined from the premises, you will see that it is invalid. (If you would like more practice with syllogisms, you can find several more "worked examples" in *Thinking Critically About Critical Thinking*, the workbook that accompanies this text.)

Here are the answers to the next three syllogisms presented on page 157:

3. From the premises you were given, is it valid to conclude that "Some lawyers are rich"?
   Nope—it's invalid.
4. From the premises you were given, is it valid to conclude that "Some coeds are good in math"?
   Yes!
5. From the premises you were given, is it valid to conclude that "All Americans should vote for health insurance"? Yes, it is.

Verbal Rules for Determining Validity

It's a peculiar thing about circle diagrams: Some people love working on them and others seem to hate them. The problem in working with them is trying all possible combinations of representations for both premises. People who prefer to think spatially seem to "see" the combinations with apparent ease, but those who prefer verbal modes of representation seem to have more difficulty. For those of you who have difficulty combining premises into circle relationships, take heart because there are verbal rules for determining if the conclusion of a syllogism is valid. These rules will work just as well as circle diagrams. Sternberg and Weil (1980) found that verbal and spatial strategies draw on different abilities and that the effectiveness of a given strategy depends on one's preferred mode of thought. There are five rules that can be used to determine the validity of a conclusion. In order to use these rules there are two additional terms that you need to learn.

There are three categories named in syllogisms, the A, B, and C, or whatever category names we substitute for them in more concrete examples. One of these categories is called the **middle term**. To determine which is the middle term, go to the conclusion. There are two categories in the conclusion; one is the subject of the sentence, the other is in the predicate. The category that is *not* mentioned in the conclusion is the middle term. It is called the middle term because it links the other two terms in the premises. Look back at Syllogism 1. The conclusion is "Some people on welfare are dishonest." "People on welfare" is the subject of this sentence, and "dishonest" is the predicate. The middle term is "poor." The middle term is in both premises, but it is not in the conclusion.

The second term that you need to know is **distributed**. A term is distributed if the statement applies to every item in the category (Govier, 1985). Consider the four

TABLE 4.3
Distributed and Undistributed Terms in the Four Moods of Syllogisms

All A are B.	A is distributed. (A is modified by "all.")
	B is undistributed. (B is undistributed because there may be some B that are not A.)
Some A are B.	Both A and B are undistributed.
No A are B.	Both A and B are distributed. (Both A and B are modified by "no.")
	(This is the same as saying that "No B are A.")
Some A are not B.	A is undistributed.
	B is distributed. (B is modified by "not.")

TABLE 4.4
Rules for Determining Validity of Conclusions
When Reasoning with Quantifiers

1. If the conclusion is negative, one premise must be negative, and conversely, if one premise is negative, the conclusion must be negative.
2. The middle term must be distributed in at least one premise.
3. Any term that is distributed in the conclusion must be distributed in at least one premise.
4. If both premises are particular, there are no valid conclusions.
5. If one premise is particular, the conclusion must be particular.
6. At least one premise must be affirmative. (There are no valid conclusions with two negative premises.)

types of category relationships shown in Table 4.3. Next to each one I've indicated which terms are distributed and which terms are undistributed. As you will see in Table 4.3, categories that are modified by "all," "no," and "not" are distributed.

Look carefully at the statement "All A are B." B is undistributed in this statement because there may be some B that are not A, so the statement is not about every B. On the other hand, consider "No A are B." In this case, B is distributed because when we say "No A are B," we are also saying "No B are A." Thus, in the second case, the statement is about all B.

For a conclusion to be valid, the syllogism must pass all of the rules in Table 4.4. If it fails on any one of them, then it is invalid.

Let's apply these rules to the syllogisms we've already solved with circle diagrams.

Syllogism 1.

A = people on welfare, B = poor, C = dishonest
All people on welfare are poor. (All A are B.)
<u>Some poor people are dishonest</u>. (Some B are C.)
Some people on welfare are dishonest. (Some A are C.)

The middle term for this syllogism is B. It is the one mentioned in both premises and is missing from the conclusion. The first rule starts "if the conclusion is negative." Because the conclusion is positive, we can immediately go on to the second rule. The second rule states that the middle term must be distributed in at least one premise. Let's check this. The middle term is B (poor people). Is it modified by "all" or "not" in either premise? It is not distributed in either premise, so we can stop here. This conclusion is invalid! But, of course, you already knew that because you discovered that it was invalid when you completed the circle diagrams.

Let's try the verbal rules with the second syllogism.

Syllogism 2.

A = parents, B = understands children, C = teachers
No parents understand children. (No A are B.)
<u>Some teachers understand children</u>. (Some C are B.)
No parents are teachers. (No A are C.)

The first rule says that if the conclusion is negative, then one premise must be negative, and vice versa. The conclusion is negative and so is one premise, so we can check the next rule.

The second rule is that the middle term must be distributed in one premise. What is the middle term? It is B, the one not mentioned in the conclusion. It is distributed in the first premise, so we can move on. The third rule is that any term distributed in the conclusion must be distributed in at least one premise. Both A and C are distributed in the conclusion. A is distributed in the first premise, but C is not distributed in a premise, so stop here. This conclusion is invalid!

Briefly, here are the answers to the remaining syllogisms.

Syllogism 3.

A = lawyers, B = smart, C = rich
Some lawyers are not smart. (Some A are not B.)
<u>Some smart people are rich. (Some B are C.)</u>
Some lawyers are rich. (Some A are C.)
fails #1: passes the first part because the conclusion is not negative; fails the second part because the first premise is negative and the conclusion is positive.
Invalid!

Syllogism 4.

All physics students are good in math. (All A are B.)
<u>Some coeds are physics students. (Some C are A.)</u>
Some coeds are good in math. (Some C are B.)
passes # 1: There are no negatives.
passes # 2: The middle term is A. A is distributed.
passes # 3: No term in the conclusion is distributed.
passes # 4: Both premises are not particular.
passes # 5: One premise is particular and the conclusion is particular.
passes # 6: At least one premise is affirmative.
Valid!

Syllogism 5.

All Americans need health insurance. (All A are B.)
<u>Everyone who needs health insurance should vote for it. (All B are C.)</u>
All Americans should vote for health insurance. <u>(All A are C.)</u>
passes # 1: There are no negatives.
passes # 2: The middle term is B. B is distributed.
passes # 3: A is distributed in the conclusion and the first premise.
passes # 4: Both premises are universal, not particular.
passes # 5: No premise is particular.
passes # 6: At least one premise is affirmative.
Valid!

Syllogisms in Everyday Contexts

Somewhere during the last section, you may have said to yourself, "Why bother!" It may seem that syllogisms are artificial stimuli created solely to make work for students and teachers. If you did have this thought, you were questioning the **ecological validity** of syllogisms. Ecological validity concerns the real-world validity or applications of a concept outside of the laboratory or classroom. In other words, do people use syllogistic reasoning in real-world contexts?

Syllogistic reasoning and the other types of reasoning like linear ordering and if, then statements are sometimes considered as a subset of problem solving. Often, when solving a problem, we begin with statements that we believe or know to be true (the premises) and then decide which conclusions we can logically infer from them.

Syllogisms also appear implicitly in normal English prose. Of course, in natural context, the premises and conclusions aren't labeled, but the underlying structure is much the same. They are especially easy to spot in legal and political arguments, and thus often appear on standardized tests for college, graduate, and law school admissions.

Here is an example of syllogistic reasoning that may seem more like the kind of syllogism you'd find in everyday contexts: The death sentence should be declared unconstitutional. It is the cruelest form of punishment that is possible, and it is also very unusual. The Constitution specifically protects us against cruel and unusual punishment.

Can you conclude from these statements that the death sentence is unconstitutional? Try to formulate these sentences into standard syllogism form (two premises and a conclusion). Use circle diagrams or the five rules to check on the validity of the conclusion. Stop now and work on this natural language syllogism.

Your syllogism should be similar to this:

Premise 1: The death sentence is cruel and unusual punishment.
Premise 2: <u>Cruel and unusual punishment is unconstitutional.</u>
Conclusion: The death sentence is unconstitutional.

If we put this in terms of A, B, and C, this roughly corresponds to:

A = the death sentence
B = cruel and unusual punishment
C = unconstitutional

This then becomes:

All A are B.
<u>All B are C.</u>
All A are C.

In its abstract form, this becomes a syllogism that can be tested with either circle diagrams or verbal rules that will determine if the conclusion validly follows from the premises. The point here is that syllogisms are often contained in everyday arguments. Medical providers are often faced with problems that take this form: Everyone with disease X will have results from the lab test of Y. Some people with results from the lab test of Y will not have disease X. Although this does not "look like" some combination of "all," "some", "no," and "some not," can you see how it is the same sort of problem with different terms to represent these relationships? Often, we don't recognize syllogistic statements because they are not neatly labeled by premise and conclusion, but if you get in the habit of looking for them, you may be surprised how frequently they can be found.

Missing Quantifiers

If there is any equality now, it has been our struggle that put it there. Because they said "all" and meant "some." All means all.

—Beah Richards (in Beilensen & Jackson, 1992, p. 22)

When syllogisms are found in everyday use, the quantifiers are often missing. Sometimes this absence is done deliberately in the hope that you will infer one particular quantifier (e.g., assume "all" instead of the more truthful "some.") Here is an example of categorical reasoning used in a presidential campaign. A presidential candidate (in the U. S. primaries) was questioned about his extramarital affairs. He responded this way: I have not been perfect in my private life, but we have had other great presidents who were also not perfect in their private lives.

Let's convert this to a categorical syllogism:

Premise 1: I am not perfect (in my private life).
Premise 2: Some great presidents were not perfect (in their private lives).
Conclusion: I will be a great president.
(implied)

In its abstract form this becomes:

A = I (the speaker)
B = people who are not perfect
C = great presidents

or

All A are B.
Some C are B.
All A are (will be) C.

The conclusion he wanted listeners to draw is that he would also be a great president. Check the validity of this conclusion either with circle diagrams or the five rules. Is the implied conclusion valid? Note also his choice of words to describe his extramarital affairs (not perfect).

In everyday language, the quantifiers may be different from those used here. "Every" and "each" may be used as substitutes for "all," and "many" and "few" may be used as substitutes for "some." It is a simple matter to change them to the quantifiers used here and then check the conclusion for its validity (Nickerson, 1986).

Here is an example (with some editing) that I recognized in a recent conversation. "People who go to rock concerts smoke dope. Jaye went to a rock concert. Therefore, Jaye smokes dope." The validity of this everyday syllogism depends on whether the speaker believes that "All people who go to rock concerts smoke dope" or "Some people who go to rock concerts smoke dope." In understanding statements like these, it's important that you specify which missing quantifier is intended. If "some" is intended, then you quickly point out that it is not valid to conclude that Jaye was among those who smoke dope. If "all" is intended, then you can question whether it is the appropriate quantifier.

Changing Attitudes with Syllogisms

The basic organization of two premises and a conclusion is frequently used to change attitudes. When used in this fashion, the first premise is a belief premise, the second premise is an evaluation of that belief or a reaction to the belief premise, and the conclusion is the attitude (Shaver, 1981). The basic structure is like this:

Belief premise
Evaluation premise
Attitude Conclusion

Consider how this works in the following example (Shaver, 1981):

Preventing war saves lives.
Saving lives is good.
Therefore, preventing war is good.

Over time, attitude syllogisms become linked so that the conclusion from one syllogism is used as the evaluation premise of another:

Defense spending prevents war.
Preventing war is good.
Therefore, defense spending is good.

In these syllogisms, the middle term (remember what this means?) becomes the reason for the conclusion. In general, the greater the number of syllogisms with the same conclusion that we believe are true, the greater the support for the conclusion. If I wanted you to conclude that defense spending is good, I'd also tell you that:

Defense spending creates jobs.
Creating jobs is good.
Therefore, defense spending is good.

The quantifiers are implicit in these syllogisms, but the underlying organization is the same. It's a matter of determining if a conclusion follows from the premises.

Common Errors in Syllogistic Reasoning

At this point in the history of psychology, when it is claimed that machines can think, it seems strange to say that people cannot.

—Ceraso and Protivera (1971, p. 400)

Some syllogisms are more difficult to solve than others. An analysis of the erroneous conclusions that people make has revealed that the errors fall into distinct

JUMP START © UFS Reprinted by Permission.

types or categories. One category of errors that we will consider here is illicit conversions.

Illicit Conversions

No, this term has nothing to do with people who make you change religions when you don't want to. It has to do with changing the meaning of a premise. When most people read statements like "All A are B," the representation they form in their mind is one in which it is also true that "All B are A" (Chapman & Chapman, 1959). As you should realize by now, "All A are B" is not the same as "All B are A." Transforming a premise into a nonequivalent form is a type of error known as an **illicit conversion**. An example of an illicit conversion in if, then reasoning is the erroneous assumption that "If A, then B" is the same as "If B, then A." In real-world terms, knowing that "all Republicans voted for this bill" is not the same as saying that everyone who voted for this bill was Republican. These are not equivalent statements.

Another common illicit conversion is the belief that "Some A are not B" also implies that "Some B are not A." The second statement is not equivalent to the first. Here are circle diagrams of these two statements. As you can see more clearly in their diagrams, they are not identical statements. To make this point clearer, consider the difference between "Some of the children are not immunized" and "Some of those immunized are not children."

A = children, B = immunized

1. Some A are not B.
    Some children are not immunized.

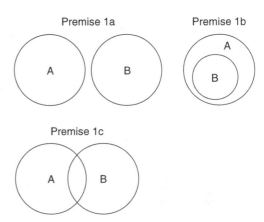

2. Some B are not A.
   Some of those immunized
   are not children.

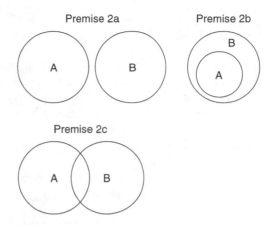

Premise 2a   Premise 2b

Premise 2c

PROBABILISTIC REASONING

The straight path of reason is narrow, the tempting byways are many and easier of access.

—Joseph Jastrow

In everyday reasoning, we don't view premises as "truths" that will necessarily require certain conclusions; instead, we think of premises as statements that either support or fail to support certain conclusions. Probabilistic reasoning occurs when we use the information we have to decide that a conclusion is probably true or probably not true. In everyday reasoning, we rely on notions of probability to assess the likelihood of a conclusion being true. Although probability is discussed in Chapter 6, it is also a reasoning skill that we need to consider in this context.

Suppose you learn that people who have untreated diabetes are frequently thirsty, urinate often, and experience sudden weight loss. You notice that you have these symptoms. Does it necessarily follow that you have diabetes? No, of course not, but these symptoms do make a diagnosis of diabetes more likely. In everyday contexts, much of our reasoning is probabilistic.

Consider this example presented by Polya (1957, p. 186):

If we are approaching land, we see birds.
Now we see birds.
Therefore, it becomes more credible that we are approaching land.

In a shorthand format this becomes:

If A, then B.
B is true.
Therefore, A is more probable than it was before we knew that B is true.

Much of our everyday reasoning is of this sort, and although A is not guaranteed with probabilistic reasoning, it does become more probable after we've told the second premise. When viewed from the perspective of if, then reasoning, we would be committing the fallacy of affirming the consequent. However, in real life we need to consider many variables and goals. Although seeing birds doesn't guarantee that land is near, I'd be getting happy if I saw birds while I was drifting and lost at sea.

Probabilistic reasoning is often a good strategy or "rule of thumb," especially because few things are known with absolute certainty in our probabilistic world. From the standpoint of formal logic, it is invalid to conclude that land is near. As long as you understand the nature of probabilities and the distinction between probabilistic and valid (must be true if the premises are true) reasoning, considering probabilities is a useful way of understanding and predicting events. When we reason in everyday contexts, we consider the strength and likelihood of the evidence that supports a conclusion and often decide if a conclusion is probable or improbable, not just merely valid or invalid. This point is explained more fully in Chapter 7 on understanding probabilities.

As much of our reasoning is dependent on the rules of probability, McGuire (1981) has coined the term **probabilogical** to describe the joint effects of these disciplines on the way we think. Accordingly, we place greater faith in conclusions when we believe that the premises are highly probable than when we believe that the premises are unlikely.

Bounded Rationality

Nothing has an uglier look to us than reason, when it is not on our side.

—Halifax (Stat Quotes http://www.stats.org/newsletters/ 0011/reasonquote.htm, retrieved January 11, 2002)

Does the fact that people often do not use the laws of logic when they reason mean that we mere mortals are illogical or irrational (not reasoned)? Many psychologists object to the idea that most people are illogical. As you have seen, people reason differently depending on the context and seem to be able to use the rules of reasoning better when the valid conclusion is one that we believe to be true than when it is not. In the real world, the content of our reasoning *does* matter, so perhaps it is not surprising that we find it difficult to reason from false or questionable premises. It seems that people are rational, but with some limitations. The term **bounded rationality** is used to describe this state of affairs (Gigerenzer & Goldstein, 1996). We usually need to reach conclusions and make decisions with incomplete information and under time limits, and we rarely have "true premises." For example, we know if we are asking permission or making an obligation, and the very different implications of if, then statements under these situations.

REASONING IN EVERYDAY CONTEXTS

Reasoning is the only ability that makes it possible for humans to rule the earth and ruin it.

—Scriven (1976, p. 2)

Syllogisms, linear orderings, disjunctions, and if, then statements are commonly found in everyday conversation. Of course, they are embedded in discourse and not labeled by premise or conclusion. They are sometimes used in ways that seem either to be deliberately misleading, or at least to capitalize on the common reasoning errors that most people make.

If you pay careful attention to bumper stickers, you'll probably be surprised to find that many are simple reasoning problems. Consider the bumper sticker I saw on a pick-up truck:

> Off-road users
> are not abusers.

The off-road users that this bumper sticker refers to are dirt bike riders who enjoy racing through open land (unpaved areas). Many people are concerned that this sport is destroying our natural resources by tearing up the vegetation. This bumper sticker is designed to present the opposing view. Notice how this is accomplished. The term "all" is implied in the first premise, when in fact "some" is true. You should recognize this as a syllogism with missing quantifiers.

Another popular bumper sticker that relies on missing quantifiers to make the point is:

> If guns are outlawed,
> only outlaws will have guns.

This is a standard if, then statement. The implied conclusion is "don't outlaw guns."

Suppose someone responded to this bumper sticker by suggesting that if guns are outlawed, approximately 80% of the crimes of violence and 90% of the petty crimes that are committed with a gun would probably be committed with a less dangerous weapon. How does an argument like this refute the if, then statement and its implied conclusion on the bumper sticker?

Here is a disjunctive argument that was common during the Vietnam War: America, love it or leave it! You may be surprised to learn that this was a slogan for those who went to fight in Vietnam. The implication was that antiwar protest meant that you didn't love America. In Chapter 5, I'll return to the use of disjunctions and ask if there really are only two options when we are given two options.

Reasoning With Diagrams

Although it seems like a lot of work to get used to thinking with diagrams, they are useful in many situations where you have to check relationships and conceptualize. The following discussion is loosely based on a discussion by Rubinstein and Pfeiffer (1980) that I have applied to the events surrounding the Los Angeles riots that occurred in 1992.

In 1992, following an unpopular verdict in which Los Angeles police officers were acquitted of the crime of beating a suspect, an event that was captured on video, a massive, bloody riot occurred. In the painful trials that followed, the prosecution attempted to show that a particular defendant was at the scene of the riot. One piece of evidence was a footprint that was at the site. The strategy for the defense was to show that many people could have left that particular foot print, but the prosecution tried to show that few people other than the defendant could have left the foot print. Look at these two diagrams.

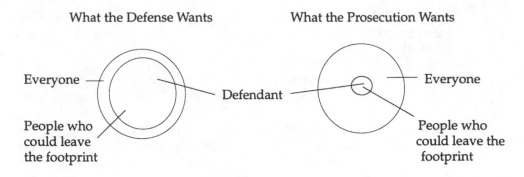

What the Defense Wants   What the Prosecution Wants

An expert from the Nike shoe company was called to testify that the print was left by a Nike sneaker. The prosecution then showed that the defendant owned a pair of Nikes in the same size as the footprint. This shrinks the size of the circle, so that few people besides the defendant would fit those particular shoes.

By contrast, the defense tried to widen the circle by showing that many people in that neighborhood wear Nike sneakers and that it was a popular shoe size. Each side, in turn, tried to widen and then narrow the circle in an attempt to persuade the jury that the defendant and few others could have left that footprint or many people could have left that footprint.

Similar strategies are used implicitly in many trials. Here is a quote from an article that appeared in the *Los Angeles Times* (Timnick, October 18, 1989). It is a description of a trial for an accused child molester: "Telling an attentive jury in Los Angeles Superior Court that the totality of evidence 'draws the ring around R. B. and P. B. closer and tighter, to the extent that you should find them guilty.'" Here the idea of drawing smaller and smaller circles was used explicitly in the prosecution's arguments. Once you get used to using diagrams as a thinking aid, you will find that you will use them often.

REASONING GONE WRONG

I hope that you are developing an appreciation for the critical importance of good thinking. If you are not yet convinced, then I expect that this section will be a "chilly awakening." In later chapters, I will continue to develop the theme that there are many people who want to persuade you to believe that something is true—for a variety of reasons. Often they will be trying to sell you something—a product, a philosophy, a political candidate or point of view, or even a new view of history. Groups that are attempting to rewrite history are called revisionists. Your only defense against the onslaught of "sales" pitches is critical thinking. I heard a revisionist speaker (someone who believes that we need to revise what we know about history) who was attempting to convince a group of young adults that slavery in the United States was "not really so bad." The presentation had all the outward appearances of a standard reasoning problem. First, listeners were asked if they agreed that people do not harm valuable property. Most nodded in agreement. Then they were told that slaves were valuable property; therefore, most slave owners took good care of their slaves. The speaker went on to say that "most slaves enjoyed being taken care of," so slavery was not as bad as we had been led to believe. The scary part of this scene was that there were many listeners who seemed to be considering this ludicrous idea or could not figure out what was wrong with it. Can you?

I hope that you are outraged at this attempt to rewrite a disgraceful part of U. S. history and to use what seems like reasoning to do it. It is true that most people do not harm valuable property, but there are massive amounts of historical evidence that slaves were often subjected to the most brutal and dehumanizing conditions. The speaker left out far too many relevant facts to make his conclusion logical. There was a seductiveness to the speaker's "logic," but it was patently wrong. There is no substitute for critical thinking.

APPLYING THE FRAMEWORK

1. What Is the Goal?

In deductive reasoning, the goal is to determine which conclusions are valid given premises or statements that we believe are true. When you identify your goal as a deductive reasoning task, you will use the reasoning skills presented in this chapter.

2. What Is Known?

In everyday prose, you will have to convert phrases and sentences into a reasoning format. You will have to determine what the premises are before you can decide whether they support a conclusion. Often quantifiers are missing and conclusions are left unstated. Sometimes you will have to consider context to decide if "if, then" really means "if, and only if, then." You will have to decide if you are reasoning with implied or explicit quantifiers, if there is a linear ordering, and whether an if, then statement is being made.

Perhaps, most importantly, you need to determine if you should be assuming that the premises are true. A conclusion is valid if it follows from the premises, but good reasoning from poor premises will not produce desirable outcomes.

3. Which Thinking Skill Will Get You to Your Goal?

The following skills to determine whether a conclusion is valid were presented in this chapter. Review each skill and be sure that you understand how and when to use each one.

- Discriminating between deductive and inductive reasoning
- Identifying premises and conclusions

- Using quantifiers in reasoning
- Solving categorical syllogisms with circle diagrams
- Solving categorical syllogisms with verbal rules
- Understanding the difference between truth and validity
- Recognizing when syllogisms are being used to change attitudes
- Using linear diagrams to solve linear syllogisms
- Watching for marked adjectives
- Using the principles of linear orderings as an aid to clear communication
- Reasoning with if, then statements
- Using tree diagrams with if, then statements
- Avoiding the fallacies of confirming the consequent and denying the antecedent
- Examining reasoning in everyday contexts for missing quantifiers

4. Have You Reached Your Goal?

This is an accuracy check on your work. When determining valid conclusions from categorical syllogisms, did you get the same answer with both the rules for syllogisms and the circle diagrams? Did you consider all combinations of representations when drawing your diagrams? Did you consciously consider common fallacies and biases so as to be sure to avoid them? Does your answer make sense?

CHAPTER SUMMARY

1. Deductive reasoning is the use of premises or statements that we accept as true to derive valid conclusions.

2. People don't approach reasoning problems according to the laws of formal logic. Instead of determining whether a conclusion logically follows from the premises as they are stated, there is a tendency to alter the premises according to one's own beliefs and then decide whether a conclusion follows from the altered statements.

3. Human reasoning is often biased by beliefs about emotional issues.

4. It is common to confuse truth with validity. Validity refers to the form of an argument and is unrelated to content. If a conclusion necessarily follows from the premises, then it is valid. The topic of truth and believability of premises are addressed in the next chapter.

5. In linear orderings, we use premises to establish conclusions about ordered relationships. A good strategy for solving linear orderings is to use a spatial representation with the items arranged in an ordered manner.

6. In if, then statements a conditional relationship is established. As in syllogisms and linear orderings, the premises that are given are used to determine valid conclusions.

7. "If" is frequently interpreted as "if and only if" in if, then statements. Although this conversion is an error according to the rules of formal logic, sometimes it is justified by the context in which it is embedded.

8. Confirmation bias is the predilection or tendency to seek and utilize information that supports or confirms the hypothesis or premise that is being considered. The "four-card selection task" is a demonstration of this robust bias.

9. Quantitative syllogisms indicate which terms belong in the categories that are specified. Statements in syllogisms can take one of four different moods: universal affirmative, particular affirmative, universal negative, and particular negative.

10. When syllogisms involve meaningful terms and categories, people often use their knowledge of the categories and their beliefs about the topics to determine which conclusions are valid instead of reasoning from the form of the syllogism.

11. Circle diagrams are useful aids for understanding relationships and checking inferences in syllogisms. The extent to which circles overlap depicts category inclusion and exclusion. An alternative to circle diagrams that many people prefer is to check conclusions for validity using the verbal rules of syllogisms.

12. The greatest difficulty in using circle diagrams is being certain that all combinations of the two premises have been represented.

13. Illicit conversions are common errors in syllogisms. The most frequent illicit conversion is to interpret "All A are B" as also meaning that "All B are A."

14. Diagrams are useful reasoning tools in many situations. The logic of circle diagrams is frequently used in legal settings and other settings in which evidence is considered.

TERMS TO KNOW

Check your understanding of the concepts presented in this chapter by reviewing their definitions. If you find that you're having difficulty with any term, be sure to reread the section in which it is discussed.

Reasoning. Has two forms: deductive and inductive. When reasoning deductively, we use our knowledge of two or more premises to infer if a conclusion is valid. When reasoning inductively, we collect observations and formulate hypotheses based on them.

Conclusion. An inferential belief that is derived from other statements.

Logic. A branch of philosophy that explicitly states the rules for deriving valid conclusions.

Valid. A conclusion is valid if it must be true if the premises are true. It "follows from" the premises.

Premises. Statements that allow the inference of logical conclusions.

Illogical. Reaching conclusions that are not in accord with the rules of logic.

Failure to Accept the Logical Task. In everyday reasoning, we alter the statements we're given according to our personal beliefs and then decide if a conclusion follows from the altered statements. We reject the logical task of deciding if a conclusion follows from the statements as they are given.

Personal Logic. The informal rules that people use to determine validity.

Pragmatic. Anything that is practical. In this context, the consideration of context and purpose when engaging in real-world reasoning tasks.

Inductive Reasoning. Observations are collected that suggest or lead to the formulation of a conclusion or hypothesis.

Deductive Reasoning. Use of stated premises to formulate conclusions that can logically be inferred from them.

Linear Ordering. Also known as linear syllogism. Reasoning that involves the inference of orderly relationships along a single dimension (e.g., size, position) among terms.

Linear Syllogism. See linear ordering.

Marked Adjectives. Adjectives that connote bias when they appear in a question (e.g., poor, dumb, or small). When asked "How poor is he," it is presumed that the response will be toward the poor extreme and not toward the rich extreme.

Unmarked Adjectives. Adjectives that are neutral in that they don't connote a particular direction when they appear in a question (e.g., big, smart, tall). When asked "How big is he?" the response could be a larger or a small number. Compare with marked adjective.

Belief Bias. Also known as confirmation bias. The interference of one's personal beliefs with the ability to reason logically.

If, Then Statements. Statements of a contingency relationship such that if the antecedent is true, then the consequent must be true.

Contingency Relationships. Relationships that are expressed with if, then statements. The consequent is contingent or dependent on the antecedent.

Conditional Logic. Also known as propositional logic. Logical statements that are expressed in an if, then format.

Antecedent. In if, then statements, it is the information given in the "if" clause appealing to your reason.

Consequent. In if, then statements, it is the information given in the "then" clause.

Tree Diagrams. Diagrams in which the critical information is represented along the branches of a "tree."

Affirming the Antecedent. In if, then reasoning, the second premise asserts that the "if" part is true.

Denying the Consequent. In if, then reasoning, the second premise asserts that the "then" part is false.

Affirming the Consequent. In if, then reasoning, the second premise asserts that the "then" part is true.

Illicit Conversion. Illicit conversions, in if, then statements occur when people believe that "If A, then B" also means "If B, then A."

Denying the Antecedent. In if, then reasoning, the second premise asserts that the "if" part is false.

Double Negation. The denial of a negative statement.

Four-Card Selection Task. A task that is often used to demonstrate confirmation biases. Subjects are required to indicate which of four cards they need to turn over in order to verify a rule about the contents of each side of the card. Overwhelmingly, subjects only select cards that will confirm the hypothesis that they are considering instead of seeking information that would disconfirm their hypothesis.

Permission Schema. Informal rules that people use when reasoning with if, then statements that pragmatically give permission.

Obligation Schema. Informal rules that people use when reasoning with if, then statements that pragmatically create an obligation.

Chained Conditional. Two if, then statements linked so that the consequent of one statement is also the antecedent of the other statement.

Combinatorial Reasoning. The use of systematic and orderly steps when making combinations so that all possible combinations are formed.

Syllogistic Reasoning. A form of reasoning that involves deciding whether a conclusion can be properly inferred from two or more statements that contain quantifiers.

Categorical Reasoning. A type of syllogistic reasoning in which the quantifiers "some," "all," "no," and "none" are used to indicate category membership.

Quantifiers. Terms like "all," "some," "none," and "no" that are used in syllogisms to indicate category membership.

Syllogism. Two or more premises that are used to derive a valid conclusion or conclusions.

Mood. Used to classify the premises and conclusions of a categorical syllogism. There are four moods that are dependent on the quantifiers used in the statements. The four moods are: universal affirmative (all A are B); particular affirmative (some A are B); universal negative (no A are B); and particular negative (some A are not B).

Universal Affirmative. The mood of statements in a categorical syllogism with the format "All A are B."

Particular Affirmative. The mood of statements in a categorical syllogism with the format "Some A are B."

Universal Negative. The mood of statements in a categorical syllogism with the format "No A are not B."

Particular Negative. The mood of statements in a categorical syllogism with the format "Some A are not B."

Circle Diagrams. A spatial strategy for determining the validity of a conclusion in a categorical syllogism. Circles are used to represent category membership.

Middle Term. In a categorical syllogism it is the term that is omitted from the conclusion and is mentioned in both premises.

Distributed. In a categorical syllogism a term is distributed when it is modified by "all," "no," or "not."

Ecological Validity. Concerns the real-world validity or applications of a concept outside of the laboratory.

Illicit Conversions. Transformations of the premises in a syllogism into nonequivalent forms (e.g., converting "All A are B" into "All B are A").

Probabilogical. Term coined to label the joint influences of probability and logic on the way we think.

Bounded Rationality. People are rational, within limits. People do not behave like logic machines, but use thinking shortcuts to save time.

5

Analyzing Arguments

Contents

Eat All Day and Still Lose Weight
Trade your old body for a new one now through an amazing scientific breakthrough. Doctors and medical technicians have made it possible for people like you and me to lose weight quickly and permanently. Tested at university labs, retested at clinics and major hospitals and acclaimed by doctors all over the world, finally there is something that helps you lose weight. If years of stubborn fat build up have been your problem, NOW AT LAST THERE IS A WAY TO ELIMINATE FAT, A WAY TO LOSE WEIGHT FAST AND EASILY. We call it XXXXXXX because it totally attacks excess fat and fluids that have plagued most people for years. . . . Everyday you will feel stronger and full of pep and energy as the excess weight you have carried for so long is carved off your body. . . . DON'T LET THIS GOLDEN OPPORTUNITY AND CHANCE OF A LIFE-TIME PASS YOU BY. Just fill out the coupon below and let it be the ticket to a slimmer you. So, what are you waiting for?

I hope that you weren't looking for a coupon for this marvelous weight loss product. The paragraph above was taken verbatim from a full-page advertisement in a popular fashion magazine. The only change that I made was to omit the name of this "miracle" diet. The name has a chemical sound to it. It's multisyllabic and ends with a number. The name sounds like a chemical formula. I had trouble selecting which advertisement I wanted to use here because there were so many that made numerous unsupported claims. Advertisements like this one can be found in most magazines and newspapers. I'll refer back to this advertisement later in this chapter when I talk about analyzing arguments and recognizing fallacies. Hold onto your money until you've read this chapter.

THE ANATOMY OF AN ARGUMENT

Neither a closed mind nor an empty one is likely to produce much that would qualify as effective reasoning.

—Nickerson (1986, p. 1)

The technical meaning of the word **argument** is different from its everyday meaning. When we use the word *argument* in everyday language, it means a dispute or a quarrel. We say two people "are having an argument" when they disagree about something in a heated or emotional way. More technically, an argument consists of one or more statements that are used to provide support for a **conclusion**. The statements that provide the support for a conclusion are called the **reasons** or **premises** of the argument. The reasons or premises are presented in order to persuade the reader or listener that the conclusion is true or probably true. Let's consider an example. Suppose that I want to convince you to stay in college until graduation. Here are some reasons (premises) that I could give. You can think of this as an addition problem with each premise summing to the conclusion.

> Premise #1: College graduates earn more money than college dropouts or people who have never attended college.
> + Premise #2: College graduates report that they are more satisfied with their lives than people who have not graduated from college.
> + Premise #3: College graduates are healthier and live longer than people who have not graduated from college.

+ Premise #4: College graduates have jobs that are more interesting and more <u>responsible than people who have not graduated from college.</u>

Conclusion: You should graduate from college.

Arguments are sometimes called "the giving of reasons." Harmon (1986) calls this process "a change in view" because the objective is to change an "old view" or belief into a "new view" or belief with reasoning.

Old View   Reasoning   New View
or Belief ————————————————————————————▶ or Belief

Every argument will have one or more premises (or reasons) and one or more conclusions. Usually, there will be several premises for one conclusion, but other combinations (one premise for several conclusions and several premises for several conclusions) are possible. **If you cannot identify at least one premise *and* at least one conclusion, then it is not an argument**. Of course, in everyday, natural-language arguments, the premises and conclusions are not labeled. They are usually embedded in extended prose. The extended prose could be a paragraph, a section or chapter of a book, or even an entire book or semester-long class.

Here are some examples of prose that are *not* arguments:

- I like my critical thinking course better than my chemistry course. (No reasons are given for this preference.)
- We drove up to the mountains, went skiing, then drove home. (This is just a descriptive list of activities linked together. There are no reasons or conclusions.)
- Buy your burgers at Burgerland. (No reasons given, but see the section below because reasons are often inferred from context in statements like this one.)
- We saw the Martians land. (This is a simple description.)
- Never trust anyone over 30. (This is an opinion without reasons.)
- Is dinner ready? (simple question.)

It may seem that it should be fairly simple to determine whether a statement or set of statements contain an argument, but in everyday language most arguments are incomplete. Sometimes the premises aren't stated, but are inferred, and other times the conclusion is unstated. Sometimes arguments are deliberately disguised so that it may appear that the speakers are not supporting some conclusion, when they really are. Consider the popular automobile advertisement that goes something like this:

More people have bought LaBaroness automobiles than any other American car.

At first glance, this seems like a straightforward declarative sentence with no reasons and no conclusion. But, the advertisers expect consumers to convert this sentence into an argument. When you hear this sentence, you presumably start generating your own reasons for the popularity of LaBaroness. If more people are buying it, it must be best and shouldn't you also buy the best? This is an example in which the listener supplies both the reasons and the conclusion. Statements very similar to this one can be found in advertisements for a diverse assortment of products including beer, beauty supplies, fitness clubs, and airlines. (The use of the comparative term "more" is discussed later in this chapter.)

If an advertiser wants to be sure that you supply the missing reasons and conclusion, the advertisement could be altered slightly so that it now reads:

More people have bought LaBaroness automobiles than any other American car. There must be some very good reasons.

Notice that a second sentence was added, but no reasons were given. It is expected that the second sentence will cue listeners (or readers) to start supplying their own reasons.

Premises

The premises are the reasons that support a conclusion. They are the "why" part of an argument. In everyday language, they can appear anywhere among a set of statements. Sometimes, the conclusion will be stated first followed by its premises. (Here is what I believe and the reasons for this belief are . . . .) Other times the conclusion may be presented last or embedded in the middle of a paragraph or other text with premises both before and after it. Premises are not always easy to recognize. There are certain key words, called **premise indicators** or **premise markers**, that often signal that what comes after them is a premise. Although premise indicators aren't *always* followed by a premise, they often are, and for this reason, it is a good idea to check for these key words when identifying premises. These terms often indicate that what follows is a reason.

> *Premise Indicators*
> because
> for
> since (when it means because and not the passage of time)
> if
> given that (or being that)
> as shown by
> as indicated by
> the reasons are
> it may be inferred (or deduced) from
> the evidence consists of
> in the first place (suggests that a list of premises will follow)
> secondly
> seeing that
> assuming that
> it follows from
> whereas

Here are some simple examples of the use of premise indicators.

- You should graduate from college **because** you will earn more money with a college degree.
- The need for the United States to send troops to Central America **is indicated by** the buildup of armed rebels in countries neighboring those with civil wars.
- **Seeing that** the current policy of supplying organ transplants is benefiting the rich, a new program is needed.

Premises can be "matters of fact" or "matters of opinion" or both. Consider, for example, the following sentences:

- All teenagers should be taught safe sex practices because of the risk of AIDS and other sexually transmitted diseases. (The reason is a matter of fact.)

- All teenagers should be taught how to knit because this will provide them with an enjoyable hobby. (The reason is a matter of opinion.)

Conclusions

The conclusion is the purpose or the "what" of the argument. It is the belief or point of view that is supported or defended with the premises. Both the premises and the conclusion are important, and both are essential components of any argument.

It is usually easier to identify the conclusion of an argument than the other components. For this reason, it is a good idea to start with the conclusion when you are analyzing arguments. There are **conclusion indicators** or **conclusion markers** that indicate that what follows is probably a conclusion. As with premise indicators, they do not guarantee that a conclusion follows them.

> *Conclusion Indicators*
> therefore
> hence
> so
> thus
> consequently
> then
> shows that (we can see that)
> accordingly
> it follows that
> we may infer (conclude) (deduce) that
> in summary
> as a result
> for all these reasons
> it is clear that

Some simple examples of the use of conclusion indicators are:

- Based on all of the reasons just stated, we **can conclude that** the flow of illegal drugs must be stopped.
- **In summary**, postal rates must be increased because we can no longer afford to run the postal system with a deficit.
- We have had very little rain this season. **Consequently**, water will have to be rationed.

Has my use of the word *simple* to describe these examples made you feel uneasy? Have you begun to expect that things will soon get more complex? If so, you are right. Natural-language is complex and so are natural-language arguments. (A natural language is a language that has evolved over time for the purpose of communication between people. Artificial languages are those languages that were created for special purposes such as computer languages.) Although all arguments *must* contain at least one argument and one conclusion, most arguments consist of additional components. Three additional components will be presented here. They are assumptions, qualifiers, and counterarguments.

Assumptions

With enough assumptions, any policy can be justified.

—Tim Brennan (January 12, 2001, from a guide to
understanding how Washington really works)

An **assumption** is a statement for which no proof or evidence is offered. Although assumptions can be either stated or unstated (implied), they are most often unstated. Advertisements and political rhetoric are good places to look for examples of stated and unstated assumptions. Let's go back to the example of the advertisement for LaBaroness, which was presented earlier in this chapter (I changed the name of the real car being advertised.):

More people have bought LaBaroness automobiles than any other American car.

The implied statement is that if more people bought LaBaroness, it must be better (in some way) than its competitors. The unstated assumption is that when large numbers of consumers make a choice, it is a good choice. There is no justification for this assumption. The implied conclusion is that you should also be making this wise choice. The advertisement could easily be altered so that the assumption is made explicitly:

More people have bought LaBaroness automobiles than any other American car. When so many people agree, it must be the right choice.

Notice that with the addition of the second sentence, the assumption is now stated explicitly. It is still an assumption because it is stated without any justification. If I had supplied some justification for this belief, then it would no longer be an assumption. Suppose I alter these statements so that they now become:

More people have bought LaBaroness automobiles than any other American car. Recent research by several well-known social psychologists and economists has shown that whenever a majority of people agree on something, they make the best choice.

Look carefully at the changes I just made. In this version, I provided a reason or justification for believing that, whenever large numbers of people make a choice, it is a good one. The research that I made up is phony, but suppose for now that it is true. The research findings become the premises or reasons for the conclusion that, whenever large numbers of people make a choice, it will be a good one. In this context, it is no longer an assumption because there are now reasons supporting it. This new conclusion then becomes the premise for the unstated conclusion that you should also buy LaBaroness. If you read the previous chapter on reasoning, this should not be a new idea for you. The idea that the conclusion from one set of statements can then become the premise for another set of statements was demonstrated in Chapter 4. In extended (longer) arguments, the conclusion from one set of statements will often become the premise in another set of statements.

The arguments that are used to build the main argument are called **subarguments**. The main argument in an extended passage is called the **main point**. The kinds of arguments that are often found in books, book chapters, and sometimes sections of chapters proceed in stages with subarguments linked to provide support for a main point.

Here is another example of an unstated assumption. The following example was taken from a catalogue that sells copper bracelets. I have altered it only slightly for this context.

For hundreds of years people have worn copper bracelets to relieve pain from arthritis. This folklore belief has persisted and copper bracelets continue to be popular. These bracelets promote close contact between the copper and your wrist.

The writers of this advertisement expect that readers will assume that copper can help alleviate the pain of arthritis and that the "medical" effect is enhanced by the close contact with the wrist. Notice that this is never stated—it can't be because there is no evidence that shows that copper has any effect on arthritis. However, this advertisement for copper bracelets is clearly written to suggest that it works. (Many people believe that it does.) Furthermore, there is a suggested assumption that the popularity of copper bracelets is due to its medical effects. Maybe they have just become fashionable, or cheaper, or better advertised, or perhaps there are just more people with arthritis who are willing to believe anything that promises to relieve their pain. We'll discuss the need to consider missing information and alternative conclusions in a later section of this chapter.

Qualifiers

A **qualifier** is a constraint or restriction on the conclusion. It states the conditions under which the conclusion is supported. An example might be helpful:

It is important that we have some indicators of what and how much students are learning in college. For this reason, a national college-level testing program is needed. However, if the national assessment is not related to the subjects taught in the college curriculum, then it will not be a valid measure of college-level learning.

Let's dissect this paragraph into its component parts:

The conclusion is: A national college-level testing program is needed.
A premise is: It is important that we have some indicators of what and how much students are learning in college. (This is the reason that supports the conclusion. It tells us why we should believe that the conclusion is true.)
An unstated assumption is: A national college-level testing program is a good way to indicate what students are learning.
A qualifier (or limiting condition) is: The conclusion is valid only when the assessment is related to what is the curriculum.

As you can see from this example, a qualifier states the conditions under which the conclusion is valid. It sets limits or constraints on the conclusion.

Counterarguments

Critical thinking requires a sense of the complexity of human issues.

—Sears and Parsons (1991, p. 64)

Sometimes, an extended argument will state reasons that support a particular conclusion and reasons that refute the same conclusion. The set of statements that refute a particular conclusion is called a **counterargument**. Let's extend the previous argument so that it now also contains a counterargument.

It is important that we have some indicators of what and how much students are learning in college. For this reason, a national college-level testing program is needed. However, if the national assessment is not related to the subjects taught in the college curriculum, then it will not be a valid measure of college-level learning. Of course, the results of a national assessment of college students could be misused in a way that would keep good students from entering graduate or professional school.

I hope that you're paying careful attention to the way the additions are altering the argument. As presented above, the conclusion, premise, assumption, and qualifier remain the same. The counterargument presents a reason for *not* having a national college-level test. The reason presented (results could be misused) is counter to the conclusion that we should have a national test—that is why these statements are called counterarguments. Even with the addition of the counterargument, the conclusion remains unchanged. The argument was written in a way that suggests that the counterargument is weaker than the main argument. The point being made is that despite the counterargument, we should still have a national test of college students—the conclusion is the same.

Does this particular example make you uneasy? Can you think of other premises that might support a different conclusion? If so, you have already begun to anticipate the content of the section on how to evaluate arguments.

DIAGRAMMING THE STRUCTURE OF AN ARGUMENT

Argument is a central feature of the resolution of scientific controversies.

Driver, Newton, and Osborne (2000, p. 287)

Arguments are a related series of statements that are made in an attempt to get the reader or listener to believe that the conclusion is true. In order to analyze or dissect an argument we need to know not only its component parts, but also how the parts are related to each other. Arguments are made up of parts that are synthesized or put together when an argument is made, and parts that can be disassembled as one way to understand them. The parts that make up an argument are premise(s), conclusion(s), assumption(s), qualifier(s), and counterargument(s). The only restriction on arguments is that each must have at least one premise and one conclusion. Beyond this, a large variety of arrangements is possible. A good way to understand the relationships among the parts of a prose passage is to draw a diagram. Diagrams are used in every chapter of this book because they require the drawer to be specific about the relationships being depicted and to think about underlying relationships. Drawing a diagram is a good general thinking strategy.

Let's consider the simplest argument with only one premise and one conclusion.

[Be sure to get plenty of aerobic exercise][1] because [aerobic exercise will help you build a strong cardiovascular system].[2]

This argument is made up of two statements. I have indicated them by putting brackets around each and numbering them "1" and "2." A **statement** is a phrase or sentence for which it makes sense to ask "Is this true or false?" The answer to this question is not relevant here; that is, it doesn't matter if the statement really is true or false, only whether it makes sense to ask if the phrase is true or false. For example, the following are *not* statements: Rinse the spaghetti. Who lives here? Is that house for sale? Wow! Commands, questions, and exclamations are not statements because it makes no sense to ask if they have a "truth value"; that is, it makes no sense to ask if they are true or false.

Look again at the simple argument in the paragraph above. Identify which of the two statements is the conclusion and which is the premise.

Conclusion: [Get plenty of aerobic exercise.] Remember, the conclusion is the statement that indicates what you should believe or what you should do. (I started with the conclusion because this is often the easiest part of the argument to identify.)

Premise: [Aerobic exercise will build a strong cardiovascular system.] This is the "why" part of the argument that gives a reason for believing the conclusion.

A diagram of this relationship shows that the conclusion is supported by the premise:

[1] [Get plenty of aerobic exercise]—the conclusion

↑

[2] [Aerobic exercise will help you build a strong cardiovascular system]—the premise

As you can see, the statement that is the conclusion [1] is at the top of the diagram and the premise [2] is holding it up. This is shown with the arrow that points from the premise to the conclusion.

Now let's consider an argument in which two different premises support one conclusion. Again, I have bracketed each statement and numbered each:

[Be sure to get plenty of aerobic exercise][1] because [aerobic exercise will help you build a strong cardiovascular system][2] and [it will lower your resting heart rate][3].

[1] Conclusion: Get plenty of exercise.
[2] Premise: Aerobic exercise will build a strong cardiovascular system.
[3] Premise: Aerobic exercise will lower your resting heart rate.

A diagram of this argument will look like this:

In this diagram, we have two premises supporting one conclusion. Both of the arrows point to the same conclusion. This is called a **convergent structure** because both premises converge onto the same conclusion; that is, they are both reasons why you should get plenty of aerobic exercise. Longer arguments will often contain several premises that support a conclusion. Let's compare this argument structure to one in which two premises are linked to each other, so that instead of both premises supporting the same conclusion, the first premise is the reason for the second premise, which, in turn, becomes the reason for the conclusion.

[It is important that you work through all of the problems in the workbook][1] because [the problems will help you to learn the skills of critical thinking.][2] We can conclude that [working the problems in the workbook will help you to learn the skills][2] based on research that shows that [active learning promotes long-term retention.][3]

In this example, we really have three different statements. The statement that I labeled [2] appears twice.

[1] *Conclusion*: It is important to work through all of the problems in the workbook. This is the conclusion—the part that tells you what to do or believe.
[2] *Premise for [1]*: Working through the problems will help you to learn critical thinking skills. This is a reason for the conclusion.
[3] *Premise for [2]*: Active learning promotes long-term retention. This is a reason for believing that working the problems will help you to learn critical thinking skills.

A diagram of this argument will look like this:

[1] [It is important to work through all of the problems in the workbook]

[2] [Working through the problems will help you to learn critical thinking skills]

[3] [Active learning promotes long-term retention]

Arguments in which the conclusion of one subargument becomes the premise of a second argument are called **chained (or linked) structures**. Can you see an important distinction between this type of argument in which [3] is a reason for [2] and [2] is a reason for [1] and the previous structure in which both [2] and [3] are reasons for [1]? Remember the old saying that a chain is only as strong as its weakest link? When arguments have a chained structure, the conclusion is only as strong as the weakest subargument. If [3] doesn't provide very much support for [2], then the conclusion [1] is weakened. By contrast, when two or more premises converge onto the same conclusion, we only increase the strength of the conclusion by adding more premises.

Let's consider an example in which there are three premises and two conclusions.

[Taylor was late for school][1] because [she overslept][2] and [she had to stop for gas.][3] [Taylor doesn't care much about school][4], therefore [she is often late.][5]

In Chapter 4 on deductive reasoning, I talked about skeleton structures—sort of fill-in-the-blank structures where it doesn't matter what gets filled in. The skeleton is the "bare bones" of an argument, the place where you hang your statements. Let's reduce this argument to its skeleton:

[1] because [2] and [3]. [4] therefore [5].

This is a good way to think about premise and conclusion indicators. Any statement that follows **because** will probably be a premise ([2] and [3]), and any statement that follows **therefore** will probably be a conclusion ([5]).

Can you see how [2] and [3] are premises for [1], and [4] is a premise for [5]?

A diagram of this argument will look like this:

This is an example of two separate arguments in the same paragraph.

Guidelines for Diagramming Arguments

In understanding complex arguments, it is wise to identify the conclusions, premises, assumptions, qualifiers, and counterarguments, and then diagram the structure of their relationship. It is often useful to turn the argument into its skeleton form, so that relationships can be seen more clearly apart from the content. This strategy is a useful aid in determining how good a particular argument is. The major difficulty in using this procedure is that complex arguments have complex structures. Sometimes there is more than one possible interpretation and, correspondingly, more than one possible diagram. Sometimes the difficulty lies in deciding if a statement is really part of a subargument or part of the main argument. In longer text, you will often have to restate premises, conclusions, counterarguments, assumptions, and qualifiers in your own words. This process can involve reducing whole chapters of books to single statements. Although this can be difficult, it is an excellent strategy for comprehension. Often the process of diagramming will reveal what's wrong or right about a certain argument. If more than one diagram of an argument is possible, then you can consider each separately. Does one diagram provide stronger support for the conclusion? Is one diagram a "truer" representation of the statements being made?

You won't want to diagram every argument you read or hear, but sometimes the issues are troublesome and important, and diagramming can be very useful in clarifying the underlying relationships among the statements. Writing and diagramming unstated premises, conclusions, and assumptions can also be very helpful in considering the strength or quality of an argument by making these components explicit and placing them in the argument framework. Like many of the other strategies presented in this book, you will have to work at learning and using the steps in analyzing arguments. However, also like the other strategies, there is good evidence that the work is worth it. Allegretti and Frederick (1995), for example, reported that college students showed significant gains on a standardized test of critical thinking after they learned how to analyze arguments.

Using Argument Structure When Writing and Speaking

In your own writing and speaking, you often need to persuade an audience that your conclusions are correct. Before you write or make an oral presentation, be sure that you can answer the following questions:

1. What is your conclusion? In other words, what is the point (or points) you want to make? Arguments are made, or constructed, from their parts, and there is no argument if there is no conclusion. Although this question is first on the list, do not start with the conclusion that you want or believe to be true and then find reasons to support it. Look at reasons and evidence that address a particular issue in as unbiased a way as possible to determine what conclusion is best supported. The idea of taking a position on a controversial issue and then finding support for that position is a close-minded approach to thinking. If an issue is controversial, then there should be support for both sides (or more than two sides), and critical thinkers should be able to cite support for multiple positions, and decide on the best conclusion by weighing all of the available evidence.
2. What are the reasons that support your conclusion? How strong are they?
3. What assumptions are you making? Are they reasonable assumptions? Should they be explicitly stated?
4. What are the conditions under which the conclusion might not be true? In other words, are qualifiers needed?
5. What are the counterarguments? Why should a reader or listener *not* believe in your conclusion? What alternative conclusions have you actively considered?
6. What's missing? Are other conclusions possible given the reasons? Are there other reasons? Other counterarguments? Other assumptions? This step requires that you look beyond the information that you are using to consider what else might be important.

ACTIVELY OPEN-MINDED THINKING

Another reason why you should learn how to analyze arguments concerns what Seech (1993) calls "points of logical vulnerability." There are some topics about which we have trouble being objective. For example, I know that it would be difficult for me to be objective about the Ku Klux Klan. This is an emotional topic for me, and I would have great difficulty concluding anything positive about this group. If I used argument analysis, especially by reducing an argument to its skeleton and then diagramming its structure, then I could assess the strength of the support for a conclusion more fairly than I could without this sort of analysis. Of course, I could still decide that any belief or action that they are advocating is wrong.

There is a theme that reoccurs in almost every chapter in this text—the pervasiveness of the confirmation bias—the bias to look for and prefer information that confirms prior beliefs (Nickerson, 1998). It is a very strong influence on the way many, perhaps all, of us think and feel, and for the most part, we are unaware of its effects. Information that supports conclusions that we believe to be true just seems better than information that doesn't. We all need to develop the conscious effort to look for and evaluate fairly evidence that is not preferred.

Think about some topic about which you have strong feelings—it could be gun control, censorship, school vouchers, innate differences between the sexes, the United Nations, the death penalty, or anything else where the conclusion (what to do or believe) is clear to you. Now suppose that you come across strong evidence that supports a different conclusion than the one you prefer—let's say it makes a strong case for allowing open access to guns and you favor strict control of gun access or you are given data that show that the death penalty increases the crime rate and you favor the death penalty. How would you respond? I suppose that you would want to know more—how the data were collected, what the data actually showed, but assume for now that there are strong data that support a conclusion you totally oppose. Now what? Baron (1993) used the term "actively open-minded" to describe people who can change a cherished belief when given good reasons to do so. It turns out that actively and honestly processing information that runs counter to prior beliefs is very difficult, but there are people who can remain open-minded enough to evaluate an argument objectively, independent of their prior beliefs (Baron, 1995; Stanovich & West, 1997). It is not impossible to be fair-minded, but it is difficult.

Historical Evidence

How do you know that World War II really happened and that it is not just a made-up story to serve as the background for Hollywood war movies? When I asked this question in class one day, a student told me that he knew that World War II really happened because his grandfather was there—his grandfather fought in the war, and it was as horrible as we have read in our history books. Based on the information we had, it was easy to conclude that the student's grandfather was a credible source of information for this topic. In addition, he had war injuries to support his story. The question may seem strange, but there are groups of people who claim that stories about World War II are exaggerated (or lies) and that there was no mass extermination of the Jews in Europe. Similarly, there are groups that claim that slavery in the United States was not so bad (as mentioned in the last chapter). In fact, there may be groups that deny everything we know about history and science. How can we honestly assess these claims? It seems that all "fringe" groups that advocate a point of view that is not well supported use similar methods in constructing their arguments.

How can we analyze historical arguments? In an outstanding analysis of the arguments used by "Holocaust deniers" (people who claim that the Holocaust never happened or that it has been exaggerated), Shermer (1997, p. 212) wrote that these groups:

1. Concentrate on any weakness in their opponents' argument instead of providing strong evidence to support their own argument;
2. Exploit errors in the opposing argument—by focusing on a mistake made by someone who supports an opposing view, they can suggest that all or most of the evidence is wrong;
3. Take quotes out of context, so that the meaning is altered;
4. Recast honest debates among scholars to make them seem as though the honest scholars disagree about fundamental issues, when in fact they may disagree only about tertiary issues; and
5. Focus on what is not known rather than what is known.

Historical arguments are correctly evaluated with the same methods that are used in anthropology, botany, geology, and every other field. Converging evidence (remember converging arguments from the earlier section?) shows that demographic data, historical records, eye-witness accounts, physical evidence, etc., all support the conclusion that the Holocaust deniers twist and distort evidence and argument to advance a racist agenda. A basic understanding of arguments—reasons, evidence, conclusions, counterarguments, etc.—can protect you from falling prey to fringe groups who are trying to advance a political agenda (often a racist agenda) that is not supported by data.

EVALUATING THE STRENGTH OF AN ARGUMENT

Advertising persuades people to buy things they don't need with money they ain't got.

—Will Rogers (1879–1935)

All arguments are not equally good or equally bad. Think about how your belief about an issue can be swayed or reinforced as each speaker in a debate presents the reasons and conclusions supporting or refuting a position. Some reasons for a particular conclusion are better than others, and sometimes, good reasons don't seem to be related to the conclusion. In this section, we consider how to evaluate the strength of an argument.

Arguments are evaluated by how well they meet three criteria. The first criterion concerns the acceptability and consistency of the premises. The second criterion concerns the relationship between the premises and the conclusion. Do the premises support the conclusion? Does the conclusion follow from them? The third criterion concerns the unseen part of the argument. What's missing that would change your conclusion? Let's consider each of these criteria in turn.

Acceptable and Consistent Premises

No man can think clearly when his fists are clenched.

—George Jean Nathan (quoted in Byrne, 1988, p. 390)

The premises are the "why" part of an argument. The premises must be **acceptable**. A premise is acceptable when it is true or when we can reasonably believe that it is true. Let's consider what this means. If I say that the sun is hot, this is an acceptable premise. I have never touched the sun, but many experts in the field have said that the sun is hot. Much of what we believe to be true comes from experts' statements and personal and common or shared knowledge. Similarly, I have no direct, first-hand knowledge of bacteria, but it is reasonable to believe that they exist. Acceptable premises are commonly acknowledged "truths" of science. I believe that California is larger than New Jersey although I have never measured them. You could probably give a long list of "facts" that are commonly believed to be true. These are examples of acceptable premises.

Premises that are false are unacceptable. Examples of false premises include: men can give birth to babies, whales can fly, all mammals are dogs, and Spanish is the primary language of Canada. I don't want to get into the philosophical considerations of how we can ever know "truth." Personal or common knowledge and expert testimony will be the guide for determining acceptability.

Unfortunately, acceptability is not an either/or proposition in which a premise is either acceptable or it is not. Sometimes, part of the job of analyzing an argument involves determining how acceptable a premise is. This may require research on your part. Suppose that you are listening to an argument about the safety of building a chemical warfare laboratory in your backyard. The corporation that wants to build the laboratory argues that the chemical warfare laboratory is safe; therefore, you have nothing to worry about. One way to decide about the acceptability of this premise is to spend some time in the library reading about the kinds of experiments conducted in such laboratories, the kinds of safety precautions that are used, and past accidents at other similar laboratories. You will also need to consider the statements of experts in this area.

In a good argument, the premises are also **consistent**. When several premises are presented to support a conclusion, they must not contradict each other. For example, an argument in which one premise states that we have to reduce unemployment in order to improve the economy and another premise states that we have to increase unemployment in order to improve the economy is an argument that contains inconsistent premises. Sometimes, when premises are inconsistent, it is possible to eliminate one of them because it is weak or faulty. If you can eliminate the inconsistency among the premises, you will be able to judge more clearly the strength of the argument.

When considering the premises of an argument, check for acceptability and consistency. When you assess the acceptability and consistency of premises, you will often have to determine the credibility of the experts who are asserting the premises.

Credibility

What makes an expert credible? In deciding who and what to believe you need to consider the source of the information. Ask yourself the following questions about an expert who is presenting the reasons for a belief:

1. Is the "expert" a recognized authority in the *same field* in which she is providing testimony? Why should you believe an expert in computer graphics when the topic concerns chemical warfare?
2. Is the expert an *independent* party in this issue? If the expert who says the laboratory is safe was hired by the corporation that owns the laboratory, then her testimony is suspect. The testimony is not necessarily dishonest or wrong, but you should be wary because a motive for personal gain may be involved.
3. What are the expert's *credentials*? Did she write several journal articles on the subject, which were then published in respected journals, or is her expertise documented with a single night school course in the topic? Is the expert current in the field? Even a renowned expert on chemical warfare from world War II will have little knowledge of advances in the field over the last 40 years.
4. Does the expert have *specific and first-hand knowledge* of the issue? She could conclude that chemical warfare laboratories are generally safe, but have no direct knowledge of the one being proposed. Did she check the plans for safety features? Does she know exactly what sorts of experiments are being planned?
5. What *methods of analysis* were used by the expert? Are there standard safety assessments for laboratories that contain dangerous chemicals? Were these used?

It is interesting to note that a similar list of variables was found in a study of what makes jurors believe experts. Legal researchers found that the most important factors in the way jurors assessed credibility were the expert's qualifications, reasoning, familiarity with the particular case and impartiality (Shuman & Champagne, 1998).

Reread the advertisement presented at the beginning of this chapter that states that we can "eat all day and still lose weight." Who are the doctors and universities that support this claim? (No names are given. You should immediately begin to question the credibility of this information.) Was their expertise in weight loss? What are their credentials? Are they independent or will they make money if you buy this product? What were the methods of analysis that were used to document the statement that it will make you feel stronger and full of pep? (None were mentioned.) Are the claims made in this advertisement credible?

Decisions about the acceptability of premises will often depend on how you evaluate the source of the information. When you have two experts who disagree, which is frequently the case, you need to understand the nature of the disagreement and their relative expertise. Are they disagreeing on research findings or the interpretation of those findings? Try to zero in on the specific points on which they disagree, so that you can scrutinize these points.

Carlson (1995) distinguished between experts with regard to matters of reality and matters of value. When the topic concerns "reality" (e.g., Do people who live near chemical warfare plants suffer from more illnesses than people who do not live near them?), then the expert can provide evidence, such as the results of studies, that support her conclusion. When the topic concerns values, the identification and role of the expert is more difficult. For example, should euthanasia be allowed? This sort of question involves issues such as whether anyone has the right to terminate his own life, and experimental data will not be useful in formulating a conclusion in this situation. A chemist might be a credible expert for questions concerning chemical warfare, but who is a credible expert for questions of euthanasia? Are the opinions of medical personnel, clergy, or ordinary citizens equally good in making these decisions? There are few guidelines for selecting credible experts in matters of value. Fischhoff (1993) is an expert on expertise. As he wisely notes, by definition, experts know more about some topic than most of us. However, expert knowledge is always incomplete and people can legitimately disagree about a wide range of topics such as which risks are worth taking.

The Credibility Crisis

The rapid, phenomenal expansion of information on the Internet has created a credibility crisis. Almost anyone can provide information on almost any topic on the Internet, and it is easily accessible with a few clicks of a mouse. Users must know how to decide if the source of the information is credible. Some sites have "seals of approval" from credible groups like the American Association for the Advancement of Science, but others are so junky that reading from them might be closer to a crime than a legitimate educational experience. Sometimes, the site looks great—spiffy graphics and scientific-sounding names—but after a few screens are read, advertisements pop up to sell you something or an obviously biased message is shown.

When evaluating information from a Web site, look for:

1. The authority—Who is sponsoring the site?, What are the authors' qualifications?
2. Accuracy—Where did the information come from? Are the data clearly labeled?

3. Objectivity—Is the site a public service or is it just a fancy "sales-pitch"?
4. Currency—When was the site last revised? Is the information still relevant?
5. Coverage—Is the information complete? (Tate & Alexander, 1996)

The crisis in credibility is not just an Internet issue. Consider the huge influence of other media, especially television and movies. Have you seen the Oliver Stone (1991) film *JFK* (Bassham & Nardone, 1997)? In the movie version, John F. Kennedy was not killed by a lone gunman, which was the conclusion reached by the Warren Commission that had been established to study this question. In the movie version of this tragic event, he was murdered by right-wing radicals at the Central Intelligence Agency and the Pentagon. According to an analysis of the information in this popular film, Newsweek labeled the film *JFK* "propaganda" that omitted important information about Lee Harvey Oswald, such as the fact that he was in a court-ordered home for disturbed boys, had made a suicide attempt when in the Soviet Union, and had attempted to assassinate a general (Bassham & Nardone, 1997). The movie was not a credible source of information, although many people believed that it was and formed their own opinion of who killed Kennedy based on the information in this film.

Premises That Support the Conclusion

Consider the following argument:

It is important that we elect a prime minister from the New Democratic Party (a political party in Canada) because the rain in Spain falls mainly on the plain.

I hope that your response to this was "huh?" The premise or reason why we should support a candidate from the New Democratic Party had nothing to do with it. The rain in Spain is unrelated to political elections in Canada. In technical terms, the premise does not support the conclusion.

In determining the relevance or relatedness between the premises and the conclusion(s), I like to use an analogy to a table. The conclusion is the top of the table and the premises are the legs. When the premises are unrelated to the conclusion, they are off somewhere in another room and cannot support the table. It is easy to detect instances in which the premises are totally unrelated to the conclusion. Other examples are more difficult as relatedness is a matter of degree. Premises can be more or less related to the conclusion.

Premises can deal with the same topic as the conclusion, yet not support the conclusion. For example, suppose I were to argue that you should get plenty of exercise because athletes get plenty of exercise. Both the conclusion and the premise concern exercise, but the premise is not a *reason for* the conclusion. Even if it is true that athletes get plenty of exercise, it may not follow that you should therefore get plenty of exercise. Maybe you have a "weak" heart and would die from exercise. The conclusion does not follow from the premise. One way of checking for the relatedness of the premise(s) to the conclusion(s) is to ask yourself if the conclusion must be true or extremely likely if the premise is acceptable. If the answer is "no," then you have to question how well the conclusion is being supported by the premise.

Determining the relatedness between the premises and the conclusion can be tricky. This is exactly the sort of determination that judges are required to make all of the time. Consider a rape case in which the defense wants to show that the woman agreed to sexual intercourse. Is her previous sexual behavior related to this issue? Most of the time, the courts have ruled that a woman's past sexual history is unrelated to whether she was coerced at the time in question, but under special circumstances, such evidence may be admissible because the judge decides that it may be related to a particular case.

The premises not only have to be related to the conclusion, they also have to be strong enough to support the conclusion. Some authors call this condition **adequate grounds**. When premises provide good support for the conclusion, we say that there are adequate grounds for believing that the conclusion is true or likely to be true.

Let's return to the table analogy. Think of the conclusion as a solid wooden table-top. A solid wooden tabletop will topple over if we try to support it with a few toothpicks. The only way to support it is to use one or more strong legs or many weaker legs that, when used together, will form a strong base of support. These possibilities are depicted in Fig. 5.1.

Let's consider some examples of strength of support.

1. [Marion and Engelbert have filed for divorce.][1] Therefore, [they plan to get a divorce.][2]

As before, I have bracketed and numbered the statements. In skeleton form, this is [1] therefore [2].

FIG. 5.1. Table analogy for understanding the strength of an argument. The tabletop is the conclusion and the legs are the premises. Strong arguments have a firm base of support.

I hope that you can see that statement [1] is a reason for statement [2], the conclusion. Because we have one reason and one conclusion, this is an argument.

The unstated assumption that they are married will be omitted from the diagram because it is not relevant to the point being made, but if it were included, it would point to [1].

Graphically, this becomes:

```
      [2]  ⎫
       ↑   ⎬  Strong
      [1]  ⎭
```

I have rated the strength of support for the conclusion as strong because I believe that filing for divorce is very strong evidence that they plan to get divorced (although there are other possibilities, which is why it is not absolutely certain).

2. [Marion and Engelbert had eggs for breakfast.][1] Therefore, [they plan to get a divorce.][2]

In skeleton form, this is still [1] therefore [2].

Because the premise is unrelated to the conclusion, it provides no support for the conclusion.

```
         [2]  ⎫
    ↑          ⎬  No Support
    [1]       ⎭
```

In this example, the reason provides no support for the conclusion. We have no reason to believe that they plan to get a divorce.

3. [Marion and Engelbert had a fight this morning.][1] Therefore, [they plan to get a divorce.][2]

The skeleton structure is still [1] therefore [2].

In this example, the premise is related to the conclusion, but the support is weak.

```
      [2]  ⎫
       ↑   ⎬  Weak Support
      [1]  ⎭
```

4. [Marion and Engelbert had a fight this morning.][1] In fact, [they fight everyday.][2] [Engelbert is moving out of their apartment and plans to move in with his mother.][3] [Marion made an appointment with a divorce attorney.][4] Therefore, [they plan to get a divorce.][5]

This example contains five statements. Statement [5] is the conclusion. The other four statements are premises for the conclusion. Let's consider each premise and decide how well it supports the conclusion.

[5]: Marion and Engelbert plan to get a divorce. This is the conclusion.
[1]: Marion and Engelbert had a fight this morning. (weak)
[2]: They fight everyday. (weak)
[3]: Engelbert is moving out to live with his mother. (moderate)
[4]: Marion made an appointment with a divorce attorney. (strong)

In this example, there are multiple premises to support the conclusion. Taken together, they provide strong support.

Look at the list of premises. With only the first one, the support for the conclusion was very weak. The addition of the second made the support somewhat stronger because there were now two separate weak premises, which are stronger together than one weak premise. As additional premises were added, support for the conclusion increased. This is another example of a convergent argument structure in which multiple premises point to (converge on) the same conclusion. Additional premises, even weak ones, increase the strength of the argument.

When analyzing the relationship between premises and a conclusion, you need to consider their relevance to the conclusion and the strength of the support that they supply. Using the table analogy, ask yourself if the tabletop has a sound base of support or if it is shaky and easy to topple over.

You may have been looking for rules or guidelines to determine the strength of support. There really are no firm rules, only guidelines. How you judge the strength of an argument depends on many personal factors, including what you already know about the topic, your personal values, and how you make judgments. Some psychologists and others have advocated for teaching children and adults about values (e.g., Sternberg, in press), which would include teaching them to view complex issues from multiple perspectives—a technique that is frequently used in critical thinking instruction, although we do not usually think of this as "teaching values." Thinking, at its heart, is still a very personal activity. Although there are many skills that you can learn that will improve how you think, we are in no danger of turning all thinking into a rigid set of steps that will make us all think the same.

Here is a good example where thoughtful people disagree. How important is a candidate's personal life in determining whether the candidate should be elected? Is it an indication that the candidate will not be honest if you know that he cheats on his spouse? Some people believe that anyone who cheats in marriage will be dishonest in other situations; others believe that the two are unrelated. Public reaction to the sexual relationship between Monica Lewinsky, a White House intern, and former U.S. President Bill Clinton showed that there were many different opinions about the relevance of this relationship to Clinton's job as president. Similarly, in Russian elections, not long ago, the leading candidate was known to have a problem with alcohol. How important would this be in your decision of whether to vote for this candidate? In answering this question, you would also want to know about the other candidates running for office and the extent of the alcohol problem, but ultimately, many people disagree over issues such as these.

Missing Components

They will try to tell you to prove you are right; I tell you to prove you are wrong.

—Louis Pasteur (1822–1895)

Most arguments are written to persuade the reader or listener that a conclusion is true or probably true. Good examples of this can be found in advertisements and political rhetoric. When you read or listen to advertisements and political claims, it is important to keep in mind the restrictions imposed on these arguments. There are laws that punish false statements by advertisers; similarly, false political statements are likely to be detected by the press or opposition party. Therefore, blatantly false statements are not usually a factor in political and advertising argument analysis, although you should remain wary of them. The bigger problem in attempts to persuade is missing and distorted claims. In other words, it is the missing parts of most arguments that are often the most important parts. In order to evaluate the quality of an argument, you need to consider what's been left out.

When evaluating an argument, consider each component separately and think about ways the statements could have been distorted and what has been omitted. Let's try this with an example that is paraphrased from a newspaper editorial written by Phyllis Schafly, a prominent spokesperson for several conservative issues. This editorial appeared in the *Washington Times* on July 21, 1993 (p. G4).

> In this commentary, Schafly argues against universal mental health care coverage. She provides an anecdote to show that mental health care is too costly and ineffective.
>
> The story is about a mechanic who "allegedly" injured his wrist. Although he had wrist surgery, he still complained of pain and "claimed" to be unable to work. He then lost his job, and with it, his insurance. During this period, his wife left him because he was beating her. Under universal mental health care coverage, he would be eligible to receive 30 days of psychiatric in-patient treatment and up to 20 sessions of out-patient therapy. Schafly concludes that this would reward his "misbehavior," and create a new welfare.

One of the best ways to think about what's missing is to change your point of view so that you now become an advocate for the "other side." In this case, try to view the argument from the perspective of someone who does not agree with the conclusion that is being advocated. What premises are missing or additional information is needed that would support an opposite conclusion? First, you should notice the use of certain words that suggest that the mechanic was not really hurt. Schafly does not know if the pain was genuine, and neither do we, but the use of terms like "allegedly" and "claims" suggests that they were not. Second, the surgery would have been performed at the same cost regardless of the mental health care coverage, so it is not relevant to the conclusion that mental health care coverage is too costly. Third, suppose that he had received the mental health care that Schafly opposes and that it helped him to return to work and stop beating his wife. Tremendous amounts of money would be saved because he could go off welfare, and the family might also have been able to survive as a unit. Of course, you can supply other possibilities. When you consider the issues from the perspective of what is not given as information, you often will arrive at a different conclusion.

Although the consideration of missing components could theoretically go on forever, the extent to which we scrutinize an argument depends on its importance. I would spend a great deal of time and effort analyzing an argument in which the conclusion concerns the safety of building a chemical warfare laboratory near my home (or someone else's home). There are many arguments in life that should be carefully evaluated, and this includes seeking and considering missing and misleading statements.

Sound Arguments

A good argument is technically called a **sound argument**. An argument is sound when it meets the following criteria:

1. The premises are acceptable and consistent. (You may have to eliminate some premises so that the others are consistent.)
2. The premises are relevant to the conclusion and provide sufficient support for the conclusion.
3. Missing components have been considered and are judged to be consistent with the conclusion.

Satisfying each of these criteria is a matter of degree. Premises are usually acceptable on some continuum from unacceptable to totally acceptable. The nature of support that they provide for the conclusion also lies on some continuum from no support to complete support. Similarly, the missing components, especially counterarguments, may weaken the argument anywhere from completely to not at all. Because all of these assessments have to be combined to decide if an argument is sound, we usually think of soundness as ranging from unsound to completely sound.

An argument is unsound if its premises are false, or if they are unrelated to the conclusion, or if a critical counterargument is missing. An argument is completely sound if the premises are acceptable and related to the conclusion in a way that guarantees the acceptability of the conclusion. Most real-life arguments fall somewhere between these two extremes. For this reason, conclusions are often preceded with probability terms like "it is likely that" or "we can probably conclude that." Here are some examples of different degrees of soundness:

Completely Sound Argument (premises are acceptable and related to the conclusion in a way that guarantees the conclusion)
All mothers are women who have (or had) children. Suzi is a woman who has a son. Therefore, Suzi is a mother.
Unsound Arguments (either the premises are unacceptable or they are unrelated to the conclusion)
All fathers have given birth to a child. Norbert has a son. Therefore Norbert has given birth to a child. (Premise is unacceptable.)
Norbert has a son; therefore, Norbert also has a daughter. (Premise is unrelated to the conclusion.)

Don't confuse the truth or acceptability of a conclusion with the soundness of an argument. A conclusion can be objectively true, even when the argument is unsound. The conclusion could be true for reasons that have nothing to do with the information stated in the argument. Here is an example of a conclusion that is objectively true embedded in an unsound argument.

The structure of the family has been changing rapidly, with more single parents now heading their own households. Consequently, the divorce rate has begun to level off and decline slightly.

The conclusion about the divorce rate is true (according to demographers), but the argument is unsound because the premise does not support the conclusion.

Complex issues rarely have one correct conclusion. More often, many conclusions are possible, and the task of analyzing an argument involves deciding which of two or more conclusions has the greater strength or support.

HOW TO ANALYZE AN ARGUMENT

1. The first step is to read or listen to the passage to determine if it contains an argument. Are there at least one premise and at least one conclusion? If not, no further analysis is needed.
2. Identify all the stated and unstated component parts: premises, conclusions, assumptions, qualifiers, and counterarguments.
3. Check the premises for acceptability and consistency. If all of the premises are unacceptable, stop here because the argument is unsound. If only some of the premises are unacceptable, eliminate them, and continue with the acceptable premises. If the premises are inconsistent with each other, decide if you can justifiably eliminate one or more. An argument cannot be sound if the premises are inconsistent or contradict each other, but you may be able to eliminate the contradiction.
4. Diagram the argument. Consider the strength of the support that each premise provides for the conclusion. Rate the strength of support as nonexistent, weak, medium, or strong. Look over the number of supporting premises. A large number of supporting premises can provide strong support for the conclusion in a convergent structure, even when separately each only provides weak support. Recall that in a linked structure a single weak link can destroy an argument.
5. Consider the strength of counterarguments, assumptions, and qualifiers (stated or omitted) and omitted premises. Do they undermine the support provided by the premises or strengthen or weaken it?
6. Finally, come to a global determination of the soundness of the argument. Is it unsound, completely sound, or somewhere in between? If it is somewhere in between, is it weak, medium, or strong?

You may be thinking that analyzing arguments is a lot of work. You are absolutely right. Diagramming and evaluating complex arguments can be as demanding as a long proof in mathematics or comprehending a complex novel. I realize that few people will formally diagram an argument in real life; however, it is a powerful and useful tool for comprehending complex arguments. Practice with diagramming arguments will aid in the analysis of other arguments even when, for time or other reasons, actual diagramming is not feasible. It will help you distinguish among the components of an argument and make judgments about its strength. When the issue is important and complex, making a diagram of its structure can be well worth the time and effort required.

A Rubric for Scoring Arguments—Even Your Own

Of course, we also present arguments to other people, and don't just analyze those that are made by other people. In a book that was written for college professors, Norris and Ennis (1989) suggested criteria that can be used to evaluate an argumentative essay. When you write your own essays or plan oral presentations, consider these criteria:

1. Do you clearly state the conclusion and define necessary terms?
2. Is the material that you included relevant to the conclusion?
3. Is the argument sound? Do the premises provide solid support for the conclusion?
4. Have you considered the credibility of your experts?
5. Is the paper well organized with different issues addressed separately?
6. Have you fairly presented alternative points of view and counterarguments?
7. Have you used good grammar and a clear style of writing?

A TEMPLATE FOR WRITING SOUND ARGUMENTS

The importance of being able to write a sound argument is recognized as a critical thinking task that is essential for success in college and in professional careers. Several different standardized examinations are requiring test-takers to write an argument as a means of assessing critical thinking and writing skills. At the present time, written arguments are required for everyone who takes the Graduate Record Examination, the selection test used for entry to most graduate schools in the United States, and the examination used for selection for entry into business schools. Here is a template for writing sound arguments.

The template is designed to help you organize your thinking on complex issues and be able to explain evidence on two or more sides of an issue, such as the evidence for and against evolutionary hypotheses of mate selection or for and against the idea that parents are important influences on their children. In completing this template, you will have to gather and assess evidence to determine the best conclusion or conclusions and not start with what you believe is true. You will need to consider both supporting and disconfirming evidence—an exercise that can help you avoid the confirmation bias. Here is an applied example:

MAKING ARGUMENTS TEMPLATE

Example 1: Does violence on television have a negative influence on children's behavior?

1. State your conclusion. (Although you may begin your formal writing here, be sure that the conclusion follows from your reasons.) As you work, this is the last part that is filled in, not the first.

2. Give three reasons (or some other number) that support your conclusion.

a.

b.

c.

3. Rate each reason as weak, moderate, strong, or very strong.

Rating for a:

Rating for b:

Rating for c:

4. Give three counterarguments (or some other number) that weaken your conclusion. Rate how much each counterargument weakens the conclusion: little, moderate, much, or very much.

a.

Rating for a:

b.

Rating for b:

c.

Rating for c:

5. List any qualifiers (limitations on the reasons for or against—for example, some evidence may be restricted to early childhood).

6. List any assumptions.

7. Are your reasons and counterarguments directly related to your conclusion?

8. What is the overall strength of your argument: weak, moderate, strong, or very strong?

Now that you have completed this worksheet, rate the overall strength of your argument.

Once the template is completed, the writing will be the easy part because you already know what you want to say and have listed your reasons and considered the strength of your argument. (If you are planning on taking any of the standardized admissions examinations that now require that you write an argument, this exercise should greatly improve your score.)

Reasoning and Rationalizing

People are irrational, short-sighted, destructive, ethnocentric, emotional, and easily misled by demagogues.

—Philip E. Tetlock (1994, p. 3)

When you evaluate arguments, you are also evaluating your own knowledge about the subject matter. There may be other counterarguments that are quite strong, but that are unknown to you. Similarly, your ratings of the strength of the components may be biased in ways that support a conclusion that you favor. Nickerson (1986) makes an important distinction between reasoning and **rationalizing**. When we rationalize, we attend to information that favors a preferred conclusion. We may selectively gather information that supports a preferred conclusion or rate counterarguments as weak because they detract from a preferred conclusion. Rationalizing also influences the nature of the missing components that we supply to an existing argument. When we add to an argument, the information that we supply is information that is readily recalled. If you've already read Chapter 2 on memory, then you are well aware of the many ways that memory can be biased. Rationalizing is usually not a deliberate process to distort the analysis of arguments, which makes it difficult to recognize and guard against. It is easier to recognize rationalizing when someone else is doing it. Perhaps the best we can do is realize that rationalization does occur and to try to be especially vigilant for rationalizing when you prefer a conclusion. When you analyze an argument, you must identify the main point that the author or speaker wants you to believe. You also have to consider both premises and counterarguments.

We tend to weigh evidence that favors a belief more heavily than evidence that disconfirms it. This bias was clearly demonstrated in a classic study in which college students served as subjects (Lord, Ross, & Lepper, 1979). Students were asked to write an essay in which they argued for or against a controversial issue such as abortion or capital punishment. The students were then given the results of experimental studies that supported a "middle of the road" point of view—that is, it was neither for nor against the controversial issue. After reading the balanced review, students who favored the "pro" position of the controversial issue believed that the objectively neutral paper supported the "pro" position. Similarly, students who favored the "con" position and then read the same objectively balanced paper believed that it favored the "con" position. Instead of bringing the two sides closer together, as might have been expected, the balanced paper drove them farther apart. Each position focused on the information that supported their own point of view and judged the evidence that ran counter to their favored position to be weak. This same finding has been found with all sorts of subject pools, including NASA scientists who favored evidence and arguments that supported their preferred hypothesis over ones that did not.

Just telling people that we tend to judge information that we favor as stronger than information that we oppose doesn't work to correct this bias. Is it any wonder why it is so difficult to get people to assess controversial issues in a fair-minded manner? Because we are not aware that we judge reasons in a way that supports what we believe to be true, it is very difficult to change the way we evaluate information. One successful attempt was accomplished by Koriat, Lichtenstein, and Fischhoff (1980). They required students to list reasons that support a conclusion and reasons that run counter to a conclusion (counterarguments), and to rate the strength of each. This should be familiar because they are the steps used in analyzing arguments. They found that students became more accurate in their assessments after this training in "giving reasons." These results have been replicated in more recent studies in which the bias for information that confirms a prior belief was reduced by requiring people to provide reasons that did not support the preferred conclusion (Lenski, 2001; Flannelly & Flannelly, 2000). The authors of one of the studies summarized their research: "critical thinking skills of students should be fostered so the students come to appreciate the importance of weighting both positive and negative evidence" (Flannelly & Flannelly, 2000). These sorts of experimental results show that the giving and assessing of reasons can have beneficial results that improve the thinking process.

PERSUASION AND PROPAGANDA

By the skillful and sustained use of propaganda, one can make people see even heaven as hell, or an extremely wretched life as paradise.

—Adolf Hitler (1889–1945; cited in Falls, 1943)

Whenever you are confronted with an argument, keep in mind that the material you are reading or hearing has been written to persuade you to do something or to believe something. Much of the communication that you receive is concerned with getting you to act or think in a certain way. Pratkanis and Aronson (1992) define **propaganda** as "mass suggestion or influence through the manipulation of symbols and the psychology of the individual" (p. 9). This broad definition is applicable to a great variety of situations. Propaganda, like beauty, is often in the eye of the beholder. It does not require that the information be false or misleading, but it does at least imply less concern for truth or rigorous argument than the sort of arguments found in scholarly journals or presented by independent parties. Frequently, the information provided is charged with appeals to emotion rather than reason.

Humans are very clever in using techniques that aim to influence others' thinking. The cleverest way to influence how someone thinks is with a well-crafted argument. If you were thinking that the work of analyzing an argument is not worth it, you have not considered the agonies of history in which people failed to analyze political arguments. Consider the evil genius of men like Joseph Goebbel, Hitler's minister of propaganda. Have you ever wondered how millions of people could be persuaded to kill millions of other people whose sole crime was believing in another religion? Of course, such evil was rooted in a long history of scapegoating, which is the practice of blaming a minority group for all of the ills in society. In order to kill so many people efficiently, it was necessary to set up "death factories" that operated with the efficiency of an assembly line, much like the factories that produce refrigerators or automobiles. First, Goebbel told lies, false reasons to support the conclusion that genocide was justified. He spread rumors about "secret books" that told about an alleged tradition of drinking the blood of innocent Christian children. Of course, there were no books, and this disgusting practice never occurred, but many people were willing to believe that it was true.

Arguments were most frequently used to persuade Nazis and others that millions of people should be slaughtered, but there were other propaganda techniques that Goebbel used, including visual images and threats of violence for anyone who didn't agree. Although other techniques are considered in more detail later in this chapter and in other chapters, I note here the particularly blatant ploy of showing pictures of Jews that were alternated with pictures of rats and roaches, so that viewers would come to associate certain facial features that are common in many Jews with disgusting rodents and bugs. (If you have studied psychology, you will recognize this technique as an application of classical conditioning.) These same sorts of techniques have been used to promote other types of equally horrific genocide. The propaganda used to justify slavery and lynchings in the United States, the slaughter of Cambodians in Asia, and the purges by Mao Tse-tung in China and Stalin in the former Soviet Union, show that propaganda has been used all over the world to encourage prejudice and killing. Why did education fail all these people in so many places around the world? For example, how did millions of Chinese, in this century, believe that Mao was their "loving father," when he was responsible for the death of millions of Chinese? Why didn't they stop to consider if the reasons they were given to support this Chinese holocaust (i.e., the cultural revolution) were not acceptable? Do you understand Hitler's now-infamous quote, "What luck for rulers that men do not think" (quoted in Byrne, 1988, p. 359)?

The Psychology of Reasons

As you now realize, an argument requires the use of reasons, and we like to have reasons for our beliefs, even when the reasons are not very good and the argument itself is weak. Three psychologists conducted a study in which they examined how people respond to the *appearance* of reasons (Langer, Blank, & Chanowitz, 1978). In this study, they had a confederate (someone working with the experimenters whose identity is not known to the true subjects) try various combinations of requests and reasons for barging ahead of people waiting in line to use a copier machine. There were three different conditions: (a) Request alone ("Excuse me, I have five pages. May I use the Xerox machine?"), (b) Request plus reason ("Excuse me, I have five pages. May I use the Xerox because I'm in a rush?"), and (c) Request plus the appearance of a reason ("Excuse me, I have five pages. May I use the Xerox machine because I have to make some copies?").

The results of this study are very interesting. In the request alone condition 60% of the people waiting said that it was okay for the confederate to make the copies. In the request plus reason condition, this figure jumped to 94%. What about the request plus appearance of a reason? In this condition, 93% of the people waiting to use the machine let the confederate go ahead. The use of the word *because* suggested that there was a reason. Remember the section on premise indicators? *Because* was listed as a word that is frequently followed by a reason. The statement "because I have to make some copies" is not a reason to let someone ahead of you in line at the copier machine. Everyone standing in line has to make some copies. It seems that we like to believe that our actions and beliefs are reasonable, that is, based on reasons. Unfortunately, even nonreasons, poor reasons, and reasons that are unrelated to the action or belief will often suffice. People who want to change how we think and act often rely on this human tendency and will deliberately use unsound reasoning to convince us that a conclusion is true.

You probably think that irrelevant reasons for a conclusion would have no effect on how people evaluate a conclusion. It seems that this should be true because irrelevant reasons are, well, irrelevant. But, psychologically, irrelevant reasons often influence what we believe and how we act even though, logically, they should not. A study of consumer decisions showed that irrelevant reasons in support of a product tend to weaken support for the product, and irrelevant reasons that run counter to a product tend to strengthen support for the product (Simonson, Nowlis, & Simonson, 1993). For example, suppose that you are a runner who is looking for good running shoes. As a salesperson, I tell you that Adibok brand is well known for their aerobic shoes, but they also make good running shoes. The fact that they are well known for their aerobic shoes should be irrelevant to the selection of running shoes, but it seems to work against this hypothetical brand. Consumers assume that if Adibok is good at making aerobic shoes, then it is less good at making running shoes. Thus, an irrelevant reason in support of this brand is psychologically converted into a reason against this brand.

Similarly, suppose that you have no interest in saunas. If I told you that the Posh Inn Hotel Chain does not have a sauna, a seemingly irrelevant reason against the Posh Inn Hotels, you would likely take this as a reason for selecting Posh Inn. Psychologically, this irrelevant reason against Posh Inn Hotels is converted into thinking that it may have something else positive that balances this irrelevant negative. In this way, a reason that should be irrelevant to your decision about Posh Inn Hotel becomes a reason for staying at Posh Inn. The point of this discussion is that people often do not behave in ways that are logical; irrelevant reasons influence how we think.

EXPLAINING AS KNOWING

"How do you know what you know?" (Kuhn, 2001). It seems that most people make judgments about their own knowledge by thinking about how well they can explain

a phenomenon. For example, in studies of how jurors decide on the guilt or innocence of a defendant, researchers found that jurors weave a story about what might
have happened at the scene of a crime and then decide how good that story is. This
mode of knowing is often labeled "explaining." Another way of knowing is to examine the strength of the evidence that supports or refutes a particular conclusion—this
is known as argument analysis. Most people use "explanations" as the primary way
of justifying claims (Brem & Rips, in press; Cheng, 1997). Consider this example:

> Which is the stronger argument?
> A. Why do teenagers start smoking? Smith says it's because they see ads that make smok-
> ing look attractive. A good-looking guy in neat clothes with a cigarette in his mouth is some-
> one you would like to be like.
> B. Why do teenagers start smoking? Jones says it's because they see ads that make smok-
> ing look attractive. When cigarette ads were banned from TV, smoking went down. (Kuhn,
> 2001, p. 4)

Answer A provides an explanation that links smoking and teens in a way that
most people think "makes sense." Answer B provides data, albeit limited, that links
smoking and advertisements. The alternative that provides evidence for the relationship is stronger than the one that merely explains, even though many people
prefer the explanation. There are many plausible explanations that could be generated, and without evidence (i.e., data) there is no good way to choose among them.
Far too many people are very confident in their knowledge of something and very
wrong (Kuhn, 2001). Think about your own understanding. How do you know
about the nature of the world? This is not meant to be an idle navel-gazing question.
If you can develop the disposition to look for evidence instead of relying on an explanation that "just seems right," you will make large gains in critical thinking.

It is important to understand that people are quite confident in their knowledge
because it makes sense to them, but "making sense" is a poor measure of the quality
of your knowing. Sometimes, it is difficult to understand why data should be preferable to explanation. Consider this example: During World War II, many Germans
refused to believe that the German army burned an entire village in Poland as they
were retreating from the Soviet front. They refused to believe it because the massacre did not make sense. Why should the German troops slaughter innocent people
in Poland? In fact, historical records (eye-witness accounts, physical evidence, written accounts, etc.) clearly show that this is what happened—the village was
destroyed by frustrated German troops who were seeking revenge for their humili-
ating loss. The evidence is more compelling than the "make sense" explanation. It is
important that we learn to value evidence when formulating conclusions. The use of
data is a critical part of critical thinking.

The preference for explanations over evidence is just one of many ways that
thinking can "go wrong." In the next section, we consider other common ways that
thinking can go astray. Unsound reasoning techniques used for the purpose of persuasion are called **fallacies**. As you go through the list of fallacies presented in the
next section, you can classify each as violating one or more of the criteria for sound arguments—the premises are unacceptable, or the premises are unrelated to the conclusion or inconsistent, or the expert is not credible, or important information is missing.

It is impossible to list every fallacy that has been employed to change how people
think. The list would be too long to be useful, with only subtle differences among
several of the techniques. Accordingly, only the most common and representative

techniques are discussed. If you understand how fallacies work in general, you'll be better prepared to recognize and defend against them. Toulmin, Rieke, and Janik (1979) call the ability to recognize fallacies "a kind of sensitivity training" because they train the reader to be sensitive to common tricks of persuasion.

Twenty-One Common Fallacies

1. Association Effects

One of the oldest principles in psychology is the notion that, if two events occur close together in time and/or space, the mind will form an association between them. Thereafter, when one occurs, the other is expected to occur. This principle has become widely used in the political arena, especially to create **guilt by association**. Suppose you read in the newspaper that a violent mass murderer endorsed a presidential candidate. This endorsement would be detrimental to the candidate, even if she did not desire it and did nothing to promote it.

A classic example of the propagandistic use of association came from a political group called "California Tax Reduction Movement." Their 1983 literature stated: "This court, dominated by Jerry Brown appointees, and having radical views close to those of Jane Fonda and Tom Hayden, has twisted the words until we don't even recognize them!" You might be wondering what Jane Fonda and Tom Hayden are doing in a sentence about the California Supreme Court. In the jargon of analyzing arguments, the premise is unrelated to the conclusion. Fonda and Hayden had no connection with the court. This literature was written with the belief that people who favor tax reductions will also be opposed to Jane Fonda and Tom Hayden. The Court is being made guilty by association with them. Although it is implied, it does not logically follow that the Supreme Court therefore has views similar to Jane Fonda and Tom Hayden. It may or may not have had such views. (Note also the use of the emotion-laden word "radical.") Whenever you see examples of associations with no justifiable connection like this one, be wary of the rest of the message. It is likely to contain an appeal to your emotions rather than to your cognition.

Just as one can have guilt by association, it is also possible to have **virtue by association**. In this instance, the names or labels attached to the person are "good" ones. Perhaps this is why certain political offices tend to run in families. People expected the Kennedy brothers to be similar as politicians because of their obvious association with each other or that the Bush children will be similar to their father, former president George Bush, Sr. This expectation is being passed onto the children and other relatives of political figures, many of whom are now involved in or considering political careers. Would you vote for or against an unknown Kennedy or Bush simply because he or she is from the same family as a former politician?

A wary recipient of messages that rely on association will ask about the nature of the association. If a candidate is a leader of the Ku Klux Klan, then associating the doctrine of the Klan with this individual is reasonable. If, on the other hand, a friend of the candidate's mother is a member of the Klan, the association is ludicrous.

2. Arguments Against the Person

Arguments against the person is the formal term for name calling or, in its Latin form, *argumentatum ad hominem*. This form of persuasion or propaganda attacks the people who support a cause, and not the cause itself. From the standpoint of argument analysis, the personal attack is irrelevant to the conclusion. For example, the Nazis believed that the theory of relativity was wrong because its discoverer was a Jew named Albert Einstein. They never considered the evidence for or against the theory, just the religion of its originator. It is basically another form of the association effect. In this case, the association that is being made is between an idea and a person. The underlying principle is that if you don't like the person who supports an idea, then you should also oppose the idea itself because the idea and the person are associated.

Suppose you were serving on a jury that had to decide which of two witnesses was telling the truth. Would you be swayed if one attorney told you to disregard one man's testimony because he had been divorced twice? Presumably not, because the man's marital status is irrelevant to the issue. Suppose you were told that one of the men had two previous convictions for lying to a jury. Would this argument against the person be relevant? I would think so. In this case, the information provided about the witness is relevant to the question of whether he is lying. Consider the strength and relevance of the argument and the purpose for which it is used, and don't be misled by irrelevant attacks on the supporters or detractors of any position.

3. Appeals to Pity

An **appeal to pity** is easy to spot. "Support this position" or "buy that product" because it needs your help. A rental car agency has made it well known that they're number 2 in their business, and therefore will try harder. They hope that consumers will root for the "underdog" and support the company that is number 2. Does this conclusion logically follow from the fact that they're number 2? No! You could also logically conclude that the number 1 company will try harder to retain their lead or that the number 2 company would have been number 1 if it had tried harder. Appeals to pity are often found in legal pleadings. A defendant's poor background or turbulent home life will often be brought up during a trial. These appeals to pity have nothing to do with the question of whether a defendant is guilty or innocent, although they may be persuasive appeals for leniency in sentencing if the defendant is found guilty. Sometimes, students use appeals to pity when attempting to persuade a teacher to raise a low grade. The grade is assigned on the quality of the work that is done, but students sometimes argue that if they work hard (or some other sad reason), the work should be graded higher than comparable work by someone who did not work as hard.

4. Popularity and Testimonials

The **popularity** technique (also known as the "bandwagon") relies on the need for conformity for its persuasive power. It is persuasive because it explains that everyone supports a position or buys a certain product. It is expected that the recipients of the message will adopt the belief or buy the product in order to feel as if she or he belongs to the groups mentioned. Implicitly, the message is "if everyone is doing it, it must be right." This fallacy was presented earlier in this chapter when we considered the advertisement for LaBaroness, the car that more people are buying than any other American car.

A variation of the popularity technique is **testimonials**. Respected politicians or movie stars endorse a belief or product. It is believed that people will want to be

Calvin and Hobbes   by Bill Watterson

similar to the people they respect, so they will choose to use the same deodorant or foot powder or support the same causes. The recipients of testimonials are expected to infer a conclusion from the information stated. It is expected that they will reason along these lines: Christie Brinkley is a gorgeous model with very few wrinkles. She uses the advertised beauty product. If I use this beauty product, like Christie Brinkley, I will have very few wrinkles. Of course, this conclusion does not follow from the first two sentences, but many people believe that it does or at least implies that it might. This fallacy is worsened when the testimonial is not even in the area in which the personality has expertise. Christie Brinkley also endorses a national newspaper. As far as I know, this is an area in which she has no expertise. She is not a credible expert in the area of journalistic quality. Yet, advertisements like these do sell products.

Sometimes, however, the popularity technique and testimonials can be valid persuasive techniques. If, for example, all of the members of an unbiased expert panel established to study the effects of a drug decide that it is unsafe, I would consider this information relevant to the question of the drug's safety because it passes the test of credibility. Similarly, if a leading educator endorses a reading text, this might properly have an impact on your evaluation of the text. Both of these examples presume that the "experts" have no personal motives for their endorsements—that is, they're not being paid for saying these things and their expertise is relevant to the position or product that they're supporting. In this case, they are credible sources of information.

5. False Dichotomy

Don't give him two sides to a question to worry him.
Give him one;
better yet, give him none!

—Ray Bradbury (*Farenheit 451*, 1950)

There are very few political or social decisions that have simple answers or that can be solved with simple choices. Yet simple slogans are the prototype or most common and representative form of persuasive techniques. **False dichotomy** is sometimes called simplification or the *black or white fallacy* because readers are asked to decide between two positions, without allowing other alternatives or "gray areas" that would combine aspects of both choices.

The following question appeared in a questionnaire that was sent by an assemblyman to his constituents (Assemblyman Montjoy Needs Your Views, 1983):

"Would you prefer that government cut spending or increase taxes?"
cut spending   increase taxes

Does this question bother you? It should. The answers to our fiscal problems are not this simple. You should ask where and how the cuts would be made and how much taxes would be increased. Perhaps "cuts" could be combined with small or temporary increases in taxes. Can you guess which answer the assemblyman prefers? Given this choice, I believe that most people would prefer to "cut spending," yet, for many, an entirely different response would result from a question that was worded differently. When you are faced with a false dichotomy or the simplification of a complex issue, don't ask yourself if the ideas are good or bad. Ask instead what is good about the ideas and what is bad about them. Consider other alternatives and combinations of ideas. Remember that one of the steps in analyzing arguments calls for supplying missing components—omitted premises, assumptions, qualifiers, and counterarguments.

6. Appeals to Pride or Snobbery

Speech was given to man to disguise his thoughts.

—Talleyrand (1754–1838; quoted in Macmillan, 1989, p. 544)

An **appeal to pride or snobbery** usually involves praise or flattery. A blatant and humorous example can be found in an advertisement that was mailed to me at home. (Notice that it begins with my name, a sure attention-getting technique.)

Dear Dr. Halpern,
You may just be the solution.
Here is the problem: How do you find the right subscribers for an extraordinary magazine that is about to be published—BUT, a magazine that isn't for everyone?
A magazine that is, in fact, for only a handful of bright, literate people, people who still in this world of instant communication love to sit down with a good book.

I'd love to believe that the publishers know me personally, and have written a magazine just for the kind of person I'd like to be. The truth is, this letter went to tens of thousands of people whose names were bought as part of various mailing lists. Clearly, they are attempting to persuade me to purchase their magazine by appealing to my pride or snobbery.

Consider the following question, which appeared as part of a "1982 Congressional Questionnaire" (Congressman Carlos J. Moorhead Reports, Summer, 1982):

In an attempt to make federal social programs more responsive to citizens' needs, less wasteful and more efficient, the Administration has proposed a New Federalism where the programs and funds—in the form of block grants—are transferred to local government for management and administration. Do you think that you, your neighbors, and your local officials have the ability to handle this new responsibility?
yes   no

Do you think that this question is slanted toward a "yes" response? The appeal to pride and snobbery is less obvious in this question than in the first example, possibly making it even more potent. The question is really, "Are you and your friends smart enough to handle X?" It doesn't matter what X is; most people believe that they are smart. The congressman has also posed the wrong question. You may be able to "handle this new responsibility" without believing that block grants are a good idea. Responses to this question were subsequently used to support the idea of block grants. Be wary of persuasive communications that include flattery. Although flattery is not in and of itself wrong, it may be used to obscure real issues.

7. Card Stacking or Suppressed Information

Card stacking or suppressed information operates as a persuasive technique by omitting information that supports the unfavored view. An automobile company recently compared the car they were advertising on television with a competitor. The advertisers stressed that their car got better mileage and cost less. What about the variables they omitted? Which car needed fewer repairs, had the more comfortable seating, or accelerated better? What about other makes of cars? Did a brand that was not mentioned exceed the advertised one on all of these dimensions? When considering persuasive information, be sure to consider what has not been stated along with the stated claims. This is another example of the need to consider the missing components in an argument.

8. Circular Reasoning

In **circular reasoning** the premise is simply a restatement of the conclusion. If you were to diagram the structure of this sort of argument, you would get a circle because the support for the conclusion is a restatement of the conclusion. Here is an example of circular reasoning:

We need to raise the speed limit because the current legal speed is too slow.

In this example, the reason given (current speed is too slow) is just another way of saying that we need to raise the speed limit. It does not support the conclusion. The conclusion would be supported with premises such as the assertion that there has been no change in the number or severity of automobile accidents with a lower speed limit or some similar statement that supports this conclusion.

9. Irrelevant Reasons

Arguments that utilize irrelevant reasons are fairly common. The Latin word for this sort of fallacy is *non sequitur*, which literally translates to "it doesn't follow." In other words, the reason or premise is unrelated to the conclusion. Of course, you recognize the importance of having relevant premises as one of the criteria for sound arguments. (If you don't, go back over the section of evaluating the quality of an argument.)

One example that comes to mind is a statement that a faculty member made at a curriculum committee meeting in which we were discussing whether we should require every student to take classes in a foreign language. The faculty member in favor of this proposal made this statement: "We should require every student to study a foreign language because it is important that we provide our students with a quality education." Look carefully at the conclusion and the premise. Is the premise related to the conclusion? Everyone on the curriculum committee believed that all students should receive a quality education, but the issue was whether all students should be required to study a foreign language. There were no reasons given as to why studying a foreign language should be a required part of a quality education. The conclusion did not follow from the reason that was given.

10. Slippery Slope or Continuum

The **slippery slope** fallacy is best described by an example. One of the arguments against court-ordered desegregation of the schools was that, if we allow the court to determine which public schools our children will attend, the court will also tell us whom we have to allow into our churches, whom we have to invite into our homes, and even whom we should marry. In this example, the action (court-ordered desegregation) lies on a continuum with the court ordering whom we should marry at an extreme end. The argument being made is that if we allow the court to have jurisdiction over events at one end of the continuum, then it will take over the other events on the continuum. For this reason, this fallacy is called either slippery slope (once you start sliding down a slope you can't stop) or the fallacy of **continuum**.

Most life events can be placed along a continuum. It does not necessarily follow that actions concerning some part of the continuum will also apply to other portions of the continuum. Let's consider a second example. The Irish believe that current U.S. immigration laws are biased against immigrants from Ireland. They have asked the U.S. immigration service to increase the quota for Ireland. Those who have argued against increasing the immigration quotas for Ireland have said that if we increase the quota for Ireland, then we'll have to increase the quota for every other country in the world, an action that they see as disastrous. Increasing the number of immigrants we accept from Ireland does not mean that we would also have to increase the quotas for other countries. The immigration office may or may not decide to alter quotas from other countries, but taking an action on behalf of one country does not mean that the other actions will follow. A more colorful name for this fallacy is "the camel's nose in the tent." It is based on the idea that if we let a camel stick its nose in the tent, the rest of the camel will soon follow.

11. Straw Person

A **straw person** is weak and easy to knock down. With a straw person argument, a very weak form of an opponent's argument is set up and then knocked down. It occurs when an opponent to a particular conclusion distorts the argument in support of the conclusion and substitutes one that is much weaker. For example, in a discussion about whether students should be evaluating their professors, one opponent to this idea offered this straw person argument: "You say that students' evaluations of their professors should be included in decisions about which professors we should be promoting. Well, I certainly don't think that the decision as to which professors get promoted should be made by students." Notice how the original argument that "student evaluations should be included in the decision-making process" was changed to "students should not be deciding which professors get promoted." The original argument was for student evaluations to be *part of* the criteria used in the decision-making process. This is not the same as having students actually make the decisions. In its changed form, the argument is easier to knock down, just like a straw person.

12. Part-Whole

Part-whole fallacies are flip sides of the same error. A part-whole fallacy is made whenever a speaker or writer assumes that whatever is true of the whole is also true of all of its parts, and whatever is true of the parts is also true of the whole. Consider some outstanding, prestigious university. (Are you thinking about your own school?) As a whole, the student body is highly intelligent, but it would be wrong to believe that every student who attends that university is therefore highly intelligent. Similarly, think of several brilliant scientists. Just because they are each brilliant doesn't mean that if we put them on a committee together (made a whole out of them), the committee would be brilliant. They may never agree or perhaps spend so much time impressing each other with how smart they are that no work would get done.

13. Appeals to Ignorance

The peculiar thing about **appeals to ignorance** is that they can often be used to support two or more totally different conclusions. This should be a clue to you that the reasoning involved is fallacious. In appeals to ignorance, the premise involves something we don't know. Our ignorance is being used to argue because there is no evidence to support a conclusion, the conclusion must be wrong. Our ignorance of a topic can also be used to support a conclusion by stating that because there is no evidence that contradicts it, the conclusion must be right. I have heard both sides argue this way in a debate on the existence of God. Believers have argued that because no one can prove that God doesn't exist, He therefore must exist. Nonbelievers have argued that because no one can prove that God exists, He therefore doesn't exist. The absence of evidence doesn't support any conclusion. The absence of evidence for one conclusion is not evidence for another conclusion.

14. Weak and Inappropriate Analogies

The topic of analogies was presented in Chapter 3, "The Relationship Between Thought and Language." It also appears later in the book in Chapters 9 and 10 on problem solving and creativity. Analogies are a basic thinking skill. We use analogies whenever we encounter something new and try to understand it by reference to something we already know. Although analogies can be extremely useful aids to comprehension, they can also be misused. Two objects or events are analogous when they share certain properties. When we argue with analogies, we conclude that what is true of one object or event is true of the other.

Consider the mother who decides that her child should not be given piano lessons because the child had dropped out of dance class. The mother formed the analogy that the child dropped out of one type of creative arts lessons and because dance class and piano lessons were similar in some ways, the child would also drop out of piano lessons. The child may or may not have continued with piano lessons, but it was a weak sort of analogy that formed the support for this conclusion. Dance class and piano lessons are similar in certain respects, but they also have many distinct differences. When considering an argument by analogy, it is important to consider the nature and the salience of the similarity relationship. It is possible that the child would have stuck with piano.

15. Appeals to Authority

I already introduced this fallacy in an informal way earlier in this chapter when I discussed expert credibility. Much of what we know and believe is based on what we learn from authorities. The fallacy of **appeals to authority** occurs when the authority we use to support the premises in an argument is the wrong authority.

If I wanted to sell you a stereo, it would be valid if I quoted from an article on stereos written by a professor of acoustics (who is an independent authority). It would be a fallacious appeal if I told you that Kobe Bryant called it the best stereo system he had ever seen. Thus, the fallacy is not in appealing to an authority on a topic, but to appealing to someone who is not a credible authority.

16. Incomplete Comparisons

"More doctors agree that Dopeys can give you the fastest pain relief." Advertisements like this one are so common that it's almost impossible to open a magazine without seeing one. Two different comparisons are made in this statement and both are incomplete. Whenever you see comparative terms ask yourself "more than what," "fastest compared to what?" **Incomplete comparisons** are missing the other half of the equation.

Incomplete comparisons often contain evaluative terms like "better," "safest," and, of course, "cleanest." This is a special case of considering missing components in an argument. How was "better" defined? How was it measured? By whom? Compared to what? There is no way to interpret claims like, "Washo will make your whole wash cleaner" without additional information. An ice cream store that I pass on my way to work has a large sign outside that states, "Voted the best ice cream." I presume that I am supposed to infer that their ice cream was voted the best, but by whom, compared to which other ice creams, what criteria were used to decide which was best, and how were the ice creams evaluated with these criteria? Every time you see a comparative claim, you should ask yourself these questions. If the answers aren't provided, then the comparison is incomplete, and the comparison is usually a meaningless ploy to get you to buy something.

17. Knowing the Unknowable

Sometimes we are given information that it is impossible to know. This is the fallacy of **knowing the unknowable**. Suppose you read in the newspapers that we need to increase the size of the police force because the number of unreported rapes has increased dramatically. A little alarm should go off when you read this: How can anyone know about the number of unreported rapes? I don't doubt that many rapes are not reported to the police or that this is an important issue. What is at question is the increase or decrease in the number when the actual number is unknowable. There are numerous times when sources give precise figures when such figures are impossible. Child abuse is another example. This is a tragic and important issue for society to grapple with, but estimates about the number of children involved can never be very accurate because much of it is undetected. Researchers can try to extrapolate from the number of child abuse cases that are treated in the emergency rooms of hospitals or that go to court, but there are no good methods of extending these known figures to unreported cases. An increase in the number of cases of rape or child abuse may be due to increased awareness and education about these crimes. An increase in reported cases could be associated with an increase, decrease, or no change in unreported cases. Again, there is no way we can know the unknowable.

18. False Cause

The fallacy of **false cause** is discussed more completely in Chapter 6, "Thinking as Hypothesis Testing," but it is also important to discuss in the context of reasoning fallacies. The fallacy of false cause occurs whenever someone argues that because two events occur together, or one follows the other closely in time, that one caused the other to occur. For example, consider the finding that as the number of churches increase in a city so does the number of prostitutes. It would be false to conclude that churches cause an increase in prostitution or that prostitutes cause more churches to be built. In fact, as the size of a city increases so does the number of churches and the number of prostitutes, as well as the number of schools, dry cleaners, volunteer agencies, and so on. Neither of them caused any of the others. They all resulted from a third factor—in this case, an increase in population. Of course, it is possible that one variable *did* cause the other to occur, but more than co-occurrence is needed to justify a causal claim.

19. Put Downs

Only a fool would endorse this candidate! No patriotic American would disagree! You'd have to be stupid to believe that! These are all examples of **put downs** (also known as belittling the opposition). An opposing viewpoint is belittled so that agreeing with it would put you in the class of people who are fools, or unpatriotic, or stupid. This technique is not so much a reasoning fallacy as it is an emotional appeal or dare.

20. Appeals to Tradition

"That's the way we've always done it." Anyone who has tried to change a policy has heard this sentence or its variant, "If it ain't broke, don't fix it." In **appeals to tradition**, the unstated assumption is that what exists is best. It may be true that current policy is better than some suggested change, but it also may not be true. There is nothing inherent in the fact that "that's the way we've always done it" that makes it a good or best way to accomplish an objective. One of the attitudes of a critical thinker that was presented in the first chapter is flexibility. Appeals to tradition deny the possibility that a different way may be an improvement.

21. False Charge of Fallacy

That's a fallacy! It seems that after some people learn to recognize fallacious reasoning, they then label everything that anyone says as a fallacy (Levi, 1991). Not every statement is a fallacy. The idea of critical thinking is to develop an amiable skepticism, not a cynical view that everything and everyone is false. It is important to know when to accept some statements as acceptable as it is to know when and what to question.

Distinguishing Among Opinion, Reasoned Judgment, and Fact

Compare the following three statements.

Britney Spears is a great singer.
Britney Spears is a great singer because she can sing a wider variety of songs than any other contemporary artist.

Britney Spears is a great singer with several different songs at the top of the chart and albums that have gone platinum.

In the first example, I have expressed an *opinion*. It is a simple assertion of a preference. I like it; I think it's best. No reasons were given to support the evaluation. Opinion reflects how an individual or group has assessed a position or product—e.g., "Vote for Max Lake; he's the best man for the job!"

The second example also expresses a preference, but in this example, the preference is supported by reasons. I like X because Y. This is an example of *reasoned judgment*. Other examples of reasoned judgment are provided throughout the chapter.

The third statement concerns factual claims. *Facts* have a verifiable truth value—e.g., Gravel-O's breakfast cereal has 100% of the recommended daily requirement of iron. Although I can't personally check the truth-value of these facts, a credible authority (e.g., the Food and Drug Administration) has verified these claims for me. Often, the distinction among fact, opinion, and reasoned judgment is a fine one. If we say that Gravel-O's is a good cereal because it has 100% of the recommended daily requirement of iron, this is a reasoned judgment based, in part, on the unstated assumption that it is good to eat cereals that contain 100% of the recommended daily requirement of iron. The distinction becomes even more difficult when you recall that opinions can serve as the premises (reasons) in an argument. Thus, when I say that Gravel-O's is a good cereal because I like its nutty taste, I have a reason to support my conclusion. If I were to add that Gravel-O's is a good cereal because I like its nutty taste and it supplies all of my iron needs for the day, the strength of my argument is increased.

"Pure" facts that are untainted by opinion are often hard to find. Take for example, your daily newspaper. Although news reporters are obligated to provide readers with facts, their opinions certainly color what they report and how they report it. Compare the way two different newspapers cover the same story. One newspaper could make it the headline on page one, thus making it important news that will be read by many, whereas the other could place it in an inside section in smaller print, thus making sure that fewer people will read the story. Look at the words used to convey the same story. A quiet night in Poland during a period of martial law could be described as "Poland Enforces Martial Law" or as "All Is Quiet in Poland." Both of these headlines could be factually correct, yet they clearly convey different ideas about Polish life.

Most news media (news magazines, newspapers, television news) are biased toward providing information that "sells." The news media often treat complex issues in a very simplistic manner with a heavy emphasis on controversies because they are more interesting than agreements. The usual rules of scientific evidence and reasoning often are abandoned in the news media where deadlines determine the news you get and interest value can drive content. The distinction between fact and opinion is becoming increasingly difficult to discern. As King (1994) notes, television programs like *Hard Copy* are supposedly "reenactments" of real events, but we never know how close the story is to reality. Add some "partially fictionalized" accounts of gruesome real-life murders and the filming of actual police arrests for entertainment shows, and the situation gets even messier. I made this point earlier when I discussed the partially fictionalized (or at least highly biased) version of the movie about the JFK assassination. The fuzzy distinction between the real and unreal gets even more difficult now that "virtual reality" computer programs are available that rival "real reality." It is a brave, new world that we are entering—one that makes critical thinking more necessary than ever.

You may be thinking that at least one source of honest facts is your textbooks. Although it is usually safe to assume that text authors do not set out deliberately to mislead students, the facts that they report are also subject to interpretation. Easily quantified and verifiable information such as the number of soldiers sent to a South American country or the size of the national deficit are probably correct or as close to correct as possible, presuming that there has been no deliberate attempt to lie. Other facts such as the sequence of events and their importance in causing a war, or strategies at political conventions, or poverty in America need to be interpreted by text authors who will decide how to describe them. The words they use, the events included or omitted, and the amount of information given, all contribute to the "factual" information that is printed. Personal bias will, of course, influence the way the ideas are presented.

It has been said that there is never just one war fought. Each side has its own version, and rarely do they agree. Unfortunately, there is always fighting somewhere around the world so that you can verify this statement for yourself. It is not unusual for each side to claim that the other fired first, or for both sides to claim victory in a battle. Obviously, in the absence of verifiable truth there is no way to know which, if either, side is presenting the facts. As before, the best way to assess the quality of the information provided is to consider the credibility of the reporter. I would prefer a report from an independent third party with first-hand and direct knowledge and appropriate credentials to a report from spokespersons from either of the sides involved in a dispute.

Advertisements make extensive use of opinions dressed up as fact. Consider the advertisements for headache remedies. Often they will show an attractive man in a white laboratory coat, obviously selected to portray a physician. He tells you that, "Speedy works fast on headache pain." Although this may seem like a fact, it is an opinion. "Fast" is a vague term, and therefore it is a matter of judgment. If the appropriate tests with a large number of people had shown that, on the average, Speedy brings pain relief in 20 minutes, this information would be a fact. If you are in doubt as to whether information is fact or opinion, check for vague or evaluative terms (fast, better, lovelier, etc.), and ask yourself how the evaluative term was defined and what type of test was conducted to support the claim. This topic is covered in more detail in Chapter 6.

Visual Arguments

He who controls images controls everything.

> —Robert Townsend (quoted in Beilensen & Jackson, 1992, p. 15)

We are living in an increasingly visual society where we get more of our information from visual displays than from words. Television is a major source of information and entertainment for many people. The average television viewer will see approximately 30,000 commercials *every* year. The message in each is mostly the same—whatever your problem is (e.g., rough elbows, teeth that do not dazzle with sparkling whiteness, overweight), you can buy a product that will solve it (Postman & Powers, 1992). Much of the persuasive message in television commercials is conveyed through the pictures that we see, often with the accompanying dialogue being of secondary importance. Images are also important in magazines, newspapers, video games, the Internet, and on billboards.

The effects of visual images are more difficult to gauge because they are often subtle. Consider a sample of cigarette advertisements. Smoking is linked to beauty, glamour, youth, health, and popularity (Kidd, 1991). A popular theme in visual cigarette advertisements is horses and the "great" outdoors. We are shown beautiful, happy people who are smoking and enjoying the good life. The horses suggest ruggedness and an unrestrained independence—just the sort of person who won't be swayed with facts that link smoking with many diseases. Careful market research pinpoints specific markets for cigarette smokers and designs images to appeal to market segments, for example, young women, with no more than a high school education, who wear jeans, and work at blue-collar jobs. The images in these ads are very different from those targeted at more educated women, who are shown reading and talking while they smoke.

Visual images are used effectively in political campaigns. Consider this description of the television advertisements that were used in a "race" for the governor in California. Wilson, the Republican incumbent, used ads that made him appear to be a leader who should not be blamed for California's woes, and Brown, the Democratic challenger, used ads in which she appeared to be a bright solution to California's problems. In Brown's television ads, California is shot in black-and-white scenes of urban decay—only Brown appears in color. By contrast, Wilson shows scenes of serial rapists and stealthy bands of illegal immigrants with Wilson's somber face appearing to be taking care of these grave problems.

Visual images can be powerful determinants of public opinion and policy. I cannot forget the pictures of starving children in Somalia, which eloquently spoke of the dire need to send U.S. troops to assist with this disaster or the image of a dead U.S. serviceman being dragged through the dusty streets of Somalia. Which image moved the United States to promptly leave Somalia? What if the images had been different? Suppose that, instead of the dead peacekeeper being dragged through the street, the media had shown pictures of Somalians receiving food and clean water—people who were alive because of the peacekeepers? The images we are shown have profound effects on how we think and feel.

Figure 5.2 shows some old propagandist images that were popular in Russia in the early and mid-20th century. Note the image of the fat, rich capitalist. His piglike face and bloated body are deliberately unattractive, and his sea of gold depicts his solitary concern with material wealth. Look also at the Soviet Army recruiter with the outstretched, pointing finger, urging Russians to volunteer. Compare him to the military recruiting posters that were popular in the United States during the same time period, a time when we all knew that "Uncle Sam wants you."

Often an image can speak more persuasively for a point of view than even the most eloquent prose. The images in Figure 5.3 were all posters from China, Germany, France, and Cuba. You don't need to be able to read the words to understand the message. Cognitive psychologists know that we have very good picture memory—a fact that is exploited in these posters. Oftentimes we do not scrutinize the images that bombard of us with the same care that we use for verbal arguments. Pay attention to the images you encounter throughout the day and consider how each is influencing what and how you think. Images are often used as nonverbal communication that reinforce stereotypes. There are women clad in bikinis in beer advertisements, images of housewives worrying about their laundry, images of African Americans smoking "uptown" cigarettes. These images are so ubiquitous that we often take them for granted. Look at and think about the images you see. Are some groups usually depicted in menial jobs on television or in advertisements?

FIG. 5.2. Images of persuasion. The piglike man surrounded with his gold was designed to represent the capitalist. It was a common image during the years when Soviet Communists needed to keep the idea that "capitalism is bad" alive. By contrast, the Soviet recruiter has his arms open to welcome all to the great cause. He bears an uncanny similarity in pose and nonverbal gestures to the American recruiting poster where we were told that "Uncle Sam Wants You."

Wer Burgerblatter liest wird blind und taub. Weg mit den verdummungsbandagen!

(Whoever reads bourgeois newspapers becomes blind and deaf. Away with the stultifying bandages!) This image is by John Heatfield, a young German, who in 1930, adopted the English-sounding name as protest against the anti-English sentiments in Germany at that time. The young Heartfield was influenced by the soldiers on the western front, who unable to get their reports passed military censors, turned to pasting photographs together in order to relate the horror of the battlefield to their friends and relatives back home. Inspired by this as well as the collage of the cubists, Heartfield and his close friend and fellow artist George Grosz, invented photomontage.

Rene Mederos, 1967
This Cuban poster shows the crushed hat of Uncle Sam as Cubans celebrated the defeat of the United States in Viet Nam.

人不犯我．我不犯人．人若犯我．我必犯人。

When China and the Soviet Union split in the 1950s, China was left without any allies. Soviet military forces were close to its borders. The dominant message was to keep foreign influences out of China.

Zhou Yuwe, 1986. "Carry out family planning. Implement the basic national policy."
In this poster, we see the message that China's strong one-child policy is on the road to a modern Westernized world. The woman and child do not seem to have Chinese features.

Honore Daumier, "La Caricature" (1832)
Daumier was sentenced to 6 months in prison for publishing this satirical drawing of King Louis-Philipe.
(from http://www.cd.sc.chu.es/FileRoom/documents/Case247/daumeier.html)

Fig. 5.3. These images originally were posters from Germany, China, Cuba, and France. Each is a visual argument—depicting a conclusion (and implied reasons) with images.

Who is used to display high fashion and who is depicted in warnings about criminal activity? It is only when you become consciously aware of the images you are viewing, that you can think critically about the visual arguments you are receiving.

How to Change Beliefs

We are constantly surrounded by individuals and groups who want to change what we think and how we act. Nearly every social interaction involves persuasion (Siegel, 1991). Advertising agencies want us to buy whatever product they are selling; political candidates want our votes; the beef council wants us to eat more beef. The list is endless. Some of these beliefs and actions are beneficial, but others are not. One of the best ways to understand the dynamics of changing beliefs is to consider the issues from the perspective of someone who wants to change the beliefs of someone else. You can use this knowledge to change beliefs or to resist change. The following list is loosely adapted from a summary of the attitude change literature.

1. Provide a credible source for the information you are presenting. The source of information should be a person or agency with the necessary expertise in the field who is independent with respect to the issue. Additional requirements for assessing the credibility of an information source are provided in this chapter.
2. Anticipate counterarguments, raise them, and provide counterexamples. This is a good technique when debating an issue before an audience. It can leave the opposition with few points to make. As you know, counterarguments weaken the support for a conclusion. This technique allows you to weaken the counterarguments.
3. Don't appear one-sided, especially when the audience may be predisposed to the opposite side. The willingness to use qualifiers and to consider counterarguments makes your position appear more credible.
4. Be direct. Tell your audience what to believe. By explicitly stating the conclusion, you eliminate the possibility that the audience will arrive at a different conclusion or not "see" the support for the conclusion that you are advocating.
5. Encourage discussion and public commitment. These variables have not been discussed in this chapter, although they appear in other places in the book. The discussion allows the audience to generate reasons and to "own" them or view them as reasons that they provided. Public commitment is a powerful motivator. If someone signs a document or speaks in favor of a position, a host of psychological mechanisms are brought into play. It is a kind of a promise to believe or act in a certain way. This technique was used extensively by Caesar Chavez and others in their attempt to get consumers to boycott grapes. (The motivation for the boycott was to protest the use of certain pesticides on the grapes.) Several years ago, I had the honor of having lunch with Caesar Chavez and a small group of students and college administrators. At lunch, he asked us all to stand up and pledge that we would not eat grapes until the growers agreed to stop using certain pesticides. The public commitment was more effective than a simple nod of the head to indicate agreement would have been. A restaurant owner in Los Angeles has borrowed this technique. A big problem for many restaurants is the large number of people who make reservations and then neither show up for the reservation nor call to cancel it. In the past, when customers called to make reservations, they were told,

"Please call if you have to cancel the reservations." Now, the person who takes the reservation asks, "Will you please call if you have to cancel the reservations?" The customer needs to make a commitment to call—and the simple act of committing seems to make a difference. The number of customers who do not cancel their reservations when they are not keeping them is greatly reduced. What a difference two words can make.

6. Repeat the conclusion and the reasons that support the conclusion several times. People prefer positions that are familiar to them. You can make the same points in several different ways. Repetition is a useful aid in recall. Thus reasons that are easily remembered (i.e., more available in memory) are more readily used to assess the strength of an argument. (The potent effects of repeated exposure are presented in Chapter 8, "Decision Making.")

7. Provide as many reasons to support the conclusion as is feasible. As you already know, one way to increase the strength of an argument is by increasing the number of reasons that support it.

8. The message should be easy to comprehend. People are negatively affected by messages they find incomprehensible (Fiske & Taylor, 1984).

9. You could use any of the 21 common fallacies presented in this chapter. But be wary, they are examples of unsound reasoning. If you want to persuade someone, your reasoning should be sound. Shoddy reasoning is detectable, and if detected, it could (and should) destroy your credibility.

10. Use vivid images that will be difficult to forget and be sure that they make your point.

APPLYING THE FRAMEWORK

Let's consider the steps in applying the general framework for thinking to analyzing arguments.

1. What Is the Goal?

You'll want to use the skills for analyzing arguments anytime you encounter attempts to persuade you or you attempt to persuade someone that a particular conclusion is either true or likely to be true. Once you become accustomed to "looking for arguments" (in its technical meaning, not in its everyday meaning) and looking at reasons, you'll be surprised how frequently you are bombarded by advertisements, political claims, and other attempts to "change your point of view." You will also need to use the information in this chapter when you make your own arguments.

2. What Is Known?

This question is about starting points in the thinking process. In analyzing arguments, you begin with statements and determine if they contain an argument. The statements are then evaluated to assess the quality of the argument. The process proceeds by identifying the conclusion and premises and systematically applying the steps of argument analysis in order to reach the goal of making a determination about how good the argument is. When you make an argument, begin with the reasons and counterarguments. Assemble the reasoning so that it supports a conclusion.

3. Which Thinking Skill or Skills Will Get You to Your Goal?

The skills of analyzing arguments involve the sequential application of "tests of goodness"—how acceptable are the premises, how much support do they provide for the conclusion, and which and how many components are missing? At a minimum, you should be able to apply the three criteria for sound arguments to any set of statements. The skills involved in analyzing arguments are ordered, with less emphasis on selecting the correct skill than on the systematic application of the entire set.

It is almost as important to be able to say why an argument is unsound as it is to be able to identify unsound arguments. You should be able to recognize the 21 fallacies presented in this chapter and explain how each of them violates one of the principles of sound arguments.

The following skills for analyzing arguments were presented in this chapter. If you are unsure about how to use any of these skills, be sure to reread the section in which it is discussed.

- Identifying arguments.
- Diagramming the structure of an argument.
- Evaluating premises for their acceptability.
- Examining the credibility of an information source.
- Determining the consistency, relevance to the conclusion, and adequacy in the way premises support a conclusion.
- Remembering to consider missing components by assuming a different perspective.
- Assessing the overall strength of an argument.
- Recognizing, labeling, and explaining what is wrong with each of the 21 fallacies that was presented.
- Recognizing differences among opinion, reasoned judgment, and fact.
- Understanding how visual arguments can be effective.
- Judging your own arguments for their strength.

4. Have You Reached Your Goal?

This is a particularly important question in analyzing arguments because one of the steps involves considering components that are not there. Have you consciously tried to restructure the argument using an opposite perspective? Are you able to make an overall judgment about the strength of the argument? Have you arrived at a sound conclusion? It is important to review the way in which you weighted the supporting premises. Often a decision to weigh a premise as either weak or moderate will have very different effects on your overall assessment of the strength of the argument.

CHAPTER SUMMARY

1. An argument is an attempt to convince the reader (or listener) that a particular conclusion is true based on the reasons presented.

2. All arguments must have at least one conclusion and one premise (reason). Arguments may also have assumptions, qualifiers, and counterarguments.

3. Arguments have structures that can be identified and diagrammed.

4. Sound (good) arguments meet three criteria: The premises are acceptable and consistent; the premises provide support for the conclusion by being relevant to the conclusion and are sufficiently strong; and missing components of the argument (e.g., assumptions, counterarguments, qualifiers, premises, and rival conclusions) have been considered.

5. When analyzing the strength of an argument, the amount of support each premise supplies to the conclusion is weighed along with the negative effects of counterarguments. Missing components are made explicit and are considered along with the stated components.

6. It is often necessary to assess the credibility of a source of information when deciding on the acceptability of a premise. There are important differences between experts for issues of fact and experts for issues of value.

7. People like to believe that their beliefs and actions are "reasoned"; however, most people are not sensitive to poor or weak reasoning. Unfortunately, there is a general preference for explanations that "make sense" over conclusions that are justified by available data. Critical thinkers need to understand the importance of data and value data-based conclusions.

8. There is a widespread bias to assign greater importance to reasons that support a conclusion that we favor than to reasons that run counter to a conclusion that we favor. This bias can be reduced by listing reasons and consciously deciding how strongly they support or run counter to a conclusion.

9. A critical part of the analysis of arguments is the consideration of missing parts and misleading statements.

10. Arguments of all sorts have been used to justify genocide and other versions of "ethnic cleansing." The techniques presented here could prevent future horrors, if people are willing to invest the time and hard work in analyzing arguments.

11. Twenty-one common techniques of propaganda were presented. Most can be categorized as types of unsound reasoning in which emotional appeals are often substituted for reasons.

12. A distinction was made among the terms "opinion," "reasoned judgment," and "fact." An opinion is an unsupported statement of preference. Reasoned judgment is a belief that is based on the consideration of premises that support that belief. Facts have a verifiable true value. It is often difficult to discern the difference among these terms in real-life settings.

13. Visual images are used to persuade. Strong images that are difficult to forget can support or refute a conclusion.

14. The beliefs of others can be changed with sound and unsound reasoning. Beware of attempts to manipulate your beliefs with shoddy reasoning techniques.

TERMS TO KNOW

Check your understanding of the concepts presented in this chapter by reviewing their definitions. If you find that you're having difficulty with any term, be sure to reread the section where it is discussed.

Argument. An argument consists of one or more statements that are used to provide support for a conclusion.

Conclusion. The belief or statement that the writer or speaker is advocating.

Reasons. The bases for believing that a conclusion is true or probably true. Note: This word may be singular or plural as there may be one or more reasons for a conclusion. When we reason (singular only), we are following rules for determining if an argument is sound.

Premises. The formal term for the statements that support a conclusion.

Premise Indicators. Key words that often (but not always) signal that the statement or statements that follow them are premises.

Conclusion Indicators. Key words that often (but not always) signal that the statement or statements that follow them are conclusions.

Assumptions. In an argument, an assumption is a statement for which no proof or evidence is offered. They may be stated or implied.

Subarguments. Arguments that are used to build the main argument in an extended passage.

Main point. The principal argument in an extended passage.

Qualifier. A constraint or restriction on the conclusion.

Counterargument. Statements that refute or weaken a particular conclusion.

Statement. A phrase or sentence for which it makes sense to ask the question, "Is it true or false?" Questions, commands, and exclamations are *not* statements.

Convergent Structures. A type of argument in which two or more premises support the same conclusion.

Chained (or Linked) Structures. Argument types in which the conclusion of one subargument becomes the premise of a second argument.

Acceptable. A standard for assessing the quality of a premise. A premise is acceptable when it is true or when we can reasonably believe that it is true.

Consistent. A standard for assessing the quality of an argument. When the premises that support a conclusion are not contradictory, they are consistent.

Adequate Grounds. A standard for assessing the quality of an argument. Occurs when the premises provide good support for a conclusion.

Sound Argument. Meets three criteria: (a) Acceptable and consistent premises, (b) premises are relevant and provide sufficient support for the conclusion, and (c) missing components are considered and evaluated.

Rationalizing. A biased analysis of an argument so that a preferred conclusion will be judged as acceptable or a nonpreferred conclusion will be judged as unacceptable. The process of rationalizing is usually not conscious.

Propaganda. Information presented by proselytizers of a doctrine or belief. The objective is to get the reader or listener to endorse the belief.

Fallacies. Unsound reasoning techniques that are used to change how people think.

Guilt by Association. The propaganda technique of associating a position or person with an undesirable position or person in order to create a negative impression.

Virtue by Association. The propaganda technique of associating a position or person with a desirable position or person in order to create a favorable impression. Compare with guilt by association.

Arguments Against the Person. A form of propaganda that attacks the people who support a cause and not the cause itself.

Appeals to Pity. A propaganda technique that asks for your compassion instead of appealing to your reason.

Popularity. A propaganda technique in which the only reason for the conclusion is that it is endorsed by "everyone."

Testimonials. An appeal in which the sole support for a conclusion is someone's unsupported opinion.

False Dichotomy. An argument in which two possible conclusions or courses of action are presented when there are multiple other possibilities. (Also known as *black or white fallacy*.)

Appeals to Pride or Snobbery. The use of praise or flattery to get its recipient to agree with a position.

Card Stacking. A propaganda technique that omits important information that might support an unfavored view.

Circular Reasoning. An argument structure in which the premise is a restatement of the conclusion.

Slippery Slope. Counterargument for a conclusion in which the premise consists of the idea that because certain events lie along some continuum it is not possible to take an action without affecting all the events on the continuum.

Continuum. Fallacy of the continuum is the same as slippery slope.

Straw Person. A type of propaganda technique in which an opponent to a conclusion distorts the argument that supports the conclusion by substituting a weaker argument.

Appeals to Ignorance. An argument in which the premise involves something that is unknown.

Appeals to Authority. Reliance on an inappropriate authority in formulating conclusions.

Incomplete Comparisons. Using evaluative terms like "better," "faster," or "cleaner" without indicating the two items that are being compared.

Knowing the Unknowable. Fallacy in which numbers are provided for events that cannot be quantified.

False Cause. Fallacy in which one event is said to have caused the other because they occur together.

Put Downs. Belittling an opposing point of view so that it would be difficult for a listener to agree with it.

Appeals to Tradition. A propaganda technique that utilizes the reason that what already exists is best.

6

Thinking as Hypothesis Testing

Contents

Suppose that the following is true: You are seriously addicted to heroin and you have two choices of treatment programs.

Program 1: This program is run by former heroin addicts. Your therapist will be a recovered addict who is the same age as you. The literature about this program states that among those who stay with the program for at least 1 year, the success rate is very high (80%). One of the biggest advantages of this program is that your therapist knows what it's like to be seriously addicted and can offer you insights from his own recovery.

Program 2: The therapists in this program have studied the psychology and biology of heroin addiction. The success rate that they provide is much lower than that provided for Program 1 (30%), but the percentage of successes is based on everyone who enters treatment. Your therapist has never been addicted to heroin, but has studied various treatment options.

This is an important decision for you. Which do you choose?

UNDERSTANDING HYPOTHESIS TESTING

Research is an intellectual approach to an unsolved problem, and its function is to seek the truth.

—Leedy (1981, p. 7)

Much of our thinking is like the scientific method of **hypothesis testing**. A **hypothesis** is a set of beliefs about the nature of the world; it is usually a belief about a relationship between two or more variables. In order to understand the world around us, we accumulate observations, formulate beliefs or hypotheses (singular is hypothesis), and then observe if our hypotheses are confirmed or disconfirmed. Thus, hypothesis testing is one way of finding out about the "way the world works." Formulating hypotheses and making systematic observations that could confirm or disconfirm them is the same method that scientists use when they want to understand events in their academic domain. Thus, when thinking is done in this manner, it has much in common with the experimental methods used by scientists.

Explanation, Prediction, and Control

All . . . by nature desire knowledge.

—Aristotle (cited in Bartlett, 1992, p. 77)

There is a basic need to understand events in life. How many times have you asked yourself questions like, "Why did my good friends get divorced when they seemed perfect for each other?" or "How can we understand why the son of the U.S. surgeon general, the chief doctor in the United States, is addicted to illegal drugs?" When we try to answer questions like these we often function as an "intuitive scientist." Like the scientist, we have our own theories about the causes of social and physical events. It is important to be able to explain why people react in certain ways (e.g., He's a bigot. She's tired and cranky after work.), to predict the results of our actions (e.g., If I don't study, I'll fail. If I wear designer clothes, people will think I'm cool.), and to control some of the events in our environment (e.g., In order to get a good job in business, I'll have to do well in my accounting course.).

The goal of hypothesis testing is to make accurate predictions about the portion of the world we're dealing with (Holland, Holyoak, Nisbett, & Thagard, 1986).

In order to survive and function with maximum efficiency, we must reduce the uncertainty in our environment. One way to reduce uncertainty is to observe sequences of events with the goal of determining *predictive* relationships. Children, for example, may learn that an adult will appear whenever they cry; your dog may learn that when he stands near the kitchen door, you will let him out; and teenagers may learn that their parents will become angry when they come home late. These are important predictive relationships because they reduce the uncertainty in the environment and allow us to exercise some control over our lives. The process that we use in determining these relationships is the same one that is used when medical researchers discover that cancer patients will go into remission following chemotherapy or that longevity is associated with certain lifestyles. Because the processes are the same, some of the technical concepts in scientific methods are applicable to practical everyday thought.

INDUCTIVE AND DEDUCTIVE METHODS

Inductive reasoning is a major aspect of cognitive development and plays an important role in both the development of a system of logical thought processes and in the acquisition of new information.

—Pellegrino and Goldman (1983, p. 143)

Sometimes a distinction is made between inductive and deductive methods of hypothesis testing (see Chapter 4 on the development of reasoning skills). In the **inductive method**, you observe events and then devise a hypothesis about the events you observed. For example, you might notice that Armaund, a retired man whom you know, likes to watch wrestling on television. Then you note that Minnie and Sue Ann, who are retired older adults, also like to watch wrestling on television. On the basis of these observations, you would hypothesize (invent a hypothesis or explanation) that older people like to watch wrestling. In this way, you would work from your observations to your hypothesis. The inductive method is sometimes described as "going from the specific to the general." In an excellent book entitled, *Induction* (Holland et al., 1986), the authors argue that the inductive process is the primary way in which we learn about the nature of the world. They state, "The study of induction, then, is the study of how knowledge is modified through use" (p. 5).

In the **deductive method**, you begin with a hypothesis that you believe to be true and then make systematic observations to see if your hypothesis is correct. Suppose that you are considering the hypothesis that old people like to watch wrestling. After developing this hypothesis, you'd look around to find out if there are many older people who like to watch televised wrestling. The deductive method is sometimes described as "going from the general to the specific." You would also want to compare the group of older people to a group of young adults to see if young adults watch wrestling less often than those who are older. After all, if almost everyone liked to watch wrestling, then there would be nothing unusual in the finding that old people like it. When you begin with a hypothesis and then collect evidence that would confirm or disconfirm it, you are using the deductive method. A critical component in hypothesis testing is that you also search for disconfirming evidence, a theme that seems to be repeated in almost every chapter in this book.

Although a distinction is usually made between these two types of reasoning, in real life they are just different phases of the hypothesis testing method. Often people observe events, formulate hypotheses, observe events again, reformulate hypotheses, and collect even more observations. The question of whether the observations or the hypothesis comes first is moot because our hypotheses determine what we choose to observe, and our observations determine what our hypotheses will be. It's like the perennial question of which came first, the chicken or the egg. Each process is dependent on the other for its existence. In this way, observing and hypothesizing recycle, with the observations changing the hypotheses and the hypotheses changing what gets observed.

If you are a Sherlock Holmes fan, you'll recognize this process as one that was developed into a fine art by this fictional detective. He would astutely note clues about potential suspects. For example, Sherlock Holmes could remember that the butler had a small mustard-yellow stain on his pants when it is well known that you don't serve mustard with wild goose, which was the main course at dinner that evening. He would use such clues to devise hypotheses like, "the butler must have been in the field where wild mustard plants grow." The master sleuth would then check for other clues that would be consistent or inconsistent with this hypothesis. He might check the butler's boots for traces of the red clay soil that surrounds the field in question. After a circuitous route of hypotheses and observations, Sherlock Holmes would announce, "The butler did it." When called on to explain how he reached his conclusion, he would utter his most famous reply, "It's elementary, my dear Watson."

Many of our beliefs about the world were obtained with the use of inductive and deductive methods, much like the great Sherlock Holmes. We use the principles of inductive and deductive reasoning to generate and evaluate beliefs. Holmes was invariably right in the conclusions he drew. Unfortunately, it is only in the realm of fiction that mistakes are never made because conclusions that result from inductive reasoning can never be known with absolute certainty. Let's examine the components of the hypothesis-testing process to see where mistakes can occur.

Operational Definitions

Scientific reasoning and everyday reasoning both require evidence-based justification of beliefs, or the coordination of theory and evidence.

—Kuhn (1993, p. 74)

An **operational definition** tells us how to recognize and measure the concept that you're interested in. For example, if you believe that successful women are paid high salaries, then you will have to define "successful" and "high salary" in ways that will allow you to identify who is successful and who receives a high salary. If you've already read Chapter 3, "The Relationship Between Thought and Language," then you should recognize the need for operational definitions as being the same as the problem of vagueness. You'd need to provide some statement like, "Successful individuals are respected by their peers and are famous in their field of work." You will find that it is frequently difficult to provide good operational definitions for terms. I can think of several people who are not at all famous, but who are successful by their own and other definitions. If you used the operational definition that requires fame as a component of success, then you would conclude that homemakers, skilled craftspeople, teachers, nurses, and others could not be "successful" based on this definition. Thus, this would seem to be an unsatisfactory operational definition. Suppose, for purposes of illustration, that this is our operational definition to classify people into "successful" and "unsuccessful" categories.

How would you operationally define "paid a high salary"? Suppose you decided on, "earns at least $1,000 per week." Once these terms are operationally defined, you could go around finding out whether successful and unsuccessful women differ in how much they are paid. Operational definitions are important. Whenever you hear people talking about "our irresponsible youth," "knee-jerk liberals," "bleeding hearts," "rednecks," "reactionaries," "fascists," or "feminists," ask them to define their terms operationally. You may find that the impact of their argument is diminished when they are required to be precise about their terms.

Many arguments hinge on operational definitions. For example, consider the debate over whether homosexuality is a mental disorder. The issue turns on the answer to operational definitions. What defines a "mental disorder"? Who gets to decide how "mental disorder" should be defined? Does homosexuality possess the defining characteristics of a mental disorder? The vitriolic arguments about whether abortion is murder can be transformed into calmer arguments over what is the appropriate definition of murder, and again the more important question, who is the right authority to define what constitutes murder. Thus, with critical thinking, explosive divisions over issues like abortion will not be resolved, but they will be changed in their character as people consider what is really being argued about. When you use operational definitions, you avoid the problems of ambiguity and vagueness. Try, for example, to write operational definitions for the following terms: love, prejudice, motivation, good grades, sickness, athletic, beautiful, and maturity.

Independent and Dependent Variables

A **variable** is any measurable characteristic that can take on more than one value. Examples of variables are gender (female and male), height, political affiliation (Republican, Democrat, Communist, etc.), handedness (right, left, ambidextrous), and attitudes toward traditional sex roles (could range from extremely negative to extremely positive). When we test hypotheses, we begin by choosing the variables of interest.

In the opening scenario of this chapter, you were asked to determine which of the two programs would more likely help you kick your heroin habit. In this example, there are two variables—type of treatment, which is the **independent variable** or the one that is under your control (Program 1 and Program 2) and recovery, which is the **dependent variable** or the one that you believe will change as a result of the different treatments (you will either [a] recover from the addiction, or [b] you won't recover from it). You want to select the program that is most likely to help you to recover. In the jargon of hypothesis testing, you want to know which level of the independent variable will have a beneficial effect on the dependent variable.

The next step in the hypothesis testing process is to define the variables operationally. Suppose we decide to define "recovery" as staying drug-free for at least two years and "not recovering" as staying drug-free for less than two years, which would include never being drug-free. It is important to think critically about operational definitions for your variables. If they are not stated in precise terms, the conclusions you draw from your study may be wrong.

Measurement Sensitivity

When we measure something, we systematically assign a number to it for the purposes of quantification. Someone who is taller than you are is assigned a higher number of inches of height than you are. If not, the concept of height would be meaningless.

When we think as scientists and collect information in order to understand the world, we need to consider how we measure our variables. For example, suppose you believe that love is like a fever, and that people in love have fever-like symptoms. To find out if this is true, you could conduct an experiment, taking temperatures from people who are in love and comparing your results to the temperatures of people who are not in love. How will you measure temperature? Suppose that you decide to use temperature headbands that register body temperature with a band placed on the forehead. Suppose further that these bands measure temperature to the nearest degree (e.g., 98°, 99°, 100°, etc.). If being in love does raise your body temperature, but only raises it one-half of a degree, you might never know this if you used headband thermometers. Headband thermometers just wouldn't be sensitive enough to register the small increment in body temperature. **Sensitive measures** can detect small changes in the variable you want to measure. You would incorrectly conclude that love doesn't raise body temperatures, when in fact it may have. As far as I know, this experiment has never been done, but it is illustrative of the need for sensitive measurement in this and similar situations.

POPULATIONS AND SAMPLES

People make innumerable decisions daily about other people that affect their lives and careers. These decisions are inevitably fraught with errors of judgment that reflect ignorance, personal biases, or stereotypes.

—W. Grant Dahlstrom (1993, p. 393)

In deciding which heroin treatment program to enter, or for that matter, which college to attend or which job to accept, you are making a bet about the future, which necessarily involves uncertainty. Hypothesis-testing principles are used to reduce uncertainty. We cannot eliminate uncertainty, but we can use the principles of hypothesis testing to help us make the best choice. In the example at the beginning of the chapter, you would have to examine and evaluate information about the success rate of both programs. You would then use this information to make your decision.

The group that we want to know about is called a **population**. Because we obviously can't study every heroin addict to determine which program has more successes, we need to study a subset of this population. A subset of a population is called a **sample**. In this example, all of the people who entered each of the programs constitute the sample. A **random sample** is a sample in which everyone in the population is equally likely to be in the sample.

Biased and Unbiased Samples

We want our sample to be representative of our population. To be representative, the addicts in our sample would need to be both female and male, from all socioeconomic levels, all intellectual levels, rural and urban areas, and so on, assuming that heroin addicts come from all of these demographic groups. We need **representative samples** so that we can generalize our results and decide, on average, that one program is more successful than the other. **Generalization** refers to using the results obtained with a sample to infer that similar results would be obtained from the population, if everyone in the population had been measured (Heit, 2000). Generalizations are valid only if the sample is representative of the population.

What happens when the sample is not representative of the population? Suppose that one program is very expensive and one is county-run to serve the poor. These are examples of **biased samples**. Because they are not representative or unbiased, you could not use these samples to draw conclusions about the population of all heroin addicts. Far too often, mistakes occur because a sample was biased. One of the biggest fiascoes in sampling history probably occurred in 1936 when the *Literary Digest* mailed over 10 million straw ballots to people's homes in order to predict the winner of the presidential election that was to be held that year (Kimble, 1978). The results from this large sample were clear-cut: The next president would be Alf Landon. What, you don't remember learning about President Landon? I'm sure that you don't because Franklin Delano Roosevelt was elected president of the United States that year. What went wrong? The problem was in how the *Literary Digest* sampled voters. They mailed ballots to subscribers of their literary magazine, to people listed in the phone book, and to automobile owners. Remember, this was 1936 and only the affluent belonged to the select group of people who subscribed to literary magazines, or had phones, or owned automobiles. They failed to sample the large number of poorer voters, many of whom voted for Roosevelt, not Landon. Because of biased sampling, they could not generalize their results to the voting patterns of the population. Even though they sampled a large number of voters, the results were wrong because they sampled in a biased way.

It is often not easy to recognize the profound effect that biased sampling can have on the information that we receive. For example, phone-in polls are very popular, probably because someone makes money from the phone calls. Suppose that a phone-in poll shows that 75% of the people who responded to a question about the death penalty were opposed to it. What can we conclude from this poll? Absolutely nothing! Polls of this sort are called *slops*, which stands for selected listener opinion polls and also describes their worth. Only people with extreme views on a topic will take the time and expense to call in their opinions. Even though these polls are usually preceded with warnings like "this is a nonscientific survey," the announcer then goes on to present meaningless results as though they could be used to gauge public opinion.

Another pitfall in sampling is the possibility of **confounding**. Confounds confuse the interpretation of results because their influence is not easily separated from the influence of the independent variable. Because patients in these two hypothetical heroin treatment programs differ systematically in more than one way—that is Program 1 provides peer counseling and the addicts in this program are very wealthy, whereas addicts in Program 2 get a different type of treatment and they are very poor—we cannot determine if any differences in recovery rate are due to the type of treatment or income levels of the patients. Because you can't separate the effect of type of treatment and income, you could not use these results to decide which treatment is more successful.

Usually, scientists use **convenience samples**. They study a group of people who are readily available. The most frequently used subjects in psychology experiments are college students and rats. The extent to which you can generalize from these samples depends on the research question. If you want to understand how the human visual system works, college students should be useful as subjects, especially if you want to know about young, healthy eyes. If, on the other hand, you want to understand sex-role stereotyping or career aspirations in adults, college students would not be a representative sample because college students tend to be less stereotyped and more career-focused than other adults. In this case, you could only generalize about college students.

In a recent election in California, there was much debate over the issue of establishing a voucher system as a means of paying for K–12 education. As you may know, some people believe that education would improve if parents received vouchers in an amount that is equal to what the state pays to educate a child in the public schools. The parents could then use this voucher to select any school that they deemed best for their children. This is a complex issue as proponents argue that the competition would improve all schools, and opponents argue that wealthy parents would supplement the voucher and send their children to private schools, whereas the poor parents would have to use the vouchers at cheaper and inferior schools. I do not want to debate the issue of vouchers here, but I do want to repeat an advertisement that was continually seen during the pre-election period. It went something like this:

> The public schools in California are doing a poor job at educating our children. Did you know that the California high school students score much lower than high school students from Mississippi on the college entrance examinations?

There are many ways the thinking in this advertisement could be criticized (including the obvious slur on the state of Mississippi), but for the purpose of this discussion consider only the nature of the samples that are being compared. Only students who are planning on attending college take the college entrance examinations. A much greater proportion of high school students in California take these examinations than those in Mississippi. Although I don't know what the actual figures are, suppose that the top 40% of California high school graduates take these exams but only the top 10% of Mississippi high school graduates take these exams. Can you see why you would expect Mississippi students to score higher because of the bias in sampling? There are other reasons why we might expect these results, which do not relate to the quality of education. California has many recent immigrants, which means many students whose English is not as good as that of native English speakers. This fact would also lower statewide averages. Again, this is a sampling problem because comparable groups that differ only on the variable of interest (state in which education was obtained) are not being made. Of course, it is possible that students in Mississippi are getting a better education than those in California, but we cannot conclude this from these data.

Sample Size

Given a thimbleful of facts, we rush to make generalizations as large as a tub.

—Gordon Allport (1954, p. 8)

The number of subjects you include in your sample is called the **sample size**. Suppose that treatment Program 1 has had six patient/subjects and Program 2 has had 10 patient/subjects. Both of these numbers are too small to determine the success rate of the treatments. (A subject is a person or animal or entity who participates in an experiment.) When scientists conduct experiments, they often use large numbers of subjects because the larger the sample size, the more confident they can be in generalizing the findings to the population. This principle is called the **law of large numbers**, and it is an important statistical law. If, for some reason, they cannot use a large number of subjects, they may need to be more cautious or conservative in the conclusions that they derive from their research. Although a discussion of the number of subjects needed in an experiment is beyond the scope of this book, it is important to keep in mind that for most everyday purposes, we cannot generalize about a population by observing how only a few people respond. Suppose this happened to you:

After months of deliberation over a new car purchase, you finally decided to buy a Chevrolet Impala. You found that both *Consumer Reports* and *Road and Track* magazines gave the Impala a good rating. It is priced within your budget, and you like its circular rear lights and "sharp" appearance. On your way out the door to close the deal, you run into a close friend and tell her about your intended purchase. "An Impala!" she shrieks. "My brother-in-law bought one and it's a tin can. It's constantly breaking down on the freeway. He's had it towed so often that the rear tires need replacing."

What do you do?

Most people would have a difficult time completing the purchase because they are insufficiently sensitive to sample size issues. The national magazines presumably tested many cars before they determined their rating. Your friend's brother-in-law is a single subject. You should place greater confidence in results obtained with large samples than in results obtained with small samples (assuming that the "experiments" were equally good). Yet, many people find the testimonial of a single person, especially if it's someone they know, more persuasive than information gathered from a large sample, especially when there is preference for the results obtained from the small sample (Klacznski, Gordon, & Fauth, 1997; Wilson & Brekke, 1994).

We tend to ignore the importance of having an adequately large sample size when we function as intuitive scientists. This is why testimonials are so very powerful in persuading people what to do and believe. However, testimonials are based on the experiences of only one person, and often that person is being paid to say that some product or purchase is good. I have an advertisement for a psychic phone line that offers "real cases" as proof that psychics are effective sources for advice on a variety of problems: "A Lancing, Michigan resident winds up with a more positive outlook in her life after one conversation . . . . And a women from Pittsburgh, Pennsylvania feels as if the psychic has reached into her soul" (*Cosmopolitan*, January 1994). The reference to a particular, unnamed person along with the name of a city and state makes these comments more personal and authentic-sounding. The more specific the information we receive, the more likely we are to believe that it is true. Give me a break!

I would like to dismiss testimonials and similar sorts of "evidence" as hogwash that no one would fall for, but I know differently. A family member spent over $300 in calls to psychics when struggling with decisions regarding her critically ill husband. This was money that she did not have for advice that was, at best, harmless, and, at worst, caused her to ignore the recommendations of the hospital staff. I later was told that psychics are not permitted to predict that anyone will die, so they gave her false hope, which made the death even more difficult to bear. I am telling you this true personal anecdote because I hope that it will be effective in causing you to think about the sort of evidence that you would need to spend hundreds of dollars for advice by a paid stranger who has no credentials or training in psychology or science.

Variability

The term **variability** is used to denote the fact that all people are not the same. Suppose that you know someone who "smoked like a haystack" and lived to be 100 years old. Does this mean that the hype about the negative effects of smoking on health is wrong. Of course not! The effect of smoking on health was determined by numerous separate investigators using large numbers of subjects. Not everyone responds in the same way, or maintains the same opinion, or has the same abilities. It is important to remember the role of variability in understanding results. Our studies can tell us, with some probability, what is generally true, but there will be individuals who do not conform to the usual pattern. There are people who smoke heavily and live to a ripe old age, but this does not mean that the studies that show that smoking causes many terminal illnesses are wrong. It just means that people are different.

Several years ago, there was much excitement over the use of laetrile, an extract from apricot pits, as a cure for cancer. Although the U.S. medical establishment found that it was worthless in the fight against cancer, many people continued to believe that it could be used as a cure. Suppose you read about someone who was diagnosed as having cancer, and this person then took laetrile. Later, this individual recovered from her cancer. What can you conclude? Would you be willing to conclude that, at least for some people, laetrile can cure or help to cure cancer? This conclusion is unwarranted. Some people recover from cancer, whereas others do not. Just as people are variable in the beliefs and attitudes that they maintain, they are also variable in the way they respond to disease. With a sample size of one, we cannot conclude that the laetrile contributed to her cure. Large-scale studies are needed that compare the survival rates of groups of people on laetrile with groups of people who used other forms of cancer treatments to decide if laetrile can be beneficial in the treatment of cancer. When these tests were conducted by the U.S. government, laetrile was found to be worthless. It's easy to see how desperate cancer patients can be misled into believing results obtained with a very small number of people.

There are many examples where people generalize inappropriately from small samples. In a recent, tragic example, the teenage son of a prominent politician in the United States committed suicide after taking a commonly prescribed acne medication. The family was absolutely convinced that the suicide was a result of depression caused by the drug, and they began an active campaign to get the drug taken off the market. In their view, their son had been a normal teen until he took the medication, and soon after taking the medication, he committed suicide. Large-scale studies did not support their belief that teens taking this drug were more likely to be depressed or commit suicide than similar teens not taking this drug. However, for the family of this teen, their own tragic experience was far more convincing than data collected on thousands of teens.

People's willingness to believe that results obtained from a small sample can be generalized to the entire population is called the **law of small numbers** (Tversky & Kahneman, 1971). In fact, we should be more confident when predicting to or from large samples than small samples. In an experimental investigation of this phenomenon (Quattrone & Jones, 1980), college students demonstrated their belief that if one member of a group made a particular decision, then the other members of that group would make the same decision. This result was especially strong when the college students were observing the decisions of students from other colleges. Thus, it is easy to see how a belief in the law of small numbers can maintain prejudices and stereotypes. We tend to believe that the actions of a single group member are indicative of the actions of the entire group. Have you ever heard someone say, "_____'s (fill in your group) are all alike?" An acquaintance once told me that all Jamaicans are sneaky thieves. She came to this conclusion after having one bad experience with a person from Jamaica. Expressions like this one are manifestations of the law of small numbers. Can you see how the law of small numbers can also explain the origin of many prejudices like racism? A single memorable event involving a member of a group with which we have little contact can color our beliefs about the other members of that group. Generally, when you collect observations about people and events, it is important to collect a large number of observations before you reach a conclusion.

There is one exception to the general principle that we need large samples in order to make valid generalizations about a population. The one exception occurs when everyone in the population is exactly the same. If, for example, everyone in the population of interest responded exactly the same way to any question (e.g., Do you approve of the death penalty?) or any treatment (e.g., had no "heart attacks" when treated with a single aspirin), then sample size would no longer be an issue. Of course, all people are not the same. You may be thinking that this was a fairly dumb statement because everyone knows that people are different. Unfortunately, research has shown that most of us tend to underestimate the variability of groups with which we are unfamiliar.

Minorities who are members of any group often report that the leader or other group members will turn to them and ask, "What do African Americans (or women or Hispanics, or Asians, or whatever the minority is) think about this issue?" It's as though the rest of the group believe that the few minority members of their group can speak for the minority group as a whole. This is a manifestation of the belief that groups other than the ones to which we belong are much more homogeneous (less variable) than the groups to which we belong. The ability to make accurate predictions depends, in part, on the ability to make accurate assessments of variability. It is important to keep the concept of variability in mind whenever you are testing hypotheses either formally in a research setting or informally as you try to determine relationships in everyday life.

SCIENCE VERSUS SCIENCE FICTION

Science is a method for understanding; it is a way of "knowing" about the world. Data (or evidence) are at the heart of the scientific method but not just "any old" data or evidence—data or evidence that were collected under controlled conditions, data that can be openly scrutinized, and data that can be replicated. Consider, for example, the hypothesis that there are psychics who can accurately predict future events. What sort of data or evidence would convince you that at least some people have psychic powers?

Amazing and Not True

I have been told by believers in psychics that they have good data—a psychic made amazingly true predictions about their life. Testimonials by one or even several people are offered as evidence that psychics exist. Believers claim that they "know" psychics have true powers because they "saw it with their own eyes." (If you have already read Chapter 2 on memory, then you know that eye-witness testimony can be highly inaccurate—an important fact, but not the main point in this discussion.) I like to remind them that they also saw Mr. Ed, the talking horse who had his own television show; do they believe that there are horses who can talk? (Actually, there are people who believe in the existence of talking horses based on the *Mr. Ed* show; Cole, 1995.)

I like to begin my college classes in critical thinking by demonstrating my own amazing psychic powers. Each semester, before the start of the first class, I check my class roster and then look up some of the students in the university records. The records include date of birth and sometimes information about siblings (if they are also students), so I can determine the astrological sign and some family information for the students enrolled in my class. I then amaze students by asking a series of questions that lead up to my ability to name students I have never met and tell them their astrological sign and some family information. (Let's see—I am getting the feeling that you are a Taurus. Your name—don't tell me—it's something like Jean or Jane, no wait, it's Jackie, isn't it? I also see a family picture with a younger sister in it. Is that correct? And her name is Latisha, right? And so on.) It is really an easy trick, yet, students wonder how I was able to know so much about people I have never met. The fact that I could tell students their name, astrological sign, and other information might look like evidence in support of psychic phenomena, and without appropriate controls, it is a very easy trick.

Cold Reading

There are many people who claim to be psychics or clairvoyants—some even claim to be able to speak with the dead. I think we can all understand the pain of grieving relatives, who really want to believe that they can talk to the dead. Televised shows have sometimes shown a portion of the séance or session with the dead. Typically, viewers will see only a few minutes of a session that may last for several hours—usually a portion where the psychic made a successful prediction like, "the person you are trying to contact—is it a parent?" What we don't see is the many instances where questions like this one are incorrect. The Australian Skeptics Society offers a cash prize of $100,000 for a proven demonstration of psychic powers. No one has collected this prize. Ray Hyman, a psychologist who studies ways to debunk psychics, explains how they "read" your mind, "speak with the dead," and other similar shows. The technique is called "cold reading." The psychic relies on body language, basic statistical information (e.g., common boys' names that start with a known letter). He offers these 13 points for amazing your own friends with cold reading (Hyman, http://www.skeptics.com.au/journal/coldread.htm):

1. Look confident—act as though you believe in what you are doing.
2. Use polls, surveys, and statistical abstracts—predict attitudes from a person's educational level and religion.
3. Stage the reading—make no excessive claims; be modest.

4. Gain the subject's cooperation—make the subject try to find truth in what you say.
5. Use a gimmick—crystal balls and palm reading are good.
6. Have a list of stock phrases available—there are fortune-telling and other manuals that have lots of good ones.
7. Use your eyes—observe clothing, jewelry, speech—these can be good hints.
8. Fish—get the subject to tell about him or herself.
9. Listen—subjects want to talk about themselves.
10. Be dramatic—ham it up for effect.
11. Pretend to know more than you are saying—subject will assume you do.
12. Flatter the subject—people love flattery.
13. Always tell the subject what she or he wants to hear.

People who talk to the dead, read palms or tea leaves, and have visited beings from other planets use similar methods when providing evidence of their unusual abilities. Remember, just because it looks like someone has made a rabbit appear from the inside of a hat does *not* mean that is what really happened. Magic tricks and science fiction can be great fun, but they are not substitutes for critical thinking. If there is only one goal that I could have for readers of this book, it is that you come to value data and evidence for the purpose of making sound decisions. It may be the most critical part of critical thinking.

DETERMINING CAUSE

Do you believe that children who are neglected become teenage delinquents?
Does jogging relieve depression?
Will a diet that is low in fat increase longevity?
Do clothes make the man?
Will strong spiritual beliefs give you peace of mind?
Does critical thinking instruction improve how you think outside the classroom?

All of these questions concern a causal relationship in which one variable (e.g., neglect) is believed to cause another variable (e.g., delinquency). What sort of information do we need to determine the truth of causal relationships?

Isolation and Control of Variables

Stop and think for a minute about the way you would go about deciding if neglecting children causes them to become delinquent when they are teenagers. You could decide to conduct a long-term study in which you would divide children into groups—telling some of their parents to cater to their every need, others to neglect them occasionally, and still others to neglect their children totally. You could require everyone to remain in their groups, catering to or neglecting their children as instructed until the children reach their teen years, at which time you could count up the number of children in each group who became delinquents. Remember, of course, that you would have to define operationally the term "delinquent." This would be a good, although totally unrealistic, way to decide if neglect causes delinquency.

It's a good way because this method would allow you to control how much neglect each child received and to isolate the cause of delinquency, as this would be the only systematic difference among the people in each group. It's unrealistic to the point of being ludicrous, because very few people would comply with your request to cater to or neglect their children. Furthermore, it would also be unethical to ask people to engage in potentially harmful behaviors.

In some experimental settings it is possible to isolate and control the variables you're interested in. If you wanted to know if grading students for coursework will make college students work harder and therefore learn more, you could randomly assign college students to different grading conditions. Half the students could be graded as pass or fail (no letter grades), whereas the other students would receive traditional letter grades (A, B, C, D, or F). At the end of the semester, all students would take the same final exam. If the average final exam score for the students who received grades were statistically significantly higher than for the students in the pass-fail condition, we'd conclude that grades do result in greater learning. (See Chapter 7 on probability for a discussion of significant differences.)

Can you see why it's so important to be able to assign students at random to either the graded or pass-fail conditions instead of just letting them pick the type of grading they want? It is possible that the students who would pick the pass-fail grading are less motivated or less intelligent than the students who would prefer to get grades or vice versa. If the students could pick their own grading condition, we wouldn't know if the differences we found were due to the differences in grading practices or due to differences in motivation or intelligence, or some other variable that differs systematically as a function of which grading condition the students select. If we cannot use random assignment, then we usually cannot make any causal claims.

Let's return to the question of whether child neglect causes delinquency. Given the constraint that you cannot tell parents to neglect their children, how would you go about deciding if child neglect causes delinquency? You could decide to find a group of parents and ask each about the amount of care he or she gives to each child. Suppose you found that, in general, the more that children are neglected, the more likely they are to become teenage delinquents. Because you lost control over your variables by not assigning parents to catering and neglecting groups, it is not possible, on the basis of this experiment alone, to conclude that neglect causes delinquency. It is possible that parents who neglect their children differ from caring parents in other ways. Parents who tend to neglect their children may also encourage drug use, or engage in other lifestyle activities that contribute to the development of teenage delinquency. A point that is made in several places in this book is that just because two variables occur together (neglect and delinquency), it doesn't necessarily mean that one *caused* the other to occur.

Three-Stage Experimental Designs

When researchers want to be able to make strong causal claims, they use a three-stage experimental design (Kimble, 1978). An experimental design is a plan for how observations will be made:

1. The first stage involves creating different groups that are going to be studied. In the example about the effect of pass-fail grading on how much is learned, the two groups would be those who receive a letter grade and those who

receive a grade of either "pass" or "fail." It is important that the two groups differ systematically only on this dimension. You wouldn't want all the students in the letter grade group to take classes taught by Professor Longwinded whereas those in the pass-fail group take classes taught by Professor Mumbles. One professor may be a better teacher, and students may learn more in one condition than the other because of this confounding variable. One way to avoid this confound is to assign half of the students in each class to each grading condition with the assignment of students to either group done at random. In this example, the students in both conditions are the subjects. A **subject** is a person, animal, or entity who serves as a participant in an experiment. Strong causal claims will involve equating the groups at the outset of the experiment. *The random assignment of subjects to groups is essential in discovering cause and effect.*

2. The second stage involves the application of the "experimental treatment." If we were conducting a drug study, one group would receive the drug and the other group would not receive the drug. Usually, the "nondrug" group would receive a placebo, which would look and/or taste like the drug, but would be chemically inert. The reason to use a placebo is to avoid any effects of subjects' beliefs or expectancies. (The topic of expectancies and the way they can bias results is discussed later in this chapter.) As discussed in an earlier section, when these sorts of controls were used to determine the effectiveness of laetrile, it was found to be worthless against cancer. In the grading example, the term "treatment" doesn't fit well, but it corresponds to taking the course under the two different grading conditions.

3. Evaluation is the final phase. Measurements are taken and two (or more) groups are compared on some outcome measure. In the grading example, final examination scores for students in the letter grade group would be compared to the scores for students in the pass-fail group. If students in one group performed significantly better than the students in the other group, then we would have strong support for the claim that one grading method *caused* students to study harder and learn more than the other.

Of course, we are not always able to equate groups at the outset and randomly assign subjects to groups, but when we can, results can be used to make stronger causal claims than in less controlled conditions.

Consider this hypothetical example:

Researchers at Snooty University have studied the causes of divorce. They found that 33% of recently divorced couples reported that they had serious disagreements over money during the two-year period that preceded the divorce. The researchers concluded that disagreements over money are a major reason why couples divorce. They go on to suggest that couples should learn to handle money disagreements as a way of reducing the divorce rate.

What, if anything, is wrong with this "line of reasoning"? Plenty. First, we have no data from a comparison group that did not divorce (i.e., no control group). Maybe 33% of all families disagree about money; maybe the number is even higher in families that stay together. Second, there is no reason to believe that disagreements over money *caused* or even contributed to divorce. Maybe couples in the process of breaking up disagree more about everything. Third, there is the problem of retrospective review, a topic that is discussed in the next section. Studies like this one are found everywhere from radio talk shows, news reports, scientific journals, and people's casual examinations of life. If you rely on the principles of hypothesis testing to interpret findings like this one, you are less likely to be bamboozled.

Using the Principles of Isolation and Control

In an earlier chapter, I presented Piaget's notion that people who have attained the highest level of cognitive development can reason about hypothetical situations. Piaget called the highest level of cognitive development the formal stage of thought. He developed several different tasks that could be used to identify people who could think at this level. If you already read Chapter 4, then you will recall the "combinatorial reasoning" task devised by Piaget. It required a planful and orderly procedure for combining objects. Another one of Piaget's tasks involved using the principles of isolation and control that are integral to hypothesis testing. Try this task.

Bending Rods.   This task is to determine which of several variables affects the flexibility of rods. Imagine that you are given a long vertical bar with 12 rods hanging from it. Each rod is made of either brass, copper, or steel. The rods come in two lengths and two thicknesses. Your task is to find which of the variables (material, length, or thickness) influence how much the rods will bend. You can test this by pressing down on each rod to see how much it bends. You may perform as many comparisons as you like until you can explain what factors are important in determining flexibility. It may help you to visualize the setup as presented in Fig. 6.1.

FIG. 6.1.   Bending rods. How would you determine whether material, length, or thickness affects rod flexibility?

What do you need to do to prove that length, or diameter, or the material rods are constructed from, or some combination of these variables is important in determining flexibility? Stop now and write out your answer to this problem. Don't go on until you have finished this problem.

Solving the Task of Bending Rods. How did you go about exploring the effect of length, diameter, and material on rod flexibility? In order to solve this problem, you had to consider the possible factors that contribute to rod flexibility, and then systematically hold constant all of the variables except one. This is a basic concept in experimental methods. If you wanted to know if material was an important factor, which rods would you test? You would bend a brass rod, a copper rod, and a steel rod of the same length and diameter. This would hold constant the length and diameter variables while testing the material variable. Some possible tests of this would be to compare flexibility among the short and wide brass, copper, and steel rods. Similarly, if you wanted to find out if length is important, you would bend a short and a long rod of the same diameter that was constructed with the same material. An example of this would be to compare the short and wide copper rod with the long and wide copper rod.

How would you decide if diameter influences rod flexibility? By now it should be clear that you would compare two rods of the same material and length and different diameters. You could test this by bending a short and wide steel rod with a short and thin steel rod. Thus, you should be able to recognize that the same principles used in hypothesis testing were needed in this task and be able to apply them correctly in order to solve this seemingly unrelated problem.

Prospective and Retrospective Research

Consider a medical example: Some health psychologists believe that certain stressful experiences can cause people to develop cancer. If this were your hypothesis, how would you determine its validity? One way would be to ask cancer patients if they had anything particularly stressful happen to them just before they were diagnosed as having cancer. If the stress caused the cancer, it would have to precede the development of cancer. When experiments are conducted in this manner, they are called **retrospective experiments**. Retrospective experiments look back in time to understand causes for later events. There are many problems with this sort of research. As discussed in Chapter 2 on memory, memories are selective and malleable. It is possible that knowledge of one's cancer will change how one's past is remembered. Moderately stressful events like receiving a poor grade in a college course may be remembered as being traumatic. Happier events, like getting a raise, may be forgotten. It's even possible that the early stages of the cancer were causing stress instead of the stress causing the cancer. Thus, it will be difficult to determine if stress causes cancer from retrospective research.

A better method for understanding causative relationships is **prospective research**. In prospective research, you identify possible causative factors when they occur and then look forward in time to see if the hypothesized result occurs. In a prospective study, you would have many people record stressful life events when they occur (e.g., death of a spouse, imprisonment, loss of a job) and then see which people develop cancer. If the people who experience more stressful events are more likely to develop cancer, this result would provide support for your hypothesis.

Most of the research we conduct as intuitive scientists is retrospective. We often seek explanations for events after they have occurred. How many times have you tried to understand why a seemingly angelic child committed a serious crime, or why a star rookie seems to be losing his touch, or why the underdog in a political race won? Our retrospective attempts at explanations are biased by selective memories and lack of systematic observations. (See the section on hindsight in Chapter 8 on decision making skills for a related discussion.)

Correlation and Cause

The process by which children turn experience into knowledge is exactly the same, point for point, as the process by which those whom we call scientists make scientific knowledge.

—Holt (1989, p. 93)

What you are about to read is absolutely true: As the weight of children increases, so does the number of items that they are likely to get correct on standardized tests of intelligence. In other words, heavier children answer more questions correctly than lighter ones. Before you start stuffing mashed potatoes into your children in an attempt to make them smarter, stop and think about what this means. Does it mean that gaining weight will make children smarter? Certainly not! Children get heavier as they get older, and older children answer more questions correctly than younger ones.

In this example, the variables' weight and number of questions answered correctly are related. An increase in one variable is associated with an increase in the other variable—as weight increases the number of questions answered correctly concomitantly (at the same time also) increases. **Correlated variables** are two or more variables that are related. If you've already read Chapter 5, "Analyzing Arguments," then you should recognize this concept as the fallacy of false cause.

People frequently confuse correlation with causation. Consider the following example: Wally and Bob were arguing about the inheritance of intelligence. Wally thought about everyone he knew and concluded that because smart parents tend to have smart children, and dumb parents tend to have dumb children, intelligence is an inherited characteristic. Bob disagreed with Wally's line of reasoning, although he concurred with the facts that Wally presented. He agreed that if the parents score high on intelligence tests, then their children will also tend to score high, and if the parents score low on intelligence tests, then their children will also tend to score low. When two measures are related in this way—that is, they tend to rise and fall together—they have a **positive correlation**. Although parents' intelligence and their children's intelligence are positively correlated, we cannot infer that parents caused their children (through inheritance or any other means) to be intelligent. It is possible that children affect the intelligence of their parents, or that both are being affected by a third variable that hasn't been considered. It is possible that diet, economic class, or other lifestyle variables determine intelligence levels, and because parents and children eat similar diets and have the same economic class, they tend to be similar in intelligence. In understanding the relationship between two correlated variables, it is possible that variable A caused the changes in variable B (A → B), or that variable B caused the changes in variable A (B → A), or both A and B caused changes in each other (A → B and B → A) or that both were caused by a third variable C (C → A and C → B).

Let's consider a different example. Many people have taken up jogging in the belief that it will help them to lose weight. The two variables in this example are exercise and weight. I've heard people argue that because there are no fat athletes (except perhaps sumo wrestlers), exercise must cause people to be thin. I hope that you can think critically about this claim. It does seem to be true that exercise and weight are correlated. People who tend to exercise a great deal also tend to be thin. This sort of correlation, in which the tendency to be high on one variable (exercise) is associated with the tendency to be low on the other variable (weight), is called a **negative correlation**. Let's think about the relationship between exercise and weight. There are several possibilities: (a) It is possible that exercise causes people to be thin; or (b) It is possible that people who are thin tend to exercise more because it is more enjoyable to engage in exercise when you are thin; or (c) It is possible that a third variable, like concern for one's health, or some inherited trait, is responsible for both the tendency to exercise and the tendency to be thin. Perhaps there are inherited body types that naturally stay thin and also are graced with strong muscles that are well suited for exercise.

If you wanted to test the hypothesis that exercise causes people to lose weight, then you would use the three design stages described earlier. If the subjects who were assigned at random to the exercise group were thinner after the treatment period than those in a no-exercise condition, then you could make a strong causal claim for the benefits of exercise in controlling weight.

Actually, the question of causation is usually complex. It is probably more accurate to use the word *influence* instead of *cause* because there is usually more than a single variable that affects another variable. A colleague suggested the following example to clarify this point (Dr. Richard Block at Montana State University): When a man is being hanged for having committed a crime, is it because someone gave him money to buy the weapon he used in the crime, or is it because someone saw him commit the crime, or is it because no one stopped him?

Illusory Correlation.   An amusing anecdote of attributing cause to events that occur together was presented by Munson (1976):

A farmer was traveling with his wife on a train when he saw a man across the aisle take something out of a bag and begin eating it. "Say, Mister," he asked, "What's that thing you're eating?"

"It's a banana," the man said, "Here, try one."

The farmer took it, peeled it, and just as he swallowed the first bite, the train roared into a tunnel. "Don't eat any, Maude," he yelled to his wife. "It'll make you go blind!" (p. 277)

Do blondes really have more fun? A popular advertisement for hair dye would like you to believe that having blonde hair will cause you to have more fun. Many people believe that they see many blondes having fun; therefore, blondes have more fun than brunettes and redheads. The problem with this sort of observation is that there are many blondes who are not having "more fun" (a term badly in need of an operational definition) than brunettes, but because they are at home or in other places where you are unlikely to see them, they don't get considered. The term **illusory correlation** refers to the erroneous belief that two variables are related when, in fact, they are not (Chapman & Chapman, 1967, 1969). Professionals and nonprofessionals alike maintain beliefs about relationships in the world. These beliefs guide the kinds of observations we make and how we determine if a relationship exists between two variables.

Let's try another example. Do you believe that you often see fat people overeating? Most people believe that they do; yet, research has shown that overweight adults tend to eat less in public places than normal-weight people. We expect to see overweight people overeating; and therefore, we believe that they do. Beware of illusory correlations when you play the role of an intuitive scientist. This phenomenon works to maintain stereotypes (e.g., redheads are hot-tempered, Scots are cheap, women can't understand math, etc.). Our beliefs about relationships between variables guide the observations we make and the way we utilize this information to formulate conclusions, many of which are incorrect.

Validity

The **validity** of a measure is usually defined as the extent to which it measures what you want it to measure. If I wanted to measure intelligence and measured the length of your big toe, this would obviously be invalid. Other examples of validity are less obvious. A popular radio commercial, touting the benefits of soup, points out that tomato soup has more vitamin A than eggs. This is true, but it is not a valid measure of the goodness of tomato soup. Eggs are not a good source of vitamin A. Thus, the wrong comparisons were made, and the measure does not support the notion that soup is an excellent food. If you've already read Chapter 5 on analyzing arguments, then you should realize that the claim that tomato soup has more vitamin A than eggs does not support the conclusion that "soup is good food." It may well be true that soup is an excellent source of vitamins, but claims like this one don't support that conclusion.

How would you react to this claim, "The Baroness is a sleek new luxury car that will provide its owner with dependable transportation for many years to come. In fact, in a recent laboratory test, the Baroness went from zero to 60 miles per hour in 7 seconds flat, beating out the six other cars in the competition." Is the acceleration speed of a car a valid index of its dependability? Probably not. Even if the figure is accurate, it is not a valid measure of dependability. If you want to know about dependability, you'll want to know about the frequency of repairs, average number of miles you could expect to drive the car before it gets turned into scrap metal, and how it performs in collisions.

Convergent Validity

When several different measures all converge onto the same conclusion, the measures are said to have **convergent validity**. If, for example, you wanted to measure charisma—the psychological trait that is something more than charm that people as diverse as Jodie Foster, Bill Cosby, and Lucy Liu are said to possess, you'd need convergent validity for your measure. People who scored high on your charisma test should also be the ones who are selected for leadership positions and have other personality traits that are usually associated with charisma. If the class wallflower scored high on your test of charisma, you'd need to rethink the validity of your test.

Intuitive scientists also need to be mindful of the need for convergent validity. Before you decide that your classmate, Willa Mae, is shy because she hesitates to talk to you, you need to determine if she acts shy with other people in other places. If she frequently speaks up in class, you wouldn't want to conclude that she is a shy person because this inconsistency in her behavior would signal a lack of convergent validity. The idea of convergent validity is very similar to the topic of convergent argument structures that was presented in the previous chapter. If you have already read Chapter 5 on analyzing arguments, then you should recall that the strength of an argument is increased when many premises support (or converge on) a conclusion. This is exactly the same situation as when several sources of evidence support the same hypothesis. The language used in these two chapters is different (support for a conclusion versus support for a hypothesis), but the underlying ideas are the same: The more reasons or evidence we can provide for believing that something is true, the greater the confidence we can have in our belief.

Illusory Validity

Everyone complains of his memory and no one complains of his judgment.

—La Rochefoucauld (1613–1680)

Both professionals and nonprofessionals place great confidence in their conclusions about most life events, even when their confidence is objectively unwarranted. Overconfidence in judgments is called **illusory validity**. In an experimental investigation of this phenomenon, Oskamp (1965) found that as clinicians were given more information about patients, they became more confident in the judgments they made about patients. What is interesting about this result is that they were not more accurate in judgment, only more confident that they were right. Why do people place confidence in fallible judgments? There are several reasons why we persist in maintaining confidence in our judgments. A primary factor is the selective nature of memory. Consider this personal vignette: As a child, I would watch Philadelphia Phillies baseball games on television with my father. As each batter would step up to home plate, my father would excitedly yell, "He's going to hit a home run, I just know it!" Of course, he was usually wrong. (Phillies fans had to be tough in the 50s and 60s.) On the rare occasions when a Phillies batter actually did hit a home run, my father would talk about it for weeks. "Yep, I knew as soon as he stepped up to home plate that he would hit a home run. I can always tell just by looking at the batter." In this instance, and countless others, we selectively remember our successful judgments and forget our unsuccessful ones. This tends to bolster confidence in the judgments we make.

A second reason for the illusion of validity is the failure to seek or consider disconfirming evidence. (See Chapter 8 on decision making for an additional discussion of this phenomenon.) This is the primary reason why people tend to believe that variables are correlated when they are not. Suppose that you have the job of personnel officer in a large corporation. Over a period of a year, you hire one hundred new employees for your corporation. How would you go about deciding if you're making good (valid) hiring decisions? Most people would check on the performance of the one hundred new employees. Suppose that you did this and found that 92% of the new employees were performing their jobs in a competent, professional manner. Would this bolster your confidence in your judgments? If you answered yes to this question, you forgot to consider disconfirming evidence. What about the people you didn't hire? Have most of them gone on to become vice presidents at General Motors? If you found that 100% of the people you didn't hire are superior employees at your competitor's corporation, you would have to revise your confidence in your judgmental ability.

Part of the reason that we fail to utilize disconfirming evidence is that it is often not available. Personnel officers don't have information about the employees they don't hire. Similarly, we don't know much about the person we chose not to date, or the course we didn't take, or the house we didn't buy. Thus, on the basis of partial information, we may conclude that our judgments are better than they objectively are.

In a scathing review of the Rorschach test, the test that is commonly known as the inkblot test because subjects are asked to tell what they see in amorphous, symmetrical blots of ink, Dawes (1994) concluded that it is not a valid measure of mental functioning. A recent review of projective tests arrived at the same conclusion (Lilienfeld, Wood, & Garb, 2000). That is, there is no evidence that it is useful in diagnosing or treating mental disorders (although it is possible to determine if someone gives unusual answers). *This means that the Rorschach has no validity.* Despite these empirical results, Dawes reports that some psychotherapists respond to this fact with, "Yes, I know that it has no validity, but I find it useful." Do you see why this is a ridiculous statement? If it has no validity, then it cannot be useful. If therapists believe that it is useful, they are fooling themselves and demonstrating the phenomenon of illusory validity. It may seem useful because they interpret the responses in ways that they believe make sense, but its only real value is as a clear demonstration of the biases that we maintain.

Why do some psychologists continue to use projective tests when many reviews of the literature show that these tests are not valid? Most psychologists genuinely want to do a good job and many believe that the tests are valid despite the lack of data to support that conclusion. They believe these tests are valid because they "feel or look right"—the results confirm what they believe to be true. Few people will cast aside their own sense of what is true for a mass of cold and impersonal data collected by and from people they don't know. In general, the scientific method is not valued when it conflicts with our personal belief system. Humans are ill-equipped to use data from large samples, perhaps because the only information that was available to us for most of the history of humankind came from personal experience or the second-hand personal experience of those we know. It is important that we use critical thinking skills for conclusions that we like and don't like.

Reliability

Both law and science must weigh the reliability of evidence, the trustworthiness
of experts, and the probability that something is true beyond a reasonable doubt.

—K. C. Cole (1995)

The **reliability** of a measure is the consistency with which it measures what it's supposed to measure. If you used a rubber ruler that could stretch or shrink to measure the top of your desk, you'd probably get a different number each time you measured it. Of course, we want our measurements to be reliable.

Researchers in the social and physical sciences devote a great deal of time to the issue of reliable measurement. We say that an intelligence test, for example, is reliable when the same person obtains scores that are in the same general range whenever she takes the test. Few of us even consider reliability when we function as intuitive scientists. When we decide if a professor or student is prejudiced, we often rely on one or two samples of behavior without considering if the individual is being assessed reliably.

Suppose that you learn that your friend Ricardo failed a college course, which all others easily passed. Could you conclude that his teacher is prejudiced? You'd need to collect many other observations of the same teacher to see how consistently or reliably Hispanic males failed his class. If there were an unusually high failure rate among Hispanic males (or whatever group you're interested in) in his class compared to their failure rate in other classes, then you'd have a strong case for the inference that the teacher is prejudiced. Without careful measurement and, in this case, a larger sample size, you cannot infer that the professor is prejudiced.

THINKING ABOUT ERRORS

To a scientist a theory is something to be tested. He seeks not to defend his beliefs, but to improve them. He is, above everything else, an expert at "changing his mind."

—Wendell Johnson (1946)

When we try to understand relationships by devising and testing hypotheses, we will sometimes be wrong. This idea is expanded on more fully in the next chapter, which concerns understanding probabilities. For now, consider this possibility: Suppose that you drive into work every day with a friend. Every morning you stop at a drive-up restaurant window and buy coffee. You decide that instead of hassling every morning with who will pay ("I'll get it"—"No, no let me"), he will flip a coin. When the outcome is heads, he will pay; when the outcome is tails, you will pay. Sounds fair enough, but on nine of the last ten days the coin landed with tails up. Do you think that your friend is cheating?

The truth is that your friend is either cheating or he is not cheating. Unfortunately, you don't know which is true. Nevertheless, you need to make a decision. You will decide either that he is cheating or he is not cheating. Thus, there are four possibilities: (a) He is cheating and you correctly decide that he is cheating; (b) He is not cheating and you correctly decide that he is not cheating; (c) He is cheating and you incorrectly decide that he is not cheating; and (d) He is not cheating and you incorrectly decide that he is cheating. With these four possibilities, there are two ways that you can be right and two ways that you can be wrong. These four combinations are shown in Table 6.1.

As you can see from Table 6.1, there are two different ways that we can make errors in any hypothesis-testing situation. These two different errors are not equally "bad." It is far worse to decide that your friend is cheating when he is not (especially if you accuse him of cheating) than it is to decide that he is not cheating when he is.

TABLE 6.1
Four Possible Outcomes for the "Who Buys the Coffee" Example

	You Decide	
	He is cheating	*He is not cheating*
The Truth is: He is cheating.	He is cheating and you decide that he is cheating. Correct Decision!	He is cheating and you decide that he is not cheating. An Error!
He is not cheating.	He is not cheating and you decide that he is cheating. A Serious Error!	He is not cheating and you decide that he is not cheating. Correct Decision!

Note. The error associated with deciding that he is cheating is more serious than the error associated with deciding that he is not cheating. Because of the difference in the severity of the errors, you will want to be more certain when deciding that he is cheating than when deciding that he is not cheating.

Thus, you would want stronger evidence to decide that he is cheating than you would want to decide that he is not cheating. In other words, you need to consider the relative "badness" of different errors when testing hypotheses.

If you take a course in statistics or experimental design, you'll find that the idea of error "badness" is handled by requiring different levels of confidence for different decisions. The need to consider different types of errors is found in many contexts. A basic principle of our legal system is that we have to be very certain that someone has committed a crime (beyond a reasonable doubt) before we can convict her. By contrast, we don't have to be convinced beyond a reasonable doubt that she is innocent because wrongly deciding that someone is innocent is considered a less severe error than wrongly deciding that someone is guilty. Similarly, when you are testing hypotheses informally, you also need to be aware of the severity of different types of errors. Before you decide, for example, that no matter how hard you study, you'll never pass some course or that the medicine you're taking is or isn't making you better, you need to consider the consequences of right and wrong decisions. Some decisions require that you should be more certain about being correct than others.

Experience Is an Expensive Teacher

Suppose that your friend shares her "secret" for curing a cold—she rubs her stomach with garlic and the symptoms of the cold go away. You are dubious, but she persists, "I know it works. I've tried it, and I have seen it work with my own eyes." I am certain that there are many people who would respond to this testimonial by rubbing garlic over their stomach, just as there are many people who willingly swallow capsules filled with ground rhinoceros penis to increase their sexual potency, megavitamins to feel less tired, and ginseng root for whatever ails them. You may even join the ranks of those who tout these solutions because sometimes your cold will get better after rubbing yourself with garlic—sometimes a desired effect follows some action (like taking capsules of ground rhinoceros penis). But, did the action cause the effect that followed it? This question can only be answered using the principles of hypothesis testing. Personal experience cannot provide the answer.

Dawes (1994) corrected the famous expression that we attribute to Benjamin Franklin. It seems that Franklin did not say that "experience is the best teacher," instead he said "experience is a dear teacher," with the word *dear* meaning expensive or costly. Sometimes, we are able to use systematic feedback about what works and what doesn't work so that we can use our experience to improve at some task, but it is also possible to do the same thing over and over without learning from experience. We are far better off using information that is generated by many people to determine causal relationships than to rely on personal experience with all of its biases and costs.

SELF-FULFILLING PROPHECIES

Science is not simply a collection of facts; it is a discipline of thinking about rational solutions to problems after establishing the basic facts derived from observations. It is hypothesizing from what is known to what might be, and then attempting to test the hypotheses.

—Rosalyn S. Yalow
(distinguished professor, City University of New York, 1988)

In a classic set of experiments, Robert Rosenthal, a well-known psychologist, and his colleague (Rosenthal & Fode, 1963) had their students train rats to run through mazes as part of a standard course in experimental psychology. Half of the students were told that they had rats that had been specially bred to be smart at learning their way through mazes, whereas the other half of the students were told that they had rats that had been specially bred to be dumb at this task. As you probably expected, the students with the bright rats had them outperforming the dull rats in a short period of time. These results are especially interesting because there were no real differences between the two groups of rats. Rosenthal and Fode had lied about the rats being specially bred. All of the rats were the usual laboratory variety. They had been assigned at random to either group. If there were no real differences between the groups of rats, how do we explain the fact that students who believed they had been given bright rats had them learn the maze faster than the other group?

The term "**self-fulfilling prophecies**" has been coined as a label for the tendency to act in ways that will lead us to find what we expected to find. I don't know what the students did to make the rats learn faster in the "bright" group or slower in the "dull" group. Perhaps the bright group was given extra handling or more food in the goal box. (When rats learn to run through mazes, they are rewarded with food when they reach the goal box.) Maybe the students given the "dull" rats dropped them harshly into the maze or were not as accurate in the records that they kept. Whatever they did, they somehow influenced their experimental results, so that the results were in accord with their expectations.

If self-fulfilling prophecies can influence how rats run through mazes, what sort of an effect will it have on everyday thinking and behavior? Earlier in this chapter, illusory correlations were discussed as the tendency to believe that events that you are observing are really correlated because you believe that they should be. Psychologists are becoming increasingly aware of the ways that personal convictions direct our selection and interpretation of facts. When you function as an intuitive scientist, it is important to keep in mind the ways we influence the results we obtain.

One way to eliminate the effects of self-fulfilling prophecies is with **double-blind procedures**. Let's consider a medical example. There are probably 100 home remedies for the common cold. How should we decide which, if any, actually relieve cold symptoms? Probably, somewhere, sometime, someone gave you chicken soup when you had a cold. Undoubtedly, you got better. Almost everyone who gets a cold gets better. The question is, "Did the chicken soup make you better?" This is a difficult question to answer because if you believe that chicken soup makes you better, you may rate the severity of your symptoms as less severe even when there was no real change. This is just another example of self-fulfilling prophecies. The only way to test this hypothesis is to give some people chicken soup and others something that looks and tastes like chicken soup and then have each group rate the severity of their cold symptoms. In this example all of the subjects are unaware or blind to the nature of the treatment they are receiving. It is important that the experimenters also be unaware of which subjects received the "real" chicken soup so that they don't inadvertently give subtle clues to the subjects. Experiments in which neither the subjects nor the experimenters know who is receiving the treatment are called double-blind experiments.

Although the chicken soup example may seem a little far-fetched, the need for double-blind procedures is critical in deciding whether any drug or treatment is working. Formal laboratory research on drugs that may be effective against AIDS or cancer always use double-blind procedures. Most people, however, do not apply these same standards when making personal decisions such as which type of psychotherapy is effective or whether massive doses of a vitamin or advice from a palm reader will improve some aspect of their life. Before you decide to see a therapist who claims to be able to improve your diabetes by manipulating your spine or to engage in screaming therapy to improve your self-confidence, look carefully for double-blind studies that support the use of the proposed therapy.

Making Sense Out of the World

Psychologists have been making the case for the 'nothing special' view of scientific thinking for many years.

—David Klahr and Herbert Simon (2001, p. 76)

As humans, we have a great need to explain—to see patterns in the dizzying array of life events and to be able to predict and prevent bad outcomes. In a study of how jurors reason, psychologists found that jurors would weave the events that were recounted during the trial into a plausible story and would then review information to see if it would fit with the story they constructed (Hastie & Dawes, 2001; Hastie & Pennington, 2000). Psychologists who study how jurors reason have found that jurors do not rely as much on evidence as the legal system instructs them to. Instead, they interpret proceedings by determining how well the information that is presented can be incorporated into a meaningful story that they constructed from the information presented during the trial. All knowledge can be thought of as a construction of the knower. Thus, this process is no different from any other ordinary cognitive process. To become better thinkers, we all need to consciously and conscientiously apply the skills used in hypothesis testing by carefully considering evidence, especially evidence that would disconfirm the narrative explanations that we rely on to make sense out of a vast array of information.

OCCULT BELIEFS AND THE PARANORMAL

Media distortions, social uncertainty, and deficiencies of human reasoning seem to be at the basis of occult beliefs.

—Barry Singer and Victor Benassi (1981, p. 49)

Do you believe in "channeling, clairvoyance, precognition, telepathy, psychic surgery, psychic healing, healing crystals, psychokinesis, astral travel, levitation, the Bermuda triangle mystery, unidentified flying objects (UFOs), plant consciousness, auras, [or] ghosts" (Gray, 1991, p. ix)? If you answered "yes" to any of these, you are not alone. A recent Gallup Poll showed that the proportion of the general population in the United States who believe in psychic and paranormal phenomena has increased over the last decade (The Gallup Organization, 2001). Belief in haunted houses, ghosts, witches, communicating with someone who has died, psychic healing, that extraterrestrial beings have visited the earth, and clairvoyance has each increased by over 5% in the last decade. One possible explanation is the increase in the number of television shows about these topics, some of which have an almost "newslike" appearance to them, including highly popular shows like *X Files* that carry the message that beings from outer space are living among us (Gibson, 2000).

Often these shows are narrated by people who appear to be honest and sincere. Few people remember the difference between actors and scientists when the actors provide a good imitation of something that looks like science.

How can we understand these beliefs when there is **no good evidence** that they have any basis in fact (Shermer, 1992; Stanovich, 1999)? In our attempt to make sense out of events in the world, we all seek to impose a meaningful explanation, especially for unusual events. Have you thought about a friend whom you haven't seen in many years and then received a phone call from him? Did you ever change your usual route home from school or work and then learn that there was a tragic accident that you probably would have been in if you had not changed your route? What about stories of people who recover from a deadly disease after they use imagery as a means of healing? We are all fascinated by these unusual events and try to understand them. Can you understand how small sample sizes (usually a single example), retrospective review (in hindsight we seek explanations that are available in memory), illusory correlations, self-fulfilling prophecies, difficulty in understanding probabilities, and other cognitive biases contribute to the popularity of paranormal beliefs? It is a fact that there is no positive evidence whatsoever for the existence of any psychic abilities. No one has collected the million-dollar prize offered by the James Randi Foundation for credible evidence of psychic or other paranormal phenomena. There are many anecdotes, but there has never been a statistically significant finding of psychic power that has been duplicated in another independent laboratory. "Anecdotes do not make a science" (Shermer, 1992, p. 19).

There are many real mysteries in the world and much that we don't understand. It is possible that someone has found a strange herbal cure for cancer, or that the lines on the palms of our hand or pattern of tea leaves in our tea cups are indicators of important life events, but if these are "real" phenomena, then they will hold up under the bright lights of double-blind, controlled laboratory testing. We can all laugh at the predictions made by various "psychics" such as the prediction that Fidel Castro would move to Beverly Hills after his government was overthrown and the many predictions about Princess Diana that included almost everything imaginable except her tragic death (Emery, 2001). We need to become much more skeptical when a friend tells us that crystals have healing powers or vitamin E can be used to revive those who have recently died. This topic is also addressed in the next chapter where I discuss how to reason with probabilities.

THINKING AS AN INTUITIVE SCIENTIST

Most people seem to believe that there is a difference between scientific thinking and everyday thinking . . . . But, the fact is, these same scientific thinking skills can be used to improve the chances of success in virtually any endeavor.

—George (Pinky) Nelson (1998)

One theme throughout this chapter is that everyday thinking has much in common with the research methods used by scientists when they investigate phenomena in their academic domains. Many of the pitfalls and problems that plague scientific investigations are also common in everyday thought. If you understand and avoid some of these problems, you will be a better consumer of research and a better intuitive scientist.

When you are evaluating the research claims of others or when you are asserting your own claims, there are several questions to keep in mind:

1. What was the nature of the sample? Was it large enough? Was it biased?
2. Are the variables operationally defined? What do the terms mean?
3. Were the measurements sensitive, valid, and reliable? Are the appropriate comparisons being made to support the claims?
4. Were extraneous variables controlled? What are other plausible explanations for the results?
5. Do the conclusions follow from the observations?
6. Are correlations being used to support causative arguments?
7. Is disconfirming evidence being considered?
8. How could the experimenter's expectancies be biasing the result?

Let's apply these guidelines to the choice of treatment programs that was presented at the opening of this chapter—the scenario presented you, as a heroin addict, with two choices of treatment programs. The first program is run by former heroin addicts and the second is run by therapists. First, what is the evidence for success rates? Although Program 1 cites a much higher success rate than Program 2, these numbers cannot be used to compare the two programs because Program 1 gives the success for those who stayed with the program at least one year, and we have no information about how many dropped out before achieving the one-year mark. Thus, the success rate for Program 1 is not a valid measure of success. We also have no information about how likely someone is to maintain recovery without treatment. In other words, there is no control group against which to measure the efficacy of treatment. Unfortunately, there is no information about the sample size because we are not told how many patients entered each program. If this were a real decision, then you would ask for this information. So far, there is little to go on.

I have found that most people like the idea that the therapist is a recovered addict who "has been there himself." The problem with this sort of qualification is that his anecdotes about "what worked for him" may be totally worthless. Dawes (1994) is highly critical of the sort of reasoning that leads people to believe that a former addict is a good choice for a counselor. As Dawes notes, the thinking that goes into this evaluation is something like this:

> The therapist was an addict.
> He did X and recovered.
> If I do X, then I will also recover.

I hope that you can see that this is very weak evidence. If you have already read Chapter 4 on reasoning, then you will recognize this as a categorical syllogism—one that is invalid. You have a single individual (sample size of one), all the biases of memory, no independent verification that X is useful, the problem of illusory correlation, and more. Of course, this individual could be an excellent therapist, but with the information that you are given, there is no reason to expect it. On the other hand, the therapist who has studied the psychology and biology of addiction should know about different treatment options, theories of addiction, and most importantly the success rates for a variety of different types of treatments based on results from large samples of addicts. This is an important point. Try posing the question that I used at the opening of this chapter to friends and relatives. You will probably find the bias toward selecting the recovered addict as a therapist.

If you scrutinize your own conclusions and those of others with the principles of hypothesis testing in mind, you should be able to defend yourself against invalid claims and improve your own ability to draw sound conclusions from observations.

APPLYING THE FRAMEWORK

In applying the general thinking skills framework to thinking as hypothesis testing, consider the following questions:

1. What Is the Goal?

You should use the skills developed in this chapter whenever you are devising hypotheses about the relationships among events and then collecting observations to test the validity of your hypotheses. There is a virtually endless number of examples when these skills are applicable. They should be used when considering social relationships (e.g., She likes it when I compliment her), physical relationships (e.g., The mercury in the tube rises when the temperature increases), treatment effects (e.g., Laughter therapy can improve the recovery rate from some dread diseases), and when functioning as a consumer of research.

2. What Is Known?

This question is about how to plan the thinking process. When thinking like an intuitive scientist, you need to begin by explicitly deciding on the nature of the hypothesis that you're testing and the way you will go about making or thinking about observations. You also need to consider the relative severity of different kinds of errors. The knowns include how you will operationalize your variables and how confident you want to be before you decide if your hypothesis is correct. In short, this step involves becoming explicit about your starting point in the thinking process. One of the most important pieces of information in determining cause is whether the subjects were assigned at random to different "treatment" groups. If not, it is extremely difficult to make valid causal claims.

3. Which Thinking Skill or Skills Will Get You to Your Goal?

The selection of the appropriate skill depends on how you've answered the previous questions. If you've decided that the hypothesis that you're testing is important enough to require a formal test, then you'll want to sample subjects in an unbiased manner and be certain that the number of subjects is sufficiently large and that measurement was accurate. Of course, I don't expect you to be testing lethal drugs based on the hypothesis-testing skills presented in this chapter. This sort of testing needs to be conducted by researchers with extensive knowledge of research and experimental design. However, you should know how to be a consumer of this sort of research and look for evidence of good hypothesis-testing methods.

The skills involved when thinking as an intuitive scientist include:

- Recognizing the need for and using operational definitions.
- Understanding the need to isolate and control variables in order to make strong causal claims.

- Checking for adequate sample size and unbiased sampling when a generalization is made.
- Being able to describe the relationship between any two variables as positive, negative, or unrelated.
- Understanding the limits of correlational reasoning.
- Seeking converging validity to increase your confidence in a decision.
- Checking for and understanding the need for control groups.
- Being aware of the bias in most estimates of variability.
- Considering the relative "badness" of different sorts of errors.
- Determining how self-fulfilling prophecies could be responsible for experimental results or everyday observations.
- Knowing when causal claims can and can't be made.

These skills should be used in your own thinking and in critiquing the thinking of others. After reading this chapter, you should be able to use these skills in any context in which they are appropriate, and even more importantly, recognizing when you need to use them.

4. Have You Reached Your Goal?

The final question to consider is whether you have reduced uncertainty: Can you predict the results of certain actions or can you make better decisions because you used the hypothesis-testing skills presented in this chapter? The ubiquitous concern for accuracy is always the final test of the quality of the decision at which you've arrived. When you function like an intuitive scientist, you will sometimes make wrong decisions because we never know "truth." But, you can minimize wrong decisions, by carefully using the hypothesis-testing skills presented in this chapter.

CHAPTER SUMMARY

1. Much of our everyday thinking is like the scientific method of hypothesis testing. We formulate beliefs about the world and collect observations to decide if our beliefs are correct.

2. In the inductive method we devise hypotheses from our observations. In the deductive method we collect observations that confirm or disconfirm our hypotheses. Most thinking involves an interplay of these two processes so that we devise hypotheses from experience, make observations, and then, on the basis of our observations, we redefine our hypotheses.

3. Operational definitions are precise statements that allow the identification and measurement of variables.

4. Independent variables are used to predict or explain dependent variables. When we formulate hypotheses, we want to know about the effect of the independent variable on the dependent variable(s).

5. When we draw conclusions from observations, it's important to utilize an adequately large sample size because people are variable in the way they respond. Most people are too willing to generalize results obtained from small samples.

6. In order to generalize about a population, the sample needs to be representative of the population. You need to ask if the sample you are using is biased in any way before making generalizations.

7. In determining if one variable (e.g., smoking) causes another variable (e.g., lung cancer) to occur, it is important to be able to isolate and control the causal variables. Strong causal claims require the three-stage experimental design that was described in this chapter.

8. In everyday contexts, we often use retrospective techniques to understand what caused an event to occur. This is not a good technique because our memories tend to be selective and malleable and because we have no objective systematic observations of the cause. Prospective techniques that record events when they occur and then see if the hypothesized result follows are better methods for determining cause-effect relationships.

9. Variables that are related so that changes in one variable are associated with changes in the other variable are called correlated variables. Correlations can be positive as in the relationship between height and weight (taller people tend to weigh more; shorter people tend to weigh less) or negative as in the relationship between exercise and weight (people who exercise a great deal tend to be thin, and those who exercise little tend to be heavy).

10. A common error is to infer a causative relationship from correlated variables. It is possible that Variable A caused Variable B, or that Variable B caused Variable A, or that A and B influenced each other, or that a third variable caused them both.

11. The belief that two variables are correlated when they are not (illusory correlation) is another type of error that is common in human judgment.

12. It is important that you use measurements that are sensitive, valid, and reliable or the conclusions you draw may be incorrect. Few people consider the importance of measurement issues when they draw everyday conclusions about the nature of the world.

13. Although many of our judgments lack validity, people report great confidence in them. This is called illusory validity.

14. Inadvertently, we may act in ways that will lead us to confirm or disconfirm hypotheses according to our expectations. These are called self-fulfilling prophecies.

TERMS TO KNOW

Check your understanding of the concepts presented in this chapter by reviewing their definitions. If you find that you're having difficulty with any term, be sure to reread the section in which it is discussed.

Hypothesis Testing. The scientific method of collecting observations to confirm or disconfirm beliefs about the relationships among variables.
Hypothesis. A set of beliefs about the nature of the world, usually concerning the relationship between two or more variables.
Inductive Method. A method of formulating hypotheses in which you observe events and then devise a hypothesis about the events you observed.
Deductive Method. A method of testing hypotheses in which you formulate a hypothesis that you believe to be true and then infer consequences from it. Systematic observations are then made to verify if your hypothesis is correct.
Operational Definition. An explicit set of procedures that tell the reader how to recognize and measure the concept in which you're interested.

(A) **Variable**. A quantifiable characteristic that can take on more than one value (e.g., height, gender, age, race).

Independent Variable. The variable that is selected (or manipulated) by the experimenter who is testing a hypothesis to see if changes in the independent variable will result in changes in the dependent variable. For example, if you want to know if people are more readily persuaded by threats or rational appeals, you could present either a threatening message or a rational appeal to two groups of people (message type is the independent variable), and then determine how much their attitudes toward the topic have changed (the dependent variable).

Dependent Variable. The variable that is measured in an experiment to determine if its value depends on the independent variable. Compare with independent variable.

Sensitive Measures. Measures that are able to detect small changes in the dependent variable.

Population. For statistical and hypothesis testing purposes, a population is the entire group of people (or animals or entities) in which one is interested and to which one wishes to generalize.

Sample. A subset of a population that is studied in order to make inferences about the population.

Random Sample. A sample in which everyone in a population has an equal chance of being selected.

Representative Sample. A sample that is similar to the population in important characteristics such as the proportion of males and females, socioeconomic status, and age.

Generalization. Using the results obtained in a sample to infer that similar results would have been obtained from the population if everyone in the population had been measured. (When used in the context of problem solving, it is a strategy in which the problem is considered as an example of a larger class of problems.)

Biased Sample. A sample that is not representative of the population from which it was drawn.

Confounding. When experimental groups differ in more than one way, it's not possible to separate the effects due to each variable. For example, if you found that teenage girls scored higher on a test of verbal ability than preteen boys, you wouldn't know if the results were due to sex differences or age differences between the two groups.

Convenience Samples. The use of a group of people who are readily available as participants in an experiment. Such samples may be biased in that they may not be representative of the population from which they were drawn.

Sample Size. The number of people selected for a study.

Law of Large Numbers. Large samples provide more reliable estimates about population characteristics than small samples.

Variability. Term to denote the fact that people (and animals) differ in the way they respond to experimental stimuli.

Law of Small Numbers. The willingness to believe that results obtained from a few subjects can be generalized to the entire population.

Subject. A person, animal, or entity who serves as a participant in an experiment.

Retrospective Research. After an event has occurred, the experimenter looks backward in time to determine its cause.

Prospective Research. A method of conducting research in which possible causative factors of an event are identified before the event occurs. Experimenters then determine if the hypothesized event occurs.

Correlated Variables. Two or more variables that are related. See positive correlation and negative correlation.

Positive Correlation. Two or more variables that are related so that increases in one variable occur concomitantly with increases in the other variable, and decreases in one variable occur with decreases in the other.

Negative Correlation. Two or more variables that are related such that increases in one variable are associated with decreases in the other variable.

Illusory Correlation. The belief that two variables are correlated, when in fact they are uncorrelated.

Validity. The extent to which a measure (e.g., a test) is measuring what you want it to.

Convergent Validity. The use of several different measures or techniques that all suggest the same conclusion.

Illusory Validity. The belief that a measure is valid (measures what you want it to) when, in fact, it is not. This belief causes people to be overconfident in their judgments.

Reliability. The consistency of a measure (e.g., a test) on repeated occasions.

Self-Fulfilling Prophecy. The tendency to act in ways that influence experimental results so that we obtain results that are consistent with our expectations.

Double-Blind Procedures. An experimental paradigm in which neither the subjects nor the person collecting data know the treatment group to which the subject has been assigned.

7

Likelihood
and Uncertainty:
Understanding
Probabilities

Contents

The jury was facing a difficult decision in the case of *People v. Collins*, (cited in Arkes & Hammond, 1986). The robbery victim could not identify his assailant. All he could recall was that the robber was a woman with a blond ponytail who, after the robbery, rode off in a yellow convertible driven by a Black man with a moustache and a beard. The suspect fit this description, but could the jury be certain "beyond a reasonable doubt" that the woman who was on trial was the robber? She was blond and often wore her hair in a ponytail. Her codefendant "friend" was a Black man with a moustache, beard, and yellow convertible. If you were the attorney for the defense, you would stress the fact that the victim could not identify this woman as the robber. What strategy would you use if you were the attorney for the prosecution?

The prosecutor produced an expert in probability theory who testified that the probability of these conditions "co-occurring (being blond *plus* having a ponytail *plus* having a Black male friend *plus* his owning a yellow convertible and so on, when these characteristics are independent) was 1 in 12 million. The expert testified that this combination of characteristics was so unusual that the jury could be certain "beyond a reasonable doubt" that she was the robber.

The jury returned a verdict of "guilty."

PROBABILISTIC NATURE OF THE WORLD

The theory of probabilities is nothing but common sense confirmed by calculation.

—La Place (1749–1827)

The legal system recognizes that we can never have absolute certainty in legal matters. Instead, we operate with various degrees of uncertainty. Juries are instructed to decide that someone is guilty of a crime when they are certain "beyond a reasonable doubt." This standard was adopted because there is always some small amount of doubt that the accused may be innocent. Jurors are instructed to operate under a different level of doubt when they are deciding about guilt or innocence in a civil case. In civil cases, they are told to deliver a verdict of guilty when the "preponderance of evidence" supports this decision. Thus, jurors are instructed to operate under two different levels of uncertainty when the case before them is criminal or civil. They need to be more certain when deciding that an accused party is guilty in a criminal case than in a civil case.

Probability is the study of likelihood and uncertainty. It plays a critical role in all professions and in most everyday decisions. All medical diagnoses and treatment decisions are inherently probabilistic, as are decisions made in business, college admissions, advertising, and research. Probability is the cornerstone of science; the laws of probability guide the interpretation of all research findings. Many of our leisure activities also rely on the principles of probability, most notably horse racing and card games. Every time you decide to take an umbrella, invest in the stock market, buy an insurance policy, or bet on a long shot in the Kentucky Derby, you are making a probability judgment. Other than the proverbial death and taxes, there is very little in life that is known with certainty. Because we live in a probabilistic world, critical thinking will require an understanding of probability.

There is good evidence that training in the use of probability will improve your ability to utilize probability values in appropriate manner. In an investigation of the use of statistical thinking in everyday reasoning tasks, researchers concluded that, "This study indicated clearly that statistical training can enhance the use of statistical rules in reasoning about everyday life and can do so completely outside the context of training" (Fong, Krantz, & Nisbett, 1986, p. 280). In other words, although the thinking skills presented in this chapter will require the use of basic arithmetic and probably some concentrated effort, it's likely that you'll be a better thinker for having worked through the problems.

Likelihood and Uncertainty

If your facts are wrong but your logic is perfect, then your conclusions are inevitably false. Therefore, by making mistakes in your logic, you have at least a random chance of coming to a correct conclusion.

> —Christie-Davies' Theorem (reference unknown, taken from a calendar)

If I flip a "fair" coin (i.e., one that is not biased, which means that either a head or tail is equally likely) into the air and ask you to guess the probability that it will land heads up, you would say that the probability of a head is 50% (or .50). This means that the coin is expected to land heads up half of the time. Although the word *probability* is used in several different ways, the definition of *probability* that is most useful in the present context is the number of ways a particular outcome (what we call a success) can occur divided by the number of possible outcomes (when each possible outcome is equally likely). It is a measure of how often we expect an event to occur **in the long run**. Success may seem like a strange word in this context, but you can think of it as the outcome in which you're interested. In this case, a success is getting the coin to land heads up. There is only one way for a coin to land heads up, so the number of ways a success can occur in this example is one. What are all the possible outcomes of flipping a coin in the air? The coin can either land heads up or tails up. (I've never seen a coin land on its edge, nor have I ever seen a bird come along and carry it off while it's flipped in the air, so I'm not considering these as possible outcomes.) Thus, there are two possible outcomes, each of which is as likely to happen as the other. To calculate the probability of getting a coin to land heads up, compute the number of ways a head can occur (1), divided by the number of possible outcomes (2), or 1/2, an answer you already knew. Because many people find it easier to think in percentages than in fractions, 1/2 is sometimes changed to 50%.

Let's try another example. How likely are you to roll a 5 in one roll of a die? As there is only one way for a 5 to occur, the numerator of the probability fraction is 1. A die is a 6-sided (cube) figure; thus there are 6 possible outcomes in one roll. If the die is not "loaded," that is, when each side of the die is equally likely to land facing up, the probability of rolling a 5 is 1/6, or approximately 17%.

What is the probability of rolling an even number in one roll of a fair die? To find this probability, consider the number of ways a success can occur. You could roll a 2, 4, or 6, all possible even numbers. Thus, there are three ways a success can occur out of six equally likely outcomes, so the probability of rolling an even number is 3/6 = 1/2.

What is the probability of rolling a whole number less than 7? If someone asked me to bet on this happening, I'd put up my house, my children, and my meager savings account to make this bet. In other words, I'd bet that this *will* happen. Let's see why. The number of ways a whole number less than 7 can occur in one roll of a die

Example

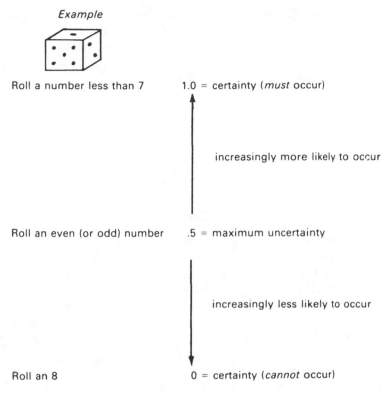

Roll a number less than 7   1.0 = certainty (*must* occur)

increasingly more likely to occur

Roll an even (or odd) number   .5 = maximum uncertainty

increasingly less likely to occur

Roll an 8   0 = certainty (*cannot* occur)

FIG. 7.1. Probability and likelihood.

is six (1, 2, 3, 4, 5, or 6), and the number of possible outcomes is six. Thus, the probability is 6/6, or 1. When a probability is equal to 1 (or 100%), it must happen; it is
certain to occur.

What is the probability of rolling an 8 in one roll of a die? Again, I'd put up
everything I own, but this time I'd bet against this occurrence. The number of ways
an 8 can occur is zero. Thus, the probability of this occurring is 0; it cannot occur.
This situation also reflects absolute certainty. Probabilities range from 0 (can never
happen) to 1 (must happen). Probability values close to 0 or 1 represent events that
are almost certain not to occur or almost certain to occur, whereas probabilities
near .5 (50%) represent maximum uncertainty, because either outcome is equally
likely, and thus there is no basis for predicting either one. This relationship is depicted in Fig. 7.1.

Odds

It is often convenient to discuss probabilities in terms of **odds**. If a friend gives you
3-to-1 odds that his school's championship tiddly-winks team will beat your
school's tiddly-winks team, this means that if four games were played, he would expect his team to win three of them. Authorities on organized sports (announcers,
sports page editors, and almost everyone else) usually express their degree of belief
in the outcome of a sporting event in terms of odds. (Betting odds like those posted
at racetracks and boxing matches refer to the amount of money that has been bet on

each contender and, thus, have a slightly different meaning from the one described here.)

To convert odds to a probability, add the two numbers that are given (e.g., 3:1 = 4), use the first number as the numerator and the sum as the denominator (3/4), and this is the equivalent probability.

The Laws of Chance

Uncertainty is an essential and integral facet of all forms of life and is, in principle, unavoidable.

—Gideon Keren and Karl Halvor Teigen (2001)

The most important phrase in the last section was "in the long run." Except for those special cases when the probability of an outcome is either 0% or 100%, we cannot know with certainty what will happen. I cannot know when I roll a die whether I will roll a 5, but, if I keep rolling a fair die for many, many trials, I do know that about 17% of the time I will roll a 5. I cannot know which roll will produce a 5, but I do know approximately how many rolls will land with a 5 showing, if I keep rolling for a long time. This is an important point. When we speak of the **laws of chance** (or laws of probability), we are referring to the ability to predict the number or percentage of trials on which a particular outcome will occur. With a large number of trials, I can be very accurate about the number of times a particular outcome will occur, but I cannot know which trials will yield a particular outcome. This means that I can make good "long-run" predictions and poor "short-run" predictions.

Let's consider insurance as an applied example of this distinction. When you buy a life insurance policy (or any other type of insurance policy), you are making a bet with the insurance company. You agree to pay a certain amount of money to the insurance company each year. They agree to pay your beneficiary a certain amount of money when you die. There are many different types of life insurance policies available, but for the purposes of this chapter, we'll consider the simplest. I'll use some simple numbers to demonstrate the statistical point that I want to make—in real life, the actual costs and payoffs are different from those used in this example. Suppose that you are 30 years old and that you agree to pay the insurance company $1,000 per year. When you die, your beneficiary will receive $20,000. You are betting with the insurance company that you will die at a fairly young age (a bet that you hope to lose) so that you will have paid them only a small amount of money and your beneficiary will receive a larger amount of money. If you die before the age of 50, you win the bet. Ignoring complications like inflation and interest, you will have paid less than the $20,000 your beneficiary will receive if you die at a young age. The insurance company, on the other hand, will win the bet if you live to a ripe old age. If you die when you are 70 years old, you will have paid them $40,000 and your dearly beloved will receive only $20,000.

Insurance companies can make money because of the laws of chance. No one knows when you or anyone else will die, but insurance companies do know how many people aged 30 (the age at which you bought your policy) will die before they reach their 50th birthday. Thus, although no one can predict accurately the age at death for any single individual, we can use the laws of chance to predict how many people will live to be any particular age.

How We Explain Chance Events

Most people can understand the laws of chance when they think about tossing a coin or rolling a pair of dice, but find it more difficult to recognize how chance operates in complicated real-world settings. Unusual events—the sort that make you say "imagine that"—are often reported in the news. Consider, for example, this newspaper headline: "Three Sisters Give Birth on the Same Day" (*Chance Magazine*, 2001). According to an article in the March 14, 2001 edition of the *Point Stevens Journal*, Karralee Morgan, Marrianne Asay, and Jennifer Hone (real people—real names—no names have been changed to protect anyone) are sisters who all gave birth on March 11, 1998 (as reported in *Chance Magazine*). It's hard to hear this story and *not* ask, "What is the probability that three sisters would give birth on the same day?" As it turns out, this is a tricky question because there are several ways of interpreting what is being asked. Consider these two possible interpretations:

> What is the probability that these three sisters (Karralee, Marrianne, and Jennifer) will all give birth on March 11, 1998?
> What is the probability that somewhere in the United States there will be three sisters (any set of three sisters) who all give birth on the same day (any day of any one year)?

Before I give you the answers, think about what is being asked and decide which of these two interpretations is more likely to occur. Did you understand that the situation described in Question 2 is *much more likely* than the situation described in Question 1? According to calculations presented in a magazine that teaches about chance events (*Chance Magazine*, 2001), the answer for Question 1 is about 1 in 50 million, but the answer for Question 2 is about 1 in 6,000. It seems likely that most people are thinking about Question 2 when they ask about the chance of three sisters giving birth on the same day, but it is easy to see why these are difficult concepts because the question is prompted by the situation in Question 1. If we want to know about any three sisters on any day in any one year (there are 365 different possible days, so there are more ways for this to happen), it is much more likely than if we mean a specific three sisters on a specific day.

Degrees of Belief

Probability is sometimes used to express the strength of a belief about the likelihood of an outcome. This is a second definition for the term probability. For example, if you interview for a job and believe that the interview went well, you might assess the probability that you will be offered the job as 80%. This probability value was not mathematically derived by calculating the number of ways a success could occur divided by the number of possible outcomes. Instead, it indicates your degree of belief that the job will be offered. It suggests a moderate to high likelihood. If someone else interviewed for the same job and believed that his chance of being offered the job was 50%, it would be obvious that he was less confident about getting the job than you were.

The use of probability to express one's degree of belief in the likelihood of an outcome is particularly prevalent at election time. Political analysts will often attach probability values to the likelihood of a candidate's election. If a political analyst gives a candidate a 30% chance of winning, she is predicting that although the candidate might win, she believes that the candidate is more likely to lose. Probability values are handy ways of quantifying confidence in an outcome.

FACTORS AFFECTING JUDGMENTS ABOUT
LIKELIHOOD AND UNCERTAINTY

*"The odds against there being a bomb on a plane are a million to one, and
against two bombs a million times a million to one. Next time you fly, cut the
odds and take a bomb."*

—Benny Hill (quoted in Byrne, 1988, p. 349)

There is a large research literature documenting the fact that most people are biased
in their assessment of probabilities. We fail to appreciate the nature of randomness
and have strong misconceptions about likelihood and uncertainty (Garfield &
Ahlgren, 1988). This is not a surprising finding given that we can only use probabilities to understand events "in the long run" and most of our everyday experiences
are based on "short-run" observations. For example, there is a large body of data
that show that, on the average, people who smoke die at a younger age than those
who don't (Paulos, 1994). Most of us can't discover this relationship on our own because we don't know the age at death for large numbers of people, but we may
know one or two people who smoked two packs a day and lived into their 90s. This
sort of personal experience would lead us to doubt the statistics that were collected
from many people. Remember though, personal experience is *not* a good way to
make many judgments about the world. Recall from the previous chapter that experience is an expensive teacher, but not a good one.

The Search for Meaning

*To live, it seems is to explain, to justify, and to find coherence among diverse
outcomes, characteristics, and causes.*

—Gilovich (1991, p. 22)

We seek causes for events that happen to us and others, but most of us rarely consider the randomness of many events. We look for patterns and meaning, a quest
that can often be helpful, but also can lead to beliefs that are groundless. For example, consider this true story: A student stopped in my office to talk with me. He told
about an "amazing thing" that just happened to him. He was a student in a class of
15 students. Each student had to make an oral presentation, and the order in which
they were to present was determined by drawing numbers from a box. "Guess who
picked number 1?" he asked excitedly. I guessed that he did. "Exactly, and do you
know the probability of that!" I did, it was 1/15 or approximately 7%. "Isn't that
amazing? Out of 15 people in the class, I picked number 1. How can you explain
that?" I attributed this not-so-amazing outcome to chance; after all, someone had to
pick number 1. He was certain that was a sign of something; maybe the "gods" had
intervened or his karma had gone berserk (whatever that means). He was looking
for a cause that could explain this event, and he never considered just plain
"chance."

There seems to be a universal need to find meaning in the vast array of everyday
events that confront us, a trait that makes it difficult to recognize chance events. You
may have heard about the controversy over the *Bible Code*, which is the title of a
book that describes how letters sampled at regular intervals (for example, every

50th letter) from the Bible had embedded in them the names of famous people and foretold events that would happen in the future (Drosnin, 1997). Statisticians howled with laughter (and scorn) at this book because chance alone would result in many words appearing in these letter strings. On the other hand, it is easy to understand how someone who does not understand concepts in probability might be persuaded by the seemingly amazing number of names and words that were embedded in long strings of letters.

The author of the *Bible Code* (Drosnin, 1997) challenged statisticians to use the same technique of letter sampling with *Moby Dick*, a book that presumably would not have embedded special messages about the future into its letter sequences. A group of Australian computer scientists (McKay, Bar-Natan, & Kalai, 1999) took up the challenge and found "M. L. King," near the phrase "to be killed by them," "Kennedy" near the word "shoot," and many more famous names and meaningful phrases (including "Princess Di" and "Lincoln") in letter strings taken from *Moby Dick*, thus showing that mere chance would result in many meaningful names and phrases embedded in long strings of letters. In general, we tend to underestimate the importance of being able to think about probabilities. In an editorial on this topic, one columnist chided the American public for making fun of a politician's poor grammar because we should be far more concerned about our politicians' math skills, especially their poor understanding of probabilities (Cole, 2001). There are many critical issues that depend on the ability to think with numbers—global warming, population growth, and the economy, to name a few.

Overconfidence

Most people ... tend to overestimate the degree to which we are responsible for our own successes.

—Simon Gervais and Terrance Odean (2001, p. 1)

By definition, there is always some uncertainty in probabilistic events. Yet, research has shown that people tend to be more confident in their decisions about probabilistic events than they should be. Consider an example that Daniel Kahneman, a researcher in this area, likes to use. When he and his coauthors began working on a text on decision making, they were fairly confident that they would have it completed within a year, despite the fact that they knew that most books like the one they were writing take many years to complete. They believed that they would beat these "odds." In fact, it took them several years to complete the text.

In an experimental investigation of the **overconfidence phenomenon**, people were asked to provide answers with a specified degree of confidence to factual questions (Kahneman & Tversky, 1979). Try it with this question: "I feel 98% certain that the number of nuclear plants operating in the world in 1980 was more than _____ and less than _____. Fill in the blanks with numbers that reflect 98% confidence. The researchers investigating this effect found that nearly one third of the time, the correct answer did not lie between the two values that reflected a 98% level of confidence. (The correct answer to this question is 189.) This result demonstrates that people are often highly confident when their high degree of confidence is unwarranted.

Have you ever bought a lottery ticket? Do you know what the odds are against your hitting the jackpot? The laws of probability dictate that you should expect to lose, yet countless numbers of people expect to win. In fact, a disturbing poll published in *Money* magazine revealed that almost as many people are planning for their retirement by buying lottery tickets (39%) as are investing in stocks (43%) (Wang, 1994).

People tend to be most confident in uncertain situations when they believe that they have control over the uncertain events. Many state lottery advisors are familiar with this principle of human nature and now have a lottery plan that allows the buyer to select his own number. People prefer to select their own numbers over being given a number at random because it gives them an illusion of control. The winning number is still selected randomly, but people believe they are more likely to win in the self-selection lottery. Overconfidence can be disastrous for financial investors. In a study of individual investors, two economists found that most people fail to recognize the role that chance plays in the stock market, so they tend to attribute gains to their own expertise in picking stocks and losses to external forces that they could not control. The result is that overconfident investors trade their stocks far too often because they believe that they are making wise choices (Gervais & Odean, 2001). If they could recognize the effects of random fluctuations in the stock market instead of attributing the changes to their own trading behaviors, they would have traded less often and ended up in better financial shape.

USING PROBABILITY

Without giving it much thought, we utilize probabilities many times each day. Let's start with one of the few examples where probability values are made explicit. Many people begin each day by reading the weather forecast in the morning paper. What do you do when you read that the probability of rain is 80% today? Most people will head off to school or work toting an umbrella. What if it does not rain? Can we conclude that the forecaster was wrong? The forecast of an 80% probability of rain means that out of every 100 days when the weather conditions are like those on this particular day, there will be rain on 80 of them. Thus, a probability of rain is, like all probability values, based on what we would expect in the long run. Weather experts know that 80 out of 100 days will have rain, but the forecasters cannot know with absolute certainty which days it will rain.

Suppose that you are to be married on this hypothetical day, and a magnificent outdoor ceremony is planned. Suppose that an 80% probability of rain was forecast, and it did not rain. Would you believe that something other than chance was responsible for the good weather or that the absence of rain is a good (or bad) sign for your marriage? If you would interpret the good weather as a sign from the heavens or some other astral body, then you have demonstrated the point that was just made—we seek meaning in events, even events as seemingly uncontrollable as the weather, and we rarely consider plain old chance.

The number of instances in which we are given explicit probability values that have been computed for us is relatively small. One area where this practice is growing is in the use of medical information sheets that are designed to help patients understand the risks and benefits of taking a particular drug. The Food and Drug Administration requires that all oral contraceptive medications (birth control pills) be packaged with statistical information about the health risks associated with them. To arrive at an intelligent decision based on the information provided, potential oral contraceptive users must be able to understand the statistical summaries that are presented in the medical information sheets.

The following excerpt from an oral contraceptive package insert provides an example: "For women aged 20 to 44, it is estimated that about 1 in 2,000 using oral contraceptives will be hospitalized each year because of abnormal clotting. Among nonusers in the same age group, about 1 in 20,000 would be hospitalized each year" (Ortho Pharmaceutical Corp., 1979, p. 16). Although consumers can readily assess that clotting is more likely for pill users, this information is of little practical value unless an oral contraceptive consumer can decide if 1 in 2,000 is a large or small number, i.e., "Is it a danger to me if I am taking the pill?" Two related experiments (Halpern & Blackman, 1985; Halpern, Blackman, & Salzman, 1989) have shown that most people find information like this to be relatively meaningless.

Consider the following: Suppose you read that the risk of developing heart disease is 10.5 times more likely for oral contraceptive users than for nonusers. Most people will conclude from this information that taking oral contraceptives presents a substantial risk of heart disease. Suppose now that you are told that only 3.5 women out of 100,000 users will develop heart disease. You probably would interpret this sentence as meaning that there is little risk associated with oral contraceptive use. Consider the "flip side" of this information and think about how you would assess safety if you read that 99,996.5 women out of 100,000 users will not develop heart disease. Does it seem even safer? Another way of presenting the same information is to convert it to a percentage. There is only a .0035% chance that oral contraceptive users will develop heart disease. Most people would now consider the risk associated with oral contraceptive use to be minuscule.

Which of these statements is correct? They all are. The only way they differ is the way in which the statistical information is presented, and different ways of presenting the same statistical information lead to very different assessments of safety (Halpern, Blackman, & Salzman, 1989). It is important to keep this in mind when interpreting statistical information. There is a trend to provide consumers with statistical risk information so that they can make informed safety judgments about a diverse assortment of topics including how to treat a particular type of cancer and the safety of nuclear energy. Although the topic of risk is considered in more detail later in this chapter, keep in mind that the best way to convert risk probabilities to a meaningful value is to write out all of the mathematically equivalent values (i.e., X out of Y occurrences, number of times greater risk than a meaningful comparison event, number that will die, number that will not die). Graphic representations of relative risks can also be helpful when there are many values that need to be compared simultaneously. The use of spatial arrays is touted throughout this book (e.g., circle diagrams when interpreting syllogisms, graphic organizers to comprehend complex prose, tree diagrams for use in making sound decisions). One advantage that they confer in this situation is that they reduce the memory load in working memory and allow us to consider several different alternatives "at a glance."

Games of Chance

People love to play games. From Las Vegas to Atlantic City, and in all of the small towns in between, and in many other countries in the world, people spend countless hours and dollars playing games of chance, skill, and semiskill. For many people, the only serious consideration they have ever given to probability is when playing games of chance.

DRABBLE By Kevin Fagan

DRABBLE © UFS

Cards

Card playing is a ubiquitous pastime, with small children playing "fish" and "old maid," and their older counterparts play canasta, bridge, poker, pinochle, black jack, hearts, and too many others to mention. The uncertainty inherent in card games adds to the pleasure of playing (although the camaraderie and pretzels and beer also help).

Good card players, regardless of the game, understand and utilize the rules of probability. Let's apply the definitional formula for probability to card games. For example, how likely are you to draw an ace of spades from a deck of 52 cards? The probability of this happening is 1/52, or approximately 2%, because there is only one ace of spades and 52 possible outcomes. How likely are you to draw an ace of any suit from a full deck of cards? If you've been following the probability discussion so far, you'll realize that the answer is 4/52, or approximately 8%, because there are four aces in a 52-card deck.

Although some professional card players claim to have worked out careful plans that will help them to change the odds of winning in their favor, it is not possible to "beat the house" for most card games, no matter how good a player one is. It is always difficult to tell the extent to which these stories of successful gamblers are hype. Professional gamblers often enjoy bragging about their winnings and conveniently forget about the times when they lost. Furthermore, most of the self-proclaimed expert gamblers are selling their "winning system." I hope that you recall from the chapters on reasoning and analyzing arguments that when an "expert" stands to gain from the sale of a product, the expert's opinion becomes suspect.

According to Gunther (1977), Vera Nettick (who is a real person) is a lucky lady. While playing a game of bridge, she was dealt a hand that contained all 13 diamonds. Breathlessly, she won a grand slam with the once-in-a-lifetime card hand. Any statistician will be quick to point out that every possible combination of cards will be dealt to somebody sooner or later. Thus, Vera Nettick's hand was no more unusual than any other card hand, although it certainly is more memorable. Can you guess how often such a hand would occur? Gunther (1977) figured this out as follows:

> There are roughly 635 billion possible bridge hands. Of these, eight might be called "perfect" hands, though some are more perfect than others. To begin with, there are four perfect no-trump hands. Such a hand would contain all four aces, all four kings, all four queens, and one of the four jacks. Any of these four hands would be unequivocally perfect, because no bid could top it. Slightly less perfect, in descending order, are hands containing all the spades, all the hearts, all the diamonds, and all the clubs. If there are eight of these perfect hands in a possible 635 billion, the statistical probability is that such a hand will be dealt one in every 79 billion tries, give or take a few.

Now all we have to do is estimate how many games of bridge are played every year and how many hands are dealt in each game. Using fairly conservative estimates, it turns out that a perfect hand should be dealt to some lucky bridge player, somewhere in the United States, roughly once every three or four years. (p. 30)

Actually, Gunther's figures are too low, because new decks of cards are organized in ascending order by suits so that one or two "perfect" shuffles will produce "perfect" bridge hands (Alcock, 1981). (A perfect shuffle occurs when, following a "cut," there is a one-to-one interweaving of cards from each half of the deck.) And, of course, none of these calculations address the possibility of cheating, which would change the probabilities because each possible combination of cards would no longer be equally likely. Consider the two card hands shown in Fig. 7.2. Every possible combination of cards is equally likely when the cards are dealt at random. This topic is also discussed in Chapter 8, "Decision Making."

Roulette

Roulette is often thought of as an aristocratic game. It is strange that it has gained this reputation, because it is a game of pure chance. Unlike most card games, there is no skillful way to play roulette. As you probably know, roulette is played by spinning a small ball inside a circular array of numbered and colored pockets. Eighteen of the pockets are red; 18 are black; and 2 are green. Players can make a variety of bets. One possible bet is that the ball will land in a red pocket. What is the probability

FIG. 7.2. Which of these two card hands are you more likely to be dealt from a well-shuffled deck of cards?

of this event when the ball is equally likely to land in any pocket? There are 18 red pockets out of 38 pockets (possible outcomes); therefore, the probability of the ball landing in a red pocket is 18/38. Because this is a number less than .5, we know that it will land in a red pocket slightly less than half of the time. Thus, if you kept betting on red, you would lose slightly more often than you would win. Suppose now you bet on black pockets. Again, the probability would be 18/38; and again, if you continue to bet on black pockets, you will lose more often than you win. Of course, sometimes you will win, and at other times you will lose, but after many spins—in the long run—you will lose at roulette.

The odds or probability of winning at any casino game are always favorable to the "house," otherwise, casinos could not stay in business. Actually, there is one person who has been able to "beat" the roulette odds. One of my heros is Al Hibbs, a scientist who gained fame for his work at the Jet Propulsion Laboratory in Pasadena, California, where much of the work on the U. S. space program is done. When he was a student, he used his knowledge of probability to run his original stake of $125 up to $6,300 at the Pioneer Club in Reno. Here's how he did it: Hibbs knows that although every number in a roulette wheel should be equally likely to occur, all manufactured devices have imperfections. These imperfections make some numbers more likely to occur than others. Hibbs and a friend recorded the results of 100,000 spins of a roulette wheel to find the numbers that occurred most often. Accordingly, they bet on these numbers. Unfortunately, none of us can duplicate his success, because the wheels are now taken apart and reassembled with different parts each day. Thus, although each wheel is still imperfect, the imperfections differ from day to day.

Computing Probabilities in Multiple-Outcome Situations

We are often concerned with the probability of two or more events occurring, such as getting two heads in two flips of a coin or rolling a 6 at least once in two rolls of a die. These sorts of situations are called **multiple outcomes**.

Using Tree Diagrams

Although it is relatively easy to understand that the probability of getting a head on one flip of a fair coin is 1/2, it is somewhat more difficult to know intuitively the probability of getting four heads in four flips of a fair coin. Although an example of flipping a coin may seem artificial, it is a good way of showing how probabilities combine over many trials. Let's figure it out. (Follow along with me, even if you are math-phobic. The calculations and mathematical thinking are relatively easy, if you work along with the examples. Do *not* look at the next several figures and exclaim, "no way, I'll just skip it." It is important to be able to think with and about numbers.)

On the first flip, only one of two possible outcomes can occur; a head (H) or tail (T). What can happen if a coin is flipped twice? There are four possible outcomes; a head on the first flip and a head on the second (HH); a head on the first flip and a tail on the second (HT); a tail on the first flip and a head on the second (TH); and a tail on the first flip and a tail on the second (TT). Because there are four possible outcomes and only one way to get two heads, the probability of this event is 1/4 (again, assuming that the coin is fair, that is, that getting a head is as likely as getting a tail). There is a general rule, the "and rule," for calculating this value in any situation.

When you want to find the probability of one event *and* another event (a head on the first and second flip), you multiply their separate probabilities. By applying the "and rule," we find that the probability of obtaining two tails when a coin is flipped twice is equal to $1/2 \times 1/2$, which is $1/4$. Intuitively, the probability of both events occurring should be less likely than either event alone, and it is.

A simple way to compute this probability is to represent all possible events with **tree diagrams**. Tree diagrams were used in Chapter 4 on reasoning when we figured the validity of if, then statements. In this chapter, we will add probability values to the "branches" of the tree to determine the probability of different combinations of outcomes. Later in this book, I will return to tree diagrams once again as a way of generating creative solutions to problems.

On the first flip, either an H or T will land facing up. For a fair coin, the probability of a head is equal to the probability of a tail, which is equal to .5. Let's depict this as follows:

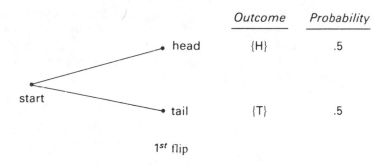

When you flip a second time, either an H on the first flip will be followed by an H or T, or a T on the first flip will be followed by an H or T. The probability of a head or tail on the second flip is still .5. Outcomes from a second flip are added as "branches" on a tree diagram.

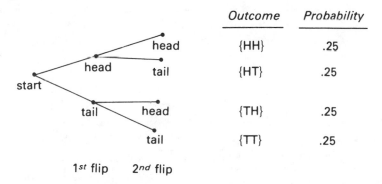

As you can see from this tree, there are four possible outcomes. You can use this tree to find out the probability of other events. What is the probability of getting exactly one H in two flips of a coin? Because there are two ways for this to occur (HT) or (TH), the answer is 2/4 or 1/2. When you want to find the probability of two *or* more different outcomes, add the probability of each outcome. This is called the "or rule." Another way to ask the same questions is, "What is the probability of getting either a head followed by a tail (1/4) *or* a tail followed by a head (1/4)?" The correct procedure is to add these values, which equals 1/2. Intuitively, the probability of

two or more events occurring should be higher (more likely) than the probability of
any one of them occurring, and it is.

We can only use the "or rule" and the "and rule" when the events we're interested in are **independent**. Two events are independent when the occurrence of one
of them does not influence the occurrence of the other. In this example, what you get
on the first flip of a coin does not influence what you get on the second flip. In addition, the "or rule" requires that the outcomes be mutually exclusive, which means
that if one occurs, the other cannot occur. In this example, the outcomes are mutually exclusive because we cannot obtain both a head and a tail on any single flip.

Let's get away from the artificial example of coin flipping, and apply the same
logic in a more useful context. I'm sure that every student has, at some time or other,
taken a multiple-choice test. (Some students like to call them multiple-guess tests.)
Most of these tests have five alternative answers for each question. Only one of these
is correct. Suppose also that the questions are so difficult that all you can do is guess
randomly at the correct answer. What is the probability of guessing correctly on the
first question? If you have no idea which alternative is the correct answer, then you
are equally likely to choose any of the five alternatives, assuming that each alternative is equally likely to be correct. Because the sum of all possible alternatives must
be 1.0, the probability of selecting each alternative, when they are equally likely, is
.20. One alternative is correct, and four are incorrect, so the probability of selecting
the correct alternative is .20. A tree diagram of this situation is shown here.

	Outcome	Probability	
Correct	{C}	.2	
Incorrect	{I}	.2	Probability
Incorrect	{I}	.2	of being
Incorrect	{I}	.2	incorrect
			on the first
Incorrect	{I}	.2	question = .8.

start   1st Question

What is the probability of getting the first two multiple-choice questions correct
by guessing? We'll have to add a second branch to a tree that will soon be very
crowded. To save space and to simplify the calculations, all of the incorrect alternatives can be represented by one branch labeled "incorrect." The probability of being
incorrect on any single question is .8:

	Outcome	Probability
Correct	{CC}	.04
Incorrect	{CI}	.16
Correct	{IC}	.16
Incorrect	{II}	.64

The probability of two correct questions by guessing is .2 × .2, which equals .04. That means that this would happen by chance only 4% of the time. Suppose we extend our example to three questions. I won't draw a tree, but you should be able to see by now that the probability is .2 × .2 × .2 = .008. This is so unusual that it would occur less than 1% of the time by chance. What would you conclude about someone who got all three of these questions correct? Most people (professors are people, too) would conclude that the student wasn't guessing, and that she really knew something. Of course, it is possible that the student was just lucky, but it is so unlikely that we would conclude that something other than luck was responsible for the outcome we obtained.

Let me point out a curious side to this kind of reasoning. Consider the plight of Sara. She took a 15-question multiple-choice test in which every question had five alternatives. Sara got all 15 questions wrong. Can you determine the probability of this happening by chance? I won't draw the tree diagram to depict this situation, but it is easy to see that the probability of being wrong on one question is .80; therefore, the probability of being wrong on all 15 questions is $(.80)^{15}$. This is .80 times itself 15 times, which equals .0352. Because this would happen by chance only 3.52% of the time, can Sara present the argument to her professor that something other than chance determined this unusual result? Of course, Sara can make this argument, but would you be willing to believe her if you were her professor? Suppose she argued that she must have known the correct answer to every question. How else could she have avoided selecting it in all 15 consecutive questions? I don't know how many professors would buy her assertion that getting all 15 questions wrong demonstrates her knowledge, even though identical reasoning is used as proof of knowing correct answers when the probability of getting all the questions correct is about the same. (In this example, the probability of getting all 15 questions correct just by guessing is $[.20]^{15}$, which is a number far less than .0001.) Personally, if I were the professor, I'd give Sara high marks for creativity and for her understanding of statistical principles. It is possible that Sara did know "something" about the topic, but that "something" was systematically wrong. I'd also point out to her that it is possible that she was both unprepared and unlucky enough to guess wrong 15 times. After all, unusual events do happen sometimes.

Before going on to the next section, be sure that you understand how tree diagrams are used to compute probabilities and to consider all possible outcomes. I'll be returning to these diagrams later in this chapter. Once you learn how to use them, you'll be surprised at how many possible applications there are for tree diagrams.

Conjunction Error—Applying the "And Rule"

The following problem was posed by Tversky and Kahneman (1983, p. 297):

> Linda is 31 years old, outspoken and very bright. She majored in philosophy. As a student, she was deeply concerned with issues of discrimination and social justice, and also participated in anti-nuclear demonstrations.

For the following list of statements, estimate the probability that it is descriptive of Linda.

A. Linda is a teacher in elementary school.
B. Linda works in a bookstore and takes yoga classes.

C. Linda is active in the feminist movement.
D. Linda is a psychiatric social worker.
E. Linda is a member of the League of Women voters.
F. Linda is a bank teller.
G. Linda is an insurance salesperson.
H. Linda is a bank teller and is active in the feminist movement.

Stop now and estimate the probability for each statement.

The short paragraph about Linda was written to be representative of an active feminist, which is Statement C. Thus, if we rely on common stereotypes of the "typical feminist," C would seem to be a likely description. Look at Statements F (bank teller) and H (feminist *and* a bank teller). How did you rank these two sentences? Most people believe that H is more probably true than F. Can you see why F *must be* more likely than H when being a bank teller and being a feminist are independent of each other? There are some bank tellers who are not active in the feminist movement. When determining the probability of both of two events occurring, you multiply the probabilities of each one occurring (the "and rule"). Thus, the probability of two events *both* occurring must be less likely than the probability of one of these events occurring. In Tversky and Kahneman's (1983) study, 85% of the subjects judged Statement H to be more probable than Statement F. The error of believing that the occurrence of two events is more likely than the occurrence of one of them is called the **conjunction error**.

For those of you who think better with spatial arrays, let's represent this problem with circle diagrams, a form of representation that was used with syllogisms in Chapter 4 on reasoning. Draw one circle to represent every bank teller in the world, and a second circle to represent every feminist. The two circles have to overlap somewhat because there are some bank tellers who are feminists. This area of overlap is shaded in Fig. 7.3. As you can see in Fig. 7.3, the shaded area that represents all people who are *both* bank tellers and feminists must be smaller than the circle that represents all bank tellers because there are bank tellers who are not feminists.

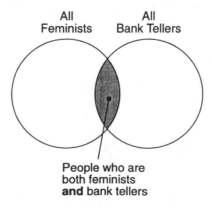

FIG. 7.3. The two circles represent "All Feminists" and "All Bank Tellers." The intersection of these two circles shows those individuals who are both feminist and a bank tellers. Because there are feminists who are not bank tellers and bank tellers who are not feminists, the area of their overlap must be smaller than either set alone.

Now that you understand the conjunctive error, try the next question (also taken from Tversky and Kahneman, 1983, p. 308):

A health survey was conducted in a sample of adult males in British Columbia, of all ages and occupations.
Please give your best estimate of the following values:
What percentage of the men surveyed have had one or more heart attacks? _____
What percentage of the men surveyed both are over 55 years old and have had one or more heart attacks? _____

Stop now and fill in the blanks above with your best estimate of these values.

Over 65% of the respondents believed that a higher percentage of the men would be both over 55 and have had a heart attack than the percentage of men who reported that they had a heart attack. Do you recognize this as another example of a conjunction error? The probability of two uncertain events both occurring cannot be greater than the probability of just one of them occurring.

There are some psychologists who object to all of the emphasis on the ways people make mistakes in their thinking (Gigerenzer, Todd, & the ABC Research Group, 2000). They argue that most of us think pretty well, given real-life circumstances, which include limited time to think through problems and limited information. Most of the time, we rely on heuristics, which are "rules of thumb" or shortcuts for thinking. Gigerenzer and his colleagues consider problems like the "Linda" problem to be "tricks." In this case, we are asked to make a decision about one person, when the probability data refer to the population of all bank tellers and all feminists. He argues that it is not irrational to use "typicality information" (e.g., the typical feminist has certain traits) when making a "best guess" about one person. This is an area where psychologists disagree about what is rational or reasoned thinking and is likely to continue to be a hotly debated topic in the next several years. The point made by Gigerenzer and others who are more optimistic about the quality of human cognition is certainly valid. Many of the examples that show how poorly most of us think seem artificial or lack important information that we normally would consider. Like many of psychology's debates, each side seems to have part of the answer. Under some circumstances, people are easily misled and thinking goes wrong in predictable ways, but under other circumstances, people can think fairly well. The situation is like the proverbial glass that is both half-full and half-empty. Regardless of your personal opinion about this debate, it is true that with hard work, we can all learn to think better—a fact that should make both the optimists and pessimists very happy.

Cumulative Risks—Applying the "Or Rule"

It should be obvious that the probability of getting three questions correct by chance when there are five alternatives will be much smaller than the probability of getting just one question correct by chance and that the probability of getting at least one question correct by chance out of three questions will be higher than the probability of getting one question correct when there is only one question. The kinds of examples presented so far were deliberately simple. Let's see how this principle applies in real-world settings.

Most real-life risks involve repeated exposure to a risky situation. Consider driving. The probability of having an accident in one car ride is very low. But what happens to this probability when you take hundreds or thousands of car rides? According to the "or rule", this is the probability of an accident on the first *or* second *or* . . . . nth car ride. In an interesting study of how people understand the concept of cumulative risk, Shaklee (1987) gave subjects different probability values that supposedly corresponded to the yearly risk of a flood. Subjects then had to estimate the likelihood of a flood in 1 month, 5 years, 10 years, and 15 years. Only 74% of her subjects knew that the likelihood of a flood increased with intervals over 1 year. Among those who gave higher probability values for intervals over 1 year, most seriously underestimated the **cumulative probability**.

Let's consider a similar example. In the case of contraception, a method that is 96% effective per year will result in an average of four pregnancies per 100 couples per year. Assuming a constant failure rate over time, we would expect even more women would become pregnant when using this method for a period of 5 years, and an even greater number when using this method over 15 years (Shaklee, 1987). In a study with college students, only 52% realized that the number of expected pregnancies would increase over time, and most of them significantly underestimated the number of pregnancies with a contraceptive method that is 96% effective.

The message here should be clear: When you are determining risk, it is important to understand whether the value you are being given is per some unit of time (e.g., 1 year) and how cumulative risks increase with repeated exposure. It seems that many people do not understand the concept that cumulative risks are greater than one-time risks.

EXPECTED VALUES

Which of the following bets would you take if you could only choose one of them?

1. The Big 12
   It will cost you $1 to play. If you roll a pair of dice and get a 12, you'll get your $1 back, plus another $24. If you roll any other number, you'll lose your $1.
2. Lucky 7
   It will cost you $1 to play (same cost as above). If you roll a "lucky 7" with a pair of dice, you'll get your $1 back, plus another $6. If you roll any other number, you'll lose your $1.

Stop now and select either item 1 or 2.

Most people choose item 1, reasoning that $24 if a 12 is rolled is four times more than they can win if a 7 is rolled, and the cost is the same for each bet. Let's see if this thinking is correct.

In order to decide which is the better bet, we need to consider the probability of winning and losing and the corresponding value of each. There is a formula that will take these variables into account and yield the **expected value** (EV) for each gamble. An expected value is the amount of money you would expect to win on each bet if you continued playing over and over. Like all probability values, it depends on what would happen **in the long run**. The formula for computing an expected value (EV) is:

EV = (probability of a win) × (value of a win) + (probability of a loss) × (value of a loss)

Let's consider the EV for Choice 1. We'll begin by computing the probability of rolling a 12 with a pair of dice. There is only one way to roll a 12, and that is with a 6 on each die. The probability of this happening when the dice are fair is $1/6 \times 1/6 = 1/36 = .028$. (Because we are interested in finding the probability of a 6 on the first *and* the second die, we use the "and rule," and multiply.) Thus, we'd expect to roll a 12 about 2.8% of the time. What is the probability of not rolling a 12? Because we are certain that you will either roll a 12 or not roll a 12 (this covers all possible events), you can subtract .028 from 1.00. The probability of not rolling a 12 is .972. (You could also arrive at this figure, with some small rounding differences, by calculating the probability of each of the 35 other possible outcomes—each will be 1/36—and adding them together.) (see Fig. 7.4.)

Using these probability values, the EV formula for Choice 1 becomes:

EV   = (Probability of a 12) × (Value of a 12) +
(Choice 1) (Probability of *not* getting a 12) × (Value of *not* getting a 12)

EV   = [(.028) × ($24)] + [(.972) × (−$1)]
(Choice 1)

EV   = $.672 −$.972
(Choice 1)

EV   = −$.30
(Choice 1)

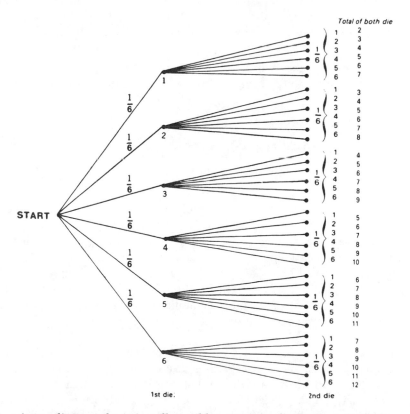

FIG. 7.4.   A tree diagram depicting all possible outcomes of rolling a pair of dice.

Let's review what happened in this formula. If you rolled a 12, you'd win $24, which is the value associated with this win. If you rolled a number other than a 12, you'd lose the $1 you paid to play this game, thus −$1 is the value associated with this loss. The probability of a win was multiplied by the value of a win. The probability of a loss was multiplied by the value of a loss. Then, these two products were added together. The EV of this bet is −$.30, which means that in the long run, if you continue playing this game many times, you could expect to lose, on the average, $.30 for every game played. Of course, on any single game, you'd either lose $1 or win $24, but after many, many games you would have lost an average of $.30 per game. If you played 1,000 games, making the same bet each time, you'd be $300 poorer.

How does this compare with Choice 2? To calculate the EV of Choice 2, we'll begin by computing the probability of rolling a 7. How many ways is it possible to roll a 7 with a pair of fair dice? You could get a 1 on the first die and a 6 on the second; a 2 and a 5; a 3 and a 4; a 4 and a 3; a 5 and a 2; or a 6 and a 1. Thus, there are 6 possible ways to roll a 7 out of 36 possible outcomes. The probability of any one of these outcomes is $1/6 \times 1/6$, which equals $1/36$. (This is the probability of rolling, e.g., a 1 on the first die and a 6 on the second die.) Thus to determine the probability of one number followed by a second number you would apply the "and rule". Because you are now concerned with the probability of a 1 followed by a 6 *or* a 2 followed by a 5 *or* a 3 followed by a 4 *or* a 4 followed by a 3 *or* a 5 followed by a 2 *or* a 6 followed by a 1, you should recognize the second step as a case where the "or rule" is needed. Because there are six possible combinations, you would add $1/36$ six times (which is, of course, the same as multiplying it by 6). Thus, the probability of rolling a 7 with a pair of dice is $6/36$ ($1/6$ or .167). The probability of not rolling a 7 is $1 - .167$, which equals .833. Now we calculate the EV of Choice 2:

$$\begin{aligned} \text{EV} &= (\text{Probability of a 7}) \times (\text{Value of a 7}) + \\ \text{(Choice 2)} &\quad (\text{Probability of not getting a 7}) \times (\text{Value of not getting a 7}) \end{aligned}$$

$$\begin{aligned} \text{EV} &= [(.167) \times (\$6)] + [(.833) \times (-\$1)] \\ \text{(Choice 2)} \end{aligned}$$

$$= (\$1.002 - .833)$$

$$= \$.169, \text{ or approximately } \$.17$$

This means that if you continued to gamble on Choice 2, you would win an average of $.17 for every game played. Thus, after 1,000 games, you could expect to be $170 richer. Of course, as in Choice 1, you would never actually win this amount on any single game; this is what would result if you continued playing many, many games. This is what would happen in the long run.

Even though you might have originally thought otherwise, Choice 2 is the better choice because of the relatively high probability associated with rolling a 7. Seven has a high probability because there were six possible combinations that would add up to a 7.

There is a party game that is based on the principle that the more ways an event can occur, the more likely it is to occur. Suppose you get a random sample of 40 people together in a room. Estimate the probability that two of them share the same birthday. You may be surprised to learn that the probability is approximately .90. Can you figure out why it is so high? There are many, many ways that 40 people can share the same birthday. To figure out the exact probability, you would take all combinations of 40 people, 2 at a time. Thus, we'd have to start with the combination of Person 1 with Person 2, then Person 1 with Person 3, and so on until Person 1 is matched with Person 40, then we'd begin again matching Person 2 with Person 3, 2 with 4, on until 2 is matched with 40. This whole process would have to be repeated until everyone of the 40 people is matched with every other one. Because there are so many possible combinations of any two people sharing any birthday in the year, this "coincidence" is more probable than it may have seemed at first. The probability of two people sharing a common birthday is over .50, when there are 23 people and over .75 when there are 32 people (Loftus & Loftus, 1982). You can use this knowledge to make wagers at parties or at any gathering of people. It's a fairly good bet when the number of people is close to 40. Most people find it hard to believe that the probability is so high.

You can also use your knowledge of probability to improve your chances in other situations. Take, for example, Aaron and Jill, who have been arguing over who should take out the garbage. Their mother agrees to help them settle this matter by picking a number from 1 to 10. The one whose number comes closer to the one selected by their mother will win the dispute. Aaron goes first and picks 3. What number should Jill select to maximize her chances of winning? Stop now and decide what number she should select. The best number for Jill to pick is 4. If her mother were thinking of any number greater than 3, Jill would win with this strategy. Thus, she can change the probability of winning in what seems like a chance situation.

SUBJECTIVE PROBABILITY

We usually do not deal directly with known or objective probabilities, such as the probability of rain on a given day or the probability of developing heart disease if oral contraceptives are taken. Yet, every day we make decisions using our best estimate of the likelihood of events. **Subjective probability** refers to personal estimates of the likelihood of events. This term is in distinction from **objective probability**, which is a mathematically determined statement of likelihood about known frequencies. Psychologists who have studied subjective probability have found that human judgments of probability are often fallible, yet we rely on them to guide our decisions in countless situations.

Gambler's Fallacy

The "Wheel of Fortune" is a popular game at fairs, casinos, amusement parks, and on television game shows. It consists of a large wheel, that can be spun. The wheel is divided into many numbered sections, much like a roulette wheel. A rubber marker indicates the winning number.

Suppose that your friend, Vanna, decides to approach the Wheel of Fortune in a scientific manner. She sits at the Wheel of Fortune and records when each number comes up as the winning number. Suppose Vanna has recorded the following series of winning numbers: 3, 6, 10, 19, 18, 4, 1, 7, 7, 5, 20, 17, 2, 14, 19, 13, 8, 11, 13, 16, 12, 15, 19, 3, 8. After examining these numbers very carefully, she proclaims that a 9 has not appeared in the last 25 spins; therefore, she plans to bet heavily on number 9, because it is now much more likely to occur. Would you agree with her that this is a good bet?

If you responded "Yes," you have committed a very common error in understanding probability. The Wheel of Fortune has no memory for which numbers have previously appeared. If the wheel had been built so that each number is equally likely to win, then a 9 is equally likely on each spin, regardless of how frequently or infrequently it appeared in the past. People believe that chance processes like spinning a Wheel of Fortune should be self-correcting so that if an event has not occurred in a while it is now more likely to occur. This misconception is called **gambler's fallacy**.

Gambler's fallacy can be found in many settings. Consider a sports example. A "slumping" batter who hasn't had a hit in a long while is sometimes believed to be more likely to have a hit because he is "due" one. A sports enthusiast, who is a friend of mine, told me the following story about Don Sutton, a former pitcher for the Dodgers. One season, Sutton gave up a great many runs. He predicted that this "slump" would be followed by a "correction" so that he would end up the season at his usual average. Unfortunately, there is no correction for chance factors and, because he had such a poor start to the season, he ended the season below his usual average.

Often, people will continue to believe in gambler's fallacy even after it has been explained to them. Students have told me that although they can understand on an intellectual level why gambler's fallacy must be wrong, on an intuitive or "gut" level, it seems that it ought to be right. Understanding probability often requires that we go against our intuitive hunches because they are often wrong. Let's try another example.

Wayne and Marsha have four sons. Although they really don't want to have five children, both have always wanted a daughter. Should they plan to have another child, because they are now more likely to have a daughter, given that their first four children were boys? If you understand gambler's fallacy, you'll recognize that a daughter is as likely as a son on the fifth try, just as it was on each of the first four. (Actually, because slightly more boys than girls are born, the probability of having a boy baby is slightly higher than the probability of having a girl baby.)

Gambler's fallacy also has a flip side, the belief that random events run in streaks. Consider the following two scenarios:

A. A basketball player has just *missed* 2 or 3 of the last shots in a row. She is about to shoot again.
B. A basketball player has just *made* 2 or 3 of the last shots in a row. She is about to shoot again.

Is she more likely to make the basket in A or B?

Gilovich (1991) asked questions like this one to knowledgeable basketball fans and found that 91% believed that the player was more likely to be successful in B than in A. In other words, they believed that players shoot in streaks. In order to determine whether there is any evidence to support the "belief in streaks," Gilovich analyzed data from the Philadelphia 76ers. He found:

- If a player just made a shot, 51% of the next shots were successful.
- If a player just missed a shot, 54% of the next shots were successful.
- If a player made two shots in a row, 50% of the next shots were successful.
- If a player missed two shots in a row, 53% of the next shots were successful.

These data show no evidence that players shoot in streaks. Yet, interviews with the 76ers players themselves showed that they *believe* that they shot in streaks. It is very difficult to convince people that chance is exactly that—it doesn't self-correct or run in nonrandom streaks.

Base-Rate Neglect

Charlie is anxious to experience his first kiss. If he asks Louise to go to the movies with him, he's only 10% sure that she'll accept his invitation, but if she does, he's 95% sure that she'll kiss him goodnight. What are Charlie's chances for romance?

Initial or *a priori* probabilities are called the **base rate**. In this problem, the first hurdle that Charlie has to "get over" is getting Louise to go out with him. The probability of this occurring is 10%. It is important to think about this figure—the base rate. Ten percent is a fairly low value, so it is likely that she will not go out with him. He wants to know the probability of two uncertain events occurring—she both goes out with him *and* she kisses him. Before we start to solve this problem think about the kind of answer you would expect. Will it be greater than 95%, between 95% and 10%, or less than 10%?

To solve this problem, we'll use a tree diagram to depict the possible outcomes and the probability associated with each. Of course, it is not likely that Charlie or any other Romeo-wanna-be will actually compute the probability values or draw a tree diagram for determining the probability of this momentous event, but this example demonstrates how likelihoods combine. Maybe he'll decide that the probability of a kiss from Louise is so small that he'll opt for Brunhilda, who is both more likely to accept his offer of a date and succumb to his romantic charms. Besides, anyone who has actually estimated probability values for romance might also want to be more precise in his estimates of two or more events.

We'll start with a tree diagram that first branches into "Louise accepts his date" and "Louise declines." A second branch will be drawn from the Louise accepts his date node indicating whether he gets kissed or not. Each branch should have the appropriate probability labels. Of course, if Louise declines his invitation, Charlie definitely won't get kissed. The branch from the "Louise declines" node is thus labeled 1.00 for "Charlie doesn't get kissed."

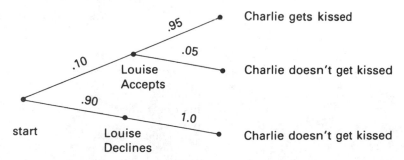

According to the "and rule" for finding the probability of two (or more) events, the probability that Louise will kiss Charlie goodnight is:

$$.10 \times .95 = .095$$

Are you surprised to find that the objective probability is less than the low base rate of 10% and much less than the higher secondary or subsequent rate of 95%?

Most people are. Hopefully, you recognized that any value greater than 10% would have been indicative of a conjunction error. Recall from the earlier section on conjunction errors that the probability of two uncertain events both occurring (Louise accepts *and* kisses Charlie) must be less than the probability of either event alone. Most people ignore (or underestimate) the low base rate and estimate their answer as closer to the higher secondary rate. In general, people tend to overestimate the probability of two or more uncertain events occurring. This type of error is known as **base-rate neglect**. Of course, in real life, estimates of probabilities for events like having a date accept your invitation and then the probability that she or he will kiss you are not very exact, so it may be a bit of a stretch to ask poor Charlie, in this example, to compute the combined probabilities of both of these events actually happening. Other situations in which probabilities are calculated from population values, like the "probability of getting malaria if you travel in a tropic country during a rainy summer" and the "probability of having a reaction to malaria medicine" may be a more realistic example where you might want to calculate joint probabilities. But, in either case, it is important to understand that, if one event occurs rarely, the likelihood of that event plus another one will be even less than the rare one alone.

MAKING PROBABILISTIC DECISIONS

Most of the important decisions that we make in life involve probabilities. Although decision making is discussed more fully in Chapter 8, let's consider how tree diagrams can be an aid for decision making.

Edith is trying to decide on a college major. She attends a very selective university that has independent admissions for each of its majors. She is seriously thinking about becoming an accountant. She knows that the accounting department accepts 25% of the students who apply for that major. Of those accepted, 70% graduate and 90% of those who graduate pass the national accounting examination and become accountants. She would like to know what her chances are of becoming an accountant if she pursues the accounting major.

To answer this question, draw a tree diagram with branches that represent the "path" for success in accounting.

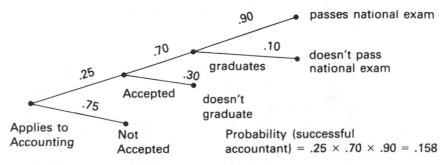

From the preceding diagram, you can see that the probability of becoming a successful accountant is equal to .25 × .70 × .90, which is .158. At this point, Edith might want to consider other options. For example, she could consider applying to both the accounting major and to the education major. She could recalculate her chances for success in one of these majors, both of these majors (if this is a possible option for her), and neither of these majors.

This example assumes that we have no additional information on which to base Edith's chances of success. Suppose instead that we know that Edith has excellent math skills. Shouldn't this sort of information change the probabilities involved and make it more likely that Edith be admitted, graduate, and succeed in a math-related occupation? Intuitively, the answer is "yes." Let's see how the problem changes by considering José's probability for success in the following example.

Combining Information to Make Predictions

José has always wanted to be an actor. Accordingly, he plans to sell his worldly possessions and head for a career in the "Big Apple" (the loving nickname for New York). Suppose that you and José both know that only about 4% of all aspiring actors ever "make it" professionally in New York. This value is the base rate; it is based on information that is known before we have any specific information about José. Stop and think about this figure—the base rate. It tells us that very few aspiring actors become professionals in this field. In other words, the chance of success is low. Suppose that you had no additional information about José. What value would you predict as his chance of success? If you said 4%, right on! In the absence of any other information, use the base rate.

José tells you not to worry, because 75% of those who are successful have curly hair and can sing and tell jokes well. Because he has curly hair, is a good singer, and is a hilarious comedian, he feels confident that he will soon be sending 8×10 glossy pictures of himself to his fan club members. This second value is called the secondary; it is the probability value that relates specific information about characteristics that are associated with José and with an outcome. We'll use these two probability values to decide if José's optimism is warranted. Exactly how likely is he to succeed? Before you continue, make a probability estimate for his chance of success. Remember, probabilities range from 0 to 1, with 0 meaning he will definitely fail and have to return to Peoria, and 1 meaning he will definitely succeed on Broadway. Stop now and make a subjective probability judgment of his chance for success.

Can you think of a way of objectively finding his chance of success? In order to arrive at an objective probability, you'll need to know another number, one that is often ignored—the percentage of those who fail and have the attributes that are associated with success (in this case, curly hair and the ability to sing, dance, and joke). Few people realize that they need to consider this value in assessing the probability of success. For ease of reference, I'll call the attributes that are associated with success (curly hair, ability to sing and tell jokes) "curly hair," and the absence of these attributes, I'll call "not curly hair." Suppose that 50% of those who fail have these attributes. Once again, tree diagrams can be used to determine probabilities in this context. Let's begin at a starting point and consider all possible outcomes. In this case, he will either succeed or fail, so we'll label the first branches "succeed" and "fail." As before, we'll put the probability of each event along the appropriate branch:

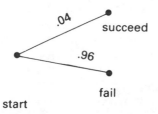

These two probabilities (.04 and .96) sum to 1.0, because they include all possibilities. One of these two possibilities must occur, so they will add up to 1.0 to indicate absolute certainty.

José knows that 75% of those who succeed have curly hair. In this example, what we are trying to find is the probability of a certain outcome (success) *given that* we already have information that is relevant to the probability of that outcome. Let's add a second branch to the tree diagram, branching off from the succeed node and the fail node. There are four different probabilities involved in this example: the probability of succeeding and having curly hair, the probability of succeeding and not having curly hair, the probability of failing and having curly hair, and the probability of failing and not having curly hair. These four possibilities are shown in the next tree diagram.

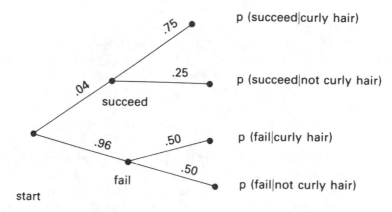

Because 75% (.75) of those who succeed have curly hair, and 25% (.25) do not have this attribute, the sum of all probabilities from a tree node must sum to 1.0. Similarly, 50% of those who fail have curly hair, whereas 50% of those who fail do not possess this attribute. Because we are considering everyone who fails, these values must also sum to 1.0.

Once the tree diagram is drawn, it is a simple matter to compute José's objective probability of success. As before, multiply along each branch to find the probabilities. In this case, we would multiply the values along each branch of the tree diagram and compile the information in a chart:

P[Succeed & Curly Hair]	= .04 × .75 =	.03
P[Succeed & Not Curly Hair]	= .04 × .25 =	.01
P[Fail & Curly Hair]	= .96 × .50 =	.48
P[Fail & Not Curly Hair]	= .96 × .50 =	.48
		1.0000

To determine José's true chance of success, we need to divide the proportion who succeed and have curly hair (.03) by the total proportion who have curly hair (.48 + .03 = .51). We are trying to *predict* José's success based on the knowledge that he has curly hair and that some proportion of all people with curly hair are successful. Of all of those with curly hair (.51), what proportion of them succeed (.03)?

$$\frac{\text{Proportion who succeed and curly hair}}{\text{Total proportion of people with curly hair}} = \frac{.03}{.03 + .48} \approx .06$$

Thus, José's chances for success are 50% higher (6% vs. 3%) than they are for any unknown, aspiring actor, but they are still very low. Knowing that he has certain attributes that are associated with success improved his probability of success above the base rate, but the improvement was very small.

You may find it easier to follow the logic of these calculations by putting the information in a table format.

	Succeed	Fail	Row Totals
Curly hair, etc.	0.03	0.48	0.51
No curly hair, etc.	0.01	0.48	0.49
Column Total	0.04	0.96	1.00

Are you surprised to find that his chance of success is so low given that the posterior or secondary probability value was so high (75%)? Most people are. The reason that José has such a slim chance of becoming an actor is because so few people, in general, succeed. The probability value José obtained was close to the a priori, or base rate, of success among all aspiring actors. Because so few actors, in general, succeed, José, and any other would-be thespian, has a low chance for success. In general, most people overestimate success when base rates are low and underestimate success when base rates are high. In the earlier example concerning Edith, we

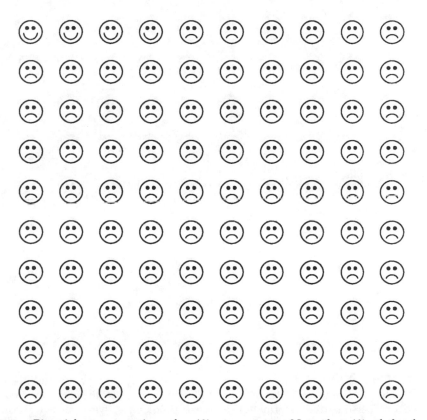

FIG. 7.5. Pictorial representation of a 4% success rate. Note that 4% of the faces are smiling, which represents the base rate—4% of all aspiring actors succeed. If we had no personal information about José, his expected probability of success would be 4%.

had only base-rate information to use in predicting success. By contrast, we had additional information about José that allowed us to improve upon the base rate when predicting his success, although because of the low rate of success for actors in general, the improvement was slight.

For those of you who prefer to think spatially or think in terms of frequencies instead of probabilities, think about a group of 100 people, 4 of whom are successful actors (4%) and 96 are not (96%). This group is shown in Fig. 7.5. Four of the 100 "people" depicted are smiling—these represent the successful actors. If you had no other information to use to predict success for José, you would use this base-rate information and give him a 4% probability for success.

Now let's consider the additional information. Three of the four of those who are shown smiling have curly hair (3/4 or 75%); whereas, half (50%) of those who are not smiling have curly hair. This information is combined with the base-rate information. It is depicted in Fig. 7.6 with the addition of curly hair to the successful and unsuccessful actors. Of the 4 smiling faces, 3 have curly hair (75%), and of the 96 frowning faces, 48 (50%) have curly hair.

By examining these figures, it should be easy to see that what we are doing mathematically is finding the proportion of smiling faces with curly hair relative to all of

FIG. 7.6. Pictorial representation of the relative proportion of successful and unsuccessful actors who have the same attributes of José. These are depicted by the addition of curly hair. When we use personalized information to make predictions, we form a fraction of the proportion of those who are successful and have the attribute (smiling and curly hair) *over* the total proportion who have the attribute (curly hair). In this case, 3 smiling faces with curly hair form the numerator and the 51 faces that have curly hair form the denominator.

the faces with curly hair in order to use this information about José to predict his success. Graphically, this is 3 smiling faces with curly hair as a proportion (or fraction) of the 51 faces that have curly hair:

$$3/51 \approx 0.06$$

To review, when you are calculating the probability of an outcome, given that you have information that is relevant to its probability, you will:

1. Draw a complete tree diagram, with the base-rate information (e.g., success or failure) as the first set of nodes. Use the secondary information to draw the second set of nodes.
2. Make a chart with all combinations of the base-rate information and secondary information as the rows in the chart.
3. Multiply probabilities across each of the branches of the tree diagram and fill in each row of the chart with these values.
4. Form a ratio (fraction) with the probability value from the branch that you are interested in (e.g., success given that he has curly hair) as the numerator and the sum of this value and the other branch that contains the same conditional statement (e.g., failure given that he has curly hair).
5. Check your answer. Does it make sense? Would you expect, as in this example, that the probability of success is higher than the base rate because we know something about the individual that is associated with success? (If we knew that José had some trait that was associated with failure, we would predict that his chance of success would be less than the base rate, but with low base rates, it probably won't be much less.)

Let's try a more realistic example: There are many diseases that occur with low base rates in the population. Medical test results must be interpreted in light of the relevant base rates for each disease. Medicine, like most other disciplines, is a probabilistic science, yet few physicians receive training in understanding probabilities. Failure to utilize base-rate information can lead to improper diagnoses. Base-rate neglect is a pervasive error in thinking about probabilistic outcomes. Consider Dreman's (1979) summary of a large body of research on this effect: "The tendency to underestimate or altogether ignore past probabilities in making a decision is undoubtedly the most significant problem of intuitive predictions in fields as diverse as financial analysis, accounting, geography, engineering, and military intelligence. The implications of such consistent errors and cognitive biases are enormous, not only in economics, management, and investments, but in virtually every area where such decision-making comes into play" (cited in Myers, 1995, p. 278).

Thinking With Frequencies

A common response to problems like the one with José is that the problem is too difficult. In fact, even though many physicians have to interpret laboratory tests where the information is similar to that in the José problem, many the physicians admit that they do not understand how they can use probability information to make important decisions about the health of their patients. Many people find it easier to think about probabilities in situations like this one by imaging frequencies (Gigerenzer & Hoffrage, 1995; Lovett & Schunn, 1999). Here is a real-life example that was used by Gigerenzer and his colleagues who looked for ways to make computing probability information easier to understand. Everyone was given the same opening paragraph:

> To facilitate early detection of breast cancer, women are encouraged from a particular age on to participate at regular intervals in routine screening, even if they have no obvious symptoms. Imagine you conduct in a certain region such a breast cancer screening using mammography. For symptom free women aged 40 to 50 who participate in screening using mammography, the following information is available for this region:

After reading this paragraph, half of the physicians in the study were given the probability format and half were given the frequency format. Here is the same information in two different formats (Gigerenzer & Hoffrage, 1995).

> *Probability Format*: The probability that one of these women has breast cancer is 1%. If a woman has breast cancer, the probability is 80% that she will have a positive mammography test. If a woman does not have breast cancer, the probability is 10% that she will still have a positive mammography test. Imagine a woman (aged 40 to 50, no symptoms) who has a positive mammography test. What is the probability that she actually has breast cancer?
> _____? (fill in your answer)
> *Frequency Format*: Ten out of every 1,000 women have breast cancer. Of these 10 women with breast cancer, 8 will have a positive mammography test. Of the remaining 990 women without breast cancer, 99 will still have a positive mammography test. Imagine a sample of women (aged 40 to 50, no symptoms) who have positive mammography tests. How many of these women actually have breast cancer? _____ out of _____?

How did you go about answering these questions?
For the probability format:

Test ⟍ Cancer	Lab test shows cancer	Lab test does not show cancer	Row Totals
Has cancer	$.01 \times .80 = .008$	$.01 \times .20 = .002$	.01
Does not have cancer	$.99 \times .10 = .099$	$.99 \times .90 = .891$	.99
Column Totals	.107	.893	1.00

Probability: has cancer given that/test shows "has cancer" $= \dfrac{.008}{.008 + .099} = 7.5\%$

Frequency: $\dfrac{\text{number who have cancer and positive test}}{\text{Number with positive test}} = \dfrac{8}{107} = 7.5\%$

The researchers found that when this information was given in the probability format only 10% of the physicians could reason correctly, but when the information was given in the frequency format, 46% reasoned correctly. The ability to combine probability information is an important thinking skill—decisions about treatment options depend on how people understand numbers. With practice, we can all think better with numbers. (Additional problems are shown in the workbook, *Thinking Critically About Critical Thinking*, that accompanies this text.)

Nonregressive Judgments

Harris is a new student at Rah-Rah State University. The average grade point average (GPA) for all students at Rah-Rah is 2.8. Harris is new to this college and has not yet taken any exams. Although we have no information about Harris specifically, what would be your best guess that his grade point average will be?

Stop here and make your best guess for his grade point average.

After his first set of midterm exams, Harris has a midterm GPA of 3.8. Given this new information, what would you now predict for Harris' GPA at the end of the school year? Most people readily answer the first question with 2.8, the average GPA for all students at Rah-Rah. This is a correct answer, as in the absence of any specific information, the average for all students, the population at Rah-Rah, is the best estimate for anyone. Most people answer the second question with 3.8. Unfortunately, this is not the best answer. Although it is true that someone who scores high on midterms will also tend to score high on finals, the relationship is not a one-to-one or perfect relationship. In general, when someone scores extremely high on some scale, she or he will score closer to the average the second time. Thus, the best prediction for Harris' GPA at the end of the school year will be less than 3.8 and greater than 2.8. (The actual value can be mathematically determined, but the calculations are beyond the scope of this book.) This is a difficult concept to understand, because most people find it to be counterintuitive.

It may be useful to think about a sports example. Consider your favorite athletes. Although they may have a truly exceptional performance one day, most often they will perform closer to average, but still above average on other days. After all, no one bowls all perfect games or bats 1,000. Sports enthusiasts will recognize this principle as the "sophomore slump." After an outstanding first year at a sport, the star will usually perform closer to average during her second year. Another example that may help to clarify the concept is an often-used one about fathers' and sons' heights. In general, very tall fathers will have sons that are closer to average height (although still above average) than the fathers are. This phenomenon is called **regression toward the mean**. (Mean is just another term for average—it is computed by adding up all the values you're interested in and dividing by the number of values.)

Earlier in this chapter, I talked about the laws of chance. No one can predict accurately the height of any particular individual. But, in the long run—that is, with many, many extremely tall fathers—most of their sons' heights will show regression toward the mean. Thus, as before, we can make better predictions by knowing about the laws of chance, but we won't always be accurate. It is important to understand this concept whenever dealing with probabilistic events.

Kahneman and Tversky (1973) studied what can happen when regression toward the mean is not understood by professionals. Israeli flight instructors were told that they should praise their students when they successfully performed difficult flight patterns and maneuvers and that they should criticize exceptionally poor performance. Based on what you've just learned about regression toward the mean, what, in general, should happen after a pilot performs extremely well? Subsequent maneuvers should be closer to average, or less than exceptional, because the performance moved or regressed toward the mean (average). Conversely, what should you expect to happen following very poor performance? Again, subsequent maneuvers should tend to be more average, or in this case, they would improve, although they may still be less than average. The Israeli flight instructors did not understand regression toward the mean and erroneously concluded that praise led to poorer performance and criticism improved it.

Let's consider another example of regression to the mean. Regression to the mean is ubiquitous, yet few people ever recognize it. Suppose that you learn of a self-help group for people with children who seriously misbehave. (There really are such groups.) Most parents will enter these groups when their child's behavior is at its worst because most parents will seek help only when the behavior is extremely bad. After a few weeks in the program, many parents report an improvement in their child's behavior. Can we conclude that the program probably worked to help parents control their children's behavior? Think regression to the mean! If parents entered the program when the behavior is extremely bad, then no matter what they do, including nothing at all, the child's behavior will most likely regress toward the mean. In other words, if a child is extremely misbehaved, it is statistically true that the child will move toward the average on measures of behavior. We would not predict angelic or even average behavior, just some improvement or movement toward the mean. Because this is a statistical prediction, sometimes, we will be wrong, but on the average and in the long run, we will be right with this prediction. Thus, we cannot conclude anything about the effectiveness of this program unless we conduct a true experiment of the sort that was described in the last chapter. We might randomly assign children and families to these groups and to "no-treatment control groups" and then determine if the children in the self-help group were significantly better behaved than those who received no treatment. We must be able to randomly assign families to groups before we can conclude that the self-help group was helpful in improving the child's behavior. Once you start looking for regression to the mean, you will be surprised how many events in life are best explained by "moving toward the average" and not to other causes.

RISK

If we examine data from thousands of communities around the United States or around the world, we will find that some communities have exceptionally high rates of some sorts of cancers, birth defects, brain tumors, unexplained deaths, and other maladies. How can we know if there are links between these high rates of illness and toxic substances such as pesticides in the water, magnetic fields from electrical power lines, or chance?

The notion of frequency, or how often an event occurs, is inherent in the definition of probability. If an event is frequent, then its occurrence is highly probable. To determine the risk involved with a disastrous event, we need first to determine the frequency with which it occurs. Because most disastrous events are rare (e.g., plane crashes, leaks from nuclear plants) and, in some cases, take years before they are evident (e.g., cancers from environmental hazards), determining their frequency is a very difficult task. To understand how people make judgments involving risks, we need to understand how they determine the frequency of real-life risky events. Several researchers (Lichtenstein et al., 1978) have focused on the way people judge the frequency of lethal (deadly) events. They studied these phenomena by asking college students and members of the League of Women Voters to decide which of two possible causes of death is more probable for several pairs of lethal events. To understand their experiment and their results, let's try a few examples. For the following pairs of items, indicate which is the more likely cause of death, and then estimate how much more likely your choice is than the other event:

A. Asthma   or   Tornado
B. Excess Cold   or   Syphilis
C. Diabetes   or   Suicide
D. Heart Disease   or   Lung Cancer
E. Flood   or   Homicide
F. Syphilis   or   Diabetes
G. Asthma   or   Botulism
H. Poisoning by Vitamins or   Lightning
I. Tuberculosis   or   Homicide
J. All Accidents   or   Stomach Cancer

Researchers found that although, in general, people were more accurate as the differences in the true frequencies of occurrence between the events increased, they made a large number of errors in estimating the relative frequencies of the events. Their subjects overestimated the frequencies of events that occurred very rarely and underestimated the frequencies of those events that occurred very often. In addition, lethal events that had received a great deal of publicity (e.g., airplane crashes, flood, homicide, tornado, botulism) were overestimated, whereas those that were undramatic, silent killers (e.g., diabetes, stroke, asthma, tuberculosis) were underestimated. It seems that publicized events were more easily brought to mind and this biased judgments of their frequency. Hazards that are unusually memorable, such as a recent disaster or an event depicted in a sensationalized way on the news like a major plane crash or botulism in undercooked hamburgers, distort our perceptions of risk. This was clear when a few incidents of shootings in high schools in the United States was immediately followed by anxious parents who took their children out of public high schools and enrolled them in private schools. Of course, the shooting death of high school students was extremely tragic, but these same parents would allow their children to drive when they were sleepy or never instructed them about ways to prevent sexually transmitted diseases, both of which are far more likely to occur than a school shooting. The more salient events were perceived to be the greater risk than the less publicized but more likely dangers of an automobile accident or sexually transmitted disease. In Chapter 2, I made the point that memory is an integral component of all thinking processes. What we remember is a major influence on how we think. The importance of being mindful of possible biases in memory when evaluating thought processes is seen in this quote:

> ...our society most often makes judgments about hazardous activities for which adequate statistical data is lacking, such as recombinant DNA research or nuclear waste disposal. We suspect that the biases found here (overestimation of rare events, underestimation of likely events, and an undue influence of drama or vividness) may be operating, indeed, may even be amplified in such situations. (Lichtenstein et al., 1978, p. 577)

It is not surprising that we tend to overestimate the probability of events that receive excessive coverage in the media. We rely on the information that is available to us to make decisions, and we are usually not aware when that information is biased or sensationalized (Fischhoff, 1993). Homicides are routinely part of every news broadcast and every newspaper; deaths from heart disease or automobile accidents are rarely mentioned in these contexts because they are far too common.

Assessing Risks

How do the experts make decisions that involve potentially disastrous outcomes? How can we as informed citizens and voters make less risky decisions? Questions like these are timely, but not easy to answer.

The goal of risk assessment is to find ways to avoid, reduce, or manage risks (Wilson & Crouch, 1987). Risk is associated with every aspect of life. For example, approximately 200 people are electrocuted each year in accidents involving home wiring or appliances, and 7,000 people die each year in U.S. homes as a result of falls (most of these people are over 65). Yet, few of us would interpret these risks as great enough either to forgo electricity or stop walking in our homes. Other risks are clearly too large to take. Few of us, for example, would decide to cross a busy freeway wearing a blindfold. And still other risks are largely unknown, such as the release of a new chemical into the environment or the development of a new technology. Wilson and Crouch (1987) suggested several ways of estimating risks that voters and consumers should consider when deciding if an action or a technology is safe enough:

1. One method of risk assessment involves examining historical data. For example, to understand the risk of cancer due to exposure to medical X-rays, there are data that indicate that for a given dose per year (40 mrem) there is an expected number of cancers (1,100). This sort of risk information can be compared to other known risks so that consumers can decide if the benefits of medical X-rays outweigh the risks.
2. The risk of a new technology for which there are no historical data can be computed when the occurrence of the events are independent by calculating the risk of separate components and multiplying along the branches of a decision tree. This method of calculating probabilities was presented in an earlier section of this chapter. A well-known example is the probability of a severe accident at a chemical plant.
3. Risks can also be calculated by analogy. (The use of analogies as an aid to problem solving is discussed more fully in the following two chapters.) When animals are used to test drugs, the experimenter is really using an analogy to extrapolate the risk to humans.

Biases in Risk Assessment

Psychologists and others who study the way people determine if something is "too risky" know that most of us fall prey to common biases when we assess the "murky psychometrical stew" (Paulos, 1994, p. 34) that constitutes the numerical information and misinformation that we need to interpret. Here are some common biases (Wandersman & Hallman, 1993):

1. When a risk is voluntary, it is perceived to be less risky than one that is not voluntary. For example, cosmetic surgery is often believed to be safer than a nonelective surgery. After all, patients choose to undergo cosmetic surgery, so they must rationalize that it is "safe enough."
2. Natural risks are believed to be less hazardous than artificial ones. For example, many people believe that naturally occurring toxins in our food are less

dangerous than ones that are caused by pesticides or preservatives that are added.

3. Memorial events in which many people are harmed at once are perceived as riskier than more mundane and less vivid events. An example of this effect is the large number of people who are terrified of plane crashes, but give little thought to automobile safety.

4. Events over which we have some perceived control are believed to be safer than those over which we don't have control. Most people tend to feel safer when they are driving an automobile than when others are driving because most of us believe that we are better-than-average drivers.

5. Phenomena that are not observable and are associated with spectacular dreaded outcomes (DNA technology, radioactive waste, AIDS, and nuclear reactors) are believed to be riskier than phenomena that involve known risks or less dreaded outcomes (smoking, auto accidents, dynamite, and handguns; Slovic, 1987).

It is clear that personal risk perceptions are not the same as scientific risk estimates. Experts in risk assessment perceive risks based on annual mortality so that the event that results in the greater number of deaths is judged to be the greater risk. Experts, for example, ranked motor vehicles as riskier than nuclear power (because more people are expected to die from motor vehicle accidents); whereas, samples of college students and members of the League of Women Voters ranked nuclear power as the greater risk (because it is an example of a spectacular dreaded outcome).

A major difficulty in interpreting low-probability risks like flood or a nuclear accident is that the figures involved are not readily meaningful. Knowing that a particular risky event occurs in 1 in 10,000 individuals is difficult to interpret. We need to be able to convert this information into an answer to the question, "Is this likely to happen to me?" One suggestion for making this sort of information more meaningful is to convert all such risks to a standard "risk per hour" metric (Slovic, Fischhoff, & Lichtenstein, 1986). For example, suppose you learned that the risk involved in taking a motorcycle trip is the same as the risk of being 75 years old for 1 hour. Would this type of information be helpful in interpreting the risk of a motorcycle trip in a meaningful way? Although information of this sort might be useful for judging comparative risk (motorcycle trip compared to hang gliding), it may not be useful by itself because it is still difficult to understand what is meant by the risk of being 75 years old for 1 hour.

As voters and as consumers we face countless decisions about a large and diverse array of topics, which include nuclear energy, food irradiation, surgical procedures, air and water quality, and drug use. An informed decision will always require careful consideration of the information that is relevant to risk assessment (e.g., historical data, risk by analogy, and risks of separate components) as well as an understanding of the way subjective estimates of risk are biased.

Here are the answers to the questions about the probability of lethal events we follow along with the true frequency of each event (rate per 100,000,000). Check your answer and see if you made the common errors of overestimating events that are more memorable and likely to affect many people at one time (like a plane crash) and underestimating those risks over which we believe we have some control (like driving an automobile).

More Likely	Rate	Less Likely	Rate
A. Asthma	920	Tornado	44
B. Syphilis	200	Excess Cold	163
C. Diabetes	19,000	Suicide	12,000
D. Heart Disease	360,000	Lung Cancer	37,000
E. Homicide	9,200	Flood	100
F. Diabetes	19,000	Syphilis	200
G. Asthma	920	Botulism	1
H. Lightning	52	Poisoning/Vitamins	.5
I. Homicide	9,200	Tuberculosis	1,800
J. All Accidents	55,000	Stomach Cancer	46,600

STATISTICAL USE AND ABUSE

There are three kinds of lies: lies, damned lies, and statistics.

—Disraeli (1804–1881)

When we want to find out something about a group of people, it is often impossible or inconvenient to ask everyone in the group. Suppose you want to know if people who donate blood to the Red Cross are, in general, kind and generous people. Because you can't examine everyone who donates blood to determine how kind and considerate she or he is, you would examine a portion of the population, which is called a **sample**. A number calculated on a sample of people is called a **statistic**. ("Statistics" is also the branch of mathematics that utilizes probability theory to make decisions about populations.)

Statistics are found everywhere, from baseball earned run averages to the number of war casualties. Many people are rightfully suspicious of statistics. A small book by Huff (1954) humorously illustrates many of the possible pitfalls of statistics. The book is entitled *How to Lie With Statistics*. In it, he rhymes the following message: "Like the 'little dash of powder, little pot of paint,' statistics are making many an important fact look like what she ain't" (p. 9). But, the real message is that you won't be bamboozled with statistics if you understand them.

On the Average

What does it mean to say that the average American family has 2.1 children? This number was computed by finding a sample of American families, adding up the number of children they have and dividing by the total number of families in the sample. This number could provide an accurate picture of American families, as most may have about two children, with some having more and others less, or it could be very misleading. It is possible that half of the families had no children and half had four or more children, thus misleading the reader into believing that most families had "about" two children, when in fact none did. This is like the man who had his head in the oven and feet in the freezer and reports that, on the average, he's quite comfortable. It is also possible that the sample used to calculate this statistic was not representative of the population—in this case, all American families. If the sample consisted of college students or residents in Manhattan, the number obtained would be too low. On the other hand, if the sample was taken in rural farm areas, the number obtained may be too high. When samples are not representative of the population, they are called **biased samples**. The statistics calculated on biased samples will not yield accurate information about the population.

Averages can also be misleading, because there are three different kinds of averages. Consider Mrs. Wang's five children. The oldest is a successful corporate executive. She earns $500,000 a year. The second is a teacher who earns $25,000 a year. Child 3 is a waiter who earns $15,000 a year. The other two are starving artists, each earning $5,000 a year. If Mrs. Wang wants to brag about how well her children turned out, she could compute an arithmetic average, which is called the **mean**. The mean is what most people have in mind when they think about averages. It is the sum of all of the values divided by the total number of values. The mean income for Mrs. Wang's children is $550,000/5 = $110,000. Certainly, anyone who is told this figure would conclude that Mrs. Wang has very successful and wealthy children.

The reason that the mean income for Mrs. Wang's children was so high is because there is one extreme score that inflated this type of average. Averages are also called **measures of central tendency**. A second kind of measure of central tendency is the **median**. It is not affected by a few extreme scores. To compute the median, the values are lined up in ascending or descending order. The middle value is the median. For Mrs. Wang's children, this would be:

$5,000; $5,000; $15,000; $25,000; $500,000.

The middle value, or median, is the third value of $15,000. Thus, she could also claim that her children earn, on the average, $15,000. (When there is an even number of values, the median is equal to the mean of the middle two values.)

Mrs. Wang can honestly claim that her children earn, on the average, $110,000 or $15,000. The point of this discussion is that you should be wary of average figures. To understand them, you need to know whether the average is a mean or median as well as something about the variability of the data and the "shape" of the distribution (the way the numbers "stack up.").

Precision

Suppose I tell you that a scientific survey was conducted on the length of workdays for office workers. Furthermore, this study found that the mean workday is 8.167 hours long. Does this sound impressive and scientific? What if I told you that most office workers work about 8 hours a day? Most of you would say, "I know that. Why did they bother?" The point is that we are often impressed with precise statistics, even when the precision is unwarranted.

Let me give you an example from a prestigious weekly news magazine. It is important that the magazine readers accept the articles as truthful and authoritative. A few years ago, a news magazine ran an article about the health hazards associated with dog droppings in New York City. To give the reader an idea of the magnitude of the problem, they presented the daily weight of New York City dog droppings in pounds, accurate to two decimal places (the nearest .01 pound!). I have no idea how they arrived at that figure, nor do I even want to think about how they collected their data. I do know that they could not measure it that accurately. Of course, the impression that is created with such precise statistics is that the news magazine is a carefully researched journal that can be trusted for the information it provides.

A more humorous example of overprecision comes from one of America's most famous authors, Mark Twain. He once reported that the Mississippi River was 100 million and 3 years old. It seems that 3 years earlier, he learned that it was 100 million years old.

Significant Differences

If you wanted to know the mean height of all women, you could select a sample of 100 women, measure their height, and compute the mean. Suppose you took another sample of 100 women and computed their mean height. Would you expect the means of these two samples to be exactly the same? No, of course not, because there could be expected to be small differences or fluctuations between these values. Each value was computed on different women, and each will yield a slightly different mean value.

If someone measured a sample of women who belong to sororities and found that their mean height is 5'5" and then measured women who don't belong to sororities and found their mean height to be 5'4 1/2", would you conclude that sorority sisters are taller than nonsorority women? I hope not, because small differences between groups can be expected to occur just by chance, especially when the **sample size**, or number of people in the sample, is small. There are statistical procedures to determine if a difference computed on two or more samples is likely to have happened by chance. If it is very unlikely to be a chance occurrence, it is called a **significant difference**.

The question of whether a change is meaningful also applies to populations as well. If your college enrollment went from 15,862 to 15,879, would the administrators be justified in concluding that the increase in enrollment is meaningful? The answer to this question depends on many other variables. If the enrollment figure has been edging up slowly every year for the last 5 years, then these figures may represent a slight, but steady, trend. On the other hand, the relatively small increase could be due to chance fluctuations and may not represent a meaningful trend. Because of chance factors, it could just as easily have gone down. Similarly, a change in the unemployment rate from 10.0% to 9.9% may be nothing more than random fluctuation, or it may be signaling the end of an economic quagmire. You can expect that Democrats and Republicans will interpret these figures differently depending on who is in office at the time.

Extrapolation

Extrapolation occurs when a value is estimated by extending some known values. If the number of psychology majors over the last 5 years at Podunck University was approximately 150, 175, 200, 225, and 250, respectively, then most people would feel comfortable about the prediction that the number of psychology majors next year will be approximately 275.

Extrapolation can be wrong, and sometimes even ridiculous. For example, suppose we were to examine the drop in the size of American families between 1900 and 1950. By extrapolation, we would predict that the average family size will soon be zero, and then become a negative number. This is, of course, an inconceivable idea! This is like saying that if the times for the 100-meter dash keep decreasing, eventually someone will run it in zero seconds and then in negative time.

Bamboozled by Statistics

How can you turn pure fat in a concoction that is 96% fat-free? No, it's not magic; in fact, it's easy. If you take two pats of butter and eat them, 100% of the calories are from fat. But, if you drop the same two pats of butter into a glass of water and drink this revolting concoction, then you have created a 96% fat-free drink (i.e., 96% water)! You would ingest the same number of calories, all of them from fat, but the 96% fat-free drink sounds healthier.This is why products that are labeled "percentage fat-free" are bogus health foods labeled in a way that is intended to misinform (Nutrition Action Newsletter, 1991).

Many of the statistics that we routinely rely upon are woefully wrong. Bozell (1993) has questioned the accuracy of the data that we are given by the media. For example, he cites a CBS reporter who warned that heterosexual AIDS increased by 30% in 1992 alone. But, according to Bozell, the Center for Disease Control reported that heterosexual AIDS increased 17% in 1992, down from an increase of 21% in 1991. Similarly, he quotes an NBC news anchor, who claimed that right now in the United States there are 5 million people who are believed to be homeless, yet the Census Bureau in 1990 counted 220,000 homeless. These are big differences, but how can we determine which of these statistics is closer to the truth?

First, it is important to develop the habit of questioning the statistics that we are given. How were they collected and who collected them? It is difficult, for example, to count accurately the number of homeless because they don't have convenient addresses or phones. How were the two estimates of this number derived? Did the data collectors sample from downtown New York or from Salt Lake City? Do you have any reason to believe that the data are being deliberately misused? For example, a conservative political group with an obvious agenda, Concerned Women for America, ran an advertisement in national newspapers in which they advocated a ban on gays and lesbians in the military. In support of their position, they reported a study that found "homosexual behavior to be promiscuous, compulsive, and uncontrollable" (quoted in Boxall, 1993, p. A18). The ad went on to claim that the "typical homosexual" had at least 68 sex partners each year! Are you wondering where and how this statistic was obtained? I hope so. The "study" was over a decade old that deliberately sought highly promiscuous gay males and therefore is not representative of gays in general. If you question the statistics that you routinely are exposed to, you are less likely to be misled by crooked statistics.

APPLYING THE FRAMEWORK

Let's consider the steps in applying the general framework for thinking to understanding and using probabilities.

1. What Is the Goal?

Whenever you are making decisions about uncertain events, you will need to consider the skills developed in this chapter. This is particularly true whenever you are given probability values or when degrees of belief are presented or implied. This situation exists in most of the problems that we solve and decisions that we make because they often involve future events that can never be known with certainty.

2. What Is Known?

In setting up the problem, you need to know if the probability values you are being given were derived objectively or subjectively. You need to look for ways that these values could be biased. Has the desirability of an outcome influenced the probability values assigned to it? Although the topic of considering the credibility of a source of information was presented in Chapter 5 on analyzing arguments, it is also relevant in this context. Before you begin the process of using probabilities, you need to assess the quality of the information that you have. Because we frequently persuade others with probability values, you need to consider how the numbers that are being presented relate to the argument that is being offered.

When determining what is known, look for information that can be used in computing probability estimates. For example, if a probability of a risk is given, is it per year, per exposure (e.g., X-ray), or per lifetime? Is there additional information available that can be combined with base rates so that a more accurate prediction can be made?

3. Which Thinking Skill or Skills Will Get You to Your Goal?

Numerous thinking skills have been presented for use when working with probabilistic events. One of the most useful is drawing a tree diagram complete with probability values on each branch. This method allows you to "see" and objectively compute the likelihood of multiple outcomes. When you are combining information with base-rate information, it is important to form the appropriate ratios so as to avoid the problem of base-rate neglect. Other skills require recognition of the type of error that frequently occurs (e.g., conjunction error, failure to consider cumulative risks) and use of the "or" and "and "rules to improve probabilistic decision making.

Because there are so few things in life that are known with certainty, the skills for understanding and using probabilities should be used frequently. After reading this chapter, you should be able to use the following skills:

- Compute expected values in situations with known probabilities.
- Recognize when regression to the mean is operating and adjust predictions to take this phenomenon into account.
- Use the "and rule" to avoid conjunction errors.
- Use the "or rule" to calculate cumulative probabilities.
- Recognize and avoid gambler's fallacy.
- Utilize base rates when making predictions.
- Use tree diagrams as a decision-making aid in probabilistic situations.
- Adjust risk assessments to account for the cumulative nature of probabilistic events.
- Understand the differences among mean and median.
- Avoid overconfidence in uncertain situations.
- Understand the limits of extrapolation.
- Use probability judgments to improve decision making.
- Consider indicators like historical data, risks associated with different parts of a decision, and analogies when dealing with unknown risks.

4. Have You Reached Your Goal?

The reason for considering probabilities is to quantify and reduce uncertainty. You will have reached your goal when you can attach more accurate probability values to uncertain events.

CHAPTER SUMMARY

1. Because few things are known with certainty, probability plays a crucial role in many aspects of our lives.

2. Probability is defined as the number of ways a particular outcome (what we call a success) can occur divided by the number of possible outcomes (when all outcomes are equally likely). It is also used to indicate degrees of belief in the likelihood of events with unknown frequencies and previous frequency of occurrence.

3. In general, people tend to be more confident about uncertain events than the objective probability values allow.

4. Mathematically equivalent changes in the way probability information is presented can lead to dramatic changes in the way it is interpreted.

5. Tree diagrams can be used to compute probabilities when there are multiple events (e.g., two or more flips of a coin). When the events are independent, the probability of any combination of outcomes can be determined by multiplying the probability values along the tree "branches."

6. Expected values can be computed that will take into account the probabilities and values associated with a loss and a win in betting situations.

7. Subjective probabilities are our personal estimates of how likely events with unknown frequencies will occur. These values are distorted systematically when people believe that they have some control over probabilistic events.

8. Most people fail to consider the cumulative nature of the likelihood of risky events.

9. People judge events that are dramatic and more publicized to be more likely than events that are less dramatic or less well known. In general, people overestimate frequent events and underestimate infrequent ones.

10. There is a tendency to ignore base-rate information especially when making predictions that involve combining information.

11. Few people realize that if a person scores extremely high or low on one measure, she or he will tend to score closer to average on the second measure.

12. There are two measures of central tendency that are frequently used—the mean and median. Each is computed with a different mathematical formula.

13. There are several systematic biases that operate when most people assess risks. These include downgrading the probability of voluntary risks and those over which we have some perceived control and overestimating risks that are artificial, memorial, and unobservable.

14. Many people erroneously believe that statistics that are expressed in precise numbers (e.g., many decimal places) are highly credible.

15. Extrapolation occurs when a value is estimated by extending a trend from known values.

TERMS TO KNOW

Check your understanding of the concepts presented in this chapter by reviewing their definitions. If you find that you're having difficulty with any term, be sure to reread the section where it is discussed.

Probability. The number of ways a particular event can occur divided by the number of possible outcomes (when all outcomes are equally likely). It is a measure of how often we expect an event to occur *in the long run*. The term is also used to express degrees of belief and previous frequency of occurrence.

In the Long Run. Refers to the need for numerous trials in order to derive accurate estimates of the proportion of outcomes that will be a "success."

Odds. A mathematical method for indicating probability that is commonly used in sporting events.

Laws of Chance (or Probability). The ability to predict the number or percentage of trials on which a particular outcome will occur.

Overconfidence Phenomenon. The tendency for people to be more confident in their judgments of probability than the objective probability values allow.

Multiple Outcomes. Refers to the probability of an event occurring in two or more trials such as getting two heads in two flips of a coin.

Tree Diagrams. Branching diagrams that may be used to compute probabilities by considering all possible outcomes in a sequence of events.

Independent Events. Two or more events are independent when the occurrence of one event does not affect the occurrence of the other events.

Conjunction Error. Mistaken belief that the co-occurrence of two or more events is more likely than the occurrence of one of the events.

Cumulative Probabilities. The probability of an event occurring over many trials.

Expected Value. The amount of money you would expect to win in the long run in a betting situation. The mathematical formula for determining expected values is the probability of winning times the value of winning plus the probability of losing times the value of losing.

Subjective Probability. Personal estimates of the probability or likelihood of uncertain events.

Objective Probability. Mathematically determined statements about the likelihood of events with known frequencies.

Gambler's Fallacy. The mistaken belief that chance events are self-correcting. Many people erroneously believe that if a random event has not occurred recently, it becomes more likely.

Base Rate. Initial or a priori probability that an event will occur.

Base-Rate Neglect. Pervasive bias to ignore or underestimate the effect of initial probabilities (base rates) and to emphasize secondary probability values when deciding on the likelihood of an outcome.

Regression Toward the Mean. In general, when someone scores extremely high or low on some measure, she or he will tend to score closer toward the mean (average) on a second measurement.

Sample. A subset of a population that is studied in order to make inferences about the population.

Statistic. A number that has been calculated to describe a sample. (In its plural form it is the branch of mathematics that is concerned with probabilities and mathematical characteristics of distributions of numbers.)

Biased Sample. A sample that is not representative of the population from which it was drawn.

Mean. A measure of central tendency that is calculated by taking the sum of all the values divided by the total number of values. Also called the average.

Measures of Central Tendency. Numbers calculated on samples or populations that give a single number summary of all of the values. Two measures of central tendency are the mean and median.

Median. A measure of central tendency that is calculated by finding the middle value in a set of scores.

Sample Size. The number of people selected for a study.

Significant Difference. A difference between two groups or observations that is so large that it probably didn't occur by chance.

Extrapolation. The estimation of a value from a trend suggested by known values.

8

Decision Making

Contents

Making Sound Decisions
  A Framework for Decision Making
  Good Decisions and Subjective
  Utility
  Descriptive and Prescriptive
  Processes
Pitfalls and Pratfalls in Decision
Making
  Failure to Seek Disconfirming
  Evidence
  Overconfidence
  Availability Heuristic
  Representativeness Heuristic
  Wishful Thinking (Pollyanna
  Principle)
  Entrapment
  Psychological Reactance
  Liking
    Reciprocity
  Mere Exposure Effect
  Emotional States
  Mindlessness
Evaluating Consequences
  Assessing Desirable and Undesirable
  Consequences

Elimination by Aspects
Preparing a Worksheet
  Framing the Decision
  Generating the Alternatives
  Listing the Considerations
  Weighing the Considerations
  Weighing the Alternatives
  Calculating a Decision
    Overall Assessment
    Dimensional Comparison
    2/3 Ideal Rule
    The Problem with Numbers
  Dilemmas in Decision Making
Postdecision Commitment and
Evaluation
  Cognitive Dissonance
    Foot-In-the-Door
  Hindsight and Forethought
Applying the Framework
Chapter Summary
Terms to Know

Six doctors in white hospital coats approach your bed. No one is smiling. The results of the biopsy are in. One doctor explains that the cells were irregular in shape; they appeared abnormal. It seems that the tumor was not clearly malignant, but not clearly normal either. They probably removed the entire tumor. It's hard to be certain about these things. You have some choices. You could leave the hospital this afternoon and forget about this unpleasant episode, except for semiannual checkups. There is an above-average chance, however, that some abnormal cells remain and will spread and grow. On the other hand, you could choose to have the entire area surgically removed. Although this would be major surgery, it would clearly reduce the risk of cancer.

How do you decide what to do? Your first response is probably to ask the doctors what they recommend. But if you do, it's likely that you won't receive a consensus of opinion. Often physicians disagree about the best way to treat a disease, especially when there are many options as in the case of complicated diseases like cancer or AIDS. It is possible that some will believe that the risk of cancer is small enough to warrant the wait-and-see decision (why rush to operate?); others will believe that immediate surgery is the best decision (better safe than sorry). Ultimately, the decision is yours.

Of course, not all decisions are a matter of life and death. We are constantly making minor decisions without much thought, such as what to wear, what to eat for breakfast, which pen to buy, and when to go to sleep. Everyone is faced with a lifetime of decisions, and some of them have major and far-reaching consequences. In this chapter we are concerned with life's major decisions. Major decisions include medical decisions like the one at the beginning of this chapter, whether to marry, whom to marry, if and when to have children, what kind of occupation to choose, how to spend your hard-earned dollars, etc. These are all personal decisions that virtually everyone has to make. We also must decide on a host of political and business issues like whether to support off-shore drilling for oil, when to increase a company's inventory, which stock to invest in, how to negotiate a contract, which party to support during political upheaval, and how to increase profits. In this chapter, you will learn skills designed to help you make sound decisions. To accomplish this, we look at the way psychologists and others study decision making, examine common pitfalls and fallacies in the decision-making process, consider the risks involved, and develop a general strategy or plan that you can use when faced with a major decision.

Decision making always involves making a choice among a set of possible alternatives. If you've read the previous chapters in this book, then you've already encountered several sections on how to make intelligent choices. In Chapter 5 on analyzing arguments, for example, you considered the way in which reasons support or refute a conclusion. When analyzing arguments, you make many decisions about the relevance and accuracy of information and how well the reasons that are provided support an action or a belief. In Chapters 6 and 7 on hypothesis testing and using probabilistic information, we learned about drawing tree diagrams, collecting information, and computing likelihoods to make decisions. Because decision making is a central theme in critical thinking, different aspects of it are presented throughout this book.

MAKING SOUND DECISIONS

Decisions per se, *take place when a goal is specified, when information is gathered and judged, when values are used to choose the best solution, and when detailed plans are made and evaluated.*

—Wales and Nardi (1984, p. 1)

The decision-making process is frequently stressful. Ask anyone you know who has recently made an important decision and you will most likely be told about sleepless nights, loss of appetite (or excessive eating), irritability, and generalized feelings of anxiety. Autobiographical and biographical accounts of decision-making stress can be found in the books written by and about several past presidents and many key figures in history. Theodore C. Sorensen (1965) in his book, *Kennedy* tells of the stress John Kennedy faced during the Berlin blockade crisis, and a book written by Richard M. Nixon before his presidency, appropriately titled *Six Crises* (1962), tells about the stress caused by his early political decisions. More recently, the world watched as U.S. President George W. Bush had to decide how to respond to the horrific attacks on the World Trade Center in New York and the Pentagon in Washington, D.C. The response had to have the effect of making similar attacks in the future much less likely, and also conveying to the people of the world that it was a counterattack against a terrorist group and not against a religious group. World leaders face crises that can make our own personal crises look insignificant by comparison, although they can feel just as difficult when our personal decisions will have important consequences for ourselves and others we care about. Most of us can only imagine the pressures involved when military or large-scale economic decisions have to be made.

It may seem that one way to cope with the stress of decision making is to avoid making decisions whenever possible. Although avoidance is one way of handling stressful decisions, it is seldom a good way. Every time you find yourself avoiding a decision, remember that, in most cases, avoiding a decision is, in fact, making one without any of the benefits of a carefully thought-out consideration of the problem.

A Framework for Decision Making

*Results from past research have indicated that poor decisions with regard to
drugs, alcohol, and other issues involving personal risks often stem from poor
decision-making strategies.*

—Knight and Dansereau (1992, p. 1)

There is a common model or framework that can be used to organize our thinking about decision making. It will be extended in Chapters 9 and 10, which are concerned with solving problems and thinking creatively. The three topics that are discussed in these chapters—decision making, problem solving, and creative thinking—have a great deal of overlap in the way they are conceptualized. Sometimes, the term "decision making" is used when the task requires the decision maker to select the best alternative from among several possibilities, and the term problem solving is used when the task requires the problem solver to generate alternatives. This sort of distinction is arbitrary, and in real life, it is often difficult to decide if the task requires the generation of alternatives or the selection of alternatives. This sort of distinction will not be used here because I do not believe that it is useful.

Take the time to examine Fig. 8.1 carefully. It contains the essential components of a framework for understanding and improving decision making, problem solving, and creative thinking. In Fig. 8.1, the process of making a decision is depicted as a series of boxes, each of which represents a different component, and several arrows that show the recursive nature of the process. These boxes are set in a large oval, which represents the context in which the decision is being made. The first stage in making a decision is the identification or realization that a decision is

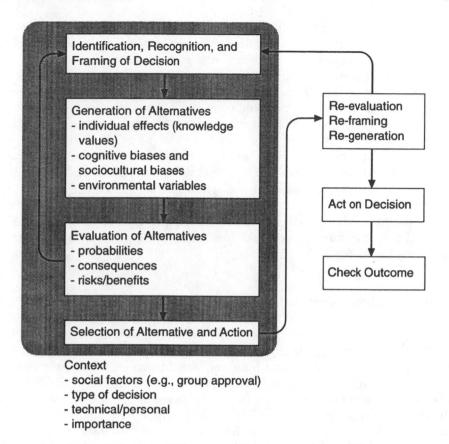

FIG. 8.1. A multiprocess model of decision making. Each of the boxes represents a stage in the decision-making process. The arrows show that the process is recursive with frequent recycling through the stages (e.g., generating alternatives may be followed by reframing the decision). The rectangular boundary represents the effects of context.

needed. This is followed by the generation of two or more alternatives that would satisfy a goal or desired outcome that is implied by the decision. Usually each alternative has several pros and cons associated with it, or, in the language of decision making, costs and benefits. The task for the decision maker is to choose the "best" alternative. The consideration of what is "best" requires an evaluation phase in which "best" often turns out to be multidimensional—best for whom? best by what criteria? best in the immediate future or long term?

Decisions also involve uncertainty because we cannot know in advance the consequences of our actions. Much of the difficulty when making decisions lies in judging which alternative is most likely to turn out best. Decisions usually have to be made with missing information and involve guesses and predictions about future events. It is also a recursive or recycling process because the nature of the decision may change as more alternatives are generated and evaluated. The decision also requires an action, although it may not be an overt movement—you could decide whom or what to believe, or to do nothing at all. All of these processes occur in a context that influences what happens and relies heavily on the information you bring with you to the decision and the information that you obtain during the decision-making process. For example, you may make a different decision if you are being observed by your friends than if you were alone (context effect), and an expert in a field may reach a different decision than a novice (effect of prior knowledge). Personal values are also a strong influence on the way the decision is phrased, the alternatives that are generated, and the way they are evaluated.

In the medical scenario at the beginning of this chapter, the decision maker must take into account the likelihood of developing cancer at some time in the future, the risks and pain of surgery, the pros and cons of various treatment regimens, and personal factors such as feelings about quality-of-life issues. When you decide which stock to invest in, you must consider what the economy might be like in the years to come. Similarly, the decision whether to have children requires that you think about what your life will be like with children who don't even exist yet. Most of life's important decisions involve competing goals; multiple players whose decisions will, in turn, affect the choices that you have; time constraints; and uncertain and changing contexts (Cannon-Bowers, Salas, & Pruitt, 1996). Not surprisingly, psychologists can offer guidelines for making good decisions, but they do not have an exact prescription that will work for all decisions.

Good Decisions and Subjective Utility

Decision making is an active process. The decision maker takes responsibility for her or his own future. After all, you are in the best position for determining how you want to spend your life and how you should make the business and professional decisions that will ultimately reflect on you. Good decision makers are more likely to get the good jobs and make favorable decisions about their personal lives as well. Recall from the first chapter that critical thinking was defined as the use of those skills or strategies that increase the probability of a desirable outcome. But, the quality of a decision needs to be judged on the basis of what was known or should have been known at the time the decision was made; sometimes, good decisions will have undesirable outcomes and sometimes poor decisions will have good outcomes. Although many famous instances of good decisions (profitable investments, successful army maneuvers) and bad decisions (Watergate, the U.S. attempt to rescue American hostages in Iran) come to mind, it is important to realize that a decision should be judged to be good or bad before the outcome is known, not after the fact. For example, most Americans would have agreed that President Carter made a wise decision to rescue American hostages in Iran, if it had been successful and no lives were lost. However, because it failed and eight Americans were killed, it is now seen as a bad decision. Thus, there is an important distinction between how good a decision is when it is being made and its outcome. You could decide to bet your life savings on a horse race (a bad decision), and "get lucky." Of course, good decisions will result in desirable outcomes much more frequently than poor decisions will.

Often, we will never know if the best decision was made. If you are a college senior who must decide between a lucrative career in accounting or a more personally rewarding career as a high school English teacher, you may never be sure if you picked the better option because you can only speculate about the career you didn't select. Robert Frost, the famous American poet, captured this feeling in his poem about a traveler who comes to a fork in the road. The traveler can never know about "the road not taken."

Good decision makers will have more desirable outcomes than poor decision makers, but what makes an outcome desirable? This is a difficult question to answer because people have different values and different goals. In deciding on a career path, it seems obvious that decisions must reflect the individual predilections of each person making this decision, just as we would not all want to marry the same person or live the same life. Somehow, we need to weigh personal values, probabilities of success, costs, and benefits to determine which choice is the best balance of these and other difficult-to-quantify variables (Baron, 1997). The term **subjective utility** refers the value of a particular choice to an individual. It is a personal assessment about a choice (subjective), which is one reason why decision making will never be an exact science like mathematics.

Before a decision can be made, the individual must realize that a decision is needed and that there are several possible alternatives. Let's consider an example. Monica is taking several demanding college courses. She needs to supplement her income by working part time and has family obligations as well. Her free time is virtually nonexistent. Monica needs to consider alternatives to her current lifestyle. She must decide how to juggle all of these commitments and still have some time left for herself. Monica has to realize that she can change her life. Too often this first step is missed and inertia sets in. Simply stated, the problem is that Monica has too many responsibilities and this is making her feel anxious and stressed. The best solution will give her more time for herself and still allow her to fulfill her responsibilities; the way she decides to balance these competing demands will depend on her personal value system (e.g., importance of spending time with her family versus the amount of money she "needs" to maintain a lifestyle that she wants). As these are essentially conflicting goals, the best decision will probably involve a compromise that will only partially satisfy each goal. It is not likely that she will find a course of action that will allow her to fill her days with leisure activities while maintaining high grades, earning money, and caring for her family.

The objective criterion for a good decision is that it has high subjective utility for the person making the decision. Some possible good decisions for Monica include finding a higher paying job or reducing her expenses so she would need to work fewer hours, beginning a more efficient study program, taking a lighter course load, and visiting her family less frequently. You may be surprised to find that with a little effort several possibilities occur to you that you might otherwise never have considered.

Devoted "Trekkies," (fans of the television and movie series called *Star Trek*) can recall many stories in which the plot involved particularly clever decision making. Consider, for example, the Trekkie-classic movie *Star Trek II: The Wrath of Khan*. In the opening scene, an attractive pointy-eared Vulcan is facing a serious problem. A sister spaceship has wandered into enemy territory and has sent a distress signal. If she does not go in to save them, they will perish; if she does, she risks enemy attack. She nervously decides to follow them into enemy territory and is immediately apprised that her starship is under attack. We soon learn that this is a computer-simulated drill designed to test the decision-making skills of future Starfleet commanders and that only one person has made the correct decision in this drill. Of course, it is Captain James T. Kirk, the hero of this series. The question of interest is whether to attempt to save the sister ship by entering enemy territory and thus risk enemy attack. Captain Kirk did neither—he redesigned the computer problem so that he would have additional choices with more favorable outcomes. For him, the problem was "how to change contingencies in a mock drill." For others, the problem had been "how to save the sister starship without being attacked." Captain Kirk made a superior decision because he defined the problem in a unique way. His unusual and excellent alternative made this decision very creative, a topic that is discussed in a later chapter. Some may say that he cheated or "copped out" by redesigning the simulation, but perhaps, he would use his ability to define problems in a unique way if he were out in space and that's what makes him an outstanding Starfleet commander. The point being made here is that often there are alternative ways of formulating what the decision requires, and some formulations will result in more favorable outcomes than others. Different formulations will lead to different solutions.

Descriptive and Prescriptive Processes

*Whenever there is a simple error that most laymen fall for, there is always a
slightly more sophisticated version of the same problem that experts fall for.*

—Amos Tversky (quoted in Gardner, 1985, p. 360)

Researchers who study decision making look at what people do when they are making a decision, often contrasting what people actually do with what they should do in order to maximize the probability of a good decision. This is the difference between a descriptive and a prescriptive account of the process. Any program that is designed to help people make better decisions will have to take into account what typically is right and wrong with most decisions, and then provide a systematic way of eliminating or reducing common errors and increasing those processes that underlie good decisions. With so many processes involved and so many decisions that need to be made, it is easy to find ways that decision making goes wrong.

Baron (1990) categorizes all thinking into "search" and "inference" stages. The search occurs when we have to generate alternatives, and to a lesser extent when we decide what constitutes a good decision. The inference relates to the kinds of judgments that are made and the way information is used. Thinking goes wrong when the search process misses some good alternatives or when the inference is incorrect (e.g., selecting an alternative that really will not solve the problem or will create other problems).

The alternatives that people generate are tied to the way memory is structured and accessed (Payne, Bettman, & Johnson, 1993). An oft-repeated theme throughout this book is the pervasive influence of memory on all aspects of thinking. The sort of alternatives that are generated will depend on what we can recall in the particular situation. Decision making is also constrained by the amount of cognitive effort that is invested in the processes of generation and evaluation. We don't want to spend huge amounts of time and energy in making most decisions, so we rely on shortcuts that sometimes lead to poor decisions. The idea is to be flexible so that the cognitive effort is proportional to the importance of the decision.

A **fallacy** is an error or mistake in the thinking process. An example of common thinking fallacies among trained professionals can be found in research with nurses conducted by Smedslund (1963) and more recently reconfirmed by Berger (1995) with a sample of physicians. Smedslund presented trained nurses with a deck of cards, which supposedly contained information gleaned from the files of 100 patients. Each card indicated whether a patient had a particular disease and whether a particular symptom was present or absent in the patient. Thus, there were four possible combinations for each patient. The patient (a) has the disease and has the symptom, (b) does not have the disease and does not have the symptom, (c) does not have the disease but has the symptom, and (4) has the disease but does not have the symptom. The task for the nurses was to determine if there is a relationship between the symptom and the disease. The number of cases in each of these four

	Has the Disease	Doesn't Have the Disease	Marginals for Rows
Has the Symptoms	37/100 = 37%	33/100 = 33%	70/100 = 70% have the symptoms
Don't Have the Symptoms	17/100 = 17%	13/100 = 13%	30/100 = 30% don't have the symptoms
Marginals for Columns	54/100 = 54% have the disease	46/100 = 46% doesn't have the disease	100% in both directions

a. Of everyone with the symptoms, 52% (37/70) have the disease. This means that if you have the symptoms, you are about as likely to have the disease as to not have the disease.
b. Of everyone with the disease, 68% (37/54) have the symptoms. This means that if you have the disease, you have about a 2/3 probability of having the symptoms.
c. Of everyone who does *not* have the disease, 72% (33/46) have the symptoms. This means that if you do *not* have the disease, there is over a 2/3 probability of having the symptoms.
d. Of everyone who does *not* have the symptoms, 56% (17/30) have the disease. This means that if you do *not* have the symptoms, there is greater than 50% probability that you have the disease.

FIG. 8.2. Number of patients within each disease/symptom category. Is there a relationship between the disease and the symptoms? Look carefully at the numbers in the marginals and think about the kind of information that they provide about the possibility of a disease–symptom relationship.

categories is shown in Fig. 8.2. Stop now and look over the data presented in Fig. 8.2. Do you think that there is a relationship between the symptom and the disease?

Overwhelmingly, the nurses concluded that there was a symptom–disease relationship, basing their decisions on the fact that 37 patients had both the disease and the symptom and 13 had neither the disease nor the symptom. They tended to ignore the 33 cases in which the symptom was present without the disease and the 17 cases in which patients had the disease, but not the symptom. These trained nurses and, more recently, a sample of physicians, routinely ignored half of the available information. The correct decision should have been that there was no relationship because there was a high probability of the disease without the symptom and the symptom without the disease. You can see this by looking at the marginals, the numbers at the end of the rows and columns. Think about the meaning of these probability values and see how they support the conclusion that there is no relationship. If you just finished reading Chapter 7 on likelihood and uncertainty, you should be able to see how the probability data that are used to make decisions in this context rely on the same thinking principles that were discussed in the likelihood and uncertainty chapter. Decisions very often involve probabilistic information, and decision-making errors using probabilities, like the one described here, are prevalent in the everyday thinking of people from all walks of life. We need to examine common decision-making fallacies because a skilled decision maker will need to know what to avoid as well as what to do.

PITFALLS AND PRATFALLS IN DECISION MAKING

Great moments in history all turned on someone's judgment as to what should be done and someone's decision to do it.

—Arkes and Hammond (1986, pp. 211–212)

A pitfall is a danger or difficulty that is not easily avoided. If you've ever spent long afternoons at the beach, you've probably seen bratty kids creating pitfalls. They dig holes in the sand and cover them with newspaper so that unsuspecting sun lovers will fall into them. The word *pratfall* needs no formal definition for fans of comedians who are famous for their frequent pratfalls. The American Heritage dictionary defines a pratfall as "a fall on the buttocks." Put these terms together and you will realize that unless common pitfalls in decision making are avoided, the decision maker will slip and fall on the part of the anatomy that is featured on blue jeans commercials. Let's examine some of the common fallacies or pitfalls in decision making.

Failure to Seek Disconfirming Evidence

Some of the worst disasters nations have known are traceable to faulty
judgments or distorted perceptions of their political leaders.

—Kruglanski (1992, p. 455)

Suppose you have a friend who is always working on crossword puzzles, anagrams, mazes, and other similar problems from puzzle books. He corners you one day with the following problem:

> I'm going to give you a series of numbers. This series conforms to a simple rule. You have to figure out what the rule is. The way to do this is by coming up with your own series of numbers. I'll tell you whether your own series conforms to this rule. You can give me as many series of numbers as necessary to discover the rule. When you believe that you know the rule, tell it to me and I'll let you know if you're right.

Reluctantly you agree to participate. You are given the following number series:

$$2 \quad 4 \quad 6$$

Stop right now and think how you would go about generating other number series that conform to the same rule as this one.

This problem was actually presented to many subjects in an experiment conducted by Wason (1960, 1968). He found that most people had difficulty with this task. Suppose that you believe that the rule is "any continuous series of even numbers." To test this rule most subjects would try series like "14, 16, 18." The experimenter would respond that this series conforms to the rule. To be certain most subjects would try again with another series, "182, 184, 186." Again the experimenter would respond affirmatively. Confidently, the subject would announce the rule, "Any continuous even series of numbers." The experimenter then informs the subject that this is not the correct rule.

Typically, subjects will try again, this time thinking up a new rule that will describe the correct number series. Suppose, this time the subject decides to try out the rule "the middle number is halfway between the other two." Now the subject asks about the series "50, 100, 150." The experimenter answers that this series is correct. The subject tries again "1006, 1007, 1008" and is told that this also conforms to the rule. Even more confident this time, the subject announces that the correct rule is "the middle number is halfway between the other two." The experimenter tells him that this is not the correct rule.

Have you discovered the correct rule by now? It is "increasing whole numbers." After almost an hour of working on this problem one of Wason's subjects came up with this rule: "The rule is that either the first number equals the second minus two, and the third is random but greater than the second, or the third number equals the second plus two, and the first is random but less than the second." You can imagine how this poor subject felt when he was told that this rule was incorrect.

Why is this problem so difficult? In all of the sample number series I've given and most of the ones people actually try, the number series conform to the rule they have in mind. There is an infinite number of possible number series that conform to the correct rule, "numbers in increasing order of magnitude." What subjects should have done is try out series that would disconfirm the rule they were trying out. For example, if you believed that the correct rule is "any continuous series of even numbers" you should try the series "1, 2, 4." If the experimenter tells you that you are correct, then you know that the rule "any continuous series of even numbers" must be wrong.

The tendency to seek information that agrees with the ideas we have is called **confirmation bias**. We have a bias or predilection to look for confirming information. Another interesting example of the confirmation bias or failure to seek disconfirming evidence is discussed in Chapter 4 on the development of reasoning skills. This example reflects the same error that was described in the previous section in which the nurses failed to consider evidence that disconfirmed the hypothesis that the symptoms and disease were related. This bias is pervasive; examples can probably be found in every applied setting. For example, a recent study of how jurors reach decisions about the guilt or innocence of a defendant shows that they construct a likely story about what probably happened at the scene of the crime. They then look for information that was revealed during the trial that is consistent with their story (Kuhn, Weinstock, & Flaton, 1994). Thus, jurors also rely heavily on evidence that confirms their beliefs.

What can we infer from the bias to seek confirming evidence? Suppose someone confronts your best friend with "the opportunity of a lifetime." A dynamic saleswoman offers him the chance to invest in a new corporation that will manufacture and sell computers that are so small they will fit in your wallet. It sounds good, but he's unsure. Prudently he decides to do some investigating. He checks out ten computer companies that are listed on the New York Stock Exchange. He finds that IBM is a large profitable corporation. If he had only invested in IBM when it was just being formed, he'd be a rich man today. He can already imagine himself lighting cigars with $10 bills. What advice would you give your friend?

Hopefully, you would point out to him that he only looked for evidence that supports the decision to invest in the corporation as only substantial corporations are listed on the stock exchange. He also needs to seek evidence that would disconfirm this decision. He should find out how many new computer corporations with big dreams have gone bankrupt and how many have not gone bankrupt in the last 10 years. He also should attempt to estimate the future market for wallet-sized computers.

Another real-life (nonlaboratory) example can be drawn from medical decision making. Imagine a young physician examining a sick patient. The patient is complaining of a high fever and sore throat. The physician must decide on a diagnosis from among myriad possible diseases. The physician decided that it may be the flu. She asks the patient if he feels "achy all over." The answer is "yes." The physician asks if the symptoms began a few days ago. Again, the response is "yes." It should be clear to the reader that the physician should also be seeking evidence that would disconfirm the flu diagnosis. She should also ask about patterns of symptoms that are not usually associated with the flu, like a rash or swollen joints or flesh-eating bacteria.

The confirmation bias is a pitfall in decision making. Wason claims that it is prevalent in the thoughts and research of scientists. In fact, a large-scale study of NASA scientists showed a strong confirmation bias (Mynatt, Doherty, & Tweney, 1978). (And yes, these are rocket scientists!) We all need to be trained to seek and examine data that are inconsistent with the ideas we are considering. There is good evidence that when people are required to consider counterevidence, they make better decisions (Koriat, Lichtenstein, & Fischhoff, 1980). In general, people spend resources (time, effort, money) looking for the wrong sort of information to inform their decisions—we need to deliberately seek information that would run counter to a preferred choice (Bastardi & Shafir, 2000).

Overconfidence

Overconfidence is a decision-making pitfall that is related to the bias to seek confirming evidence. In general, most people do not see the need to improve the way they make decisions because they believe that they are already making excellent decisions. The unwarranted belief that we are usually correct is a major, real-life barrier to critical thinking. The tendency to be overconfident about the quality of our thinking is a theme that runs through several chapters in this book. Most people believe that they think well—it's other people whose thinking needs improvement. After all, if most people are very confident that they are making the correct decision, why should they exert the time and effort to learn and apply the skills of critical thinking?

Why do we tend to believe that we are good decision makers? In part because we cannot remember other alternatives that might have led to better decisions (e.g., I can't think of any reasons why I might not be right) and because we can never know about the outcomes that would have resulted from other decisions (Holyoak & Simon, 1999). Furthermore, we tend to remember more positive aspects of an option we select than of one we do not select, even when the options were manipulated experimentally to control for these differences (Mather, Shafir, & Johnson, 2000). In a discussion of political decision making, Kruglanski (1992) lists ambition, status seeking, delusions, and prejudice as some of the reasons for bad decisions. If these less-than-ideal motives are added to politicians' overly confident belief that the decisions they make are usually right, it is easy to explain some very bad political decisions.

Availability Heuristic

A **heuristic** is any "rule of thumb" that we use to solve problems. It won't always give us the right answer, but it is a helpful aid. Psychologists usually distinguish between heuristics and algorithms. An **algorithm** is a procedure that will always yield the correct answer if you follow it exactly. Let's try a simple example from mathematics to clarify these terms. Remember the procedures you learned in solving long-division problems. Given a problem like $176\sqrt{7019}$, you were first told to estimate about how often 176 would "go into" 701, as it is unlikely that you ever learned the time tables for 176. You might estimate it to be about 4 times. The problem thus far would look like this:

$$176\overline{)7019} \quad \overset{4}{}$$

You would check out this estimate with the appropriate multiplication.

$$\begin{array}{r} 4 \\ 176\overline{)7019} \\ 704 \end{array}$$

Oops, too large!

Once you have realized that 4 was too large you would probably try 3. This procedure is a heuristic. It is a guide or aid to help you find the correct answer, but it doesn't always work perfectly as seen in the above example. On the other hand, an algorithm always leads to the correct answer. If you want to find the area of a rectangle that is 3 feet long and 2 feet wide you will always get the correct answer if you use the formula: length × width, or in this case, 3 feet × 2 feet = 6 square feet. The use of an appropriate algorithm is an example of cognitive economy, a topic that was introduced earlier in this book. We don't need to use mental effort and "reinvent" ways to find the area of a rectangle when there is a ready-to-use algorithm that we can call upon for the correct answer.

There are many situations in which we use both heuristics and algorithms. In cooking, for example, a recipe is an algorithm. If the recipe is followed exactly, the result should always be the same dish that is described in the cookbook. When cooks ad lib by adding additional seasoning or when they create a new recipe, they are using their general knowledge about the types of flavors that go together. This is an example of a heuristic. Heuristics or "rules of thumb" are frequently used by a decision maker without the realization by the decision maker that they're being used.

Availability is a commonly used heuristic. The term availability heuristic was coined by two prominent psychologists, Daniel Kahneman and Amos Tversky (1973; Tversky & Kahneman, 1974), who conducted numerous experiments on decision making and, in the process, provided a catalog of thinking errors. In order to understand the availability heuristic, consider the following questions:

1. Are there more words in the English language that begin with the letter *r* or have the *r* in the third position?
2. Would you expect the 2000 census to show that there are more librarians or farmers in the United States?
3. Are there more deaths due to homicide or due to diabetes-related diseases?

If you answer the first question like most people, you believe that there are more words that start with the letter *r* than there are words with *r* in the third position. In answering this question most people find that they can think of more words that start with *r* (rice, root, room, roam, religion, rhinoceros, rye) than have *r* in the third position (bird, torrid, horror, hero). In the jargon of psychology, words starting with the letter *r* are more available (in memory) than words with *r* in the third position. That is, they come to mind more easily. If you answered "words that start with *r*," you were wrong. According to Berger (1995), the English language contains many more words with *r* in the third position than in the first position. It is just more difficult to think of them because it is easier to retrieve words from memory by the first letter than by the third. Earlier in this chapter I talked about the pervasive influence of memory in every aspect of critical thinking. This is another example of the way in which the kinds of memories we retrieve can determine how decisions are made.

If you have already read Chapter 7 on likelihood and uncertainty, then you already know that there has been a backlash against the idea that humans are poor thinkers. In recent years, there has been more emphasis on accuracy in everyday thinking than in errors in thinking (e.g., Gigerenzer & Goldstein, 1996; Hammond, 1996; Hoffrage, Hertwig, & Gigerenzer, 2000). Systematically, Gigerenzer and his colleagues have examined each of several thinking biases to show that under some conditions, thinking is fairly accurate. For example, in a study where participants were asked to compare the frequency of letters in the first or second position of words, frequency judgments were more accurate than when comparisons were made for letters in the first or third position of words (except for letters that were either very frequent or very infrequent). The conclusion from this line of research is that accuracy in judgments depends on the way questions are asked, what is being compared, and a host of other variables. The goal of this book is to improve thinking, not to argue how good most of us are as thinkers—we can all always improve.

Your answer to the second question probably depends on whether you live in an urban or rural area. Most city dwellers believe that there are more librarians than farmers in the United States. After all, few city dwellers have ever met a farmer whereas they probably know, or at least know of, several librarians. Actually, there are many more farmers in the United States than there are librarians, a fact that was more likely to be answered correctly by readers from rural farm regions. This is another example of how the use of the availability heuristic can lead to the wrong decision.

Most residents of large cities probably believe incorrectly that there are more deaths due to homicide than to diabetes. The reason for this is not difficult to understand. Pick up any newspaper or watch television news on any day and there is likely to be a report of one or more homicides. Although you may know only a few people who have diabetes and may not know personally anyone who has been murdered, you've heard or read about many homicide victims, so there seems to be more of them. A study of people who watch many violent television shows found that these people believe that they are more likely to be a victim of a violent crime than those who don't watch these shows (Gerbner, Grass, Morgan, & Signorielli, 1980). Presumably they maintain this belief because examples of violent crimes are more readily available in their memory. This finding has important implications because it would be expected to affect how frequent viewers of televised violence vote on crime-related propositions and how they make decisions like buying a home burglary alarm, keeping a gun in the house, or going out at night.

The availability heuristic can be found in many applied settings. Its influence can best be understood with an example: In a medical text written by Gifford-Jones (1977), the author discusses the difficult medical decision concerning whether women in their late thirties or early forties should have their ovaries removed when they are having a hysterectomy. Like all difficult decisions, there are pros and cons associated with each alternative. In discussing how this decision is often made, Gifford-Jones (1977, pp. 174–175) wrote:

> I recall operating some time ago with a former professor of gynecology at Harvard. He was in a rather philosophical mood and was pondering the pros and cons of what to do with the ovaries. "Sometimes whether or not I remove the ovaries depends on what has happened to me in the last few weeks," he said. "If I've watched a patient die from cancer of the ovary, I often remove them. But if I've been free of this experience for a while, I'm more inclined to leave them in."

The availability heuristic is frequently seen in other medical examples. It is not unusual for a pediatrician whose own children suffer from severe allergies to be especially vigilant about possible allergic reactions in his patients. This may or may not be a good thing. The best physician is one who has a broad scope of experience with a large variety of illnesses so that he has a large number of medical diagnoses available to him.

Prejudice and stereotypes may also exist, at least in part, because of the human tendency to utilize readily available information. Although prejudice and stereotypes were discussed more fully in Chapter 2 on the development of memory skills, it is easy to see how availability plays a role in establishing and maintaining prejudice and stereotypes. If a minority person is convicted of a heinous crime, many people will distrust other members of the same minority. The thousands of honest hard-working minority persons are forgotten or overlooked. Their existence is overshadowed by the salient criminal.

Availability has been carefully studied in the laboratory by research psychologists because it plays a role in decisions that are made in a wide range of settings. In another experiment by Tversky and Kahneman (1974), groups of college students were given one of the two following arithmetic problems:

$$8 \times 7 \times 6 \times 5 \times 4 \times 3 \times 2 \times 1 = ?$$

or

$$1 \times 2 \times 3 \times 4 \times 5 \times 6 \times 7 \times 8 = ?$$

The college students examined either the first or second row of numbers for 5 seconds. Their task was to estimate the product because 5 seconds was not enough time to solve the problem. Students who were given the first problem, the one beginning with large numbers, gave an average estimate of the product to be 2,250. Students who were given the second problem, the one beginning with small numbers, gave an average estimate of the product to be 512. The correct answer is 40,320. Thus, when the problem began with large numbers the estimated answer was large compared to the problem that began with small numbers. The estimate differences between the ascending and descending series demonstrates that judgments were systematically biased toward the most readily available information.

Representativeness Heuristic

Suppose that a young man in a pinstripe suit, black shirt, and white tie comes up to you and asks if you'd like to make some money by betting on whether a coin lands on "heads" or "tails." (If you have already read Chapter 7, you may recall a similar sneaky character.) You look at him dubiously. He explains that it's really quite simple. He'll flip one coin six times. All you have to do is bet on the pattern of heads and tails that will result from six tosses of a coin. Although there are many sequences possible, you decide to concentrate on three of them. Using the letter "H" to represent heads and "T" to represent tails, on which of the following three outcomes would you bet?

H-T-H-T-T-H
H-H-H-T-T-T
H-T-H-T-H-T

If you responded like most other people, then you selected the first series of heads and tails, probably because it seemed more similar to a random or chance pattern of heads and tails. In fact all three series are equally likely. Any series of heads and tails taken six at a time is as likely to occur as any other. The above example demonstrates the belief that an outcome of a random process should look like or be representative of randomness. Because our common-sense notion of randomness is that of a process without a pattern, we tend to think that H-T-H-T-H-T is not as likely to occur from six tosses of a coin as a more random-looking series. This, however, is not true. (What some people find even more surprising is that H-H-H-H-H-H is as likely to occur as H-T-H-T-H-T.)

Of course, you're more likely to get approximately equal numbers of heads and tails after many coin flips than you are to get mostly or all heads or mostly or all tails because there are more possible patterns that yield these outcomes. For example, there is only one pattern of outcomes that will correspond to six heads (H-H-H-H-H-H), whereas there are many ways to get three heads and three tails in six flips of a coin (e.g., H-H-H-T-T-T; H-T-H-T-H-T; T-T-T-H-H-H; H-T-H-T-H-T; etc.). Each series or pattern of heads and tails is equally likely. This concept is also discussed in Chapter 7.

To clarify the **representativeness heuristic**, which is the belief that any member of a category should "look like" or have the traits associated with its category, let's try another example. Suppose you get a letter from an old friend from whom you haven't heard in many years. He tells you that he is the proud father of six children—three girls and three boys. After trying to consider what life is like with six children, you then wonder about their birth order. Which of the following orders do you think is more likely (with "G" standing for girl and "B" standing for boy):

B-B-B-G-G-G
       or
B-G-G-B-G-B

If you've followed the discussion so far, you will realize that although the second series appears to be more representative of a random process, they are, in fact, equally likely.

Wishful Thinking (Pollyanna Principle)

Quite often people will overestimate their chances for success or the likelihood of a desired outcome. Halpern and Irwin (1973) found that when participants in an experiment wanted an event to occur (they would win money), they believed that it was more likely to occur than when its occurrence would have been unfavorable (they would lose money). It seems that humans are an optimistic species. The tendency to believe that pleasant events are more likely than unpleasant ones is a manifestation of **wishful thinking**, the idea that if we want something to happen it will. This has also been called the Pollyanna Principle in honor of the protagonist of a 1913 novel who always found something to be happy about, no matter how bleak the situation.

A large fast-food hamburger chain is basing a promotional gimmick on wishful thinking. The corporation that made golden arches an integral part of American life is offering a game that pays off with large sums of money. Some lucky Big Mac hamburger consumer will match up small game coupons for the grand prize. A blitz of television advertising shows lucky burger eaters exclaiming over the money they've won. Apparently, the lure of winning must sell more hamburgers, or it would have been discontinued. It must be assumed that people grossly overestimate their chance of winning the prizes. The actual estimated probability of winning the grand prize is less than a million to one. As required by law, these odds are posted (in fine print) on the posters that announce the game, yet they are routinely ignored and thought to be more favorable than they actually are. Few of us can appreciate astronomical odds like this one. You're probably more likely to find a needle in a haystack. Yet, because of wishful thinking, many people will line up for hamburgers and a chance to win.

Optimism is a potent human trait that often directs how we think and act. Seligman (1991) identified optimism as a critical element in political elections. It seems that candidates who are optimistic about the future are more likely to garner winning votes than those who are pessimistic. He found that in 9 out of 10 presidential elections in the United States, the candidate who gave the more optimistic speeches won the election. Optimism may be a wonderful human trait, but not when it distorts the decision-making process. Good decisions rely on realistic assessments of likelihood, not optimistic ones. Failure to consider seriously unpleasant outcomes can lead to disastrous consequences.

Entrapment

Suppose you were offered the opportunity to bid on a $1 bill. You and some friends can make bids, and the highest bidder will pay the amount bid and get $1 in return. The only hitch is that both the highest bidder and second highest bidder must pay the amount they bid, but only the highest bidder will receive the dollar in return. Suppose that you agree to play and that you continue to raise your bid until you have offered 80 ¢. Now a friend bids $1. What do you do? You will probably decide to bid $1.05 for the $1 because you'll certainly lose 80 ¢; unless you continue to increase your bid. Shubik (1971) has found that people will continue to bid amounts over $1 to win the dollar bill in an attempt to keep their losses at a minimum in this game.

What has happened in this game is **entrapment**, a situation in which an individual has already invested money, time, or effort and decides to continue in this situation because of the initial investment. Entrapment is also called **sunk costs** because of the importance that we attach to the costs we have already "sunk" into a course of action. People commonly fall prey to entrapment. Consider Fred's decision about his automobile. He has already replaced the muffler, brakes, and ignition system when he finds out that his car needs a new transmission. Because he has already invested so much money into his car, he feels "trapped" into replacing the transmission instead of buying a new car. Or consider another common example. Everyone has had the frustrating experience of calling on the phone for some information and being put on "hold." After listening to the irritating strains of "elevator music" for several minutes, you need to decide whether to hang up or continue waiting. Many people continue to wait because of the time they've already invested.

Making decisions in light of previous investments requires that the individual consider *why* the investment has been so high either in terms of money or time, and whether, at this point in time, the car is worth the additional sum of money or the phone call is worth an additional 10 minutes on "hold." Examples of entrapment are commonly found in government budget hearings (Fischer & Johnson, 1986). One argument in favor of continuing to support the development of the MX missile is that the millions of dollars that have already been spent on it would be lost if we decided to discontinue the project. Sometimes, politicians and others will try to minimize the appearance that they have wasted money by continuing to fund projects that should be discontinued (Arkes, 1996). If more people were vigilant for sunk costs, we would save money and other valuable resources that could be put to better uses.

In a study of how people respond in sunk-costs situations, researchers asked subjects open-ended questions about common decisions (Larrick, Morgan, & Nisbett, 1990). Consider this one:

> You and a friend just spent $7 each to see a movie. About a half hour into the movie, you both realize that it is "two thumbs down"—a really bad movie. What do you do? List some good reasons for staying until the end of the movie, then list some good reasons for leaving after a half hour.

Stop now and try this demonstration.

Look over your reasons. Of course, you just read about entrapment, so you are not a naive subject, but review the answers that you gave anyway. If you listed the fact that you spent $7 as a good reason for staying, you are demonstrating the fallacy of entrapment. If you listed as a good reason for leaving the fact that the movie is a waste of time, then you receive partial credit for recognizing the cost of staying. If you also listed the fact that you could be doing something better with your time, then you would get credit for recognizing that by staying you would also be losing out on doing some better activity. Let's go over the reasoning again because I have found that many students have difficulty with this concept:

You already spent the $7 for the movie. No matter what you decide to do at this point in time, the money is gone, and you are down by $7, so it should not be relevant to your decision. You lost $7, no matter what you decide to do. At a half-hour into the movie, you have a decision to make. If you stay, you will not only have to endure a bad movie, but you will also miss out on a more pleasurable activity that you could be doing. Thus, there is a dual cost to staying—seeing a bad movie and missing out on some better activity. Try out this example with some friends or family. Explain the fallacy of entrapment to them.

Psychological Reactance

Our emotional states have a major impact on the kinds of decisions that we make (Kavanaugh & Bower, 1985). We select alternatives that seem "best" to us, and our determination of what's best is not always based on sound rational criteria. One example of the effect of emotional states on the kinds of decisions people make has been labeled **psychological reactance**, which is resistance arising from restrictions of freedom. Consider this example (Shaver, 1981): It's been a bitterly cold winter and you can hardly wait for a much deserved spring break. One of your close friends is planning on basking in the Fort Lauderdale sun. Another friend can't wait to hit the slopes in Vail. Both friends have asked you to join them in their spring break revelry. As you consider the options, you begin to favor the bikini-clad vacation when your Florida-bound friend tells you that you *must* go to Florida with him. How does this loss of freedom affect your decision?

Logically, it would seem that being told that you must do what you want to do would have no effect on your decision, but many people do not react this way. Some people would react to this loss of freedom by deciding to go skiing instead. The extent to which psychological reactance affects a decision depends on the number of freedoms that are being threatened and the source of the threat. There are also large differences among individuals in the extent to which they are prone to reactance. Consider how you will probably respond when you are told what to do in different situations. If you are likely to do the opposite, no matter what you are told to do, then you are demonstrating reactance and will sometimes make poor decisions because of this tendency. Whether you're dealing with your parents, an employer, or a foreign government, psychological reactance can interfere with the decision-making process by causing you to select a less desirable alternative.

Liking

It should seem obvious that people select alternatives that have been evaluated positively along some dimension. This point will be made more explicitly later in this chapter; however, it is important to consider here some of the factors that influence positive evaluations. In other words, what are some factors that determine liking?

Reciprocity

When assessing the pros and cons of various alternatives, our subjective feelings about the alternatives play a large role in decision making. Simply put, we choose people and actions that we like. Reciprocity is one determinant of what and whom we like. We tend to like people who like us. In Cialdini's (1993) delightful book about myriad influences that affect our thoughts and actions, he tells about the "World's Greatest Car Salesman." The super salesman seems to differ from other more mundane sellers in several ways, but the most interesting is his strange habit of correspondence. Super salesman sends a card to each of his more than 13,000 former customers each month. Can you guess the message on this card? No, it's not a list of maintenance tips or repair coupons. In fact, every card every month contains the same message: "I like you." Twelve times a year, every former customer receives the same obviously impersonal message. It seems to work. When the time comes to decide where to purchase another car, these former customers are reminded of their "friend" who likes them. Reciprocity of liking apparently has a powerful effect on decision making in this context.

The psychological literature is full of other examples of the influence of reciprocity on decisions. For example, you are much more likely to buy a product if I give you a free sample than if I don't. The next time you are in the supermarket when samples are being given away, watch how people respond to the covert pressure to buy the product they have just tasted. You'll find that a surprisingly high number will buy the product. People seem to feel that they owe something in exchange for the "free" sample. Political favors are blatant examples of reciprocity-induced liking as are charitable requests that are accompanied by "gifts" like address labels, key rings, and stamped return envelopes.

Mere Exposure Effect

Suppose that you walked into a voting booth on a primary election day and were faced with the following choice:

County Solicitor (Choose One)

Myron Jones
John Adams
Victor Light

Unfortunately, you have not kept up with local politics, and are unfamiliar with the record of any of these candidates. Which candidate would you vote for? Studies indicate that you probably chose John Adams.

In an election in New Hampshire about 10 years ago, John Adams, an unemployed cab driver who did not campaign, won the Republican nomination for the state's First Congressional District. Why did John Adams, a man who spent no money on his campaign and who never gave a speech, win his party's nomination? Psychologists believe that when voters were confronted with three names they didn't recognize, they picked the one linked in history with a political figure. Hence, prior exposure creates a sense of familiarity, which in turn can enhance your liking for the stimulus, a phenomenon known as the **mere exposure effect**.

Political commercials often operate on this principle. They repeatedly hark, "Vote for Brandon Lee, He's the One!" Such commercials give absolutely no information about the candidate. They rely on the well-documented effect that familiarity will enhance liking. Based on this principle, repetition was commonly used in Nazi Germany and North Korean prison camps during World War II in an attempt to make their political ideologies more palatable to the prisoners.

What should you do if you face unknown candidates' names in a voting booth? If you can't vote intelligently for an office, skip that section and vote for the offices with which you're familiar. Intelligent voters ask themselves, "What do I know about these candidates?" and do not fall prey to a familiar sounding name.

Emotional States

Like many cognitive psychologists, I often forget the critical role that emotions play in the thinking process. (Astute readers will probably recognize this as due to the availability heuristic.) Intuitively, we all know that emotions are important. For example, would you ask your boss for a raise if you knew that she just had a fight with her husband? Of course, your boss's relationship with her husband should be irrelevant to whether you get a raise, but a bad mood tends to spill over and affect unrelated decisions. So does a good mood. In an investigation of the way mood influences the way decisions are made, Bower (1994) found that interviewees for a job were rated higher when the interviewers were given good news prior to the interview than when they were given bad news. In a laboratory study of the way negative events affect the decisions people make, subjects were required to keep their hand in a bucket of ice water—a condition that is known to be stressful. They were then asked to provide their opinions of various people. The researchers found that the decisions these subjects made were much more hostile than in a control condition in which they did not have the physical stressor caused by keeping a hand in ice water (Berkowitz & Thome, 1987).

It is easier to recognize the effect of emotions on the way we think than it is to correct for it. It is important that we all consider how our own moods may be affecting the quality of the decisions that we make, and we may also try to influence the mood of others who will be making decisions that affect us.

Mindlessness

People often think they are making carefully calculated decisions when they are not. Cost-benefit analyses usually take place after the fact.

—Langer (quoted in Coughlin, 1993, p. A9)

Although we may believe that we are rational, thoughtful people, Langer (1989, 1994) found that many of the decisions that we make are **mindless**, that is, without conscious thought about what we are doing. For example, she told about a time when she presented a credit card to a store clerk. The clerk looked at the card and then told her that she had not yet signed it. (It was a new card.) Langer then signed the card and signed the charge slip. The clerk mindlessly checked the two signatures to see if they matched. (She had just seen her sign both.) This simple example serves to show that many of the actions that we take are done without conscious thought. Langer argues that mindlessness is a bad habit, and that with effort, we can and should be more consciously aware of what we are doing and why we are doing it.

EVALUATING CONSEQUENCES

Murphy's Law: Anything that can go wrong, will.
Comment on Murphy's Law: Murphy was an optimist.

If you return to Fig. 8.1, you'll see that evaluation is done repeatedly as new alternatives are generated, the decision is phrased differently, and the consequences of alternatives are considered. Decision making always involves uncertainty because we are thinking about the way different actions will have some future effect. The decisions that we make have implications for the future, and the future inherently involves unknowns. For this reason, the principles involved in assessing likelihood and uncertainty that were presented in Chapter 7 are an integral part of the decision-making process.

Research on how people typically deal with uncertainty has shown that the usual response is to ignore it (Hogarth, 1988). Although this may reduce the immediate complexity of a decision, it is obviously a maladaptive procedure that could lead to catastrophic results. It is possible to reduce the number of unknowns in any situation. This will almost always involve some work by the decision maker, but if the decision is an important one, it will be time well spent. Let's consider a common example. Most of us will purchase several automobiles in our lifetimes. For a majority of Americans, this will represent the second largest expenditure that they will make, exceeded only by a home purchase. The quality of this decision can be improved with a little research. You can determine which automobile variables are important to you and gather relevant data about each car you are considering for possible purchase.

Almost any decision can be improved with a little research that would reduce the uncertainty. For example, if you are uncertain about the safety of genetically altered foods, an afternoon at the library reading both pro and con materials should allow you to make a much more informed decision about this important issue.

Assessing Desirable and Undesirable Consequences

We can understand judgment as the quality of analysis, reflection, and ultimately insight that informs the making of politically consequential framing decisions.

—Renshon (1992, pp. 481–482)

The decision maker must always be aware of the risks and benefits associated with taking or not taking a particular course of action. The way consequences are evaluated will depend on the context. For example, the consequences of *not* taking an umbrella will be greater if you are heading off for a business meeting where showing up dry is important than if you are taking the dog for a walk and then returning home.

If you live in an apartment near a college campus, you are well aware of the "joys" associated with apartment hunting. Rental units are often in short supply in college communities and are priced in a range that strains the typical student's budget. Students may find themselves considering an apartment that lacks the amenities they were hoping for at a price that is really above their income. The risk associated with turning the apartment down is that they might not find another apartment within walking distance to the college campus. The risks associated with renting the apartment must also be considered. What if they find that they really can't afford to keep up the monthly rental payments? The decision maker has to decide which risk is greater and the likelihood of each occurring. Obviously, both risks need to be assessed very carefully and additional alternatives considered. Perhaps a cheaper apartment can be found in another section of town with good public transportation to campus, or perhaps a roommate can be found to share the rent.

A poignant example of failure to assess risks adequately can be found in an analysis of the United States' military actions just prior to the attack on Pearl Harbor. Admiral Kimmel, Commander in Chief of Naval Operations in the Pacific, had received several warnings from Washington that a Japanese attack in the Southwest was possible. He decided to downplay the probability of an attack on Pearl Harbor because he believed that other naval sites were more likely targets. Quite by accident, and almost an hour before the attack, two army privates spotted on a radar screen large numbers of unidentified aircraft flying toward Pearl Harbor. Realizing that these could be Japanese bomber planes, they reported the presence of the unidentified aircraft to the Army's radar center.

Let's consider the plight of the officer on duty at the radar center. The United States was not at war with Japan. He had never received the recent warning that a Japanese attack was imminent. He had to decide whether the unidentified objects on the radar screen belonged to the United States or Japan. There were costs and risks associated with either choice. If he had erroneously decided that they were Japanese planes, he would have been responsible for recalling personal "leaves" for large numbers of servicemen and women and creating havoc and panic on the military base. There were also large financial costs involved in preparing for anti-aircraft maneuvers. Because he assessed the possibility of a Japanese attack to be low, he told the two privates to forget about the objects detected by radar. He decided that they were probably the Army B-17s that were expected to arrive some time that day. With the unfortunate benefit of hindsight, it is clear that he failed to assess adequately the risks associated with each decision. The result was the worst naval disaster in U.S. history with over 2,000 lives lost. Even though he believed that an attack was unlikely (wishful thinking), he should have realized that the risks were too great to justify his decision. Decisions made under extreme risks need careful scrutiny and not an off-hand dismissal. In this case the risks associated with deciding that the planes belonged to the United States were many times greater than those associated with the decision that they were Japanese bombers.

Research has shown that the Pearl Harbor scenario is not unusual. Whenever extreme risk is associated with a course of action, there is a tendency to minimize the unfavorable consequences (Janis & Mann, 1977). This is sometimes called **biased discounting**—the bias or predilection to discount or reduce perceived risk or its probability. It often operates along with wishful thinking, which causes the decision maker to assess the probability of a desirable outcome too high, the failure to seek disconfirming evidence, which is the tendency to ignore evidence that would not support your favored hypothesis, and overconfidence in the quality of the decision that was made. These tendencies, taken together, allowed the radar officer to bolster his decision to ignore the unidentified objects by rationalizing either that even if they were Japanese bomber planes they probably would not do much damage or it was extremely unlikely that they were Japanese aircraft. A more recent example in which the failure to consider the consequences of certain decision alternatives can be seen in an analysis of the Gulf War that involved the United States, Iraq, and Kuwait. The researcher who conducted the Gulf War analysis found many similarities to the decisions that were made at Pearl Harbor (Renshon, 1992). I expect that many analyses of the horrific attacks on the World Trade Center and Pentagon will be forthcoming, all with the goal of understanding how the attacks could have happened and how better thinking and preparation can prevent similar attacks in the future.

When making decisions, many people prefer risks associated from not acting to the risks associated with taking action. The bias or preference for inaction is known as **omission bias** (Baron, 1994). Consider the decision to vaccinate your child against some dread disease. Many parents will decide not to vaccinate their children even when the risk of serious illness or death from the vaccine is extremely small and the risk of getting a serious disease or dying is many times higher if the child is not vaccinated. There is a consistent bias in which the cost of "doing nothing" is not adequately assessed (Pence, 2001).

ELIMINATION BY ASPECTS

Let's return to the earlier problem of deciding which automobile to buy. With so many automobiles on the market, where do you begin? Most people begin decision-making processes of this sort with a strategy known as **elimination by aspects**, although few people know it by this name (Tversky, 1972). An individual who is concerned about unemployment in the U.S. car industry would begin by eliminating cars that are not manufactured in the United States. In this instance, the aspect under consideration is the place in which the automobile is manufactured. At this point, most people will decide which features (or aspects) of automobiles are important to them. Suppose that you are on a limited budget so that cost is an important feature to you. You would probably determine the cost of various models of Fords, Plymouths, Chevrolets, and other U.S. autos. Models that cost more than your price ceiling would be eliminated.

Let's suppose further that frequency of repair is another important variable. Of course, no one can tell you how frequently the car you choose will need repair, but you can reduce some of the uncertainty associated with this variable by finding out how often other models similar to the ones you are considering have needed repair in the past. This information is available in consumer periodicals in every library. If some of the models that you are still considering are judged as "worse than average" on the frequency of repairs, then presumably these would be eliminated from further consideration. The elimination by aspects strategy would be recycled repeatedly until the decision maker is left with a few possible models from which to choose. Typically, small and seemingly insignificant differences will come into play to complete the process—for example, "I'm tired of shopping," or "Let's just take this one," or "The dealer will include at no extra cost furry dice to hang from the rearview mirror if I buy this model," or "I can drive this one home today." The use of small and relatively inconsequential factors to close the decision is an example of mindlessness, a topic that was discussed earlier in this chapter. Most consumers are not aware that something as "small" as free fuzzy dice tilts the balance of what had been a prudent process.

The method of elimination by aspects can be used in many contexts. Political candidates, for example, can be thought of as choices that vary along several criteria. If you decide that the issues that are important to you include a strong military defense, reduction of taxes, and school prayer, then you could rank each of these candidates along these aspects and eliminate the candidates who don't share your views. You would have to determine which of these aspects is most important if you find that none of the candidates shares all of your views about these important issues. Elimination by aspects is "fast and frugal" reasoning (Gigenzer, Todd, & the ABC Research Group, 1999; Gigenzer & Goldstein, 1996). It is one of several "shortcuts" in reasoning where the decision maker does not carefully weigh a large amount of data, but relies instead on a quicker (and some would say "dirtier") method of reaching a decision. It is much faster than the worksheet method that is presented next, and it works well when there are time constraints or when the decision does not warrant the extensive work of a worksheet.

PREPARING A WORKSHEET

*The time is ripe for a major national and international effort to include thinking
and decision-making in school curricula.*

—Baron and Brown (1991, p. 6)

We have clear evidence that decision-making biases do not go away just by telling
people not to make them, but decision making can be improved with effective training programs (e.g., Payne, Bettman, & Johnson, 1993; Rittle-Johnson & Alibali, 1999).
Researchers have found that the best way to make an important decision involves
the preparation and utilization of a decision worksheet. The purpose of a worksheet
is to optimize decision making. Psychologists who study **optimization** compare the
actual decision made by a person to a theoretical "ideal" decision to see how similar
they are. Proponents of the worksheet procedure believe that it will yield optimal
(best) decisions. Although there are several variations on the exact format that a
worksheet can take, they are similar in their essential aspects. Worksheets require
framing the decision in a clear and concise way, listing many possible alternatives
that would achieve a desired goal, listing the relevant considerations that will be affected by the decision, determining the relative importance of each consideration,
and mathematically calculating a decision. The end product of the worksheet procedure is a single numerical summary of each possible solution or alternative. In
theory, the alternative with the highest number of points emerges as the best decision,
but more usually, the careful consideration of alternatives and their probabilities and
value to the decision maker leads to a decision before the entire process is completed
because it helps to clarify values and keeps the decision maker focused on the task.

Most important problems are multifaceted with several different ways of framing
the decision, and many alternatives to choose from, each with unique advantages
and disadvantages. One of the benefits of a pencil-and-paper decision-making procedure is that it permits us to deal with more variables than our immediate processing ability would allow. If you've already read Chapter 2 on utilizing memory,
you'll recall (I hope) that working memory is limited in the number of pieces of information it can deal with at one time. A worksheet can be especially useful when
the decision involves a large number of variables with complex relationships.

Let's consider the worksheet procedure with a realistic example for most college
students: "What will I do after graduation?" A hypothetical student, Evan, has several postgraduation opportunities. He is contemplating the following: (a) a job in a
large fashionable department store where he will train to be a buyer; (b) a teaching
position in an inner-city school, probably a fifth or sixth grade class; (c) a graduate
school degree in business administration; (d) a law school degree; and (e) a year off
to "bum around" Europe. A decision-making worksheet will be very important in
helping him choose the best alternative. Notice that I did not say "correct" alternative
because there are many possible good alternatives for real-life, complex decisions.

Framing the Decision

The first step in making a sound decision is the realization that a decision needs to
be made. A decision-making worksheet begins with a succinct statement of the
problem that will also help to narrow it. Thus, the problem for Evan becomes "What

will I do after graduation that will lead to a successful career?" If Evan words his decision this way, he has already decided that his decision will involve long-range goals and not immediate ones. It is important to be clear about this distinction because most often long-range goals will involve a different decision than short-range ones. Thus the options of attending graduate or law school are really statements about working in business or as a lawyer and not decisions about school per se.

The importance of this first step cannot be overemphasized. The entire decision-making process depends on the way the problem is defined. If Evan had posed the problem as "How can I best earn a good living?" he would find that the process would focus on monetary considerations. Similarly, the process would change if he posed the problem as, "Should I go to graduate school?" Research with business managers has shown that the ability to redefine business problems is an important characteristic of good decision making in management (Merron, Fisher, & Torbert, 1987). The way the decision is framed will determine the alternatives that are generated and the way they are evaluated. This is an important point. If you are worried about world hunger, you could frame the decision about what to do about it several ways: How can we produce enough food to feed all the people in the world? How can we adjust the world population so that it does not exceed the food supply? How can we move food from wealthy countries to poor ones? How can we develop non-food alternatives that are nutritious? Each of these decisions will suggest different alternatives.

Similarly, be mindful of the way others have framed decisions for you. The media may adhere to all guidelines of fairness and still present decisions in ways that limit broader considerations. For example, I recently served as a juror on a complex trial where the attorney for the defense framed the question for the jury as "Why should you believe the alleged victim?" By contrast, the attorney for the prosecution framed the question for the jury as "Is there sufficient evidence that the defendant committed the alleged crime?" Each of these "decision frames" led to the consideration of different types of evidence. The jury had to be aware of the differences in framing and attempt to see the decision about guilt or innocence from several different perspectives as we conducted our deliberations.

A worksheet procedure can have many important applications for social problems. Consider the contemporary problem of violence, which is filled with numerous decision points. It seems that it should be possible to teach aggressive children and adults to reframe their problems in ways that suggest nonviolent alternatives. For example, instead of asking, "How can I get even with a classmate?" the child could be trained to ask, "How can I improve a bad situation?" Perhaps a thoughtful, creative reader will devise an educational program that teaches children, and perhaps even politicians, to reframe decisions so that nonaggressive alternatives are generated.

Generating the Alternatives

The next step is to write out in separate columns across the top of the worksheet all possible alternatives that could solve the problem. You'll need a large sheet of ruled paper or a computerized spreadsheet because it would make no sense to cut the worksheet process short because you ran out of space on your paper. It is important that you don't evaluate the alternatives at this stage; however, this is not the place for fiction either. If you are tone deaf, this is not the time to fantasize about a career in the opera. Allow room for two columns under each alternative that will be used later for calculations. Thus far, Evan's worksheet would look something like this:

TABLE 8.1
What Will I Do After College That Will Lead to a Successful Career?

Alternatives	Dept. Store Buyer	Teacher—Inner-City School	Graduate School—Business	Law School	"Bum" in Europe for a Year

Evan notices while drawing up his worksheet that these alternatives are not all mutually exclusive. There's no reason why he can't decide to travel around Europe for a year and then select a career goal; besides, a vacation in Europe is not a long-range plan and the decision currently being made is for life career goals. He decides at this point to erase the fifth alternative because it seems to require a separate decision from the other four. He also remembers at this point that his father always hoped that Evan would want to run the family-owned lumber business after his graduation from college. Although this is not an appealing idea to Evan, he substitutes it as an additional choice because the rules for this step of the process do not allow for evaluation.

Listing the Considerations

The decision Evan makes will have multiple effects. His feelings about making a personal contribution to society, his income and his future lifestyle, his parents' and friends' opinions of him, the quality of his workday, and many other variables are at stake. If Evan were married with children, the impact of each decision on his spouse and children would also need to be considered. At this point Evan should cover the alternatives and list on the left-hand side of his worksheet the considerations or variables that will be affected by his decision. The worksheet would now look like Table 8.2.

Before proceeding, Evan should now put the worksheet away and mull over the way the decision was framed and the alternatives and the considerations that he listed. Often people find that in the course of worksheet preparation they think of new alternatives and discover which considerations are important to them. It is also a good idea to ask other people you trust if they can think of additional alternatives and considerations. Considerations and alternatives that are not listed on the worksheet will not be considered, so it is extremely important to list all the relevant alternatives and considerations. This is another vulnerable point in the decision-making

TABLE 8.2
What Will I Do After College That Will Lead to a Successful Career?

Alternatives	Dept. Store Buyer	Teacher—Inner-City School	Graduate School—Business	Law School	Run Family Lumber Business
Considerations					
Desire to Help Society					
Income					
Parents' Opinions					
Friends' Opinions					
Interest in the Work					

process—failure to consider possible alternatives. Don't cut this part of the decision-making process short. It is important.

Be sure, however, that you don't let other people make the decision for you. Suppose that Evan's friend suggests that Evan seriously pursues his interest in music and becomes a jazz musician. In addition, Evan thinks up several additional considerations, which he lists on his worksheet. He also decides that as he is planning for his future, he should realistically consider his chances for success at each alternative. (See Table 8.3.)

Listing all relevant considerations is an important part of the worksheet process. Janis and Mann (1977) believe that poor decisions often result from failures to think through all of the relevant considerations. They suggest that considerations be listed under four categories—gains and losses for self, gains and losses for significant others, self-approval and disapproval, and social approval and disapproval, to avoid overlooking important considerations.

Weighing the Considerations

It is almost always true that the considerations are not equally important to the decision maker and therefore need to be weighed accordingly. A 5-point scale in which 1 = of slight importance, 5 = of great importance, and the numbers 2, 3, and 4 reflect gradations of importance between these end points can be used to quantify the relative importance of each consideration. Weighing considerations is a personal matter. It is likely that each of us would assign weights somewhat differently. If Evan felt that his desire to help society was moderately important to him, he would rate it a 3. Similarly, if he believed that income was more than moderately important to him, but less than "of great importance," he would rate it a 4. The appropriate weights are placed alongside each consideration.

After assigning numbers (the weights) to each consideration you should stop to survey the weights. If Evan rated "friend's opinions" with a larger number than "parents' opinions," this reflects how he feels about their relative opinions. This is a good way to clarify which considerations are most important to you. It is a good way to consider your own values.

TABLE 8.3
What Will I Do After College That Will Lead
to a Successful Career?

Alternatives	Dept. Store Buyer	Teacher— Inner-City School	Graduate School— Business	Law School	Run Family Lumber Business	Jazz Musician
Considerations						
Desire to Help Society						
Income						
Parents' Opinions						
Friends' Opinions						
Interest in the Work						
Prestige of Occupation						
Employment Security						
Amount of Vacation and Free Time						
Likelihood of Success						

It is not unusual to find that the process ends here because the decision maker realizes which alternatives are important and does not need to complete the process.

Weighing the Alternatives

Now is the time to think carefully about each alternative and determine how well each satisfies the considerations listed. The alternatives will be weighed using the numbers -2, -1, 0, $+1$, and $+2$. A positive number indicates that it is favorable or "pro" the consideration with $+2$ indicating that it is highly favorable and $+1$ indicating that it is somewhat favorable. A negative number will be used if an alternative is incompatible with or "con" a consideration, with -2 indicating that it is highly incompatible and -1 indicating that it is somewhat incompatible. Zero will be used when an alternative is neither favorable nor unfavorable to a consideration.

We'll use Evan's worksheet to demonstrate how to weigh alternatives. First, Evan has to contemplate how becoming a department store buyer will satisfy his desire to help society. Certainly it won't hurt society, but it probably won't help it either. Evan believes that although it may create additional jobs in related industries (fashion, sewing, etc.), this is not really what he had in mind when he thought about helping society; therefore, he rates it a zero on this consideration. This number is placed under "Department Store Buyer" in the left-hand column on the first row. Subsequent ratings will be placed directly below this number. If he does eventually become a buyer for a large department store, he probably will earn a satisfactory income. He certainly won't be rich, but it will be enough money to allow him to live comfortably; therefore, he gives it a $+1$. Both his parents and friends will consider it to be a moderately good job, so he rates it a $+1$ on both these considerations. He believes that it should be very interesting work and rates it a $+2$ on "interest in the work." It should be a moderately prestigious occupation and thus rates a $+1$ in this category. Unfortunately, it probably won't offer much employment security because department store sales are tied to the economy, which seems to fluctuate erratically; he therefore rates it -1 on "employment security." A department store buyer is required to work a 40-hour or more workweek with only a few weeks a year for vacation, thus rating a -2 on vacation and free time. He notes that he is moderately likely to succeed as a department store buyer, so he rates it $+1$ on this consideration.

It is usually necessary to gather more information at this stage of the decision-making process. Evan may need to phone the local school district to find out what the median salary is for school teachers. He also might seek the advice of his college advisor to determine if he has the math skills needed to succeed in business administration. We know that the way alternatives are evaluated is influenced by feelings, which, in this case, is perfectly rational because the choice is a personal one, and Evan's feeling about the alternatives should be part of the decision-making process (Overskeid, 2000).

Each alternative is rated in a similar manner by thinking how well it satisfies the objectives of each consideration. When he completed weighing the alternatives, Evan's worksheet looked like Table 8.4.

Calculating a Decision

If you have carefully followed the worksheet procedure this far, you've realized that it requires numerous decisions before even coming close to yielding the one you

TABLE 8.4
What Will I Do After College That Will Lead to a Successful Career?

Alternatives		Dept. Store Buyer	Teacher— Inner-City School	Graduate School— Business	Law School	Run Family Lumber Business	Jazz Musician
Considerations							
Desire to Help Society	(3)	0	+2	0	+1	0	0
Income	(4)	+1	−1	+2	+2	0	−1
Parents' Opinions	(2)	+1	0	+1	+2	+2	−1
Friends' Opinions	(3)	+1	+2	0	+1	−1	+2
Interest in the Work	(5)	+2	+2	+1	0	−1	+1
Prestige of Occupation	(1)	+1	−1	+2	+2	−2	+1
Employment Security	(3)	−1	−2	0	+1	+2	−2
Amount of Vacation and Free Time	(2)	−2	+2	−2	−2	+1	+2
Likelihood of Success	(5)	+1	+1	−1	−1	+2	−2

want to make. By now Evan has decided what type of decision he's making (long range), listed all the alternatives and all the considerations that he believes to be necessary, decided how important each consideration is to him and how well each alternative satisfies the objectives of each consideration.

There are three different strategies for calculating a decision at this point. They are overall assessment, dimensional comparison, and the "2/3 Ideal Rule." Each utilizes a different criterion for selecting the best decision from a worksheet.

Overall Assessment

An **overall assessment** of the various weights is obtained by determining how well each alternative satisfies the considerations taken as a whole or overall. This is calculated by multiplying the weight previously assigned for each consideration by the value assigned to how well an alternative satisfies that consideration. For example, Evan has rated his desire to help society a 3 and the department store buyer alternative a 0 on this consideration. The first cell of the worksheet is 3 × 0 = 0. This result, 0, is placed in the right-hand column under "Department Store Buyer." Continuing down to the next consideration, we see that Evan rated income as 4 and the department store buyer alternative +1 on income. Because 4 × 1 = 4, he would place a 4 in the right-hand column below Department Store Buyer and next to "Income." This procedure is repeated for each alternative. The right-hand column for each alternative is then added yielding a total score for each alternative. This procedure is demonstrated in Table 8.5.

Perusal of the worksheet will now show that based on an overall assessment, the alternative with the highest total score is "Teacher—Inner-City School." You will also notice that the alternative to become a department store buyer obtained a fairly high score that was close to a winning alternative. Thus far, it seems that Evan should seriously be thinking about a career as a teacher.

Dimensional Comparison

In a **dimensional comparison** strategy each consideration (the "dimensions") is examined to find which alternative has the highest score. For example, if "Desire to

TABLE 8.5
What Will I Do After College That Will Lead to a Successful Career?

Alternatives		Dept. Store Buyer		Teacher— Inner-City School		Graduate School— Business		Law School		Run Family Lumber Business		Jazz Musician	
Considerations													
Desire to Help Society	(3)	0	0	+2	6	0	0	+1	3	0	0	0	0
Income	(4)	+1	4	−1	−4	+2	8	+2	8	0	0	−1	−4
Parents' Opinions	(2)	+1	2	0	0	+1	2	+2	4	+2	4	−1	−2
Friends' Opinions	(3)	+1	3	+2	6	0	0	+1	3	−1	−3	+2	6
Interest in the Work	(5)	+2	10	+2	10	+1	5	0	0	−1	−5	+1	5
Prestige of Occupation	(1)	+1	1	−1	−1	+2	2	+2	2	−2	−2	+1	1
Employment Security	(3)	−1	−3	−2	−6	0	0	1	3	+2	6	−2	−6
Amount of Vacation and Free Time	(2)	−2	−4	+2	4	−2	−4	−2	−4	+1	2	+2	4
Likelihood of Success	(5)	+1	5	+1	5	−1	−5	−1	−5	+2	10	−2	−10
			18		20		8		14		12		−6

Help Society" is examined, you will see that "Teacher—Inner-City School" had the highest rating among all the other alternatives; therefore, it would "win" on this consideration and get one point. Looking at "Income" you will see that both "Graduate School—Business" and "Law School" were assigned +2 on this dimension. In the event of ties each winning tied alternative is awarded one point. If each consideration is examined in a similar manner, the following number of considerations won for each alternative will result:

Number of Considerations Won

Department Store Buyer	Teacher— Inner-City School	Graduate School— Business	Law School	Run Family Lumber Business	Jazz Musician
1	4	2	3	3	2

As seen here, the alternative "Teacher—Inner-City School" scored highest among the alternatives on four considerations. Thus, the results of the dimensional comparison strategy agree with the overall assessment results. Notice that both "Law School" and "Run Family Lumber Business" won three considerations each, yet scored fairly low on the overall assessment.

2/3 Ideal Rule

The **2/3 Ideal Rule** was suggested by Carkhuff (1973). It requires the decision maker to calculate an overall assessment total for a perfect or ideal alternative. If an ideal alternative were added to Evan's worksheet, it would rate +2 on each consideration because it would be highly favorable to each consideration. A total overall score for an ideal alternative can be arrived at by adding all of the consideration weights and multiplying the total by 2 as seen here:

$$3 + 4 + 2 + 3 + 5 + 1 + 3 + 2 + 5 = 28$$
$$28 \times 2 = 56$$

The reasoning behind the 2/3 Ideal Rule is that a best alternative may not be good enough if it fails to measure up to 2/3 of an ideal solution. Thus, according to this rule a minimally acceptable alternative would score an overall 37.5 ($2/3 \times 56 = 37.5$). If you turn back to the completed worksheet, you'll see that the highest total was for the teacher alternative and it rated, by the overall assessment method, a 20 (considerably less than the 37.5 required by this rule). Evan has several choices at this point. He can disregard the 2/3 Ideal Rule (which is likely if he is pleased with the decision to become a teacher), or he can expand and recycle the process by generating additional considerations and alternatives until he reaches a consensus with all three calculating procedures.

The 2/3 Ideal Rule is based on the idea that some alternatives are "good enough" while others are not. Searching for alternatives that are good enough is called **satisficing** (Marsh & Shapira, 1982; Tversky & Kahneman, 1981) and refers to terminating the decision making process when an alternative that is "good enough" to satisfy most of the important considerations is found. The decision making process cannot go on forever, so at some point, the decision maker will have to decide that one alternative is "good enough." The problem really is *when* to terminate the process, and there are no simple answers to this question. Important decisions like the one considered in this example should be given the time and effort they deserve. Often, better decisions are possible if the decision maker would invest more time and effort into generating alternatives and listing considerations.

The Problem with Numbers

One problem in using worksheet procedures to make decisions is the reliance on subjective estimates—estimates of the probability of success, estimates of the importance of consideration, and estimates of the extent to which an alternative is favorable or unfavorable for a consideration. Although a large table of numbers can look very scientific, the end result is only as good as the numbers that go into the calculations (cf., Baron, 1997). Sometimes, small differences in how you assess probabilities or values can change the outcome. So, it is important that you think about the worksheet procedure as an aid or "decision-making helper," not an absolute determinant of what you do. It should help you to clarify your values, force you to think systematically about multiple variables, and aid in the generation of additional possible alternatives. Ideally, the decision will become clear as you work on the worksheet so that it is more of a process for making a decision than an absolute determinant of what you decide.

Dilemmas in Decision Making

The decision maker will often encounter dilemmas in calculating a decision. It is not unusual for two or more alternatives to have exactly the same high score or for one alternative to obtain the highest total with the overall assessment and a different one with the dimensional comparison. This can always be remedied by generating additional considerations and repeating the process until an alternative emerges as best. It is also possible to combine two or more alternatives. For example, Evan could become a buyer in a department store and volunteer to tutor children on weekends. This would allow him to realize his desire to help society while maintaining the benefits of the buyer alternative. Sometimes the decision maker will abandon the worksheet before it's completed because the process helped to clarify the issues and led directly to a decision without the calculations.

Certainly, the worksheet procedure requires a great deal of work, as its name implies. You might be wondering if there is any evidence to suggest that it's worth the extra effort—that it actually leads to better decisions. Yes, there is. Mann (1972) randomly selected 30 high school seniors (15 females and 15 males) from a college preparatory program to participate in an experimental investigation of the worksheet procedure. He taught them how to prepare a worksheet that would help them make decisions about college. The procedure he used was similar to the one presented here, but not identical to it. He also employed a "control group" of 20 students who were not taught the worksheet procedure. Mann contacted the students approximately 6 weeks after they notified the colleges about their decision concerning which college they planned to attend. The group that had received worksheet training (the experimental group) had less postdecision stress and anxiety and were happier about the decisions they made than the control group. Mann also reported that they had considered possible unfavorable consequences of their decision more carefully than the control group. Thus, if something does go wrong, they will more likely be prepared for it than those in the group without worksheet training.

Additional evidence that supports the validity of the worksheet procedure comes from a study by Wanous (1973). He conducted an experiment to study the employment decisions of telephone operators. One group of prospective telephone operators was shown a film that portrayed both the positive and negative aspects of the job whereas a control group was shown the standard training film that stressed only the positive aspects. All subjects in both groups decided to accept the employment offer to become telephone operators. One month later, subjects who had viewed the "balanced" presentation reported that they were happier with their decision than the other telephone operators who had viewed the standard one-sided film. In addition, significantly fewer subjects from the experimental group were thinking about quitting their job than from the control group. In a similar vein, Janis and Mann (1977) reported several studies in which the worksheet procedure has been utilized in health decisions (e.g., elective surgery) with beneficial outcomes.

More recently, Knight and Dansereau (1992) used a decision-making worksheet with college students who were presented with a story about "Chris," a student who had to make decisions about alcohol and other drug use. The students who were required to complete a worksheet showed evidence of better decisions regarding alcohol and drug use than a control group that did not receive training with worksheets. I don't know if these college students will actually make better real-life decisions about alcohol and other drug use, but other studies with decision-making worksheets suggest that they will. One of the benefits of the worksheet procedure is that it allows people to feel more confident about difficult decisions and better prepared for decision-making situations because they are required to evaluate alternatives in a systematic manner.

POSTDECISION COMMITMENT AND EVALUATION

To begin with it was only tentatively that I put forward the views that I have developed . . . but in the course of time they have gained such a hold upon me that I can no longer think in any other way.

—Sigmund Freud (1856–1939)

The decision-making process doesn't end with the decision. Once a course of action has been selected, the decision maker must make detailed plans to carry it out and needs to remain committed to the decision. However, if a major change occurs in the evaluation of the consideration, then the process should be repeated. For example, if Evan were unexpectedly offered a lucrative contract to become a jazz musician, he would be wise to reconsider this alternative. Success at this alternative would now seem much more likely and a large income would be assured. Decision making is not a static process. Our major life decisions will have to be reconsidered whenever a major variable changes.

Commitment is also important in decision making. Once a course of action has been decided upon, we tend to view it as the "obvious" correct alternative, often forgetting the effort that went into the decision. Consider how commitment shapes behavior. In a radio interview, one restaurant owner was discussing the problem of getting reservations on Valentine's Day (although the example applies to any day). He said that one major problem is the large number of people who make reservations, but never show up or even bother to cancel them, so restaurant seats are empty while diners are turned away. He said that two simple words drastically reduced the number of "no shows" he had at his restaurant. In the past, the person taking the reservations would end each call with a cheery, "Please phone to cancel your reservations if you cannot make it." Instead, she asked, "Will you please phone to cancel your reservations if you cannot make it?" By asking "will you," the caller had to make a verbal commitment to canceling the reservation, which according to this unnamed restaurant owner, greatly reduced the number of "no shows" at his restaurant.

Cognitive Dissonance

Most of the time, people find that they are pleased with their decisions. This finding has been of considerable interest to research psychologists. Leon Festinger (1964), a famous research psychologist, proposed his theory of **cognitive dissonance** to explain this phenomenon. It is based on the idea that people like their beliefs, attitudes, and actions to be consistent, and when they are not consistent, an unpleasant internal state arises—dissonance. Dissonance needs to be reduced. If you believe that it is wrong to smoke marijuana and you attend a party where you smoke marijuana, you will feel uncomfortable because your actions and beliefs are not in agreement. They are not consistent with each other. In order to reduce the discomfort of cognitive dissonance, which is an unpleasant internal state, you will generally change your beliefs and conclude that you did the right thing because "marijuana probably isn't so bad after all." In general, the theory of cognitive dissonance has received considerable experimental support. In one study (Brehm, 1956) subjects rated the desirability of several gifts (e.g., toaster, coffee maker). They were then asked to choose between two gifts that they had rated as equally desirable. After a decision had been made, subjects rated the rejected gift as being much less desirable than the one they chose. The theory of cognitive dissonance would have predicted this result because subjects would now believe that they must like the selected object much more than the rejected one in order to maintain consistency. It seems that once a decision is made the alternatives that were not selected will seem much less attractive than the one that was.

The theory of cognitive dissonance can be applied in a number of situations. It can be used to explain the famous fable The Fox and the Sour Grapes. The story goes something like this: A hungry fox spies grapes hanging high overhead. After repeated unsuccessful attempts to reach them, he decides that they were probably sour and walks away. Like the human subjects described in this section, he downplayed the desirability of the object he didn't obtain.

The theory of cognitive dissonance only applies when a conscious decision has been made. If you were coerced in some way, there would be no dissonance. Suppose that you were required to write an essay on some topic that you are opposed to, like the inferiority of a racial or ethnic group, or why drugs should be available to elementary school children. If you were coerced into doing this, there would be no need to change your attitudes to keep them consistent with this behavior. However, if you voluntarily decided to write such an essay, then cognitive dissonance theory would predict a change in your attitude toward the position you took in the essay. This is a major theory in social psychology that explains why people are usually satisfied with the decisions they make. It is easy to see how it contributes to the unwarranted confidence that most people have in their decisions.

Foot-in-the-Door

Cognitive dissonance can be used to understand a common persuasive technique know as the **foot-in-the-door**. The phrase comes from common parlance among door-to-door salespeople who claimed that they could make a sale if only they could get a "foot-in-the-door"—get the prospective customer to allow the salespeople to make their sales pitch. Research on the use of this technique shows that if people agree to a small request—like signing a petition in favor of safe driving—later, they are more likely to agree to a larger request—like donating money to a safe driving campaign (Cialdini, Trost, & Newsom, 1995). People are more willing to agree to an inconvenient or costly request when it follows a smaller or less costly request that is consistent with the larger one. It seems that many people reason that they must really care about the issue or topic because they already showed their support with a smaller action.

Hindsight and Forethought

Hindsight bias is a cheap price we have to pay for a much larger gain: a well-functioning memory that we do not need—such as outdated knowledge—and that constantly updates our knowledge, thereby increasing the accuracy of our inferences.

—Ulrich Hoffrage (quoted in Azar, 2000, p. 29)

The term **hindsight** is probably not a new one for you. After a decision has been made and the relevant events occur, well-meaning friends will often tell you they could have predicted the consequences of your decision. If you have ever been divorced (or have exchanged confidences with someone who has), there were probably several acquaintances, who claimed to have known all along that, "he (or she) was no good for you." Events appear different with the benefit of hindsight. Forethought is the opposite of hindsight. There should be fewer unfortunate consequences if decisions are carefully thought out before they are made.

In experimental investigations of hindsight, most participants erroneously believed that they could have predicted the consequences of historical and personal decisions before they occurred. In our earlier analysis of the Pearl Harbor disaster, it seemed obvious that the only possible decision was to assume that the aircraft belonged to the Japanese. It should be remembered that we analyzed the disaster with the full knowledge of the ensuing events. Hindsight occurs only when poor or wrong decisions have been made. It is seldom that good decisions are analyzed after the fact. Forethought and hindsight are qualitatively different. At the time of the decision (forethought) there is doubt and deliberation, but following the unfavorable consequences of the decision (hindsight) there is often a great sense of certainty that the future should have been predicted more accurately.

An example of the power of hindsight occurred in 1974 when an editorial in a Eugene, Oregon, newspaper called upon the local prison warden to resign. A "convicted murderer, bank robber, and all-around bad actor" had been given a 4-hour pass to leave the state penitentiary (Fischoff, 1975). Instead of returning, he kidnapped and murdered an Oregon couple. With the benefit of hindsight—that is, with the full knowledge of the result—does it seem that the warden should have known that this would happen? Given the disastrous outcome it was a wrong decision, but was the result obvious or even likely before the pass was granted? The convict had been a model prisoner before the pass was granted. Do you think that the warden should have been required to resign?

Hindsight is of little value in the decision-making process. It distorts our memory for events that occurred at the time of the decision so that the actual consequence seems to have been a "foregone conclusion." Thus, it may be difficult to learn from our mistakes. Retrospective (after the fact) review, on the other hand, can be a valuable aid in improving future decisions. Unlike hindsight, it does not involve a faulty reconstruction of the information available at the time of the decision so that the consequence appears obvious.

There are plenty of examples of the hindsight bias whenever a political decision results in a disastrous outcome. For example, you may recall the tragic end to the Branch Davidians in Waco, Texas, in 1993. Attorney General Janet Reno ordered that federal agents take over the compound following a lengthy siege and the shooting of several federal agents by the members of this religious cult. At least 15 children in the Davidian compound were killed by their parents during an apparent murder/suicide frenzy that occurred when the Davidians were attacked by the federal agents. Did Reno make a bad decision? It is clear that the decision had a bad outcome, but given what was known at the time the decision was made, should she have reasonably expected that the Davidians would kill each other if the agents stormed the compound? Federal agents are involved in many activities, with very, very few ever resulting in disaster. There were no good reasons to have predicted that these religious parents would kill their children and then each other. Dawes (1993) points out how the news media used their knowledge of this salient, improbable, and painful outcome to cloud their understanding of the factors that were available at the time the decision was made.

Like many of the thinking skills and biases that are presented in this book, hindsight bias shows up in many different contexts and often goes unrecognized. Consider the plight of every clinical psychologist. Psychologists and other therapists are legally bound by a law called "Tarasoff," which requires that they warn appropriate authorities if a patient tells them about plans to hurt someone. (Actually, the law is more complicated than this simple description implies.) The problem for therapists is determining what constitutes a credible threat that needs to be reported. In one study, a group of adults was given a scenario that described the treatment of a potentially violent patient. The scenarios were all the same, but there were three different "endings"—one group of adults read that the patient had become violent, another group read that the patient had not become violent, and the third group was not given any information about the patient's behavior. As predicted, the adults who were told that the patient became violent were much more likely to believe that the patient's violent behavior was foreseeable from the therapy sessions than the adults who read the same scenarios, but were given a different ending (LaBine & LaBine, 1996). Of course, none of the adults who made these judgments had any awareness of the hindsight bias. Hindsight bias is difficult to correct because we are usually not aware when it is operating. The next time a major disaster follows from a decision, pay careful attention to the way the decision is analyzed by the news media and the political party that is likely to gain from this tragedy. Ask yourself if the outcome could have reasonably been predicted prior to the decision.

It is a good idea to determine what went wrong if a poor decision has been made or if a good decision had a negative consequence, as long as we do not fall prey to hindsight.

Immediately after the tragic bombing of a federal building in Oklahoma in 1995, numerous political pundits proclaimed that they knew that a disgruntled militia was a serious threat to society. *After* it happened, we all "could see it coming."

APPLYING THE FRAMEWORK

In applying the general thinking skills framework to decision making, consider the following questions:

1. What Is the Goal?

The skills involved in decision making should be used whenever you are faced with selecting the best alternative among a set of alternatives. Examples of situations that require the use of these skills include personal, professional, and political decisions. The process starts with the recognition that a decision is needed and then a careful consideration of how it should be framed. Because a common failure occurs in the generation of a limited number or limited scope of alternatives, exert time and effort on this stage of the process. The time and effort should be proportional to the importance of the decision. Think through positive and negative consequences of various alternatives.

2. What Is Known?

The entire decision-making process is predicated on the belief that you are selecting from among a set of alternatives. If you have no alternatives, then there is no decision. Similarly, the process requires that you frame the decision in several ways so that you can generate a range of alternatives. A decision can only be as good as the information on which it is based. If you do not know much about a problem, then you cannot select intelligently from a set of solutions. Probably the greatest difficulty with making decisions is the failure to consider alternatives that aren't listed on a worksheet or aren't made conscious in some other way. Good decisions will require information gathering and assessment before the selection of alternatives begins.

3. Which Thinking Skill or Skills
Will Get You to Your Goal?

The kind of skill you select when you are confronted with an important decision depends upon the nature of the problem. Some of the skills involve avoiding common fallacies like the failure to seek disconfirming evidence or the reliance on available information to assess the likelihood of an outcome. If the decision has potentially negative consequences, then the positive and negative results of a course of action have to be compared to each other and to those associated with other alternatives.

The weighing of considerations to calculate relative importance and likelihood is helpful whenever there are multiple alternatives and the decision is an important one.

The following decision-making skills were developed in this chapter:

- Listing alternatives and considering the pros and cons of each.
- Reframing the decision so as to consider different types of alternatives.
- Recognizing the need to seek disconfirming evidence and deliberately seeking disconfirming evidence.
- Understanding the way that information that is readily recalled or information that appears representative of a random process can influence how decisions are made.
- Considering how overly optimistic assessments bias the selection of alternatives.
- Recognizing arguments that are based on entrapment and considering why the costs have been high.
- Being mindful of the way liking can affect the evaluation of alternatives.
- Evaluating positive assessments of alternatives that are based on reciprocity or familiarity.
- Seeking information to reduce uncertainty when making risky decisions.
- Preparing a decision-making worksheet for important decisions.
- Understanding the distinction between the quality of a decision and its outcome.
- Understanding the way emotional states like reactance and anger can affect the way we evaluate alternatives and behaving in ways that minimize their effects.
- Recognizing that hindsight analysis of a decision is usually biased and of limited value.

4. Have You Reached Your Goal?

The process of making a decision could, theoretically, go on forever. Most decisions, however, have deadlines. After you have carefully considered various outcomes, you need to take an overview of your decision and then follow through and act on it. Does the decision seem right? Are you satisfied with the process and outcome? As stated in the chapter, because of the uncertainty inherent in decisions, sometimes good decisions will have poor outcomes. When this happens, scrutinize the nature of the outcome. Was there a consideration that you failed to consider at the time the decision was made? Can you learn from the negative outcome? Can you imagine the consequences of an alternative you rejected?

CHAPTER SUMMARY

1. Decision making is an active process that begins with a clear definition of the decision and a set of alternative solutions from which to choose.

2. One way to improve decisions is to frame them several ways. Additional alternatives can emerge by changing the focus of what is being decided on.

3. Few people ever receive formal instruction in thinking skills, and even trained professionals commit common decision making fallacies.

4. A common error in decision making is the failure to seek disconfirming evidence.

5. People often rely on heuristics or "rules of thumb" to help them make decisions. The availability heuristic or reliance on events that are readily recalled is a common decision-making heuristic. When time is limited or the decision does not merit a large investment of time or effort, there are many heuristics (thinking shortcuts) that often work quite well.

6. Because of the widespread but erroneous belief that the laws of chance are self-correcting, many people believe that "random-looking" sequences of outcomes are more probable outcomes of a random process than orderly sequences of outcomes.

7. Unwarranted optimism can also lead to poor decisions because it prevents realistic assessment of both desirable and undesirable consequences of a decision.

8. People often fall prey to entrapment. They find it difficult to reverse their decision after having invested large amounts of time or money.

9. Decisions are often biased by emotional states like psychological reactance (the resistance to a loss of freedom), mood, and liking induced by reciprocity and familiarity.

10. Risky decisions require special care. There is often a tendency to downplay the likelihood of a disastrous outcome.

11. When the alternatives vary along several dimensions, decisions are sometimes made by eliminating alternatives until only one or two choices remain.

12. Important decisions can be optimized by preparing a worksheet in which alternatives and considerations are listed and weighed in a table format.

13. People are most often satisfied with the decisions that they make, possibly because cognitive dissonance works to maintain consistency between actions and beliefs and because they cannot think of any reason why they might be wrong. Thus, we reason that if we decided on a course of action it must have been the best one.

14. After the consequences of a decision have occurred, there is a great sense of certainty that the consequences should have been obvious. Hindsight is a ubiquitous phenomenon that distorts how we perceive the information that was available before the decision was made.

15. There is an important distinction between a good decision that is based on the information that is available when the decision is being made and its outcomes. Sometimes, good decisions will have undesirable outcomes because of the inherent uncertainty in most important decisions.

TERMS TO KNOW

Check your understanding of the concepts presented in this chapter by reviewing their definitions. If you find that you're having difficulty with any term, be sure to reread the section in which it is discussed:

Subjective Utility. The value of a choice to an individual who is making a decision.

Fallacy. An error or mistake in the thinking process.

Confirmation Bias. The predilection to seek and utilize information that supports or confirms one's hypothesis or beliefs while ignoring disconfirming information.

Overconfidence. An unwarranted confidence in the quality of decisions that are being made.

Heuristic. A general "rule of thumb" or strategy that we use to solve problems and make decisions. Although it doesn't always produce a correct answer, it is usually a helpful aid. Compare with algorithm.

Algorithm. A problem-solving or decision-making procedure that will always yield the solution to a particular problem if it is followed exactly. Compare with heuristic.

Availability Heuristic. A decision-making "rule of thumb" that is used when estimates of frequency or probability are made based on the ease with which instances come to mind; for example, many college students believe that there are more professors in America than farmers because they can think of more professors whom they know than farmers.

Representativeness Heuristic. A decision-making "rule of thumb" in which the determination of a sample's likelihood is made by noting its similarity to a random process. If it "looks like" a random process, it is judged to be more probable than if it appears orderly or patterned.

Wishful Thinking. People tend to overestimate their chances of success or the likelihood of a desirable outcome.

Entrapment. A situation in which an individual has already invested much money, time, or effort and therefore decides to continue in this situation because of the money, time, or effort that has already been invested.

Psychological Reactance. Resistance arising from restrictions of freedom. Some people will select a less preferred alternative if they are told that they must select the preferred alternative.

Mere Exposure Effect. Very often, repeated exposure to a stimulus will enhance your liking for it.

Mindlessness. Making decisions with little or no conscious effort.

Biased Discounting. Predilection to discount or reduce the magnitude or probability of risk.

Omission Bias. The preference for risks associated with *not* taking an action over risks associated with acting.

Elimination by Aspects. A decision-making strategy in which choices are sequentially eliminated if they fail to meet one or more considerations.

Optimization. Making the best possible decision in any situation.

Overall Assessment. A method of calculating a decision from a worksheet. The alternative with the highest worksheet total would be selected. Compare with dimensional comparison and 2/3 Ideal Rule.

Dimensional Comparison. A method for calculating a decision from a worksheet. The alternative that has "won" the greatest number of considerations would be selected. Compare with overall assessment and 2/3 Ideal Rule.

2/3 Ideal Rule. A method for calculating a decision from a worksheet. Only alternatives whose worksheet totals are at least 2/3 as large as the ideal choice would be chosen. Compare with dimensional comparison and overall assessment.

Satisficing. Terminating the decision-making process when an alternative that is "good enough" to satisfy most of the important considerations is found.

Cognitive Dissonance. A theory based on the notion that people want their beliefs, attitudes, and actions to be consistent. When they are not consistent, an unpleasant internal state arises—dissonance—which needs to be reduced. We reduce dissonance by changing our beliefs and attitudes so that they are in accord with our actions.

Foot-in-the-Door. A two-stage persuasive technique. People are more likely to comply with a large request if they first comply with a smaller, but related, request.

Hindsight. Reevaluation of a decision after it has been made and its consequences have occurred with the belief that the consequences should have been known before the decision was made.

9

Development of Problem-Solving Skills

Contents

Suppose you're driving alone at night on a long, dark stretch of freeway that is infrequently traveled when you suddenly hear the familiar "thump-thump" of a very flat tire. You pull onto the shoulder of the road and begin the unpleasant task of changing a tire, illuminated only with the light of the moon and a small flashlight. Carefully, you remove the lug nuts and place them in the hubcap by the roadside. A speeding motorist whizzes past you, hitting the hubcap and scattering the lug nuts across the dark freeway and out of sight. Here you sit, a spare tire in one hand, a flat tire propped against the car, and no lug nuts, on a dark night on a lonely stretch of freeway. To make matters worse, a cold rain is beginning to fall. What would you do?

One of my students told me that this incident actually happened. He went on to elaborate that the flat tire occurred alongside a large mental institution near our college. While the hapless motorist sat pondering his problem, he attracted the attention of several "residents" of the institution, who gathered near the motorist along the chain link fence that separated them. One resident offered this solution to the motorist's problem: Remove one lug nut from each of the other three tires and use them to attach the spare. Each tire should hold securely with three lug nuts until the motorist reaches a gas station. The grateful motorist thanked the institution resident and then asked, "How'd you think of such a good solution to this problem?" The resident replied, "I'm not dumb, I'm just crazy!"

I doubt if this exchange ever really occurred. After this problem appeared in the earlier editions of this book, students from many different countries wrote to tell me that they heard the same story, but with the poor motorist breaking down near their school. In any case, virtually everyone agrees that the resident offered a good solution to the motorist's predicament. Why was it so difficult for the motorist to solve the problem? Why did the solution seem so easy and obvious after it was revealed? How did the resident come up with such a good solution?

WHAT IS A PROBLEM?

Even now there are few schools that encourage the young or old to think out
questions for themselves. And yet, life is a continuous problem for the living,
and first of all we should be equipped to think, if possible.

—Clarence Darrow (1936, p. 25)

Everyone has problems, so it would seem that it would be an easy word to define. We all know a problem when we see one, but how would you define the general term "problem"? Psychologists think of **a problem** as a gap or barrier between where you are and where you want to be. You have a problem if you cannot think of a way of getting around the gap or barrier so that you can reach the place you want to be or when there appears to be many ways around the gap or barrier, but you do not know which of the apparent paths will actually lead to the goal. This definition of a problem is graphically represented in Fig. 9.1. As you will see later in this chapter, the way a problem is represented can influence how or whether you can solve it. Be sure that you understand the way the word *problem* is visually defined in Fig. 9.1.

There is a gap or barrier separating you from where you want to be. This is a problem.

FIG. 9.1.   A visual representation of a "problem." To solve the problem, you need to find a way to get over the gap or around the barrier that is keeping you from the place (or state) where you want to be.

ANATOMY OF A PROBLEM

Finding the right answer is important, of course. But more important is developing the ability to see that problems have multiple solutions, that getting from X to Y demands basic skills and mental agility, imagination, persistence, patience.

—Mary Hatwood Futrell, President, NEA
(cited in Heiman & Slomianko, 1986, p. 18)

Consider this more mundane problem that differs in several important ways from the "lug nut" problem presented at the start of this chapter: Keith has to catch a 9:00 a.m. plane for Philadelphia, and he's already behind schedule. The quickest route to the airport is the freeway, except when the traffic is heavy. The traffic is almost always heavy with commuters during the morning rush hour. There is a back road route that might be a good one, if the road along the river isn't flooded. The road is frequently closed because of flooding after heavy rains. As you can probably guess, it rained last night. The surface street route is the longest. If Keith chooses this route, he may miss his plane. Of course, if he spends too much time pondering this problem, he'll surely miss his plane. Which route should he take?

To understand any complex phenomenon, like problem solving, we need a model or theoretical framework that we can use to study and understand how people solve all sorts of problems. A model is an as, if statement. This means, let's examine the phenomenon that we want to know about "as if" it were something else. In an earlier chapter, I suggested that you think about memory as if it consisted of stages in a computer program and to think of different kinds of memory as different ways of slicing a pizza. Theoretical models of this sort are useful for organizing what we know about thinking and for suggesting new types of research and ways to improve the process we are trying to understand.

In their classic book, Newell and Simon (1972) conceptualized all problems as being composed of the same basic parts or structures. Their idea is that problems can be understood by reducing them to their anatomical parts. According to this view, the **anatomy of a problem** can be thought of as having a starting or initial state (Keith's home) and a final or goal state (the airport). All of the possible **solution paths** from the **initial state** to the **goal state** comprise the **problem space**. In solving a problem, people search through the problem space to find the best path from the initial state to the goal; that is, they consider all of the alternatives that would lead to the goal and select the best one.

In addition to an initial state, a goal state, and the paths connecting them, there are **givens**—information and rules that place constraints on the problem. The givens include the knowledge needed to reach the goal and the need to select the best route. This information can be explicitly stated or implicitly assumed. Two implicit givens in the problem presented earlier were the knowledge that Keith would drive a car to the airport and that he would either take the freeway route, back-road route, or surface-street route. This anatomy or framework for conceptualizing problems has proven useful in understanding the process of problem solving. The anatomy of the airport problem is schematically shown in Fig. 9.2. We return to the airport problem later in the chapter as different problem-solving strategies are considered.

Problems differ in many ways, including difficulty and where in the problem space the gap occurs. In the airport problem, the difficulty lies in choosing the path (route) that would get Keith to the goal in the shortest time. In the lug nut problem, the difficulty was in generating any solution path. The initial state was a spare tire with no lug nuts; the goal was mounting the spare tire to the car securely enough to drive the car. The problem in both scenarios was the apparent absence of paths to the goal.

Consider Rubik's cube as a difficult problem. The goal for a Rubik's cube is to align each small colored square so that each of the six sides of the cube will be a uniform color. This is a prohibitive problem because there are millions of combinations of possible moves (paths to the goal). The "trick" is to determine which combination of moves will lead to the goal. In this sort of problem, the difficulty lies in reducing the number of possible paths so that only potentially correct ones will be chosen. Newell and Simon (1972) calculated that the average 40-move chess game has 10^{120} paths. This number is so large that it is almost impossible for most of us to imagine! Perhaps this is why we view great chess masters with such awe. They have the knowledge to avoid blind paths (bad moves) that won't lead to the goal (winning) and to select the best combination of moves.

Although problem solving, decision making, and creativity are discussed in separate chapters in this book, there is considerable overlap among these topics. Many

FIG. 9.2. The anatomy of the airport problem. Givens: Keith will drive to the airport. He will take one of these routes. He must take the fastest route.

decisions are involved in solving a problem; generating satisfactory solution paths often requires considerable creativity. The division among these topics is for ease of presentation. All of the chapters in this text are interrelated in that they represent arbitrary ways of "cutting up the thinking pie." The information presented in the other chapters will also contribute to your understanding of problem solving.

STAGES IN PROBLEM SOLVING

The aim of heuristics is to study the methods and rules of discovery and invention. . . . Heuristic, as an adjective, means "serving to discover."

—Polya (1945, pp. 112–113)

In 1926 Graham Wallas examined anecdotal accounts of creative scientists and concluded that problem solving progresses in a series of stages. Although there is disagreement among psychologists as to whether all problem solving is done in qualitatively different stages, a brief review of the hypothesized stages may prove useful to us as problem solvers.

The first stage is **preparation or familiarization**. This includes the time spent in understanding the nature of the problem, the desired goal, and the givens. This is a crucial part in problem solving because a correct solution cannot be generated without an adequate understanding of the problem. The second stage is the **production stage**. During this stage, the problem solver produces the solution paths that define the problem space. **Judgment or evaluation** is the third stage. During this stage, individuals evaluate the solution paths in order to select the best one. The fourth stage is a strange one that may or may not occur, depending on the problem. Sometimes when we can't find a solution path, we stop working on the problem, at least for a short while. The period when we're not actively considering the problem is called the **incubation stage**. There are many reports from famous scientists that a solution came to them during the incubation phase—seemingly "out of the blue." Because of the fascination incubation holds for most people, it deserves separate consideration.

Incubation

Have you ever had the experience of working unsuccessfully on a problem, then having the solution come to you sometime later when you were not consciously thinking about it? If so, then you have experienced incubation effects first hand. The term incubation suggests a mother hen sitting on great ideas that are about to hatch.

The idea of an incubation phase is attractive to most people. It represents one of the few instances in which we may get something for nothing. An oft-cited example of incubation comes from the writings of the famous French mathematician Poincare (1929):

> Then I turned my attention to the study of some arithmetical questions apparently without much success and without a suspicion of any connection with my preceding researches. Disgusted with my failure, I went to spend a few days at the seaside, and thought of something else. One morning, walking on the bluff, the idea came to me, with just the same characteristics of brevity, suddenness and immediate certainty, that the arithmetic

transformations of indeterminate ternary quadratic forms were identical with those of non-Euclidean geometry. (p. 388)

Incubation is a poorly understood phenomenon. If your employer found you sitting with your feet propped on your desk, gazing out the window, she probably would not be pleased to learn that you were "incubating" on company time. A familiar experience is having a correct answer come to you immediately after turning in an exam or paper. This is most likely the result of incubation. It's a good idea to work well ahead of deadlines to allow ample time for incubation effects to occur. We don't know how people are able to produce solutions during time-outs. There is no evidence that people continue to work on the problem at an unconscious level, although some people have suggested that this is how incubation occurs. Most likely, the time-out period serves to dissipate fatigue and allow individuals to get out of sets or ruts in their thinking processes so that they can view the problem from a different perspective.

Herbert A. Simon (1977), the Nobel Prize-winning psychologist, has attempted to explain incubation as due, in part, to selective forgetting. He suggested that when we are working on a problem we rely on a relatively small number of concepts held in a limited capacity short-term or working memory. (See Chapter 2 on Memory for a detailed discussion of this concept.) When we're not working on a problem, the information held in short-term memory is quickly forgotten. If this information was not productive for discovering a solution, then having forgotten it will be beneficial to finding a good solution. There is good evidence that when we are trying to recall a name or word that we know we know, but can't recall (that frustrating tip-of-the-tongue feeling), successful retrieval will often occur sometime later, when we are not actively trying to remember the name or word (e.g., Burke, MacKay, Worthley, & Wade, 1991).

It's a good idea to put aside a problem that you're having difficulty solving and return to it at a later time (Smith & Blankenship, 1991). This is especially good advice during an exam when you can skip a difficult problem and move on to solve other ones that are easier. At least you'll be sure of getting credit for the easier problems, but watch your time limits carefully so that you can correctly finish as many problems as possible in the allotted time. (Of course, it's also a good idea to work on the problems worth the most points first to maximize your exam score.)

Insight

Did you ever have the solution to a problem come to you "in a flash"? Sudden knowledge of the solution is called **insight** or the "Aha!" experience. Insightful solutions can occur during periods of incubation or while actively working on a problem. It is metaphorically referred to as switching on a lightbulb in the head. Insight experiences are common. I have found them to occur frequently in the statistics classes that I teach. Often students will ponder over a problem or listen attentively to a lecture, then suddenly they'll break into a broad grin and exclaim, "Now I understand!" A law school student once told me that she spent the first three-fourths of her first year in law school in an intellectual fog. She really felt that she understood very little about the basic concepts. Then, something "clicked" and she suddenly understood the reasoning that went into legal principles. It's as if a little light went on that illuminated the concepts. Her insight led to a successful legal career.

Reprinted with special permission of NAS, INC.

Persistence

"I have a bias, which leads me to believe that no problem of human relations is ever insolvable."

—Ralph Bunche (quoted in Beilensen & Jackson, 1992, p. 31)

Although persistence doesn't usually appear as a stage in problem solving, it is probably the most important variable in determining success. An individual who persists at a problem is much more likely to solve it than an individual who gives up. Persistence is close to Levine's (1994) idea of "intimate engagement" (p. 3), the willingness to work on a problem in an involved and concentrated way. For example, suppose that you are given a problem to solve in mathematics. It should be obvious that if you give up as soon as you find that the solution isn't immediately apparent, you will not perform as well in solving the problem as someone who continues to work on it.

Think about the anatomy of the problems that I just described. Suppose that you cannot find a path from the initial state to the goal. Giving up will assure failure. Several studies have shown that terminating the search through the problem space too early in the problem-solving process is a leading reason for failure in problem solving.

Heller, Saltzstein, and Caspe (1992) compared the way experienced physicians go about solving the problem of making an accurate diagnosis with the way novice physicians make a diagnosis. When you visit a physician, you are there because you have a problem. You need to find the cause for your symptoms, so that the symptoms and the underlying cause can be treated. Novice physicians terminated their search for a cause as soon as they found a plausible alternative. By contrast, the senior physicians persisted in their search through the problem space even after they found a possible cause. Similar results were found when students who were successful in solving problems in a genetics class were compared to unsuccessful students. The most salient difference between the successful and unsuccessful problem solvers was the tendency to consider more options; that is, the good problem solvers persisted longer than the poor problem solvers when searching for solutions and continued to work on the problem after a plausible solution was found (Smith, 1988).

The same results were found in studies of mathematical problem solving. When college students are given mathematical problems to solve, most will try to recall a solution for a similar problem (retrieval from memory of a familiar solution) instead of trying to reason from their knowledge of mathematics (Lithner, 2000). Those who continue to work on the problem when they cannot readily recall a solution are more successful than those students who "give up." This is an important point: In order to become a good problem solver, you must be willing to work at the problem and to search the problem space for solution paths even when none are obvious or a plausible one has been found.

WELL-DEFINED AND ILL-DEFINED PROBLEMS

Here is Edward Bear, coming downstairs. Now, bump, bump, bump, on the back of his head, behind Christopher Robin. It is, as far as he knows, the only way of coming downstairs, but sometimes he feels that there really is another way, if only he could stop bumping for a moment and think of it.

—A. A. Milne (*Winnie-the Pooh*, 1926, p. 3)

Problems come in all shapes and sizes. Consider the following two problems:

1. The parallelogram problem (after Wertheimer, 1959). Some time back in fifth or sixth grade, you learned that in order to find the area of a rectangle you should multiply the height by the length. Now you are given the following parallelogram that is 4″ long and 2″ high. What is its area?

2. Write a poem expressing the joy you feel when spring flowers bloom.

Do these problems seem qualitatively different to you? The parallelogram problem has a single correct answer. Have you figured it out? Wertheimer (1959) suggested that the correct answer lies in perceptual reorganization, or seeing the problem in a new way. The new way consists of seeing the parallelogram in terms of a rectangle and two triangles. Thus, the parallelogram becomes:

Once the problem is restructured this way, it is only a short leap to figure out that the area of the parallelogram can be found with the same formula for the area of a rectangle because the two triangles can be fit together so that a new rectangular figure is formed with a 4″ length and a 2″ height. In the present example, the area of the parallelogram is 2″ × 4″ = 8 square inches. There is no other correct answer. The goal (correct answer) is **well defined**, as is the path to the goal.

Writing a poem is a different sort of problem. The goal (a beautiful poem) is ill defined, as there are many forms a poem can take. There are countless ways to write a poem. The greatest difficulty in this case lies in evaluating the quality of the end product. The goal is uncertain in **ill-defined** problems, thus part of the difficulty lies in determining if the problem has been solved.

Most of the problems that confront people outside of school are ill defined. The problem solver must decide how to define the goal and then evaluate how well the goal has been attained. By contrast, many of the problems that students are asked to solve in school are well defined, that is, there is a single correct answer. Other examples of ill-defined problems are: creating a way to increase sales for a business; finding more effective ways to study; writing a clear, easy-to-read textbook; saving money for college tuition; building a better mousetrap; de-escalating the nuclear arms race; getting a date with the attractive newcomer at your school; and improving the environment. In ill-defined problems, the goal may be vague or incomplete, which makes the generation of solution paths difficult and their evaluation even more difficult.

One of the best ways to approach ill-defined problems is to make the goal explicit. It is usually possible to state the goal in several different ways for ill-defined problems. For example, the problem of increasing sales can be reidentified as the problem of increasing profits because the real goal is to find ways to make more money. When stated in this form, the problem changes from its initial conceptualization. Solution paths can now include ways to cut losses, reduce inventories, or collect bad debts. The best way to approach ill-defined problems is to specify multiple goals in objective terms so that a variety of solution paths can be considered. This sort of exercise will suggest additional solutions and can improve the way you search for solutions.

Sometimes the distinction between well-defined and ill-defined problems blurs. Consider again the problem of getting Keith to the airport on time. If the problem is selecting among the three routes to the airport, it is well defined, but if other solution paths and goals are possible, for example fly to the airport, or take a different plane from a nearer airport, or take the subway, then the problem becomes somewhat more difficult to define. Even when a problem seems to be well defined, it is useful to consider whether other goal states would solve the problem, and, if so, what sorts of solution paths are possible with different goals.

PROBLEM PLANNING AND REPRESENTATION

In the mathematics and science courses I took in college, I was enormously irritated by the hundreds of hours that I wasted staring at problems without any good idea about what approach to try next in attempting to solve them. I thought at the time that there was no educational value in those "blank" minutes and I see no value in them today.

—Wickelgren (1974, p. ix)

Recent research in problem solving has focused on the importance of devising a plan for finding and selecting solutions. Planning is a higher order thinking skill that is used to direct and regulate behavior. A plan provides a structure that problem solvers can use in a step-by-step manner to help them reach the desired goal.

Multiple Statements of the Goal

Stating the goal in many different ways, which results in multiple goal states, even when the problem appears to be well defined, is an example of a planful approach to problem solving. The generation of multiple goal states will increase the size of the problem space and provide more opportunities for finding a good solution. This sort of plan is **transcontextual**, which means that it can be used in any context with any sort of problem (Ceci & Ruiz, 1993). Here is an example of this approach:

Various opinion polls have identified "fear of crime" as the number 1 concern of most Americans. Not too surprisingly, politicians have made crime a major part of their campaign pledges. Fear of crime is an important and ill-defined problem. Suppose we turn this problem into a clearly articulated goal.

Goal #1: Reduce crime. Given this goal, what are some possible solutions or paths of action that will move our society from its present start state of "fear of crime" toward the goal of reducing crime? Here are two possible solutions that (might) move us toward the goal of reducing crime:

- Make capital punishment a national law
- Incarcerate criminals for life if they are convicted of three major crimes

Now, let's restate the goal in other ways and see how each restatement of the goal suggests different solutions. One approach for restating the goal state is to view the problem from different perspectives. What is a goal state for those citizens who are potential victims of crime?

Goal #2: Make life safer for honest citizens. This sort of goal shifts solutions from the criminals to the potential victims of crime. Some possible solutions that come to mind for attaining this goal:

- Provide better security for honest citizens
- Teach everyone self-defense
- Organize anticrime groups in every neighborhood

Goal #3: Reduce the number of criminals. Given this goal, solutions now focus on numbers rather than methods and on the criminals instead of the honest people in the community. For example,

- Send criminals to Siberia
- Return to gallows and public floggings to send a strong anticrime message to would-be criminals
- Begin community programs that act as a deterrent to a life of crime (e.g., improve education and sports programs)

Goal #4: Change people's perceptions so that they no longer fear crime. This sort of goal will not affect the actual crime rate, rather it will change how people think about crime. Some possible solutions for this goal:

- Give everyone drugs that reduce anxiety (so they no longer fear crime)
- Provide information that shows that the crime rate is really very low (this could be true or false; either would satisfy this goal, although lying is obviously unethical)

Goal #5: Reduce violent crimes. This goal also shifts how we think about the problem because it concerns the degree of violence instead of the number of crimes, number of criminals, or how people feel about crime. Some possible solutions:

- Make it illegal to own a gun
- Legalize drug use

Another way to generate goal states is to view the problem from the perspective of the criminals. What would it take to get them not to engage in crime? It soon becomes clear that crime is not a homogeneous category, and different sorts of actions are needed for different sorts of crimes. Suppose that you were a car-jacker. What would prevent you from hijacking cars? Would having a job make a difference? What if you abused your spouse? What would work to stop spousal abuse?

Of course, some of these possible solutions are ludicrous, such as sending criminals to Siberia or giving everyone anti-anxiety drugs, and others are unethical. The idea behind this example is that new perspectives on a difficult problem emerge when we are forced to state an ill-defined goal in several ways. It is likely that several solutions can be used together so that America's number 1 fear is alleviated. Try this sort of exercise with other difficult problems. You may be surprised to find that you can think of different categories of solutions by specifying qualitatively different sorts of goals and by viewing the problem from different perspectives. Restating the goal in multiple ways and considering different perspectives are two examples of using a plan to solve problems. Although plans for solving problems can vary in complexity, most will consist of five basic steps: (a) recognition that a problem exists (This is an important stage that often is the mark of creativity, a topic that is addressed in the next chapter. Consider any major change, such as the change from horse and buggy to motorized vehicles. For most of the pre-automotive world, horses worked very well, and the proposition that they could be replaced by a box on wheels that constantly broke down and needed fuel to run, was ludicrous. Few people saw any problem with travel by horse and therefore did not see a problem that needed to be solved); (b) construction of a representation of the problem that includes the initial and goal states; (c) generation and evaluation of possible solutions; (d) selection of a possible solution; and (e) execution of the possible solution to determine if it solves the problem.

Unfortunately, some or all of the steps will have to be repeated if the goal is not attained. Problem solving is not a simple or linear process. It often requires changes in the representation of the problem or redefinition of the goal as well as generation of numerous possible solutions and reevaluation of the possible solutions. Bransford and Stein (1993) use the acronym IDEAL to stand for these five steps: I (Identify the problem); D (Define and represent the problem); E (Explore possible strategies); A (Act on the strategies); L (Look back and evaluate the effects of your activities). General problem-solving approaches are used in many situations. For example, basic principles in problem solving are being used to help couples avoid divorce by teaching them how to solve their marital problems (Bodenmann, 1997) and in management training programs in many corporations where managers are taught to act like problem solvers (O'Loughlin & McFadzean, 1999).

A major goal of The Productive Thinking Program (Covington, Crutchfield, Davies, & Olton, 1974), one of the oldest and most popular programs designed to help children "learn to think," was to develop the habit of planning a solution strategy. Figure 9.3 shows a few sample frames from this program that emphasize the need to approach problems in an orderly manner.

Representation of the Problem Space

There is little doubt that diagrammatic representations considerably help humans solve certain classes of problems.

Patrick Oliver (2001, p. 63)

FIG. 9.3. Advice for children on how to devise a problem solving plan. (From The Productive Thinking Program by Covington, Crutchfield, Davies, & Olton, 1974, Lesson 6, p. 17).

The best way to solve a problem is to devise the best representation. In an extensive set of studies of the way scientists think about difficult problems, Dunbar (1998) found that, when scientists represented a problem, they naturally included those features of the problem that they thought would be important in solving the problem, with systematic differences among the representations reflecting different beliefs about the nature of the problem. Consider, for example, an economics problem like a high rate of unemployment. Members of different political parties will represent the same problem in different ways because they have different beliefs about the cause of the problem. The same sort of representational differences were found in studies of the way scientists solve problems in their academic discipline. According to Dunbar, the molecular biologists who recently identified a gene for some types of breast cancer were successful in their quest for this elusive gene because they used a different representation for this genetics problem than the unsuccessful scientists.

Mayer (in press) found that good visual representations can help readers comprehend difficult text. Readers who have already read Chapter 2 on memory will recognize this finding as an example of the principle that visual and verbal information work together to enhance memory. (If you don't remember this principle, try drawing a diagram that shows the two systems working together along with a verbal summary of the principle.) One principle of good thinking that appears in almost every chapter of this book is to use multiple representational systems—that is, adding diagrams to printed text and using verbal descriptors with spatial information.

In discussing the way good representations are constructed, Newell (1983) said that "Memory must be tickled," a phrase that I have often used because I believe that it is a critical consideration in how we think. Every time you think, your knowledge about the problem must be accessed and utilized. Every problem solver must be able to make inferences from problem statements to build an adequate problem representation—one in which missing and conflicting information is made obvious and critical relationships are easy to grasp.

Try this example: Draw a representation and write an algebraic formula that corresponds to the following statement:
There are six times as many students as professors at this university.
If you are like many college students, you drew a diagram like this one:

This translates into 6S=P.

If I gave you the number of students, you could use this formula to find that number of professors and vice versa. Can you see why the formula derived from this representation is wrong? The formula states that there are more professors than there are students, rather than the reverse! The reason that so many students have difficulty with this problem and others like it lies in the way in which the words are translated into a diagram. The juxtaposition of the words "six times the number of students" seems to automatically suggest that the number of students should be multiplied by six. Mayer found a significant improvement in the mathematical problem-solving skills of college students after only 3 hours of training on how to devise correct representations (Lewis & Mayer, 1987). It is difficult to overstate the importance of a good representation when solving problems.

The following sections contain suggestions for devising good representations and demonstrate the intimate relationship between the representation and the solution to the problem. Good representations share certain characteristics. They take advantage of spatial locations to group information in a visual format; they also act as a check on how well you understand the problem. Let's try some examples of ways to represent problems.

Write It Down

All problems are initially represented in your head. It is a good idea to get the paths and goals on paper or into some other concrete form. This tactic will reduce the memory load and allow you to view the problem visually. The simplest example of the aid provided by a pencil and paper is a straightforward multiplication problem. Solve the following problem without writing anything:

$$976 \times 893$$

Of course, you would consider this a ridiculous request because it is a simple problem with paper and pencil and a difficult one to perform in your head because of the demands on working memory. Whenever there are several facts or different options to keep track of, it is a good idea to use paper and pencil.

Draw a Graph or Diagram

"A bear, starting at point P, walked one mile due south. Then he changed direction and walked one mile due east. Then he turned again to the left and walked one mile due north, and arrived exactly at the point P he started from. What was the color of the bear?" (Polya, 1957, p. 234).

Does this problem seem strange or even impossible to you? If you draw a simple "map" of the bear's route, it will be a pie-shaped wedge. Where on earth is this possible? Think about a globe. Did you just say "Why, of course, point P must be the North Pole" to yourself? Once you realize that you're at the North Pole, this problem becomes easy to solve. The bear must be white, because only polar bears live at the North Pole.

Consider the following problem:

A venerable old monk leaves the monastery at exactly 6:00 a.m. to climb a winding mountain trail to the solitude of the mountain peak. He arrives at exactly 4:00 p.m. After spending the night in sleep and prayer, he leaves the mountain peak at exactly 6:00 a.m. and arrives at the monastery at exactly 4:00 p.m. There are no constraints on the speed at which he walks. In fact, he stops several times along the way to rest. Is there some point on the mountain trail that he passes at exactly the same time each day?

Stop and think about this problem for a moment. Does it seem like a difficult one? There are two ways to consider this problem that will make the answer seem simple, but before you go on, decide how you would go about solving this problem, and then solve it. As you can probably guess, a good representation of the central elements of the problem will be an important determinant of the solution.

One solution is to draw a graph of the monk's ascent and descent. The graph can take any shape because you know nothing about his hourly progress. The graphs of the ascent and descent should appear as in Fig. 9.4.

Now, superimpose the two graphs and see if there must be some point where the graphs intersect. If there is, then there is some time when the monk passed the same point at the same time on each day. This is shown in Fig. 9.5.

Drawing a graph provides a clear picture of the results. Actually, an easier way of solving this problem involves changing the representation and restating the facts in the problem in an equivalent, but different, form. Assume two people traverse the same mountain path at the same time on the same morning. If one starts at the monastery and the other starts at the mountain peak, both leaving at 6:00 a.m. and both arriving at their opposite destinations at 4:00 p.m., it is obvious they must meet somewhere along the path no matter how often each chooses to rest and reflect. Thus, with a change in representation, a difficult problem can become trivial.

I recently taught a laboratory course in experimental psychology. In that course, college students were required to conduct experiments, gather data, and interpret their data in meaningful ways. Although the students were taught the statistical methods needed for data analysis, I found that when they graphed their results they obtained a much better understanding of the phenomenon they investigated. They were able to use their experimental results to formulate sound conclusions because they understood the nature of their findings. The students found that a simple graph

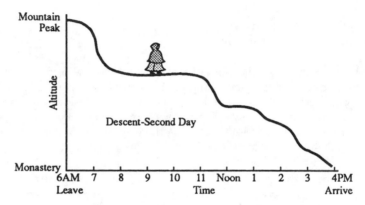

FIG. 9.4. Graphs of the monks ascent and descent. The graphs can take any shape because the monk can rest as often as he wishes when he climbs the hill and when he descends.

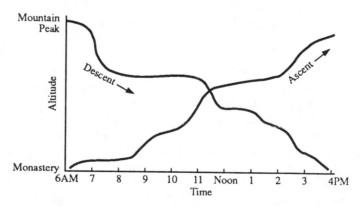

FIG. 9.5. By superimposing the ascent and descent graphs, it is easy to see that there must be some place at which the graphs intersect. Thus, there must be a place on the mountain trail that the monk crosses at the same time each day.

was a more valuable tool for comprehension than the elaborate statistical procedures that they were required to use.

Graphs and other kinds of diagrams are especially useful comprehension strategies in mathematical and scientific problem solving. For example, a common problem in undergraduate statistics courses requires finding the area between two points
under a certain kind of curve called a "normal" or "bell-shaped" curve. This problem can be difficult or confusing for students, but it becomes easy if they draw the
curve and shade in the area they want to find. In fact, I don't give my statistics students the algebraic rules for finding the appropriate area. Students find it easier to
figure it out for themselves from the diagrams they draw.

Consider the geometry problem that was posed by Kohler (1969). You are given
only information in Fig. 9.6 and the fact that the radius of the circle is 5″. Can you
find the length of line L in inches?

One of the reasons that this is a difficult problem is that in the pictorial representation line L appears most saliently as the hypotenuse of two right triangles, the
triangle with sides LDX, and the triangle with the other two sides defined by the in-
tersecting horizontal and vertical radii. How can you change this diagram so that
the solution can be obtained? Consider the information given. Because the only
length given in this diagram is the radius of the circle, it is likely that this will be
needed in solving the problem. Try drawing in additional radii around the circle as
shown in Fig. 9.7. Does this help to suggest the solution?

Look carefully at the quadrant containing L. Can you find another line equal in
length to L? If you think of L as the diagonal inside a rectangle with sides D, X, and
the unlabeled sides formed by the intersection of the horizontal and vertical radii,
the other diagonal in the rectangle must be the same length as L. The other diagonal
must be the radius; thus, line L, like the radius, is also 5″ long. Although the initial
representation of the problem was somewhat misleading, a solution was found with
the appropriate operations.

Of course, there was no way of knowing at the outset that moving the radii
around the circle would lead to the answer. It was obvious, however, that the answer
would depend on the radius in some way, because it was the only measurement

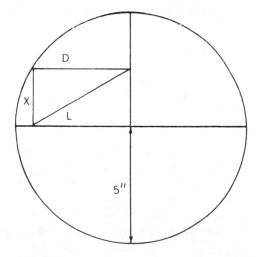

FIG. 9.6. Using only the Information given in this figure, can you determine the length of
line L? (Problem adapted from Köhler, 1969)

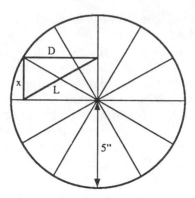

FIG. 9.7. Additional radii have been drawn over Fig. 9.5 as an intermediate step toward a solution. Can you use the additional radii to find the length of the line L?

given, and the goal was to find the length of line L. The operations used to transform the givens into solution paths involved the knowledge you brought with you to the problem. If you did not know that the two diagonals in a rectangle must be equal, then you could not have solved the problem. Good problem solvers utilize a solid knowledge base that is built up over a lifetime of educational experiences—ones that are accumulated both inside and outside of the classroom. The best strategy for solving problems is to know a great deal about a great many topics.

Let's try another example in which graphs or diagrams will simplify the search for a solution path. Problems like this one were frequently used in the Analytical Reasoning Test portion of the Graduate Record Examination, a test that is used in admissions decisions for many graduate schools. In a study of the predictive validity of these tests for graduate students in Yale's psychology department, Sternberg and Williams (1997) found that scores on the analytic test were significantly correlated with the ratings given to graduate students by Yale faculty several years later (at least for the male students in their sample).

> To save money and their sanity, Melvin, Brock, Marc, and Claire decide to form a baby-sitting cooperative. They agree to baby-sit for each other's children with the understanding that when one of them stays with another's children, the recipient will repay the sitter with an equal number of baby-sitting hours. They decide to tally baby-sitting hours at the end of the month. During the month, Melvin sat with Brock's children 9 hours, Marc sat with Melvin's children 3 hours, and Claire stayed with Melvin's children 6 hours. Marc baby-sat 9 hours with Claire's children and Brock baby-sat 5 hours with Claire's children. Which of these people has 12 hours of baby-sitting time due to him or her?

A good diagram of the relationship among these four people is clearly needed. The relevant givens will involve the four people and the number of hours owed to each. Let's start with the first sentence, "Melvin sat with Brock's children 9 hours." Thus, Brock owes Melvin 9 hours of baby-sitting at the end of the month. The operation being used is the transformation of number of hours spent baby-sitting into number of hours owed to each sitter. A simple diagram of this relationship is:

                          9 hours
    Brock ——————————————————————————→ Melvin

The next sentence translates into "Melvin owes Marc 3 hours and Melvin owes Claire 6 hours."

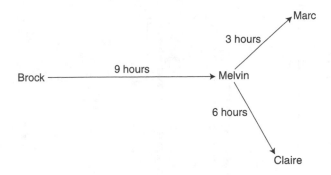

Then, changing the third sentence so that it reflects what is owed, Claire owes Marc 9 hours and Claire owes Brock 5 hours.

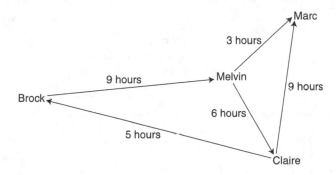

It is easy to see from this diagram that only Marc is owed 12 hours of baby-sitting, 3 hours from Melvin and 9 hours from Claire. A good diagram of the hours owed is essential in finding the solution to this problem.

There are several other ways of representing the information in the baby-sitting co-op problem that will display all of the essential relationships, and thus also give the correct answer. When a colleague (Dr. Susan Nummedal at California State University, Long Beach) posed this problem to her students, she found that they devised a variety of representations to solve the problem. One student used a simple bar graph to keep track of the number of hours sat by each participant. This representation is shown in Fig. 9.8.

Other students used a variety of table formats. One listed the number of hours "gave" as a positive number and "received" as a negative number because it was owed. Another student split the information into "sitter" and "sat for" categories, then filled in a table of information summing across the columns for the total number of "sat for" hours for each participant, and summing down the rows for the total number of "sitter" hours for each participant. These representations are offered in Tables 9.1 and 9.2, respectively.

As a baby-sitting co-op problem demonstrates, there are often many ways of representing a given problem. As you work through the problems in this chapter, try a variety of representations. A good representation will present all of the relevant information in a way that it can be readily understood and assimilated. Good representations provide the necessary solution paths to the goal.

FIG. 9.8.   Alternative form representation

TABLE 9.1
**A Table Format for Representing
the Information in the Babysitting
Co-op Problem**

	Gave	Received	Total Due
Melvin	+9	−3, −6	0
Marc	+3, +9		12
Claire	+6	−9, −15	−8
Brock	+5	−9	−4

TABLE 9.2
**An Alternative Table Format That Can Be Used to Represent
the Information in the Babysitting Co-op Program**

		Sitter				Total Number
		Melvin	Marc	Claire	Brock	of Hours Sat For
	Melvin		3	6		9
Sat For	Marc					0
	Claire		9		5	14
	Brock	9				9
Total Number of Hours Sat		9	12	6	5	

Try a Hierarchical Tree

Hierarchical trees are branching diagrams. They are most frequently used to assess mathematically the probability or likelihood of uncertain outcomes. (See Chapter 4 on reasoning for the use of tree diagrams in solving if, then problems and Chapter 7 on probability for the use of decision trees in calculating probabilities.) Hierarchical trees or tree diagrams can be useful aids in decision making and problem solving. In this context, they are called decision trees. If the problem you're working on is fairly complex, with each possible solution path requiring subsequent additional paths, a hierarchical tree or tree diagram should be considered.

Here is a classic problem that has a long history in the psychological literature on problem solving. Although the problem is a medical one, no specialized knowledge is needed to solve it:

> Suppose you are a doctor faced with a patient who has a malignant tumor in his stomach. It is impossible to operate on the patient, but unless the tumor is destroyed the patient will die. There is a kind of ray that can be used to destroy the tumor. If the rays reach the tumor all at once at a sufficiently high intensity, the tumor will be destroyed. Unfortunately, at this intensity the healthy tissue that the rays pass through on the way to the tumor will also be destroyed. At lower intensities the rays are harmless to healthy tissue, but they will not affect the tumor either. What type of procedure might be used to destroy the tumor with the rays, and at the same time avoid destroying the healthy tissue? (Duncker, 1945, pp. 307–308)

Research has shown that this is a difficult problem to solve (and modern medical advances since 1945 make new solutions possible). Although a variety of solutions were attempted, the best solution is to use several weak rays, each coming from different places outside the body focused so that they would meet and summate at the tumor site. In this manner, the healthy tissue won't be hurt by the weak rays, and the tumor will receive a high level of radiation. This solution was formulated from a broader category of solutions that included having each ray grow stronger as it reached the tumor.

One subject's search for solution paths is shown in Fig. 9.9 in a hierarchical tree diagram. Note that the goal is explicitly stated at the top of the tree. General broad strategies are listed one level below the goal, with more specific ways of satisfying each strategy on lower levels.

Another example of using trees to solve problems is the familiar use of family trees. Estate lawyers, who often face a tangled web of family relationships, need to be able to determine the relations among family members in order to handle wills and estate taxes. Multiple spouses, cohabitation, stepchildren, half-siblings, and out-of-wedlock births can make the difficult matter of inheritance a legal nightmare.

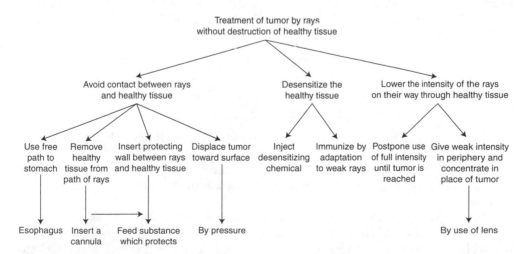

FIG. 9.9. A hierarchical tree diagram of one subject's attempted solutions to Duncker's X-ray problem. (After Duncker, 1945).

Make a Matrix

A **matrix** is a rectangular array of facts or numbers. It is really just a fancy word for a chart. When the givens in a problem can be broken down into categories, a matrix may be a good method of representation. Consider the problem posed by Whimbey and Lochhead (1982):

> Three men—Fred, Ed, and Ted—are married to Joan, Sally, and Vickie, but not necessarily in that order. Joan, who is Ed's sister, lives in Detroit, Fred dislikes animals. Ed weighs more than the man who is married to Vickie. The man married to Sally breeds Siamese cats as a hobby. Fred commutes over 200 hours a year from his home in Ann Arbor to his job in Detroit. Match up the men with the women they married. (p. 67)

What are the categories of information given in this problem? The givens concern husbands and wives. Set up a three-by-three matrix and fill in as much of it as you can with the information given above:

	Joan	Sally	Vickie
Fred			
Ed			
Ted			

Because Joan is Ed's sister, she cannot be his wife, so fill in a "NO" in the Joan–Ed cell of the matrix. Skip the next two statements for the time being and go on to the statement that Ed weighs more than the man married to Vickie; therefore, Ed is not married to Vickie. Ed must be married to Sally. So far the matrix appears as below:

	Joan	Sally	Vickie
Fred		NO	
Ed	NO	YES	NO
Ted		NO	

Peruse the problem for more clues. Have you found the important one? Fred lives in Ann Arbor and Joan lives in Detroit; therefore, we would conclude that they're probably not married. Because Fred is not married to Joan or Sally, he must be married to Vickie. Who's left for Ted? Joan must be married to Ted.

The completed matrix:

	Joan	Sally	Vickie
Fred	NO	NO	YES
Ed	NO	YES	NO
Ted	YES	NO	NO

(Additional problems like this one can be found in the workbook that accompanies this text, *Thinking Critically About Critical Thinking*.)

Admittedly, this is an artificial problem, not much like the ones we encounter in real life. Let's consider a more practical application of the matrix form of problem representation:

There is considerable controversy over the issue of vitamin C as a deterrent for the common cold. How would you decide if vitamin C prevents colds? Most probably, you would give vitamin C to some people and not others and count the number of colds in each group. Suppose you found the following results: 10 people who took vitamin C did not catch a cold; 4 people who took vitamin C caught a

	Vitamin C			
	Took Vitamin C	Didn't Take Vitamin C		
Caught a cold	4	6	Total number who caught a cold: 10	Of those who caught a cold, % who took vitamin C: 40%
				Of those who caught a cold, % who didn't take vitamin C: 60%
Didn't catch a cold	10	8	Total number who didn't catch a cold: 18	Of those who didn't catch a cold, % who took vitamin C: 55.5% (10/18)
				Of those who didn't catch a cold, % who didn't take vitamin C: 44.4% (8/18)
	Total number who took vitamin C: 14	Total number who didn't take vitamin C: 14	Total number in the study: 28	

cold; 8 people who didn't take vitamin C didn't catch a cold; and 6 people who didn't take vitamin C caught a cold. What would you conclude?

Because we have categories of information (took or didn't take vitamin C and caught or didn't catch a cold), a matrix displaying the appropriate values will help us to understand the givens.

By examining every cell of the matrix, you can determine if vitamin C prevented colds. To see if vitamin C worked, you need to consider how many of those who caught a cold had taken vitamin C. The answer is 4 out of 10, or 40%. You also need to consider how many of those who didn't catch a cold had taken vitamin C. The answer is 10 out of 18, or 55.5%. Few would be willing to conclude from these data that vitamin C helped to prevent colds from these data. (Research concepts are discussed more fully in Chapter 6 and 7 on thinking as hypothesis testing and probability. Statistical tests are used to decide if these numbers are significantly different.) By representing the information in a matrix, the results can be more easily determined. This is essentially the same problem that was discussed in Chapter 8 on decision making when the nurses and physicians had to decide if there was a relationship between a disease and a set of symptoms. Given the overlap among the topics, you would expect that techniques that are useful in one context would also be useful in related contexts.

Manipulate Models

It is often a good idea to make a concrete representation for abstract problems. I'm sure that you've seen an architect's model for a planned complex like a shopping center, office building, or college campus. The miniature buildings and walkways are not made because architects love doll-sized buildings. Although they are often made to communicate architectural plans to others who are not skilled at reading blueprints, the miniature models also help the architect solve problems. With the movable parts, she or he can move the buildings to find the best way to place them before construction begins.

Let's try a problem where making a model will help in finding a solution. There are two groups of beings on a mythical planet in a far-away galaxy: they are Hobbits and Orcs. One day three Hobbits got lost while exploring the homeland of the Orcs. The Hobbits could get home safely if they could cross the river that separates their two homelands. The Orcs agreed to help the Hobbits cross the river, but the only boat they had could hold only two beings at a time, and the Hobbits could not let themselves ever be outnumbered by the Orcs or the Orcs would eat them.

Your problem is to figure out a sequence of moves that will carry all three Hobbits to the other side of the river and return all three Orcs on their own side. The constraints are that only two beings can fit in the boat at one time, and if at anytime the Orcs on one shore outnumber the Hobbits, you'll have to start over.

This would be an impossible problem to solve without some external form of representation. Use some small objects to represent the Hobbits and Orcs and move them across an imaginary river. Three large paper clips for the Hobbits and three small paper clips for the Orcs will work well. You'll have to imagine that you are transporting them in a boat. Be sure to write down all of your moves. Plan to take as long as 10 to 15 minutes to solve this problem. As you work toward the solution, be aware of how you're thinking about the moves. Don't go on until you've worked through the problem.

The complete sequence of moves needed to move the Hobbits is shown in Fig. 9.10. One of the greatest difficulties with this problem is the need to move all three Orcs across the river, a situation that is not desired, in order to move the Hobbits without allowing them to become outnumbered. Problems of this sort have come to be known as **detour problems** because the path to the goal is not a direct linear one. Intermediate steps are required that seem directly opposite to the goal— in this case, moving all three Orcs to the opposite side of the river when the desired goal is to have all of them on the side from which they originated. It is important to recognize that the route to a goal will often involve detours.

As a more realistic example, consider Leon's goal to become very wealthy. One solution path to the goal may involve going deeply into debt in order to finance his education. Even though going deeply into debt is seemingly antagonistic to becoming wealthy, it may be a necessary detour. Be sure to consider solution paths that involve detours when faced with difficult problems.

Select the Best Representation

It is a good idea to utilize an external form of representation (e.g., paper and pencil, a model) whenever there are more than a few givens that need to be manipulated. The immediate or working memory span can quickly become overloaded. If you have already read Chapter 8 on decision making, you will recognize the importance of writing down alternatives and considerations so that you can reduce the load on working memory and allow the problem solver to generate more alternative solutions. Experimental results or almost any other pattern of numbers should always be graphed. If your problem is mathematical or spatial, a diagram is likely to

Fig. 9.10. Steps needed to move three Hobbits across the river using a boat that will hold only two beings without allowing the Orcs to ever outnumber the Hobbits.

be helpful. Diagrams can help to disentangle any situation in which the givens have many complex interrelationships. Diagrams can make important relationships explicit, a fact that can often lead directly to the goal. Hierarchical trees are a natural form of representation when the material itself forms a hierarchically arranged structure. Matrices are likely to be useful when the givens can be grouped into categories for meaningful comparisons. "Mock-ups" or miniature models can aid in problem solving when movement and placement of the givens determine the solution. Often the way a problem is represented can mean the difference between a solution or nonsolution (Posner, 1973). If you find that one form of representation isn't fruitful, try a different one.

PROBLEM-SOLVING STRATEGIES

Solving problems can be regarded as the most characteristically human activity.

—Polya, p. ix (1981)

It does no good to tell someone who is faced with a problem that he should plan a solution, if he has no idea how to plan. The steps look deceptively simple—generate and evaluate possible solutions. But what if you can't think of any solutions? There are several strategies that can be used in a systematic manner to help you generate solutions. Although no single strategy can guarantee perfect solutions every time, learning how to use several different strategies can give you direction and confidence when presented with a new problem.

Schoenfeld (1979) found that many mathematicians and scientists claimed to use specific strategies and rules when solving problems in their academic disciplines. Many of the scientists and mathematicians believed that their students would solve problems better if they learned some basic skills for attacking problems. In addition, several researchers have found that instruction in general problem-solving skills can improve problem-solving ability (e.g., Lithner, 2000). You can think of the following strategies or problem-solving aids as ways to plan a solution.

Means-Ends Analysis

Most often progress toward the goal is not made along a single well-paved road. When the goal is not immediately attainable, we often need to take detours or break the problem down into smaller problems, called **subproblems**, each with its own goal, called a **subgoal** (Catrambone, 1998; Dunbar, 1998). Like all of the strategies for solving problems, selecting and utilizing subgoals requires planning. The procedure by which people select subgoals and use them to progress toward the goal is called **means-ends analysis**. This is a general, often powerful method for problem solving. The problem is first broken down into subgoals. Operations that will reduce the distance between the problem solver's current state and the subgoal are then used. In this manner, the problem solver will move closer and closer to the goal. Work through the following examples in order to clarify this concept.

The first step in means-ends analysis is to enumerate appropriate subgoals and to select the most promising one. Suppose that during a game of chess you decide that a good subgoal is to put the opposing king in check. The goal, of course, is to win the game, but it will be necessary to work toward subgoals to attain the goal. Putting the opposing king in check is the immediate "end" toward which you're working. You now need to select the "means" for obtaining that end, hence the term "means-ends analysis." In order to achieve your subgoal, determine the current state position of your pieces. Then identify any difference between where your pieces are and where you want them to be. Operations would be selected that would reduce this difference, and place the opposing king in check. Suppose no single move can achieve this subgoal. The means-ends analysis procedure would recycle, this time selecting a smaller subgoal, perhaps moving another piece out of the way. The constant recycling of these two processes—setting subgoals and reducing distances—will allow you to make progress toward the goal.

A favorite problem of psychologists that can be used to demonstrate means-ends analysis is the Tower of Hanoi problem. The name of this puzzle is derived from an

FIG. 9.11.   Start state and goal for the Tower of Hanoi problem. Use the strategy of means-ends analysis to solve this problem.

interesting legend. Suppose that there are 3 pegs and 64 disks, each one a different size, stacked on one of the pegs in size order. It may help to think of the disks as 64 different size doughnuts that can stack one on top of each other on the pegs. The task is to transfer all of the disks from the first peg to the third peg using the middle peg as an intermediary. The rules for moving disks include moving only one disk at a time and never placing a disk on top of a smaller one. The legend around this task is that there are monks in a monastery near Hanoi who are working on this puzzle, and when they complete it the world will come to an end. Even if this legend were true, you would have little cause for worry because if they were to make perfect moves at the rate of one per second, it would take close to a trillion years to complete this task (Raphael, 1976).

Because you probably don't want to spend quite that much time solving the Tower of Hanoi, you can try a simplified version of it using only three disks. You can easily work this problem using any three coins of different sizes (a quarter, penny, and dime will work well) and three small sheets of paper. Stack the coins with the smallest on top and largest on the bottom on one sheet of paper. The task is to move the coins from the first piece of paper to the third so that they will be in the same size order. You may move only one coin at a time. All three pieces of paper may be used in solving the problem. Write down all of the moves you make in solving this problem. The initial and goal states are shown in Fig. 9.11.

In a means-end analysis of the Tower of Hanoi problem, one obvious subgoal is to get the quarter on the third piece of paper. This cannot be done immediately because the dime and penny are on it; therefore, a second subgoal needs to be considered. A second subgoal is to end up with the penny on the quarter. This can be accomplished when the penny is on the second paper and the quarter is on the third paper. This subgoal cannot yet be pursued because the dime must be moved first. In this manner, subgoals or ends are considered along with the means to accomplish them. A complete solution with all of the moves is shown in Fig. 9.12. If you try the problem with four or five coins instead of three, you'll find that it gets much more complicated, although the strategy remains the same. A quick search on the Internet will show several sites that have computerized versions of the Tower of Hanoi problem for those of you who want to try it with many more disks than show here.

Working Backwards

Means-ends analysis is a forward-looking strategy, which means that all of the planning is done by considering operations that move you closer to subgoals and, ultimately, the final goal. Sometimes it is a better strategy to plan operations by **working backwards** from the goal to your present or initial state. The simplest example of this can be found in the paper-and-pencil mazes that many children love to solve.

Some of these mazes have several possible paths leading away from the start box and only one correct path ending in the goal box. Even young children realize that

FIG. 9.12. Solution to the Tower of Hanoi problem. Notice how subgoal are planned and obtained in reaching the goal.

they can solve the maze more quickly if they work the maze backward, beginning from the goal and drawing their path to the start box. An example of this type of maze is shown in Fig. 9.13.

Working backward is a good strategy to use whenever there are fewer paths leading from the goal than there are leading from the start. Of course, mazes aren't the only situation when working backward is good strategy. Consider the following problem. "Water lilies on a certain lake double in area every 24 hours. From the time the first water lily appears until the lake is completely covered takes 60 days. On what day is it half covered?" (Fixx, 1978, p. 50).

The only way to solve this problem is to work backwards. Can you solve it with this hint? If the lake is covered on the 60th day and the area covered by the lilies doubles every day, how much of the lake is covered on the 59th day? The answer is half. Thus, by working backward, the problem is easy to solve. A **forward-looking strategy** with this problem will ensure insanity.

It is often a good idea to combine forward and backward strategies. If you are faced with the task of solving proofs in geometry and trigonometry, a combination of forward and backward strategies may often prove most useful. You can start from the goal, transforming expressions on each line, and then alternate operations between the start state and the goal until the solution path meets somewhere between the two.

Simplification

You turn the problem over and over in your mind; try to turn it so it appears simpler . . . . Is the problem as simply, as clearly, as suggestively expressed as possible?

—Polya (1981)

Problems that are difficult to solve are often complex in nature. A good way to approach such problems is to strip away as much of the complexity as possible in

FIG. 9.13. Working backward is a good strategy when there are fewer paths from the goal than from the start.

order to reduce them to a simple form. Often, the best form of representation can perform the task of **simplification** because it will allow you to "see" the solution in an efficient way.

Suppose you are faced with the classic cat-in-the-tree problem. According to common folklore, cats can climb up trees, but not down. (There is no more truth to this than to the notion that elephants are afraid of mice.) Suppose that you are faced with the task of retrieving a cat from the top branch of a 10-foot-tall tree. The only ladder you have is 6 feet long. You'll need to place the base of the ladder 3 feet from the trunk of the tree to steady it. Will you be able to reach the cat?

Like most problems, a good way to approach this problem is to diagram the given facts. A diagram of this problem has been drawn in Fig. 9.14. Once the information is presented in a diagram format, it is easy to perceive the problem as a simple geometry problem: What is the hypotenuse of a triangle whose two other sides are 10 feet and 3 feet long? At this point, you'd need to rely on previously acquired knowledge about triangles to recognize and solve this problem. When the topic is thinking, there is no substitute for a good education to provide the foundation and

FIG. 9.14.   The cat-in-the-tree problem. Once the information is drawn in a diagram form, it is easy to see that it is a simple geometry problem.

raw materials for thought. It is thought and knowledge that are needed for good thinking.

The formula for finding the hypotenuse of a right triangle is:

$$a^2 + b^2 = c^2$$

Substituting the appropriate values in the previous equation:

$$10^2 + 3^2 = c^2$$
$$100 + 9 = c^2$$
$$109 \quad\;\; = c^2$$
$$\sqrt{109} \;\; = c$$
$$10.4 \quad\;\; = c$$

Thus, the ladder would need to be 10.4 feet long to reach the top. But wait, could you redraw the problem using the information given to find out if you could still use the 6-foot ladder to reach the cat? See Fig. 9.15 for a slightly different diagram of the problem.

The same formula can be used, but now the unknown is not the hypotenuse, but another one of the sides of the right triangle.

Rearranging the terms will yield:

$$a^2 + b^2 = c^2$$
$$a^2 \quad\;\;\; = c^2 - b^2$$

FIG. 9.15. If the cat-in-the-tree problem is changed so that the unknown value is how high a 6-foot ladder will reach if it is placed 3 feet from the trunk, a different answer is obtained.

$$a^2 = 6^2 - 3^2$$
$$a^2 = 36 - 9$$
$$a^2 = 27$$
$$a = \sqrt{27}$$
$$a = 5.2$$

Thus, the top rung of the ladder will touch the tree 5.2 feet above the ground. Will you be able to reach the cat? Draw yourself near the top rung of the ladder. If you are over 5 feet tall, you should have no trouble reaching the cat if you are standing on the top or second rung. In fact, you won't even have to reach up.

Simplification is a good strategy when the problem is abstract or complex or contains information that is irrelevant to finding a solution. Often, simplification will work hand in hand with selecting the optimal form of representation because a good representation will often simplify a problem. But caution is needed when trying to simplify. Although it worked in this example, sometimes the attempt to simplify a complex problem will lead to solving a problem that is different from the one you have.

Generalization and Specialization

When confronted with a problem, it is sometimes helpful to consider it as an example of a larger class of problems (**generalization**) or to consider it as a special case (**specialization**). The form of problem representation that is most compatible with the generalization and specialization strategy is the tree diagram. Most goals can be classified as both a subset of a larger category and as a heading for a smaller one. Let's work an example to clarify what this means. As a furniture designer, you are given the problem of designing a chair that will be especially well suited for reading. How would you go about solving this problem?

As you probably realized, this is an ill-defined problem. The difficulty is largely centered on evaluating which of several possible chairs will best satisfy the goal. Use a tree diagram to classify chairs in general, and "chairs for reading" in particular. Although there are many possible diagrams, one example is presented in Fig. 9.16.

I hope that you worked through this problem and drew your own tree diagram. As you can see in Fig. 9.16, thinking about "chairs for reading" as a subset of the category "chairs" can help you to incorporate other features of chairs in your design while custom tailoring the chair with some of the possibilities that are unique to "chairs for reading." Thus, the process of generalization and/or specialization can help you to consider your problem from both broad and narrow perspectives.

Random Search and Trial-and-Error

Recall that the anatomy of a problem consists of a start or initial state, a goal, and solution paths leading from the start state to the goal. One strategy for searching among possible solution paths is **random search**. Although this probably seems like a nonstrategy or "un-strategy," in some cases it will work quite well. When there are very few possible solution paths, random search will lead to the goal in a short time. A truly random search would mean that there is no systematic order in which the

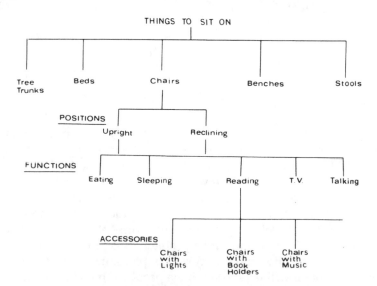

FIG. 9.16.   Possible tree diagram for the problem of designing a chair for reading.

possible paths are explored and no memory for paths already tried. A systematic **trial-and-error** search through the problem space (contains the paths, goal, and start state) is preferable. Trial-and-error search is best applied to well-defined problems with few possible solution paths. Simple, short anagrams are good candidates for these search methods. Unscramble the following letter to form an English word:

THA

Because there are only six possible orders for these three letters (THA, TAH, HTA, HAT, ATH, AHT), trying each one until a solution is found is fairly straight-forward and simple strategy. If you used a truly random search, you would not keep track of which letter orderings you used and would repeat some until the cor-rect order was found. Systematic trial-and-error is almost always superior to ran-dom search, although only slightly better when there are very few possibilities.

Both trial-and-error and random search are poor strategies when the number of possible paths increases, because of the sheer number of possible combinations. Often, in larger problems, it is helpful to eliminate some of the paths and then search among a smaller subset with a trial-and-error strategy.

Rules

Some kinds of problems, like series problems, depend on **rules**. Once the underly-ing principles are established, the problem is solved. Most problems in mathematics and the physical sciences follow rules. *A good way to discover rules is to look for pat-terns in the givens or subgoals.* Problems requiring rule discovery are often used on tests of intelligence.

Complete the following pattern:

ABBACCCADDDDA

This is a fairly simple series problem. The next six letters are EEEEEA. Certain patterns are common in problems of this sort. To detect them, count the number of repeating symbols, look across the series for repetitions at long intervals, try simple additions and subtractions, etc. This is not a trivial problem. The decoding of enemy war messages during World War II was a major factor contributing to our victory. The United States and British governments employed many professional decoders whose job it was to find rules that could be used to decipher German and Japanese military messages.

Suppose that there is intelligent life in outer space, and that they are also wonder-ing about us. How would they let us know that they exist? Some scientists, science fiction authors, and members of the general public believe that they would make their presence known by sending messages. No one believes that these messages would be in English, or Chinese, or Samoan, or any other Earth language. They would send messages in their own native tongue or native whatever if they don't have tongues. How would we on Earth recognize such messages? The U. S. military has decided that if we are being sent messages from outer space the one distin-guishing characteristic of these messages would be a rule-governed "grammar" or patterned repetition. As strange as this may seem, the military does monitor outer space for anything that seems like a patterned communication. So far, they haven't received any and we can continue to believe, for the time being at least, that we are the most intelligent beings in space (or that the more intelligent beings do not want us to know they are out there, or that they can't reach us, or they don't want to reach us).

Hints

Hints are additional information that is given after an individual has begun to work on a problem. Often the hint provides additional information that is important to your solution. Sometimes a hint will require that you change the way you have been approaching the problem or limit the number of possible solutions. A common example of the use of hints is the "hot-cold" game played by children. An object is hidden in a room. The child who is "it" wanders around the room while the other children yell "hotter" if she is moving closer to the hidden object and "colder" if she is moving away from the hidden object. In this problem, the child who is "it" should take one small step at a time continuing in the same direction when the hint is "hotter" and trying a slight change in direction when the hint is "colder." Research on the way people use hints has shown that general hints like "think of new ways of using objects" do not facilitate the problem solution (Duncan, 1961). The more specific the hint, the greater the benefit derived from it.

One of psychology's favorite problems is the two-string problem. Imagine walking into a room with two strings hanging from the ceiling. The strings are too far apart for you to reach both at the same time, yet your task is to do exactly that. This situation is depicted in Fig. 9.17.

The best solution to the two-string problem involves setting one string in a swinging motion, usually by tying a heavy object to the end of one string to serve as a weight, so that the problem solver can reach the string as it swings toward him. When researchers provided hints for the problem solver by pretending to accidentally bump against one string to get it swinging, most of the problem solvers hit upon this solution, but few were consciously aware that they utilized this hint (Maier, 1931).

In one experimental investigation of how people use hints, researchers had subjects learn pairs of words so that if the experimenter said one word, the subject would respond with its pair. (This is called paired-associates learning.) One of the pairs that the subjects learned was "candle box." After learning the list of paired-associates, subjects were given Duncker's (1945) candle problem, which involved affixing a candle to a wall by using a box as the candle-holder (see Fig. 1.1 in Chapter 1). Did this hint help them to solve this problem? In general, their performance on this task was improved only if they were told by the experimenter to think about the pairs of words they had learned as a problem-solving aid (Weisberg, DiCamillo, & Phillips, 1978). They did not spontaneously use this hint to solve the problem, most likely because they were unaware that it was a hint. Research has confirmed these results with other types of problems (Perfetto, Bransford, & Franks, 1983). In general, it seems that hints are helpful only when the problem solver perceives the hint as a possible solution aid.

Good problem solvers will seek out hints. Gathering additional information can be thought of as hint-seeking behavior. It is almost always a good strategy to get all

FIG. 9.17. The two-string problem. How could you reach both strings at the same time? (After Maier, 1930)

of the information that you can about your problem. The additional givens will help you to restructure the problem space and provide direction so that solution paths may be found more easily.

Split-Half Method

The **split-half method** is an excellent search strategy when there is no a priori reason for selecting among a sequentially organized set of possible solution paths. Suppose, for example, that there is a stoppage in the plumbing system that prevents water from coming out of your kitchen faucet. The stoppage is somewhere between the place where your pipes connect with the other pipes on your street and your kitchen faucet. How would you search for the pipe stoppage while making as few holes as possible in the pipe?

In this example, the solution (the place where the pipe is stopped) lies somewhere along a linear route. The best way to search in this problem is the split-half method. Because this problem requires that you break the pipe each place you search, you want to search as efficiently as possible. Begin halfway between the street connection and your kitchen sink. If you find that water can still run freely at this point, you know that the stoppage is between this point and your sink. If this happens, look again half-way between this point and your kitchen sink. If the water is still running freely at this point, then you'll know that the stoppage is closer still to the sink and you'll look again midway between that point and your sink.

Suppose that on your first attempt you find that the water is not running at this point. Then the stoppage must be between the street and this midpoint. Your next search would be midway between the current search point and the street connection. In this manner, you would continue searching until the stoppage is found. This is a good method anytime you have a problem that is structurally similar to this one, such as trying to locate a break in the electrical wiring in your home or auto.

You can use the split-half method to play a party game called "Guess Your Age." (I made this game up.) Your friends can pretend to be any age. You can guess the age of anyone between 0 and 100 with no more than seven guesses. How would you do it? Begin with the age that is midway between 0 and 100, which, of course, is 50. The player would have to respond by telling you if the age she is thinking of is older or younger than 50. Thus, she would respond with "younger" or "older." Suppose that she responds, "younger." What age should you guess next? You'd pick the age midway between 0 and 50, which is 25. Suppose she now responds, "older." Your third guess should be halfway between 25 and 50. Because we're only concerned with whole numbers, your next guess would be 38. If she now responds younger, you'd guess 32, as this number is midway between 25 and 38. If the next response is older, you'd guess 35 (midway between 32 and 38). If the response is younger, you'd guess 33. At this point you know that she is pretending to be either 33 or 34. Thus, any age can be guessed with at most seven guesses. Try this method out with some friends. It will be good practice in using the split-half strategy. Consider this strategy whenever there are several possible equally likely solutions aligned along a single dimension.

Brainstorming

"The best way to have good ideas is to have lots of ideas."

—Linus Pauling (cited in Goertzel & Goertzel, 1995, p. 274)

Brainstorming is fun. It was originally proposed by Osborn (1963) as a method for group problem solving, but it's also useful for individuals working alone. Brainstorming is useful in generating additional solution paths and thus should be considered whenever the difficulty involves finding solution paths. The goal of brainstorming is to produce a large number of possible solutions. Problem solvers are encouraged to think up wild, unusual, imaginative ideas and to write them all down, no matter how silly they seem. The underlying principle is that the greater the quantity of ideas, the greater the likelihood that at least one of them will be good. To foster creative use of imagination, rules include no criticism or ridicule, even when the ideas may appear ridiculous. Judgments about the worth of the ideas are deferred until a later evaluation phase. Sometimes parts of the various ideas are combined or refined to improve upon them.

Brainstorming can be done in large or small groups or alone. After the brainstorming session, the list of possible solutions can be perused to find ones that will solve the problem in light of the problem constraints, which often include financial and time limitations and/or ethical considerations. Brainstorming was used effectively by a food manufacturer faced with the problem of finding a better way to bag potato chips. The problem solvers (corporate executives) were asked to think up the best packaging solution they had ever seen. Someone said that bagging wet leaves was the best packaging solution he had ever seen. If you attempt to bag dry leaves they crumble and don't fit into trash bags well, but if you hose them down before bagging them you can use fewer bags and fill them more easily with less empty space in each bag. Following this lead, they tried wetting potato chips and then putting them into bags. The result was disastrous—the potato chips dried into tasteless crumbs. But this idea ultimately led to the popular potato chip that comes stacked in a can. The identical chips are formed from a liquid potato mixture that is cooked into chip-shaped molds. In this manner, a wild and not-too-good solution (wetting potato chips) was parlayed into a highly successful product. It's true—the original potato chip problem remains to be solved, but the executives were quite happy with the new potato chip product.

Contradiction

The best solution to many problems often involves contradictory properties. For example, consider the problem of the perfect pizza box—one that keeps the pizza hot, but doesn't allow steam to collect inside the box so that the crust doesn't get wet and soggy. These are contradictory properties—keep the pizza covered so it stays hot *and* don't let the steam condense and turn the crust soggy. The next time you send out for a pizza, examine the box. Most pizza boxes represent a compromise between these two properties—the lid is closed to keep it hot, but it also has small vents to allow some of the steam to escape. The result is a compromise solution. The pizza gets cold sooner because the vents let cold air in, and the pizza gets only a little soggy because the amount of condensed moisture is limited.

One suggestion for solving any problem that involves contradictions is to never compromise; instead, devise a solution that satisfies all of the desirable properties of a good solution. Sure, but how? In the pizza box problem, Valdman and Tsourikov (cited in Raia, 1994) designed a box with "dimples" (raised dots) on the bottom so that the moisture would condense below the crust and not on it, while trapping hot air below the pizza to serve as additional insulation. Valdman and Tsourikov have designed a computer-assisted program that suggests ways to satisfy contradictions in any problem without compromising. They culled the files of the U.S. Patent Office and discovered over 200 general principles that can be used alone or in combination to solve a wide range of problems. The program begins by asking for a clear definition of the type of problem that is being solved. It is looking for general principles (e.g., the need for insulation and eliminating condensation, without regard to pizza). Solutions are suggested from its computerized bank of solutions based on other problems that involve similar sorts of contradictions. They call their algorithm (steps used to solve a problem) the theory of inventive problem solving. Although their advertisements for this commercially available software program make fantastic claims of success, additional studies by unbiased researchers are needed before we can evaluate its efficacy. Using their basic ideas, we can all imagine an optimal solution to any problem and then find ways to satisfy seemingly contradictory properties of the optimal solution.

Here is another example of a problem involving contradictions. Consider the problem of picking tomatoes. Mechanical tomato pickers are cheap and fast, but they bruise the tomato. A compromise would be to pad the arms of the mechanical picker or slow down the process so that fewer tomatoes are bruised. But, the cardinal rule of the theory of inventive problem solving is to never compromise. An even better idea, one that won't require the picker to slow down or bruise the tomatoes, is to develop a tomato with a thicker skin so that it won't bruise when it is picked by the clumsy and fast-moving machine (The Cognition and Technology Group at

Vanderbilt, 1993). Thus, the apparent contradiction (pick tomatoes fast with a machine and do not allow bruising) was resolved without compromise.

Analogies and Metaphors

We can scarcely imagine a problem absolutely new, unlike and unrelated to any formerly solved problem; but if such a problem could exist, it would be insoluble. In fact, when solving a problem, we should always profit from previously solved problems, using their result or their method, or the experience acquired in solving them.

—Polya (1945, p. 92)

Gick and Holyoak (1980, p. 306) ask, "Where do new ideas come from?" Many scientists and mathematicians respond that their ideas or solutions to problems come from recognizing analogies and metaphors drawn from different academic disciplines (Hadamard, 1954). In fact, it seems that the most common form of inference is made by noting similarities (**analogies** and metaphors) between two or more situations. Like hints, the analogy must be recognized as relevant in the problem being considered and then modified for the particular situation.

Consider the following problem:

> A small country fell under the iron rule of a dictator. The dictator ruled the country from a strong fortress. The fortress was situated in the middle of the country, surrounded by farms and villages. Many roads radiated outward from the fortress like spokes on a wheel. A great general arose who raised a large army at the border and vowed to capture the fortress and free the country of the dictator. The general knew that if his entire army could attack the fortress at once it could be captured. His troops were poised at the head of one of the roads leading to the fortress, ready to attack. However, a spy brought the general a disturbing report. The ruthless dictator had planted mines on each of the roads. The mines were set so that small bodies of men could pass over them safely, since the dictator needed to be able to move troops and workers to and from the fortress. However, any large force would detonate the mines. Not only would this blow up the road and render it impassable, but the dictator would then destroy many villages in retaliation. A full-scale direct attack on the fortress therefore appeared impossible. (Gick & Holyoak, 1980, p. 351)

To help you solve this problem, I'll also give you a hint. The solution is analogous to one discussed earlier in this chapter, although the context is entirely different. Stop for a few minutes and attempt to work on this problem. Think about the problems presented earlier. It should help if you draw a diagram.

The solution to this problem is analogous to the one used in the inoperable stomach tumor problem. In that problem (Duncker, 1945), the best solution involved sending weak rays through the body simultaneously from several different points so that they would converge on the tumor as depicted here.

Similarly, the army could be divided into small groups that would attack the fortress from all sides. Did you recognize that these problems were essentially similar in form and could be solved with the same solution? In a study of the use of diagrams as an aid in analogical problem solving, Pedone, Hummel, and Holyoak (2001) found that by animating the diagram so that the arrows moved in to a central point, college students were more likely to use the display as a retrieval cue that helped in solving the X-ray and fortess problems. It seems that these diagrams work best when problem solvers have their attention drawn to the structure of the problem so that they can recognize that these two types of problems have similar structures, even though they have very different surface characteristics (content).

Gordon (1961), originator of a group called "Synectics," presented guidelines for the use of analogies in solving problems. The term "Synectics" was taken from a Greek term that means joining together different and apparently unrelated elements. Gordon suggests that we consider four different types of analogies when faced with a problem:

1. Personal Analogy

If you want to understand a complex phenomenon, think of yourself as a participant in the phenomenon. For example, if you want to understand the molecular structure of a compound, think of yourself as a molecule. How would you behave? What other molecules would you want to attach yourself to? Get away from reliance on scientific notations and actually pretend to be a molecule bouncing in a compound. You may see relationships from this perspective that you were blind to when acting as a scientist.

The use of personal analogies is especially well suited for solving a wide range of conflict problems. If each side of a conflict can imagine how the problem appears to the other side, including acceptable goals, new solutions can become apparent. Both sides can identify common interests and use them to invent options that they both find acceptable (Bernstein, 1995; Fisher & Ury, 1991).

2. Direct Analogy

Compare the problems you're working on with several problems in other domains. According to Gordon, this method was used by Alexander Graham Bell: "It struck me that the bones of the human ear were very massive indeed, as compared with the delicate thin membrane that operated them, and the thought occurred that if a membrane so delicate could move bones relatively so massive, why should not a thicker and stouter piece of membrane move my piece of steel. And the telephone was conceived" (Gordon, 1961, p. 41).

A particularly fertile area for analogies is biology, where many solutions to biological problems have been evolving since the first life form appeared on Earth. When a Synectics group was faced with the problem of devising a bottle closure that could be used with glue or nail polish, the analogy they used was the biological closure of the anus (rectum). Apparently, this solution worked quite well. (You can think about this the next time you use a bottle of LePage's mucilage.)

3. Symbolic Activity

This solution strategy utilizes visual imagery. Its goal is to get away from the constraints of words or mathematical symbols. Students who utilized imagery to

Reprinted with special permission of King Features Syndicate.

visualize the tumor problem and the fortress problem were most likely to notice spontaneously that the two problems were analogous. If you work on generating a clear image of a problem, you may "see" a solution that had been overlooked.

4. Fantasy Analogy

In your wildest dreams, what would you want of a solution? An example of this is to imagine two small insects that would automatically zip your jacket or a silk worm that would spin silk rapidly to keep you warm when the temperature drops. These are fantasy analogies. Like brainstorming, a fantasy analogy can result in wild, impractical solutions that can later be modified to practical, workable ones.

Although it is clear that analogies are important aids in problem solving, it is rare for most people to notice a potential analogy spontaneously (VanLehn, 1989). If you are able to diagram the underlying relationships, as in the preceding problem, or to state the general rules, as in the contradictions problem, you are more likely to notice structural relationships and find useful analogies. Novice problem solvers are less likely to perceive structural similarities between problems that have different contents than more experienced problem solvers (Davidson & Sternberg, 1998).

Consult an Expert

"If at first you don't succeed, try, try, again. Then quit. No use being a damned fool about it."

—W.C. Fields (quoted in Teger, 1979, p. XIV)

Often in life, we don't have to solve problems alone. Sometimes the best way to solve a problem is to let experts do it for us, or at least help us with solving the problem. People seek accountants for help with their tax problems, attorneys for their legal problems, and physicians for their health problems. We elect officials to handle the problems of running our country and rely on military experts to wage wars. These people became experts in their field by obtaining the appropriate knowledge in their subject area and through repeated applications of this knowledge to real-world problems. Consulting an expert is often an excellent solution strategy. Their greater experience and knowledge will allow them to solve many problems in their area of expertise much more efficiently than a novice. If you decide to consult an expert, the problem becomes: (a) how to know somebody who is an expert; and (b) how to select which "expert" to use. Once you've passed these hurdles, your problems still aren't over. You need to be sure that the expert has all of the facts and has considered all of the relevant alternatives. Listen carefully to the expert's analysis of the risks and alternatives, but make the decision yourself. An expert is a problem-solving aid, not the solution. For some guidelines in recognizing an appropriate expert, consult Carlson (1995) and review the section on authorities in Chapter 4 on reasoning.

Select the Best Strategy

Twelve different strategies have been presented as aids in problem solving. When confronted with a problem, how do you know which to use? It is important to keep in mind that these strategies are not mutually exclusive. It will often be best to use them in combinations. The best strategy, or strategies, depends on the nature of the problem. After all, if you are taking an exam, you could be expelled if you consult the paper of an "expert" student sitting next to you.

Along with each strategy, I presented some guidelines for its appropriate use. In general, a few higher level "strategies for selecting strategies" include:

1. If the problem is ill defined, restate the goal or the problem in several different ways.
2. When there are very few possible solutions, a trial-and-error approach will work well.
3. If a problem is complex, try simplification, means-ends analysis, and generalization and specialization.
4. When there are fewer paths leading away from the goal than there are from the start state, work backwards.
5. If you can gather additional information, do it. Look for and utilize hints, and consult experts with specialized knowledge.
6. If there is an ordered array of equally likely alternatives, try the split-half method and seek rules.
7. If the problem is a lack of possible solution paths, brainstorm to generate alternative solution paths.
8. Problems in design and engineering are good candidates for devising solutions that seem, at first, to require contradictions in their solution.
9. Using analogies and metaphors and consulting an expert are widely applicable to all sorts of problems, but be prepared to use visualization and to deliberately seek analogies in order to recall an analogous solution.
10. Remember that these are only guidelines to solving problems. The best way to be an expert problem solver is to practice solving lots of problems.

PROBLEM-SOLVING PROBLEMS

Clinging to the past is the problem. Enhancing change is the answer.

—Gloria Steinem (1994)

There are many possible reasons why people find some problems difficult, perhaps even impossible to solve. Sometimes we're stuck in "thinking ruts" and cannot seem to think our way out of them. Two of these "ruts" are functional fixedness and mental set.

Functional Fixedness and Mental Set

Recall the two-string problem presented earlier in this chapter. The task was to grasp simultaneously two strings that hung from the ceiling. The correct solution involved setting one string into motion, perhaps by tying a heavy object like a pair of pliers to its end to serve as a weight. One reason why this was such a difficult problem is functional fixedness. Subjects were fixated or "stuck" on the usual function of a pair of pliers and have difficulty thinking of them as having a different function.

Another example of **functional fixedness** was presented in Chapter 1, the introduction. In a classic problem, subjects were asked to attach a candle to the wall so that it could be burned, using only a box of thumbtacks and some matches. Subjects had difficulty thinking of the box as a candle holder because they saw it in terms of its usual function—a container for thumbtacks.

Mental set refers to the problem solver's state of mind. It is a general term for the inability to think of a new solution or new type of solution for familiar problems. I think of functional fixedness and mental state as "ruts in one's thinking." They are predispositions to think and respond in certain ways. To demonstrate how powerful some sets can be, work on the nine-dot problem in Fig. 9.18. Stop now and work on this problem.

The difficulty posed by the nine-dot problem comes from a perceptual set imposed by the square arrangement. Most people attempt to solve the problem by staying within the imaginary boundary formed by the outer dots. If you extend your lines beyond this imaginary boundary, you'll find that the problem is easy to solve. In addition, most people attempt solutions in which the line goes through the center of each dot. One solution to the nine-dot problem is shown in Fig. 9.19.

There are several other solutions to the nine-dot problem. Each of them involves breaking set in some way. Two solutions (Adams, 1979, pp. 25–26) are presented in Fig. 9.20. A few other more exotic solutions, including one submitted by a 10-year-old girl, which consists of one very fat line drawn through all nine dots can be found in Adams' (1979) gem of a book, *Conceptual Blockbusting*. The set of staying within the rectangular area is pervasive and difficult to break. Strategies that get you to view problems in novel ways, like the personal analogy strategy, are good ways to work on set-breaking solutions.

FIG. 9.18.   The nine-dot problem. Using no more than four straight lines and without lifting your pencil from the paper, draw a line through all nine dots.

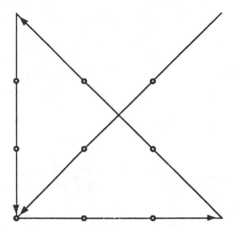

FIG. 9.19. One possible solution to the nine-dot problem. Note that the solution involves breaking "set." Most people assume that the lines must form a square and that each line must pass through the center of each dot.

Misleading and Irrelevant Information

My father used to love this riddle:

> Suppose you are a bus driver. On the first stop you pick up 6 men and 2 women. At the second stop 2 men leave and 1 woman boards the bus. At the third stop 1 man leaves and 2 women enter the bus. At the fourth stop 3 men get on and 3 women get off. At the fifth stop 2 men get off, 3 men get on, 1 woman gets off, and 2 women get on. What is the bus driver's name?

Could you answer this question without rereading the problem? The bus driver's name is, of course, your name because the riddle began, "Suppose you are a bus driver." All of the information about the rest of the passengers was irrelevant. Often information that is irrelevant to the problem serves to mislead problem solvers down dead-end paths. Real-life problems often involve deciding what information is relevant. To avoid being misled by information, be clear about the goal state. Simplification will sometimes help in separating the relevant from the irrelevant givens.

Let's try another example:

> If you have black socks and brown socks in your drawer mixed in the ratio of 4 to 5, how many socks will you have to take out to make sure of having a pair of the same color?" (Fixx, 1978).

Think about this problem. What is relevant? What is irrelevant? The answer is three socks because any two must match if there are only brown and black socks. The information about the ratio of socks is irrelevant and misleading. Imagine yourself actually picking socks from a drawer and this problem will be easier to solve.

A common attribute of ill-defined problems is that they potentially involve a huge amount of information. Consider the very real-world problems in international relations such as, "How can we influence Russia so that it cleans up its environmental hazards?" or "How can we provide food for the countless numbers of people who go hungry in the United States and the rest of the world?" The "problem," with broad problems such as these, requires the selection of information that could lead to the desired goal. Unlike the motorist problem that I presented at the opening of

FIG. 9.20. Other possible solutions to the nine-dot problem. (From Adams, 1979; Reprinted by permission from W. W. Norton.)

this chapter, the difficulty is not in the absence of paths to the goal, but in too many possible paths. Which path is most likely to be the best? How can we choose among the better options? There are no simple answers for these questions, which is why we continue to have environmental threats and hunger.

Worldview Constraints

Often we fail to solve problems because of the **worldview constraints** placed on us by our social class, nationality, or political views. Consider the following problem:

A ping pong ball 1″ in diameter falls into a 3″ length of pipe that is 1 1/8″ in diameter. The pipe is firmly affixed to the concrete pavement. It is extremely important to remove the ball. You and some friends are faced with this task. All you have is some fine wire and your collective abilities to solve this problem. What do you do?

Most people approach this task by attempting to bend fine wire into tweezers to pluck it up. A better solution is to urinate into the pipe so that the ball will float to the top. This probably never occurred to you because it is not an acceptable thought for most people in our society. Although this has never been verified, it would probably be an easier task for people in other societies where urination is not considered as private an act as it is in our society.

I received a first-hand lesson in the ways in which worldviews influence problem solving during the semester that I spent at Moscow State University in Russia. Russia is a country emerging from communism, and a communist solution to a problem is very different from a capitalist solution. Under communism, the state is expected to solve problems like inflation, unemployment, and the supply of consumer goods; whereas, under capitalism these sorts of problems are handled largely by the private sector. It is difficult to imagine the tremendous effect that culture has on the way we think without an extended experience in a culture other than the one you know best. It is for this reason that I tout the educational benefits of extended foreign travel. It can change your own worldview and help you to appreciate the extent to which the problems we identify and the solutions we generate are influenced by cultural factors.

APPLYING THE FRAMEWORK

The general thinking skills framework that we've been using throughout the book is particularly applicable to problem solving.

1. What Is the Goal?

One of the first steps in solving a problem is to be explicit about the goal. This is relatively easy for well-defined problems (e.g., How many ounces are in a pound?). Most problems, however, are ill defined and can have multiple goals. Being explicit about the goal and considering alternative goals will force you to cast the problem in the thinking skills framework and to begin goal-directed thinking.

2. What Is Known?

This is part of the preparation or familiarization process. The knowns or "givens" determine the nature of the problem. It is often possible to improve on what is known by gathering additional information. Once you have a clear determination of the knowns, you can use that information as a guide to selecting the best representation and best problem-solving strategy.

3. Which Thinking Skill or Skills Will Get You to Your Goal?

Twelve different kinds of strategies or skills were presented in this chapter along with general guidelines such as restating the goal and selecting a representation.

You need to select strategies that are most likely to solve the problem. A trial-and-error approach to selecting a strategy is, itself, a poor strategy. Guidelines were presented for evaluating strategies depending on the nature of the problem.

The skills for planning and solving problems that were presented in this chapter are applicable to almost any problem. After reading this chapter you should be able to:

- Plan and monitor a strategy for finding a solution.
- Identify any problem as either well defined or ill defined and adjust your solution plan according to the type of problem.
- Use graphs, diagrams, hierarchical trees, matrices, and models as solution aids.
- Devise a quality representation of a problem.
- Select the problem-solving strategies that are appropriate for the problem.
- Use all of the following strategies: mean-ends analysis, working backwards, simplification, generalization and specialization, random search and trial-and-error, rules, hints, split-half method, brainstorming, contradiction, analogies and metaphors, and consulting an expert.
- Demonstrate an awareness of functional fixedness so as to avoid it.
- Distinguish between relevant and irrelevant information.
- Understand how worldviews can constrain the problem-solving process.

4. Have You Reached Your Goal?

The final step in problem solving is an assessment of the quality of the solution. In well-defined problems, this question becomes: Is your solution the correct one? In ill-defined problems, the solution has to evaluated qualitatively both in an absolute sense (Does it alleviate or reduce the problem?) and in a relative sense (Is it the best alternative?).

CHAPTER SUMMARY

1. All problems can be conceptualized as being composed of "anatomical" parts that include a start state, a goal state, and paths leading from the start to the goal. This entire structure is called the problem space. You have a problem when there is a gap or barrier between where you are (start state) and where you want to be (goal state).

2. It is common to divide the problem-solving process into four stages: preparation or familiarization; production; judgment or evaluation; and incubation. Incubation is an optional stage that does not always occur. Persistence is a critical trait of good problem solvers.

3. Problems can be classified along a continuum ranging from well defined to ill defined. Well-defined problems have explicit paths and goals. Ill-defined problems are subject to multiple interpretations and judgments about the goal state. Most of the problems encountered in life are ill defined.

4. Solution strategies need to be planned. A plan for solving a problem will include the construction of a representation and the generation and evaluation of possible solutions.

5. An invaluable aid in solving problems is to devise an external form of representation. The best representation to choose will depend on the type of problem.

6. Twelve different strategies for generating and evaluating solutions were presented. Often several will be used together in solving a problem. General guidelines were offered for the appropriate use of each.

7. There are four common sources of difficulty that problem solvers encounter. Functional fixedness refers to the failure to utilize items in unusual ways. Mental set, which is closely related to functional fixedness, refers to the predisposition to respond to any situation in a fixed way. Misleading and irrelevant information can "derail one's trail of thought" and can lead you down blind paths. The constraints imposed upon us by our society cause us to view problems from our own narrow frames of reference.

TERMS TO KNOW

You should be able to define or describe the following terms or concepts. If you find that you're having difficulty with any term, be sure to reread the section in which it is discussed.

A Problem. A problem is defined as a state where there is a gap or barrier between where the problem solver is and where she or he wants to be.

Anatomy of a Problem. Newell and Simon (1972) have conceptualized all problems as consisting of parts or components—an initial state, a goal state, and solution paths that link the initial state to the goal state.

Solution Paths. Methods or means for solving problems. Routes that lead from the initial state to the goal state in a problem.

Initial State. The starting or beginning place in a problem. A problem is solved when the problem solver can find "paths" from the initial state to the goal.

Goal State. The desired end state in a problem. When a problem solver finds "paths" to the goal, the problem is solved.

Problem Space. All possible paths from the initial state to the goal state in a problem.

Givens. Information or rules that place constraints on the problem.

Preparation of Familiarization Stage. The first stage in problem solving, which includes the time spent in understanding the nature of the problem, the desired goal, and the givens.

Production Stage. The second stage in problem solving. During this state, the problem solver produces the solution paths that define the problem space.

Judgment or Evaluation Stage. The third stage in problem solving during which time the problem solver evaluates the solution paths in order to select the best one.

Incubation. A period in problem solving when the problem solver is not actively working on the problem. Sometimes people report that a solution comes to them during this "time-out" period.

Insight. Sudden knowledge of a solution to a problem. Also known as the "Aha!" experience.

Well-Defined Problems. Problems with a single correct answer.

Ill-Defined Problems. Problems with many possible correct answers. The difficulty with these problems lies in evaluating possible solutions to decide which one is best. Often the goal in these problems is vague or incomplete.

Transcontextual. A problem-solving strategy that is useful in any context with any sort of problem. An example of a transcontextual strategy is to state the goal four different ways whenever a problem is encountered.

Hierarchical Trees. Branching diagrams that serve as a representational aid in solving problems. Instances of categories provide the "nodes" of the trees.

Matrix. A rectangular array of numbers that is used as a means of representing problems that contain categories of information.

Detour Problems. Problems in which the path to the goal is not a direct linear one. Intermediate steps are required that seem directly opposite the goal.

Subproblems. When difficulty is encountered in solving a problem, it can be broken down into several smaller problems or "subproblems."

Subgoal. When difficulty is encountered in solving a problem, it can be broken down into several smaller problems called "subproblems." Each subproblem has its own goal, called a "subgoal."

Means-End Analysis. A general problem-solving strategy in which operations are used to reduce the distance between the problem solver's current state and the nearest possible subgoal or goal.

Working Backwards. A problem-solving strategy in which operations are planned that move from the goal to the present or initial state. This method is usually contrasted with the forward-looking strategy.

Forward-Looking Strategy. A problem-solving strategy in which all of the planning is done by considering operations that move the problem solver closer to subgoals and the goal. This method is usually contrasted with working backwards from the goal.

Simplification. A problem-solving strategy in which as much of the complexity as possible is removed from the problem in order to facilitate a solution.

Generalization. A problem-solving strategy in which the problem is considered as an example of a larger class of problems.

Specialization. A problem-solving strategy in which the problem is considered as a special case drawn from a larger set of problems.

Random Search. A problem-solving strategy in which all possible solution paths from the initial state to the goal are considered in an unsystematic (random) manner. This method is usually contrasted with trial-and-error search.

Trial-and-Error. A problem-solving strategy in which all solution paths from the initial state to the goal are searched systematically. This method is usually contrasted with random search.

Rules. The principles that underlie some problems. For example, solutions to problems that require a prediction of the next element in a series depend on the discovery of their rules.

Hints. Additional information that is given after an individual has begun to work on a problem.

Split-Half Method. A problem-solving strategy that is useful when there is no a priori reason for selecting among a sequentially organized set of possible solution paths. The method consists of continually selecting a point that is halfway between the present state and the goal as a systematic means for "guessing" at the solution.

Brainstorming. A group or individual method for generating solution paths for problems. Problem solvers are encouraged to think up wild, imaginative solutions and to defer judgment on these solutions until a later time when they may be modified or combined. The goal is to produce a large number of possible solutions.

Analogies. A problem-solving strategy in which similarities are noted between two or more situations, while simultaneously discerning that there are also differences; for example, by noting similarities between two different problems, the problem solver may discover that similar solutions are applicable.

Personal Analogy. A problem-solving strategy suggested by Gordon (1961) in which you think of yourself as a participant in the phenomenon that you want to understand.

Direct Analogy. A problem-solving strategy suggested by Gordon (1961) in which you note similarities between your problem and related problems in other domains.

Symbolic Activity. The deliberate use of visual imagery or other symbolic representation as a problem-solving aid.

Fantasy Analogy. A problem-solving strategy suggested by Gordon (1961) in which problem solvers utilize their imagination to conceptualize ideal solutions.

Functional Fixedness. A type of mental set in which individuals only consider the usual use (function) of objects.

Mental Set. Predispositions to think and respond in a certain way.

Worldview Constraints. Limitations on the way we approach problems placed on us by our social class, nationality, or political views.

10

Creative Thinking

Contents

The history of civilization is essentially the record of man's [and woman's]
creative ability.

—Osborn (1963, p. ix)

I spent a morning at a special summer program for "mentally gifted kids," the ones who score within the top one or two percent of all children in their age group on intelligence tests. Every morning, the second to tenth graders gather in a small auditorium to contemplate a "thought for the day," work on a puzzle, plan activities, and gripe about the usual things all kids gripe about. The puzzle for the day was "How can you take one away from 9 and get 10?" The kid sitting next to me whispered, "Do you know the answer?" After a few seconds thought, I gloated with a "Yes" response, pleased as punch that I could keep up with this elite group of short people.

Many hands shot up in response to the puzzle. The first child to answer was a tiny, red-headed girl, reminiscent of Charlie Brown's heartthrob. "It's easy," she said as she walked confidently to the chalkboard. "If you take away a negative one, the effect will be the same as addition." As she spoke, she wrote the following on the board:

$$9 - (-1) = 9 + 1 = 10$$

I was amazed. Why hadn't I thought of that? A second hand went up and a young boy on the verge of adolescence explained another answer: "In Roman numerals, nine is written 'IX,' so if you take 'I' (one) away, you'll end up with 'X,' the Roman numeral for 10."

Another child responded with a sheepish grin, saying that, "This is a little silly, but, if you write 'q' and take the one, or vertical line, away and place it in front of the changed number, you'll have '10.'" I don't know why this was a silly answer—it was the one I had been thinking of.

Still more hands were up, anxious to demonstrate more ways to answer the puzzle. One child wrote out the word "NINE," then erased the second letter (the i that looked like a one), which left her with a "N NE." If you count the number of straight lines left in these letters, there are 10 (three in each "N" and four in the "E").

Actually there were even more answers, but I lost track as I sat with my mouth gaping open, trying to follow each explanation. How did the children come up with so many creative answers?

DEFINING CREATIVITY

A psychology of man is impossible without understanding man's ability to
create.

—Arasteh and Arasteh (1976, p. 3)

Creativity is a difficult word to define. We say that someone "is creative" when she has produced an outcome or a product that is both unusual and appropriate (or meaningful or useful or particularly good). Thus, creativity is defined by two aspects of its consequence (novelty and quality) and not the process that led to the consequence.

Both the unusualness and appropriateness criteria require judgments: How unusual is the idea and how well does it meet some objective? Because both of these criteria vary along quantitative dimensions, creativity exists in degrees. This means that any action or thought can be more or less creative. Creativity is not a single trait that people either have or don't have. Creative thinking involves cognitive processes that occur in a context. These processes involve novelty in one or more of the processes that lead to creative outcomes—ways of identifying that a problem exists, defining a problem, generating and evaluating possible solutions, and judging how uniquely and how well the problem is solved.

Suppose that you are invited to supper at your friend Hazel's house. You know that she is an adventuresome cook and therefore you look forward to the meal with relish. The main dish is an original concoction of hot dogs and fruit salad in a cold mustard sauce. (This part is a true story. I was once served this at a friend's house.) The coup de grace is a dessert that she made in her new ice cream maker—liver- and brussel sprout-flavored ice cream. Although these are unusual dishes, few people would willingly eat them. Most of us would not judge these culinary delights as creative because they do not satisfy the criterion that the idea or product be good or useful.

One problem with our working definition of creativity concerns the terms "unusual" and "good" or "useful" because satisfaction of these criteria is a matter of judgment, and people will often disagree. This means that creativity exists in the eyes of the observer, although there are also good data showing that experts in a field (e.g., visual arts, music, science) generally show good agreement in the creativity ratings they assign to creations in their field (e.g., paintings, musical scores, research findings; Sternberg & Lubart, 1996). It's easy to see why creativity has been an elusive topic. Someone or some group must judge an act or idea as unusual and good or useful before it can be labeled creative, and there will often be disagreement on the way these attributes are judged. Judgments of creativity also change over time so that a "zany" idea at one time in history (e.g., the earth revolves around the sun and not the reverse) may come to be viewed as "monumental" at some time later.

Prince (1970, p. i) offered a somewhat poetic definition of creativity, which, I believe, is itself creative. Consider his definition:

CREATIVITY: an arbitrary harmony, an expected astonishment, a habitual revelation, a familiar surprise, a generous selfishness, an unexpected certainty, a formidable stubbornness, a vital triviality, a disciplined freedom, an intoxicating steadiness, a repeated initiation, a difficult delight, a predictable gamble, an ephemeral solidity, a unifying difference, a demanding satisfier, a miraculous expectation, an accustomed amazement.

Gardner (1989) has added an additional requirement to his definition of creativity. Gardner wants creativity to include the idea that the creative individual *regularly* solves problems or fashions products that are creative. This additional requirement would remove "luck" from the creative process because luck or random actions cannot explain regular results. However we choose to define creativity, we need it, and we all possess it to some extent. Our everyday lives are more pleasurable because of our creative actions; the arts depend on it for their existence; science and mathematics could not progress without it. Every time we express a complex thought or fill a blank piece of paper with our words, we are creating; when we do it particularly well in an unusual way, then we are creative.

Lateral and Vertical Thinking

Vertical thinking is concerned with digging the same hole deeper. Lateral thinking is concerned with digging the hole somewhere else.

—DeBono (1977, p. 195)

The distinction between lateral and vertical thinking was first made by DeBono (1968, p. 11). It is best illustrated with a short story that is probably an old fable that has been told for many generations:

> Many years ago when a person who owed money could be thrown into jail, a merchant in London had the misfortune to owe a huge sum to a money-lender. The money-lender, who was old and ugly, fancied the merchant's beautiful teenage daughter. He proposed a bargain. He said he would cancel the merchant's debt if he could have the girl instead.
>
> Both the merchant and his daughter were horrified at the proposal. So the cunning money-lender proposed that they let Providence decide the matter. He told them that he would put a black pebble and a white pebble into an empty money-bag and then the girl would have to pick out one of the pebbles. If she chose the black pebble, she would become his wife and her father's debt would be cancelled. If she chose the white pebble, she would stay with her father and the debt would still be cancelled. But if she refused to pick out a pebble, her father would be thrown into jail and she would starve.
>
> Reluctantly the merchant agreed. They were standing on a pebble-strewn path in the merchant's garden as they talked and the money-lender stooped down to pick up the two pebbles. As he picked up the pebbles, the girl, sharp-eyed with fright, noticed that he picked up two black pebbles and put them into the money-bag. He then asked the girl to pick out the pebble that was to decide her fate and that of her father.

What would you do if you had been the girl? If you think about this problem in a careful, logical, straightforward way, you're using **vertical thinking**, a type of thinking that will not be much help in this situation. Typical "vertical thinking" answers are: let the girl sacrifice herself or expose him for the crook he is. Consider DeBono's suggested solution: The girl should fumble when she draws the pebble from the bag, dropping it onto the pebble-strewn path. She should then tell the villain that they can determine the color of the pebble she took by seeing the color of the one left in the bag. Because the remaining pebble must be black, the money-lender will be forced to admit that she had chosen the white pebble or expose himself as a crook.

Virtually everyone agrees that this is both a good and unusual answer to the girl's dilemma. **Lateral thinking** is a way of thinking "around" a problem. "Lateral thinking generates the ideas and vertical thinking develops them" (DeBono, 1968, p.6). Lateral thinking, then, is sometimes used as a synonym for creative thinking or idea discovery, whereas vertical thinking is the refinement and improvement of existing ideas.

The world's most famous fictional detective, Sherlock Holmes, often exhibited lateral thinking. One of my favorite examples was Holmes' response to an idea by his faithful assistant, the good Dr. Watson. Watson pointed out that a certain dog would not be at all helpful in solving a mystery because the dog had done nothing on the night of the murder. Sherlock cleverly noted that the dog was extremely important in solving the mystery precisely because he had done nothing on the night of the murder because dogs would be expected to bark or become excited at the sight of strangers or of violent struggles.

Creative Genius or Pedestrian Process?

"The human mind treats a new idea the way the body treats a strange protein; it rejects it."

—P. B. Medawar (quoted in Byrne, 1988, p. 16)

Are creative individuals qualitatively different from the rest of us, or do we all have (to some extent) what it takes to create something great? Increasingly, psychologists have come to believe that there is "nothing special" about creative giants like Einstein, Madame Curie, and Mozart and that the creative process can be understood as an extension of common everyday thinking processes. Weisberg (1988, 1993) has championed the everyday view of creativity in his analysis of the antecedents of creative thinking. For example, he presents a brief biography of Alexander Calder (1898–1976), a popular artist who is best known for his brightly colored mobiles. Calder invented the mobile as an art form. As a child, Calder used wire to make jewelry for his sister. His parents were artists who made certain that he had art lessons and was surrounded with both sculpture (his father's profession) and drawings (his mother's profession). He visited the studios of Piet Mondrian, an abstract artist who used strong, primary colors and abstract designs in his work. It is easy to see how these life experiences led to an art form in which brightly colored abstract patterns were strung together and hung in space. The creative act was the assimilation of these diverse forms and influences—one that, at least in hindsight, could have been predicted from Calder's life experiences.

The view that even great creative products can be produced by almost anyone with at least slightly above-average intelligence and expertise in a discipline is gaining in popularity. For example, Hayes (1989) noted that there are no cognitive abilities that separate creative and noncreative people. According to this view, most of us have "what it takes" to be highly creative. From a cognitive perspective, creative thinking uses thought processes that are quite ordinary. We can all come up with "novel products of value" (Weisberg, 1993, p. 4). All we need to do is learn how— and there's the rub!

Sensitivity, Synergy, and Serendipity

Creative thought is innovative, exploratory, venturesome.

—Kneller (1965, p. 6)

Creativity has been described as the three Ss: sensitivity, synergy, and serendipity (Parnes, Noller, & Biondi, 1977). **Sensitivity** is the use of our senses, our "windows to the world" that we use to touch, smell, taste, and see. It has been suggested that highly creative people may experience the physical world with greater intensity than the rest of us, although I don't know of any data to support this possibility. It does seem that creative thinking involves the "noticing" or remembering of some critical aspect of the environment or a problem that the rest of us overlooked. One of the benchmarks of a creative person is the ability to find problems and not just solutions to them. Look at Fig. 10.1. This is called "Boring's Wife-and-Mother-In-Law." Can you guess why? Look closely. Can you see both an old woman and a young woman in the picture?

Count the prongs on Fig. 10.2. Do they disappear as you count them? This is an impossible figure—impossible because it can't ever exist, except in the artist's mind.

FIG. 10.1. Boring's Wife-and-Mother-In-Law. Can you see both an old woman and a young woman in this picture?

FIG. 10.2. An impossible figure. Try to count the prongs.

In creating each of these figures, the artists displayed a sensitivity to details that is both unusual and appropriate. Perhaps these are examples of heightened sensitivity to visual stimuli.

Synergy is the bringing together of seemingly disparate parts into a useful and functioning whole. It is close to Koestler's (1964) notion of **bisociative thinking** in which two previously unconnected "frames of reference" are amalgamated. If you can take ideas from different domains and bring them together so that they work successfully in a new context, you have demonstrated synergy. Examples of synergy can be found in the brief biography of Calder, which was presented earlier, who brought together his experiences with wire objects, bright colors, and abstract drawing to create his wildly popular mobiles.

Gordon (1961) suggested that one way to promote creativity is to bring people from diverse fields together to find problems and to create solutions, the two mainstreams of the creative process. In order to bring together diverse ideas, you need to have a broad range of experiences and knowledge. Creativity is enhanced when groups are composed of diverse team members (Jackson, 1996). One argument for a liberal arts education is that it provides the breadth of knowledge needed to view the world from different perspectives and to permit the combination of ideas across domains of knowledge.

According to von Oech (1983), Johannes Gutenberg conceived of the printing press by combining two previously unconnected ideas—the wine press and the coin punch. The purpose of the coin punch was to leave an impression on a small area such as a coin. By contrast, the wine press applied pressure over a large area in order to squeeze the juice out of grapes. One day Gutenberg put the coin punch under the wine press and found that he could get images on paper. This simple, but original, combination resulted in the printing press and literally changed the world by making books widely available.

Serendipity is a unexpected discovery that is unplanned. Biographies of great scientists often contain accounts of serendipitous events, some of them seemingly preposterous. I have often felt that focusing on serendipity did the scientist a great injustice. A new miracle drug may have been the result of an accidental spill, but it was the prepared scientist who could appreciate the results of the accident that created the drug. The scientist was able to select the relevant information from the accident so that it could be used in a novel way instead of simply labeling it a mistake and forgetting about it. Although serendipity may have contributed to a creative act, the persistence, motivation, and hard work on the part of the creator allowed the serendipitous event to occur. Serendipity may play a role in great scientific discoveries, but such fortuitive "accidents" seem most likely to occur in the laboratory at 2 a.m.

Consider how an artist friend of mine combined sensitivity, synergy, and serendipity to create a new form of art. Robert Perine, a San Diego artist (who also created the beautiful and novel depiction of "The Thinker" on the cover of this book), decided to incorporate the glass that is used to cover pictures into the pictures themselves. He cut odd-shaped glass coverings and placed them over his watercolor paintings to see how the beveled edges in the glass would refract the paint beneath it and give it a glossy, shimmering appearance. It was a simple idea that brought together the framing process and the picture itself in a new art form that incorporates the picture and the glass used to protect it. Creative ideas often seem simple and surprising. Like Calder's union of jewelry design and bright abstract painting to create his mobiles, and Gutenberg's union of the coin press and wine press to create the printing press, this contemporary artist brought together two known processes (framing and painting) in a novel and useful way with a creative outcome.

Jokes, puns, and witticisms could also be considered as a form of creative expression. A joke brings together two ideas that are not usually combined: Did you hear the one about the two former schoolmates who meet unexpectedly for the first time in 25 years? As they caught up on the details of their lives, one asked the other if he had any children. Sorrowfully he replied, "Yes, one living and one married." The listener was expecting the phrase "one living and one dead" and the surprise juxtaposition of "living and married" is the humorous element in this joke. Laughter is often the response to original ideas also. The surprising combination of elements (synergy) makes for good jokes and creative ideas.

Creativity as Investment Theory: Buy Low; Sell High

Even in companies that pride themselves on their encouragement of wacky,
creative thinkers—outside-the-box requires them to be wacky and creative in the
right sort of way—and to think outside the appropriate box.

—Peter Martin (2001, July 17, p. 10)

Suppose you were to decide right now to "do something creative." Where and how would you begin? Would you search popular and scholarly media to identify emerging trends, such as the development of smaller computers, more powerful drugs, or faster means of transportation, and apply your knowledge and skills in one of these areas? If so, then you would be exhibiting a not-very-creative approach to deciding which ideas or products to pursue. Sternberg and Lubart (1995, 1996) maintain that creative people make unusual decisions about the topics and products in which they are willing to invest their own time and effort; those of us who are not recognized as creative may have made errors in selecting the topic that is worth pursuing. Creative people work on topics that are unpopular at the time; they make creative contributions to the field, and then move on to another unpopular topic. In this way, creativity is like the classic mantra of finance, "buy low; sell high." In other words, creative people invest in unpopular topics (topics where there is low interest) and move on to another unpopular topic when the first one gains in popularity (leave the area when interest is high). The definition of creativity requires "something unusual," so creative people, by definition, buck the crowd instead of following it.

The investment theory of creativity addresses an important question in the world of ideas—what is worth thinking about? In Chapter 9 on problem solving, the problem finding (or identifying) is similar to the idea of deciding how to invest cognitive resources. Finding the right problem to solve (or a problem worth solving) is at least as important as deriving a successful solution. Problem solving and creativity are closely related topics. Creative problem solvers (and finders) will have knowledge about the topic, sufficient intellectual ability (i.e., intelligence), an encouraging environment, an appropriately flexible thinking style, a personality that is open to new ideas, and the motivation to persist at a task.

Creativity as a System

A scientific theory or other product is creative only if the innovation gains the
acceptance of a field of experts and so transforms the culture.

—Nakamura and Csikszentmihalyi (2001, p. 337)

Creativity will involve more than just knowledge about a field or the willingness to propose a novel idea. There are many different ways of examining this strange creature we call "creativity." Some psychologists have adopted a systems approach to creativity, which means that they believe it is the confluence of many different types of variables that make creativity more or less probable. Of course, the creative individual is central to the process, but she or he works in a domain of knowledge (e.g., art, physics, decorating, teaching, horse breeding, and any other domain you can think of). The contributions of an individual to a domain are judged by the people in the field—the art critics, funding agencies for physics research, editors of decorating magazines, etc. The people in the field act as the gatekeepers for a domain—they decide what is and is not valued. Docents in art museums often tell stories of artists who died penniless because their unusual style was not recognized as genius until after their death. Of course, they never mention those dead, penniless artists whose art is still not recognized as having value—and may never be. The role of the gatekeepers to a domain is critical in understanding creativity because these influential people can spur creativity or stifle it, depending on their own views of what is novel and appropriate for their domain. In a fascinating case study of these influences, Naka-mura and Csikszentmihalyi (2001) recount an interview with Linus Pauling, a scientist who won a Nobel Prize for his work in the fields of organic chemistry and nuclear disarmament and ignoble scorn for his work on the role of vitamin C in preventing colds. This fascinating account emphasizes the importance of variables that are beyond the control of a creative individual.

CREATIVITY AS A COGNITIVE PROCESS

The man with a new idea is a Crank until the idea succeeds.

—Mark Twain (1897, aka Samuel L. Clemens)

If the creative act is "nothing special," then we should be able to understand it and predict when it will occur using a common cognitive framework. Several different psychologists have suggested that creativity is as "simple" as problem solving, except that the problem or the solution are novel and appropriate. According to this view, creative thinking is a multistage process that consists of identifying a problem, deciding what is important about the problem, and arriving at a novel way of solving it. Perkins (1988) stresses the processes of searching and selecting as integral to creative acts, but these are the same processes that were used to understand more mundane problem solving and decision making. "Creativity" brings together many topics that have been addressed in earlier chapters; yet, it is also more elusive and mysterious because, by definition, we cannot tell anyone how to create the "unusual." What makes the processes of identifying problems, searching for solutions, selecting the most promising ones, and conveying the outcome, creative?

Stretching and Rejecting Paradigms

A **paradigm** is an example that is used as a pattern. In psychology it usually refers to an experimental setup, but it can be anything. In this context, it is used to mean "a usual way of thinking or responding." Consider this example: Suppose that you are a manufacturer of golf clubs. Like all manufacturers, you want to sell more golf clubs. Paradigmatic thinking about this problem might lead you to increase your advertising budget so that advertisements for your golf clubs reach more people (McFadzean, 2000). If you stretch the paradigm, you might start to think that instead of reaching more people with your advertisements, you want to target buyers of golf clubs, so you would plan your advertising to reach fewer people, but a more select group. If you reject the paradigm, you change the nature of the problem that is being solved. Callaway Golf, a U. S. manufacturer of golf clubs, did exactly that (Kim & Mauborgne, 1999). Their creative idea—"Big Bertha Golf Clubs." What, you don't know about Big Bertha? Instead of making golf clubs that would compete with other well-known brands of golf clubs, they made new golf club aimed at a new golf-playing audience—people who don't play golf. The creative people at Callaway thought about all of the people at country clubs who play tennis instead of golf because these tennis players find the idea of using a tiny club to hit a tiny ball too daunting a task. After all, the head of a tennis racket is much larger than the head of golf club, so it should be easier to hit a tennis ball with the large head of a tennis racket than a tiny golf ball with a small head of a golf club (other things being equal, which, of course, they are not). Callaway saw a business opportunity that no one had seen. A golf club with a large head makes playing golf less difficult and more fun for people who do not play golf. Thus, they combined the larger head of the tennis racket with the shaft of a golf club to create Big Bertha—a profitable move that expanded the market for golf clubs. This creative act involved rejecting the business-as-usual paradigm.

It is useful to conceptualize creative thinking within the framework that was developed in the chapter on problem solving (Chapter 9). A problem exists when there is a discrepancy between where the problem solver is and the desired end state or goal. A solution is a plan for attaining the goal. Guilford (1977) described the relationship between problem solving and creativity this way: ". . . problem-solving and creative thinking are closely related. The very definitions of those two activities show logical connections. Creative thinking produces novel outcomes, and problem-solving produces a new response to a new situation that is a novel outcome. Thus, we can say that problem-solving has creative aspects."

The Problem of Problem Definition

All of our great inventors were problem finders. They recognized problems that the rest of the world never saw. For example, why did people need electric lights when gas worked well, or why should we even want to travel in a metal box propelled with a new-fangled engine when horses were more reliable (at that time)? We all studied the great inventors of the past, people like Benjamin Franklin, George Washington Carver, and Thomas Edison. Present-day inventors also find problems. An "Invention Convention" is held annually in the United States to highlight the creative talents of current inventors. Some of the items first displayed at this convention are a double-headed toothbrush that can brush both sides of the teeth at the same time, a portable hot water shower that can be used for camping because it is lightweight and relies on the sun to heat the water, bedroom slippers with headlights, and an electric box that makes and bakes a loaf of bread—all you do is pour in the ingredients. These have all become commercial successes, which means that the general public believes that they are good solutions to a problem that most of us never knew existed. How many of these can you identify—'*The Blair Witch Project*,' which used internet marketing to make a low-budget film a commercial success; "Cows on Parade," a promotion that brought more than 2 million visitors to Chicago to view brightly painted, whimsical, fiberglass cows in various locations around the city; "Viagra," a drug developed to enhance the sexual abilities of men (and vastly increase profits of the manufacturer); "America Online," an online Internet service that offered services that no one before ever thought were needed (Ryan, 2001). These examples are so deeply ingrained in American culture that it is hard to believe that these are just some of the many creative ideas and products developed in the last two decades. In every case, someone saw an opportunity that the rest of us missed. What can we learn from these and other creative successes?

Selecting Relevant Information

Virtually every creative act involves a novel way of defining a problem and selecting information that is relevant to reaching the goal. We usually think of creativity in the arts and sciences, but it can and should exist in a host of everyday settings that range from planning your finances so that your money lasts until the end of the month to getting your teacher to accept a late paper.

Consider a couple seeking marriage counseling. The wife complains that her husband spends too much time at work, and if he really loved her, he would spend more time at home. The husband complains that he has a great deal of pressure at the office and that he has to work long hours to "get ahead." If his wife loved him more, she would understand. There are multiple possible ways to define their problem. They could pose the problem as: "Should we get a divorce?" But, other possible problem definitions include: (a) How can we find ways to spend more time together? (b) How can we assure each other that we are still in love? (c) How can the husband "get ahead" while spending less time at work? (d) How can they learn to adjust to the present situation? (e) Is "getting ahead" an important goal? (f) What can the wife do so that she doesn't feel lonely and resentful when her husband is at work?

If you consider the problem for a few more minutes, you can come up with many other problem definitions. The nature of the solution will change every time the problem is redefined. The selection of relevant information to help you reach a goal is related to your knowledge of the problem space (topic). In this example, you would need to know more about the couple to help them find a good solution. Suppose that you know that the wife is an aspiring artist. You could suggest that she pursue her art interests so that she would feel less lonely and deserted. Alternatively, if you know about the availability of other jobs for the husband, you could suggest that he change jobs. In fact, therapists who have adopted this technique report that they can help families overcome destructive conflicts by teaching them how to discover creative solutions to their interpersonal problems (Carson, 2001).

Lateral thinking or "thinking around a problem" is really just another term for "redefining the problem." In the story about the clever girl who knew she was being offered two black pebbles, she didn't conceptualize the problem as "What should I do when I pick the black pebble?" Instead, she redefined the problem as "How can I avoid the appearance that I picked up the black pebble?" It's not so much "thinking around the problem" as it is redefining the problem so that it can be solved in a favorable way. This point was also made in the previous chapter on problem solving. In a review article of research and theory on creativity, Mumford and Gustafson (1988) noted that creativity is related to "information that is seemingly irrelevant to the solution of the problem at hand" (p. 30). By focusing on the fact that the pebbles on the path were black and white and therefore she could drop one without its being identified, the heroine of this short story was able to generate a novel solution.

Generation, Exploration, and Evaluation

Creativity is a puzzle, a paradox, some say a mystery.

—Margaret A. Boden (1990, p.vii)

If creative thinking is just a variant of everyday problem solving, then there should be general principles that can be applied across domains of knowledge. Are the creative dancer, scientist, teacher, and writer all using the same sorts of processes in their creation despite the fact that they are using different modes of expression with very different problems? Although there are obvious differences, they all have to generate possible solutions to their problem and explore the "problem space," a term that was defined in the problem-solving chapter as all of the possible goals and ways of getting from the start point to the goal. Finke, Ward, and Smith (1992) have posited a two-phase model that they call **geneplore**, named for the repeated cycles of generation and exploration that are part of every problem-solving process. Creative individuals need to be involved and committed so that they continue the processes long enough to allow a creative solution to emerge. Levine (1994) calls the willingness to work on a problem "intimate engagement," a term that connotes the close links among motivation, hard work, time on task, and willingness to explore possibilities.

Evaluation is also a creative act because the problem solver must be able to recognize when a good solution has been obtained (Doolittle, 1995). Effective evaluation is needed to terminate the process or the problem solver can be caught in unending loops of exploration and generation. Notice that a problem-solving view of creativity also entails all of the other stages of cognition. A successful exploration of the problem space requires that the problem solver be able to notice and remember critical aspects of the problem. Thus, as in all of thinking "memory must be tickled."

Although it is clear that memory is an important component of both creative and noncreative problem solving, the utilization of memory must differ in some way between these two processes. When thinking creatively, the memory task is more than retrieval of a known fact; it involves a broader search, with fewer constraints on the type and breadth of information retrieved (Bink & Marsh, 2000). In fact, one detrimental effect of expertise is the finding that the ability to retrieve a well-known solution or response may hinder creativity (Sternberg & O'Hara, 1999). Thus, experts, who can retrieve solutions to problems as readily as we might retrieve an arithmetic fact, are less likely to consider additional possible solutions than the novice who needs to think through a solution. This model of creative thinking offers two possibilities for those who are interested in enhancing creative thinking—(a) conduct broad searches of memory, or in other words, do not stop thinking about a problem as soon as a solution has been found, and (b) practice synthesizing information that has been retrieved (i.e., remembered or "thought of") so that information can be combined in novel ways.

Insight and Incubation

Not surprisingly, both the terms "insight" and "incubation" were discussed in Chapter 9 on problem solving. Insight was described as the sudden awareness of a solution; incubation was described as period of time when an individual is not actively working on a problem that is followed by a successful solution. These two stages in the problem-solving process are often associated with creative solutions. Although these are both "hidden" processes that are seemingly mysterious, it is possible to examine them within the framework of a general cognitive model.

I hope that you can recall from Chapter 2 on memory, the idea that the information people store in memory is connected in weblike networks. For example, your information about flowers is connected such that what you know about roses is (metaphorically) stored close to your information about petunias, azaleas, and other flowers. If you know a great deal about flowers, then you have an extensive and highly interconnected network of information. If you grew up in the tropics, then your knowledge of flowers is probably very different from that of someone who grew up in Antarctica because you probably would have very different information about flowers. The interconnectedness of knowledge is important here. According to a network model of memory, all of your knowledge about flowers is also connected to your knowledge of water and sun, which in turn are connected to many different types of information. Theoretically, if you start at any point in this giant interconnected web, you could trace your way to any other place in the web. A hypothetical schematic of a section of someone's knowledge network is shown in Fig. 10.3.

When a new idea suddenly comes to someone, it means that he has successfully traveled his personal knowledge network from one place to another—the new idea representing the connection between two previously unconnected nodes. Think about someone you love. What sorts of ideas and images come to mind? Does the image of a rose seem appropriate? If so, it may be because I brought your knowledge of roses to mind in the last paragraph and the path from your love to that of roses was "activated." Does the phrase, "My love is like a red, red rose" have any meaning for you? Does the sudden association of your love and roses seem insightful?

Psychologists call the "thinking about" or the "reminding" process spread of activation to denote the idea that the activity that was begun when I told you to think about a loved one, spread to your knowledge of roses. People with large knowledge nets will have more places for the activation to spread, and the best way to have a

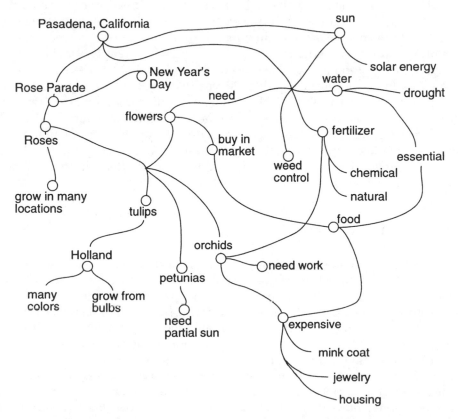

FIG. 10.3. An example of the way information in memory is interconnected in a giant weblike knowledge structure. Creativity involves "noticing" or making unusual connections.

large knowledge net is to have a large number of interconnected knowledge structures. There is no substitute for knowledge about a topic; just as there is no substitute for the ability to use the information stored in memory in thoughtful ways. If you want to be more creative in the sciences, for example, you would need to acquire knowledge about the field so that relevant information will be available for solving problems about science. We use our knowledge nets for new ideas, and skimpy nets yield few ideas. It is the ability to use the information stored in memory that allows us to create by going beyond what we have learned.

Let's consider what else is happening when you solve a problem. Suppose that you are reading a murder mystery in which the prime suspect is the hero, and hence, unlikely to be the murderer. You are focusing on another character who, you believe, "did it." Dutifully, you generate possible solutions and explore the problem space, but to no avail. You cannot connect your prime suspect to the murder scene, so you "forget" about the problem and resume other activities. In other words, you create a period of incubation. Then, when you return to the book, you "see" that it was not your prime suspect, but some other character. Using the jargon of the problem-solving literature, you were fixated on one solution type (finding a way to link your suspect to the crime) and the incubation period allowed you to "forget" this type of solution so that other more profitable paths could be pursued—sort of a release from fixation.

Good problem solvers know how to search through a large problem space, so as to make it an efficient process. When there are a large number of possible paths to a goal, good problem solvers use heuristics, or search plans, to "prune the search tree" (Boden, 1990, p. 78). If you have an extensive knowledge net concerning some topic, then you have more potential paths or links among concepts and more retrieval cues that can help you remember and select relevant information when it is needed.

Analogical Thinking

Analogy is inevitable in human thought.

—Oppenheimer (1956, p. 129)

Analogies underlie much of our everyday thinking, our artistic expressions, and scientific achievements. Sternberg (1977, p. 353) has noted, "reasoning by analogy is pervasive in everyday experience. We reason analogically whenever we make a decision about something new in our experience by drawing a parallel to something old. When we buy a new goldfish because we liked our old one, or when we listen to a friend's advice because it was correct once before, we are reasoning analogically." Thinking involves the ability to note resemblances or correspondence between two objects, while simultaneously discerning that there are also differences. When you use analogies you observe that two entities are similar with respect to some property, and dissimilar with respect to others. Analogies are discussed in several chapters in this book because they are pervasive in human thought.

We utilize analogies to make sense of the world. They help us to understand new events by relating them to ones already known; they allow us to communicate our thoughts; they are the foundations of creative thinking. Analogies are one way of making the unfamiliar known. Analogies are always imperfect because they imply a similarity between objects and events that are not identical. In evaluating and creating analogies, carefully consider the nature of the comparison. If I say that you are like your brother because you both have two eyes, you would certainly object because the number of eyes one has is not a relevant dimension for comparison. However, if I say that you are like your brother because you are both passive and stingy, you might still object, but the nature of the comparison is a relevant one.

One of the most famous creative uses of analogy is seen in the story of Archimedes, a famous Greek mathematician, physicist, and inventor (287–212 B.C.). He was given the task of determining if the crown of King Hiero II was pure gold—the only kind of crown worthy of a king. According to the legend, Archimedes did not know how to solve this problem because of the irregular shape of the crown. One day, while lowering himself into a bathtub full of water, the tub overflowed. The answer was immediately obvious. Like his body, a solid gold crown would displace a volume of water identical to that displaced by a bar of gold that was equal in weight to that of the crown. Because gold is denser than silver, an object (like a crown) would displace less water than another object of the same weight that had been mixed with silver. The story goes on to say that in his excitement he ran naked through the street yelling, "Eureka, I have found it!" He found that Hiero's crown displaced more water than an equal weight of gold, thus showing that the crown had been alloyed with silver (or some other metal less dense than gold). He had a true creative insight mediated by the analogy of his body displacing his bathtub water and the knowledge that a gold crown would displace a predetermined volume of water. (In some versions of the story, the crown was pure gold and the king was very happy, so don't take the story literally.)

Although the use of analogies from distant domains is a common theme in discussions of creativity, in fact, the spontaneous noting of similarities in very different contexts is not a common occurrence. As discussed in Chapter 9 on problem solving, analogical transfer is more likely to occur when we learn to think about the structure of a problem (e.g., displace water as a form of measurement) instead of the surface or domain features (how is a gold crown like taking a bath). Perhaps it is because it is unusual that it figures prominently in our belief about creativity—which requires an unusual outcome or process.

Making the Familiar Strange

Although the usual function of analogies is to make the unfamiliar familiar, Gordon (1961, 1976), the founder of a creative technique known as synectics, suggests that we reverse the process for creative results. Gordon (1976) suggests that we use analogies and metaphors by trying "strange new contexts in which to view a familiar problem" (p. 251). Gordon suggests, as an example, that we consider a naive student examining a fish's heart for the first time. Because the student knows nothing about anatomy, the context is strange, yet the flow of blood through the heart may remind him of a filter system for a local swimming pool. The student's analogy is a creative contribution to his understanding of anatomy.

Gordon has suggested four specific types of analogies for use when attempting to solve a problem creatively. They are personal analogy, direct analogy, symbolic analogy, and fantasy analogy. Each is described in Chapter 9 on the development of problem-solving skills. Analogies can also be used creatively to find problems. For example, executives at Bradford Associates (Westport, Connecticut) spent an afternoon sipping martinis and brainstorming about possible new products that would be marketable. As they were enjoying their own liquid refreshments, they decided that the time had come "for a six-pack that a dog could ask for by name." They are now marketing a chicken-flavored soft drink for dogs known as "Arf'n'Arf." Here is a clear example of the use of analogies to find problems (the need for a doggie soft drink). Similarly, a popular dog product is now being developed for people. Many dogs enjoy munching on bone-shaped biscuits that help to keep their teeth and gums healthy. A similar biscuit that will help humans to keep their gums and teeth healthy is now available on some market shelves.

Bionics is a special type of analogy. It relies on analogies from nature that can be adapted to human problems. For example, special properties of the eyes of beetles have suggested a new type of ground speed indicator for airplanes, and the principles of adhesion used by cockleburs have served as the prototype for Velcro-type closures. Bionics is also concerned that the broad impact of solutions be considered because borrowing another analogy from nature, small changes in our ecological system can result in disastrous consequences to other life forms in the food chain. Papanek (1977) calls this the "total-chain-of-design idea." It requires the creative consideration of entire systems and interrelationships of parts.

Weber and Perkins (1992) conceptualize the creative process as finding ways to bridge different problem spaces, so that solutions can be applied and modified across domains of knowledge. Consider modern surgery to unclog clogged arteries. A thin tube is threaded into the artery. When the clog is reached, a small "balloon" is inflated in the artery to open the clogged area. This is the same technique that has been used by plumbers to open clogged pipes. Thus, cardiac surgeons are saving lives with a common problem-solving technique that was designed for plumbing. Many creative acts involve adapting solutions from one field for use in an unrelated field.

Remote Associations Test

There is a test of creativity that rests on the notion that creative people can form connections between seemingly very different topics. Mednick and Mednick (1967) have created a test to tap this dimension of creativity. It is called the Remote Associations Test or RAT for short. Test takers are given three words and are asked to come up with a fourth word that relates to all three. As an example, what word relates to:

RIVER   NOTE   BLOOD

Can you come up with the relational word? (The answer is bank—river bank, bank note, blood bank.) Try some other remote associations similar to the ones on the RAT:

1. BOARD   DUCK   DOLLAR
2. FILE   HEAD   TOE
3. BOILED   LID   FLOWER
4. BALL   MALARIA   BUTTER
5. CLASS   STAGE   SOCCER

(The answers are at the end of the chapter.)

Do creative people come up with remote associations when they think creatively? It seems that some do, but there is very little direct evidence that tests like the RAT can predict creativity in natural contexts. An invention by Michael Reynolds of Taos, New Mexico, seems to epitomize this type of thinking. He combined his knowledge of the high cost of housing with the problem of soda cans littering the countryside and the proverbial lightbulb went on. He made these remote associations and constructed a house of aluminum soda cans. For his second house, he is filling the cans with water so that the solar-heated cans of water can supplement his home energy needs.

ENCOURAGING CREATIVITY

One of the objections I hear to setting forth creativity as a goal for higher education is, 'We can't all be Einsteins.' This is undeniable; it is also irrelevant.

—Hutchings (1986, p. 14)

There has been considerable debate over the question of whether it is possible to make people more creative by providing them with special experiences that are designed to enhance creativity. There is a sizable research literature that shows that it is possible. This notion is not really a surprising conclusion given that creative thinking shares many features with everyday sorts of problem solving, and the evidence reviewed in the first chapter and several places throughout this book showed that improved thinking is a possible outcome of education. In a review of the research literature on creativity, Baer (1993) cautiously concluded that there are many variables that are involved in the enhancement of creative thinking.

What are the many variables that are important in determining when and how much creativity can be enhanced?

The Person, the Problem, the Process

Discovery consists of looking at the same thing as everyone else and thinking something different.

—Albert Szent-Gjorgyi (Nobel Prize winner in medicine; quoted in von Oech, 1983, p. 7)

It is clear that creativity is not something that exists in an all-or-none fashion. People are more or less creative, just as they are more or less athletic or good-looking or prejudiced. The question of whether there is some inborn or inherited trait that is associated with high creativity has been difficult to answer. Most of the research has centered on the relationship between creativity and intelligence. Are intelligent people the most creative people?

In general, people with above average scores on intelligence tests tend to be creative, whereas those with low IQ scores tend not to be; but the relationship is not a perfect one. It is not true that the very smartest people are always the most creative. There is a certain minimum intelligence that is needed to be creative, but beyond the minimal level, IQ doesn't seem to matter much. Even if you're not a particularly intelligent person, you may have great creative potential. In addition, we all have different abilities. A person with a broad knowledge net about football strategies and skill in running and throwing is more likely to be a creative football player than an individual who has little knowledge of the field and is clumsy with a football, but the second individual may be more creative in an unrelated domain of knowledge such as poetry or ballet.

Creativity as a Goal

We want creative citizens, who can take responsibilities and who are able to solve problems that do not yet exist today.

—Olli-Pekka Heinonen (Finland's minister of education, quoted in Shavinina, 2001, p. 292)

The easiest way to enhance creativity is to value it. In an experimental study, Shalley (1991) found that college students who were told that creativity was valued produced more creative products (had creativity goals) than students who had been told that they were being judged on the number of products they produced (had productivity goals) or told nothing about expectations for creativity or number produced. The underlying idea behind this research was that most people pay more attention and exert more effort if they have clear goals. It seems that people will be more creative when they are told to be creative. This is probably not a surprising result to the college students who are reading this. After all, how often are students encouraged or even permitted to be creative in school? Most often, the learning goal in school is to be able to repeat back something that was learned in class or to be able to apply a skill in an appropriate setting. Apparently, we can be more creative if we are expected to be creative.

Environmental Factors

People will be most creative when they feel motivated primarily by the interest, enjoyment, satisfaction, and challenge of the work itself—not by external pressures.

—Hennessey and Amabile (1988, p. 11)

Creative thinking, like all activities, takes place in a social context—a fact that is often overlooked in the cognitive literature. Amabile (1996, 1997, 2001) has studied the environmental-social factors that can encourage or discourage creativity. Like other researchers in the field of creativity, she concluded that much of what happens in school and work settings is not conducive to the development of creativity. She found that creative individuals often view their work as a labor of love. They work long hours because they are impelled by their curiosity and their own desire to achieve a goal. Hard work is a repeated theme among those who study the creative process. This sort of motivation is called **intrinsic motivation** because it comes from within the individual. By contrast, much of the motivation provided at school and work is **extrinsic motivation**, which is motivation that comes from others, such as promises of a good grade or money. According to Amabile, the best way to promote creativity is to arrange the environment so as to maximize intrinsic motivation. Six conditions that tend to kill intrinsic motivation are (a) constant evaluation, (b) surveillance, (c) reward, (d) competition, (e) restricted choice (e.g., limited choice of materials to use), and (f) an extrinsic orientation toward work.

Most school and work environments tend to be heavily weighted towards the negative end of these six factors; teachers and supervisors watch while students and employees work, competition is either overt or covert, but almost always present, and the workers receive grades or payment for their efforts. It is impossible to avoid extrinsic motivators completely as there will always be deadlines, competition, and restrictions, for example. Despite these realities, it is possible to design school and work environments to foster creativity by reducing the focus on extrinsic motivators and emphasizing the intrinsic rewards of the creative process. Environmental factors like these are only part of the creativity equation—creativity needs more than a conducive environment to flourish. In addition to changes in the environment, creativity training also needs a skills component. No one can become a creative scientist or great author or talented artist without the factual knowledge and technical skills that are relevant to their chosen field. There is no substitute for knowledge.

Not surprisingly, blanket statements like "external rewards hinder creativity" have been challenged by several researchers who found that, at least sometimes, external rewards can stimulate creative responses. For example, in Nakamura and Csikszentmihalyi's (2001) case study of the life of Linus Pauling, it is clear that Pauling changed the focus of his work to organic chemistry because he was given grant money for research in organic chemistry. He then went on to make highly creative advances in this new field of study, so the extrinsic motivation provided by the grants did not seem to diminish his creative genius; instead the grants refocused his creativity in a new domain. In a study of the effects of extrinsic rewards on creativity, researchers found that there are many other variables that influence creativity and, under some conditions, external rewards like providing money for creative outcomes, can enhance creativity (Eisenberger & Cameron, 1998). The effect of intrinsic rewards on creativity remains a contested area of research.

There is at least one conclusion on which everyone can agree: A quality education (both inside and outside of school) will give you the basis for the remote associations or divergent thoughts or novel ideas. Creative people need a head filled with thoughts and facts in order to create with them. The inferences from Amabile's work are clear: cultivate a love of learning, reward your own creative efforts, take the college courses that will fill your mind with new thoughts (and not just the easiest courses offered). Creative endeavors result from hard, intellectual work that is self-motivated and self-monitored. Don't be afraid to engage in it.

Personality Factors

Multiple studies have found that the primary determinant of new product failure is an absence of innovativeness.

—Sethi, Smith, and Park (2001, p. 73)

There are certain personality factors that are consonant with creativity. Because creativity (as we have defined it) requires an unusual or novel act, the creative individual must not be swayed by a need for conformity nor be resistant to change. In order to persist in doing or thinking the unusual, the creative person will also need to have enough self-confidence so as not to be dissuaded from a pursuit when others denigrate or deride it. There also needs to be a love or joy with pursuits that are cognitively complex. Perhaps there is some validity to the notion of the "eccentric" artist or scholar. If you read the first chapter of this book, you will recognize that these are dispositions of critical thinkers—not surprisingly, I return to some of the same themes that were presented in the first chapter as I near the end of this book.

The creative person must be self-motivated so that he or she will persist at a task. Sometimes, school experiences tend to favor the noncreative students, as many traditional assignments don't call for creative responses. Creative people may have to create their own rewards for their actions and find satisfaction in the creative process itself. The ability and willingness to take risks and to tolerate ambiguity is also needed for creative acts. When we try to do things differently, we sometimes fail. Most of the great discoveries in modern times were initially met with ridicule and repeated failure (a horseless carriage, a machine that could fly, etc.). We need to teach children and learn for ourselves that failure is an important part of life and that every great success was built upon previous failures. Creative people are able to "slow down" and take the time to review and rethink their usual way of doing things and resist quick closure on problems (Larson, 2001). In the first chapter of this book, I made the case for the importance of a critical-thinking attitude. The same themes are repeated in this chapter on enhancing creativity. The only seeming contradiction comes from recent research on creativity in teams. Team cohesion seems to be detrimental to creativity (Sethi, Smith, & Park, 2001). If team members are quick to agree with each other (high cohesion), then unusual solutions or conclusions will never emerge from a team because usual and common outcomes will be generated most often. We need teams that foster and encourage dissent (in a positive way). Group leaders who insist on consensus are inadvertently stifling creativity. If everyone in a group agrees, then it is likely that only one person is doing the thinking. Of course, it can be uncomfortable to "go against the crowd," yet creative people are able to be a lone dissenter. In order to be an effective dissenter, creative people often persuade group members to consider seriously his or her unusual perspective. In real-life settings, social skills are vital for successful ideas.

In a study of creative people (Barron, 1958), writers, artists, musicians, and mathematicians were given a battery of tests to determine if they had any personality traits in common. In general, these highly creative individuals were nonconforming, unconventional, and generally less concerned with "making a good impression." One contemporary American hero is the recently deceased Richard Feynman. Feynman was the Nobel prize-winning physicist who became famous in the nonscientific world when he investigated the tragic explosion of the Challenger. He demonstrated that "O" rings, rubber circular gaskets used on the Challenger, get brittle when they get cold. His simple test consisted of dunking an "O" ring in ice water and showing that it could crack when cold. The attitude of risk taking and nonconformity is exemplified by the title of an autobiographical book about his life entitled *What Do You Care What Other People Think?* (1989). Of course, this does not mean that if you become nonconforming and unconventional, you'll then become highly creative, but it suggests that a more open-minded and less self-conscious approach to life's problems can pay off. Feynman also demonstrated a natural curiosity and immense breadth of knowledge. His interests weren't limited to physics and extended to many domains including the arts and music.

I had the great honor to meet this remarkable man. I recall with great clarity a time when I sat next to him at an informal dinner party. He remarked to my daughter, who was young at that time, that growing old was a peculiar thing. When he was my daughter's age, he could never get enough dessert, and now that he is old and can have all the dessert he wishes, he no longer wants it! At the time, I thought that this was an odd discussion between a child and older man, but now I think it was just part of the eccentricity that marked his genius.

STRATEGIES FOR CREATIVE THINKING

The nation that neglects creative thought today will assuredly have its nose ground into the dust of tomorrow.

—Fred Hoyle (1915–2001, astronomer and physicist)

Creativity has never been given the attention it deserved in standard educational settings. Over four decades ago, Lowenfeld (1962) called creativity "education's stepchild," a fact that remains true today. There seems to be no place in the traditional school curriculum for creativity training. There have been many programs developed with the specific goal of training people to be creative in order to fill this gap, probably because leaders in the corporate and manufacturing worlds know that they must produce new and better products than the competition, or they will find themselves working for the competition.

Basic Principles

Although there are considerable differences among creativity-training programs, they all share some basic common principles:

1. Teach students to think of different ways to accomplish an objective and then how to select the best one.
2. Provide plenty of examples and exercises to model and practice creative skills.
3. Teach students how to ask relevant questions and how to discover when a problem exists.
4. Evaluate the quality of an idea by its consequences.
5. Reward original and relevant ideas, but be certain to keep the reward secondary to the enjoyment of the creative process. Let students know that their ideas are valuable.
6. Provide unstructured situations. Teach them the value of persistence when they fail.
7. Provide students with a tangible plan for finding solutions. This means that they should be trained in ways that will help them to make relevant information that they have stored in memory accessible and to find ways to bridge areas of knowledge. Plans include recognizing puzzling facts, seeking information, generating possible solutions, changing perspectives, and restating the goal.
8. Restrain from labeling or categorizing problems or solutions too quickly in the problem-solving process because labeling tends to encourage fixation, the opposite sort of set that is needed for flexible thinking.
9. Create the expectation that creative outcomes result from hard work, persistence, a broad knowledge base, and the willingness to continue thinking after a satisfactory solution or answer has been found.
10. Encourage risk taking and nonconformity, along with a repertoire of responses that are needed for teamwork.

You may be thinking that there is no such thing as "strategies for creative thinking" because creativity involves breaking rules, not following them—a sort of a free activity. Bailin (1987) has argued against this notion of creativity. As she noted, most creative actions take place within a framework of rules. Even the most beautiful sonnet contains 14 lines of specified meter and rhyme, all great ballets are performed with the principles and techniques of dance, and all scientific discoveries are made by experts who are knowledgeable in their field. In order to depart from a framework or to bend the usual rules, the creative individual must have some knowledge of convention as well as some guidelines for unconventional thinking.

Productive Thinking Program

One of the first and best-known creative training programs was developed by Covington, Crutchfield, Davies, and Olton in 1974 for fifth and sixth graders. The program consisted of a workbook in which the brother-and-sister team of Jim and Lila had to solve a series of detective stories. The reader, along with Jim and Lila, had to formulate hypotheses, gather evidence, and ask questions in order to solve the crime. If you've already read Chapter 6, "Thinking as Hypothesis Testing", you'll recognize this sequence as the steps used in experimental methods of discovery. All along Jim and Lila were guided by a wise "Uncle John" who would provide hints and explain their mistakes. This program was discussed briefly in Chapter 9 on problem solving.

One of my favorite stories from the Productive Thinking Program concerns a missing jewel. As guests arrived at a party, they brought wrapped gifts for the wealthy hostess. Suddenly, the lights went out, and when they went on again a valuable jewel was missing. Lila and Jim had to determine what had happened to the jewel. No one could have left or entered the room as the door had remained locked. The window was opened, but there were no footsteps in the fresh snow that covered the ground. Later we learn that there is a feather on the floor and that one of the boxes has a hole in the bottom. Have you solved the crime by now? A trained pigeon was taken from a wrapped box and used to transport the jewel to an accomplice. The pigeon escaped with the jewel by flying through the open window.

It takes Lila and Jim a while to find and put together the clues in order to solve this crime. Crutchfield (1966) believes that with direct training with stories like this one, children can learn to think more creatively. The reader engages in the discovery process along with the protagonists, and may even solve the problem before Lila and Jim. A modern version of this sort of student involvement in using clues and solving problems that are embedded in realistic situations is now on interactive computer discs. For example, *The Adventures of Jasper Woodbury*, an interactive educational program that teaches mathematics and other sorts of problem-solving skills was developed by the Technology Group at Vanderbilt University (Van Haneghan, Barron, Young, Williams, Vye, & Bransford, 1992). It includes many of the principles that are discussed in this chapter. The Jasper Woodbury series has been constantly evaluated over the last 10 years for its effectiveness in teaching mathematical problem-solving skills. The researchers report generally positive results (*http://peabody. vanderbilt.edu/ctrs/lsi/research.htm*).

Several other programs have recently arrived on the market or are scheduled for release in the near future. Although many of these programs are promising, potential users are urged to ask for the evidence that they actually work as promised. It is very difficult to find solid evidence that children trained with these methods actually grow up to be more creative adults or that they ever apply these skills in real-life settings. This is, of course, the real goal of any thinking skills program—use of the skills in unrelated situations. The teacher was an important variable in any program's success because it is what students are asked to do with information that is important in determining the outcome.

There are some popular programs that claim to increase creativity, but unless there are solid data to back up these claims, you are not thinking critically if you accept the claims at face value. Mall bookstores have rows of books that lure readers who want to be more creative to "try on different hats" and to stimulate different ways of thinking by "thinking outside of the box"—quick claims that offer little in the way of empirically validated findings (DeBono, 1985, 1992). Critical thinkers look for evidence to support claims—especially when the claim is that thinking can be improved.

Quantity Breeds Quality

Since 1990 30% of (Glaxo Wellcome's) revenues has come from new products . . . Glaxo Wellcome aims to increase research and development productivity threefold to produce 20 new compounds from exploratory research each year, leading to the launch of three significant new products annually.

—Sue Godfrey (executive director, Glaxo Wellcome, 2001, p. 1)

The notion that if you have lots of ideas, some of them will be good is the major thrust of **brainstorming**. Brainstorming was discussed in Chapter 9 on the development of problem-solving skills as a way to find solution paths that solve problems. It is a creative way to generate solution paths and is often used in creative problem solving. Brainstorming is a way of producing a list of ideas that can subsequently be evaluated. Although brainstorming can be done individually, it is more commonly considered a group activity. The only rule of brainstorming is that all judgment be deferred until some later time so that no one hesitates to offer unusual or off-beat ideas. Osborn (1963) offers many examples in his book, *Applied Imagination*. For example, Osborn reports that a 15-minute brainstorming session at American Cyanamid Corporation produced 92 ideas, or more than six ideas per minute. This was an average of eight ideas per participant. Simonton (referenced in Begley, 1993) found that creative people had many more bad ideas and many more good ideas than their less creative peers because they had many more ideas overall.

The quantitative advantages of brainstorming are without question. But do more ideas necessarily imply better ones? Often, the best ideas result from the combination (synergy) and alteration of the ideas listed. The atmosphere of deferred judgment is clearly consistent with the discussion on environment presented earlier in the chapter. It encourages risk taking and unconventionality, both of which are prerequisites to creative thinking. At the very least, brainstorming is fun. It is a recommended strategy for enhancing creative thought because it incorporates several of the principles for creative thinking, but the evidence that brainstorming produces more high-quality ideas than other techniques is still limited.

Osborn had a group of parents brainstorm on how to get their children to watch less television and read more books. Read carefully through the list of ideas the parents came up with. It seems to me that some combination of these ideas would surely be effective.

1. Pull plug in TV set.
2. Break up the set.
3. Set a definite time for looking at TV.
4. Arouse interest in books.
5. Acquire a bad horizontal tube.

6. Reorient antenna in order to get bad reception.
7. Select a book that has been seen on TV.
8. Set example by reading yourself.
9. Buy a portable radio for children.
10. Evaluate TV programs.
11. Encourage visits to library.
12. Have the children write book reports.
13. Give money for movies.
14. Donate a TV to library.
15. More outdoor companionship with parents.
16. As a result of seeing TV story (say Robinson Crusoe) children given same book to read and do research on.
17. Start reading aloud to them when young.
18. Read them good books.
19. Make reading as convenient as TV.
20. Give them their own bookcase in room.
21. Give records for Hi-Fi.
22. Give subscriptions to children's magazines.
23. Select books suitable to age.
24. Get them interested in daily newspapers, even if only the comics.
25. Help them with their homework.
26. Select type of news they read.
27. Discuss with them the books they have read.
28. Have them read to you.
29. At PTA meeting, have subject discussed with teachers; get teachers to recommend books.
30. Encourage group reading.
31. Buy them a good dictionary.
32. Always answer questions if you can.
33. Buy a good children's encyclopedia.
34. Institute games requiring the use of words and general knowledge.
35. Get local schools to have course in fast reading and good reading.
36. Have children checked physically—there may be some reason why they are unable to read.
37. In addition to their allowance, give them a fee for each good book that they read.

Creative Ideas Checklist

Another method for producing creative ideas is to present people with a checklist of diverse categories or adjectives or questions that could conceivably apply to the question or problem at hand. These lists are called **creative ideas checklists**. By forcing people to change the type of answer that they are considering, flexibility in thinking is encouraged. Doolittle (1995) found that the use of many different types of solutions is more important in creative problem solving than just having many different solutions that all involve the same category of response. In order to understand this distinction, consider a problem that involves moving A to B. There may be many different ways to move A (car, boat, roller skates), but a flexible list would include other categories of responses such as having them meet in the middle or moving B or moving both to point C, or solving the problem without moving either A or B.

In one study of the use of lists to stimulate creative ideas, Davis and Roweton (1968) gave students the following list, which was labeled "Aids in Thinking of Physical Changes":

a. Add or Subtract Something
b. Change Color
c. Change the Materials
d. Change by Rearranging the Parts
e. Change Shape
f. Change Size
g. Change Design or Style

Students who were given this list were told to, "List as many physical changes as you can for a thumbtack." Davis and Roweton reported that the group that had received the checklist produced a greater number of ideas and more creative ideas than a control group that had not been given the checklist. A cookie manufacturer began making "reverse" chocolate chip cookies—chocolate cookies with white chocolate chips. They have become an overnight financial and taste success. You should recognize this simply as (d) in the above list—a change by rearranging the parts. This simple creative act has paid well for its innovator.

Perhaps the most famous checklist is a generalized one that can be applied in a variety of situations. Whiting (1958, p. 62) attributes this list to Osborn.

Put to Other Uses? New ways to use as is? Other uses if modified?

Adapt? What else is like this? What other idea does this suggest? Does past offer parallel? What could I copy? Whom could I emulate?

Modify? New twist? Change meaning, color, motion, odor, form, shape? Other changes?

Magnify? What to add? More time? Greater frequency? Stronger? Larger? Thicker? Extra value? Plus ingredient? Duplicate? Multiply? Exaggerate?

Minify? What to substitute? Smaller? Condensed? Miniature? Lower? Shorter? Lighter? Omit? Streamline? Split up? Understate?

Substitute? Who else instead? What else instead? Other ingredient? Other material? Other process? Other power? Other place? Other approach? Other tone of voice?

Rearrange? Interchange components? Other pattern? Other layout? Other sequence? Transpose cause and effect? Change pace? Change schedule?

Reverse? Transpose positive and negative? How about opponents? Turn it backward? Turn it upside down? Reverse roles? Change shoes? Turn tables? Turn other cheek?

Combine? How about a blend, an alloy, an assortment, an ensemble? Combine units? Combine purposes? Combine appeals? Combine ideas?

Although there are many such lists, a third one worth considering is from Parnes (1967, p. 231) who suggests that you ask yourself these idea-spurring questions when you're looking for new ideas:

1. Effects on objective?
2. Individuals and/or groups affected?
3. Costs involved?
4. Tangibles involved (material, equipment, etc.)?
5. Moral or legal implications?

6. Intangibles involved (opinions, attitudes, feelings, aesthetic values, etc.)?
7. New problems caused?
8. Difficulties or implementation and follow-up?
9. Repercussions of failure?
10. Timeliness?, etc.

In a recent twist on the idea of lists that stimulate creative thinking, McGuire (1997) listed several techniques for finding creative hypotheses that are worth pursuing. The research literature in psychology and other sciences is huge, but much of it involves problems that are trivial (at least in the opinions of some people). How can researchers find and recognize those research problems that are potentially important? His long list of strategies for answering this question includes: (a) *counterexamples* or thinking about ways the opposite would be true (e.g., instead of thinking that bad parents cause neurosis suppose bad parenting causes good mental health); (b) *reverse causal direction* (e.g., instead of hypothesizing that coffee causes headaches maybe having headaches leads people to drink coffee); (c) *push an example to an extreme* (e.g., if children's use of grammar shows that they learn general grammatical rules what would perfect grammar in children suggest?); (d) *extrapolate from similar problems* (e.g., older adults can improve their memory for names with mnemonics so perhaps they could improve their memory for locations with mnemonics); (e) *shift attention to the opposite end of a problem* (e.g., instead of thinking about the cost of a new technology think about its benefits); and (f) *pay attention to outliers or unusual responses* (what it is about Person X that led her to respond differently from the other participants). McGuire's list is considerably longer than the sample items presented here, but these examples should demonstrate the main idea of manipulating how one thinks to discover hypotheses that are potentially important enough to warrant empirical investigation. He notes that he has only informal data on the effectiveness of these strategies and calls for more research on the important problem of finding out which techniques can enhance creativity.

Although the purpose of creative ideas checklists is to create novel ideas, it is also possible that they could have an inhibiting effect. If you only considered the possibilities on a small checklist, you could miss other ideas by narrowing your search to ones that are suggested by the list. These lists cannot be used as algorithms that would always lead to a creative response, but may be helpful as heuristics to help get a stalled thinking process moving again.

We've all had the experience at one time or another of being "stuck," when ideas don't seem to flow. If you go through these checklists, pondering each item, you're bound to get your thoughts flowing again. Using the cognitive framework introduced earlier, they all provide probes for searching knowledge networks so that different sorts of information can become available for use.

Attribute Listing

More innovation is the key weapon for UK companies to outperform world competitors.

—McHardy and Allan (2000, p. 496)

In **attribute listing**, every characteristic or quality of the item or situation is listed and then examined for possible modification or recombination. Let's try an example.

Suppose you want to make something really different for dinner tonight. In fact, you want to make a food that no one else in the world has ever tasted before. How would you go about doing this? First, you could list many different foods:

eggs
hot dogs
baked Alaska
stewed tomatoes
steak Tartare
chocolate pudding
etc.

Alongside each food, you would list several of its attributes, such as shape, consistency, color, texture, odor, temperature, etc. You'd then randomly pair attributes to come up with a new food. You might think of the "soft and shimmery" attribute of jello and the cold, hard attribute of ice cream and combine the two so that you'd freeze the jello or whip the ice cream. Attribute listing is a good procedure for fashion design. You could list every part of a dress, for example, and every attribute of that part. A partial example is:

Dress Part	Attribute
collars	pointed, rounded, none, Nehru
sleeves	raglan, short, rolled, long
waist	cinched, gathered, dropped, loose
skirt	full, straight, ruffled, pointed

A talented dress designer could combine possible dress attributes, coming up with thousands of unique designs (e.g., a dress with a Nehru collar, short sleeves, gathered waist and ruffled skirt.) This unique combination shows why I should stay out of fashion design—although the resulting dress would be unusual, it would probably not pass the evaluative test for creativity—appropriate or good.

Crovitz's Relational Algorithm

Those of you who have already read Chapter 8 on the development of decision making skills know that an algorithm is a step-by-step guide that leads to a solution. Crovitz's (1970) **Relational Algorithm** is a solution guide that relies on changing the relations among items. Crovitz lists 42 "relational words" (p. 100). They are:

about	at	for	of	round	to
across	because	from	off	still	under
after	before	if	on	so	up
against	between	in	opposite	then	when
among	but	near	or	though	where
and	by	not	out	through	while
as	down	now	over	till	with

When you are in need of a creative solution, you have only to try different ways of "relating" the elements. Crovitz uses Duncker's classic X-ray problem as an example.

Although this problem was described in Chapter 9 on the development of problem-solving skills, I'll present it again briefly. The problem is to get rid of an inoperable stomach tumor with X-rays without harming the healthy tissues. However, when the radiation is intense enough to destroy the tumor, it will also harm the healthy tissue surrounding it. The best solution involves using several weak rays through different parts of the body so that they will summate on the tumor. Crovitz demonstrates how the relational algorithm can be used to find a solution to this and other problems. The procedure is fairly simple. Form a sentence with each relational word using it as it might relate to the tumor. For example:

1. Take the rays **through** the esophagus.
2. Take the sensitivity **from** the tissues.
3. Take tissue **off** the tumor.
4. Take strong rays **after** weak rays.
5. Take a shield **on** stomach walls.
6. Take the tumor **across** the stomach.
7. Take a cannula **through** the stomach wall.
8. Take the power **from** the rays.
9. Take the tumor **to** the exterior. (Crovitz, 1970, p. 102).

Crovitz claims that this method works well because it forces the individual to consider new relationships among the parts of the problem.

Plus, Minus, Interesting

Plus, Minus, Interesting (PMI) is a plan for beginning the problem-solving process that was suggested by DeBono (1976). When you are searching for a solution to an intractable problem, one way to begin is to list all of the "givens" in a problem and all possible solutions (even ones that are unrealistic) and to consider for each what is positive about it, what is negative about it, and what makes it interesting. The idea behind this process is that a careful and methodic consideration of various components of different solutions and other aspects of the problem will help the problem solver to find new solutions by highlighting positive aspects and eliminating negative ones. The use of the "interesting" category will help the problem solver to consider what makes a solution interesting, and thereby lead to the consideration of additional alternatives. It is a plan for seeking information that may be relevant to a solution, and like all of the other strategies, it provides a guide for exploring knowledge nets.

Activating Inert Knowledge

All of the strategies for creative thinking are designed to increase the "flow of ideas." Psychologists call this improving **ideational fluency**. In PMI, for example, the problem solver is given a plan for generating ideas. She is told the kind of information she should consider (givens and possible solutions) and how to evaluate them. Earlier in this book, I talked about the importance of tickling memory. This is particularly important when you seem to have "run out of ideas." There are several simple plans that can be employed when this happens. For example, in a study described by Perkins (1985), children were instructed to list words that they might use when writing a composition about a selected topic. The children were given a few minutes to complete this prewriting task. The researchers reported that after only a few hours of training with this method, the children were writing longer and better passages. Let's consider the simple elegance behind this procedure. By listing topic-relevant words, the students were required to think about their knowledge of the topic *before* they began to write. They made their knowledge about the topic more available for use in their composition. It forced them to plan their response.

Writing is one of the most creative tasks that we can be asked to do. Students and even prolific authors often complain about "writer's block." This simple method, which is applicable at all levels, should help to eliminate writer's block because it is a way of activating one's knowledge of the topic so that it can be used. I have used it in several college classes that I teach with good results.

Browsing

In our society we have great institutions that function as repositories for ideas. They are called libraries. Wicker (1981) suggests that we "probe library sources" to generate new ideas. Pick up newspapers and magazines, case histories and biographies, scholarly journals, joke books, and even children's literature. Use a broad range of sources. You can't make "remote associations" or borrow ideas from other fields if your own knowledge is confined to a narrow discipline. This technique is easier than ever because there are many quality library resources available online, so we can "browse" in our jammies late at night, but be careful—there is also a great deal of worthless and even harmful junk on the Internet. Be sure that you can tell the difference between scholarly and applied research and unsubstantiated "hot air" that is blowing around on the Internet.

Use qualitative and quantitative information. Census reports can suggest new problems because they succinctly state what people are doing, where they are doing it, what they are eating, how they are living, and how they are dying. Learn something new every day. If you pick up a journal at random and read one new article a day, you'll be surprised at how the newly acquired information crops up in everyday contexts. You can also browse with quality television shows like *Nova*, *60 Minutes*, and *National Geographic*. They contain a wealth of fascinating information on almost any topic of interest. Don't forget to go to museums, art galleries, theater, and the opera. If you feel that you can't afford these outings, remember that many have a "free day" once a month and offer reduced rates for students, the elderly, and groups.

Visual Thinking

When Mozart was asked where he got his ideas he said, "Whence and how they come I know not; nor can I force them."

—(quoted in Vernon, 1970, p. 53)

Creative thinking often calls for images. The musician must first "hear" the sounds before she places the notes on paper; the poet must hear the rhyme before it is written; the painter must see the forms before his first brush stroke; and the chef must "taste" the combination of ingredients before the new recipe is created. It does seem that there are certain creative acts for which words are inadequate. Most people report that, at least some of the time, they think in images. An **image** is a picture-like representation in the mind. (See Chapter 2 on the development of memory skills for discussion of imagery.)

Gonzalez, Campos, and Perez (1997) examined the relationship between imagery and creativity. They gave high school students tests of imagery and spatial ability and the Torrence Test of Creative Thinking. They found positive relationships between imagery and creativity, which were stronger for the students with high IQs than for students who score within the average range on intelligence tests. Other researchers have suggested a relationship between creativity and imagery. The rationale behind this proposed relationship is that good imagers should be able to "see" problems in ways that should help them to generate solutions that are different from their peers who are low in the ability to create images. A suggested method for solving problems is to draw a diagram, thus transforming a verbal problem into a visual one. Adams (1979) calls visual thinking an "alternative thinking language." It is an alternative to verbal-based thought. Adams suggests that we each take a drawing course to improve our ability to see and, in turn, to think creatively. He claims that we can improve our visual thinking with practice, but like many similar claims, the evidence is not presented in a form that can be scrutinized.

Imagine the following (Adams, 1979, p. 91):

1. A pot of water coming to a boil and boiling over;
2. Your Boeing 747 being towed from the terminal, taxiing to the runway, waiting for a couple of other planes, and then taking off;
3. Your running cow changing slowly into a galloping racehorse;
4. An old person you know well changing back into a teenager;
5. A speeding car colliding with a giant feather pillow;
6. The image in (5) in reverse.

Putting It All Together

Several different strategies or methods to produce creative thoughts have been presented. It would be naive to believe that if you can recite each of these methods, you will automatically have creative thoughts. They are merely guidelines for hard work, and some of us will have to work harder than others.

It is clear that creative thinking is a skill that can be cultivated (Shalley, 1991). The strategies presented in this chapter are the plans for developing that skill. You may be wondering, "Where do I begin?" You begin with a problem or a need. For some, creative ideas will immediately seem to flow; for others it will be more like pulling teeth. If you find yourself "out of fresh new ideas," try the techniques listed above. Visualize the situation, use analogies and metaphors, consider relations, list attributes, mull checklists, and brainstorm. The creative process within you should ignite with some help from these strategies.

APPLYING THE FRAMEWORK

In applying the general thinking skills framework to creative thinking, consider the following questions.

1. What Is the Goal?

The creative process is defined by its outcome. The goal in thinking creatively is the production of a novel and appropriate response. Often it also involves the identification of a novel problem. The creative problem solver knows which problems are solvable and worth solving. In the language of investment theory, they buy low and sell high (become interested in the problem when the general interest level is low and move on to other problems when the problem becomes popular).

2. What Is Known?

A point that was made in this chapter is that one cannot be creative in a vacuum. You need the knowledge and skills of a domain to be creative. There is no substitute for information about the problem. You may have the potential to become a truly great architect or writer, but without knowledge of these fields, it is unlikely that you will design an innovative structure or write a truly great novel. In the problem about the merchant's daughter that was told in this chapter, there would have been no creative answer if she had not used her knowledge about the dishonest money lender to watch closely when he picked up the pebbles. Similarly, a careful consideration of the particular aspects of any problem is needed for finding problems and for finding solutions. Begin the creative process by listing the "givens."

3. Which Thinking Skill or Skills Will Get You to Your Goal?

This is really the question of how can we be creative. Numerous skills were suggested to guide the creative thinking process. The skill you select will depend on the nature of the problem. For example, visualizing the problem is more likely to be helpful with problems that have a spatial aspect to them such as geometry problems or terrain problems. The skill of generating a list of topic-relevant words can be helpful in a variety of situations, but seems particularly well suited for writing and composing. Creative thinking checklists are useful in design problems; whereas "plus, minus, interesting" can be used anytime you find that you don't know how to begin finding a solution. The following creative thinking skills were developed in this chapter. Review each skill and be sure that you understand how to use each one.

- Defining a problem in multiple ways.
- Brainstorming to increase the number of ideas produced.
- Working with people from different backgrounds in order to increase the probability of bisociative thinking.
- Considering the physical changes listed in the creative ideas checklist.
- Arranging the environment to maximize intrinsic motivation.
- Encouraging an attitude of risk taking.
- Evaluating possible solutions using the questions suggested by Parnes (1967).
- Listing and combining attributes to devise a novel product.
- Forming sentences about the problem using relational words.
- Evaluating solutions and other aspects of the problem along the dimensions of plus, minus, interesting.
- Listing terms that are related to the problem before you attempt a solution.

- Gathering additional information.
- Using analogies to make the unfamiliar known and distorting analogies to make the familiar unknown.
- Visualizing the problem.
- Using the hypothesis generating suggestions made by McGuire (counterexamples, opposites, anomalous data, and the others.)
- Discouraging group cohesiveness so unusual thoughts can be considered.

4. Have You Reached Your Goal?

Because the creative process is judged by its outcome, the solution or product will need to be evaluated along the twin dimensions of originality and appropriateness. The evaluation is also a component in the creative process. If it fails on either of these dimensions, then the thinking process will have to begin again until a creative outcome is produced.

CHAPTER SUMMARY

1. Creativity involves the dual notion of unusual or unique and good or useful. It always involves judgment, and people may not agree on which actions or outcomes deserve to be labeled "creative."

2. DeBono has made a distinction between vertical thinking and lateral thinking. Vertical thinking is logical and straightforward, whereas lateral thinking is a creative way to think "around" a problem.

3. An increasingly popular view in psychology is that creative individuals are not qualitatively different from the rest of us. We all have the ability to be creative.

4. Virtually all creative acts will involve novel ways of defining a problem and the selection of relevant information.

5. Creativity has been described as a blend of sensitivity, synergy, and serendipity. It is as if a fortuitous event brings together remote ideas in a person who is sensitive to their combination.

6. Creativity can be understood as a cognitive process that involves using the information stored in memory to go beyond what is learned from experience. Cognitive psychologists describe the process as a spread of activation through a knowledge network with repeated cycles of generation and exploration.

7. Although it is true that, in general, intelligent people are more creative than less intelligent people, it seems that a minimal level of intelligence is all that is needed for creative expression.

8. Analogies are often part of the creative process in which solutions are adapted from different domains of knowledge.

9. Creative people tend to be self-motivated, persistent, tolerant of ambiguity, self-confident, and willing to take risks.

10. Intrinsic motivation seems to be one of the best predictors of creative behavior. In order to encourage the production of creative outputs, the environment should be designed to support intrinsic motivation.

11. Several strategies to foster creative thinking were presented. Brainstorming is based on the supposition that if you have many ideas some of them will be good. Each item on a checklist of creative ideas can be applied to a problem to see if a creative

spark is struck. Crovitz's relational algorithm relies on changing the relations among the parts of a problem to arrive at a solution. The PMI strategy encourages novel solutions by requiring the problem solver to evaluate various aspects of the problem. Analogies and metaphors tune us in to similarities and differences that can be valuable in creating novel solutions. Visual thinking seems to be involved in many sorts of creative endeavors—especially the arts and sciences. The easiest way to foster creativity is to value it.

12. All of the strategies to enhance creativity involve searching an individual's knowledge net so that remote ideas can be associated, analogies applied across domains of knowledge, and information that is stored in memory can become available.

TERMS TO KNOW

You should be able to define or describe the following terms and concepts. If you find that you're having difficulty with any term, be sure to reread the section in which it is discussed.

Creativity. The act of producing something that is original and useful.

Vertical Thinking. Thinking that is logical and straightforward. Used in the refinement and development of ideas. Compare with lateral thinking.

Lateral Thinking. Thinking "around" a problem. Used to generate new ideas. Sometimes used as a synonym for creative thinking. Compare with vertical thinking.

Sensitivity. Responsiveness to the information we perceive through our senses, which includes "noticing" stimuli that may be critical to a creative solution.

Synergy. The bringing together of seemingly disparate parts into a useful and functioning whole. Creative thinking often seems to involve such combinations.

Bisociative Thinking. Bringing together two previously unassociated ideas or "frames of reference."

Serendipity. A happy, unexpected discovery.

Paradigm. An example that is used as a pattern.

Geneplore. Term coined by Finke, Ward, and Smith (1992) to denote the cycles of generation and exploration that are part of the creative process.

Bionics. The use of analogies from nature that can be adapted to human problems.

Intrinsic Motivation. Inherent desire to engage in a task for its own sake and without regard for reward or punishment.

Extrinsic Motivation. Engaging in a task in order to receive reward or to avoid punishment.

Brainstorming. A group or individual method for generating solution paths for problems. Problem solvers are encouraged to think up wild, imaginative solutions and to defer judgment on these solutions until a later time when they may be modified or combined. The goal is to produce a large number of possible solutions.

Creative Ideas Checklists. Lists that suggest ways to generate creative ideas by varying a problem's components and relationships among the components.

Attribute Listing. A method of generating creative solutions in which every characteristic or quality of the item or situation is listed and then examined for possible modification or recombination.

Relational Algorithm. A method for generating creative ideas that relies on changing the relations among items using relational words such as "on," "between," "under," and "through."

Plus, Minus, Interesting. De Bono's (1976) plan for searching for a solution by noting positive, negative, and other interesting aspects of the solutions being considered.

Ideational Fluency. The process of generating many ideas in order to solve problems.

Image. A picture-like representation in the mind.

Answers to remote associations presented earlier in the chapter: 1. Bill, 2. Nail, 3. Pot, 4. Fly, 5. Coach.

11

The Last Word

Thinking is like loving and dying:
Each must do it for him (her) self.

—Anonymous

You may find that this is your favorite chapter because it is essentially a blank chapter. As you worked your way through this book, you learned information that should help you to become a better thinker. This is especially true if you also worked your way through the exercises, questions, and reviews in the Exercise Book that accompanies this text. Each chapter dealt primarily with one type of thinking category. This was necessary because a large block of information needed to be broken down so that it could be presented in manageable units. Unfortunately, thinking doesn't break into neat and separate categories and mixed sorts of skills are needed in most situations. Memory must always be accessed, the type of representation and the words we use will influence how we think, evidence always needs to be considered, thinking must be logical, and so on. As you go through life, you will need to use all of the skills that you practiced and improved upon in each of the chapters. But, most importantly, you need to adopt the attitudes and dispositions of a critical thinker. You need to find problems that others have missed, support conclusions with good evidence, and work persistently on a host of problems. I hope that your encounters with this book will help you become a better thinker.

This is also a good time to step back and reflect on the definition of critical thinking that was presented in the first chapter and the broad categories of information and strategies in the following chapters. Does the working definition of critical thinking seem like it captured the multiple dimensions of complexity that are inherent in critical thinking? Can you and will you use some of the thinking skills in your own life—to make decisions, read about and plan research, understand the structure of a written passage, think creatively, remember more effectively, and more? Are you more likely to have a desirable outcome because of something that you learned? Have you adopted at least some of the attitudes of a critical thinker?

Although this is a nonchapter, there is a corresponding chapter in the Exercise Book, *Thinking Critically About Critical Thinking*, that requires you to select and integrate thinking skills as you think through a variety of problems. As you work on these problems, try to put the entire text together in some way that is useful and meaningful to you. You are what and how you think. Be sure to act on your thoughts and to use them to advance yourself and to improve even a small corner of the world. Think well and with great wisdom. The future depends on it.

Reprinted with special permissions of King Features Syndicate.

References

Adams, A., Carnine, D., & Gersten, R. (1982). Instructional strategies for studying content area texts in the intermediate grades. *Reading Research Quarterly, 18*(1), 27–55.

Adams, J. L. (1979). *Conceptual blockbusting: A guide to better ideas.* New York: Norton.

Alcock, J. E. (1981). *Parapsychology: Science or magic?* Oxford, England: Pergamon.

Allegretti, C. L., & Frederick, J. N. (1995). A model for thinking critically about ethical issues. *Teaching of Psychology, 22,* 46–48.

Allport, G. W. (1954). *The nature of prejudice.* Cambridge, MA: Addison-Wesley.

Amabile, T. M. (1996). *Creativity in context: Update to the social psychology of creativity.* Boulder, CO: Westview.

Amabile, T. M. (1997). Motivating creativity in organizations: On doing what you love and loving what you do. *California Management Review, 40,* 39–58.

Amabile, T. M. (2001). Beyond talent: John Irving and the passionate craft of creativity. *American Psychologist, 56,* 333–336.

American Psychiatric Association. (1994). *Diagnostic and statistical manual of mental disorders.* Washington, DC: Author.

American Psychological Association. (1992). Learner-centered psychological principles: Guidelines for school redesign and reform. *The Psychology Teacher Network, 2,* 5–12.

Anderson, B. F. (1980). *The complete thinker: A handbook of techniques for creative and critical problem solving.* Englewood Cliffs, NJ: Prentice-Hall.

Arasteh, A. R., & Arasteh, J. D. (1976). *Creativity in human development.* New York: Schenkman.

Aristotle. (1954). Rhys Roberts (Trans.). *Rhetoric III* (1410b, 1st Modern Library ed.). New York: Modern Library (exact wording varies by translation).

Arkes, H. R. (1996). The psychology of waste. *Journal of Behavior and Decision Making, 9,* 213–224.

Arkes, H. R., & Hammond, K. R. (1986). Law. In H.R. Arkes & K.R. Hammond (Eds), *Judgement and decision making: An interdisciplinary reader* (pp. 211–212). Cambridge, MA: Cambridge University Press.

Asimov, I. (1989, March 31). Combatting US scientific illiteracy. *Los Angeles Times,* p. 8.

Atkinson, R. C. (1975). Mnemotechnics in second-language learning. *American Psychologist, 30*(8), 821–828.

Azar, B. (2000, May). Blinded by hindsight. *Monitor on Psychology,* pp. 28–29.

Baddeley, Λ. D. (1986). *Working memory.* Oxford, England UK: Clarendon Press/Oxford University Press.

Baddeley, A. D. (1992). Working memory. *Science, 255*(5044), 556–559.

Baddeley, A. D., & Andrade, J. (2000). Working memory and the vividness of imagery. *Journal of Experimental Psychology: General, 129*(1), 126–145.

Baer, J. (1993). *Creativity and divergent thinking.* Hillsdale, NJ: Lawrence Erlbaum Associates.

Bahrick, H. P., & Hall, L. K. (1991). Lifetime maintenance of high school mathematics content. *Journal of Experimental Psychology: General, 120*(1), 20–33.

Bahrick, H. P., Hall, L. K., & Berger, S. A. (1996). Accuracy and distortion in memory for high school grades. *Psychological Science, 7*(5), 265–271.

Bailin, S. (1987). Creativity and skill. In D.N. Perkins, J. Lochhead, & J. Bishop (Eds.), *Thinking: The second international conference* (pp. 323–332). Hillsdale, NJ: Lawrence Erlbaum Associates.

Baron, J. (1987). An hypothesis about the training of intelligence. In D. N. Perkins, J. Lochhead, & J. Bishop (Eds.), *Thinking: The second international conference* (pp. 60–67). Hillsdale, NJ: Lawrence Erlbaum Associates.

Baron, J. (1990). Harmful heuristics and the improvement of thinking. In D. Kuhn (Ed.), *Developmental perspectives on teaching and learning thinking skills* (pp. 28–47). New York: Basel, Karger.

Baron, J. (1993). Why teach thinking?—An essay. *Applied Psychology: An International Review, 42*, 191–214.

Baron, J. (1994). Nonconsequentialist decisions. *Behavioral and Brain Sciences, 17*, 1–42.

Baron, J. (1995). My side bias in thinking about abortion. *Thinking and Reasoning, 1*, 221–225.

Baron, J. (1997). Biases in the quantitative measurement of values for public decision. *Psychological Bulletin, 122*, 72–88.

Baron, J., & Brown, R. V. (1991). *Teaching decision making to adolescents*. Hillsdale, NJ: Lawrence Erlbaum Associates.

Barron, F. (1958). The psychology of imagination. *Scientific American, 199*, 151–166.

Bartlett, F. C. (1932). *Remembering: A study in experimental and social psychology*. Cambridge, England: Cambridge University Press.

Bartlett, J. (1980). Familiar quotations: A collection of passages, phrases, and proverbs traced to their sources in ancient and modern literature (15th and 125th anniversary eds.). Boston: Little, Brown.

Bartlett, J. (1992). *Familiar quotations* (17th ed.), Boston: Little, Brown.

Bassham, G., & Nardone, H. (1997). Using the film JFK to teach critical thinking. *College Teaching, 45*, 10–11.

Bastardi, A., & Shafir, E. (2000). Nonconsequential reasoning and its consequences. *Current Directions in Psychological Science, 9*(6), 216–219.

Begley, S. (1993, June). The puzzle of genius. Newsweek, pp. 46–49.

Beilensen, J., & Jackson, H. (1992). *Voices of struggle, voices of pride*. White Plains, NY: Peter Pauper Press, Inc.

Benjamin, A. S., Bjork, R. A., & Schwartz, B. L. (1998). The mismeasure of memory: When retrieval fluency is misleading as a metamnemonic index. *Journal of Experimental Psychology: General, 127*, 55–68.

Berger, D. (1995). Errors in judgments and decisions: Understanding our cognitive fallibilities. In P. Foster (Ed.), *Critical Thinking: Views and values in college teaching* (pp. 48–68). Riverside, CA: La Sierra University Press.

Berkowitz, L., & Thome, P. R. (1987). Pain expectation, negative affect, and angry aggression. *Motivation and Emotion, 11*, 183–193.

Berlin, B., & Kay, P. (1969). *Basic color terms: Their universality and evolution*. Berkeley: University of California Press.

Bernstein, D. A. (1995). A negotiation model for teaching critical thinking. *Teaching of Psychology, 22*, 22–24.

Beyth-Marom, R., Dekel, S., Gombo, R., & Shaked, M. (1985). *An elementary approach to thinking under uncertainty*. Hillsdale, NJ: Lawrence Erlbaum Associates.

Bink, M. L., & Marsh, R. I. (2000). Cognitive regularities in creative activity. *Review of General Psychology, 4*, 59–78.

Blasko, D. G. (1999). Only the tip of the iceberg: Who understands what about metaphor? *Journal of Pragmatics, 31*(12), 1675–1683.

Block, R. A. (1985). Education and thinking skills reconsidered. *American Psychologist, 40*, 574–575.

Boden, M. A. (1990). *The creative mind: Myths & mechanisms*. New York: Basic Books.

Bodenmann, G. (1997). Can divorce be prevented by enhancing the coping skills of couples? *Journal of Divorce & Remarriage, 27*, 177–194.

Bollag, B. (1997) *School-reform effort grows in Eastern Europe* [Web Page]. URL http://chronicle.com/search97cgi/s97_cgi? [2000, December 28].

Boring, E. G. (1932). Intelligence as the tests test it. *New Republic, 35*, 35–37.

Bousfield, W. A. (1953). The occurrence of clustering in the recall of randomly arranged associates. *Journal of General Psychology, 49*, 229–240.

Bower, G. (1994, May 25). *Electronic communication from Marina Volkov at the Federation of Behavioral, Pyschological, and Cognitive Sciences*, federation@apa.org

Bower, G. H. (1972). Mental imagery and associative learning. In L. Gregg (Ed.), *Cognition in learning and memory*. New York: Wiley.

Bower, G. H. (1970). Organizational factors in memory. *Cognitive Psychology, 1*, 18–46.

Bower, G. H., & Cirilo, R. K. (1985). Cognitive psychology and text processing. In *Handbook of discourse analysis* (Vol. 1, pp. 71–105). New York: Academic Press.

Bower, G. H., & Clapper, J. P. (1989). Experimental methods in cognitive science. In M. I. Posner (Ed), *Foundations of cognitive science* (pp. 245–301). Cambridge, MA: MIT Press.

Bower, G. H., & Clark, M. C. (1969). Narrative stories as mediators for serial learning. *Psychonomic Science, 14*, 181–182.

Boxall, B. (1993, October 12). Statistics and science can be trusted to suit debate. *The Los Angeles Times*, p. A18.

Bozzell, L. B., III. (1993, July 21). Exposing statistical myths. *The Washington Times*, p. 64.

Bradbury, R. (1950). *Fahrenheit 451*. New York: Simon & Schuster.

Braine, M. D. (1978). On the relation between the natural logic of reasoning and standard logic. *Psychological Review, 85*(1), 1–21.

Bransford, D. (1979). *Human cognition: Learning, understanding and remembering*. Belmont, CA: Wadsworth.

Bransford, J. D., Arbitman-Smith, R., Stein, B. S., & Vye, N. J. (1985). Improving thinking and learning skills: An analysis of three approaches. In J. W. Segal & S. F. Chipman (Eds.), *Thinking and learning skills: Volume 1. Relating instruction to research* (pp. 133–206). Hillsdale, NJ: Lawrence Erlbaum Associates.

Bransford, J. D., Brown, A. L., & Cocking, R. R. (Eds.). (1999). How people learn: Brain, mind, experience and school. National Research Council Commission on Behavioral & Social Sciences & Education. Committee on Developments in the Science of Learning. Washington, DC: National Academy Press.

Bransford, J. D., & Johnson, M. K. (1972). Contextual prerequisites for understanding: Some investigations of comprehension and recall. *Journal of Verbal Learning & Verbal Behavior, 11*(6), 717–726.

Bransford, J. D., Sherwood, R., Vye, N., & Rieser, J. (1986). Teaching thinking and problem solving: research foundations. *American Psychologist, 41*(10), 1078–1089.

Bransford, J. D., & Stein, B. S (1993). *The ideal problem solver: A guide for improving thinking, learning, and creativity* (2nd ed.). New York: Freeman.

Brehm, J. W. (1956). Postdecision changes in the desirability of alternatives. *Journal of Abnormal and Social Psychology, 52*, 384–389.

Brem, S., & Rips, L. (in press). Explanation and evidence in informal argument. *Cognitive Science*.

Brennan, J. (1993 May). Why polls can be poles apart. *The Los Angeles Times*, p. A5.

Brennan, T. (2001 January). An academic's guide to the way Washington really works. *The Chronicle of Higher Education*, p. B11.

Brim, O. G., Jr. (1966). High and low self-estimates of intelligence. In O. G. Brim, R. S. Crutchfield, & W. H. Holtzman (Eds.), *Intelligence: perspectives 1965*. New York, Harcourt, Brace & World.

Brooks, L. W., Simutis, Z. M., & O'Neil, H. F., Jr. (1985). The role of individual differences in learning strategies research. In R. F. Dillon (Ed.), *Individual differences in cognition* (Vol. 2, pp. 219–251). New York: Academic Press.

Bross, I. D. J. (1973). Languages in cancer research. In G. P. Murphy, D. Pressman, & E. A. Mirand (Eds.), *Perspectives in cancer research and treatment* (pp. 213–221). New York: Alan R. Liss.

Brown, A. L., & Campione, J. C. (1990). Communities of learning and thinking or a context by any other name. In D. Kuhn (Ed), *Developmental perspectives of teaching and learning thinking skills. Contributions to human development* (Vol. 21, pp. 108–126). Basel, Switzerland: Karger.

Bruer, J. T. (1993). *Schools for thought: A science of learning in the classroom.* Cambridge, MA: MIT Press.

Bruner, J. S. (1957). On going beyond the information given. In J. S. Bruner (Ed.), *Contemporary approaches to cognition* (pp. 41–69). Cambridge, MA: Harvard University Press.

Bucciarelli, M., & Johnson-Laird, P. N. (1999). Strategies in syllogistic reasoning. *Cognitive Science, 23,* 247–306.

Bugliosi, V. (1978). *Till death do us part.* New York: Bantam Books.

Burke, D. M., MacKay, D. G., Worthley, J. S., & Wade, E. (1991). On the tip of the tongue: What causes word finding failures in young and older adults? *Journal of Memory and Language, 30,* 542–579.

Byrne, R. (1988). *One thousand nine hundred eleven best things anybody ever said.* New York: Fawcett.

Cannon-Bowers, J. A., Salas, E., & Pruitt, J. S. (1996). Establishing the boundaries of a paradigm for decision-making research. *Human Factors, 38,* 193–205.

Carey, J., Foltz, K., & Allan, R. A. (1983). The mind of the human machine. *Newsweek.*

Carkhuff, R. R. (1973). *The art of problem solving.* Amherst, MA: Human Resource Development Press.

Carlson, E. (1995). Evaluating the credibility of sources: A missing link in the teaching of critical thinking. In D. F. Halpern & S. G. Nummedal (Eds.)., Psychologists Teach Critical Thinking [Special issue]. *Teaching of Psychology, 22,* 39–41.

Carroll, D. W. (1986). *Psychology of language.* Belmont, CA: Brooks/Cole.

Carroll, L. (1971). *Through the looking glass.* London: Oxford University Press (Original work published 1872).

Carson, D. (2001). Innovative treatments in couples and family therapy. *Annals of the American Psychotherapy Association, 4,* 13–14.

Catrambone, R. (1998). The subgoal learning model: Creating better examples so that students can solve novel problems. *Journal of Experimental Psychology: General, 127,* 355–376.

Ceci, S. J. (1996). *On intelligence: A bioecological treatise on intellectual development.* Cambridge, MA: Harvard University Press.

Ceci, S. J., & Ruiz, A. I. (1993). Inserting context into our thinking about thinking: Implications for a theory of everyday intelligent behavior. In M. Rabinowitz (Ed.), *Cognitive science foundations of instruction.* Hillsdale, NJ: Lawrence Erlbaum Associates.

Center for Media and Public Affairs. (*Merchandizing Mayhem: Violence in popular culture 1998–1999.* [Web Page]. URL http://www.cmpa.com/archive/viol98.htm [2002, February].

Ceraso, J., & Protivera, A. (1971). Sources of error in syllogistic reasoning. *Cognitive Psychology, 2,* 400–410.

Champagne, A. B. (1992). Cognitive research on thinking in academic science and mathematics: Implications for practice and policy. In D. F. Halpern (Ed), *Enhancing thinking skills in the sciences and mathematics* (pp. 117–134). Hillsdale, NJ: Lawrence Erlbaum Associates.

Chance Magazine. (Spring, 2001). Three sisters give birth on the same day, pp. 23–25.

Chance, P. (1986). *Thinking in the classroom: A survey of programs.* New York: Teachers College Press.

Chang, J. (1993). *Wild swans: Three daughters of China.* New York: HarperCollins.

Chapman, L. J., & Chapman, J. P. (1959). Atmosphere effect re-examined. *Journal of Experimental Psychology, 58,* 220–226.

Chapman, L. J., & Chapman, J. P. (1967). The genesis of popular but erroneous psychodiagnostic observations. *Journal of Abnormal Psychology, 72,* 193–204.

Chapman, L. J., & Chapman, J. P. (1969). Illusory correlation as an obstacle to the use of valid psychodiagnostic signs. *Journal of Abnormal Psychology, 74,* 271–280.

Cheng, P. W. (1997). From covariation to causation: A causal power theory. *Psychological Review, 104,* 367–405.

Cheng, P. W., & Holyoak, K. J. (1985). Pragmatic reasoning schemas. *Cognitive Psychology, 17*(4), 391–416.

Chesler, P. (1972). *Women and madness.* New York: Doubleday.

Chi, M. T., Glaser, R., & Farr, M. J. (Eds.). (1988). *The nature of expertise*. Hillsdale, NJ: Lawrence Erlbaum Associates.

The Chronicle of Higher Education. (1987). p. A2.

The Chronicle of Higher Education. (1994). p. A8.

The Chronicle of Higher Education. (2000) *Survey finds that most Americans want college to prepare them for a job* [Web Page]. URL http://chronicle.com/search97cgi/s97_cgi? [2000, December 28].

Cialdini, R. B. (1993). *Influence: Science and practice* (3rd ed.). Glenview, IL: Scott Foresman.

Cialdini, R. B., Trost, M. R., & Newson, J. T. (1995). Preference for consistency: The development of a valid measure and the discovery of suppressing behavioral implications. *Journal of personality and social psychology, 69,* 318–328.

Clark, H. H., & Haviland, S. E. (1977). Comprehension and the given-new contract. In R. O. Freedle (Ed.), *Discourse production and comprehension*. Norwood, NJ: Ablex.

Clemens, S. L. (1897). *Following the equator*. Hartford: The American Publishing Co.

Clinton's message to USA's students: Learn to earn. (1994 February). *USA Today International Edition*, p. 6A.

The Cognition and Technology Group at Vanderbilt. (1983). Toward integrated curricula: Possibilities from anchored instruction. In M. Rabinowitz (Ed), *Cognitive science foundations of instruction* (pp. 33–56). Hillsdale, NJ: Lawrence Erlbaum Associates.

Cohen, D. (2000) *With Asian economies on the rebound, the region's colleges are also upbeat* (April 27) [2000, December 28].

Cohen, M. S., Freeman, J. T., & Wolf, S. (1996). Metarecognition in time-stressed decision making: recognizing, critiquing, and correcting. *Human Factors, 38*(2), 206–219.

Cole, K. C. (1995 June). Finding the truth is a slippery thing. *Los Angeles Times*, p. B2.

Cole, K. C. (2001 June). Leaders; Poor math skills add up to bad public policy. *Los Angeles Times*, p. 8.

Collett, P. (1994) *A new university for Pakistan* [Web Page]. URL http://chronicle.com/search97cgi/s97_cgi? [2000, December 28].

Connor-Greene, P. A. (2000). Assessing and promoting student learning: Blurring the line between teaching and testing. *Teaching of Psychology, 27,* 84–88.

Conway, M. A., Cohen, G., & Stanhope, N. (1991). On the very long-term retention of knowledge acquired through formal education: Twelve years of cognitive psychology. *Journal of Experimental Psychology: General, 120*(4), 395–409.

Coughlin, E. K. (1993, November). When people make up their minds, psychologist says, they often do not really make up their minds at all. *The Chronicle of Higher Education*, p. 9.

Covington, M. V., Crutchfield, R. S., Davies, L. B., & Olton, R. M., Jr. (1974). *The productive thinking program*. Columbus, OH: Charles E. Merrill.

Crovitz, H. F. (1970). *Galton's walk: Methods for the analysis of thinking, intelligence and creativity*. New York: Harper & Row.

Crutchfield, R. S. (1966). Creative thinking in children: Its teaching and testing. In O. G. Brim, Jr., R. S. Crutchfield, & W. H. Holtzman (Eds.), *Intelligence: Perspectives 1965, The Terman-Otis Memorial Lectures*. New York: Harcourt, Brace & World.

Cull, W. L. (2000). Untangling the benefits of multiple study opportunities and repeated testing for cued recall. *Applied Cognitive Psychology, 14,* 215–235.

Cybernation International. *The People's Cybernation* [Web Page]. URL http:// www.cybernation.com/victory/quotes/thoughtsandthinking.html [2002, January 15].

Dahlstrom, G. W. (1993). Tests: Small samples, large consequences. *American Psychologist, 48*(4), 393–399.

d'Angelo, E. (1971). *The teaching of critical thinking*. Amsterdam: Gruner.

Damer, T. E. (1987). *Attacking faulty reasoning* (2nd ed.). Belmont, CA: Wadsworth.

Dansereau, D. F. (1995). Derived structural schemas and the transfer of knowledge. In A. McKeough, J. Lupart, & A. Marini (Eds.), *Teaching for transfer: Fostering generalization in learning* (pp. 93–121). Mahwah, NJ: Lawrence Erlbaum Associates.

Dansereau, D. F. (2001). (personal communication).

Darrow, C. (1932). *The story of my life*. New York: Charles Scribner's Sons.

Davidson, D., & Sternberg, R. J. (1998). Smart problem solving: How metacognition helps. In D. J. Hacker, J. Dunlosky, & A. C. Graesser (Eds.), *Metacognition in educational theory and practice* (pp. 47–65). Mahwah, NJ: Lawrence Erlbaum Associates, Inc.

Davidson, J. (1996). Choosing when it's confusing. *Vital Speeches, 63*(3), 84–90.

Davis, G. A., & Roweton, W. (1968). Using idea checklists with college students: Overcoming resistence. *Journal of Psychology, 70*, 221–226.

Davis, M., & Hult, R. E. (1997). Effects of writing summaries as a generative learning activity during note taking. *Teaching of Psychology, 24*, 47–49.

Dawes, R. M. (1993, June). Finding guidelines for tough decisions. *The Chronicle of Higher Education*, p. 40.

Dawes, R. M. (1994). *House of cards: Psychology and psychotherapy built on myth*. New York: The Free Press.

Day, R. S., Rodin, G. C., & Stoltzfus, E. R. (1990). *Alternative representations for medication instructions: Effects on young and old adults*. Paper presented at the 3rd Cognitive Aging Conference, Atlanta.

DeBono, E. (1968). *New think: The use of lateral thinking in the generation of new ideas*. New York: Basic Books.

DeBono, E. (1976). *Teaching thinking*. London: Temple Smith.

DeBono, E. (1977). Information processing and new ideas—lateral and vertical thinking. In R. B. Noller, A. M. Biondi, & S. J. Parnes (Eds.), *Guide to creative action: Revised edition of creative behavior guidebook*. New York: Scribner's.

DeBono, E. (1985). *Six thinking hats*. Boston: Little-Brown.

DeBono, E. (1992). *Serious thinking: Using the power of lateral thinking to create new ideas*. New York: HarperCollins.

De Lopez, R. S. (1992 June). Promote thinking, say university leaders. *The News*, Mexico City, p. B4.

Decyk, B. N. (1994). Using examples to teach concepts. In D. F. Halpern (Ed.), *Changing college classrooms: New teaching and learning strategies for an increasingly complex world* (pp. 39–63). San Francisco: Jossey-Bass.

Dees, S. M., & Dansereau, D. F. (2000). *TCU guide maps: A resource for counselors*. Fort Worth, TX: Texas Christian University, Institute of Behavioral Research.

deGroot, A. D. (1966). Perception and memory versus thought: Some old ideas and recent findings. In B. Kleinmuntz (Ed), *Problem solving: Research, method, and theory*. New York: Wiley. p. 114

deGroot, A. D. (1983). Heuristics, mental programs, and intelligence. In R. Groner, M. Groner, & W. F. Bischof (Eds), *Methods of heuristics* (pp. 109–129). Hillsdale, NJ: L. Erlbaum Associates.

Dewey, J. (1933). *How we think: A restatement of the relation of reflective thinking to the educative process*. Boston: Heath.

Dews, S., & Winner, E. (1999). Obligatory processing of literal and nonliteral meanings in verbal irony. *Journal of Pragmatics, 31*(12), 1579–1599.

Diamond, R. M. (1997). *Curriculum reform needed if students are to master core concepts* [Web Page]. URL http://chronicle.com/search97cgi/s97_cgi? [2000, December 28].

Donovan, J. J., & Radosevich, D. J. (1998). A meta-analytic review of the distribution of practice effect: Now you see it, now you don't. *Journal of Applied Psychology, 84*, 795–805.

Doolittle, J. H. (1995). Using riddles and interactive computer games to teach problem solving. In D. F. Halpern & S. G. Nummedal (Eds.), Psychologists teach critical thinking [Special Issue]. *Teaching of Psychology, 22*, 33–36.

Dreman, D. (1979). *Contrarian investment strategy: The psychology of the stock market success*. New York: Random House.

Driver, R., Newton, P., & Osborne, J. (2000). Establishing the norms of scientific argumentation in classrooms. *Science Education, 84*, 287–312.

Drosnin, M. (1997). *The bible code*. New York: Simon & Schuster.

Drysdale, W. (1887). *Proverbs for plymouth pulpit*. New York: D. Appleton and Company.

Dunbar, K. (1998). Problem solving. In W. Bechtel (Ed.), *A companion to cognitive science* (pp. 289–298). London: Blackwell.

Dunbar, K. (2001). The analogical paradox: Why analogy is so easy in naturalistic settings yet so difficult in the psychological laboratory. In D. Gentner & K. Holyoak (Eds.), *The analogical mind: Perspectives from cognitive science* (pp. 313–334). Cambridge, MA: The MIT Press.

Duncan, C. P. (1961). Attempts to influence performance on an insight problem. *Psychological Reports, 9*, 35–42.

Duncker, K. (1945). On problem solving. *Psychological Monographs* (Whole No. 270).

Eisenberger, R., & Cameron, J. (1998). Reward, intrinsic interest, and creativity: New findings. *American Psychologist, 53*, 676–679.

Ekman, P. (1992). *Telling lies: Clues to deceit in the marketplace, politics and marriage*. New York: Norton.

Emery, G. (2001). *Failed psychic predictions for 1998: Psychic report card dubious once again* [Web Page]. URL http://wysiwyg//17/www.csicop.org/article/psychic-predictions/1998.html [2001, July 3].

Eylon, B. S., & Linn, M. C. (1988). Learning and instruction: An examination of four research perspectives in science education. *Review of Educational Research, 58*(3), 251–301.

√ Facione, P. (1991). Teaching and college-level critical thinking skills. *Paper Presented at the 11th Annual International Conference on Critical Thinking and Educational Reform. Sonoma, CA*.

√ Facione, P. A., Facione, N. C., & Giancarlo, C. A. (2000). The disposition toward critical thinking: Its character, measurement, and relationship to critical thinking skill. *Informal Logic, 20*(1), 61–84.

Falls, C. (1943). *Ordeal by battle*. New York: Oxford University Press.

Ferguson, G. (1981). Architecture. In N. L. Smith (Ed.), *Metaphors for evaluation: Sources of new methods*. Beverly Hills, CA: Sage.

Festinger, L. (1964). *Conflict, decision and dissonance*. Palo Alto, CA: Stanford University Press.

Feynman, R. (1989). *What do you care what other people think?* New York: Bantam.

Finke, R. A., Ward, T. B., & Smith, S. M. (1992). *Creative cognition: Theory, research, and applications*. Cambridge, MA: Bradford.

Fischer, G. W., & Johnson, E. J. (1986). Behavioral decision theory and political decision making. In R. R. Lau & D. O. Sears (Eds.), *The 19th Annual Carnegie Symposium on Cognition: Political Cognition* (pp. 55–65). Hillsdale, NJ: Lawrence Erlbaum Associates.

Fischer, S. C., & Spiker, V. A. (2000). *A framework for critical thinking research and training*. (Report Prepared for the U. S. Army Research Institute).

Fischhoff, B. (1975). Hindsight does not equal foresight: The effect of outcome knowledge on judgment under uncertainty. *Journal of Experimental Psychology: Human Perception and Performance, 1*, 288–299.

Fischhoff, B. (1993). Controversies over risk: Psychological perspective on competence. *Psychological Science Agenda, 6*, 8–9.

Fisher, R., & Ury, W. (1991). *Getting to "yes": Negotiating agreement without giving in* (2nd ed.). New York: Penguin.

Fisher, R. P. (1995). Interviewing victims and witnesses of crime. *Psychology, Public Policy, & Law, 1*(4), 732–764.

Fiske, S. T., & Taylor, S. E. (1984). *Social cognition*. New York: Random House.

Fiske, S. T. (1993). Controlling other people: The impact of power on stereotyping. *American Psychologist, 48*(6), 621–628.

Fixx, J. F. (1978). *Solve it*. New York: Doubleday.

Flannelly, L. T., & Flannelly, K. J. (2000). Reducing people's judgment bias about their level of knowledge. *Psychological Record, 50*, 587–600.

Fletcher, M. (2000, March). Why crime is down in America. *Milwaukee Sentinel*, [retrieved online at http://www.jsonline.com/news/editorials/mar00/fletcher26032500.asp].

Fogelin, R. J. (1987). *Understanding arguments, an introduction to informal logic* (3rd ed.). New York: Harcourt Brace.

Fong, G. T., Krantz, D. H., & Nisbett, R. E. (1986). The effects of statistical training on thinking about everyday problems. *Cognitive Psychologist, 18*(3), 253–292.

Fox, L. S., Marsh, G., & Crandall, J. C., Jr. (1983). *The effect of college classroom experiences on formal operational thinking.* Paper presented at the 1983 Annual Convention of the Western Psychological Association, San Francisco.

Frammolino, R. (1993 December). Most college GEDs fail simple tests, study finds. *The Los Angeles Times*, pp. A41, A43.

Freud, S. (1930). *Civilization and its discontents.* Newark, DE: the Hogarth Press.

The Gallup Organization. (*Americans' belief in psychic and paranormal phenomena is up over the last decade* [Web Page]. URL http://www.gallup.com/poll/releases/pr010608.asp). [2001, July 3].

Gardner, H. (1983). *Frames of mind: The theory of multiple intelligences.* New York: Basic Books.

Gardner, H. (1985). *The mind's new science: A history of the cognitive revolution.* New York: Basic Books.

Gardner, H. (1989). *To open minds.* New York: Basic Books.

Gardner, H., Krechevsky, M., Sternberg, R. J., & Okagaki, L. (1994). Intelligence in context: Enhancing students' practical intelligence for school. In K. Mc Gilly (Ed.), *Classroom Lessons: Integrating cognitive theory and classroom practice* (pp 105–127). Cambridge, MA: MIT Press.

Garfield, J., & Ahlgren, A. (1988). Difficulties in learning basic concepts on probability and statistics: Implications for research. *Journal for Research in Mathematics Education, 19*(1), 44–63.

Garnham, A., & Oakhill, J. (1994). *Thinking and reasoning.* Oxford, England: Blackwell.

Gazzaniga, M. S., Ivry, R. B., & Magnun, G. R. (1998). *Cognitive neuroscience: The biology of the mind.* New York: Norton.

Geiselman, R. E., & Fisher, R. P. (1985, December). Interviewing victims and witnesses of crime. *Research in Brief, National Institute of Justice*, 1–4.

Gentner, D., & Gentner, D. R. (1983). Flowing water or teeming crowds: Mental models of electricity. In D. Gentner & A. L. Stevens (Eds.), *Mental models.* Hillsdale, NJ: Lawrence Erlbaum Associates.

Gentner, D., & Holyoak, K. J. (1997). Reasoning and learning by analogy: Introduction. *American Psychologist, 52*(1), 32–34.

Gerbner, G., Grass, L., Morgan, M., & Signorielli, N. (1980). *Violence profile No. 11: Trends in network television drama and viewer conceptions of social reality.* Philadelphia: Annenberg School of Communication.

Gervais, S., & Odean, T. (2001). Learning to be overconfident. *The Review of Financial Studies, 14*, 1–27.

Gibson, S. (2000). X-files and X-fictions. *Skeptic, 8*, 8–10.

Gick, M. L., & Holyoak, K. J. (1980). Analogical problem solving. *Cognitive Psychology, 12*, 306–355.

Gifford-Jones, W. (1977). *What every woman should know about hysterectomy.* New York: Funk & Wagnalls.

Gigerenzer, G., & Goldstein, D. C. (1996). Reasoning the fast and frugal way: Models of bounded rationality. *Psychological Review, 103*, 650–669.

Gigerenzer, G., & Hoffrage, U. (1995). How to improve Bayesian reasoning without instruction. *Psychological Review, 102*, 684–704.

Gigerenzer, G., Todd, P. M., & the ABC Research Group. (2000). *Simple heuristics that make us smart.* New York: Oxford University Press.

Gilbreth, F. B. (1963). *Cheaper by the dozen.* New York: Crowell.

Gillette R. (1987, December). Exotic ways to learn doubted by U.S. study. *The Wall Street Journal*, pp. 1, 32.

Gilovich, T. (1991). *How we know what isn't so: The fallibility of human reason in everyday life.* New York: Macmillan.

Glaser, R. (1984). Education and thinking: The role of knowledge. *American Psychologist, 39*(2), 93–104.

Glaser, R. (1992). Expert knowledge and processes of thinking. In D. F. Halpern (Ed.), *Enhancing thinking skills in the sciences and mathematics* (pp. 63–75, ix, 155). Hillsdale, NJ: Lawrence Erlbaum Associates.

Glucksberg, S., & Weisberg, R. W. (1966). Verbal behavior and problem solving: Some effects of labeling in a functional fixedness problem. *Journal of Experimental Psychology, 71*(5), 659–664.

Godfrey, S. (2001). Are you creative? *Glaxo Wellcome Newsletter*, p. 1.

Goertzel, T., & Goertzel, B. (1995). *Linus Pauling: A life in science and politics*. New York: Basic Books.

Goleman, D. (1995). *Emotional intelligence*. New York: Bantam Books.

Gonzalez, M. A., Campos, A., & Perez, M. J. (1997). Mental imagery and creative thinking. *Journal of Psychology, 131*, 357–364.

Gordon, W. J. J. (1961). *Synectics*. New York: Harper & Row.

Gordon, W. J. J. (1976). Metaphor and invention. In A. Rothenberg, & C.R. Hausman (Eds.), *The creativity question*. Durham, NC: University Press.

Govier, T. (1985). *A practical study of argument*. Belmont, CA: Wadsworth.

Graf, P., & Komatsu, S. I. (1994). Process dissociation procedure: Handle with caution. *European Journal of Cognitive Psychology, 6*(2), 113–129.

Gray, W. (1991). *Thinking critically about new age ideas*. Belmont, CA: Wadsworth.

Greenwald, A. G. (1992). New Look 3: Unconscious cognition reclaimed. *American Psychologist, 47*, 766–779.

Greenwald, A. G., Spangenberg, E. R., Pratkanis, A. R., & Eskenazi, J. (1991). Double-blind tests of subliminal self-help audiotapes. *Psychological Science, 2*(2), 119–122.

Guilford, J. P. (1977). *Way beyond the IQ*. Buffalo, NY: Creative Education Foundation.

Gunther, M. (1977). *The luck factor*. New York: Macmillan.

Hadamard, L. (1954). *The psychology of invention in the mathematical field*. Princeton, NJ: Princeton University Press.

Halpern, D. F. (1985). The influence of sex-role stereotypes on prose recall. *Sex Roles, 12*(3–4), 363–375.

Halpern, D. F. (1987). Analogies as a critical thinking skill. In D. Berger, K. Peydek, & W. Banks (Eds), *Applications of cognitive psychology: Computing and education* (pp. 75–86). Hillsdale, NJ: Lawrence Erlbaum Associates.

Halpern, D. F. (1994). A national assessment of critical thinking skills in adults: Taking steps toward the goal. In A. Greenwood (Ed.), *The national assessment of college student learning: Identification of the skills to be taught, learned, and assessed* (pp. 24–64). Washington, DC: U. S. Department of Education, National Center for Education Statistics.

Halpern, D. F. (Ed). (1994). *Changing college classrooms: New teaching and learning strategies for an increasingly complex world*. San Francisco: Jossey-Bass.

Halpern, D. F. (1995). The skewed logic of the bell-shaped curve. [Special Issue]. Race & IQ. *Skeptic, 3*, 64–71.

Halpern, D. F. (1998). Teaching critical thinking for transfer across domains: Dispositions, skills, structure training, and metacognitive monitoring. *American Psychologist, 53*, 449–455.

Halpern, D. F. (2000). *Sex differences in cognitive abilities* (3rd ed.). Mahwah, NJ: Lawrence Erlbaum and Associates, Inc.

Halpern, D. F. (in press). Why wisdom? *Educational Psychologist*.

Halpern, D. F., & Blackman, S. (1985). Magazines vs. physicians. The influence of information source on intentions to use oral contraceptives. *Women and Health, 10*, 9–23.

Halpern, D. F., Blackman, S., & Salzman B. (1989). Using statistical risk information to assess oral contraceptive safety. *Applied Cognitive Psychology, 3*, 251–260.

Halpern, D. F., & Collaer, M. L. (in press). Sex differences in visuospatial abilities: More than meets the eye. In P. Shah & A. Miyak (Eds.), *Higher-level visuospatial thinking and cognition*. Cambridge: MA: Cambridge University Press.

Halpern, D. F., Hansen, C., & Riefer, D. (1990). Analogies as an aid to understanding and memory. *Journal of Educational Psychology, 82*(2), 298–305.

Halpern, D. F., & Irwin, F. W. (1973). Selection of hypotheses as affected by their preference values. *Journal of Experimental Psychology, 101*, 105–108.

Halpern, D. F., & Nummedal, S. G. (1995). Closing thoughts about helping students improve how they think. *Teaching of Psychology, 22*(1), 82–83.

Hammond, K. R. (1996). *Human judgment and social policy: Irreducible uncertainty, inevitable error, unavoidable injustice.* New York: Oxford University Press.

Hanson, N. R. (1958). *Patterns of discovery.* Cambridge, England: Cambridge University Press.

Harman, G. (1986). *Change in view: Principles of reasoning.* Cambridge, MA: MIT Press.

Harris, R. J. (1977). Comprehension of pragmatic implications in advertising. *Journal of Applied Psychology, 62*(5), 603–608.

Harris, S. B. (1993). The resurrection myth in religion, science, and science fiction. *Skeptic, 2*, 50–59.

Hasher, L., & Zacks, R. T. (1984). Automatic processing of fundamental information: The case of frequency of occurrence. *American Psychologist, 39*(12), 1372–1388.

Hastie, R., & Dawes, R. (2001). *Rational choice in an uncertain world: The psychology of judgment and decision making.* Thousand Oaks, CA: Sage.

Hastie, R., & Pennington, N. (2000). Explanation-based decision-making. In T. Connelly, *Judgment and decision making: An interdisciplinary reader.* New York: Cambridge.

Hayes, J. R. (1989). Cognitive processes in creativity. In J. A Glover, R. R. Ronning, & C. R. Reynolds (Eds.), *Handbook of creativity* (pp. 135–145). New York: Plenum.

Heiman, M., & Slomianko, J. (1986). *Critical thinking skills.* Washington, DC: National Education Association.

Heit, E. (2000). Properties of inductive reasoning. *Psychonomic Bulletin & Review, 7*(4), 569–592.

Heller, R., Saltzstein, H. D., & Caspe, W. (1992). Heuristics in medical and non-medical decision-making. *The Journal of Experimental Psychology*, 211–235.

Henle, M. (1962). On the relation between logic and thinking. *Psychological Review, 69*, 366–378.

Hennessey, B. A., & Amabile, T. M. (1988). The conditions of creativity. In R. J. Sternberg (Ed.), *The nature of creativity: Contemporary psychological perspectives* (pp. 11–38). Cambridge, MA: Cambridge University Press.

Herrmann, D. J., & Gruneberg, M. M. (1999). *How to cure your memory failures.* London: Blandford.

Herrnstein, R. J., Nickerson, R. S., de Sanchez, M., & Swets, J. A. (1986). Teaching thinking skills. *American Psychologist, 41*, 1279–1289.

Herrnstein, R. J., & Murray, C. A. (1994). The bell curve: Intelligence and class structure in American life. New York: The Free Press.

Hoffrage, U., Hertwig, R., & Gigerenzer, G. (2000). Hindsight bias: A by-product of knowledge up-dating? *Journal of Experimental Psychology: Learning, Memory, and Cognition, 26*, 566–581.

Hogarth, R. M. (1988). *Judgment and choice: The psychology of decision.* Chichester, England: Wiley.

Holland, J. H., Holyoak, K. J., Nisbett, R. E., & Thagard, P. R. (1986). *Induction: Processes of inference, learning, and discovery,* Cambridge, MA: MIT Press.

Holley, C. D., Dansereau, D. F., McDonald, B. A., Garland, J. D., & Collins, K. W. (1979). Evaluation of a hierarchical mapping technique as an aid to prose processing. *Contemporary Educational Psychology, 4*(3), 227–237.

Holt, J. (1964). *How children fail.* New York: Dell.

Holt, J. (1989). *Learning all the time.* Reading, MA: Addison-Wesley.

Holyoak, K. J., & Simon, D. (1999). Bidirectional reasoning in decision making by constraint satisfaction. *Journal of Experimental Psychology: General, 128*, 3–31.

Hostetler A J. (1988). Army eyes novel learning methods. *The American Psychological Association Monitor, 19*, 7.

Huff, D. (1954). *How to lie with statistics.* New York: W. W. Norton & Company.

Hummel, J. E., & Holyoak, K. J. (1997). Distributed representations of structure: A theory of analogical access and mapping. *Psychological Review, 104*, 427–466.

Hunt, E. B. (1989). Cognitive science: Definition, status, and questions. *Annual Review of Psychology, 40*, 603–629.

Hunt, E. B. (1995). *Will we be smart enough? A cognitive analysis of the coming workforce.* New York: Russell Sage Foundation.

Hunt, M. (1982). *The universe within: A new science explores the human mind.* New York: Simon & Schuster.

Hutchings, P. (1986). Some late night thoughts on teaching creativity. *American Association for Higher Education, 39*, 9–14.

Hyman, R. (2001). *Australian Skeptics Guide to "Cold Reading"* [Web Page]. URL http://www.skeptics.com.au/journal/coldread.htm [2002, January 20].

Izawa, C. (1993). Efficient learning: The total time, exposure duration, frequency, and programming of the study phase. In C. Izawa (Ed), *Cognitive psychology applied* (pp. 15–42). Hillsdale, NJ: Lawrence Erlbaum Associates.

Izawa, C., & Hayden, R. G. (1993). Race against time: Toward the principle of optimization in learning and retention. In C. Izawa (Ed.), *Cognitive psychology applied* (pp. 15–41). Hillsdale, NJ: Lawrence Erlbaum Associates.

Jackson, S. E. (1996). The consequences of diversity in multidisciplinary work teams. In M. A. West (Ed.), *Handbook of work group psychology* (pp. 53–76). Chichester, England: Wiley.

Jacoby, L. L., Kelley, C. M., & Dywan, J. (1989). Memory attributions. In H. L. Roedinger III & F. I. M. Craik (Eds), *Varieties of memory and consciousness: Essays in honour of Endel Tulving* (pp. 391–422, xx, 445). Hillsdale, NJ: Lawrence Erlbaum Associates.

James Randi Educational Foundation. (*One Million Dollar Paranormal Challenge* [Web Page]. URL http://www.randi.org/research/index.html [[February 2, 2002]].

James Rogan Communications. (1993). *Bits & Pieces*, p. 7.

James, W. (1890). *The principles of psychology.* New York: Holt.

Janis, I. L., & Mann, L. (1977). *Decision making: A psychological analysis of conflict, choice, and commitment.* New York: The Free Press.

Jensen, A. R. (1980). *Bias in mental testing.* New York: Free Press.

Jepson, C., Krantz, D. H., & Nisbett, R. E. (1993). Inductive reasoning: Competence or skill? In R. E. Nisbett, *Rules for reasoning* (pp. 70–89). Hillsdale, NJ: Lawrence Erlbaum.

Johnson-Laird, P. N., Legrenzi, P., & Legrenzi, M. S. (1972). Reasoning and a sense of reality. *British Journal of Psychology, 63*(3), 395–400.

Johnson-Laird, P. N., & Wason, P. C. (1970). A theoretical analysis of insight into a reasoning task. *Cognitive Psychology, 1*(2), 134–148.

Johnson-Laird, P. N., & Wason, P. C. (1977). *Thinking: Readings in cognitive science.* Cambridge, England: Cambridge University Press.

Johnson, M. K., & Raye, C. L. (1981). Reality monitoring. *Psychological Review, 88*(1), 67–85.

Johnson, W. (1946). *People in quandries: The semantics of personal judgement.* New York: Harper & Row Publishers.

Jones, E. A., Dougherty, B. C., Fantaske, P., & Hoffman, S. (1995). *Identifying college graduates' essential skills in reading and problem-solving: Perspectives of faculty, employers and policymakers.* (Contract No. R117G10037/CDFA84.117G.). University Park: U.S. Department of Education/OERI.

Jones, E. A., Hoffman, S., Moore, L. M., Ratcliff, G., Tibbetts, S., & Click, B. A. (1995). *National assessment of college student learning: Identifying college graduates' essential skills in writing, speech and listening, and critical thinking. (NCES 95–001).* Washington, DC: U.S. Government Printing Office.

Juge, M. L. (2000 March). What's in a name? More than meets the eye. *The Chronicle of Higher Education*, p. B4.

Kahane, H. (1980). *Logic and contemporary rhetoric: The use of reason in everyday life* (2nd ed.). Belmont, CA: Wadsworth.

Kahane, H. (1992). *Logic and contemporary rhetoric: The use of reason in everyday life* (6th ed.). Belmont, CA: Wadsworth.

Kahneman, D., & Tversky, A. (1973). On the psychology of prediction. *Psychological Review, 80*, 237–251.

Kahneman, D., & Tversky, A. (1979). Prospect theory: An analysis of decision under risk. *Econometrica, 47,* 263–291.

Kavanaugh, D. J., & Bower, G. H. (1985). Mood and self-efficacy: Impact of joy and sadness on perceived capabilities. *Cognitive Therapy & Research, 9,* 507–525.

Kellogg, R. T. (1990). Effectiveness of prewriting strategies as a function of task demands. *American Journal of Psychology, 103*(3), 327–342.

Keren, G., & Teigen, K. H. (2001). Why is $p = .90$ better than $p = .70$? Preference for definitive predictions by lay consumers of probability judgements. *Psychonomic Bulletin & Review, 8,* 191–202.

Kidd, V. (1991). An analysis of the California tobacco education campaign's visual anti-smoking messages. *Feedback, 32,* 14–18.

Kim, W. C., & Mauborgne, R. (1999). Strategy, knowledge, innovation and the knowledge economy. *Sloan Management Review, 40,* 41–54.

Kimble, G. A. (1978). *How to use (and misuse) statistics.* Englewood Cliffs, NJ: Prentice-Hall.

King, A. (1989). Effects of self-questioning training on college students' comprehension of lectures. *Contemporary Educational Psychology, 14*(4), 366–381.

King, A. (1992). Facilitating elaborative learning through guided student-generated questioning. *Educational Psychologist, 27*(1), 111–126.

King, A. (1994). Inquiry as a tool to critical thinking. In D. F. Halpern (Ed), *Changing college classrooms: New teaching and learning strategies in an increasingly complex world* (pp. 13–38). San Francisco: Jossey-Bass.

King, P. M., & Kitchener, K. S. (1994). *Developing reflective judgment: Understanding and promoting intellectual growth and critical thinking in adolescents and adults.* San Francisco: Jossey-Bass.

Klaczynski, P. A. (1993). Reasoning schema effects on adolescent rule acquisition and transfer. *Journal of Educational Psychology, 85*(4), 679–692.

Klaczynski, P. A., Gordon, D. H., & Fauth, J. (1997). Goal-oriented critical reasoning and individual differences in critical reasoning biases. *Journal of Educational Psychology, 89*(3), 470–485.

Klahr, D., & Simon, H. A. (2001). What have psychologists (and others) discovered about the process of scientific discovery? *Current Directions in Psychological Science, 10,* 75–79.

Klauer, K. C., & Meiser, T. (2000). A source-monitoring analysis of illusory correlations. *Personality & Social Psychology Bulletin, 26,* 1074–1093.

Kneller, G. F. (1965). *The art and science of creativity.* New York: Holt, Rinehart & Winston.

Knight, K., & Dansereau, D. F. (1992). Tools for drug and alcohol education: Using decision worksheets in personal problem solving. *Journal of Drug Education, 22*(3), 261–271.

Koestler, A. (1964). *The act of creation.* London: Hutchinson.

Kohler, W. (1969). *The task of Gestalt psychology.* Princeton, NJ: Princeton University Press.

Koriat, A., Lichtenstein, S. F., & Fischhoff, B. (1980). Reasons for confidence. *Journal of Experimental Psychology: Human Learning and Memory, 6,* 107–118.

Kosonen, P., & Winne, P. H. (1995). Effects of teaching statistical laws on reasoning about everyday problems. *Journal of Educational Psychology, 87,* 33–46.

Kronholm, M. M. (1993). *The impact of a developmental instruction approach to environmental education at the undergraduate level on reflective judgment.* Unpublished doctoral dissertation, Southern Illinois University, Carbondale, IL.

Kruglanski, A. W. (1992). On methods of good judgment and good methods of judgment. *Political Psychology, 13,* 455–475.

Kuhn, D., Weinstock, M., & Flaton, R. (1994). How well do jurors reason? Competence dimensions of individual variation in a juror reasoning task. *Psychological Science, 5,* 289–296.

Kuhn, D. (1993, January). Connecting scientific and informal reasoning. *Merrill-Palmer Quarterly,* pp. 74–103.

Kuhn, D. (2001). How do people know? *Psychological Science, 12*(1), 1–8.

La Place, M. (1951). *A philosophical essay on probabilities* (exact wording varies by translation). New York: Dover Publications, Inc.

La Rochefoucauld. (1959). The maxims of La Rouchefoucauld. Louis Kronenberger (Trans.). New York: Random House.

LaBine, S. J., & LaBine, G. (1996). Determination of negligence and hindsight bias. *Law & Human Behavior, 20,* 501–516.

Langer, E. J. (1989). *Mindfulness.* Reading, MA: Addison-Wesley Pub. Co.

Langer, E. (1994, July). *Improving the quality of thinking in a changing world.* Paper presented at the Sixth International Conference on Thinking. Cambridge, MA.

Langer, E. J. (2000). Mindful learning. *Current Directions in Psychological Science, 9,* 220–223.

Langer, E. J., Blank, A., & Chanowitz, B. (1978). The mindlessness of ostensibly thoughtful action: The role of "placebic" information in interpersonal interaction. *Journal of Personality and Social Psychology, 36,* 635–642.

Larrick, R. P., Morgan, J. N., & Nisbett, R. E. (1990). Teaching the use of cost-benefit reasoning in everyday life. *Psychological Science, 1,* 362–370.

Larson, C. F. (2001). Management for the new millennium—the challenge of change. *Research Technology Management, 6,* 10–12.

Lawson, T. J. (1999). Assessing psychological critical thinking as a learning outcome for psychology majors. *Teaching of Psychology, 26,* 207–209.

Leedy, P. D. (1981). *How to read research and understand it.* New York: Macmillan.

Lehman, D. R., Lempert, R. O., & Nisbett, R. E. (1988). The effects of graduate training on reasoning: Formal discipline and thinking about everyday-life events. *American Psychologist, 43*(6), 431–442.

Leive, C. (1994). Miss America. *Glamour,* pp. 234–237, 275–281.

Leming, J. S. (1998). Some critical thoughts about the teaching of critical thinking. *Social Studies, 89*(2), 61–66.

Lenski, S. D. (2001). Intertextual connections during discussions about literature. *Reading Psychology, 22,* 313–335.

Levi, D. S. (1991). *Critical thinking and logic.* Salem, MI: Sheffield.

Levine, M. (1994). *Effective problem solving.* Englewood Cliffs, NJ: Prentice-Hall.

Lewis, A. B., & Mayer, R. E. (1987). Students' misconceptions of relational statements in arithmetic word problems. *Journal of Educational Psychology, 79,* 363–371.

Lichtenstein, S., Slovic, P., Fischoff, B., Layman, M., & Combs, B. (1978). Judged frequency of lethal events. *Journal of Experimental Psychology: Human Learning & Memory, 4*(6), 551–578.

Lilienfeld, S. O., Wood, J. M., & Garb, H. N. (2000). The scientific status of projective techniques. *Psychological Science in the Public Interest, 1,* 27–66.

Lithner, J. (2000). Mathematical reasoning and familiar procedures. *International Journal of Mathematical Education in Science & Technology, 31,* 83–96.

Loftus, E. F. (1975). Leading questions and the eyewitness report. *Cognitive Psychology, 7,* 560–572.

Loftus, E. F. (1979). *Eyewitness testimony.* Cambridge, MA: Harvard University Press.

Loftus, E. F. (1993). The reality of repressed memories. *American Psychologist, 48*(5), 518–537.

Loftus, G. R., & Loftus, E. F. (1982). *Essence of statistics.* Monteray, CA: Brooks/Cole.

Lopes, L. L. (1982). Doing the impossible: A note on induction and the experience of randomness. *Journal of Experimental Psychology: Learning, Memory, & Cognition, 8*(6), 626–636.

Lorayne, H. (1975). *Remembering people.* New York: Stein & Day.

Lorayne, H., & Lucas, J. (1974). *The memory book.* New York: Stein & Day (Also published in paperback by Ballantine Books, 1975).

Lord, C., Ross, L., & Lepper, M. (1979). Biased assimilation and attitude polarization: The effects of prior theories on subsequently considered evidence. *Journal of Personality and Social Psychology, 37,* 2098–2109.

Lovett, M. C., & Greenhouse, J. B. (2000). Applying cognitive theory to statistics instruction. *The American Statistician, 54,* 196–209.

Lovett, M. C., & Schunn, C. D. (1999). Task representations, strategy variability, and base-rate neglect. *Journal of Experimental Psychology: General, 128*(2), 107–130.

Lowenfeld, V. (1962). Creativity: Education's stepchild. In S. J. Parnes & H. F. Harding (Eds.), *A source book from creative thinking.* New York: Scribner's.

Macmillan Publishers. (1989). *Macmillan dictionary of quotations*. New York: Author.

Maier, N. R. F. (1931). Reasoning in humans II: The solution of a problem and its appearance in consciousness. *Journal of Comparative Psychology, 12*, 181–194.

Mann, L. (1972). Use of a "balance sheet" procedure to improve the quality of personal decision making: A field experiment with college applicants. *Journal of Vocational Behavior, 2*, 291–300.

Marsh, J. G., & Shapira, Z. (1982). Behavioral decision theory and organizational decision theory. In G. R. Ungson, & D. N. Braunstein (Eds.), *Decision making: An interdisciplinary inquiry*. Boston, MA: Kent.

Martin, P. (2001 July). Life after the myth. *Financial Times*, p. 10.

Mather, M., Shafir, E., & Johnson, M. K. (2000). Misremembrance of options past: Source monitoring and choice. *Psychological Science, 11*, 132–138.

Matlin, M. (2002). *Cognition* (5th ed.). Orlando, FL: Harcourt College Publishers.

Mayer, R. E. (1987). *Educational psychology: A cognitive approach*. Boston: Little, Brown.

Mayer, R. E. (in press). Cognitive theory and the design of multimedia instruction: An example of the two-way street between cognition and instruction. In D. F. Halpern & M. G. Hakel (Eds.), *From theory to practice: Applying the science of learning to the university and beyond. New directions for teaching and learning*. San Francisco: Jossey-Bass.

Mazzoni, G. A. L., Loftus, E. F., Seitz, A., & Lynn, S. J. (1999). Changing beliefs and memories through dream interpretation. *Applied Cognitive Psychology, 13*(2), 125–144.

McCormick, C. B., & Levin J. R. (1987). Mnemonic prose-learning strategies. In M. A. McDaniel & M. Pressley (Eds), *Imagery and related mnemonic processes* (pp. 392–406). New York: Springer-Verlag.

McFadzean, E. (2000). Techniques to enhance creative thinking. *Team Performance Management, 6*, 62–72.

McGuire, W. J. (1981). The probabilogical model of cognitive structure and attitude change. In R. E. Petty, T. M. Ostrom, & T. C. Brock (Eds.), *Cognitive responses in persuasion* (pp. 392–406). Hillsdale, NJ: Lawrence Erlbaum Associates.

McGuire, W. J. (1997). Creative hypothesis generating in psychology: Some useful heuristics. *Annual Reviews of Psychology, 48*, 1–30.

McHardy, P., & Allan, T. (2000). Closing the gap between what industry needs and what HE provides. *Education and Training, 42*, 496–508.

McKay, B., Bar-Natan, D., & Kalai, G. (1999). Solving the bible code puzzle. *Statistical Science, 14*, 150.

McKeachie, W. J. (1992). Update: Teaching thinking. In D. J. Stroup & R. Allen (Eds.), *Critical thinking: A collection of readings*. Dubuque, IA: Brown.

McKinnon, J. W., & Renner, J. W. (1971). Are colleges concerned with intellectual development? *American Journal of Psychology, 39*, 1047–1052.

Mednick, S. A., & Mednick, M. T. (1967). *Remote associates test: Examiners manual*. Boston: Houghton Mifflin.

Mehrabian, A. (2000). Beyond IQ: Broad-based measurement of individual success potential or "emotional intelligence." *Genetic, Social, & General Psychology Monographs, 126*(2), 133–239.

Merron, K., Fisher, D., & Torbet, W. R. (1987). Meaning making and management action. *Groups & Organizational Studies, 12*, 274–286.

Meyer, B. J. F., & Poon, L. W. (2001). Effects of structure strategy training and signaling on recall of text. *Journal of Educational Psychology, 93*(1), 141–159.

Miller, J. E., Jr. (1972). *Words, self, reality: The rhetoric of imagination*. New York: Dodd, Mead.

Milne, A. A. (1926). *Winnie the Pooh*. New York: Dutton.

Morgan, J. J. B., & Morton, J. T. (1944). The distortion of syllogistic reasoning produced by personal convictions. *Journal of Social Psychology, 20*, 39–59.

Moss, J. (1950). *How to win at poker*. Garden City, NY: Garden City Books.

Mumford, M. D., & Gustafson, S. B. (1988). Creativity syndrome: Integration, application, and innovation. *Psychological Bulletin, 103*, 27–43.

Munby, H. (1982). *Science in the schools*. Toronto: University of Toronto.

Munson, R. (1976). *The way of words*. Boston: Houghton Mifflin.

Mussweiler, T., & Strack, F. (2000). The use of category and exemplar knowledge in the solution of anchoring tasks. *Journal of Personality & Social Psychology, 78*(6), 1038–1052.

Myers, D. G. (1995). *Psychology*. New York: Worth.

Mynatt, C. R., Doherty, M. E., & Tweney, R. D. (1978). Consequences of confirmation and disconfirmation in a simulated research environment. *Quarterly Journal of Experimental Psychology, 30*(3), 395–406.

Nakamura, J., & Csikszentmihalyi, M. (2001). Catalytic creativity: The case of Linus Pauling. *American Psychologist, 56*, 337–341.

National Commission on Excellence in Education. (1983). *A nation at risk: The imperative for educational reform*. Washington, DC: Author.

National Education Goals Panel. (1991). *The national education goals report: Building a nation of learners*. Washington, DC: U. S. Printing Office.

National Research Council. (1994). *Learning, remembering, and believing: Enhancing human performance*. Washington, DC: National Academy Press.

Neisser, U. (1982). *Memory observed: Remembering in natural contexts*. San Francisco: Freeman.

Neisser, U., Boodoo, G., Bouchard, T. J. J., Boykin, A. W., Brody, N., Ceci, S. J., Halpern, D. F., Loehlin, J. C., Perloff, R., Sternberg, R. J., & Urbina, S. (1996). Intelligence: Knowns and unknowns. *American Psychologist, 51*(2), 77–101.

Nelson, G. P. (1998 April). You don't have to be a rocket scientist to think like one. *Star Tribune*, p. A14.

Nelson, T. O. (1996). Consciousness and metacognition. *American Psychologist, 51*, 102–116.

Nelson, T. O., & Narens, L. (1990). Metamemory: A theoretical framework and new findings. *The Psychology of Learning and Motivation, 26*, 125–141.

Neubert, G. A., & Binko, J. B. (1992). *Inductive reasoning in the secondary classroom*. Washington, DC: NEA Professional Library, National Education Association.

Newell, A. (1983). The heuristic of George Polya and its relation to artificial intelligence. In M. G. R. Groner, & W.F. Bischof (Eds.), *Methods of heuristics* (pp. 195–243). Hillsdale, NJ: Lawrence Erlbaum Associates.

Newell, A., & Simon, H. A. (1972). *Human problem solving*. Englewood Cliffs, NJ: Prentice-Hall.

Nickerson, R. S. (1987). Why teach thinking? In J. B. Baron, & R. J. Sternberg (Eds), *Teaching thinking skills: Theory and practice* (pp. 27–37). New York: Freeman.

Nickerson, R. S. (1998). Confirmation bias: A ubiquitous phenomenon in many guises. *Review of General Psychology, 2*(2), 175–220.

Nickerson, R. S. (1986). *Reflections on reasoning*. Hillsdale, NJ: Lawrence Erlbaum Associates.

Nickerson, R. S., & Adams, M. J. (1979). Long-term memory for a common object, *Cognitive Psychology, 11*, 287–307.

Nisbett, R. E. (1993). *Rules for reasoning*. Hillsdale, NJ: Lawrence Erlbaum Associates.

Nixon, R. M. (1962). *Six crises*. Garden City, NY: Doubleday.

Norman, D. A. (1976). *Memory and attention: An introduction to human information processing*. New York: Wiley.

Norman, D. A. (1988). *The psychology of everyday things*. New York: Basic Books.

Norris, S. P. (1992). *The generalizability of critical thinking: Multiple perspectives on an educational ideal*. New York: Teachers College Press.

Norris, S. P., & Ennis, R. H. (1989). *Evaluating critical thinking*. Pacific Grove, CA: Critical Thinking Press & Software.

Noveck, I. A., & Politzer, G. (1998). Leveling the playing field: Investigating competing claims concerning relative inference difficulty. In M. D. S. Braine & D. P. O'Brien (Eds.) *Mental logic* (pp. 367–384). Mahwah, NJ: Lawrence Erlbaum Associates, Inc.

Nutrition Action Health Letter (1991, July/Aug). *Eater's Digest*, p. 13.

O'Loughlin, A. & McFadzean, M. E. (1999). Toward a holistic theory of strategic problem solving. *Team Performance Management, 5*, 103–120.

Oliver, P. (2001). Diagrammatic reasoning: An artificial intelligence perspective. *Artificial Intelligence Review, 15*, 63–78.

Oppenheimer, J. R. (1956). Analogy in science. *American Psychologist, 11*, 127–135.

Ortho Pharmaceutical Group. (1979). *The pill—After your doctor prescribes* . . . Raritan, NJ: Author.

Orwell, G. (1949). *1984*. New York: Harcourt, Brace.

Osborn, A. F. (1963). *Applied imagination: Principles and procedures of creative problem solving.* New York: Scribner's.

Osgood, C. E. (1953). *Method and theory in experimental psychology.* New York: Oxford University Press.

Oskamp, S. (1953). *Method and theory in experimental psychology.* New York: Oxford University Press.

Overskeid, G. (2000). The slave of the passions: Experiencing problems and selecting solutions. *Review of General Psychology, 4*(3), 284–309.

Paas, F. G. (1992). Training strategies for attaining transfer of problem-solving skill in statistics: A cognitive-load approach. *Journal of Educational Psychology, 84*, 429–434.

Palincsar, A. S., & Brown, A. L. (1984). Reciprocal-teaching of comprehension-monitoring activities. *Cognition and Instruction, 1*, 117–175.

Papanek, V. J. (1977). Tree of life: Bionics. In S. J. Parnes, R. B. Noller, & A. M. Biondi (Eds.), *Guide to creative action: Revised edition of creative behavior guidebook.* New York: Scribner's.

Parducci, A. (1968). The relativism of absolute judgments. *Scientific American, 219*(6), 84–90.

Park, D. C. (1992). Applied cognitive aging research. In F. I. M. Craik & T. A. Salthouse (Eds.), *The handbook of aging and cognition* (pp. 449–493). Hillsdale, NJ: Lawrence Erlbaum Associates.

Parnes, S. J. (1967). *Creative behavior workbook.* New York: Scribner's.

Parnes, S. J., Noller, R. B., & Biondi, A. M. (1977). *Guide to creative action: Revised edition of creative behavior guidebook.* New York: Scribner's.

Patterson, M. E., Dansereau, D. F., & Wiegmann, D. A. (1993). Receiving information during a cooperative episode: Effects of communication aids and verbal ability. *Learning & Individual Differences, 5*(1), 1–11.

Paulos, J. A. (1994). Commentary: Counting on dyscalculia. *Discovery*, 30–36.

Payne, J. W., Bettman, J. R., & Johnson, E. J. (1993). *The adaptive decision maker.* Cambridge, England: Cambridge University Press.

Peck, J. (1986). Not killing is a crime? In B. Lown & E. Chazov (Eds.), *Peace: A dream unfolding* (p. 146). Ontario, Canada: Sommerville House Books Ltd.

Pedone, R., Hummel, J. E., & Holyoak, K. J. (2001). The use of diagrams in analogical problem solving. *Memory & Cognition, 29*, 214–221.

Pellegrino, J. W., & Goldman, S. R. (1983). Developmental and individual differences in verbal and spatial reasoning. In R. F. Dillon & R. R. Schmeck (Eds.), *Individual differences in cognition* (pp. 137–180). New York: Academic.

Pence, G. E. (2001, January). Setting a common, careful policy for bioethics. *The Chronicle of Higher Education*, p. 20.

Perfetto, G. A., Bransford, J. D., & Franks, J. J. (1983). Constraints on access in a problem solving context. *Memory & Cognition, 77*, 562–571.

Perkins, D. N. (1988). Creativity and the quest for mechanism. In R. J. Sternberg & E. E. Smith (Eds.), *Psychology of human thought.* New York: Cambridge.

Perkins, D. N. (1985). Postprimary education has little impact on informal reasoning. *Journal of Educational Psychology, 77*, 562–571.

Perkins, D. N., & Grotzer, T. A. (1997). Teaching intelligence. *American Psychologist, 52*(10), 1125–1133.

Pinkley, R. L., & Northcraft, G. B. (2000). *Get paid what you're worth: The expert negotiator's guide to salary and compensation.* New York: St. Martin's Press.

Pitt, J., & Leavenworth, R. (1968). *Logic for argument.* New York: Random House.

Pogrow, S. (1992). A validated approach to thinking development for at-risk populations. In C. Collins & J. Mangieri (Eds), *Teaching thinking: An agenda for the twenty-first century* (pp. 87–101). Hillsdale, NJ: Lawrence Erlbaum Associates.

Poincare, H. (1929). *The foundations of science*. New York: Science House.

Polya, G. (1945). *How to solve it: A new aspect of mathematical method*. Princeton, NJ: Princeton University Press.

Polya, G. (1957). *How to solve it: A new aspect of mathematical method*. Garden City, NY: Doubleday.

Polya, G. (1981). *Mathematical discovery* (Combined ed.). New York: John Wiley & Sons.

Posner, M. I. (1973). *Cognition: An introduction*. Glenview, IL: Scott, Foresman.

Postman, N., & Powers, S. (1992). *How to watch TV news*. New York: Penguin.

Potts, G. R. (1972). Information processing strategies used in the encoding of linear orderings. *Journal of Verbal Learning and Verbal Behavior, 11*, 727–740.

Powell, D. (1985). *The wisdom of a novel: A dictionary of quotations*. New York: Garland.

Pratkanis, A. R., & Aronson, E. (1992). *Age of propaganda: The everyday use and abuse of persuasion*. New York: W. H. Freeman.

Prince, G. M. (1970). *The practice of creativity*. New York: Harper.

Quattrone, G. A., & Jones, E. E. (1980). The perception of variability within in-groups and out-groups: Implications for the law of small numbers. *Journal of Personality and Social Psychology, 38*, 141–152.

The Quoteaholic. *Galileo* [Web Page]. URL *www.quoteaholic.com* [2002, January 15–20].

Raia, E. (1994, June 2), Russian style. *Purchasing*, pp. 28–29.

RAND Corporation. (1992). Health care and the uninsured: Who will pay? *RAND Research Review, XVI*, 6–8.

Raphael, B. (1976). *The thinking computer: Mind inside matter*. San Francisco: Freeman.

Reber, P. J., & Kotovsky, K. (1997). Implicit learning in problem solving: The role of working memory capacity. *Journal of Experimental Psychology: General, 126*(2), 178–203.

Regents of the University of California. *How much information?* [Web Page]. URL *http://www.sims.berkeley.edu/how-much-info/* [2001, January 30].

Reisberg, D. (2001). *Cognition*. New York: W. W. Norton & Company.

Renshon, S. A. (1992). The psychology of good judgment: A preliminary model with some applications to the Gulf War. *Political Psychology, 13*, 477–495.

Resnick, L. B. (1985). Cognition and instruction: Recent theories of human competence. *Psychology and Learning* (pp. 127–186, 243).

Restak, R. M. (1988). *The mind*. New York: Bantam Books.

The Review. *Science and Pseudoscience Review in Mental Health* [Web Page]. URL http://www.pseudoscience.org/definitions-pseudo.html [1920].

Reyes, R. M., Thompson, W. C., & Bower, G. H. (1980). Judgmental biases resulting from differing availabilities of arguments. *Journal of Personality & Social Psychology, 39*(1), 2–12.

Rhoads, K. (1997). *What's in a frame*? [Web Page]. URL www.influenceatwork.com [2002, February 10].

Rips, L. J. (1988). Deduction. In R. J. Sternberg & E. E. Smith (Eds.), *The psychology of human thought* (pp. 116–152). New York: Cambridge University Press.

Rips, L. J. (2001). Two kinds of reasoning. Psychological Science, 12, 129–134.

Rittle-Johnson, B., & Alibali, M. W. (1999). Conceptual and procedural knowledge of mathematics: Does one lead to the other? *Journal of Educational Psychology, 91*(1), 175–189.

Roediger, H. L. (1990). Implicit memory: Retention without remembering. *American Psychologist, 45*(9), 1043–1056.

Roediger, H. L. I., & Bergman, E. T. (1998). The controversy over recovered memories. *Psychology, Public Policy, & Law, 4*(4), 1091–1109.

Rokeach, M. (1960). *The open and closed mind: Investigations into the nature of belief systems and personality systems*. New York, Basic Books.

Rosch, E. (1977). Human categorization. In N. Warren (Ed.), *Studies in cross-cultural psychology* (Vol. 1). New York: Academic Press.

Rosenthal, R., & Fode, K. L. (1963). The effect of experimental bias on the performance of the albino rat. *Behavioral Science, 8*, 183–187.

Ross, J., & Laurence, K. A. (1968). Some observations on memory artifice. *Psychonomic Science, 13*(2), 107–108.

Rothenberg, A. (1979). *The emerging goddess: The creative process in art, science, and other fields.* Chicago: University of Chicago Press.

Rubinstein, M. F., & Pfeiffer, K. R. (1980). *Concepts in problem solving.* Englewood Cliffs, NJ: Prentice-Hall.

Ryan, M. (2001). Top 10 ideas of marketing. *Advertising Age, 72,* 6–8.

Sadler, W. A. Jr., & Whimbey A. (1985). A holistic approach to improving thinking skills. *Phi Delta Kappa, 67,* 199–202.

Salovey, P., & Sluyter, D. J. (1997). *Emotional development and emotional intelligence: Educational implications.* New York: Basic Books.

Sapir, E. (1960). *Culture, language and personality.* Berkeley: University of California Press.

Schacter, D. L. (1999). The seven sins of memory: Insights from psychology and cognitive neuroscience. *American Psychologist, 54*(3), 182–203.

Schafly, P. (1993 July). A mental health care nightmare. *The Washington Times,* p. G4.

Schauble, L., & Glaser, R. (1990). Scientific thinking in children and adults. In D. Kuhn (Series Ed., Vol. Ed.), *Contributions to human development: Vol. 21. Developmental perspectives on teaching and learning thinking skills* (pp. 9–27). New York: Basel, Karger.

Schmidt, H. G., Peeck, V. H., Paas, F., & van Breukelen, G. J. P. (2000). Remembering the street names of one's childhood neighbourhood: A study of very long-term retention. *Memory, 8*(1), 37–49.

Schmolck, H., Buffalo, E. A., & Squire, L. R. (2000). Memory distortions develop over time: Recollections of the O.J. Simpson trial verdict after 15 and 32 months. *Psychological Science, 11*(1), 39–45.

Schoenfeld, A. H. (1979). Can heuristics be taught? In J. Lochhead & J. Clement (Eds.), *Cognitive process instruction: Research on teaching skills,* Philadelphia: Franklin Institute Press.

Schoenfeld, A. H. (1985). *Mathematical problem solving.* Orlando, FL: Academic Press.

Schoenfeld, A. H., & Herrmann, D. J. (1982). Problem perception and knowledge structure in expert and novice mathematical problem solvers. *Journal of Experimental Psychology: Learning, Memory, & Cognition, 8*(5), 484–494.

Science in the Public Interest. (2000). Bar exams: Energy bars flunk. *Nutrition Action Health Letter, 27,* 10–12.

Scriven, M. (1976). *Reasoning.* New York: McGraw-Hill.

Seamon, J. G., Williams, P. C., Crowley, M. J., Kim, I. J., Langer, S. A., Orner, P. J., & Wishengrad, D. L. (1995). The mere exposure effect is based on implicit memory: Effects of stimulus type, encoding conditions, and number of exposures on recognition and affect judgments. *Journal of Experimental Psychology: Learning, Memory, & Cognition, 21,* 711–721.

Sears, A., & Parsons, J. (1991). Towards critical thinking as an ethic. *Theory and Research in Social Education, 19*(1), 45–68.

Seech, Z. (1993). *Open minds and everyday reasoning.* Belmont, CA: Wadsworth.

Seligman, M. (1991). *Learned optimism.* New York: Knopf.

Sethi, R., Smith, D. C., & Park, C. W. (2001). Cross-functional product development teams, creativity, and the innovativeness of new consumer products. *Journal of Marketing Research, 38,* 73–85.

Shaklee, H. (1987). *Estimating cumulative risk: Flood and contraceptive failure.* Twenty-Eighth Annual Meeting of the Psychonomic Society, Seattle, WA.

Shalley, C. E. (1991). Effects of productivity goals, creativity goals, and personal discretion on individual creativity. *Journal of Applied Psychology, 7*(2), 179–185.

Shaver, K. G. (1981). *Principles of social psychology.* Cambridge, MA: Winthrop.

Shavinina, L. V. (2001). A new wave of innovations in psychology: High intellectual and creative education multimedia technologies. *Review of General Psychology, 5,* 291–315.

Shermer, M. (1992). Anecdotes do not make a science: The skeptics reply. *Skeptic, 1,* 18–19.

Shermer, M. (1997). *Why people believe weird things: Pseudoscience, superstition, and other confusions of our time.* New York: W. H. Freeman.

Shubik, M. (1971). The dollar auction game: A paradox in noncooperative behavior and escalation. *Journal of Conflict Resolution, 15,* 109–111.

Shuman, D. W., & Champagne, A. (1998). Removing the people from the legal process: The rhetoric and research on judicial selection and juries. *Psychology, Public Policy, & Law, 3*(2–3), 242–258.

Siegal, E. (1991, May). Persuasion and decision-making. *APS Observer*, p. 8.

Simon, H. A. (1977). The psychology of scientific problem solving. In H.A. Simon (Ed.), *Models of discovery*. Dordrecht, Netherlands: D.Reidel.

Simon, H. A., & Kaplan, C. A. (1989). Foundations of cognitive science. In I. Posner (Ed.), *Foundations of cognitive science* (pp. 1–47). Cambridge, MA: The MIT Press.

Simonson, I., Nowlis, S. M., & Simonson, Y. (1993). The effect of irrelevant preference arguments on consumer choice. *Journal of Consumer Psychology, 2*, 287–306.

Singer, B., & Benassi, V. A. (1981). Occult beliefs. *American Scientist, 69*, 49–55.

Slovic, P. (1987). Perception of risk. *Science, 236*, 280–285.

Slovic, P., Fischhoff, B., & Lichtenstein, S. (1986). Knowing with certainty: The appropriateness of extreme confidence. In H. Arkes & K. R. Hammond, *Judgement and decision making: An interdisciplinary reader* (pp. 397–416). New York: Cambridge University Press.

Smedslund, J. (1963). The concept of correlation in adults. *Scandinavian Journal of Psychology, 44*, 165–173.

Smith, L. (1992, June). Rick's place revisited. *The Los Angeles Times*, p. A1.

Smith, M. U. (1988). Successful and unsuccessful problem solving in classical genetic pedigrees. *Journal of Research in Science Teaching, 25*(6), 411–433.

Smith, S. M., & Blankenship, S. E. (1991). Incubation and the persistence of fixation in problem solving. *American Journal of Psychology, 104*(1), 61–87.

Snyder, M., & Uranowitz, S. W. (1978). Reconstructing the past: Some cognitive consequences of person perception. *Journal of Personality & Social Psychology, 36*(9), 941–950.

Soler, M. J., & Ruiz, J. C. (2000). The spontaneous use of memory aids at different educational levels. *Applied Cognitive Psychology, 10*, 41–51.

Solorzano, L. (1985). Think! Now schools are teaching how. *U.S. News & World Report*.

Sorensen, T. C. (1965). *Kennedy*. New York: Harper & Row.

Spellman, B. A., & Holyoak, K. J. (1992). If Saddam is Hitler then who is George Bush? Analogical mapping between systems of social roles. *Journal of Personality & Social Psychology, 62*(6), 913–933.

Stahl, N. N., & Stahl, R. J. (1991). We can agree after all! Achieving consensus on critical thinking using the delphi technique. *Roeper Review, 14*(2), 79–88.

Stanovich, K. E. (1999). *Studies of individual differences in reasoning*. Mahwah, NJ: Lawrence Erlbaum Associates, Inc.

Stanovich, K. E., & West, R. F. (1999). Discrepancies between normative and descriptive models of decision making and the understanding/acceptance principle. *Cognitive Psychology, 38*(3), 349–385.

Stanovich, K. E., & West, R. F. (1997). Reasoning independently of prior belief and individual differences in actively open-minded thinking. *Journal of Educational Psychology, 89*(2), 342–357.

Steinem, G. (1994). *Moving beyond words*. New York: Simon & Schuster.

Sternberg, R. J. (1977). Component processes in analogical reasoning. *Psychological Review, 84*, 353–373.

Sternberg, R. J. (1982). Who's intelligent? *Psychology Today, 16*, 30–33, 35–39.

Sternberg, R. J. (1992). Ability tests, measurement and markets. *Journal of Educational Psychology, 84*, 134–140.

Sternberg, R. J. (1999). The theory of successful intelligence. *Review of General Psychology, 3*(4), 292–316.

Sternberg, R. J. (in press). Why schools should teach for wisdom: The balance theory of wisdom in educational settings. *Educational Psychologist*.

Sternberg, R. J., & Lubart, T. I. (1995). *Defying the crowd: Cultivating creativity in a culture of conformity*. New York: Free Press.

Sternberg, R. J., & Lubart, T. I. (1996). Investing in creativity. *American Psychologist, 51*, 677–688.

Sternberg, R. J., & O'Hara, A. (1999). Creativity and intelligence. In R. J. Sternberg (Ed.), *Handbook of creativity* (pp. 251–272). New York: Cambridge University Press.

Sternberg, R. J., & Weil, E. M. (1980). An aptitude strategy interaction in linear syllogistic reasoning. *Journal of Educational Psychology, 72*(2), 226–239.

Sternberg, R. J., & Williams, W. (1997). Does the graduate record examination predict meaningful success in the graduate training of psychologists? A case study. *American Psychologist, 52*, 630–641.

Stewart, J. K. (1985). From the director. *National Institute of Justice: Research in brief.* Washington, DC: US Department of Justice.

Swanson, H. L. (1990). Influence of metacognitive knowledge and aptitude on problem solving. *Journal of Educational Psychology, 82*(2), 306–314.

Taplin, J. E., & Staudenmayer, H. (1973). Interpretation of abstract conditional sentences in deductive reasoning. *Journal of Verbal Learning & Verbal Behavior, 12*(5), 530–542.

Tate, M. A., & Alexander, J. (1996). Teaching critical evaluation skills for World Wide Web resources. *Computers in Libraries, 16*, 49–52.

Teger, A. I. (1979). *Too much invested to quit: The psychology of escalation of conflict.* New York: Pergamon.

Tetlock, P. E. (1994). The psychology of futurology and the future of psychology. *Psychological Science, 5*, 1–4.

Texas Library Association. *Knowledge is Power* [Web Page]. URL *http://www.txla.org/groups/godort/kip-award.html* [2002, January 29].

Time. (1998, June 1). Sounds like, smells like, feels like, p. 25.

Timnick, Lois. (1989). *McMartin defense urges jury to end years of 'vile allegations'* [Web Page]. URL www.latimes.com [2002, January 15–2002].

Toulmin, S., Rieke, R., & Janik, A. (1979). *An introduction of reasoning.* New York: Macmillan.

Tulving, E. (1972). Episodic and semantic memory. In E. Tulving & W. Donaldson (Eds), *Organization of memory.* New York: Academic Press.

Tutu, D. (1986). How to eat an elephant. In B. Lown & E. Chazov (Eds.), *Peace: A dream unfolding* (p. 216). New York: Academic Press.

Tversky, A. (1972). Elimination by aspects. A theory of choice. *Psychological Review, 79*, 281–299.

Tversky, A., & Kahneman, D. (1971). Belief in the law of small numbers. *Psychological Bulletin, 76*, 104–110.

Tversky, A., & Kahneman, D. (1983). Extensional versus intuitive reasoning: The conjunction fallacy in probability judgement. *Psychological Review, 90*, 293–315.

Tversky, A., & Kahneman, D. (1981). The framing of decisions and the psychology of choice. *Science, 211*, 453–458.

Tversky, A., & Kahneman, D. (1974). Judgment under uncertainty: Heuristics and biases. *Science, 185*, 1124–1131.

Tversky, B. (1973). Encoding processes in recognition and recall. *Cognitive Psychology, 5*, 275–287.

Tweney, R. D., & Chitwood, S. T. (1995). Scientific reasoning. In S. E. Newstead & J. S. B. T. Evans (Eds.), *Perspectives on thinking and reasoning: Essays in honour of Peter Wason* (pp. 241–260). Hillsdale, NJ: Lawrence Erlbaum Associates.

Van Haneghan, J., Barron, L., Young, M., Williams, S., Vye, N., & Bransford, J. (1992). The "jasper" series: An experiment with new ways to enhance mathematical thinking. In D. F. Halpern (Ed.), *Enhancing thinking skills in the sciences and mathematics* (pp. 15–38, ix, 155). Hillsdale, NJ: Lawrence Erlbaum Associates.

VanLehn, K. (1989). Problem solving and cognitive skill acquisition. In M. Posner (Ed.), *The foundations of cognitive science* (pp. 527–580). Cambridge, MA: MIT Press.

Vaughan, J. L. (1984). Concept structuring: The technique and empirical evidence, In C. D. Holley & D. F. Dansereau (Eds.), *Spatial learning strategies: Techniques, applications, and related issues* (pp. 127–147). New York: Academic Press.

Vernon, P. (1970). *Creativity: Selected readings.* Harmondsworth, England: Penguin.

von Oech, R. (1983). *A whack on the side of the head.* New York: Warner Books.

Vosniadou, S., & Orotony, A. (Eds). (1989). *Similarity and analogical reasoning*. Cambridge, England: Cambridge University Press.

Vygotsky, L. S. (1978). *Mind in society*. Cambridge, MA: Harvard University Press.

Wales, C. E., & Nardi, A. (1984). *Successful decision-making*. Morgantown, WV: Center for Guided Design.

Walsh, J. (1981). A plenipotentiary for human intelligence. *Science, 214*, 640–641.

Wandersman, A. H., & Hallman, W. K. (1993). Are people acting irrationally? Understanding public concerns about environmental threats. *American Psychologist, 48*, 681–686.

Wang, P. (1994). How to retire with twice as much money. *Money*, pp. 77–84.

Wanous, J. P. (1973). Effects of a realistic job preview on job acceptance, job attitudes, and job survival. *Journal of Applied Psychology, 58*, 327–332.

Wason, P. C. (1968). On the failure to eliminate hypotheses: A second look. In P. C. Wason & P. N. Johnson-Laird (Eds.), *Thinking and reasoning*. Baltimore: Penguin.

Wason, P. C. (1960). On the failure to eliminate hypotheses in a conceptual task. *Quarterly Journal of Experimental Psychology, 12*, 129–140.

Wason, P. C. (1969). Structure simplicity and psychological complexity. *Bulletin of the British Psychological Society, 22*, 281–284.

Weber, R. J., & Perkins, D. N. (Eds.). (1992). *Inventive minds: Creativity in technology*. New York: Oxford University Press.

Wegner, D. M., Wenzlaff, R., Kerker, R. M., & Beattie, A. E. (1981). Incrimination through innuendo: Can media questions become public answers? *Journal of Personality & Social Psychology, 40*(5), 822–832.

Weisberg, R. W. (1988). Problem solving and creativity. In R. J Sternberg (Ed.), *The nature of creativity: Contemporary psychological persepctives* (pp. 148–177). New York: Cambridge University Press.

Weisberg, R. W. (1993). *Creativity: Beyond the myth of genius*. New York: Freeman.

Weisberg, R., Dicamillo, M., & Phillips, D. (1978). Transferring old associations to new situations; A nonautomatic process. *Journal of Verbal Learning and Verbal Behavior, 17*, 219–228.

Wertheimer, M. (1959). *Productive thinking*. New York: Harper.

Whimbey, A. (1976). *Intelligence can be taught*. New York: Bantam.

Whimbey, A., & Lochhead, J. (1982). *Problem solving and comprehension: A short course in analytic reasoning*. Philadelphia: Franklin Institute Press.

Whiting, C. S. (1958). *Creative thinking*. New York: Reinhold.

Whorf, B. (1956). *Language, thought, and reality*. Cambridge, MA: MIT Press.

Wickelgren, W. (1974). *How to solve problems*. San Francisco: Freeman.

Wicker, A. W. (1981). *Getting out of our conceptual ruts: Strategies for generating new perspectives on familiar research problems*. Paper presented at the 1981 annual convention of the Western Psychological Association, Los Angeles.

Williams, W., Blythe, T., White, N., Li, J., Sternberg, R., & Gardner, H. (1996). *Practical intelligence for school handbook*. New York: HarperCollins.

Wilson, R., & Crouch, E. A. C. (1987). Risk assessment and comparisons: An introduction. *Science, 286*, 267–270.

Wilson, T. D., & Brekke, N. (1994). Mental contamination and mental correction: Unwanted influences on judgments and evaluations. *Psychological Bulletin, 116*, 117–142.

Zimbardo, P. G., & Leippe, M. R. (1991). *The psychology of attitude change and social influence*. New York: McGraw-Hill.

Author Index

A

Adams, A., 120
Adams, J. L., 388, 425
Adams, M. J., 53
Ahlgren, A., 270
Alcock, J. E., 275
Alexander, J., 198
Alibali, M. W., 331
Allan, R. A., 6
Allan, T., 421
Allegretti, C. L., 192
Allport, G. W., 61, 238
Amabile, T. M., 413
Anderson, B. F., 141
Andrade, J., 73
Arasteh, A. R., 397
Arasteh, J. D., 397
Arbitman-Smith, R., 98
Arkes, H. R., 265, 315, 324
Aronson, E., 207
Asimov, I., 4
Atkinson, R. C., 74
Azar, B., 341

B

Baddeley, A. D., 67, 73
Baer, J., 412
Bahrick, H. P., 80
Bailin, S., 416
Bar-Natan, D., 271
Baron, A. L., 13
Baron, J., 194, 313, 314, 329, 331, 338
Barron, F., 415, 417
Barron, L., 58
Bartlett, F. C., 62
Bartlett, J., 26, 232
Bassham, G., 198
Bastardi, A., 318
Beattie, A. F., 48
Beecher, H. W., 107
Begley, S., 418
Beilensen, J., 170, 221, 354
Benassi, V., 256

Benjamin, A. S., 70
Berger, D., 314, 319
Berger, S. A., 80
Bergman, E. T., 63
Berkowitz, L., 327
Berlin, B., 107
Bernstein, D. A., 385
Bettman, J. R., 314, 331
Beyth-Marom, R., 79
Bink, M. L., 407
Binko, J. B., 4
Biondi, A. M., 400
Bjork, R. A., 70
Blackman, S., 113, 273
Blank, A., 208
Blankenship, S. E., 353
Blasko, D. G., 97
Block, R. A., 10, 11
Blythe, T., 22
Boden, M. A., 409
Bodenmann, G., 358
Bollag, B., 5
Boodoo, G., 22
Boring, E. G., 23
Bouchard, T. J. J., 22
Bousfield, W. A., 57
Bower, G. H., 42, 57, 73, 89, 121, 123, 124, 125, 324
Boxall, B., 303
Boykin, A. W., 22
Bozell, L. B. III, 303
Bradbury, R., 213
Braine, M. D., 150
Bransford, D., 69
Bransford, J. D., 54, 58, 66, 69, 94, 98, 358, 380, 417
Brehm, J. W., 340
Brekke, N., 239
Brem, S., 210
Brennan, J., 117
Brennan, T., 187
Brim, O. G., Jr., 21
Brody, N., 22
Brooks, L. W., 50
Bross, I. D. J., 31
Brown, A. L., 69, 94, 120

Subject Index